W9-ASB-133

THE TWENTIETH-CENTURY MIND

III

1945–1965

THE TWENTIETH-CENTURY MIND

in three volumes

I: 1900–1918
II: 1918–1945
III: 1945–1965

# THE TWENTIETH-CENTURY MIND

History, Ideas, and Literature in Britain

EDITED BY

C. B. Cox and A. E. Dyson

III

1945–1965

OXFORD UNIVERSITY PRESS
LONDON OXFORD NEW YORK
1972

*Oxford University Press*

LONDON OXFORD NEW YORK
GLASGOW TORONTO MELBOURNE WELLINGTON
CAPE TOWN IBADAN NAIROBI DAR ES SALAAM LUSAKA ADDIS ABABA
DELHI BOMBAY CALCUTTA MADRAS KARACHI LAHORE DACCA
KUALA LUMPUR SINGAPORE HONG KONG TOKYO

Paperback edition ISBN 0 19 281124 X
Clothbound edition ISBN 0 19 212193 6



First published as an Oxford University Press paperback, and simultaneously in a clothbound edition, by Oxford University Press, London, 1972



*Printed in Great Britain*
*by Richard Clay (The Chaucer Press), Ltd.,*
*Bungay, Suffolk*

# CONTENTS

# Introduction

## I

In 1954 C. S. Lewis delivered his inaugural lecture at Cambridge as Professor of Medieval and Renaissance English Literature. He argued that the greatest of all divisions in the history of the west is 'that which divides the present from, say, the age of Jane Austen and Scott'. No precise dating of this division is possible. No one could point to a year or decade in which the change indisputably began, but 'somewhere between us and the Waverley Novels, somewhere between us and *Persuasion*, the chasm runs'. This belief that twentieth-century man is a unique creature, embroiled in a quite new cultural situation, is common to a large number of modern writers.

As might be expected, there is much disagreement about the essential characteristics of this new sensibility. In the Introduction to the second volume of *The Twentieth-Century Mind*, we discussed the pessimism of the 1920s, the sense in Yeats or D. H. Lawrence of living at the end of an era of civilization. Typical of those years was Oswald Spengler's *The Decline of the West*. The horrors of trench warfare obviously made an ineradicable impact on the human imagination; Virginia Woolf used the same image as Lewis when she described the outbreak of war in 1914 as 'like a chasm in a smooth road'. Since 1945 there has been much talk about the psychological effects on man of the concentration camps and the threat of nuclear war. In *The Liberal Imagination* (1951), Lionel Trilling argues that there is in western civilization a growing disgust for life, and that this means that the individual as an aesthetic object can perhaps no longer command our best attention. The fiction writer turns towards satire or fantasies of the absurd. The reaction of the modern novelist to this situation is discussed in detail in Professor Malcolm Bradbury's chapter. According to Trilling, this predicament brings problems different in kind from those confronted by Freud and the great writers of the past:

> . . . society's resistance to the discovery of depravity has ceased; now everyone knows that Thackeray was wrong, Swift right. The world and the soul have split open of themselves and are all agape for our revolted inspection. The simple eye of the camera shows us, at Belsen and Buchenwald, horrors that quite surpass Swift's powers, a vision of life turned

back to its corrupted elements which is more disgusting than any that Shakespeare could contrive, a cannibalism more literal and fantastic than that which Montaigne ascribed to organized society. . . . before what we now know the mind stops; the great psychological fact of our time which we all observe with baffled wonder and shame is that there is no possible way of responding to Belsen and Buchenwald. The activity of mind fails before the incommunicability of man's suffering.

That the concentration camps have formed a new consciousness in western man is a view which occurs repeatedly in the works of George Steiner. In *Language and Silence* (1967) he asks: 'Has our civilization, by virtue of the inhumanity it has carried out and condoned . . . forfeited its claims to that indispensable luxury which we call literature?' How can we accept Matthew Arnold's faith in the civilizing influence of art now we know that a 'man can read Goethe or Rilke in the evening, that he can play Bach and Schubert, and go to his day's work at Auschwitz in the morning'? The poet is tempted by silence. In the words of Theodor Adorno, a European Jew: 'No poetry after Auschwitz'.

This cultural pessimism has not gone unchallenged. The historian Geoffrey Barraclough has written: 'The pessimism which sees all change as change for the worse is a recurrent theme of history, which history has recurrently refuted.' Frank Kermode, whose views are outlined in our chapter on literary criticism, has shown how 'crisis ethics' are to be found in many times and places in the history of western civilization. But, although we may agree with Barraclough and Kermode to reject the more extravagant claims of cultural pessimism, it is undeniable that the predicament of twentieth-century man differs in certain fundamental ways from that of previous centuries.

C. S. Lewis outlines various developments that distinguish modern man from his predecessors. He believes a major change has taken place in political attitudes. In his view, both dictatorships and democracies in modern times depend upon 'government by advertisement'. We no longer talk of our 'rulers'; the usual word now is 'leaders'. We live in an age of 'appeals', 'drives', 'campaigns', and the mass media, through popular newspapers, radio, film, and television, are exploited by pressure groups and politicians to sway public opinion.

Far more significant, according to Lewis, is the transformation in our modes of life and thought brought about by machines. The importance of the new technologies has repeatedly been stressed in our previous volumes, and here Professor Ian Hunter deals specifically with new psychological problems of the interaction of man and machines. Since 1945 there has been growing understanding of communication processes, and of central significance, of course, is our increasing reliance on the computer. Lewis argues that machines persuade us to accept instinctively a belief in progress. The ordinary person thinks in terms of old machines being superseded by new and better ones. In his own life he proceeds from bicycle to cheap car to expensive car, from radio to television to colour television. Our moods, therefore, tend not towards conservation of what we already possess, but instead we assume that everything is provisional and soon to be replaced. It could be argued that since Lewis gave his lecture in 1954 there have been signs of a reversal of these assumptions. The hydrogen bomb and the dangers of germ warfare have provoked a profound distrust of science. The pollution of the environment has led to a new concern for ecology, and the word 'conservation' now attracts fashionable approval. In his chapter on physics, Professor Cole tells us that the cost of the new technology is so enormous that we may be reaching the limit of the knowledge we can afford. The conflict of attitudes to the machine is summed up in popular feelings about the space probes. That men should walk on the moon is a great triumph of progress and man's power to use nature for his own purposes. At the same time the huge cost of these enterprises seems out of proportion when we consider the tragic unsolved problems of starvation and overpopulation in so many areas of the world.

Of all the changes in the twentieth century discussed by Lewis, the most important is that we now live in a post-Christian era. In his chapter on theology, Dr. David Pailin draws attention to the difficulties of the Church in presenting its faith as a serious option to a world racked with doubt, uncertainty, and despair underneath a fading veneer of affluent complacency. According to Lewis, we are not relapsing into paganism, for we are not returning to the worship of a plurality of gods. Christians and pagans have much more in common with each other than either has with a post-Christian: 'The gap between those who worship different gods is not so wide as that between those who worship and those who do not.'

The new twentieth-century sensibility emerges most clearly in the arts. Lewis starts by emphasizing the declining influence of our classical heritage. For Edward Gibbon in the eighteenth century the partial loss of ancient learning and its recovery at the Renaissance were both unique events, but, Lewis writes, 'we have lived to see the second death of ancient learning.' In the twentieth century something which was once the possession of all educated men has shrunk to being the technical accomplishment of a few specialists. The new generations of undergraduates are almost entirely out of touch with the values and significance of Greek and Latin culture.

Lewis concentrates specifically on the loss of contact with ancient learning, but many recent writers link this breakdown to a complete loss of confidence in the power of reason. For George Steiner, 'the house of classic humanism, the dream of reason which animated western society, have largely broken down.' In the Introduction to our first volume, we outlined changes taking place, particularly in psychology, philosophy, physics, and anthropology, which challenged the optimistic belief that man's reason would gradually bring Utopia on earth, and that reality was a harmonious whole tending towards perfection. Franz Kafka's writings depict with frightening clarity man's nightmare isolation in a universe beyond his comprehension. In this volume, Professor Bradbury describes the novelist's concern with the metaphysical worries consequent upon loss of meaning and identity in modernized society, and in all the chapters in the arts section we find emphasis on despair and madness, the irrational and the absurd.

Central to these changes are new attitudes towards language. In the arts we find a growing uncertainty about the value of words and their relation to things, a lack of confidence resulting in some cases in the belief, as with Marshall McLuhan (see p. 455), that verbal forms are in decay. For C. S. Lewis, the strangeness of the Dadaists and the Surrealists, the difficulties of a poem such as *The Waste Land*, mark a kind of art generically different from the forms and conventions which existed from Homer to George Eliot. Before 1900, trust in language was reflected in the doctrine of *mimesis*, the assumption that there is a representative inter-relation between language and the facts of the world. In our chapter on literary criticism, we discuss how recent manifestations in the arts deliberately throw doubt on the mimetic accuracy of language. Eliot's *The Waste Land* is a typical case. In this poem, the words float together in uncertain relationships, with themselves, with the objective world, with Eliot's private sensibility. In Eliot we often detect a prevalent note of parody, an ironic tone which undermines the authority of the assertions. This use of parody to explore the uncertainties of language is seen in its most extreme form in the exuberant fictions of Nabokov, in *Pale Fire*, for example.

## II

And so to define the uniqueness of the twentieth century we can point to the growth of the mass media, the importance of machines, the decline of Christian belief, the loss of the classical heritage, the cult of the irrational in the arts. In conclusion we may risk one final attempt at a general summary. Modern writers continually express their sense of the age in images of fragmentation, the outsider, the refugee, the alien, the exile. Many writers have themselves been culturally displaced persons; Conrad, Pound, Eliot, Joyce, Beckett, and Nabokov are obvious examples. Post-Darwin man tends no longer to feel at home in his environment, no longer to find creation and nature explicable except as nightmare. New developments in the sciences challenge our confidence in reason and the mind. In his chapter on chemistry, Dr. Jarlath Ronayne comments on how science has lost its belief that it can uncover absolute truth; instead it can only substitute an ability to describe objectively the veil of appearance which covers reality. Distrust of grand claims for the dignity and significance of man produces a reductive quality in much thought and art, as in the continued influence of behaviourism. Dr. Raymond Plant's chapter on philosophy describes the kind of thinking about language which, at its most extreme, finds metaphysics or, for example, the formulations of words in Plato, a meaningless activity. The *reductio* of language is the subject-matter of much of Beckett's writing. Steiner writes of this:

> Beckett's *reductio* of language—*Echo's Bones*, the title of his early book of verse, is a perfect designation—relates to much that is distinctive of modern feeling. . . . There are passages in Beckett nearly interchangeable with the 'language exercises' in Wittgenstein's *Investigations*; both stalk the vapid inflations and imprecisions of our common speech. *Act Without Words* (1957) is to drama what *Black on Black* is to painting, a display of reductive logic. Beckett's silences, his wry assumption that a rose may indeed be a rose but that only a fool would take so scandalous a proposition for granted or feel confident of translating it into art, are akin to monochrome canvases, Warhol statics, and silent music.*

But Steiner goes on to point out a difference, for there is in Beckett 'a formidable inverse eloquence'. A typical contradiction, as in Kafka or Pinter, lies in the modern artist's creative zeal in communicating the impossibility of communication.

This contradiction reveals something basic about the modern

* *Extraterritorial* (1972), p. 14.

mind. In his chapter on poetry, Dr. Patrick Swinden argues that we tend to distrust myths of resolution, completeness, and organic unity, and that this explains the grotesque qualities of Ted Hughes's recent poetry. Although this is true, the twentieth century has witnessed a variety of attempts to discover a new co-ordinating myth, a continual search for some type of unity of being. In his chapter on drama in our second volume, Mr. Walter Stein suggested that the essential components of modern experience were Utopian aspirations and fascinated fixations on their collapse; this is particularly seen in responses to Marxism. We might rephrase this and say that essential to twentieth-century experience is a desire for synthesis, together with a despairing recognition of the difficulty of the quest. The longing for some general thesis into which all aspects of human life can be fitted explains the popular response to 'myth-makers' such as Frazer, Freud, and Marx, or more recently, D. H. Lawrence, Marcuse, and McLuhan. In the 1930s Dr. Leavis seemed to offer his apostles such a unifying myth, in his emphasis on a 'great tradition' which the elect must keep alive in these barbaric times. This moral purpose found it difficult to come to terms with the qualities of anarchy and absurdity in modern art. With the decline of this faith in the saving power of literary criticism, students have turned to linguistics, sociology, and anthropology, with their global pretensions, for a myth of unity.

In his chapter on structural anthropology, Dr. Eric Sharpe describes Claude Lévi-Strauss's search for the unconscious structure underlying all institutions and customs, and how he satisfies those anthropologists who, dissatisfied with the fragmentation imposed by field-work, are trying to discover a lost synthesis. In Dr. Roger Fowler's chapter on linguistics, he outlines Noam Chomsky's belief that study of language involves study of the whole nature of man. Mr. Stephen Mennell shows how since 1945 sociology has become a cult, which, particularly in its Marxist forms, offers some kind of final synthesis. All these examples suggest a common psychological desire for a unifying vision.

But the facts continually oppose such 'concord fictions'. Professor Cole shows how physics has become a gigantic structure with specialisms within specialisms that in many ways act against a deep understanding of the data themselves. To some degree the twentieth-century mind must be a specialist mind, involved in modes of thought comprehensible only to a small minority. The breakdown of classical and Christian traditions deprives us of any organized centre of thought. In our view, there is a deep human resistance to this fact, a natural longing for community and relationship. This impulse towards unity can be highly dangerous; it can create a kind of authoritarianism which imposes conformity by force. Hitler's Germany is the prime example. On the other hand, it is right that we should continue to seek for some total explanation of our predicament, for some philosophy of man by which to live.

This tension between fragmentation and unity is profoundly expressed in the works of our two greatest modern poets, Yeats and Eliot. In Yeats we find a peculiar contemporary phenomenon. The artist creates myths, his unifying 'Vision', yet much of his poetry at the same time ironically exposes the inadequacy of the myth. Yeats's 'The Circus Animals' Desertion' conveys this conflict most powerfully:

> Those masterful images because complete
> Grew in pure mind, but out of what began?
> A mound of refuse or the sweepings of a street,
> Old kettles, old bottles, and a broken can,
> Old iron, old bones, old rags, that raving slut
> Who keeps the till. Now that my ladder's gone,
> I must lie down where all the ladders start,
> In the foul rag-and-bone shop of the heart.

T. S. Eliot is similarly preoccupied with the conditions for the unification of experience. In his early poetry, subject and object, mind and things, exist in a fluid, uncertain relation. After his conversion to Christianity, he finds that the fragmentary can only have meaning in relation to the timeless, to the Word, to Christ:

> We shall not cease from exploration
> And the end of all our exploring
> Will be to arrive where we started
> And know the place for the first time.

In this connection, it seems likely that the central insights of the Christian tradition have been less damaged by the modern confusions and disasters considered here, than many humanists have supposed. Christianity has always recognized man's power for evil, as well as for goodness; it has been as far removed from Utopianism as from despair. Intellectually, it has been in tune with scepticism about the value of reason; from St. Paul through St. Augustine to Pascal and T. S. Eliot, many great Christian minds have denied that unaided reason can sustain, or save, man. Again, Christianity was at home in crisis and persecution, in the catacombs and in exile, long before it was at home in the great civilization it helped to build. It is optimistic humanism which has been undermined by the ferment and uncertainty of twentieth-century thought.

## III

In these volumes we try to give the reader information and ideas to help him overcome the prison of specialization. But we do not pretend that completeness is ever possible. As we explained in our introduction to the first volume, our aim is not to achieve the comprehensive coverage of an encyclopedia. We believe that every student must make a centre for himself in some specialized discipline, and then work outwards into other subjects, reading major works, relating ideas to the central areas of thought in which he is an expert, continually aware of the extent of his own ignorance.

In this volume we have no chapter on historiography. We consulted various historians, and they all agreed that we are too close to post-1945 events for such a chapter to be written with proper objectivity. As usual, the history chapters, and also the theology and philosophy chapters, are mainly confined to Britain. Since 1945 the disciplines of linguistics, sociology, and anthropology have assumed increasing importance, so each is given a separate chapter. Developments in the sciences are international, so the chapters on physics, chemistry, and biology give a general survey. Contributors have been encouraged not to confine themselves rigidly to the prescribed dates; in this volume Professor Waddington takes up his account of biology from the 1920s, where, at a convenient dividing line, his chapter ended in our first volume. We have asked the authors to concentrate on a few major themes, accepting that many important developments must be omitted. In the literature chapters we again deal mainly with Britain, though American writing is becoming more influential. The volume ends with Mr. Edward Lucie-Smith's comprehensive summary of the other arts.

C. B. Cox<br>
*March 1972* A. E. Dyson

# I

# History: Political and Diplomatic

W. CARR

## I

Great Britain emerged triumphant but exhausted from the ordeal of the Second World War. Hitler was dead, and Germany, broken and defeated, lay at the mercy of the victorious Allied Powers. That the victory was dearly bought was quickly apparent. Large areas of Europe, especially in the east, were utterly ravaged by war, and the old balance of power, on which the continent had rested since the days of Bismarck, was completely destroyed in the closing stages of the conflict. Russian soldiers had entered Warsaw, Prague, Budapest, and Bucharest, and were stationed on the line of the river Elbe in the very heart of Germany. In the west the United States of America, by virtue of its enormous military and economic power, dominated the political scene from the Pacific Ocean to Paris. East of Suez the impact of the war was no less profound. The Japanese 'New Order' in Asia, although short-lived, had helped to undermine still further the basis of the old colonial empires acquired by the European Great Powers at the end of the nineteenth century. It was soon evident that the old order could not be restored in its entirety in Asia, Africa, or the Middle East any more than in Europe, and attempts to put the clock back proved unavailing in the long run. In the course of the next two decades the peoples in this part of the world succeeded for the most part in throwing off the colonial yoke; in doing so they altered the whole balance of world power and ended the age of European primacy for ever.

It was symptomatic of the new mood of the British people in 1945 that Winston Churchill (1874–1965), the embodiment of wartime Britain's will to victory, suffered a decisive defeat in the general election. His party, the Conservatives, won only 213 seats compared with 393 for the Labour party led by Clement Attlee (1883–1967), a modest but tenacious politician who had been deputy Prime Minister in the war Cabinet. The new Labour Government, which Attlee headed for the next five years, faced a herculean task of recovery and reconstruction. At home it was committed to an ambitious programme of social reform and economic change which earned it a permanent place in British history. Abroad British policy had to be reshaped to fit the vastly altered circumstances of a post-war world from which many of the familiar landmarks had disappeared.

Formidable obstacles stood in the way of this bold programme. The economic cost of the war had been tremendous; a quarter of Britain's overseas assets had been sold to pay for essential wartime imports; a massive external debt of over £3,500 million had been incurred mostly to Commonwealth countries for services rendered; and many valuable export markets had been lost. The result was a huge deficit on the balance of payments in 1945. This could not easily be rectified because of the dominance of the American economy in the western world. In the absence of alternative sources of supply, Britain, like the rest of Western Europe, found herself completely dependent on the American continent for vital food and raw materials at a time when the world was suffering from an acute dollar shortage. The situation worsened still further when Lend-Lease, American aid which Britain had received since 1941, was abruptly terminated by an administration anxious to return to normalcy at once and blissfully unaware of the degree to which the west was now dependent on the American colossus. Britain clearly needed a period of uninterrupted peace in which to recover economically and to carry out the basic reorientation of foreign policy forced upon her by the changed pattern of world politics. Yet barely two years after Field Marshal Montgomery (b. 1887), the British commander in Europe, accepted the surrender of the German armed forces on Lüneberg heath, Britain was drawn into a new power struggle between the United States and Russia which destroyed the high hopes of peace, committed her to a heavy rearmament burden, and seriously retarded economic recovery.

Though diminished in economic and financial stature, Britain by virtue of her role as a world power still sat at the top table in 1945. In those days it was fashionable to depict Britain as the centre of three concentric circles. The first was the association with the new Commonwealth which began to take shape when India, Pakistan, and Ceylon obtained their independence but decided to maintain ties with Britain. The second was the association with Europe to which Britain could never be wholly indifferent and which had plunged her into major wars twice within twenty-five years. Finally, the link with the United States, the dominant member of the Atlantic community: much was made of the 'special relationship', the product of the community of language and culture among the English-speaking peoples, which Britain hoped would enable her to exert influence over American policy. At the same time there was much sympathy in Britain for the sufferings of the Russian people during the war and admiration for their courageous resistance to Hitler, sentiments which helped to weaken the old fear and suspicion of communism. Therefore the new Labour Government felt particularly well placed to remain on good terms with the United States and with Russia, and indeed to act as a bridge between the capitalist and communist worlds.

This was avowedly the objective of the new Foreign Secretary, Ernest Bevin (1881–1951), former leader of the giant Transport and General Workers' Union and the incarnation of the English trade union movement with all its virtues and vices. Bevin was a vigorous, forthright, and earthy figure, Churchillian in stature and personality, a tough negotiator, not without vision but impatient of temperament and unused to the subtle nuances of international politics. That he lacked some of the qualities desirable in a foreign minister is clear, but in retrospect it would seem that the chances of successfully steering a middle course between Moscow and Washington were slight, particularly as Britain was weak economically and beset with serious problems of adjustment in the Middle and Far East.

Even during the war the relations between the United States and Russia were uneasy. Profound ideological differences were barely masked by wartime co-operation, and in the closing stages of the struggle the old fears and suspicions revived on both sides. Superficially, it seemed that the world in 1945 was dominated by two 'super-powers', both immensely strong. In fact Russia emerged fearfully mauled from the war, acutely aware of her own weakness and desperately in need of peace. Initially the Russian leader, Josef Stalin (1879–1953), was probably willing enough to co-operate with the United States and Britain in order to prevent a recrudescence of German militarism. But he remained deeply suspicious of American military power and resented her refusal to share the secrets of atomic power with wartime allies. Nor could Stalin understand western criticism of his policy in Eastern Europe, in view of the Churchill–Stalin agreement in October 1944 which had, in effect, partitioned Europe into spheres of influence.* The United States, on the other hand, was irritated by the cautious, tortuous diplomacy of the Russians and deeply alarmed by Stalin's evident determination to

* Russia was given a 90-per-cent interest in Romania, and a 75-per-cent interest in Bulgaria, Britain a 90-per-cent interest in Greece, and each power had a 50-per-cent interest in Hungary.

remain master of Eastern Europe at all costs. Impatient for quick results, anxious to make the world safe for democracy and free enterprise and to 'bring the boys home' as quickly as possible, the Americans were correspondingly slow to appreciate the deep historical and political roots of Russian policy.

However, in the immediate postwar years it was Britain, not the United States, who clashed most frequently with Russia. In September 1945 when the Council of Foreign Ministers* met in London to discuss the conclusion of peace treaties with ex-enemy states, the Soviet Foreign Minister, Vyacheslav Molotov (b. 1890), demanded that Tripolitania, a former Italian colony in North Africa, be placed under Russian trusteeship in order to give Russia a merchant shipping base in the Mediterranean. Probably Molotov, whose intransigent diplomacy did much to wreck this and subsequent conferences, was only seeking a bargaining counter and had no serious intention of establishing Russia as a Mediterranean power. But this proposal, taken in conjunction with Stalin's demand during the Potsdam conference in July for a base at the Straits, alarmed Bevin. '. . . You cannot help being a little suspicious if a Great Power wants to come right across . . . the throat of the British Commonwealth,' he commented later† in a revealing aside which showed that despite his oft-repeated aversion to power politics, he was as determined as Churchill to protect traditional British interests in the Middle East.

Events in 1946 deepened Bevin's conviction that Russia was deliberately delaying a general peace settlement in the interests of world communism. In January there were acrimonious debates on Persia, Greece, and Indonesia in the Security Council of the newly formed United Nations Organization. Russia's failure to honour a wartime agreement and withdraw her troops from northern Persia set the alarm bells ringing in London. When Britain criticized Russian policy in Persia, Russia retaliated with sharp attacks on British policy in Greece and Indonesia. The Soviet representative, deputy Foreign Minister Andrei Vyshinsky (1883–1954), accused Britain of seeking to impose fascism on Greece by postponing a national plebiscite promised in 1945. He was equally critical of the use of British forces to restore Dutch rule in Indonesia in the teeth of bitter nationalist opposition; the fact that the local British commander tactlessly employed Japanese troops to disarm the nationalists exacerbated the situation. Rather foolishly, Bevin refused to

* Britain, France, Russia, and the United States.

† *Hansard*, vol. 415, col. 1342 (7 Nov. 1945).

permit a United Nations mission of inquiry to visit Indonesia, an action which seemed to reinforce Soviet suspicions of 'British imperialism'.

Some encouraging progress was made in the summer of 1946 towards the conclusion of peace treaties with Italy, Finland, Hungary, and Romania. But when the Council of Foreign Ministers met in December to discuss the German problem, serious disagreements soon disrupted the meeting. On the vital question of reparations the Anglo-American and Russian positions were fundamentally opposed, each side interpreting the key Potsdam agreement* to suit itself. Russia, in an effort to make good the fearful devastation caused by the German invaders, was stripping her zone of occupation of industrial potential and taking reparations from current production regardless of the effects on Germany as a whole. Britain and the United States, anxious to restore the German economy in the interests of European recovery, insisted that Germany must be treated as an economic unit and that reparations must not be a first charge on current production. Meanwhile, the cost of supporting the population in the British zone of occupation reached £80 millions, a heavy burden on the precarious balance of payments. To lighten the load, Britain agreed to the integration of the British and American zones in January 1947, a step immediately denounced by Russia as a breach of the Potsdam agreement and a move towards the creation of an anti-Soviet bloc.

Despite his deep suspicion of Soviet policy, Bevin had not given up hope of playing a mediatory role between Russia and the United States. These hopes were finally dashed with the onset of the Cold War in the spring and summer of 1947. It began with Greece, a British responsibility under the Churchill–Stalin agreement of 1944. British forces helped to put the Greek monarchists in power at the end of the war because Churchill felt that a right-wing government in Greece would counterbalance the forces of change in Eastern Europe. Greek politics were highly volatile and by the autumn of 1946 a new civil war had broken out. The strain of supporting the Greek government against the Communist-led National Liberation Front (E.A.M.) proved too great for Britain. After the worst snow storm for fifty years paralysed British industry at the end of January 1947, the Government reached an historic decision. In February

* The Potsdam conference agreed that the four powers would occupy and administer Germany, each in its own zone of occupation. Germany was to be disarmed, demilitarized, and de-Nazified, and arrangements were made for the collection of reparations.

Bevin informed Washington that Britain could no longer stay in Greece or continue to give aid to Turkey. This led to an equally dramatic change in American policy. In March 1947 President Harry S. Truman (b. 1884) announced that the United States would give military and economic assistance to Greece and Turkey in order to protect 'free peoples who are resisting attempted subjugation by armed minorities and by outside powers'. This was a turning point in postwar history; the American retreat from Europe, which had begun with the end of the war, was over at last. But the ideological coloration of the President's declaration was singularly unfortunate; it could hardly fail to inflame the delicate diplomatic situation and widen the gulf between the capitalist and communist worlds. As the announcement was made on 12 March, two days after the opening of the Foreign Ministers' Conference in Moscow, it is not surprising that the deliberations deadlocked and ended in complete failure in May.

Another decisive event was in the making. By the summer of 1947 Western Europe was on the point of complete economic collapse. In July the dominance of the American economy was plainly revealed when Britain, in accordance with the stringent terms of the American loan of 1945, made sterling freely convertible and removed discrimination against dollar goods. A serious financial crisis ensued and within a month Britain's reserves were so sadly depleted by the flight from sterling that the Government was obliged to reverse the decision. However, help was on its way across the Atlantic. On 5 June the new American Secretary of State, General George C. Marshall (1880–1959), in a major speech at Harvard University held out the prospect of economic assistance on condition that the countries of Europe were prepared to co-operate in a joint programme to apply aid when it was given to them.

Bevin seized the offer with alacrity and took the initiative in calling interested states to a conference in Paris under his chairmanship. Eager to utilize this opportunity of improving the climate of international affairs, and with the agreement of the French Foreign Minister, Georges Bidault (b. 1900), Bevin extended an invitation to Russia. True, Marshall subsequently admitted that he had intended to include Russia in his invitation.* But it is highly unlikely that the Americans, who were already terminating credits to Communist countries, would have offered aid to Russia on terms acceptable to

* That was probably the intention of George Kennan (b. 1904), chairman of the policy-planning staff of the State Department whose report formed the basis of the Marshall offer.

the Soviet government. Molotov came to Paris for a preliminary meeting with Bevin and Bidault but did not stay long. He was suspicious of an integrated recovery programme, fearing that the capitalist west would insist on the abandonment of ambitious Soviet plans for the industrialization of Eastern Europe. That the United States would exert immense political influence over states in receipt of aid seemed axiomatic. In any case, as Marxists believed in the imminent collapse of American capitalism, the wisest course was surely to stand aloof and allow economic chaos to engulf Western Europe. When Molotov broke off the discussions and left Paris, Europe reached the parting of the ways. Fifteen states including Britain formed the Organization for European Economic Cooperation (O.E.E.C.) and staged an impressive recovery with the help of massive injections of American aid. Eastern Europe, however, increased its dependence on the Soviet Union. In July, Russia signed trading agreements with her Communist neighbours. And in September the Cominform, successor to the old Comintern, was formed to co-ordinate the work of Communist parties in Eastern and in Western Europe where Communists withdrew from the French and Italian coalition governments in protest against the European Recovery Programme (E.R.P.).

It was generally assumed in the west that Russia was preparing an all-out economic and political offensive against the capitalist powers. In January 1948 Attlee referred to communism as a new form of imperialism inimical to the welfare and way of life of the peoples of Europe, while Bevin emphasized the need for concerted action by Western Europe to meet this new peril. Events in Czechoslovakia strengthened the belief that communism was entering a more aggressive phase. The Communists, who held key posts in the Czech coalition government, expected to lose support in the forthcoming general election. Taking advantage of a dispute with non-Communist colleagues, the Communist premier, Klement Gottwald (1896–1953), formed a new government on 21 February 1948, consisting largely of Communists and fellow travellers. Simultaneously police detachments and workers' militia units paraded ostentatiously through the streets of Prague. President Eduard Beneš (1884–1948) approved the new government which still included Jan Masaryk (1886–1948), a devoted democrat, a friend of the west, and the son of the first president of Czechoslovakia. On 6 March Masaryk fell to his death in mysterious circumstances. In April the Czech Socialists were incorporated in the Communist party and in May a National Front of Communists and Socialists received a massive majority at the polls for a thoroughgoing socialist programme. The fact that Czechoslovakia was virtually inside the Communist camp before the bloodless *coup d'état* and that the Communists enjoyed much popular support was overlooked in the west, where it was readily assumed that the Communists were now bent on upsetting the established order by force in all countries.

The mounting tension between east and west was accentuated by differences of opinion over Germany. When the four foreign ministers met in Moscow in March 1947 the atmosphere was tense and the chances of agreement slight. The reparations deadlock could not be broken. East and West Germany were going their separate ways, the former organized on socialist lines whereas in the latter the free-enterprise system had been restored. No progress was made on the future political structure of a united Germany. Russia favoured a centralized state, a proposal which aroused western suspicions that she was preparing the ground for a Communist *coup d'état* at a later date; on the other hand western proposals for a federal structure were rejected by Molotov, who claimed that the west was seeking to strengthen anti-Soviet elements in Germany.

The division of Germany deepened after the Moscow conference. In May 1947 a German economic council was set up by the United States and Britain, partly for reasons of efficiency but also to involve the Germans in the management of their own affairs again. To increase production in the western zone Britain and the United States permitted a substantial increase in German steel production, which had been frozen at a very low level by the four powers in 1946.* After another abortive four-power conference, this time in London in December 1947, Bevin's objections to separate political institutions for West Germany weakened. In February 1948 the Benelux countries, Holland, Belgium, and Luxembourg, joined with Britain, France, and the United States at the London conference to discuss the future status of the Ruhr and the creation of a separate West German government.

Predictably Russia denounced all these actions as flagrant breaches of the Potsdam agreement. She retaliated in kind. A Russian-sponsored economic council was set up in the eastern zone and a Communist-dominated people's council for unity was asked to draft a constitution for a separate East German state. On 19 March 1948, in angry protest against western policy, the Russian commander-in-chief, Marshal Vasily Sokolowsky (b. 1897), stormed out of the

* France, fearful of a German military revival, opposed this upward revision of the level of industry agreement.

Allied Control Council, the co-ordinating body set up in Berlin in 1945 to supervise the four zones of occupation.

Early in June the London conference reached agreement on the internationalization of the Ruhr and announced the calling of a constituent assembly to draft a West German constitution. By now the need for currency reform was acute both in the western and eastern zones. Having failed to obtain Russian agreement to a common currency for the whole of Germany, the western powers introduced a new currency into the western zones on 18 June but not into their sectors of Berlin. On 23 June Russia retaliated by ordering a currency reform in the eastern zone which also applied to Berlin. In an attempt to accommodate Russia the western powers offered to accept the *Ostmark* in their sectors of Berlin, with certain safeguards. When Russia refused, they introduced the new *Deutschmark* into West Berlin. Russia replied by imposing a complete blockade on West Berlin. Early in January 1948 the Russians began to interfere with American and British traffic to Berlin. On 23 June all road and rail traffic was suspended and on 10 July all canal traffic ceased, ostensibly for technical reasons. Only an air corridor remained open. Much to the surprise of the Russians, Britain and the United States decided to use this corridor to fly in essential supplies of food and raw materials, a remarkable technical operation which was maintained day in and day out for the next ten and a half months.

In the non-Communist world the Berlin blockade was condemned as a callous and brutal attempt to break the spirit of the courageous Berliners, and to force the western powers out of the city. At the height of the crisis Bevin declared that Britain would stay in Berlin whatever the provocation, an attitude fully endorsed by the Americans without whose support the air lift could not have been maintained throughout the winter.* In the face of determined resistance Stalin, having no desire to challenge the western powers in the air, gave way. In May 1949 Russia lifted the blockade and recognized the right of the western powers to stay in Berlin in return for another round of four-power talks on Germany which quickly ended in deadlock.

Already in March 1948 a fifty-year pact against aggression had been signed in Brussels by Britain, France, Holland, Belgium, and Luxembourg. The United States welcomed this pact and indicated their readiness to underwrite the defence of Western Europe, much to Bevin's satisfaction. Thus in April 1949 the Benelux pact was merged into the larger North Atlantic Treaty Organization (NATO)

* Bevin estimated the American share in the operation at 60 per cent.

in which the United States and Canada pledged military support to the Benelux countries, Britain, France, Italy, Denmark, Norway, Iceland, and Portugal in the event of aggression. The new alliance ended an era of American isolation. No longer could the Americans rely on British naval supremacy to protect them from potential aggressors as they had done throughout the nineteenth century. The weakness of Europe and the power of Russia convinced the United States that a military presence in Europe was essential in the interests of national security.

## II

In the summer of 1950 the attention of the world switched to the Far East. British commitments in Asia had altered radically since the end of the war. By the end of 1947 India, Pakistan, Ceylon, and Burma had become independent, all except the latter opting to stay in the British Commonwealth. However, Britain still remained a power of some consequence east of Suez, with vast commercial and economic interests and bases at Singapore and Hong Kong. So important were her interests in Malaya that Britain was prepared in 1948, at a time of financial difficulty, to commit 100,000 men to a successful struggle against Communist guerrillas. That did not deter her from recognizing the Peking government when the Communists came to power in October 1949, for, unlike the United States administration, the British government believed that ideological differences should not be allowed to obscure diplomatic realities.

American suspicion of Communist China dominated the events of 1950. Since 1945 Korea had been divided, with the Communists controlling the north and anti-Communists the south. The two Koreas coexisted uneasily until 25 June 1950, when North Korean forces suddenly invaded the south. The United States at once promised military assistance to South Korea. Twenty-four hours later the Security Council, in the absence of the Russian delegate, endorsed American military intervention and widened it into a United Nations operation. Britain, as a member of the U.N. as well as a power interested in the stability of South-East Asia, sent a token force to Korea but inevitably the brunt of the fighting over the next three years fell on American shoulders.

The Korean War deepened western fears of Russia. It was widely supposed that North Korea would not have risked war without encouragement from Moscow, and that Russia might well launch a surprise attack in Western Europe. The fears proved groundless but some tense moments lay ahead. When American forces moved into North Korea and approached the Yalu River frontier with China, Chinese fears of the United States mounted. In November, Chinese troops, ostensibly volunteers, intervened in the war and drove the Americans back. The flamboyant and politically inept General Douglas MacArthur (1880–1964), former head of the Allied occupation forces in Japan and now commander of the United Nations forces in Korea, was eager to bomb Chinese targets and wanted to use Chinese Nationalist forces from the island of Formosa in the war. In November 1950 Attlee, deeply concerned by talk about the use of atomic bombs in Korea, flew to see President Truman. Attlee's expression of alarm on that occasion at the prospect of war with China may well have strengthened Truman in his determination not to allow soldiers to dictate policy. Finally, in April 1951, MacArthur was recalled by the President after being warned repeatedly not to express disagreement with government policy.

The Korean War plunged Britain into grave difficulties. In September 1950 the Government decided to spend £3,600 million on armaments over the next three years; in February 1951 this was increased to £4,700 million, an intolerable burden for the straitened British economy. Essential raw materials were in short supply and rising in price as a result of feverish American stock-piling, while a shortage of machine tools made it virtually impossible to fulfil the programme. To meet part of the cost the new Chancellor of the Exchequer, Hugh Gaitskell (1906–63), imposed charges on spectacles and dentures. In protest the Minister of Labour, Aneurin Bevan (1897–1960), resigned, being accompanied by Harold Wilson (b. 1916), President of the Board of Trade, and John Freeman (b. 1915), parliamentary secretary to the Ministry of Supply. This started a feud in the Labour party which weakened its electoral prospects and only ended when Bevan defended Gaitskell at the party conference of 1957 against those who demanded unilateral renunciation of Britain's hydrogen bomb. Bevan argued forcefully in 1951 that massive rearmament would weaken the free world, straining the British economy beyond endurance and crippling the welfare state which was, he believed, the only sure defence against communism. Born in the year of Queen Victoria's Diamond Jubilee, Bevan, one of the great radical figures in the British labour movement, was profoundly convinced that Britain still had a special role to play in world affairs; she could not play it 'tagging along behind the Americans all the time', as he put it, but only if she was strong-minded enough to mediate between capitalist America and socialist Russia.

Attlee's Government had achieved great things since 1945. Substantial progress had been made towards the creation of a welfare state. Overseas Britain adapted herself to postwar realities, although not without great difficulty as the troubles in Palestine and Malaya indicate. And with American aid the British economy was coming into balance by 1949. The Korean War cast a dark shadow over these achievements, and undermined the Government's position. Rearmament precipitated a major financial crisis; gold and dollar assets worth £850 million were lost in the second half of 1951. The sudden death of Ernest Bevin in April 1951 sorely weakened the Government at a critical moment; the tenure of the new Foreign Secretary, Herbert Morrison (1888–1965), was a singularly unhappy one, coinciding with crises in relations with Iran and Egypt. In October, Attlee appealed to the country. Although the total Labour vote was higher than ever, the Conservatives gained 321 seats to Labour's 295 and formed a government under the ageing Churchill. In fact no dramatic changes of policy occurred. Despite their talk of 'setting the people free', the Conservatives retained many controls after the 'bonfire' of 1953–4 and preserved the essential fabric of the welfare state. Abroad they were loyal members of NATO although it is significant that Churchill adjusted the pace of rearmament in 1952, a belated testimony to the correctness of Bevan's analysis.

This was a tense period in international affairs. As the Korean War dragged on the attitude of the United States to world communism hardened appreciably. Many Americans, bewildered by the victory of communism in China, listened with relief to the politically illiterate and rabidly anti-Communist Senator Joseph McCarthy (1909–57), who accused 'pseudo-Communists' in high places of betraying American interests. This feverish mood found expression in 1952 in the passage of the McCarran Act imposing security checks on British citizens as on other foreign nationals visiting the United States. In November the Republicans won the presidential election. General Dwight D. Eisenhower (1890–1969), an upright soldier with limited political gifts, became President, and John Foster Dulles (1888–1959) took over the State Department. An able and dedicated anti-Communist, Dulles was a fierce critic of Truman's 'containment' policy. During the presidential campaign Dulles advocated a 'liberation' policy designed to 'roll the Communists out of Eastern Europe'. In office Dulles redefined American strategy in terms of 'massive retaliation', declaring in January 1954 that the United States would not hesitate to employ nuclear weapons to stop a

Russian land offensive in Europe. This new and dangerously intransigent mood aroused deep concern outside the United States, and many observers feared that the polarization of the world around Washington and Moscow must surely end in war.

The prophecies of doom were confounded for two main reasons. In the first place, Stalin died in March 1953, after ruling Russia with an iron hand for a quarter of a century. His successors began to pursue less rigid policies at home and abroad where it was apparent that Stalin's clumsy and aggressive tactics had merely alerted the imperialist powers and retarded the advance of communism. Secondly, it was dawning on the policy-makers in Washington and Moscow alike that nuclear weapons had transformed international affairs. In September 1949 Russia exploded her first atomic bomb and in August 1953 her first hydrogen bomb. The result was a state of nuclear deadlock; neither power dared use its new weapons to settle disputes when the outcome was likely to be a thermonuclear war engulfing aggressor and victim together. Because of this the United States made no attempt to interfere in Central Europe either in 1953 when disturbances occurred in East Germany or in 1956 at the time of the Hungarian revolution.

Logically this meant that the 'super-powers' must learn to live together in one world. On this strictly utilitarian basis contacts between east and west developed slowly but surely in the second half of the 1950s. Sir Winston Churchill played a leading role in breaking the ice. In May 1953, eager to exploit what he sensed was a favourable moment in world affairs, he called on his own initiative for a summit conference. The Americans were much more sceptical of Russian intentions, fearing a trap to retard the consolidation of NATO. However, they eventually agreed to test Russian intentions and in February 1954 the four foreign ministers met in Berlin to discuss the German and Austrian problems. Little progress was made at Berlin, but the presence of the Russians at the conference table was an encouraging omen. In May 1955 hope rose higher when the four powers finally signed a peace treaty with Austria. In July another four-power conference met at Geneva, this time with the four heads of state in attendance. Again no agreement was reached, but the cordial atmosphere, the 'Geneva spirit' as it was called, encouraged the foreign ministers to meet again later in the year. On the other hand, although the worst of the Cold War seemed to be over, there was no relaxation of military vigilance on either side. Indeed in 1955 Britain decided to manufacture the hydrogen bomb, a decision supported by the Labour opposition on the ground that without the bomb Britain would be far too dependent on the United States in an emergency.*

The mid-1950s saw a significant revival of British influence in world affairs. The Foreign Secretary, Anthony Eden (b. 1897), established a considerable reputation as a successful negotiator in the best traditions of the old diplomacy. His first opportunity arose in 1954 when the western alliance was shaken by a severe internal crisis. In 1950, when the danger of Russian aggression in Europe seemed very great, Britain and France bowed reluctantly to American pressure for the rearmament of West Germany. However, to allay French fears of a revival of German militarism, it was agreed that, although West Germany would be completely independent, the new German units would form part of an integrated European army. In opposition Churchill had commended the idea to West European statesmen; in office he was as unwilling as the Labour opposition to integrate British defence forces with those of the 'Six', i.e. the six West European countries who formed in 1951 the European Coal and Steel Community. Five of the six were prepared to go ahead without Britain. France was at first hesitant. Then in 1954 she totally rejected the concept of an integrated army, feeling that, in the absence of Britain, German units would soon dominate it. And as the danger of war in Europe receded there seemed less justification for entanglements with the old enemy, Germany. The French decision precipitated a serious crisis in the western alliance. Off-stage Dulles warned of an 'agonizing reappraisal' of American policy if the European army was stillborn. Churchill and Eden were in complete agreement with Dulles when he insisted that the occupation of West Germany must be ended and that she must participate in western defence on a basis of absolute equality with other powers. But how could France be reconciled to this? At this critical point Eden made a lightning tour of the West European capitals, which was followed by a conference in London. His efforts were crowned with success. It was agreed that West Germany become a completely sovereign state and join NATO. At the same time, to ensure some degree of control over German armaments without overt discrimination against Germany, a new organization called the West European Union, composed of the Brussels treaty powers with the addition of Germany and Italy, was created to supervise the arms levels of all

* Attlee's cabinet decided in principle to manufacture a British atomic bomb. The Conservatives confirmed the decision. The test explosion of the first British atomic bomb occurred in October 1952 and the test of the first hydrogen bomb in 1957.

members. As a further reassurance to France, Eden promised to keep four divisions and a tactical air force permanently in Europe, a pledge which might have changed the course of history had it been made in 1936. The rearmament of West Germany did not pass unchallenged in the east, where the Warsaw pact was established to co-ordinate the defence arrangements of the East European bloc.

Eden also played an important role in Far Eastern diplomacy in 1954. Since the end of the war France had faced increasing difficulties in her former colonial possessions in Indo-China. In 1949 she set up a sponsored state of Vietnam but was still unable to suppress the Communist-led Viet Minh nationalist movement. Once communism had triumphed on the Chinese mainland, the Americans, who had previously frowned on the activities of the 'French imperialists', decided that Indo-China was, after all, a focal point in the struggle for the soul of Asia and started to give aid to the French. President Eisenhower declared in a famous phrase that if Indo-China was lost to communism, South-East Asia would fall 'like a set of dominoes'. By the spring of 1954 the French were in desperate straits, with Viet Minh forces surrounding their main defences at Dien Bien Phu. Dulles was ready to give further assistance to France. But when he advocated joint air and naval action by the interested powers, Churchill and Eden rejected the dangerous proposal and opted firmly for a negotiated settlement. As the Berlin conference had agreed to further discussions on Korea and Indo-China, representatives of Britain, Communist China, France, Russia, and the United States met at Geneva in April. Early in May Dien Bien Phu fell, a heavy blow to French morale in Asia. However, for once France read the signs correctly and a prominent radical, Pierre Mendès-France (b. 1907), was elected Prime Minister with a mandate from the National Assembly to negotiate a compromise settlement. After weeks of negotiation in which Eden played a prominent part agreement was reached. In July the fighting ceased, Vietnam was in effect partitioned into a Communist north and a non-Communist south, Laos and Cambodia were neutralized, and free elections promised for the whole of Vietnam in 1956. This was the best settlement obtainable in the circumstances. But, as it undoubtedly represented a considerable victory for communism, the United States was deeply offended by what she regarded as British and French readiness to compromise vital principles. Dulles left Geneva in a 'holier-than-thou' mood and refused to be a party to the agreement. The most he would promise was not to use force to disturb the settlement.

Prior to the conference Dulles had pressed for the immediate creation of a Far Eastern defence system comparable to NATO. Eden counselled caution, being anxious not to jeopardize the chances of a political settlement in Indo-China. But once the conference was over he helped Dulles bring the South-East Asia Treaty Organization into being. At Manila in September 1954 Australia, Britain, France, New Zealand, and the United States pledged themselves to resist aggression in South-East Asia. However, of the Asiatic countries only Pakistan, Thailand, and the Philippines agreed to join. The others, led by India's Prime Minister, Pandit Nehru (1889–1964), remained suspicious of American policy; up to a point they sympathized with China, a fellow Asiatic oppressed in the past as they had been by white powers; and most of all they wished to avoid involvement in Cold War strategies certain to distract their attention from the fight against poverty and illiteracy. Dulles, on the other hand, saw world politics as a titanic struggle between the forces of good (capitalism) and the forces of evil (communism). He dismissed with contempt all who refused to take sides. That Eden showed some concern for the susceptibilities of neutralist Commonwealth countries during the Indo-Chinese crisis, was further evidence in the American Secretary of State's eyes of British 'softness' towards communism.

It is surprising in view of his constructive statesmanship in 1954 that Eden should have plunged Britain into the disastrous Suez adventure two years later. As Prime Minister, after Churchill's resignation in 1955, Eden paid great attention to the Middle East, an area of considerable strategic importance to Britain. Since the war the growing power of Arab nationalism had weakened her position; in 1953 she agreed to withdraw from the Sudan and in 1954 from the Canal Zone. Dulles, alarmed by the prospect of a military vacuum in the area, succeeded in persuading Pakistan, Iraq, Iran, and Turkey to join with Britain and the United States in a new military alliance, the Baghdad pact, in 1955. Inevitably American intervention provoked Russian counter-action. She embarked upon a grand political and economic campaign in the Middle East, skilfully exploiting the resentment most Arab states felt for the Baghdad pact powers. In September 1955 Colonel Gamal Abdel Nasser (1918–1970), dictator of Egypt and the natural leader of the Arab world, concluded an arms deal with Czechoslovakia, much to the alarm of the west. When it was rumoured that he had accepted Russian aid to build the mighty Aswan dam, Dulles retaliated in July 1956 by withdrawing an American offer to help finance this project. Eden quickly followed suit. Nasser retorted by nationalizing the Suez Canal, a dramatic gesture calculated to rally the Arab world round Egypt.

Britain, the largest single user of the Canal, was deeply disturbed by Nasser's action, which she immediately condemned as a breach of international law. To some extent fears about access to the Canal were justified after the bitter disputes with Egypt in the 1950s; a country which had steadfastly denied Israeli ships access to the Canal since 1948 might conceivably treat vital British oil cargoes in like manner. Behind these natural anxieties lurked deep-seated resentment of the dwindling power of Britain since 1945, envy of American ascendancy, and much contempt for Egyptian pretensions especially among ex-servicemen. That explains why such a large cross-section of the British public readily accepted Eden's somewhat exaggerated view of Nasser as another Hitler who must be brought to heel at once if law and order were to be preserved in the Middle East.

Negotiations between Egypt and the main Canal users brought no satisfaction to Britain, who insisted on international control of the waterway. On 25 October 1956 a new explosion rocked the Middle East when Israel, alarmed by Arab military preparations, advanced towards the Canal. It is not clear what knowledge, if any, Eden had of the collusion between France and Israel which preceded the attack. What is not in doubt is that Eden and the French Foreign Minister, Christian Pineau (b. 1904), were swift to seize an opportunity of dealing with Nasser. On 30 October an Anglo-French ultimatum was sent to Israel and Egypt ordering the belligerents to withdraw to positions ten miles east and west of the Canal respectively. When Egypt refused to obey, British and French forces landed at Port Said on 5 November after an intensive bombardment.

It was quickly apparent that Britain and France had blundered badly. World opinion turned decisively against them. The United Nations General Assembly condemned the attack while Russia threatened reprisals on London unless Britain withdrew. Most serious and unexpected was the reaction of the United States. Although Eden and Dulles had been on bad terms for some time, the former had never anticipated American opposition to the use of force; after all, the United States had not hesitated to intervene in Guatemala in 1954 when she thought her vital interests were at stake. Not only did the Americans support the Russian demand in the United Nations for an Anglo-French withdrawal, but Washington actually threatened economic sanctions unless Britain gave way. On 6 November Britain announced a cease-fire and by the end of the year all British and French forces had left Egypt.

Absolutely nothing had been gained by the Suez war. Nasser was stronger than ever. International control of the Canal was out of the question, and as the Egyptians had blocked the Canal when the invasion commenced, Western Europe experienced an oil shortage for several months. British prestige in the Middle East suffered an incalculable blow. The Commonwealth was deeply divided and many members resented Britain's failure to consult them. Eden's political career came to an abrupt end. Already a sick man, a factor of some importance in explaining his conduct, he resigned in January to be succeeded by the Chancellor of the Exchequer, Harold Macmillan (b. 1894).

The Suez crisis undoubtedly marked the nadir of British prestige in the postwar world. Curiously enough it left no permanent scars either on the domestic or on the international scene. At home the Conservatives, led with consummate skill by Macmillan, a colourful and highly intelligent political operator, won the 1959 general election with an increased majority over their Labour opponents; Conservative conduct in 1956 played virtually no part in the election campaign, which concentrated on the material benefits of the affluent society. The Commonwealth survived Suez and the breach in Anglo-American relations was repaired when Macmillan and Eisenhower met in Bermuda in March 1957. To some extent this *rapprochement* was facilitated by a clouding over of the international scene. The savage repression of the Hungarian revolution in November 1956 revived old fears of Russian behaviour, and after an uneasy pause in 1957 tension between east and west started to mount again and culminated finally in the Cuban crisis of 1962, which brought the world nearer to war than it had been since 1948.

In October 1957, on the eve of the fortieth anniversary of the Russian revolution, Russia proudly launched the first earth satellite. The *bleep bleep* of Sputnik I as it circled the globe was not only an impressive tribute to Soviet technology but had strategic implications of the highest order. No longer could America rely upon automatic and absolute nuclear superiority in a crisis. Theoretically American cities were now exposed to Soviet missiles. Massive retaliation ceased to be a viable policy (if it ever had been), as Dulles quietly admitted in December in the influential journal *Foreign Affairs*. Profoundly shaken by this realization, America strove desperately to close the 'missile gap'* and retain absolute superiority in this field. After several failures she succeeded in December in

* In fact, as Kennedy discovered when he became President in January 1961, the United States still possessed a very considerable lead over Russia in missiles.

launching an intercontinental ballistic missile. Meanwhile, in order to adjust the 'balance of terror' in America's favour, Eisenhower secure Macmillan's approval for the stationing of intermediate-range missiles in Britain. In December the NATO Council confirmed the American decision to arm NATO with tactical nuclear weapons. It was also agreed that American intermediate-range missiles be stationed in Italy, Greece, and Turkey.

No doubt the new American nuclear policy in Europe and particularly the possibility of West Germany acquiring nuclear weapons gave some cause for alarm to Russia. But fear of Germany was not the chief determinant of Soviet policy now directed by the ebullient and jovial Nikita Khrushchev (1894–1971), First Secretary of the Central Committee of the Communist party since 1955 and Premier since 1958. A confident and assured character, thoroughly convinced of the ultimate victory of world communism, Khrushchev was intent on consolidating Russia's hold over Eastern Europe, which had been badly shaken by the events of 1956. He was especially anxious to strengthen the position of East Germany, the weakest Russian satellite, and hoped to persuade the western powers to recognize the existence of two German states and leave them to negotiate reunification at a later date. To attain these objectives Khrushchev tried in the first half of 1958 to arrange a summit conference. Having failed in this, he changed his tactics and started to probe the weak link in the western position: Berlin. In November he suddenly demanded the setting up of a free city of West Berlin, a proposal which implied the withdrawal of the western garrisons. Failing agreement on this, Khrushchev threatened to hand over Russia's occupation rights to the East Germans and leave the three western powers to negotiate rights of access to Berlin with a sovereign East German state. The three powers firmly resisted what they regarded as an alarming revival of Stalinist tactics. In fact Khrushchev was as careful as Stalin had been to avoid a direct confrontation with the west in Berlin, and continually postponed the signature of a peace treaty with East Germany in the hope that his mixture of bluster and conciliation would weaken the western stand.

Up to a point the bluff worked. The western powers finally agreed to negotiate with Russia on the German question. This was largely Macmillan's doing. In the first place his twelve-day visit to Moscow in February 1959 aroused only scepticism and suspicion in Washington, Paris, and Bonn. But he persevered in his efforts and eventually persuaded Eisenhower to agree to a preliminary meeting of the four foreign ministers. In May the death of the intransigent Dulles removed a formidable obstacle to a *détente.** Although little progress was made on the question of reunification when the foreign ministers met at Geneva, nevertheless the conference was in sight of agreement on an interim statute guaranteeing western rights in Berlin. In September Khrushchev visited the United States and the cordial atmosphere surrounding his meeting with Eisenhower at Camp David seemed to augur well for the future. Finally, in December 1959 a summit conference was agreed to by the western powers, although Macmillan, in response to French and German pressure, was obliged reluctantly to abandon his plan for a controlled arms zone in Germany.

It was a false dawn. When the long-awaited conference met in Paris in May 1960, the climate changed again. Khrushchev's enthusiasm for a summit had evaporated, possibly as a result of pressure from Stalinist elements in the party presidium and from the Chinese, who persisted in regarding any negotiation with the west as a sign of weakness. When an American U2 reconnaissance plane was shot down over Russia on 1 May, Khrushchev had an excuse for breaking up the meeting. On 9 May the new Secretary of State, Christian Herter (1895–1966), publicly defended this violation of Soviet air space as necessary to verify that Russia was not secretly planning an attack on the free world. Three days later President Eisenhower endorsed Herter's ill-advised remarks. Macmillan worked hard to prevent the collapse of a conference on which he had pinned his hopes of a general *détente* in Europe. He managed to persuade Eisenhower to announce the suspension of U2 flights and, as a gesture of appeasement, to promise not to renew them. But the President's advisers set their face against a public apology and the punishment of those guilty, as Khrushchev demanded. The Soviet Premier refused to begin formal discussions and left Paris the next day, but not before he had denounced the west in forthright terms at a dramatic press conference.

## III

The international situation remained unsettled throughout 1960 and into 1961. Macmillan, disillusioned by the summit failure, was content to let the newly elected President of the United States, John F. Kennedy (1917–63), take the lead in handling Russia. An able, idealistic, and powerful leader, the new President, though by no

* Shortly before his death there were signs of a more flexible attitude on Dulles's part towards German reunification.

means averse to negotiation, was firmly determined to resist Soviet expansionism. His first meeting with Khrushchev in Vienna in June 1961 did not lighten the gloom. Khrushchev reiterated his demand for a demilitarized West Berlin and threatened to sign a peace treaty with East Germany by the end of the year. Kennedy left Vienna convinced that Russia was ready to risk war over Berlin. As the tension mounted in July, he ordered a substantial increase in America's fighting forces, and declared unequivocally in a major speech that the United States intended to defend the rights of the west in Berlin, 'the great testing place of western courage', at all costs. By this time the East German government faced an acute internal crisis caused by the steady flow of refugees to the western sectors. In the end Walter Ulbricht (b. 1893), minister-president of the German Democratic Republic, was forced to act, and on 13 August he walled off East Berlin from the rest of the city. After this dramatic gesture, revealing all too plainly the essential bankruptcy of the Ulbricht regime, the tension abated somewhat, perhaps because Khrushchev began to realize that the western powers could not be intimidated into leaving Berlin. After a final dramatic confrontation between American and Russian tanks at 'Checkpoint Charlie', in the heart of Berlin, Khrushchev announced that Russia would not, after all, sign a peace treaty with East Germany.

When the great confrontation between Russia and the United States occurred in 1962, it was caused not by another Berlin crisis but by events in the Caribbean. Cuba had been a thorn in the side of the United States ever since the radical revolutionary Fidel Castro (b. 1927) came to power in 1959. Castro's sweeping agrarian reforms and the increasing dependence of Cuba on the Communist world exacerbated relations with the United States. President Kennedy had already suffered one sharp reverse over Cuba. On coming to power he was confronted with plans for the invasion of Cuba by anti-Castro forces supported by the Central Intelligence Agency (C.I.A.). Reluctantly he allowed the invasion to proceed but without American air cover. When the invaders landed at the Bay of Pigs they were wiped out. Following this, Castro's ties with Moscow increased. In September 1962 Cuba signed a security pact with Russia. Then on 14 October a U2 reconnaissance plane photographed Russian medium- and intermediate-range missile sites under construction in Cuba and the crisis exploded on the world.

The realization that Russia had turned NATO's flank and was now in a position to reduce American cities to piles of radioactive rubble shocked the American people and galvanized Kennedy into action. On 22 October, in order to prevent further missile equipment reaching Cuba, the President announced a complete blockade of the island, demanded the removal of the missiles, and threatened Russia with nuclear retaliation if missiles were ever fired from Cuban soil. As twenty-five Russian ships steamed across the Atlantic towards the line of American blockade ships around Cuba, the tension reached unbearable proportions. U Thant (b. 1909), Secretary-General of the United Nations, intervened in a desperate attempt to avoid war. He asked Khrushchev to stop further missile shipments, and Kennedy to raise the blockade, the legality of which U Thant doubted. Khrushchev was willing to accede to this request but Kennedy would not raise the blockade. On 26 October the crisis deepened further when the White House announced that work on the missile sites was being accelerated. In the next forty-eight hours White House spokesmen raised the stakes by making it clear unofficially that American military action to remove the missiles was imminent. But while deliberately increasing the pressure on Russia, Kennedy simultaneously offered Khrushchev an olive branch, taking up a private offer made by the Russian leader on 25 October to remove the missiles under United Nations supervision provided that the blockade was lifted and that the United States guaranteed the independence of Cuba. When Khrushchev accepted the offer on 28 October, the crisis was over and the world moved away from the brink of war.

Curiously enough relations between Russia and the United States improved steadily after the crisis. Kennedy, despite a notable victory over Russia, showed commendable restraint and welcomed the possibility of a real *détente* between the nuclear giants. At the same time Khrushchev seemed to recognize at last that provocative policies leading to the brink of war were too dangerous in the nuclear age; and as the gulf between China and Russia deepened, he, too, saw some merit in improving relations with the United States. Macmillan was able to play some part in facilitating the *rapprochement*, especially in the field of disarmament where he encouraged Kennedy's efforts to negotiate a ban on the testing of nuclear devices. The efforts were crowned with success in August 1963 when Russia, the United States, and Britain signed a test-ban treaty. This was followed by the creation of a direct teleprinter circuit, the so-called 'hot line', between Washington and Moscow for use in future emergencies. By 1967 Russia and the United States had even succeeded in working out a draft convention to prevent nuclear proliferation, for it was now tacitly agreed in White House and Kremlin alike that the spread of nuclear weapons could only jeopardize the fine balance on which peace rested.

The Cuban crisis registered the continuing decline in Britain's status as a world power. During the crisis Kennedy informed his NATO allies of American intentions but he did not consult them; perhaps it could not have been otherwise when the vital interests of the United States were at stake. But inevitably the coinage of the 'special relationship' with America depreciated still further; war or peace had depended on the nerves of two men, the Premier of the Soviet Union and the President of the United States, while Britain stood by helplessly on the touch line.

Heavy expenditure on nuclear weapons over the years had failed to give Britain any more influence over American policy than that exerted by non-nuclear powers. Indeed in April 1960 Britain had already admitted her inability to maintain an independent deterrent. The abandonment of 'Blue Streak' marked the end of British attempts to produce her own missile. Shortly afterwards Britain entered into an agreement with the United States for joint production of an improved missile, the 'Skybolt'. Immediately after the Cuban crisis British dependence on America was emphasized once more when the United States suddenly cancelled the 'Skybolt' programme, as they had found a more reliable delivery vehicle in the Polaris missile launched from submarines. In an attempt to maintain some semblance of independence in the nuclear arms field, Macmillan negotiated the Nassau agreement with President Kennedy in the Bahamas in December 1963. Certainly Macmillan could claim that he had persuaded the President to sell Polaris missiles to Britain and to concede Britain's right to use them in a national emergency. But it was also agreed that the British submarines carrying these missiles would have to form part of a multilateral force which would be under effective American control.*

There were other signs of a continued decline in British influence in world affairs in the 1960s. Early in 1965 the war in Vietnam, which started as small-scale guerrilla activity in the south in 1958, became more intense. In July President Lyndon Johnson (b. 1908) committed more American forces to the struggle against the Vietcong. In October 1964 the Labour party had won the British general election by a narrow margin, more because of mounting dissatisfaction with Conservative policies at home than out of any positive

* In that these nuclear weapons could only be used with the consent of all the participating members, of whom the United States was the most important.

desire on the part of the electorate for socialist policies.* There was no change in foreign policy. The new Government, led by Harold Wilson, an earnest, able, and artful politician, quickly accepted the American version of the fighting as an act of aggression by Communist North Vietnam rather than as a tragic civil war. Despite Wilson's much-publicized midnight telephone calls to the White House, the fact remained that Britain could exert little influence over United States policy. By the mid-1960s disillusionment with the special relationship was fairly widespread in Britain, a factor of some importance in turning Britain towards Europe.

When the French Foreign Minister, Robert Schuman (1886–1963), launched his plan for an integrated coal and steel community in 1950, the Labour Government remained aloof. Attlee and his colleagues were afraid that the element of supranationalism involved would remove vital economic decisions from British hands. They were confident, too, that Britain, being a world power, had no need to commit herself wholeheartedly to Europe. Ten years later the picture was very different. The European Economic Community founded in 1957 was fast becoming a powerful force (even if it was not nearly so dynamic as ardent advocates of British entry pretended) and a market of growing importance for British goods.

By this time significant changes had occurred in the Commonwealth. In the 1950s Churchill and Eden resisted the mounting pressure for independence in Kenya and Cyprus. But Macmillan, with his customary perceptiveness, recognized the historical inevitability of the processes at work in Africa. Indeed, he greatly accelerated them with his reference to 'the wind of change . . . blowing through the continent' in a masterly speech at Cape Town in 1960. Within two years nearly all the remaining colonial territories became independent: Nigeria and British Somaliland (1960), Sierra Leone (1961), Uganda (1962), Tanganyika, Zanzibar, Kenya, and Gambia (1963). As nearly all of them opted to remain in the Commonwealth, the balance of power swung away from the old white dominions towards the black nations. The significance of this was brought home sharply in 1961 when the newly proclaimed Republic of South Africa decided not to press for continued membership in the Commonwealth in view of strong criticism of her racial policies from several members. On the face of things the Commonwealth was stronger than ever before, a great family of nations 600 million strong, white and coloured, rich and poor, bound by a common

* Labour won 317 seats, the Conservatives 304, and the Liberals 9, giving Wilson an overall majority of 5.

belief in basic human values and well placed to exert great influence on world affairs.

Appearances were illusory. In fact many of the black states were by no means in agreement with British policy; there was much criticism of Britain's cautious attitude towards South Africa and especially of her handling of the Rhodesian problem after that country's unilateral declaration of independence in November 1965. Nor could it be denied that economic ties between Britain and the Commonwealth, although still significant, were a declining asset. As the Commonwealth nations developed diversified economies they needed more capital than London could supply, as well as larger markets for their produce than those in Britain. Thus while inter-Commonwealth trade stagnated, trade between the Commonwealth and the Common Market grew rapidly. And in matters of defence the older white dominions, Canada, Australia, and New Zealand, looked not to Britain but to the United States for protection; as early as 1951, in the ANZUS pact, from which Britain was excluded, the United States had assumed major responsibility for the defence of Australia and New Zealand.

At first Britain tried to obtain the economic benefits of Common Market membership without the political disadvantages of integration by advocating the creation of a much wider free trade area. Negotiations with the Six to this end failed. Whereupon in 1959 Britain formed the European Free Trade Area (EFTA) with Austria, Denmark, Norway, Sweden, Portugal, and Switzerland, a development which divided Europe into two rival economic blocs. Finally, in 1961, Macmillan grasped the nettle firmly and applied to join the Common Market. Well ahead of public opinion on this issue, the Prime Minister played down the political consequences of membership and made great play of the economic advantages to be gained. During the negotiations with the Six in 1962 Britain fought hard to protect Commonwealth trading interests and to retain the considerable advantages of cheap food imports from Commonwealth producers. In the end the application failed, not because Britain was unwilling to make very heavy sacrifices at the expense of countries such as New Zealand, but for purely political reasons. General de Gaulle (1890–1970), President of France after 1958, was pathologically suspicious of British ties with the United States. The Anglo-American nuclear agreement at Nassau aroused his wrath and probably for that reason, in January 1963 he imposed his veto on the negotiations—yet another poignant illustration of the extent to which Britain's future was dependent on the good-will of other countries.

The election of a Labour Government in 1964 did not dispel the uncertainty surrounding Britain's role in the world. Initially the Government was lukewarm towards Europe, because Wilson thought that Britain still had a role to play east of Suez as a peace force extinguishing 'brush fires', as he put it. It was the serious economic plight of Britain in 1965 and 1966 which blew the Government off this course and compelled it, reluctantly, to agree to far-reaching reductions in overseas commitments which dealt a severe blow to lingering hopes of remaining a great world power. The process of disengagement from imperial commitments which began in Greece in 1947 continued at an accelerated pace under Wilson and for much the same reason. In the end he arrived at the same conclusion as Macmillan and made formal application to join the Common Market in 1967. There was a significant change of attitude compared with 1961, partly because public opinion was much more favourable to a British application. Wilson placed the emphasis not on the economic advantages of membership, about which the Government was somewhat reserved, but on the necessity of being part of a larger political unit which would be capable of playing an effective role in world affairs, mediating in the disputes between east and west, and assisting the developing countries in their struggle against poverty and disease.

This bold attempt to find a new identity for Britain as the leader of Europe was frustrated in December 1967 by another veto from General de Gaulle. The setback proved to be only temporary, for the Conservative Government that came to power in June 1970 reopened negotiations with the Six, and when this chapter was written British entry into Europe appeared virtually certain to take place in January 1973.

Summing up and looking back over the two decades reviewed in this chapter, it is apparent that the old relationships between Britain, the United States, the Commonwealth, and Europe have undergone radical and permanent alteration. The special relationship with the United States counts for much less today; the Commonwealth has come of age and diversified its interests even though it still retains considerable significance as a diplomatic grouping. Britain's relations with Europe, seen in the long term, have increased steadily in importance both economically and politically. Prophecy is not the province of the historian. But it is reasonable to suppose that the story of Britain's relations with Europe, as indeed with any international grouping, will continue to be an evolving one. It may well be that Britain can retain some important Commonwealth links despite entry into the E.E.C. Integration in a United States of Europe is likely to remain a distant possibility. And the impact on the Community of its enlargement from six to possibly ten may accelerate welcome changes transforming it gradually into a more flexible and wider association in keeping with Britain's empirical political traditions.

## FOR FURTHER READING*

An excellent account of British foreign policy in this period is F. S. Northedge, *British Foreign Policy: The Process of Adjustment 1945–61* (1962). Also good is C. M. Woodhouse, *British Foreign Policy since the Second World War* (1961). There are stimulating references in W. N. Medlicott, *Contemporary England 1914–64* (1967) and in D. Thomson, *England in the Twentieth Century* (Penguin 1965). For detailed accounts of foreign political development the *Survey of International Affairs*, published annually since 1947 by Chatham House under various editors, is quite indispensable. See also P. Calvocoressi, *World Politics since 1945* (1968) and D. Crowley, *The Background to Current Affairs* (4th ed., 1966). For British politics the *Annual Register*, ed I. S. Macadam, should be consulted.

There are many books on the Cold War, most of which try to allocate responsibility for it in varying proportions to the shortcomings of American or Russian policy. D. Horowitz, *From Yalta to Vietnam* (1965), a well-documented account, and K. Ingram, *History of the Cold War* (1953) are sympathetic to Russia, while D. Donnelly, *The Struggle for the World* (1965) and D. Rees, *The Age of Containment 1945–1965* (1967), a volume in the Making of the Twentieth Century series, take the American side. W. H. McNeill, *America, Britain and Russia: Their Co-operation and Conflict 1941–46* (1953) and L. Halle, *The Cold War as History* (1967) are both scholarly analyses of its origins.

Works on British political personalities include: C. R. Attlee's terse autobiography, *As it Happened* (1954), and F. Williams, *A Prime Minister Remembers* (1961), which is based on interviews with Lord Attlee; H. Morrison, *An Autobiography* (1960); A. Bevan, *In Place of Fear* (1952), a highly interesting political treatise; A. Bullock, *The Life and Times of Ernest Bevin*, I (1960), a standard work; *Hugh Gaitskell 1906–1963*, ed. W. T. Rodgers (1964), a series of appreciative essays. Four volumes of H. Macmillan's autobiography have appeared, *The Winds of Change 1914–1939* (1966), *The Blast of War 1939–1945* (1967), *Tides of Fortune 1945–1955* (1969), and *Riding the Storm 1956–1959* (1971); also E. Hughes, *Macmillan: Portrait of a Politician* (1962) and A. Sampson, *Macmillan: A Study in Ambiguity* (Penguin 1967). Harold Wilson has produced an account of his administration, *The Labour Government 1964–1970: a Personal Record* (1971). Last, but by no means least, is the delightful autobiography of 'Rab' Butler, *The Art of the Possible: the Memoirs of Lord Butler* (1971).

* Place of publication, in this and following reading lists, is London unless otherwise indicated.

For the Suez crisis *The Memoirs of the Rt. Hon. Sir Anthony Eden: Full Circle* (1960) contain much original material and are essential. The most recent account is Hugh Thomas, *The Suez Affair* (1967). M. and S. Bromberger, *Secrets of Suez* (1957) contains revelations from French sources.

On Britain's relations with Europe see J. Pinder, *Britain and the Common Market* (1961) and M. Camps, *Britain and the European Community 1955–63* (Princeton, 1965).

2

# History: Economic and Social

SIDNEY POLLARD

## I

The British economy at the end of the war represented an unusual combination of factors of production. Its capital equipment was run down, neglected, and in part wrecked, and its distribution was much distorted by the urgent needs of total war. By contrast, the fully employed labour force was animated by a very high morale, and was soon to be augmented by the millions returning from the armed services. The economic outlook was, at one and the same time, promising and depressing, a challenge and a despair.

A similar contrast emerged from an examination of the general setting of the economy in postwar Britain. Among the factors lending their support to optimism was the remarkable development, under the stimulus of military need, of new scientific and technological marvels, of which the nuclear bombs dropped on Japan were the most awful examples, together with an immense growth potential for them in a peacetime world. Against this, however, stood the experience of the aftermath of every major victorious war, the last occasion being in 1919–20, when the release from the fighting had led to a febrile boom, beginning as a restocking boom but ending in a purely speculative demand inflation, and ushering in, on its collapse, a severe and lasting depression, which brought in its wake much unemployment of men and resources. It was, in fact, not in Britain alone, but among all the Allies, that the awareness of this earlier experience conditioned economic thinking and planning, and as the years pass it becomes increasingly difficult to recall to what an enormous extent economic policy in the immediate postwar years was, therefore, geared to the events of the 1920s and to the fear of renewed mass unemployment that would follow the expected short-lived boom, rather than to the realities of the late 1940s.

Finally, the public was also aware of the differences from any previous situation. There had been great destruction and great deprivation, on a scale quite different from any that had gone before, and Britain, Europe, and the world were crying out for the goods and services which only the advanced economies could produce, and could produce only inadequately even if they could be going at full blast. It looked, therefore, from this point of view, as though there would be enough work for everyone capable of useful employment, for far longer than was the case after 1918. At the same time, the British public entered upon the years of reconstruction with the live consciousness of the need for economic and social improvement, the belief, fostered in wartime, that victory over the external foe would be matched by the conquest of the internal evils which had caused so much needless suffering in the inter-war years. The enthusiastic reception accorded to the Beveridge Report of 1942, and the remarkable political swing to the left in 1945, were eloquent proofs of this, and demanded a diversion of particularly scarce resources to new social purposes.

It was against the background of these diverse pressures that the Government and its economic advisers had to attempt the delicate task of permitting output to rise without jeopardizing employment and stability. They had to hand one means denied to their predecessors, a rudimentary understanding of the workings of the economy as developed by Keynes in the 1930s. It had been applied in the later years of wartime budgeting, and incorporated into the official policy of all the main parties by the White Paper on *Employment Policy* in 1944,* which made the maintenance of a high level of employment an avowed aim of Government. Whether it was the application, and much greater refinement and understanding, of Keynesian techniques which saved Britain and the world from the 1930s type of depression in the postwar years, or whether more credit should be given to the much greater gap of unsatisfied demand existing after 1945 than in the earlier period, the larger expenditure on arms and on aid, and the pressure maintained by trade unions and similar bodies, is an issue on which it is possible to disagree. There can be no doubt, however, that by the early 1950s it was becoming increasingly clear that the economy, far from settling down around a mean level of 14 per cent of unemployment, as in the inter-war years, was fluctuating round a state of continuous inflation and generally high pressure of demand. In consequence, the main policy issues turned away from questions of unemployment, and towards the rate of growth. With unemployment rarely exceeding 2 per cent (except in regional pockets of much higher levels), economic welfare became, as so often before in western history, dependent on total output. Despite great apparent outward changes, the social structure and the income distribution of Britain remained

* Cmd. 6527.

remarkably stable in those twenty peacetime years. Economic success was therefore measured by the size of the cake, rather than by changes in its shares.

The outstanding feature of the period was that the size of the cake grew. The sense of material well-being, the assurance of economic progress to the point at which moralists began to deplore the prevailing materialism, and the absence of stirring social issues at home, became diffused among nearly all classes, only a small, if significant, minority having failed to share in them. This included old-age pensioners, widows, some members of large families, and some men in irregular employ: a group characterized largely by misfortune or a temporary phase in their lives rather than by permanent social position. For all but this submerged group, hunger, cold, and inadequate clothing were banished for the first time in history. Even medical attention and education now became potentially available to all, though in these respects the rise was a more continuous one since pre-war days. Over most of this period, the majority were inclined to agree with the political slogan that they had 'never had it so good'.

At the base of the greater material comfort was the greater output of home industry. The export of commercial and financial services or the earnings of foreign investments, which once played so large a part in British wealth, dwindled into marginal significance at most. In this period it was real production, productivity, and real incomes that grew together, each one depending on the others. The rate of growth, around a compound 2–3 per cent a year, was much below that achieved by other comparable countries, but it was higher than most optimists had dared to hope in 1945 and it was as great, if not greater, than that achieved in any comparable period in the past. It was the basic economic fact of the postwar years. Moreover, we are likely to underestimate the benefits derived, since the statistics on which the rate is calculated leave out such factors as the improvement in the environment, or changes in capacity or quality of performance of notionally similar consumer goods.

In order to achieve this result, British industry was transformed in one long haul of continuous adaptation. The war had done a great deal to acclimatize managers and workers to an atmosphere of change, and to the new role of scientists and technologists both as originators of change and as controllers of processes, increasingly taking the place of traditional skills and practical experience. The enhanced role played by this type of professional innovation, a new source of initiative independently generated within the body economic, is perhaps the most striking discovery of our time. It clearly has not yet reached its limits. In 1964–5, about £771 million was spent on scientific research and development, 61 per cent of which was accounted for by private industry, 25 per cent by the Government, and the rest mainly by public institutions, such as universities and public corporations. It represented 2½ per cent of the national income, compared with the £300 million, or 1·8 per cent of the national income, spent in 1955–6.

The war contributed greatly to the creation of this new role, and some of the war-based and science-based industries have seen the most spectacular break-throughs, as well as the most rapid rates of progress. Air transport, for example, has been revolutionized by the jet engine, by radar and other electronic control devices, and by the application of discoveries in metallurgy, all of which were speeded or developed during the war. Land transport has been completely transformed by the motor road vehicle, which in many respects has become the most typical product of the mid-twentieth century: in its mass production, its role as a status symbol and as a luxury turned into a necessity, its effect on mobility, its link with a whole network of related technical improvements, and its threat to the amenities of society as a whole. Though in essence the motor vehicle is a development of the inter-war years, registrations rose from 2,559,000 in 1945 to 12,873,000 in 1965, or five-fold since the war. Even railways, though a declining sector (train miles fell from 539 million to 290 million in 1945–65), saw a major technical change in the replacement of steam by diesel and electric traction, and the widespread adoption of electronic control mechanisms.

Atomic power, first applied to peaceful uses when the Calder Hall reactor began to generate electric power in 1956, earth satellites, and many of the marvels of the chemical and pharmaceutical industries were also among the consequences of feverish wartime research and development programmes. The effects of new technologies, whether developed in war or in the years of peace that followed, were however not limited to a few industries, but permeated virtually all of the productive sectors of the economy. Agriculture, for example, benefited by the discoveries of chemistry, by soil science, the biological sciences, and mechanical engineering, among others, and was thus able to keep up its output while employment fell from 1,041,000 in 1945 to 497,000 in 1965 *—the sharpest drop in any single employment group. The coal industry, another area of declining employment, was nevertheless the scene of striking technical progress,

* The figures are for the total working population in agriculture, forestry, and fishing, but the first forms much the largest section.

though much of it consisted in spreading to the majority of the pits the best practices applied in the most advanced ones before the war, and closing most of the others. Again, plastics and artificial fibres have transformed a whole range of capital and of consumption goods, and the gaily coloured, light, and purpose-made materials which are being substituted ever more freely for natural fibres, wood, and metals are as characteristic for the industrial changes of recent years as the grey and black of iron, steel, and coal were for the industrial revolution of the past. As for the other large category of goods used in everyday consumption, food and drink, new methods of preparation and preservation have greatly enlarged the range available at any one time and place, though in this case the quality may not have survived entirely unscathed.

Among capital goods industries, civil engineering, when given the opportunity by large-scale contracts, achieved both spectacular new results and sharp reduction in costs by new techniques and new methods of organization. Even building, perhaps the most conservative industry of all, became in part receptive to labour-saving and mass-production methods, as well as the utilization of new materials.

Changes in British industry belie the view of Britain as a stagnant, conservative economy, though it must appear such by comparison with the fastest-growing economies, like those of Japan or Germany. To bring about even the British rate of growth, there had to be movement and mobility within industries as well as between them. The extent of the flight from agriculture has been noted above; mining, in 1945–65, lost about 170,000 of its total working population; cotton and allied spinning and weaving employed 360,000 in 1937, 317,000 in 1951, and 135,000 in 1965. Against this, construction gained nearly 1 million in 1945–65, the distributive trades 850,000, other services (run down by the war, and somewhat affected by a change in classification) by nearly 3·5 million, and shipbuilding, engineering, and metals by 1·3 million. Again, while the output of all industry rose by 107 per cent, and of manufacturing industry alone by 121 per cent between 1946 and 1965, the index for chemicals rose by 235 per cent, for vehicles by 171 per cent, for engineering and electrical products by 173 per cent, and for gas, electricity, and water by 165 per cent. By contrast, the output of coal fell from 187 million tons in 1947 to 180 million tons in 1965, having risen to its postwar peak of 214 million tons in 1952; and cotton and allied textile spindles in place fell from 25·8 million ring equivalents in 1945 to 5·5 million in 1965, looms from 480,000 to 127,000 in the same period.

Much of this continued the trend of the pre-war years and it was, similarly, accompanied by high geographical mobility, away from Scotland, the North, and Wales, and towards the Midlands, London, and the South generally. Between 1946 and mid-1965, something like 3 per cent of the population, or 1½ million, had transferred from the first group of regions to the second, and since the movement was superimposed on the intra-regional figures, the degree of mobility must be considered substantial. Between the wars, this kind of movement had been welcomed in many quarters, as a voluntary and 'natural' means of relieving the pressure of localized high unemployment, and providing labour for the growth areas. Since 1945, however, it has been viewed with mixed feelings. For the magnetism exacted by the Midlands and the South caused increasing congestion, leading to rising economic and social costs there, while wasting social capital in the areas losing the population and delaying their possible rehabilitation. Above all, this costly mobility seems unable to even out the inequality between the regions and perhaps even helps to aggravate it, for the North and the West, the areas of the older industrialism, continue to show higher unemployment rates, lower wages and incomes per head, and poorer social facilities. Legislation and administrative action since the war have therefore been designed to take industry to these regions, and to control new building elsewhere. The Town and Country Planning Act of 1947, the Distribution of Industry Act of 1958, and the Local Employment Act of 1960, among others, which give powers to influence the decisions of private industrialists, have been supplemented by positive directives, as in the case of the siting of the new continuous steel strip mills. Yet migration continues, sensitive as ever both to social and economic stimuli.

There has necessarily also been industrial and social mobility. The men in the expanding motor-car works of Coventry, Luton, or Dagenham came, not only from other regions, but also from other industries, and often from other skills. Indeed, the concept of 'skill' itself, undermined by the new machine technology and by growing provisions in technical colleges and organized training schemes in place of simple apprenticeship, is beginning to undergo a change, to refer to intelligent adaptability as much as to the acquisition of a fixed corpus of skill. A new chapter in the financing of formal training opened with the Industrial Training Act of 1964, which is gradually being applied to all major industries, and authorizes the compulsory levying of all firms to finance training schemes approved by the industry as a whole.

At the same time, the numbers of 'white-collar' workers were growing apace, both in the offices, laboratories, and managerial hierarchies of the day's more complex industries, and in the service industries such as commerce, finance, and distribution. Between 1951 and 1959 alone, according to Guy Routh's calculations, professional workers increased by 26 per cent, clerical workers by 21 per cent, but manual workers by only 4 per cent. In those years, to be sure, the pay differential between them and the 'blue-collar' manual workers narrowed considerably, and made the former increasingly willing to join their associations to the T.U.C., but much of the social difference still survived, in monthly rather than weekly pay, in canteen facilities, or in the treatment during temporary illness or redundancy, and the move from one to the other is still widely held to constitute a 'rise'. Millions of families have, in the nature of things, experienced this rise in their own lifetime, and are enjoying the satisfaction of having 'risen' by their own efforts, without the full consciousness that they are merely part of a very large sweep of social change.

Finally, industrial change was also accompanied by consolidation and further concentration of industrial power. In some instances, as in a few spectacular 'take-over bids', and in the creation of personal empires in the newspaper, real estate, and retail distribution field, this concentration has been much in the public eye. But ordinarily the process went on quietly behind the scenes, creating combinations by financial control, by holding companies or by other means that may leave the original name and its associated good-will intact. There has also been a striking further increase in the proportion of share capital held by insurance companies, unit trusts, and similar institutions: in 1965, insurance companies held over £4,300 million of the capital of private companies, and were increasing their holdings by a net £300 million a year. With the number of shareholders typically running into thousands, these are often much the largest blocks of holdings, and in recent years insurance companies have shown signs of departing from their traditional neutrality towards the management of firms in which they hold an interest. Some form of collaboration of firms with the identical major shareholder cannot, therefore, be entirely ruled out.

The attitude of the State towards this concentration has been understandably ambivalent, encouraging the potential economies of rationalization, while attempting to minimize the risk of monopolistic powers over markets, labour, or local amenities. In some cases, as in 1959–60 in the aircraft manufacturing industry, which has the

Government and public boards as its major customers and faces powerful foreign competition, the Government actively encouraged mergers and the creation of monopolistic groups under private control. In general, however, successive administrations of both parties have pursued an active policy to break restrictive practices. The Monopolies and Restrictive Practices Commission was set up in 1948, largely to report on industries referred to it by the Board of Trade. A further Act of 1956 put teeth into the legal provisions, enacting, on the one hand, the compulsory registration of all restrictive trading agreements, and on the other hand setting up the Restrictive Practices Court, to decide on individual agreements referred to it. At the same time, however, individual producers were given specific powers to enforce the resale price maintenance (r.p.m.) of their own goods. The effects of this legislation were mixed. Nearly half of the over 2,000 agreements registered were abandoned (or had the restrictions removed) at once or after an adverse test case decision. Yet the court could work its way through the agreements only very slowly, and several of them were, in fact, allowed to stand. On the opposite side, the newly strengthened power over r.p.m. has been largely nullified by the ability of supermarket operators and other low-cost retailers to give discounts, forcing others to do likewise, and by the growing practice of large retailing firms to market their own branded product, so that far fewer goods were sold under r.p.m. in 1965 than in 1956. The Commission, for its part, also uncovered a few spectacular cases of monopolistic profiteering, in which Government pressure and the accompanying publicity led to sharp price reductions.

The shrinking markets in the bad years before the war had led to market sharing, 'rationalization', and destruction of productive capacity. For the full-employment, inflationary economy of the postwar years, the drive to create competitive conditions, and the emphasis on expansion and the conquest of new markets, were similarly appropriate, particularly until the early 1950s, when there was ample demand everywhere. Later on, foreign markets became more difficult, because more competitive, but the buoyancy at home remained. There were, it is true, substantial fluctuations in the economy in 1945–65, some of which will be noted below, but there was nothing to correspond to the trade cycle hard-core unemployment with which the world had become familiar in the previous century or more, and there was no re-emergence of that million and a half of unemployed men in Britain alone.

Instead, there was inflationary pressure. Dammed up during the war years, it was carefully contained in the late 1940s and, being fed by new streams, it never totally subsided. The speed of the price rises varied, but the direction remained upward. Between 1947 and 1965, on one official set of figures, the cost-of-living index rose by about 102 per cent, i.e. it more than doubled. In retrospect, over a bare twenty-year period, this seems a very substantial price inflation, but as it proceeded by only a few per cent per annum, it never looked like getting out of hand.

The inflation had curiously little effect on the savings habits of any except a small minority of the very wealthy or the speculators. Securities redeemable at par in cash naturally lost in attractiveness, for example, and equities protected from inflation (not to mention pictures or jewellery) became more desirable to hold, but on the whole, savings continued to accumulate even at rates of interest which were, when the erosion of capital value by inflation has been taken into account, wholly negative.

The effects of the price rise on the distribution of incomes was much more important. *Rentiers*, pensioners, and others living on fixed incomes suffered most. Owners of land rent-fixed for long periods also tended to see their increases lag behind the price level, except for those landlords fortunate enough to own building land or land in city centres, whose property was often increased in value beyond the dreams of avarice by social forces quite outside their control. Wages not only kept in step with prices, but over the period as a whole shared fully in the increase of real incomes per head; salaries varied greatly, but in general did less well than wages. Farm incomes fluctuated violently, influenced by outside factors, such as the farm-price reviews and the subsidies, but in general were exceptionally high in the immediate postwar years, to fall back by the early 1960s to more traditional comparable levels. Profits, the residual incomes, did relatively well, as always in times of rising prices.

While the share of wages in total incomes rose slightly above the 40 per cent around which it had fluctuated for the past century, the differentials between skilled and unskilled, which had been narrowed still further in the Second World War, failed to widen again after: by the 1960s, unskilled wage rates were around 85 per cent of those of skilled workers, and actual earnings around 80 per cent. Other anomalies had inevitably crept in when a steady money wage increase of around 5 per cent a year was required merely to keep real wages constant. Railway workers, for example, traditionally paid less than comparable tradesmen elsewhere because of their job security, failed to gain compensating wage increases when security lost its value and when dismissals became a possibility in this declining industry. Any chances of compensating wage rises in other 'secure' occupations, like urban passenger transport or nursing, were reduced by the influx of immigrant labour with poor bargaining power. By contrast, wages in the growth industries, like coal in the 1940s and motor manufacture in the 1950s, which had to be well above the average to induce workers to move into them, stayed high even after the rapid recruiting drive was over. In any case, the growing share of overtime and piece earnings in the total, and the 'wages drift', i.e. the payment of wages above the agreed rates, further distorted relative positions. A consistent wages or incomes policy, that would attempt to align different occupations by some common-sense criteria, and relate increases to production available, proved impossible to draw up, let alone enforce, though mooted repeatedly in different quarters.

Wage and salary levels were clearly among the key cost factors entering into the inflationary spiral. Whether their rise, in monetary terms, was cause or effect of inflation, whether in other words the price rise was one induced by 'cost-push' or 'demand-pull', was hotly debated in those years: in retrospect, it seems that each was the dominant factor over part of the period. A result of the British experience, however, was that a framework came to be accepted within which a trade union, for example, could safely ask for wage increases at fairly regular intervals and receive them, since higher costs could be passed on, and these would lead, in turn, to demands for higher wages. Trade unions, now enlarged by additional members and some amalgamations since the 1930s, and accustomed by wartime practice to engage in joint industry-wide bargaining, followed each other in regular 'rounds' of wage demands, echoed by other trades until it was the first one's turn again. The incomes of other classes showed the same volatile upward trend in an era of virtually full employment of resources.

Money wages increases were not wholly inflationary, for in part they were matched by productivity increases. But such increases in output per man-hour or man-shift were by no means spread evenly among the different industries and occupations. They were, in general, most marked in the mass-production industries and least evident in personal services, and the widening differentials between labour-intensive and capital-intensive industries, which are found in all progressive economies, were clearly evident in the changes of relative prices. Thus between 1948 and 1962, while the price of motor vehicles rose by 25 per cent and of radio and electrical goods by 60 per cent, food prices rose by 79 per cent, those of communication services by 89 per cent, and of other services by 69 per cent.

An industrial situation which many workers came to accept, however doubtfully and however slow they were to forget the searing experience of the pre-war years, that there were always jobs to be had and that dismissal was no longer an ultimate deterrent, required new concepts of discipline and incentive. Scientific management enjoyed an unwonted vogue, and the concept of the worker as a full human being whose co-operation has to be sought rather than enforced, spread from the best firms to the average. A significant by-product was the difficulty of recruiting men to the position of foremen, as the pay differential was being eroded at the same time as much of the authority. Yet men were reluctant to give up their protective and restrictive trade practices, evolved in less fortunate days and based on the fear of redundancy, and the events of 1966–7 have shown that they were not entirely unjustified. By the end of the 1945–65 period there came to be some signs in individual trades such as shipbuilding or printing that unions even in declining industries could adapt rather than restrict, but a total change of heart would require a break-through in the environment, an eager acceptance of change by all sectors of the population, and this has not occurred either in expanding or in contracting industries.

The total rise in real incomes, paralleling that of total output and amounting to around 60–70 per cent over the twenty years, lifted the families of most men in full employ well above subsistence levels and into what some Americans have called 'the age of mass consumption'. Put differently, since 1945 the increases in consumption expenditure were found to only a small extent in such items as food, or other necessities such as clothing. Instead, families spent their additional margins of income increasingly on non-necessities, and among these particularly on those commodities which could meet the opportunities of rising demand by falling relative prices, achieved precisely by their growing markets and the opportunities of mass production.

The motor-car, which even in 1945 was still a middle-class status symbol, became by the 1960s a near-necessity for clerical and skilled manual workers, and is destined to spread wider still, while two-car families are becoming common among the middle classes. Already about one-half of all families possess a car. Similarly, well over three-quarters of all households possess radio and TV sets and electric vacuum cleaners, about half possess washing machines and sewing machines, and electric or gas cookers have become well-nigh universal. Between 1946 and 1965, the quantity of food consumed rose by 57 per cent and of clothing by 94 per cent, but the volume of sales of furniture and household goods, radio and electrical goods rose by 177 per cent, of electricity by 413 per cent, and of motor-cars by 1,288 per cent.* As part of the same affluence, however, expenditure on some 'luxuries' which did not fall in relative price, such as dining out or holidays abroad, also increased spectacularly. There can be little doubt that figures of this magnitude represent a change in the style of living for the majority of the population in the space of less than twenty years. On the one hand, many of these innovations freed housewives from the worst of the domestic chores, and allowed them to go out to work with less detriment to their homes, and the continued high figure of females at work, about one-third of the working population, has itself led to important social changes. On the other hand, the new potential freedom to act or to enjoy one's leisure exerts a profound influence on many lives, particularly on the young who are, like the mass-production goods they favour, becoming increasingly classless.

Consumption of this kind reacts fairly quickly to income, and even the more durable goods, which are generally acquired by some hire-purchase method, can reflect short-term changes in prosperity. Housing, however, and the general amenities of an urban environment, cannot. As a result, the rehabilitation of British housing has not kept pace with the general prosperity. A costly building programme, it is true, has erected some 5½ million dwellings since 1945, including those built for local authorities, for other public bodies, and privately, and represents around one-fifth of total gross fixed capital formation year by year. One family in three now lives in a postwar dwelling. Yet the combination of a growing and shifting population consisting of an increasing number of separate households, the natural decline of old property, assisted often by the neglect of their owners who were discouraged by rent control, and, lastly, rising standards of expectation which make formerly marginal residences no longer acceptable, created new demands for housing throughout the period almost as fast as old ones were being met. The housing shortage was much less severe in 1965 than it was in 1945, after the capital running-down of the war years, but it was serious still, and, it may be remarked in parentheses, in this it was representative of other social capital, like hospitals, schools, and

* Current national consumers' expenditure at constant (1958) prices, according to the National Income Blue Books.

roads, all of them much improved and enlarged in the twenty post-war years, yet all much further behind needs and expectation than any equivalent provisions of the private, profit-making sector.

There were several distinct stages in the building programme, partly determined by the incentives provided by governments of different political complexion. The postwar Labour Government favoured council housing, and little private building took place. In the 1950s private building, particularly for sale to middle-class owners rather than for renting, was much encouraged by different Conservative Ministers, and formed a growing share in a growing total: by 1958, investment in dwellings in the private sector for the first time exceeded that in the public sector by a substantial margin, and in the early 1960s approached nearly double its level. From 1964 onwards, however, municipal building was again favoured and private building fell sharply. In the early postwar years, the building pattern followed that of the 1930s and, apart from the bomb-damage replacement, tended to concentrate on suburban estates, usually around both edges of the 'green belts' which were among the positive achievements of the Town and Country Planning Acts. The resulting sprawl, inconvenience, and loss of agricultural land, as well as the dereliction of the inner areas of cities and towns, were beginning to lead to a reappraisal by the late 1950s, and it may be that the Barbican scheme in London, and the attempts of such other cities as Liverpool and Sheffield to site new dwellings near the urban centres, will be more widely followed in the future. An alternative solution was tried with the creation of wholly 'new towns' under the New Towns Act of 1946. Twenty-one such towns in Great Britain (and one in Northern Ireland) have been set up under their Development Corporations, and under the terms of the 1959 Act, four of them were found sufficiently mature to be transferred to the newly created (Central) Commission for New Towns. By the end of 1965, well over £400 million had been advanced for their construction. On the whole they have proved successful commercially, and were not without some achievements socially. Among a second generation of such towns planned at the end of the 1945–65 period were some that were to become large cities and major regional centres in their own right.

The new affluence described here, however, was not universal, though it has become much more widespread and by the 1960s embraced a broad band within the income pyramid, of perhaps 10 million households among the lower middle classes and the skilled and semi-skilled workers, who were certainly outside it in the 1930s.

Certain groups persistently remained below it, and their numbers were in 1955–65 rising rather than declining. In part, no doubt, the rise in numbers may have been illusory, since it is merely the shortfall from a rising standard, yet there is sufficient absolute measurement in the concepts of nutrition, or the 'national assistance' level, to point to the persistence of real poverty and want in an affluent society. A recent estimate puts the totals falling below that acceptable level as 7 to 8 million persons, of whom the largest categories include 3 million persons in low-wage occupations or with very large families, 2½ million persons of pensionable age, ¾ million mothers and children without fathers, ¾ million in families whose breadwinner is disabled, and ½ million dependent on an unemployed person. Out of this larger number, the persons actually living below the basic assistance rates, widely agreed to be inadequate, were estimated to number 2½ million, in the not unfavourable year 1960.

After the major reform of the welfare provisions in 1946–7, no new means were tried throughout the whole of the following period to deal with this apparently intractable one-seventh of the population: on the contrary, some measures, such as the relaxation of rent control, were bound to aggravate the problem still further. Some of the main categories of people in want, like those of old age or suffering incapacity or unemployment, were such that few working-class families could deem themselves immune from them. The problem, therefore, was not merely that of a submerged seventh, but of a much larger number at critical periods in their lives.

## II

No account of the development of the British economy in 1945–65 can limit itself to home affairs. The context of world trade and production continued to be of major significance even if perhaps in a manner different from that of the inter-war years. In the early postwar years, the major new adverse factors were the loss of overseas investments, and the relative decline of the gold and currency reserve as a proportion of the overseas trade it has to finance. In more recent years, it also appeared that the failure of home production, and its efficiency, to grow at the same rate as those of other leading countries had reacted adversely on the export performance.

In the course of the war, about one-quarter of Britain's overseas investment had to be sold off, and the remainder was matched, by 1945, by an almost exact equivalent of around £3,500 million of British debts to other countries accumulated during the war years.

In terms of annual payments, there was still a positive net balance, since British investments returned higher yields than the largely official holdings of foreign owners, but it was greatly reduced from the £175 million net which 'interest, profits, and dividends' had yielded in 1938. To that extent, production had to be directed to exports in place of living off past investments.

In the late 1940s, the problem was aggravated by a worsening in the terms of trade, requiring a still larger volume of exports to pay for the same quantity of imports. Indeed, it was calculated by the British planners that, in order to pay for the pre-war volume of imports in these adverse conditions, as well as permitting some slight resumption of capital exports and/or a strengthening of the reserves, exports would have to rise by 75 per cent over the pre-war volume. This target, unrealistic though it seemed at the time, was reached by 1950, while imports were held at around 10 per cent below the pre-war figure. Yet even this surprisingly successful performance was not enough to ease the foreign balance of payments, for the terms of trade worsened further, government expenditure abroad continued much higher than had been allowed for, and there was also a substantial leak or flight of capital abroad. Exports continued to mount, and the balance continued weak, throughout the period of the Korean War, which further sent up the costs of raw materials and others of our normal imports.

From 1952 onwards the terms of trade began to move in Britain's favour, and despite occasional fluctuations continued their upward trend to 1965, thus greatly alleviating, in one respect, the strain on the balance of payments, since the necessary imports required a progressively smaller volume of exports. At the same time, however, sales abroad became increasingly more difficult, as foreign competition arose to meet a more discriminating market. The problem of exports, therefore, changed from that of sparing sufficient from the starved home market, to the more normal commercial one of selling in a competitive and price-conscious environment.

In some respects, the export performance was not discreditable after 1950 either. As a proportion of the gross national product, the exports of goods rose from 10·3 per cent in 1938 to 10·9 per cent in 1946 and 15·5 per cent in 1965, exports of goods and services together from 14·0 per cent to 16·4 per cent and to 21·1 per cent. These proportions to some extent indicate the effort and the adjustment involved. Growth has been particularly satisfactory in chemicals, machinery, and transport and communications equipment. Yet the growth of the national product itself has been slow compared with that of other countries, and the comparative export achievements, therefore, similarly disappointing. Thus, in 1950, Britain accounted for 28 per cent of the export of the five leading countries, the U.S.A., Britain, Germany, France, and Japan. By 1959 this had dropped to 21 per cent, and by the first two quarters of 1965 to 18 per cent. The British share of the total world market has dropped similarly, and in some commodities, like shipbuilding, it has slumped drastically. The decline is strongly associated with the fact that British export prices, like British prices in general, have tended to rise faster than those elsewhere. There has been no marked regional trend in the relative loss of overseas markets: apart from a fall in exports to the Common Market countries, and rise in exports to EFTA countries, which are accounted for by the tariff barriers and preferences respectively, the loss has been fairly uniform throughout the world.

In absolute terms, however, exports grew and were, by the 1960s, higher than ever before, as well as constituting a larger proportion of home output than in any other major economy. Out of these exports it proved possible to pay not merely for a heavy burden of government expenditure overseas, but also to engage once more in a considerable amount of overseas investment, which had virtually come to a halt in the inter-war years. In the 1950s, these net investments exceeded, on average, £240 million a year (of which £150 million was private investment), so that the portfolio held abroad may have risen by well over £3,000 million since the war. Certainly 'property income from abroad' has risen, according to the official statistics, from £292 million in 1946 and £788 million in 1955 to £1,518 million in 1965, or more than five-fold, while prices little more than doubled. At the same time, however, investments in Britain by other countries appeared on a substantial scale for the first time in nearly two centuries. American capital was particularly strongly represented, and achieved a powerful or dominant influence in certain industries, like motor manufacture or oil refining: United States investment here has been estimated at $619 million in 1943 and $4,194 million in 1960, but other countries were also active. One official estimate puts private British investment abroad in the course of the five years 1961–5 at $4,564 million, but foreign investment here at no less than $3,354 million. Total 'property income paid abroad' rose from £166 million in 1946 to £715 million in 1965.

The total effect of all these disparate influences was to make the British economy far more vulnerable to any excess of imports over exports not fully covered by 'invisible earnings' from services, or overseas investment, than at any time before. This effect has been further aggravated by the failure of the current reserve in gold or dollars to grow in step with the volume of trade and finance: a weakness from which other countries, notably the United States since about 1960, were also inclined to suffer. In Britain, for example, while the volume of foreign transactions rose from under £2,000 million in 1946 to over £8,000 in 1965, or four- to five-fold, the reserve remained constant at somewhere just above £1,000 million. It meant that instead of acting as a buffer, evening out temporary excesses of payments due one way or the other, the reserve had become, relatively, so small that it could hardly be used at all: for in a period of loss, out-payments were taken as a sign of weakness which immediately caused large withdrawals of funds and credits from speculative centres abroad and threatened to turn every minor retreat into a rout. It should be added that the reserve was even more vulnerable than it need have been, because it was in effect the reserve for the whole of the sterling area, and subject therefore to stresses emanating from outside this country as well as from within.

This was particularly unfortunate since the rise in home prices seemed to have settled down at a level permanently out of step, or out of equilibrium, with the rest of the world. Thus when full employment obtained in Britain, together with a satisfactory growth rate, imports rose sharply without an immediate parallel expansion in exports or in any other earnings of foreign currency, and a drain on the reserve began, accompanied by adverse effects on the exchange rate of the pound sterling. No postwar Government was prepared to allow these movements to continue for any length of time, or to reverse them by any means other than a deflation sufficiently sharp to achieve a cut in imports, possibly a rise in exports, and a restored foreign balance. It thus appeared possible for Britain to have an annual growth rate of around 4 per cent *or* to balance her foreign payments, but not to do both at the same time. Basically, this was the general framework of the 'stop–go' policies which, between 'go' years of around 4 per cent growth and 'stop' years of around 0–1 per cent growth, achieved an average growth of around 2½ per cent a year.

The similarity with the pre-war depression years, in which the problem also appeared to be the inability of Britain to sell sufficient exports to keep the home economy buoyant, was superficial and misleading. The plain fact was that the world of the 1940s was so conscious of the economic tragedy of the 1930s as to bend all efforts to avoid a repetition of the mistakes made then. In the event, the mass unemployment and destruction of capital were avoided. Much to their own surprise, the leading nations maintained full employment and a high level of demand throughout, despite occasional fluctuations, and intractable pockets of unemployment in certain industries or regions in the U.S.A., Belgium, Italy, and elsewhere. How far the international economic organizations set up after the war were responsible for this success is debatable, but there can be no doubt that they have provided a framework of international economic co-operation, in the non-Communist world at least, which significantly affected the action of each individual state.

Among the most important of the early creations were the International Monetary Fund, the World Bank (1944), and the General Agreement on Tariffs and Trade (1947). The first created a fund, provided by the contributions of member states in gold, dollars, and their own currency, on which members could draw to correct temporary payment unbalances. The second provided for long-term loans, mainly to less developed countries. G.A.T.T. laid down certain standards of conduct and, in particular, prohibited certain kinds of discrimination in international trade. Each of them took great care not to infringe the sovereignty of member countries, and each agreement allowed for emergency action at a time of acute unbalance, yet the total effect of them was the avoidance of the kind of selfish and self-defeating policies which had worsened the effects of world depression in the 1930s. At the same time, the hopes of the sponsors for a major and progressive liberalization of world trade have not been fully realized. Countries in balance-of-payments difficulties, such as the developing nations after the price falls of the early 1950s, the U.S.A. (at times), and, above all, the United Kingdom, could not be expected to dismantle their often complex and delicate systems of protection. Countries with large surpluses, like Germany and France, found it impossible to adopt the nineteenth-century British method of massive foreign investment; instead, they accumulated gold, reducing the central reserves of the sterling and dollar areas in the process and making them less secure.

Within Europe, however, economic collaboration went much further. The Organization for European Economic Co-operation (O.E.E.C.) was set up in 1948 to distribute Marshall funds and to lower trade barriers; in 1950 the European Payments Union (EPU) was formed as a mechanism for settling balances multilaterally, and making available intra-European credits: in 1958 its place was taken by the European Monetary agreement. Meanwhile, the first limited steps of the 'Schumann Plan', which had created the Coal and Steel

Community of 1953, had been greatly extended by the treaty of Rome, concluded in 1957. Under its terms, the six countries concerned, namely Germany, France, Italy, Belgium, Holland, and Luxembourg, began in 1958 a 12–15 years' process (since speeded up) of reaching by stages a completely free 'common' internal market among themselves, and a unified tariff towards the outside world. The treaty of this European Economic Community, E.E.C., also necessarily involved the progressive equalization of other economic activities among the 'Six', including social, fiscal, and colonial policies.

Britain, in common with some other countries, was invited to join at the time, but remained outside. Among the reasons for this were her links with the sterling area and the cheap food producers of the Commonwealth and overseas regions generally; an agricultural support policy working by subsidies rather than by tariffs; and Britain's unwillingness to give up her sovereignty over such matters as immigration, investment, and social policies, which appeared to be the minimum corollaries of joining the E.E.C. Nevertheless, the emergence of a large unified market of around 180 million souls, including some of the wealthiest and most rapidly growing economies of the western world, presented certain threats which the United Kingdom thought to minimize by an association of her own, the European Free Trade Area, EFTA, also known as the 'Seven', consisting of the three Scandinavian countries, Switzerland, Austria, and Portugal, besides Britain.* This group, set up in 1959, looked from the beginning to be less permanent and less viable than the rival E.E.C. It is geographically scattered, and has been growing less successfully than the E.E.C., and all the other partners combined do not add up to the British home population. Further, EFTA did not aim at a common tariff, or at common social policies, merely at free trade among its members. The initial impression that EFTA was a mere temporary bargaining counter against the E.E.C. was partly dispelled by its success in matching the accelerated internal tariff reductions of the latter, step by step, without losing cohesion. Yet it seemed likely that if Britain did eventually obtain admission into E.E.C.,† EFTA would be dissolved without much ceremony, several of the other members would join with her, and those prevented by their status of neutrality from doing so would seek other forms of association.

* Finland adhered later.

† See W. Carr's account in chapter 1, pp. 25–6, of the political background to the E.E.C. negotiations.

These negotiations serve to illustrate the extent to which governments, in Britain as abroad, had been participating in economic decision-making since the war. The postwar Government had inherited an almost complete apparatus of economic control, covering imports, production, investment, prices, and incomes. A large part of this was dismantled as soon as conditions permitted, and, with a slight relapse in 1950–2, because of the Korean War, the process of abolishing 'direct controls' was, in the main, completed by 1954, including both raw material controls and consumer rationing. Yet a powerful system of steering or indirect control remained and became part of the accepted scene of the postwar years.

Only a few areas of its operation can be mentioned here, and they but briefly. Investment, as one of the keys to the future, remained under fairly severe control throughout. Home capital formation was freed from direction in 1959, but overseas investment continued to require government sanction. On the positive side, finance to smaller firms was made available via the Industrial and Commercial Finance Corporation, set up in 1946 and reorganized in 1959; to bridge the temporary needs of larger firms, the Finance Corporation for Industry was sponsored, using funds supplied largely by the banks. At the same time, investment at home was encouraged by varying tax concessions.

Industrial relations also emerged from the war within a tight strait-jacket of control which was not entirely lifted at once. The pre-war Trade Boards were transformed into more aptly named Wages Councils in 1945 and were given greater powers, while the originally separate bodies for road haulage and catering workers were merged into the general scheme in 1959. Including agriculture, covered by separate Boards, nearly 6 million workers were then nominally covered by statutory wage fixing. In addition, the Government from time to time exerted direct influence on the wage negotiations in nationalized industries, and on the salary rates of public employees, such as school teachers, whose pay terms were normally settled by independent authorities.

These groups, over which there was some direct control (and including the Civil Service) embraced well over 40 per cent of the employed population, but beyond them, some initiative and control over the terms and conditions of employment remained for all workers. Compulsory arbitration by Statutory Order 1305 was carried over into the peace years, and even in 1951, when the order was repealed to permit strikes and lockouts once more, a new Order, No. 1376, preserved, somewhat illogically, the provisions of compulsory arbitration by the Industrial Disputes Tribunal, whose awards had legal force. This, in fact, was repealed in 1958, and all that remained under the Terms and Conditions of Employment Act of 1959 was the power to enforce 'recognized conditions' of employment in certain cases.

These measures dealt with piecemeal individual application by separate trades. But wages were also influenced in the aggregate. Early in 1948, the Government issued a statement on *Personal Incomes, Costs and Prices*,* in which it attempted to deal with the mounting internal inflationary pressure by demanding a standstill of profits and rents, and exhorted trade unions to accept a virtual standstill in wages also. This exhortation, coming from a Labour Government, did inhibit wage demands by trade unions for nearly two years, but loyalty and the belief in the efficacy of such voluntary restraint were progressively eroded by continuing price rises, and most of the 1950s saw a free-for-all in which trade unions, like other groups, settled down to demand and receive regular increases, only the nationalized industries attempting from time to time to stem the tide in what the Government saw as the national interest of containing inflation. In 1956 the Government again, with the help of the British Employers' Confederation, sought to stabilize wages by means of direction and exhortation, but on this occasion failed to carry the T.U.C. with it. In the following year the Council on Productivity, Prices and Incomes was set up, but as it had few powers and little logic in the prevailing system of free bargaining, its attempts to relate incomes to output and discourage purely inflationary cost rises achieved little beyond the accumulation of useful information, and the delay in pay increases to the members of some weaker trade unions. By 1965, the control of incomes was felt to be more necessary still, and a National Board for Prices and Incomes was created, which received further powers by the Act of 1966. In the foreign exchange crisis of 1966, the rapier of earlier methods was replaced by the club of a complete wage freeze, announced in July 1966, which stopped even wage increases granted and in the pipeline and those contractually agreed. Whatever may be thought of the appropriateness of such methods to the complex economy of the 1960s, it had at least the merit that, backed by the power of the law, it succeeded in halting rises in wage rates. It could not halt the progress of inflation, as there were no equivalent powers taken for preventing price rises, and those that existed were not used.

There was, finally, also, a many-sided Government initiative

* Cmd. 7321.

relating to industry. For example, the postwar concern with productivity led to a series of sponsored visits of selected groups of employers and trade unionists to the U.S.A. and the publication of their findings in official 'productivity reports'. Under the Industrial Reorganization Act of 1947, the scheme was expanded into the creation of Development Councils, also based on representation from both sides of industry. These did not fulfil the expectation of the Government that they would become centres of innovation and progress, and by the end of the 1950s they had petered out or been wound up; but meanwhile an increased number of government research centres was being financed, and funds made available for research in the universities and elsewhere under a reorganized Department of Scientific and Industrial Research. On a different plane, the agricultural price and marketing boards were expanded. In 1959, under the Cotton Industry Act, a levy raised for the scrapping and re-equipment of plant was supplemented by a government subsidy. The Government's action in regard to the aircraft production industry has been noted above. Influence over the location of industry has become many-sided and not without effect, and in some cases, as in the steel strip mills in 1960, or the location of new motor works in Merseyside and in Scotland, virtually amounts to a directive.

In 1962, the National Economic Development Council was set up, again with the participation of industrialists and trade unionists. Its object was to encourage and facilitate faster economic growth by a study of the factors that might encourage or inhibit it, and by influencing the decision-makers both in the Government and in the private sector to opt for policies that would promote efficiency and expansion. The N.E.D.C. had an uncertain start, but in the years 1963–4 it enjoyed considerable influence, and its 'target' of a 4 per cent annual growth rate was widely accepted as a realistic determinant of policy. Some of its specialized subdivisions, or 'little Neddies', set up for individual industries, also seemed to carry their industries with them. The new Labour Government of 1964 appeared at first to strengthen the policies and views it advocated by the creation of the Department of Economic Affairs, which had a senior Minister at its head and which was widely expected to balance the restrictive influence of the Treasury. However, the serious exchange crisis which, beginning in 1964, reached its nadir in 1966, posed yet again the alternatives of endangering the foreign balance and the pound sterling, or halting expansion, and once more the Treasury and the Bank of England, thinking financial soundness to be the primary aim, won the day, and the growth 'plans' of the Department of Economic Affairs and N.E.D.C., concerned with economic growth and prosperity, were unceremoniously jettisoned.

Most obviously representative of the new role of government in industry was the nationalization of a number of key industries after the war. Legislation was passed covering Cable and Wireless (1946), Civil Aviation (1946), Coal (1946), Electricity (1947), Transport (1947), Gas (1948), and Iron and Steel (1948). The larger part of the iron and steel industry and road haulage were later returned to private ownership, and some private civil airlines were also permitted to operate. The relations between the boards administering these different industries and the Government have gone through several phases in the first two decades of their existence, and while their diversity makes generalization difficult, the working relationship that has emerged is that the boards may enjoy a great deal of autonomy in their day-to-day management, but in the last resort are subject to the long-term and even short-term aims of Government policy. Interference and direction have been particularly felt in wages settlements, as well as in the investment programme which requires, in the capital-intensive industries concerned, constant resort to outside sources. Between 1951 and 1965, capital formation among the 'Public Corporations' totalled £11,200 million, and in 1961–5 averaged well over £1,000 million a year.

All these and innumerable similar means of influencing economic matters by government agencies, represent in some measure continuations and extensions of pre-war developments. Even the nationalized industries have their antecedents in such institutions as the Post Office or the B.B.C. Superimposed on all this, however, and representing a radically new departure in principle, was a system of new powers and purposes. This was termed 'employment policy' from its early preoccupation with securing full employment. More accurately, it was concerned with determining the degree of activity and the level of incomes within the economy as a whole, so as to keep production, incomes, and expenditure in balance, as well as foreign payments and the investment programme, while yet achieving such positively desirable aims as stability (i.e. price stability and the absence of fluctuations), full employment, and a satisfactory rise in output or 'economic growth'. In general, it would be difficult to pronounce the policy wholly a success, or to see in it much more than a series of temporary expedients reacting to a series of unexpected crises. Full employment, it is true, was preserved, though whether as a result of any deliberate policy is uncertain. Against this, inflation has been continuous and irresistible, fluctuations have been wide and disruptive, the pound sterling has been in continuous danger and had to be devalued once, the economic dependence of this country on others, particularly the U.S.A., has become so large as to impair seriously its political sovereignty, and the growth rate has been consistently the lowest among all the advanced industrial nations in the world.

The immediate postwar years opened with a large prospective balance-of-payments deficit, bridged only by the American and Canadian loans of 1946, amounting to $3,750 million and $1,250 million respectively (plus $650 million to meet outstanding Lend-Lease debts), and, in 1948–50, by Britain's share of the 'Marshall aid' offered to Europe by the U.S.A. The price of the loan, however, was a premature return to sterling convertibility in the summer of 1947, which rapidly exhausted most of the British reserves and caused the first crisis, solved by an enforced return to control as well as to austerity at home, and by Marshall aid a year after. The restrictive measures then taken were largely successful, and the release from restraint and the general expansion in 1948–9 caused a renewed outflow of sterling, aggravated, as was to become the familiar pattern, by speculative withdrawal of funds from London. As a result, severe pressure on the pound set in, and Sir Stafford Cripps (1889–1952), the Chancellor, decided to devalue the pound in September 1949.

The extent of the devaluation was drastic, from $4.03 to $2.80, and although many other countries followed suit, either to the full 30 per cent or part of the way only, the immediate problem was solved, funds flowed back, and expansion could begin again. The exchange rate was not to be tampered with again in the 1945–65 period, and on the contrary, the maintenance of the pound sterling on the new parity with the dollar became one of the cornerstones of economic policy. Threatened disequilibria in the foreign balance were to be dealt with entirely by deflation and restriction at home. The mid-1950s, benefiting by the rapid growth in prosperity of Britain's European markets and an improvement in the terms of trade, saw relative relaxation all round. By the end of the decade, the Government added to its restrictive apparatus a newly developed, and much resented, policy of interfering in collective bargaining for the purpose of holding down money wages. Also, following the Radcliffe Committee's Report,* the concept of what constituted

* *Report of the Committee on the Working of the Monetary System* (1959), Cmnd. 827.

'money' and was therefore a legitimate object of the Government's restrictive measures, was much widened. Despite these additional powers, the whole of this period was characterized by an unbroken set of cycles, expansion and exchange crises being followed by restriction, stagnation, and rectifying of the foreign balance, played out against a background of inflation at home and weakness of sterling abroad.

The crises of 1947 and 1949 have been noted already. By 1951 (true to form in the odd-numbered year), another crisis had developed, partly caused by the unexpected costs and adverse price movements of the Korean War. This time, the measures taken to restrict home demand included a rise in bank rate to 4 per cent, announced by the Chancellor in his budget of March 1952. It represented a break with a consistent policy of 'cheap money' of twenty years' duration and is to be read, in the long view, not so much as a breach with the Keynesian tradition as a recognition that inflation, rather than underemployment, had become the characteristic state of the economy.

This time, recovery did not begin until 1953, and it was not until 1955 that the next crisis erupted, leading to another 'stop'. As it was proposed to restrain the economy by monetary means rather than by direct control, on this occasion bank rate was used early, and raised in February to 4½ per cent. The budget itself was, however, still expansionist, and it was not until later in the summer (and with the autumn budget) that the 'credit squeeze' policy took shape. The year 1956 looked like bringing relief and recovery, though bank rate was now at 5½ per cent, but when some relaxation was introduced, a fresh crisis came to the boil in 1957, largely because of capital and speculative money movements, the real trade balance remaining fairly safe. Yet the September deflationary measures were sharper than had been known for some years, with bank rate at the peak of 7 per cent, and as a result, recession followed in 1958. Gradually, in 1958–9, the brakes were taken off, leading to the next expansion and crisis in 1960. This time the squeeze lasted for about two years and was followed by expansion in 1962–4, and yet another exchange crisis in 1964. Action in that instance was delayed because of the timing of the general election, and the measures taken to stave off the primary and immediate threat, i.e. the speculative attack on the pound, and to correct the underlying weakness of a trade unbalance included a 15 per cent surcharge on all imports, an increase in the bank rate back to the crisis level of 7 per cent, a loan of £347 million from the International Monetary Fund, and arrangements to borrow over £1,000 million from other central banks. Yet the imbalance continued to 1966, when measures of restriction were more drastic than any that had yet been seen in peacetime. There was no indication that these restrictions would do any more than offer temporary relief. The fundamental disequilibrium, which brings it about that every approach to full employment and rapid expansion is invariably accompanied by an adverse trade balance, could not be affected by these measures and, on the available evidence, may even be worsened by measures which halt investment and delay the modernization of industry.

Compared with this massive intervention, most other aspects of budgetary policy became of minor significance. One, however, must be noted, from time to time occupying the centre of the stage, and this was the Government's role in redistributing incomes. One detailed calculation, made for 1948–9, at the end of the egalitarian war and reconstruction years, showed that the taxation and welfare system combined transferred about £1,260 million, or 13·1 per cent of the national income, from the richer to the poorer citizens. Further, the British income-tax system had a built-in equalizing tendency during an inflation, since similar real incomes were being represented by steadily rising money incomes which took their earners into higher tax brackets. The capital gains tax, introduced in 1965, was also one to hit the rich harder than the poor. Nevertheless, a long series of measures taken during the rule of Conservative Chancellors between 1951 and 1964, of which the drastic surtax concession of 1961 was much the most important, together with the greater importance of national insurance contributions, representing a highly regressive tax, and the greater skill in tax avoidance on the part of the very rich, particularly in the fields of income tax and estate duties, have worked in the opposite direction. As a result, the redistributive effort of the taxation system as a whole at the end was less than at the beginning, and probably no higher than the 8·8 per cent calculated for 1937.

Changes in the welfare services were among the most important events in the social history of Britain in this period. The key measures were the 1944 Education Act and the immediate postwar legislation, particularly the family allowances brought into operation in 1945, and the comprehensive National Insurance Act and National Health Service Act of 1946, becoming effective in 1948. They created unified sickness and unemployment benefits, pensions, and other grants, and a system of free national medical services. The continuing need for national assistance payments to those claiming benefits under the insurance schemes, as well as to others, is eloquent proof of the inadequacy of these provisions; nevertheless, they represented a major step forward towards the ideal of a 'national minimum', and the abolition of preventable suffering. The years following those momentous statutes saw little change, and in some areas, such as in medical treatment, hospital accommodation, and education, the principle of private payment for what are clearly expected to be better provisions has survived and perhaps been extended. Indeed, it may be doubted if the building of new hospitals and schools, and the increases in the rates of grants to match the fall in the value of money, have kept pace with needs since 1948. In some fields, as in housing, where the Housing Subsidies Act of 1956 reduced subsidies and led to a sharp reduction in local council building, and where the Rent Act of 1957 permitted large increases in rent in many rented properties, the protection and welfare available to the poorer members of the community were greatly reduced in a very sensitive area, though there was some redress by the Rate Rebate Act and the Rent Act of 1965, passed by the Labour Government.

Policies on these matters were the issues over which many of the political battles of the twenty postwar years were fought. Yet, once again, the record showed that in the long run, the social and economic welfare of a country and of its major groups of citizens depends mainly on the aggregate of its production and incomes, and only to a limited degree on their distribution.

Since 1965, a low rate of investment and a low rate of economic growth have continued to hamper social progress, and to limit the freedom of manœuvre, of successive British Governments. In 1970–1, the accompanying features were reversed, and instead of full employment and a balance-of-payments deficit, the Heath Government worked with a healthy balance-of-payments surplus and heavy unemployment, approaching 5 per cent overall and around 10 per cent in the worst areas, yet the basic stagnation continued. At the time of writing, the signs point towards an early joining of the European Common Market; but unless the underlying slow growth, and the many officially induced 'stops', are overcome, that drastic step will represent but another economic opportunity lost.

## FOR FURTHER READING

The best brief general account of this period will be found in two volumes of essays edited by G. D. N. Worswick and P. H. Ady, *The British Economy 1945–1950* (Oxford, 1952) and *The British Economy in the Nineteen-Fifties* (Oxford, 1962). Though the contributors are largely the same, the two volumes differ considerably, the earlier containing much more factual material, and the later being more biased towards the discussion of economic policy. Both, however, are comprehensive in their field, authoritative, and contain excellent bibliographies. No comparable volume is available for more recent years, but a study in great depth was published by Richard E. Caves and associates, entitled *British Economic Prospects* (1968), and up-to-date trends may be followed in the official annual statistical publications, including *National Income and Expenditure* and *Annual Abstract of Statistics* (both Central Statistical Office), and, since 1958, *Statistics on Income, Prices, Employment and Production* (Ministry of Labour).

The changes in particular industries are covered in the two volumes edited by D. L. Burn, *The Structure of British Industry* (Cambridge, 1958), and, in a more summary manner, in G. C. Allen, *British Industries and their Organisation* (1959).

Comparative studies of economic growth will be found in Angus Maddison, *Economic Growth in the West* (1964), U.N. Economic Commission, *Some Factors in Economic Growth in Europe during the 1950s* (Geneva, 1964), and A. Lamfalussy, *The United Kingdom and the Six* (1963). All these are critical of the British performance, and Samuel Brittain, *The Treasury under the Tories 1951–1964* (1964) seeks to fix the blame on the constitutional factors involved in the overriding influence of the Treasury on policy, and in its financial, rather than industrial, orientation. Defences of British policy are harder to find, but some of the criticisms, at any rate, are answered by Colin Clark, *Growthmanship* (Institute of Economic Affairs, 1962 ed.), John Knapp and K. S. Lomax, 'Britain's Growth Performance: The Enigma of the 1950s', *Lloyd's Bank Review* (Oct. 1964), F. W. Paish, *Studies in an Inflationary Economy* (1962), and in some of the essays in *Economic Growth in Britain*, ed. P. D. Henderson (1966). Those competent to master complex mathematical formulae will derive much benefit from the relationships established in J. C. R. Dow, *The Management of the British Economy 1945–1960* (Cambridge, 1964) and W. Beckerman *et al.*, *The British Economy in 1975* (Cambridge, 1965).

The history and problems of financial measures are treated with great understanding in Sir Donald MacDougall, *The World Dollar Problem* (1957), C. W. McMahon, *Sterling in the Sixties* (1964), R. J. Ball, *Inflation and the Theory of Money* (1964), and the historical sections of the (Radcliffe) *Report of the Committee on the Working of the Monetary System* (H.M.S.O., 1959). The best critical summary of the latter's views is W. Manning Dacey, *Money under Review* (1960).

There is no good summary account of the history of public finance in this period, though there are several good studies of individual taxes or specific tax proposals. The best of the poor field of general histories is A. R. Ilersic, *Government Finance and Fiscal Policy in Post-War Britain* (1955). The annual *Economic Report*, published before the Budget, gives some idea of the factors influencing the Chancellor of the Exchequer. The following two collections of essays will be found to be useful introductions to the nationalized industries and the problems of their administration as well as the role they played in the economy: W. A. Robson, *Nationalised Industry and Public Ownership* (1962) and A. H. Hanson, *Nationalization: a Book of Readings* (1963).

The role of the trade unions is briefly, but intelligently, discussed in D. F. MacDonald, *The State and the Trade Unions* (1960). For a bird's-eye survey of wage changes, see K. G. J. C. Knowles and E. M. F. Thorne, 'Wage Rounds, 1948–1959', in *Bulletin of the Oxford Institute of Statistics* (Feb. 1961). There are many good summaries of the great changes in the social insurance field after the war: among the best are D. C. Marsh, *National Insurance and Assistance in Great Britain* (1951) and M. Bruce, *The Coming of the Welfare State* (1961). Initial enthusiasm has long since been replaced by more critical views of the working of welfare provisions in the 1950s and 1960s. Attacks on them in principle are still rare, but friendly criticism of their working is widespread. The best are collected in R. M. Titmuss, *Essays on the Welfare State* (1964 ed.).

# 3

# Philosophy

RAYMOND PLANT

'Like everything metaphysical, the harmony between thought and reality is to be found in the grammar of a language.' Thus Wittgenstein in his *Zettel*[1] encapsulated in one of his inimitable obscure aphorisms the preoccupations of a whole generation of philosophers. Of course, language has always been of philosophical concern—one need but think of Plato's *Cratylus*, the concerns of Herder, the insights of Hegel into language in his Jena lectures;[2] but never before in the history of thought have philosophers been preoccupied with language to the extent that they saw both the problems of philosophy and the solutions to these problems as internally connected with the linguistic habits of a society. All of this is platitudinous. What is important, however, is the fact that linguistic philosophy in Britain during the period 1945–65 was never a homogeneous movement, however much the descriptions given to it—'linguistic philosophy', 'Oxford philosophy', 'linguistic analysis'—may have implied that it constituted a dominant school working within a determinate idiom. It will be a major aim in this essay to try to illuminate the *different* approaches to language and the role of language *vis-à-vis* philosophy during this period. To do this, much attention will be paid to the major mentors of this generation of philosophers—Wittgenstein, John Austin, Gilbert Ryle, and John Wisdom. The obscure, dense, but intensely penetrating writings of Wittgenstein; the analytic incisiveness and Baconian fact-gathering of Austin; the Aristotelian urbanity of Ryle; and the tortured perplexity of John Wisdom represent not merely differences of temperament but crucial and subtle differences of philosophical perspective.

Within this heterogeneous idiom there were not only significant differences of doctrine, but towards the end of the period important changes of direction. In the late 1940s and early 1950s the emphasis was very much on piecemeal analysis in an attempt to eschew the penchant for system and metaphysics which afflicts most philosophers; but in 1959 two works, both by philosophers deeply influenced by the linguistic tradition—Hampshire's *Thought and Action* and Strawson's *Individuals*—moved towards altogether broader questions which had a Kantian and, in the case of Hampshire, even an Hegelian dimension.

The common complaint of non-philosophers against linguistic philosophy was its triviality—a broad criticism, and difficult to take very seriously. Those who made such a charge must have been ignorant of the work of, for example, Ryle and Wittgenstein on the philosophy of mind, or of Austin on determinism and its relationship to ordinary discourse. Certainly there is a great deal which is arguable in their positions, but one can hardly convict them of triviality. Perhaps, though, the criticism was meant less as applying to the results of such philosophical investigation than to the linguistic idiom itself. It was perhaps felt that philosophers were concentrating upon *mere* words and what mattered was 'life and life alone'. Philosophers lost in the labyrinth of language had let 'real life', practical activity, pass them by. Such a criticism, however, depends upon the mistaken view that language is one thing and human activity another—the implication being that philosophers ought to concentrate upon the latter and shed their preoccupation with the former. Actions, however, need to be identified; they do not exist in the void, wearing their fortunes on their faces. They are picked out through language, through descriptions. Actions in a sense embody ideas, concepts, beliefs, and to look at language is to look at the possibilities of acting in a determinate manner.* To be philosophically interested in language is to be interested in the range of possibilities of activity considered from one point of view. Actions and descriptions are not two separate or separable things: each is an aspect of the other. In such a way linguistic philosophy considered as a philosophical perspective could not be convicted on *a priori* grounds of triviality. Certainly the linguistic philosopher might direct his attention to trivial aspects of language, but that is a different issue and one which does not invalidate the approach.

## I

Probably the greatest single influence on British philosophy in the postwar period was the later work of Ludwig Wittgenstein (1889–1951). Although his later views on language and philosophy were worked out in a fairly clear-cut form in the 1930s, they were communicated in rather a secretive manner to a select band of disciples and, it must be said, votaries. His influence, therefore, although it permeated the thinking of many during the 1930s, was not felt

* This point is argued in more detail below, pp. 96–7.

explicitly until the posthumous publication of his works began in the 1950s. Wittgenstein came back to Cambridge in 1929 to resume philosophical work after his confidence in the finality of the solutions which he had worked out in the *Tractatus Logico-Philosophicus* began to be eroded. In this year he gave a paper, 'Some Remarks on Logical Form', to the Aristotelian Society, and, although his paper is still very much in the *Tractatus* idiom, the seeds of doubt may be found within it. During the 1930s he gave classes in Cambridge to selected students, some of the notes of which were published after his death as *The Blue and Brown Books* (1958). Other volumes of his work in the late 1930s and 1940s have also been published—notably *Philosophical Investigations* (1953), *Remarks on the Foundations of Mathematics* (1956), *Zettel* (1967), and *On Certainty* (1969).

In the preface to his *Philosophical Investigations*, the only work which Wittgenstein himself prepared for publication, he claimed that his later views could only be made intelligible in the light of his earlier *Tractatus Logico-Philosophicus*. Although the major doctrines argued in that work have been outlined in volume II of this series,* some of the salient points will be discussed again for the sake of setting Wittgenstein's later remarks in their correct light.

One of the most illuminating ways of approaching the *Tractatus* is through the idea that language basically has a truth-functional structure—that all meaningful complex propositions can be seen as truth functions of elementary propositions. This important thesis is argued in the following *Tractatus* propositions:

4.4 A proposition is an expression of agreement and disagreement with truth possibilities of elementary propositions.

4.41 Truth possibilities of elementary propositions are the conditions of the truth and falsity of propositions.

4.411 It immediately strikes one as probable that the introduction of elementary propositions provides the basis for understanding all other kinds of proposition.

4.51 Suppose that I am given *all* elementary propositions: then I can simply ask what propositions I can construct out of them. And there I have all propositions, and that fixes their limits.

4.52 Propositions comprise all that follows from the totality of all elementary propositions.

5\. A proposition is a truth function of elementary propositions.

Elementary propositions exist as building-blocks of complex propositions, and analysis of complex propositions brings us to

* See *The Twentieth-Century Mind*, vol. II, pp. 108–13.

elementary propositions (*Tractatus* 4.221). Language has this truth-functional, extensional structure.[3]

But what are these obviously crucial elementary propositions?

4.21 The simplest kind of proposition, an elementary proposition, asserts the existence of a state of affairs.

4.22 An elementary proposition consists of names. It is a nexus, a concatenation of names.

At this point the reader might well ask the question—why names? The answer is that the introduction of names enables the philosopher to account for the determinate sense of language. In order for elementary propositions, and thereby all propositions, to have meaning, only two alternatives are possible. The first is that the signs in the elementary proposition could be elucidated by means of another proposition; but then a question might arise over the meaning of this second proposition and this would in a sense make language a self-validating system.

2.0211 If the world had no substance then whether another proposition had sense would depend on whether another proposition was true.

If language did not in some way refer to the world, if its meaning did not come in an extra-linguistic fashion, then language would have no determinate sense. It was Wittgenstein's view that names stood in an immediate relationship with the world—the named object being the meaning of the name and thus *not* requiring *elucidation* to be meaningful. This complicated thought he put forward in the following propositions:

3.23 The requirement that simple signs be possible is the requirement that these be determinate.

3.202 The simple signs employed in propositions are called names.

3.203 A name means an object. The object is its meaning.

3.21 The configuration of objects in a situation corresponds to the configuration of simple signs in the propositional sign.

3.221 Objects can only be named. Signs are their representatives. I can only speak about them: I cannot put them into words.

Only by the postulation of elementary propositions consisting of names denoting simple objects could Wittgenstein account for the determinate sense of language given its truth-functional structure.

It seems clear that Wittgenstein, *pace* Russell,* was thinking not just of an ideal, logically perfect language, but ordinary language;

* In his Introduction to the English edition of the *Tractatus* Russell argued that Wittgenstein was concerned with 'the conditions which would have to be fulfilled by a logically perfect language'.

this hypothesis is borne out by propositions 5.5563 and 4.002 in the *Tractatus* and more particularly by the paper 'Some Remarks on Logical Form', in which Wittgenstein argues with reference to the *Tractatus* position: 'If we try to analyse *any* given proposition we shall find that in general they are logical sums, products or truth functions of simpler propositions.'[4] In his earlier work, therefore, Wittgenstein seems to be committed to the view that language has a unitary logical structure and is related to a reality external to it in a fixed way. It was from the basic doctrine that he began to move after 1929. He came to see that the simple correlation between words and objects insisted upon in the *Tractatus* was mistaken, at least as a total explanation of the determinate sense which language undoubtedly has. It is rather only within ongoing linguistic practices that we can make sense of the notion of an object, and an object of a particular sort, type, or category. A language is not given sense, life, and meaning by abstract juxtaposition between its basic components and the simple objects which these components designate. The living nature of language involves far more than this, and in his later works he struggles to indicate what this 'more' is.

Many reasons may be cited to explain Wittgenstein's fundamental shift of direction in his later work. In the first place he did not, in the *Tractatus*, pursue an actual analysis of a complex proposition into its elementary components. He did not produce an example of a name; nor did he indicate the kind of entity he had in mind as a simple object. Indeed, this was no mere accident. He considered that *qua* logician his task was purely *a priori*—to indicate the formal requirements which would have to be satisfied by a language with determinate sense. It was not his role to produce examples of names and objects which would satisfy these formal requirements. In fact in the *Tractatus* he criticized Russell for attempting to give examples on an *a priori* basis. However, by 1929, in his paper on 'Logical Form', the manifest implausibility of this Olympian detachment appeared to have registered on his mind. Now he considered the production of examples an important philosophical task, and apparently a task in which the logician could take part: 'We can only arrive at an accurate analysis by what might be called the *logical investigation* of the phenomena themselves, in a certain sense.'[5] However, once Wittgenstein became interested in the closer *empirical* study of language and linguistic practices he became aware of the falsity of some of the formal requirements set out in the *Tractatus*.

In addition, other factors might be adduced to explain the change: his experience as a teacher in Austria during the 1920s, faced with the practical task of teaching a language; the pragmatist influence of his friend, F. P. Ramsey, an influence which Wittgenstein himself acknowledged in the Preface to the *Philosophical Investigations*; and perhaps also the conventionalism and finitism of the mathematician Brouwer whose lectures Wittgenstein attended.

Whatever the influences may have been upon his mind, the beginning of the shift in his position may be seen in his *Philosophische Bemerkungen* (1965) and in lectures which he gave in Cambridge between 1930 and 1933 which were summarized by G. E. Moore, who attended them, in his *Philosophical Papers* (1959). In the *Bemerkungen* Wittgenstein was particularly concerned with the *Tractatus* doctrine that elementary propositions are independent of one another and cannot contradict one another. In the later work, he concentrated upon propositions concerning degrees of colour and argued that such propositions could not be considered truth-functionally, nor for that matter could any colour proposition be independent of other colour propositions because such propositions are exclusive.

He began to express the view that elementary propositions do not correspond to objects in a monadic, disconnected form, but rather are related to one another in groups or systems, each group of propositions having its own rules or grammar. 'Each system', so he argues, 'is, so to speak, a world'. These ideas, so crucial to his later writings, were however only very tentatively asserted in the *Bemerkungen*, but became much more clear in the 1930–3 lectures and *The Blue and Brown Books*. In these works Wittgenstein took the view that the meaning of an assertion is not primarily secured by the relationship of the components of the assertion and a set of extra-linguistic objects, but by the place of the proposition in a grammatical system. He had come to recognize very clearly that it is only *within* a set of rules, activities, grammatical conventions, and methods of projection that the correlation between a word and an object can be set up and grasped. For example, it might be thought that ostensive definition secures in a simple and immediate fashion a correlation between a word and an object. However, Wittgenstein points out, an ostensive definition has to be interpreted, the gesture made in the definition has to be understood, the *general* place of the word thus defined—e.g. a colour word—has *already* to be grasped. In all, ostensive definition presupposes a background of training which has to be present in order for the definition to make sense.[6] Only against *this* background can the relation between words and objects be understood.

The general system within which a word functions becomes for Wittgenstein more important for understanding the word's meaning than its simple correlation with objects—which, in the *Tractatus*, were considered to be the meanings of the words. Systems of words are governed by grammar. By grammar Wittgenstein does not mean precisely the same thing as a linguist might mean. For example: 'I believe falsely', 'I can feel your pain', are, for Wittgenstein, examples of assertions which go against grammar. They mean *nothing*, and therefore such assertions transgress the rules of grammar, although they would not normally be recognized by grammarians to have done so.

A great deal of orthodox philosophizing, Wittgenstein argued, broke grammatical rules in this kind of way. An example may make Wittgenstein's insistence that philosophical problems arise out of linguistic confusion clearer:

X is brown
X is good

are syntactically similar. They have a subject/predicate form. In the first case some quality is being ascribed to X, namely that it is brown. This quality is ascribed to X on the basis of normal sense experience. On the face of it, given the syntactical similarity, it would be tempting to look at the second assertion in the same way—that some quality is being ascribed to X, that some information is being given about the character of X. At this point all sorts of philosophical problems arise. What sort of quality does the word 'good' refer to, how is it to be discerned, how are disputes about its presence or absence to be resolved? All these sorts of problems, part of the stock-in-trade of moral philosophy, have their roots in the philosopher's being held captive by the form of the sentence—its subject/predicate structure. Taken in isolation from the language game of morality, apart from all other sorts and types of moral assertion—which may be pieces of advice, hortatory or minatory imperatives, expressions of emotion and attitude—this kind of problem arises. Such problems only arise 'when language goes on holiday', when the philosopher concentrates upon any one set of examples, when he nourishes himself with only a 'one-sided diet'.

Certain pictures are built into certain forms of expression[7]—in the one just discussed the picture of goodness as a kind of quality, although of a somewhat ethereal type; in other expressions we have the picture of the *mind* as a kind of private entity, or of *time* as a flowing stream. If the philosopher concentrates *only* upon such expressions, all kinds of intractable problems will arise. What he has to do to avoid these problems is to become clear about the grammar of all the types of expressions involved. Certainly philosophical problems are not just 'wished onto' language by the philosopher; they arise very naturally out of certain sorts of expressions, but what is needed is a realization of the complexity of the system of discourse from which the expression is derived and which in isolation from this complexity gives rise to the philosophical problem.

The idea that there are genuine philosophical problems to be solved by a determinate philosophical technique is for Wittgenstein a very dangerous one. Philosophical problems arise when the rules of grammar are not being observed, and when the boundaries of language are being crossed—when, for example, we ask 'What time is it on the sun?' The role of the philosopher, as conceived by Wittgenstein, is not to attempt to think such problems through to a conclusion but rather to dissolve the problem by careful attention to the grammar of the expressions involved and their role in the social and linguistic practices which give them point and purpose. Clarity about the complex uses of language and the grammar exemplified in these usages is for Wittgenstein the hallmark of the philosophical enterprise. Complete clarity, an overall view '*übersichtliche Darstellung*'[8], would entail the disappearance of philosophical problems: 'The clarity that we are arriving at is indeed complete clarity. But this simply means that philosophical problems will disappear.'[9] This clarity is directed towards the grammar of a language, a grammar which in a sense we are already aware of because it is presupposed in our very use of language. Consequently in trying to achieve this clear view the philosopher is not trying to find out anything *new*;[10] he is just trying to make explicit something which is implicitly presupposed by our activity. In this sense his work has no peculiarly *philosophical* content. There can be no philosophical doctrines, no philosophical theses: 'If one tried to advance theses in philosophy, it would never be possible to debate them, because everyone would agree with them.'[11]

Such a view of the role of the philosopher—dissolving the problems which beset him rather than attempting to solve them—does not make philosophy any easier, nor does it make it a terminable activity. It is no easier because the demand is for clarity about something extraordinarily complex, the particular use of language and its role in particular kinds of social activity. Wittgenstein, for example, tried desperately to get clear about the meaning of 'pain', i.e. the grammar of the word and its role in human life, human attitudes and reactions, and he found this difficult enough to achieve. When one considers the range of philosophical problems, it seems that the notion of complete clarity, of perspicuous representation, is a regulative one.

It is regulative for another reason too. Philosophical problems arise because we entangle ourselves in the rules of our language, and we fail to see our way round our linguistic habits. Hence philosophical problems could only be finally dissolved if language and social practices failed to develop. However, language games develop all the time; old ones become forgotten,[12] and lose their place in the life of the community. Perhaps religion and its philosophical difficulties are now going through this process. Other language games arise, bringing with them obdurate philosophical difficulties of their own. An example of a fairly new philosophical difficulty might be the following: human brains are rather like computers, so in what sense are persons like computers? A new form of human activity and its linguistic self-understanding here give rise to a whole new range of deep-seated difficulties. So even granting Wittgenstein's view of philosophy, it seems that philosophy is interminable.

Wittgenstein sometimes drew an analogy between the man beset by philosophical perplexity and the person who is mentally sick. The mentally sick person fixes upon some feature of his environment, perhaps exaggerates its importance; this leads him to misrepresent his relationships both to other people and to the world. He feels trapped and shut in by his misunderstood relationships. Therapy must consist, at least in part, in showing that his difficulty *is* one of misinterpretation, of over-concentration on just a few features of his environment. The person obsessed with philosophical difficulties is in a similar position. He misrepresents his language, and concentrates his attention only upon a few expressions. Problems then develop with which he cannot cope—'philosophical problems have the form, "I do not know my way about".' In his *Remarks on the Foundations of Mathematics*, Wittgenstein calls philosophical perplexity a sickness: 'The philosopher is the man who has to cure himself of many sicknesses of the understanding before he can arrive at the notions of a sound understanding. In the midst of life we are in death, so in sanity we are surrounded by madness.'[13] In his emphasis on this aspect of philosophical perplexity and its cure, Wittgenstein wanted to make clear that there was no analogy whatsoever between the philosopher's treatment of his problem and the scientist's approach to his questions. The scientist tells us something new, discovers new facts, brings things before our minds which we do not know. The philosopher can only successfully tackle his problem in so far as he returns to what we already know and do in an everyday use of language. Only by bringing language back to its everyday use from its metaphysical use can the saving quality of clarity be achieved:

> . . . We are most tempted to think that there are things hidden, something which we can see from the outside but which we cannot look into. And yet nothing of the sort is the case. It is not new facts about time which we want to know. All the facts that concern us lie open to view.[14]

Grammar is not hidden, does not lie behind or beyond linguistic practice, is not something over and above it any more than the rules of cricket are hidden or something over and above the game of cricket. In philosophy we have to remind ourselves of something we already implicitly know—the grammar, the rules involved in what we actually do both with and in language.

This emphasis in Wittgenstein's work upon the crucial role of rules, of the grammar of language, and less emphasis upon what might be called the external relation of language to the world, might lead to the charge of extreme conventionalism. If the meaning of language is secured through grammar, by means of rules as much as through its relation to external objects, does not this make language entirely conventional and arbitrary? Certainly Wittgenstein wants to argue that grammar has a certain force, but is not the basis of this force entirely arbitrary? Which god ordered that we should follow these rules?

The first thing to be said against this objection is that the rules are *established*; they are built into and structure an ongoing linguistic practice, so that if you want to do this kind of thing in language then you have to obey the rules which constitute the language. The rules of cricket are similarly *not* arbitrary in this sense. On the other hand, rules are arbitrary in that they cannot be finally justified. If you wished to justify the following of a linguistic practice structured by a set of grammatical rules, it would follow that you would have to give reasons based upon a description of reality, and yet what counts as *reality* and *reason* is given by the rules. We need to follow the rules of grammar to describe reality, and such description cannot therefore justify the rules: 'If I have exhausted the justifications I have reached bedrock and my spade is turned. Then I am inclined to say —this is simply what I do.'[15]

The use of the first person singular here should not mislead us. Rules cannot be followed on an individual basis, by individual commitment; they are public, checkable, and established as the basis of public acts of communication. This thesis that one cannot follow a private rule for the use of an expression or for a system of expressions has enormous consequences for Wittgenstein's views on the classical problems in the philosophy of mind.

Most people in their reflective moments must be struck by the incongruity which exists between the different types of predicates applied to persons. There are predicates which ascribe certain publicly ascertainable qualities—e.g. has black hair, is married, is six feet tall, etc.—and predicates which apparently ascribe qualities of a radically different type: qualities, moods, feelings which appear in or seem to be accessible only to the person concerned—is in pain, is thinking of a girl, is jealous. No doubt such moods, thoughts, and feelings are usually expressed either in behaviour or in self-avowal, but such external features are at the best *evidence* for the existence of inner states of mood, feeling, and sensation. The problem then arises of how it is that we have acquired the appropriate set of concepts relating to feelings, moods, sensations, thoughts, etc., if these are regarded as being internal and private, and how, once acquired, these concepts can become part of an inter-subjective system of communication. If the word 'pain', for example, is construed as the name of a private sensation, how did I acquire the word and how do I understand the word when *anyone else* uses it? For me the word 'pain' means *my* pain, my private inaccessible sensation. There have been many attempts to deal with this problem of other minds, notably through the argument from analogy, but the novelty of Wittgenstein's position here is that, trading upon his conception of language as governed by public rules, he will not allow that the problem exists in that form. Words for states of mind cannot be used primarily to refer to such inner events because we should then have to make sense of both private ostensive definition[16]—setting up the correlation of word with the appropriate inner experience, and, having done that, the idea of following a private rule.[17] Wittgenstein argues that a rule is intrinsically connected with the idea of a right and a wrong, a correct and an incorrect way of doing something—but can the notions make sense on a purely private basis? In order to know that I am using the word 'pain' correctly today I have to remember that the sensation is qualitatively the same as the sensation which I have had before, and which I referred to as 'pain'; but how can I be sure of my memory, and what indeed would this memory consist in except other images and traces requiring comparison? I cannot check that my memory is correct and so I cannot check that I am following the rule. It is, as Wittgenstein says, like buying two copies of the same morning paper to make sure that what is said is true.[18]

Rules for the use of words have to be publicly checked, which means that they have to be publicly acquired. This entails that words such as 'pain', 'jealousy', etc., have to be learned in public, behavioural contexts, and that their primary meaning cannot be given with reference to internal private states or feelings. To say this does not mean that Wittgenstein was a behaviourist. A behaviourist would categorically assert that a word such as 'pain', 'jealousy', etc., would be equivalent in meaning to a set of statements about behaviour patterns. Wittgenstein does not want to go as far as this. What he does want to say is that we could not talk about 'pain', 'jealousy', the whole gamut of 'mental' experience, unless there were some links to the behavioural patterns. At the same time he wanted to say that the relationship between behaviour and pain was not to be construed as sign and thing signified—without behaviour of certain sorts we could not have acquired the meaning of the word 'pain'. The relationship is not an external, *contingent* one as the dualist would suggest, nor is it a *necessary* one as the behaviourist or physicalist would claim. Wittgenstein refers to this link as a *criterion* which, he implies, is a *sui generis* relationship not to be identified with either the wholly necessary or the wholly contingent, the two polarities of empiricist epistemology.

It is arguable that Wittgenstein's work on the mind and its place in language represents a very significant shift in philosophical thinking. The dominant empiricist epistemology had seen language largely as a way in which we talk about the contents of our minds—ideas for Locke, impressions + ideas for Hume, sense-data for Russell and Ayer. The implication was that a man's relationship to an ongoing linguistic community is merely contingent, that we can envisage a Robinson Crusoe from birth coming to self-consciousness and language in the absence of such a community.[19] Such a thesis has had a social and political dimension in empiricism. Social and political space has been understood as an area of activity for private self-conscious individuals. For Wittgenstein, however, membership in a linguistic community is not merely contingent, but a condition of being able to speak about one's own experience at all, and thus of coming to self-consciousness. The implications for social, moral, and political philosophy of this central placing of man in society have not been worked out[20] in any way at all comparable with the way in which the individualist epistemology of Locke, for example, was worked out in his social and political writings.

Although Wittgenstein's influence upon modern British philosophy has been enormous, very few have been willing to follow him in his ideas on philosophical perplexity and its dissolution. Philosophers have taken from Wittgenstein the emphasis upon linguistic clarity but not his view that philosophical problems are not genuine. Probably only John Wisdom (b. 1904),* who eventually succeeded to Wittgenstein's chair in Cambridge, has been greatly influenced by this view of philosophical perplexity and the tendency to treat such perplexity as an illness requiring therapy and cure. Even then, Wisdom concedes far more to the metaphysician trapped by his problems and indulging in his extravagant solutions than Wittgenstein ever did. Certainly Wisdom holds that philosophical difficulties are unlike any others; they cannot be settled by observation, by normal empirical methods. Even the *behaviour* of the sceptical philosopher lecturing at 9.30 a.m. on 'The Unreality of Time' does nothing to undermine his scepticism. Very often these problems are found to have their roots in language, and yet at the same time metaphysical solutions to these obdurate but essentially pseudo-problems are not to be dismissed as *nonsense*, but as *paradoxical*. Paradoxes, as everyone knows, exaggerate. Taken literally, they are ridiculous, and yet contain a grain of truth. So the moral philosopher who says that moral judgements are meaningless has said something paradoxical—an odd state of affairs, but his assertion is not just idle, to be combated by pointing out his inconsistency. What he is perhaps doing, albeit in a wholly extravagant fashion, is trying out a feature of moral language which would be missed or by-passed at the naïve unreflective, non-philosophical, non-metaphysical level, namely that the kind of assertions made in morality are very different, and thus have a different meaning, from statements for example about material objects. We shall go wrong, therefore, if we dismiss as idle the metaphysician's talk; but we shall also go wrong if we take it too literally. The metaphysician is talking no more nonsense than the poet, nor as much sense as the scientist. The reason why the philosopher defends his paradoxes with such passion, Wisdom suggests, is not merely to produce the nugget of illumination involved in his paradoxes; there may also be unconscious causes.[2] This point, of course, links up with Wittgenstein's idea of philosophy as a sickness of the understanding. This idea of unconscious causes

* Wisdom's major writings are *Other Minds* (1952); *Philosophy and Psycho-Analysis* (1953); *Paradox and Discovery* (1965).

influencing the adoption of a particular philosophical position is linked by Wisdom to his earlier point that philosophical disputes cannot be settled by empirical observation. Something has to explain the tenacity with which particular philosophical positions are held in the absence of such evidence, and the practical, behavioural dimension with which, for example, scepticism is regarded by the sceptic as irrelevant.

Although Wittgenstein went to some pains to stress how unlike the scientific approach to a problem his way of looking at philosophy was, John Austin (1911–60), White's Professor of Moral Philosophy in Oxford and the other chief mentor of the present generation of philosophers, went to some lengths to link his view of philosophy and its role *vis-à-vis* language to an almost Baconian methodology of science. Austin was as much preoccupied with language as was Wittgenstein, but his approach differed in a significant number of ways. Their differing approach to language may be seen first in terms of their different backgrounds. Wittgenstein knew very little of the history of philosophy, and his concern with language was largely self-generated. Austin, a product of the Oxford Greats school, had been trained not only in philosophy but also in classical scholarship. Consequently he approached language partly from a non-philosophical background, with a scholarly interest in language, its grammar, syntax, and philology, that was never really a part of Wittgenstein's philosophical equipment.

The philosophical differences, however, went much deeper than this. Wittgenstein, as we have seen, rejected the idea of real, definite, soluble philosophical problems. Austin, however, seemed to imply that there were definite problems in philosophy which could be better understood and solved if only the correct method were adopted. Wittgenstein, somewhat disingenuously in the light of some of the positive positions in his later work, rejected the idea that there could be philosophical positions, theses, doctrines, and answers, and he also felt a distaste for philosophy as a profession or as an academic discipline. Austin on the other hand, though distrustful of a great deal of classical philosophizing, seemed to take the view that it was only if members of the academic discipline adopted the correct methods and joined forces with other researchers into language that the problems of philosophy could be solved. Thus between the two chief mentors of the generation of philosophers who came to be called linguistic philosophers there was very wide-ranging disagreement.

Austin's work is not very extensive; indeed most of it consists of lecture notes turned into book form by editors after his death. His published papers are included in an edition of *Philosophical Papers* (1961) published after his death and include 'Ifs and Cans' (1956), 'A Plea for Excuses' (1956), 'How to Talk—Some Simple Ways' (1953), 'Are There "*A Priori*" Concepts?' (1939), 'Other Minds' (1946), 'Truth' (1950), and 'Pretending' (1958). The posthumous books are *Sense and Sensibilia* (1962), based upon lecture courses given in Oxford during the 1950s, and *How to Do Things with Words*, the William James lectures given at Harvard in 1955 and published in 1962.

Most of these works are attempts at solutions or notes towards the solution of particular problems, but many crucial methodological remarks are made in them. Austin denied the idea that the great classical problems of philosophy—truth, freedom of the will, appearance and reality—could be confronted directly, and even hinted that they did not exist at all in that form. All these questions as they stand involve philosophers' jargon and terminology, and are, therefore, suspect. What is needed before one can even begin to approach such broad philosophical issues is an appreciation of the meaning which many of the words involved in such questions have in ordinary language. Philosophers tend not to do this; they soon take speculative flight and address themselves to these very broad questions which would perhaps not arise in that form had they been more careful about language in the earlier stages of philosophical inquiry. The consideration, often not very carefully conducted, of a situation —for example, of hallucination—soon has the epistemologist groping for words like sense-data, and then worrying about the relationship between sense-data and material objects, or whether the introduction of sense-data is a linguistic or an ontological move. If the epistemologist in this particular case, and philosophers generally, did more spadework on the circumstances which lead to the development of their problems they would perhaps not find themselves faced by such obdurate problems in the first place.

Perhaps the opening paragraph of his paper on 'Truth' captures Austin's insistence on not taking philosophical problems at their face value, and his emphasis on the need to concentrate on smaller, more manageable, but still important issues.

> 'What is truth?' said jesting Pilate, and would not stay for an answer. Pilate was in advance of his time. For 'truth' itself is an abstract noun, a camel, that is, of logical construction which cannot get past the eye even of a grammarian. We approach it cap and categories in hand: we ask ourselves whether Truth is a substance (the Truth, the Body of

Knowledge) or a quality (something like the colour red inhering in truths), or a relation ('correspondence'). But philosophers should take something their own size to strain at. What needs discussing rather is the use, or certain uses, of the word 'true'. *In vino*, possibly, '*veritas*', but in sober symposium '*verum*'.[22]

He is not concerned to say that there are no real philosophical difficulties here, but the difficulties, if they exist, must be shown to emerge from the painstaking attempt to establish important features of words such as 'true' and 'truly' in this case, or, in other problems, words such as 'voluntary', 'intentional', etc., without immediately passing to the discussion of truth or the freedom of the will. Such spadework may show that the traditional large, unmanageable question has very little to do with the actual difficulties experienced in operating in ordinary contexts with our linguistic apparatus. Such problems may then be seen as merely *philosophical* constructions.

The other aspect of this emphasis in Austin's thinking was his scepticism concerning the value of philosophical terminology. Jargon such as '*a priori*', 'analytic', 'necessary', 'sense-datum', is introduced without sufficient reason to meet extremely ill-defined needs. This is certainly shown in his attitude to the terminology of sense-data, which he considers is introduced into epistemological discussion after an extremely perfunctory analysis of the phenomena of illusion and hallucination. In Austin's view, when these phenomena are correctly discussed, there is no need to introduce the sense-datum terminology with all its attendant philosophical difficulty. This does not mean, however, that philosophical terminology is never justified. There are admittedly places in his work where he implies this, for example in the following passage from 'A Plea for Excuses':

. . . our stock of words embodies all the distinctions men have found worth drawing, and the connections they have found worth making, in the lifetimes of many generations: these surely are likely to be more numerous, more sound, since they have stood up to the long list of the survival of the fittest, and more subtle, at least to all ordinary and reasonably practical matters than you or I are likely to think up in our armchairs of an afternoon.[23]

Despite such a great respect for linguistic tradition, Austin's practice belies this statement of theory. He himself introduced terminology, for example 'locutionary force', 'illocutionary force', 'perlocutionary force', 'performative utterance', but he did imply that all jargon should be introduced *in extremis*, and then to meet a clear-cut requirement.

The advantage, according to Austin, of beginning an inquiry with an attempt to clarify the ordinary uses of words which are germane to traditional philosophical discussion, is that agreed data may well be attained and perhaps in addition something of significance in philosophy, namely 'agreeing about how to reach agreement'. If we do this kind of field work we may make progress and he cites the example of aesthetics: '. . . if only we could forget for a while about the beautiful and get down instead to the dainty and the dumpy.'[24] It is in this kind of context that Austin draws the analogy between linguistic philosophy and science. He was most explicit on this point in 'A Plea for Excuses' and in a paper read to a group of British and French philosophers. In this latter paper he says:

> We have to look for our subjects in less septic regions, those that are less bitterly disputed. For this I see three good reasons: in the first place, we may try our hand without getting too heated; in the second place, the big problems that have resisted all assaults from the front might yield if we attack them from the side; in the third place, and this seems to me by far the most important, isn't it risky to claim to know in advance which are the most important problems. . . . I believe that by standing back we shall have a better chance of seeing the peaks standing out, and of finding a good route, as we go along. The example of physics is again instructive By pottering about on one side and another with one's instruments as Faraday did, one has a better chance of happening upon something really important than by saying one fine day: 'let's attack some great problem; let's ask, for instance, what our Universe is made of.'[25]

In 'A Plea for Excuses' his justification of his preoccupation with language was more direct: '. . . there is gold in them thar hills.'[26]

So much for Austin's methodological views. Actual analyses are very difficult to summarize, since Austin was so skilled at seeing the importance and variety of usage. Among his papers, the most valuable is, perhaps, 'Ifs and Cans'. This is notable partly because of its densely packed argument and also for the tangible nature of the argument, sometimes rare in philosophical discussion.

In this paper Austin is concerned with the problem of determinism, but again he will not attack the problem directly; indeed, he seems to claim not to be able to understand what determinism is. His approach to the *broad* problem is characteristically oblique, whereas his attack on the *specific* problem which concerns him is characteristically direct. Austin discusses how far determinism is compatible with our usual ways of talking. In his *Ethics* (1952), G. E. Moore had argued that in one sense determinism is compatible with our normal ways of speaking. This was an important argument because the apparent incompatibility had always been a problem for the determinist. Moore argued that assertions which apparently imply freedom of choice, such as 'I could have done it if I had chosen', could be translated into 'I should have done it if I had chosen', with the implication that the 'if' clause refers to a causal antecedent. The point of the substitution was to show that the language of voluntary action—'I could have done it if I had chosen'—is not incompatible with a causal explanation of action. Austin, however, suggests that this substitution will not work, that 'should' cannot be substituted for 'would', and that the 'if' does not refer to a causal antecedent. Austin argues that 'could have' is the past indicative of 'can',[27] and not the subjunctive as is suggested by Moore's substitution. Typically, Austin says nothing about the large philosophical problem of free will versus determinism, but he does consider that he has demonstrated an important truth by close attention to linguistic detail, and that this is the way philosophical progress can be made.

*Sense and Sensibilia* is the most negative and destructive of Austin's writings. He is concerned in this work to make a root-and-branch attack upon the phenomenalist thesis and the terminology of sense-data: an attack based upon a close analysis of A. J. Ayer's work *The Foundations of Empirical Knowledge.* Austin tries to show that the argument from illusion which constitutes the first part of Ayer's book is based upon mis-description, a state of affairs which leads to the need to introduce the sense-datum language. A reconsideration of the initial problem and a redescription of the points raised by the argument from illusion makes the introduction of the language of sense-data both otiose and distorting.

Probably Austin's most fruitful work was, however, *How to Do Things with Words.* This work is concerned with classifying certain usages. He first distinguishes between performative utterances and constative utterances. In a *constative* (usually speaking), a fact is stated; in a *performative*, something is not described but done. To say, given the structure of our conventions, 'I promise to pay you £5' is not to *describe* something else which is going on; it is to *perform the action* of putting oneself under an obligation. Other performatives are, for example, 'I name this ship *Queen Elizabeth*', 'I give and bequeath my watch to my brother', 'I bet you 6p. it will rain tomorrow', 'I baptise you Matthew Benedict'. Performatives differ from constative statements in that they are appraised differently. Statements are true or false, but this does not apply to performatives;

the latter are rather inappropriate or infelicitous, the inappropriateness being diagnosed basically with reference to background conventions and requirements.[28]

One problem which Austin faced was how, in fact, to distinguish the two, other than on purely intuitive grounds. Certainly they cannot be distinguished grammatically because, as he points out, they may have the same grammatical form as constatives.[29] It is not a necessary condition for a performative to be a first-person indicative, for both of the following are performatives, if uttered appropriately: 'I arrest you in the name of the law'; 'You are arrested in the name of the law'. Austin was forced to try to distinguish and to demarcate performatives from constatives through the notions of a locutionary, an illocutionary, and a perlocutionary speech act. To perform a locutionary act is to utter a sentence with a certain sense and reference; an illocutionary act is such as to warn, advise, or inform, to have a certain conventional force; a perlocutionary act is one in which a particular effect is achieved: someone is convinced, deterred, misled, or whatever. Austin introduced these distinctions because to define a performative solely in terms of *doing something* in language is not particularly enlightening, since in uttering at all we are in some sense doing something. On this more complex basis, locutionary acts correspond to constatives, illocutionary acts to performatives; but at the same time he also wants to say that any single speech act includes a locutionary and an illocutionary element, and therefore no statement can be classed as wholly performative or wholly constative. The *total* speech act has both a sense and reference, and an illocutionary force. The philosophical importance of these distinctions, along with the enormous number of other distinctions made in the book, may be seen in several ways. Austin himself mentions moral philosophy, and argued that although modern moral philosophy is on the right track in looking at the use of the word 'good' in contexts such as expressing approval, commending, and grading, we shall only become really clear about the matter when we have the whole list of illocutionary acts of which these are examples. The other application of Austin's work in moral philosophy is in the distinction which many philosophers have drawn since the time of Hume between 'facts' and 'values', for with his doctrine of the locutionary and illocutionary dimension of every total speech act, Austin implied that the fact-stating and the evaluative function of language cannot be very clearly separated. It was a very great blow to philosophy when Austin died because he then seemed, after a long period of necessary spadework, to be moving towards an attempt to synthesize his researches and relate them to broader philosophical problems.

Both Austin and Wittgenstein laid the foundations of their influential postwar views in the middle and late 1930s; Wittgenstein in *The Blue and Brown Books*, Austin in discussion and in the papers 'Are There "*A Priori*" Concepts?' and 'The Meaning of a Word', and the same is true of Gilbert Ryle (b. 1900), the other dominating figure in the postwar generation of philosophers. Ryle's two major works in our period, *The Concept of Mind* (1949) and *Dilemmas* (1954), were particular and dazzling examples of a specific mode of philosophizing which he had worked out in the thirties, particularly in the paper 'Systematically Misleading Expressions'.[30] Ryle in fact appears to have been a somewhat reluctant convert to the linguistic idiom in philosophy. During his earlier Oxford career he had lectured on phenomenology and had, in fact, reviewed Martin Heidegger's *Sein und Zeit* for *Mind*,[31] a journal which he was later to edit. Ryle's acquaintance with the strong objectivizing streak in the writings of Meinong, Husserl, and Heidegger perhaps explains the point of his article 'Systematically Misleading Expressions', in which he argued that philosophers are led into bogus metaphysical difficulties because they misconceive, misconstrue, and misrepresent the idioms of ordinary speech. Because the sentences 'Mr. Baldwin is Prime Minister', 'The Queen of Hearts is a fictional character', have the same grammatical form we might be tempted to think that, since the first sentence describes an object, the second must too, although an object of a peculiar logical type. This kind of analogy had led Meinong in particular to develop a lavish ontology, containing not merely ordinary objects existing in the real world, but also objectives, desideratives, and objecta merely subsisting and providing meanings for referring expressions such as the Queen of Hearts.[32] From this position, however, paradoxes or antinomies follow. When did the Queen of Hearts marry? How old was she? etc. Such metaphysicians, such object theorists, go wrong because they mistake the actual grammar of an expression for its real or logical grammar. The role of the philosopher, as Ryle sees it, is the redescription of those statements which are philosophically puzzling and which give rise to such paradoxes and confusions. He considered it to be the role of the philosopher to attempt to correct and rectify the logical geography of an area of discourse. Clearly Ryle's account of philosophy owes something to the inspiration of Russell, particularly his theory of descriptions, which was an attempt to restate in a non-problematic fashion a sentence such as 'The present King of France is bald'. Although Ryle's account and way of doing philosophy is a great deal less formal than that of Russell, he still uses Russellian terminology, the philosopher's task being to make explicit the logical grammar or the logical syntax of a difficult expression.

This sort of conception of philosophy was brilliantly exemplified in Ryle's *The Concept of Mind*, which was an attempt to rectify the logical grammar or geography of an area of discourse where the problems are notoriously intractable. Most statements about states of mind, qualities of mind, motives, intentions, and so on are usually regarded as categorical in form: 'He is intelligent.' 'His motive for coming was jealousy.' An emphasis upon this kind of expression naturally leads to the view that states, occurrences, and moods are being ascribed to the person concerned, and further that these states and occurrences exist in a private medium, namely the mind. In Ryle's view such an analysis is mistaken, and he shows how, when it is taken seriously, all kinds of antinomies follow. For example, if an intelligent performance has to be the consequent of a mental activity of theorizing, then, Ryle argues, we can never perform intelligently:

> The consideration of propositions is itself an operation, the execution of which can be more or less intelligent, less or more stupid. But if for any operation to be intelligently executed, a prior theoretical operation had first to be performed and performed intelligently, it would be a logical impossibility for anyone ever to break into the circle.[33]

Ryle tends to attempt such *reductio ad absurdum* methods in respect of other mental operations when they are construed on a Cartesian private, inner-state model. The categorical form of our way of speaking about the mind in some sense masks the true nature of the situation. Considered on this basis, the mind is the topic of sets of propositions which are not in principle testable. They are not testable because they refer to private occurrences which are accessible only to the individual who has them. Rather, Ryle argues, such statements are better construed as covert *hypotheticals*, and it is his thesis that such an approach does more justice to the way in which we think about the exercise of qualities of mind, moods, inclinations, intentions, and so on. Understood in this way, as hypotheticals, psychological statements describe not untestable occurrences inferentially discerned, but overt activity. To say 'X is intelligent' is not to credit X's mind with some enduring quality; it is to refer to the character of his overt behaviour. It is to say 'If X were asked to do A.B.C.' (where these are conventionally regarded as tests of intelligence) 'then he would do them successfully'. 'Mental' words denoting 'intelligence', motives, feelings, emotions, etc. refer not to inner, hidden goings-on, but to a disposition to behave in certain ways.

Of course, it might be objected against Ryle's thesis that if, for example, intelligence is regarded as a disposition to behave in a particular fashion, how can we distinguish between an intelligent performance and one done merely by rote or through habit? Is there anything in the behaviour itself considered as an overt happening which allows us to draw this distinction? Surely, it might be suggested, the difference between an intelligent performance and a merely habitual or rote performance must consist in the fact that the former was preceded by certain mental operations, whereas the latter was not. Ryle argues that in order to draw these perfectly ordinary distinctions we certainly have to go beyond what is presented to us in the performance, but we do not have to make references to occurrences in people's minds; rather, we have to look at a particular exercise of intelligence in terms of that person's general disposition or propensity to act in this way. If it really is an intelligent performance it will be able to be repeated, varied to suit varied circumstances, and so on. To ascribe intelligence to someone is not to attribute a mental cause to his behaviour; it is to consider his performance in a certain light—in terms of his disposition, his propensities and bents.

Ryle also argues that the Cartesian goes wrong in looking for the 'core' of an activity in the human mind. Intelligence, for example, does not refer to one thing, a particular quality of a person's mind: it is rather a word for a whole variety of performances in different and varied contexts.[34] Those dispositions of behaviour to which 'mental' words refer are not 'single track', as, for example, the disposition of being a smoker; rather, such higher-grade dispositions are multi-track, capable of being unpacked into an indefinite number of hypotheticals. As Ryle tellingly remarks:

> When Jane Austen wished to show the specific kind of pride which characterized the heroine of *Pride and Prejudice* she had to represent her actions, words, thoughts and feelings in a thousand different situations. There is no standard type of action or reaction such that Jane Austen could say, 'My heroine's kind of pride was just the tendency to do this, whenever a situation of that sort arose.'[35]

In *The Concept of Mind* Ryle attempts this kind of analysis in respect of the most important 'mental' operations, willing, intending, wanting, acting from a particular motive, sensing, observing, imagining. His method is usually to apply the Cartesian doctrine to such operations and then deduce absurd or, at the very least, counter-intuitive conclusions from such an application in order to show that such an interpretation does not illuminate the facts. He then usually expounds the positive doctrine, an analysis in terms of dispositions, unpacked in hypothetical statements. This method fits in very closely with the view of philosophy adumbrated in his earlier 'Systematically Misleading Expressions', although the book is no mere slavish working-out of a methodological position. On the contrary, it is one of the most brilliant works of his generation.

On reading *The Concept of Mind*, however, one is sometimes struck by the ambiguity of the thesis which is being argued. On the one hand Ryle seems to want to take the very radical line and claim that there are no 'mental' experiences, no private mental happenings, no states of ourselves which only we can be in a position to observe, and that all 'states of mind' are in fact capable of being regarded as ways of performing. On the other hand he does, in his positive analysis of ways of speaking about the mind, seem to concede that the dispositional analysis will not enable us to dispense with such occurrences altogether. In his discussion of intelligence and the distinction between 'knowing how' and 'knowing that' he implies that a great deal of thinking is done, as he inimitably puts it, '. . . in internal monologue or silent soliloquy, usually accompanied by an internal cinematograph show of visual imagery . . .',[36] and, in a very significant passage in which the ambiguity or even equivocation seems clear, he argues:

> Overt and intelligent performances are not clues to the workings of minds; they are those workings. Boswell described Johnson's mind when he described how he wrote, talked, ate, fidgeted and fumed. His description was, of course, incomplete, since there were notoriously some thoughts which Johnson kept carefully to himself, and there must have been many dreams, daydreams and silent babblings which only Johnson could have recorded and only James Joyce would wish him to have recorded.[37]

The clause 'which only Johnson could have recorded' seems to bring back privacy and privileged access with something of a vengeance. Ryle may not be particularly interested in such happenings or in attempts by 'stream-of-consciousness' novelists to record them, but in a passage which begins by stating his very radical and extreme thesis he concedes, or at least appears to concede, a great deal to those views which the general position seems, on the face of it, to rule out. These examples, and others which can be given, seem to imply a restriction of Ryle's thesis, namely to the position that the dispositional analysis which he adopts is capable of making intelligible a great deal of the import of our mental vocabulary in a way that a rigidly dualist distinction between the mind and the body cannot; but at the same time mental activity cannot be rendered in this way without something being left out. It is perhaps interesting that both Ryle and Wittgenstein vacillate in their different ways on this point. Both wished to insist that our 'mental' vocabulary refers by and large to overt performance, although Wittgenstein does not go into such detail as Ryle, nor does he hold such a determinate position, but when pressed by an imaginary interlocutor on the role of inner states Wittgenstein equivocates in as confusing a way as Ryle does in the passage quoted. He says:

> 'But you will surely admit that there is a difference between pain-behaviour accompanied by pain and pain-behaviour without any pain?'—Admit it? What greater difference could there be?—'And yet you again and again reach the conclusion that sensation itself is a *nothing*'—not at all. It is not a *something*, but not a nothing either. The conclusion was only that a nothing would serve just as well as a something about which nothing could be said.[38]

This is a crucial but tantalizingly obscure remark in Wittgenstein's attempt to elucidate the grammar of this aspect of our sensation vocabulary. Both Ryle and Wittgenstein appear implicitly to assert that there are features of mental experience which are non-behavioural and non-dispositional.

*The Concept of Mind* was probably the most consistent and most determined attempt to deal with a very broad problem from within the linguistic idiom. It is certainly a good deal more robust and asserts a far more rigid position than most followers of Austin would have wished to hold on the basis of the evidence produced, and it was a great deal more clear than any of the more tortured writings of Wittgenstein on the subject.

## II

The emphasis during the 1940s and 1950s upon ordinary language and its importance to philosophy, coupled with the view that this was in a sense a revolutionary approach to the subject,* led to a period of relative neglect of the history of philosophy. There was a

* As the title *The Revolution in Philosophy* (1957), a book of essays by influential figures in philosophy during the period, would imply.

feeling that there was very little to be learned from the history of the subject. Those who followed Wittgenstein felt that a great deal of classical philosophy was the result of reflection on the metaphysical use of words in isolation from their role in a stream of life, that these problems arose only when 'language went on holiday'. Austin, on the other hand, as we have seen, felt that philosophers had couched their problems in technical terminology which was often introduced to fill a spurious need, and which then generated in a quite gratuitous manner its own philosophical difficulties. As Warnock argued, describing Austin's technique: '. . . it may be salutary to place a moratorium on discussion of the state, on virtue, on the moral law, and consider instead the difference between kindness and kindliness and exactly what it is to be tactless and inconsiderate.'[39] Only through this patient process could the large problems be made to yield to thought even if they continued to exist in their original form after this spadework. This kind of emphasis and the lingering influence of the attack on metaphysics during the 1930s led to a general distrust of what might be termed 'big-system metaphysics' of the kind to be found, for example, in Plato, Spinoza, Leibnitz, Hegel, or Bradley. Nearer the end of our period, in the late 1950s, however, there was a significant move towards broader questions, and in this renewal of interest the influence of certain classical philosophers may be discerned. Three major works come to mind in this context—*Individuals* by P. F. Strawson, in which can be seen the influence of Kant; *Thought and Action* by Stuart Hampshire, which shows the influence certainly of Wittgenstein and Austin, but also of Spinoza and Hegel; and J. N. Findlay's *Values and Intentions*, much indebted to Hegel, Meinong, Husserl, and Sartre. Indeed, it is significant that all three of these philosophers have written books on important traditional philosophers, seeing in their work very positive value. Hampshire has discussed Spinoza,[40] Strawson Kant,[41] and Findlay Hegel[42] in a very sympathetic way.

In *Individuals* Strawson (b. 1919) draws a distinction between descriptive and revisionary metaphysics. The descriptive metaphysician is concerned to describe the structure of our thought about the world, and this is, in fact, Strawson's own aim in *Individuals*, published in 1959. As such, this style of metaphysics links up with some of the ideas of Wittgenstein and Austin about the need for a description of the actual conceptual and linguistic apparatus which we bring to bear on reality. As Wittgenstein argues, 'Philosophy leaves everything as it is.' But at the same time Strawson was willing to put in a good word for revisionary metaphysics too, when he argues that the best revisionary metaphysics—the attempt to provide a better structure for our thought about the world—are 'both intrinsically admirable and of enduring philosophical utility'.[43] Unfortunately Strawson takes this interesting observation no further, and the grounds for his making it are consequently left rather obscure.

Strawson subtitles his own work an 'Essay in Descriptive Metaphysics', and attempts to distinguish it in terms of its generality from what passed at the time for conceptual or linguistic analysis. The analyst may be interested in a small group of concepts taken from perhaps a restricted form of activity; the law, or morality, for example. The descriptive *metaphysician*, however, will attempt to describe the major features of our conceptual framework taken as a whole—its presuppositions which lie hidden below the surface of normal non-philosophical operations. Against such a view of the task of metaphysics it could be argued that merely to describe the general features of a particular given conceptual framework is implicitly to take it as standard and to fail to realize that conceptual schemes and structures have a history, that they change. Strawson's answer to this objection is that as a metaphysician he is interested only in the most *general* features of our thought about the world, and that these features do not vary: '. . . there is a massive central core of human thinking which has no history—or none recorded in histories of thought; there are categories and concepts which in their most fundamental character change not at all.'[44] He considers therefore that he is justified in arguing in a wholly *a priori* manner.

In *Individuals* Strawson argues that the basic component of our conceptual system is that of a material object, or spatio-temporal particular, and that it is only through the identification of a material object that we are able to identify anything at all. *Any* identifiable particular, he argues, must be related in a unique way to a particular which can be spatio-temporally located. One *prima facie* objection to this thesis arises when we consider states of mind, for there seem to be difficulties involved in the view that states of mind are to be identified by their unique relationship to a *material* object. It is in trying to overcome this objection that Strawson makes possibly the most original contribution to philosophy in the whole work.

He considers initially the other possible ways in which states of mind might be identified, the Cartesian theory and the no-ownership theory. On the Cartesian model, states of consciousness are not identified by reference to a material object; rather they are considered to be owned by a private *mind* or ego. Whereas the body is the subject of predicates which describe corporeal characteristics, the mind is the subject to which predicates denoting states of consciousness are ascribed. Obviously, if the Cartesian position could be maintained, it would deal a very severe blow indeed to the central thesis of *Individuals*, and Strawson employs considerable ingenuity in refuting Descartes. He argues that the idea of a predicate implies that there is a range of particulars to which the predicate may be significantly, although not necessarily truly, applied. This is regarded as being true even of predicates such as 'capital of', for it is certainly meaningful, but false, to say 'New York is the capital of the U.S.A.'

In the case of predicates denoting states of consciousness, this condition of something's being a predicate does not hold if the Cartesian model of the mind is presupposed. If the word 'pain' denotes a private sensation accessible only to me, then the range of that predicate is restricted only to me.* I cannot significantly apply it to anyone else because what the word 'pain' means is 'my pain'. My pain is the only exemplar of pain. This, however, conflicts with Strawson's notion of a predicate, and he argues that in order to apply such a predicate to oneself, one must first of all have built up, from the case of others, a significant range of application. '. . . It is a necessary condition of one's ascribing states of consciousness to oneself, in the way that one does, that one should also ascribe them, or be prepared to ascribe them, to others who are not oneself.'[45] Given the incoherence of the Cartesian position once the implications of predication are understood, Strawson argues that the way to solve the problem is to treat the concept of a person as logically primitive. The word 'I' refers not to a Cartesian subject, nor to a body merely, but to a person. Corporeal characteristics are ascribed to a person's body; other predicates are ascribed to the person on the basis of his bodily behaviour. The bodily behaviour of a person is not evidence for the existence of something else—as states of a Cartesian ego—rather it is the logically adequate criterion for the ascription of such states to him as a person.

Some of the same preoccupation with identifying particulars and persons can be seen to pervade Stuart Hampshire's (b. 1914) work *Thought and Action*, published in 1959, something of an *annus mirabilis* for British philosophy. Hampshire's book is, however, very different both in style and in much of its content from Strawson's work. Probably the most fundamental form of disagreement between

* '. . . the idea of a predicate is correlative with that of a *range* of distinguishable individuals of which the predicate can be significantly, though not necessarily truly, affirmed' (*Individuals*, p. 99). There is a critique of Strawson in A. J. Ayer's *The Concept of a Person* (1963).

them is over the neutrality of the descriptive method in philosophy. Hampshire argues that the philosopher, when writing about the general structure of thought, is compelled not merely to *describe* concepts but to *choose* between applications of them. There are situations in philosophizing when one comes across an essentially disputed concept, for example that of the human person, his powers and capacities. At this point merely impartial analysis fails, since the grammar of the language, to use Wittgenstein's expression, is not decisive. Concepts such as action, responsibility, intention, and freedom are not clear-cut in ordinary usage and yet they are crucial to what we mean by a person. How they are to be employed has ultimately to be *decided* upon by the philosopher, and in this area so connected with the possibility of human thought and action, this decision is in a sense a moral one. If Hampshire is correct, we see here the breakdown of Wittgenstein's suggestion that 'philosophy leaves everything as it is' and Austin's assimilation of philosophy to scientific method.

Hampshire himself has not, in fact, shied away from making such decisions, and in both *Thought and Action* and *Freedom of the Individual* he has been much concerned with defending a particular way of employing the concept of freedom. It has often been argued, first in the seventeenth century with the rise of natural science, and again in the twentieth century with the development of the social and human sciences, that knowledge is inimical to freedom. The more we come to know about the workings of the natural world, the workings of the human body, and the powers of the human mind, the more limited and exiguous will our freedom to act become. Hampshire rejects such a view because it implicitly links freedom with random activity, whereas for him freedom is much more a case of our being able to form intentions which we are then able to carry out. If freedom is understood in *this* sense, then knowledge becomes not so much the enemy of freedom as indispensable to its exercise. The more I know about the world in which I live, the structure of social relations within which I operate, and the workings of my own mind, the more will I be able to form intentions which I shall in fact be able to carry out. I shall not be frustrated by forming intentions which cannot be carried out because I am ignorant of the nature of my social world and the powers of my mind. Knowledge will inform me of what is within my power. Freedom is the capacity to form intentions within my power, and to carry them out successfully. However broad scientific knowledge of the world, society, and myself may become, I can always, Hampshire argues, step back, put some distance between myself and such knowledge, and say, 'Given what I know, how shall I act?' No advance in science can undermine this freedom.

Although Hampshire philosophizes within the analytical linguistic idiom, his development of the idiom in new directions is plain. He has emphasized the necessity for choice between sets of disputed concepts, and the need to provide a justification for such a choice. Philosophy for Hampshire can be descriptive, scientific, and objective only up to a point; beyond that point it has to become revisionary in a way which demands not just academic but also moral commitment. This way of philosophizing links up this broader analytical and linguistic idiom with the great philosophical works of the past, particularly with Spinoza and Hegel. The revolution in philosophy widely talked about in the early 1950s is now seen to be not so revolutionary, but perhaps more interesting for not being so.

The development of the linguistic idiom in philosophy, with the emphasis upon the complexity of usage, the contextual and practical basis of meaning, and the relationship between philosophical problems and language thus conceived, led to a revision of the role of formal logic in philosophy. During the earlier part of the century, under the general influence of the writings of Frege, Russell, and the earlier work of Wittgenstein, philosophers had come to see their task as being that of logical analysis. In some sense, their purpose was to translate recalcitrant sentences which generate philosophical problems into a more formal mode, whereupon their problematic status would disappear. Probably the largest single influence here was Russell's theory of descriptions, which was regarded by F. P. Ramsey and many of his generation as a paradigm of philosophy. However, with the growing emphasis upon language and its ordinary contextual usage, there grew up the feeling that the role of logic in philosophy was really quite restricted. Although such a view is very strongly implied in many of Wittgenstein's *obiter dicta*, particularly in the *Philosophical Investigations*, much of the credit, or at least the responsibility, for this changed view on the role of logic *vis-à-vis* philosophy must lie with Strawson. His views on these matters were formulated with reference to the theory of descriptions in 'On Referring',[46] and towards logic in general in *An Introduction to Logical Theory* (1952). In his article 'On Referring', Strawson made a frontal attack upon the theory of descriptions, which had been widely regarded as a perfect example of philosophical analysis. Russell had argued in 'On Denoting'[47] that the sentence, 'The present King of

France is bald', is meaningful but false, and his theory of description was an attempt to account for this. He regarded it as a conjunction of three statements, namely:

(i) There is something which is King of France.
(ii) Whatever else is King of France is identical with that thing.
(iii) If anything is King of France, then it is bald.

This may be fully translated symbolically as:

$(\exists x)[\phi x]$.
$(y)[\phi y \supset y \equiv x] \,.\, \psi x$.

This translation* does not mention the non-existent and is to be regarded as a straightforward factual claim which is in fact false. For Strawson, however, this theory is a response to a question which would never have been framed had careful attention been paid initially to the statement. Strawson argued that Russell's basic mistake was to suppose that if a significant sentence is not being used to make a true statement, then it must be being used to make a false statement. A *sentence*, Strawson argues, is never true or false, but can be either meaningless or significant; a *statement*, on the other hand, can be true or false but not as such meaningful or meaningless. A sentence is to be understood just as a set of words, sounds, or symbols, and as such can be used to make a variety of statements. For example, 'The present King of France is bald' makes different statements depending on the context. If it were uttered in the seventeenth or eighteenth century, it would in those contexts be true or false, but taken as a sentence outside of any context at all the question of truth or falsity does not arise. Before such questions arise the statement-making context must first be understood.

This emphasis upon the totally contextual nature of language, and how the same words may be used in a wide variety of utterances, echoes Wittgenstein's insistence upon the multiplicity of language games. Logic is therefore of quite limited usefulness in philosophy. It cannot formalize contextual discourse, and yet most philosophical problems arise from such contexts. Certainly logic may be of use in situations where context does not matter, such as, for example, in mathematics and science, but it cannot cope with the complexity of informal discourse. In his *Introduction to Logical Theory* Strawson takes this view a great deal further and argues that the logical connectives defined in truth-table terms which the logician uses to refer to connectives in ordinary speech (e.g. if . . . then, not, and,

* $(\exists x)$ is the logician's symbol for 'There is an $x$'. It is usually called the existential quantifier. $(y)$ is the universal quantifier. The second symbolized line includes (ii) and (iii) above.

or) only represent a *selection* from how these are used in ordinary discourse. Strawson goes on in Chapter 8 of the work to argue the case for an informal theory of the logic of ordinary discourse—'the study of the logical features of ordinary speech'. This differs, he argues, from Austinian-style analysis in that in the attempt to answer from the case of ordinary speech such questions as ' "What are the conditions under which we use such and such an expression or class of expressions?" or "Why do we say such and such a thing and not such and such another?", we may find ourselves able to frame classifications or disclose differences broad and deep enough to satisfy the strongest appetite for generality.'[48]

Such an informal logic of language will not have the crystalline purity of classical logic, or of the propositional calculus, but it is precisely this kind of purity which, Strawson argues, has kept logic divorced from the context of ordinary speech, where most intractable philosophical difficulties are to be found.

## III

So far this essay has been concerned more with the general methodological perspectives adopted by the chief mentors of the present generation of philosophers, and how these perspectives were applied by those who developed them to particular philosophical problems and difficulties. In the field of the specific areas of philosophy, particularly moral philosophy and the philosophy of mind, a good deal of important work was produced by those who showed a general commitment to the notion of philosophical analysis, but who were not necessarily in the forefront of methodological investigation. For the purposes of this essay I shall consider two general areas. The first is the debate within moral philosophy between Richard Hare, who advocated a form of non-naturalism, and such neo-naturalists as Mrs. Foot. The other belongs to the philosophy of mind, particularly the attempt to elucidate the concept of action and the connected concepts of intention, motive, and volition.

Before the Second World War, moral philosophy was dominated by two incompatible positions: the intuitionism of Ross and Pritchard, and the emotivism expounded by A. J. Ayer in *Language, Truth and Logic*. The crucial issue separating the intuitionists from the emotivists was the status of moral discourse. For the intuitionists to make a moral judgement was to state a fact, albeit of a somewhat idiosyncratic type. They held that an action, a situation, or an event was possessed of a non-natural property, namely goodness or badness, rightness or wrongness. The presence or the absence of a non-natural quality was to be discerned through intuition, with one's mind's eye, or with one's moral sense. The moral agent was regarded as a spectator making attempts to describe his observations.

For the emotivists, on the other hand, moral judgements did not state facts at all, nor did they convey information: they were, in a *sense*, meaningless. The meaning such judgements had was regarded as emotive; they were used to evince, express, give vent to feelings and attitudes, and in such a way as to influence the actions of others. No information was being given: a feeling was being expressed. Emotivism, of course, was part and parcel of the radical empiricism of the positivists. The insistence on the emotive meaning of ethical terms was the result less of a phenomenological inquiry into the types of assertions made in moral life, than the consequence of the positivists' rigid dichotomy between the necessary and tautological on the one hand, and the contingent and synthetic on the other, coupled with the claim that all discourse with cognitive meaning has to fall into one of these two patterns. Moral language manifestly does not, and hence was regarded, on logico-metaphysical grounds, as emotive.

To many opponents of emotivism this thesis appeared not so much as an attempt to locate moral discourse on a logical map, as a recipe for social and moral irrationalism, an understandable charge in the context of the late 1930s. This charge initially had more plausibility than it warranted, in that Ayer's views on moral philosophy in *Language, Truth and Logic*, though immensely influential, were perhaps too succinctly expressed. He insisted upon the emotive, non-cognitive status of moral discourse, and left it more or less at that. The charge of irrationalism was mitigated a great deal during the war years by J. N. Findlay in 'Morality by Convention', an article published in *Mind* for 1944, and by C. L. Stevenson in *Ethics and Language*. Both these writers stressed that the feelings and the emotions which moral judgements express do not exist in the void, but arise out of and are connected with beliefs about the world. Certainly, at the purely moral, attitudinal level, disagreement is possible—*de gustibus non est disputandum*—but the beliefs on which attitudes are based can be discussed perfectly rationally. Both Findlay and Stevenson insisted that the charge of irrationality launched against emotivism should be seen in the perspective of the relation between belief and attitude.

At the same time, however, Stevenson in particular did not want to minimize the non-rational element in morality, but only wished that its location should be understood. Moral assertions are emotive, but they are much more. They do not merely *express* an individual's attitude; they also seek to *propagandize* it. Many words used in moral judgement, according to Stevenson, involve persuasive definition. A word is used in such a way that it has both descriptive and evaluative content, and in moral judgement we trade on this. 'Democracy' is a word which in our society has a strong positive evaluation built into it, but a very fuzzy descriptive meaning; consequently it is very easy to use it in a variety of different contexts to refer obliquely to features of the context and elicit approval for it. To say of a person's conduct in a meeting that it was 'undemocratic' is to express an attitude, but also to attempt to elicit an unfavourable one on the part of others by referring to his behaviour in this kind of dual descriptive/evaluative way. A contemporary political scientist has stressed how this still occurs in the case of democracy: 'Democracy is perhaps the most promiscuous word in the world of public affairs. She is everybody's mistress and yet retains her magic even when a lover sees that her favours are being, in his light, shared by many another.'[49] This distinction between the descriptive meaning of an expression, which in the case of democracy is unclear, and its emotive meaning, which interestingly enough is very strong, is very important for understanding the subsequent development of moral philosophy. Especially influential is the work of Richard Hare (b. 1919), particularly his *Language of Morals* (1952) and *Freedom and Reason* (1963).

Hare's work can best be seen as at one and the same time a reaction against some features of emotivism and a development of some of its fundamental ideas in a rather different direction. Hare apparently committed himself to moral philosophy in an attempt to find a *rational* basis for morals without at the same time abandoning subjectivism and non-naturalism.[50] He freely agrees with the emotivist that moral utterances do not convey information about the inherence or the supervention of moral qualities, but whereas the emotivist had seen the language of morals as a medium for the *expression* of feelings and the propagation of attitudes, Hare saw in morality an action-guiding basis, its status prescriptive and imperatival, shot through with a *sui generis* form of rationality, and being based ultimately not upon feeling but upon decision.[51]

At first sight it might seem that the change in emphasis from expression to guidance is slight. What is at stake in it? The answer is that this change places importance on the role of rationality in morals. If, as the emotivists assert, the function of moral discourse is both expressive and propagandist, then the notion of reason plays no intrinsic part: influence could be exercised in other ways, for example through drugs, blackmail, advertising, or hypnosis. The notion of influence does not require that there should be rational grounds for the exercise of it. The case is very different, however, with guidance. There has to be an explicit understanding of what is being offered as guidance. There can be no subtle persuasive definition, and this will involve an understanding of the grounds on which it is offered. Hence for Hare the role of rationality is intrinsic to the moral context.

Moral assertions are action-guiding although they need not have the grammatical form which attempts at guidance usually have, namely hortatory or minatory imperatives; rather, for Hare, moral assertions or moral judgements *entail* imperatives. 'X is right' is indicative in form, but it entails the imperative 'Do X' or 'Let us do X'. A moral judgement is not itself imperatival, but all moral judgements entail imperatives for Hare. He has attempted to work out an imperatival logic which would thus illuminate the structure of moral argument, and a logic which helps to understand the role of factual assertions in moral discourse. The general imperative-implying assertion above—namely 'X is right'—might be exemplified in the particular form 'It would be right to feed this man', which may be seen as a conclusion of the following explicit or presupposed piece of reasoning:

It is right to feed the starving
This man is starving
∴ it is right to feed this man.

The major premise and the conclusion both entail imperatives; one a general one, 'Let us feed the starving', the other a particular one, 'Let us feed this man'. 'This man is starving' is a factual premise. The problem then arises: what is the status of the major premise? We can see how the conclusion follows logically from the conjunction of the premises, but what about the major moral premise? (The minor factual premise is not in principle a difficulty.) Hare has two moves to make here. The first move is that the major premise may itself be the conclusion of some more general moral syllogism; the second is that it records some fundamental *decision* on my part to commit myself to this principle. It is obvious that even if the first move is made, sometime we shall be forced to take up the second.

At this point in the exposition, the reader has a right to be puzzled. It might be conceded that Hare has shown a logical connection between a particular principle of action and a general principle, and the mediating role of factual assertions; but if, in the end, major premises in practical syllogisms record decisions and commitments, is not this to come back to the irrationalism of emotivism despite the veneer of logical sophistication? Decision has merely replaced feeling. No wonder it has been argued by Hare's critics that here is a British existentialist.* We all make our moral commitments, and ultimately we cannot argue against those who make different ones.

This criticism would, however, be misconceived, because at this point Hare brings to bear the other logical feature of moral discourse, its universalizability. According to Hare, to say that something ought to be done is never to make a particular judgement; it is always to imply that whoever else is in a *relevant* situation ought to do X. 'Whoever' here is meant to include the moral agent himself as well as the rest of mankind. Similarly, to say that 'X is good' is to use a word with both a descriptive and an evaluative force. The word 'good' evaluates X, but does so in terms of certain palpable features of X which I have chosen as criteria of goodness: these constitute the descriptive meaning of 'good'. In this case too I am committed to a universalizable judgement, but by the *descriptive* meaning of the word.

Hare considers that this universalizability criterion allows one to have leverage with a moral opponent. If a man says that 'Black men or their descendants ought to be kept out of white society', this judgement, if it is to be a *moral* judgement, must be universalizable. So it is always proper to ask the person who holds such views: 'If you were found to be the descendant of a black man, would you be prepared to be treated in the same way?' Hare believes that few people would accept this: those who would may, he says, be labelled fanatics. This is in a sense an odd argument, because it does not really alter the logical basis of moral judgement, namely choice and decision; the thesis of universalizability is an attempt rather to make people aware of the logical implications of moral choice. It is, however, possible for someone to accept such an implication, and here reasons have an end. To call him a fanatic may be justified, but

* Hare's own answer to this charge of the arbitrariness of principles is as follows:

> To describe such ultimate decisions as arbitrary because *ex hypothesi* everything which could be used to justify them has already been included in the decision would be like saying that a complete description of the universe was utterly unfounded, because no further fact could be called upon in corroboration of it. This is not how we use the words 'arbitrary' and 'unfounded'. (*The Language of Morals*, p. 69.)

really the rationality of morals is a fragile veneer laid over matters of choice and decision.

A further interesting feature of Hare's theory which has attracted a good deal of comment is his doctrine of moral weakness. Moral judgements entail imperatives. We assent to a description by believing it; we assent to an imperative by acting on it. Action, not belief, is therefore the touchstone of moral sincerity. *Not* to act on a moral judgement if one is psychologically and physically able to do so is tantamount to a denial of the principle involved. Taken at its face value, therefore, there is a problem of sincerity but not of moral weakness.

The counter-objection here is that patently sincere people may be morally weak. The most quoted example in this context is St. Paul who, in the Epistle to the Romans, VI, argues: 'The good which I want to do, I fail to do; but what I do is the wrong which is against my will; . . . I want to do the right, but only the wrong is within my reach.' Some philosophers have insisted that this is a case of moral weakness, and not insincerity. Hare, however, argues that in fact St. Paul does not fulfil the requirement of being psychologically capable of acting on the imperatives which his moral views entail, and he regards this as being made clear in the context of the passage. St. Paul says: '. . . if what I do is against my will, clearly it is no longer I who am the agent, but sin that is lodging within me.' St. Paul can sincerely accept 'the law of God', but because his bodily nature operates under a different law he is 'a prisoner under the law that is in my members', and thus not a moral agent in the full sense.

The other major objection which has been raised against Hare's thesis is over the role of choice in terms of the criteria by virtue of which one uses evaluative words. According to Hare, evaluative words are used in terms of descriptive criteria—but I choose the criteria. Once chosen, I am in a sense bound by them because they allow the evaluative judgement to be universalized, but the fact remains that I choose them in the first place. Mrs. Foot and Peter Geach have argued strongly against this account of choice in morality. According to Mrs. Foot, the criteria for the use of evaluative expressions are not open to choice. In the case of human virtues and vices, if certain factual conditions are fulfilled, then the ascription of the virtue or the vice follows as a matter of course. For example, if I spit in the face of an acquaintance without cause or provocation, then it follows that I am *rude*; there is no role for choice. Someone who refuses the ascription fails to see the meaning of 'rude'. Similarly with commendation of objects. The criteria involved in calling a knife a good knife are tied to the function for which knives are specified. One cannot choose the criteria here: they are fixed by the specification of the object. Geach stresses the importance of function in morality. The nature of an object, screwdriver, cow, farmer, etc., supply criteria for ascription of evaluative terms. This thesis is extremely Aristotelian, but is involved in many objections. It might be argued that while certain human functions may be clear-cut, so that the criteria for evaluation are determinate, this does not apply to a great many important functions, for example, 'teacher'. Is a good teacher one who instils into his children self-discipline, and initiates them into the structure of an academic tradition; or one who merely acts as a guide to the free expression of personality in a wholly open and unstructured fashion? Here it seems that we must *choose* our criterion. We also have the evaluative expression, 'He is a good man.' What can be made of this? Is it reducible to a set of statements about particular functions, i.e. he is a good father, husband, teacher, Chinese clog dancer, or has man *per se* a function? Certainly Aristotle considered he had when he argued in his *Nicomachean Ethics*: 'Are we then to suppose that, while the carpenter and shoemaker have definite functions . . . man as such has none?' In a secular world in which the notion of human nature is an essentially contested concept, as we have seen Hampshire arguing, such a specifically human function is very difficult to determine.

It might also be argued that to stress the function of human beings and to regard these as central to the evaluation of persons is morally dangerous; it can lead to a narrowing of moral horizons. Gerald in *Women in Love* expresses in a rather frightening way the Aristotelian-Geach moral perspective:

> What mattered was the pure instrumentality of the individual. As a man as of a knife: does it cut well? Nothing else mattered.
>
> Everything in the world has its function, and is good or not good in so far as it fulfils this function more or less perfectly.

This emphasis upon looking at some kind of objective background to morality instead of fixing the source of moral value ultimately in individual decision-making has been transformed by Iris Murdoch in a highly significant work, *The Sovereignty of Good* (1970), into an extremely metaphysical thesis. She sees in great works of art something which will wean us away from particularity and prejudice in our moral judgements, and which will provide a universal dimension as a background for the moral life. She asserts that this cannot be found in human nature itself: that man has to look for the transcendant if he is to live morally.

The counterpoise to this thesis in a sense was an article by Professor Anscombe published in 1958[52] in which she argued that progress in moral philosophy depended upon progress in the philosophy of mind. The virtues and the vices, she maintained, are connected with human flourishing, a notion which in turn is connected with needs and wants. Only in so far as the powers of the human mind are specified in the philosophy of mind shall we know what would contribute to human flourishing. The philosophy of mind would almost provide a transcendental deduction of the virtues and the vices. Such a view, despite its initial plausibility, shows a great lack of sociological sophistication. Morality cannot be derived from a specification of human needs, for what a man is regarded as needing is basically defined by the moral context in which he lives, moves, and has his being.[53] All that the philosophy of mind can do is to elucidate in a very formal way the basic meanings of central concepts such as intention, motive, will, etc., and the relations between them.

Taken in this very formal way, the philosophy of mind has been one of the most interesting areas in philosophical discussion during our period. The major figures discussed earlier—Wittgenstein, Ryle, Austin, and Wisdom—all made signal contributions to the subject, but in addition many lines of inquiry which they only began to open up were very fruitfully exploited by other thinkers. Of course, the very idea of philosophy of mind is one which may arouse suspicion in the minds of empiricists. What can the philosopher, with no laboratory, no specific training, no apparatus, contribute to this subject, which is the preserve of empirical researchers in psychology, physiology, and perhaps linguistics? The general answer to this question must be that the philosopher is concerned with the analysis of the concepts used by these practitioners, but also, and more importantly even, the concepts used in ordering daily life in our attempts to talk about our own experiences, feelings, motives, and so on. Whatever empirical practitioners may achieve, their theories often appear to have no connection with the elucidations of these concepts in everyday life.

Perhaps the most central and, if valid, most important distinction drawn by philosophers of mind is that between action and behaviour and the different kinds of explanations relevant to each. It is possible, so the argument runs, to distinguish sheer colourless physical movement and the action which is, as it were, constituted from such physical movement. Certainly action statements are not reducible to sets of statements about physical movements. The same set of physical movements, for example those involved in forming the letters which constitute my signature, may constitute a whole range of different actions: paying a gas bill by cheque; signing a register; expressing my views on abortion in a petition; egotistical doodling and so on.[54] Actions are linked both to language and to social convention. They have to be identified and picked out by reference to the range of concepts available: concepts which in turn presuppose institutions, practices, and activities. Physical movements, on the other hand, are to be identified through neutral physiological concepts. The explanation of action is in terms of reasons which presuppose conventions; explanation of behaviour on the other hand is in terms of causes. There are no doubt great problems as to how these two sorts of explanations are to be correlated, since one cannot perform an action without one's body moving in certain ways, but notionally they are distinct.

This emphasis upon the category of human action has also led to philosophical investigation of central 'mental' concepts associated with action, such as intention, motive, and will. Very often philosophers have regarded action as distinct from a sheer physical reflex, because action is prefaced by some inner event, such as the forming of an intention, having a motive in mind, or performing an act of will. These occurrences were supposed to stand as causal antecedents to physical movements, making such movements purposive and thus not sheer reflex movements. A great deal of energy has been expended in destroying this assumption. One of the major works here has been A. I. Melden's influential *Free Action* (1961), in which he tries to account for our conceptual distinction between reflex behaviour and intentional, purposive, voluntary action. A major argument against the inner-cause view is that causal connections, at least on the Humean account, are constant contingent conjunctions between distinct existences, and such existences require independent identification. This is impossible in second- and third-person cases in the case of intentions, motives, and acts of will. I can only identify another person's intention, motive, or act of will *through* his bodily behaviour: I have no direct acquaintance with the occurrences in his mind and, furthermore, if Wittgenstein's strictures on private languages are accepted, I cannot talk about my own inner states until I have learned to identify them in the case of others. This entails that there is a conceptual connection between the specification of intentions, motives, and acts of will, and sorts and types of behaviour, which then entails that these are *not* distinct things in the requisite

Humean sense, and thus do not stand in a causal relation with one another. The distinction between action and reflex behaviour, a good many philosophers would say, has to be linked, as was suggested earlier in this discussion, with conventions. We learn to recognize actions or see behaviour as constituting a particular action through our social training, by which we are initiated into an established structure of convention, and an established set of linguistic practices.

This linking of action and convention has also led to the conclusion that the *identification* of action in certain important cases in a pluralistic society is problematic. People may bring to bear different sorts of convention in their identification of action. Where one man sees primarily an economic activity, a Calvinist may see a man gaining a sign of his election; the existence of sub-cultures with their own specific conventions and their own ways of seeing makes identification in many cases difficult. There are no brute facts about human action;[55] where we agree in identification we agree on the basis of shared convention; where we do not, the conventions have a lack of congruence.

## IV

Throughout this period in British philosophy a certain insularity reigned. Apart from one or two conferences to discuss themes of mutual interest, conferences which often turned into dialogues of the deaf, there was very little explicit influence or contact between British and continental philosophy. This was so in spite of the fact that there are clear affinities in results, if not in methods; for example, both Heidegger and Wittgenstein stress how much man's conception of himself and his world depends upon his being a part of a linguistic community. Heidegger stressed the practical nature of knowledge in *Being and Time* in a way which perhaps finds an echo in the work of Ryle; Hare has often been called the British existentialist, and despite a brisk matter-of-factness totally alien to the brooding anxiety of Sartre, the two are alike in stressing, for very different reasons, the role of choice and decision in morality. Hampshire's concern with the nature of the human mind, his emphasis upon psycho-analysis and its philosophical importance, and his attempt to make the philosophy of mind relevant to moral philosophy and aesthetics finds a reflection in the similar preoccupations of Merleau-Ponty and Sartre. However, more recently there have been more hopeful signs of dialogue. Continental philosophy has been dominated by the thought of Kant, Hegel, and Marx in a way in which British philosophy has never been; but with the development of political radicalism among students in the late 1960s there has been a resurrection certainly of interest in Marx and Hegel. Philosophy students have been convinced by French philosophers such as Goldman and Lefebvre, by Germans such as Marcuse, Adorno, and Habermas, that there is much of central philosophical importance in thinkers such as Hegel, Marx, Kant, and Fichte. It is an open question whether or not they will be able to convince their teachers.

## NOTES

[1] L. Wittgenstein, *Zettel* (1967), 12.

[2] On Hegel's linguistic insights reference might be made to R. Plant, *Hegel* (1972).

[3] There is a very good discussion of the *Tractatus* from this point of view in D. Favrholdt, *An Interpretation and Critique of Wittgenstein's 'Tractatus'* (Copenhagen, 1964).

[4] *Proceedings of the Aristotelian Society*, Supp. vol. IX (1929), 162.

[5] Ibid. 163.

[6] *V*. L. Wittgenstein, *Philosophical Investigations* (1953), paras. 28, 33.

[7] Ibid. para. 115.

[8] Ibid. para. 122.

[9] Ibid. para. 133. Cf. L. Wittgenstein, *Remarks on the Foundation of Mathematics* (1956), 109.

[10] L. Wittgenstein, *Blue Book* (1958), 6.

[11] *Philosophical Investigations*, para. 128.

[12] Ibid. para. 23.

[13] *Remarks on the Foundation of Mathematics*, IV, 53.

[14] *Blue Book*, 6. Cf. *Philosophical Investigations*, para. 126, also 325, 326.

[15] *Philosophical Investigations*, para. 217.

[16] Ibid. para. 258.

[17] Ibid. para. 265.

[18] Ibid.

[19] This is Ayer's example in 'Can There be a Private Language', *Proc. A. Soc.*, Supp. vol. XXVIIIa (1954).

[20] Some of the implications have been drawn, *v*. P. G. Winch, *The Idea of a Social Science* (1958); H. McCabe, *Law, Love and Language* (1968); Brian Wicker, *Culture and Theology* (1966).

[21] *V*. Preface to M. Lazarowitz, *The Structure of Metaphysics* (1958).

[22] J. L. Austin, *Philosophical Papers* (1961), 85.

[23] Ibid. 130.

[24] Ibid. 131.

[25] Cahiers de Royaumont: Philosophie No. IV, *La Philosophie Analytique* (Paris, 1962), 350.

[26] *Philosophical Papers*, 129.

[27] Ibid. 163. He also discusses the problem with reference to Latin. 'I could have' is sometimes equivalent to *potui*, i.e. 'I *was* in a position to'; on other occasions it may be translated by *potuissem*, i.e. 'I should have been in a position to'.

[28] *V.* particularly Lecture II for a classification of infelicities.

[29] *V.* particularly Lecture V. A simple discussion of the performative/constative distinction is to be found in Cahiers de Royaumont, op. sit., '*Performatif—constatif*', 271 ff.

[30] *Proc. A. Soc.*, XXXII (1931–2), 139–70.

[31] *Mind*, XXXVIII (1929), 355–70.

[32] For a sympathetic discussion of Meinong and of his influence on British philosophy, *v.* J. N. Findlay, *Meinong's Theory of Objects* (2nd ed., 1965).

[33] G. Ryle, *The Concept of Mind* (Penguin ed., 1963), 31. All quotations are from this edition.

[34] The general form of this thesis is extensively argued in his article 'Heterologicality', *Analysis*, XI (1950–1), 61–9.

[35] *The Concept of Mind*, 44.

[36] Ibid. 28.

[37] Ibid. 57.

[38] Wittgenstein, *Philosophical Investigations*, para. 304.

[39] G. J. Warnock, 'J. L. Austin: A Remarkable Philosopher', *The Listener*, 7 April 1960, p. 617.

[40] S. Hampshire, *Spinoza* (1951).

[41] P. F. Strawson, *The Bonds of Sense* (1966).

[42] J. N. Findlay, *Hegel: A Re-examination* (1959).

[43] P. F. Strawson, *Individuals* (1959), 9.

[44] Ibid. 10.

[45] Ibid. 99.

[46] *Mind*, 1950.

[47] In *Mind*, 1905; reprinted in *Logic and Knowledge*, ed. R. C. Marsh (1956).

[48] P. F. Strawson, *Introduction to Logical Theory* (1952), 232.

[49] B. Crick, *In Defence of Politics* (1964).

[50] W. D. Hudson, *Modern Moral Philosophy* (1970), 157.

[51] This aspect of Hare's work is discussed most fully in Chapter IV of *The Language of Morals*.

[52] G. E. M. Anscombe, 'Modern Moral Philosophy', in *Philosophy*, XXXIII (1958).

[53] *V.* the reply to Anscombe in D. Z. Phillips and H. O. Mounce, 'On Morality's Having a Point', *Philosophy*, XL (1965).

[54] For an argument of this sort *v.* A. MacIntyre, 'A Mistake about Causality in Social Science', in *Philosophy, Politics and Society*, Ser. II, ed. P. Laslett and W. G. Runciman (1964).

[55] *V.* G. E. M. Anscombe, *Intention* (1957), section 23, and 'On Brute Facts', *Analysis*, 1958.

## FOR FURTHER READING

The notes contain references to most of the main works published by those who exercised most influence in philosophy during the period. Among general surveys J. Passmore's book, *A Hundred Years of Philosophy* (1968), is unsurpassed. *British Analytical Philosophy*, ed. Bernard Williams and A. Montifiore (1966), is not a survey but a selection of essays by influential analytical philosophers who attempt not so much to talk about analytical techniques as to apply them to a whole range of questions. The book also contains an interesting introduction by Williams and Montifiore, and a good comparative article on Wittgenstein and Austin by D. F. Pears. *The Revolution in Philosophy*, edited by A. J. Ayer (1957), is an attempt by several of its leading practitioners to interpret the development and role of analytical philosophy. A general attack on the movement may be found in E. Gellner's notorious *Words and Things* (1959), which was refused a review in *Mind* by Ryle, an action which led to a long and acrimonious correspondence in *The Times*. The consequences of this rumpus are interestingly discussed by Ved Mehta in *The Fly and the Fly-bottle* (1963).

The later work of Wittgenstein has attracted several major commentaries, the first of which was by David Pole, *The Later Philosophy of Wittgenstein* (1958). Other more comprehensive works are G. Pitcher, *The Philosophy of Wittgenstein* (Englewood Cliffs, N.J., 1964); K. T. Fann, *The Philosophy of Wittgenstein* (Oxford, 1967); D. F. Pears, *Wittgenstein* (1971). The last volume is probably the best. There is also a very interesting collection of articles edited by G. Pitcher in *Wittgenstein* (1968).

Several philosophers have attempted to apply Wittgenstein's insights more systematically to particular philosophical problems, particularly Peter Winch in his *The Idea of a Social Science* (1958), and his article 'Understanding a Primitive Society' in the *American Philosophical Quarterly*, 1964. Whereas Winch has looked at sociological and anthropological understanding from a Wittgensteinian point of view, D. Z. Phillips has concentrated upon religion, particularly in *The Concept of Prayer* (1967) and *Faith and Philosophical Understanding* (1971). An analysis of the importance of Wittgenstein's work for theology is to be found in W. D. Hudson, *Ludwig Wittgenstein* (1968).

General studies on Austin in book form are few. There is a collection of essays edited by K. T. Fann, *The Philosophy of J. L. Austin* (1970), and M. Furberg, *Locutionary and Illocutionary Acts* (The Hague, 1963). Ayer has replied to Austin's critique of his views on sense-data in 'Has Austin Refuted the Sense Datum Theory?' in *Metaphysics and Common Sense* (1969). There is a good collection of essays on Gilbert Ryle in *Ryle*, ed. O. Wood and G. Pitcher (1971).

The work of Hampshire on the philosophy of mind and upon moral philosophy has been extensively criticized by Iris Murdoch in *The Sovereignty of Good* (1970). The role of Hampshire's work as a foil to Miss Murdoch's own conceptions is discussed at some length in A. S. Byatt's *Degrees of Freedom: The Novels of Iris Murdoch* (1965).

The vexed question of the relationship between logic and philosophy has attracted a good deal of attention. Strawson's opinions express what a great many modern British philosophers feel, but by no means all of them. P. T. Geach, A. N. Prior, and C. Lejewski, all from different points of view, have insisted upon the importance of logic for philosophy—Geach even in the ambiguous implication of the title of his *Logic Matters* (1971), and Prior by his practice in *Past, Present and Future* (Oxford, 1967) and *Papers on Time and Tense* (1968), and his posthumous *Objects of Thought* (Oxford, 1971). Lejewski has attempted to emphasize the importance for philosophical problems of the logical systems developed in the 1930s in Poland, particularly in his 'Leśniewski's Ontology' in *Ratio* (1961) and in 'Logic and Existence', published in a volume of general interest on this topic—*Logic and Philosophy*, ed. G. Iseminger (New York, 1968).

Moral philosophy has been a very fertile field for philosophical work during this period. A good general survey is G. J. Warnock, *Contemporary Moral*

*Philosophy* (1967). W. D. Hudson has drawn together many of the most influential papers of the period in a valuable volume *The Is/Ought Question* (1969). A companion volume, *Weakness of Will*, edited by G. Mortimer (1970), contains articles on Hare's theories on assenting to a moral principle. Alasdair MacIntyre, *A Short History of Ethics* (1967), discusses the development of modern moral philosophy and has an interesting discussion of the differences between Hare and the neo-naturalists. P. G. Winch, *Moral Integrity* (Oxford, 1970), is a fine statement of the opposite position to that found in Professor Anscombe and Mrs. Foot's work. R. W. Beardsmore in *Moral Reasoning* (1969) and D. Z. Phillips and H. O. Mounce in *Moral Practices* (1970) take up analogous positions from a basically Wittgensteinian point of view.

In the philosophy of mind a series of *Studies in Philosophical Psychology*, edited by R. Holland, have been very influential indeed. G. E. M. Anscombe, *Intention* (Oxford, 1957), is probably the most influential discussion of a particular concept; C. Taylor, *The Explanation of Behaviour* (1964), is an extremely interesting work and also slightly out of line with the mainstream argument about the explanation of action encountered during our period. Taylor argues that the question of whether human behaviour is explicable mechanistically or teleologically is in fact an empirical and not a conceptual issue. Alasdair MacIntyre, 'The Antecedents of Action' in *British Analytical Philosophy* (cited above), also casts some doubts upon the action/behaviour–reasons/causes distinction.

The revival of interest in continental philosophy is perhaps best manifested in translation. Lukàcs's *History and Class Consciousness* was translated in 1971; Goldmann's classical study on Jansenism and its role in French society and influence on Racine, *The Hidden God*, has been published in English, as has his study, *Immanuel Kant* (1972), and his short work, *The Human Sciences and Philosophy* (1969). There is at the moment a growing interest in the works of M. Merleau-Ponty on the philosophy of mind, particularly his *Structure of Behaviour* (1968) and *The Phenomenology of Perception* (1962), and in the writings of Jurgen Habermas on philosophy and social thought, particularly the selection from his *Technik und Wissenschaft als Ideologie* which has been published in *Towards a Rational Society* (1971) and *Knowledge and Human Interests* (1971). Also of significance in this revival of interest in continental thought is the *British Journal of Phenomenology and Existentialism*, edited from the Philosophy Department in the University of Manchester.

# 4

# Theology

DAVID A. PAILIN

In November 1939 William Temple (1881–1944) wrote in *Theology* that future theologians 'must dig the foundations deeper' and 'be content with less imposing structures' than their predecessors. While he was confident that 'one day theology will take up again its large and serene task, and offer to a new Christendom its Christian map of life', he considered that 'that day can barely dawn while any who are now already concerned with theology are still alive'.[1] A quarter of a century later it could not be claimed with any conviction that 'that day' had begun to dawn. In the intervening years, as we shall see, various types of theological activity were pursued. Some of these may lead to the desired dawn but as yet none of them can be judged to provide more than possibly fruitful lines for further exploration.

In the immediate postwar years the Church felt that it had something significant to say to a world whose values had been disturbed by the war. Church leaders expected an end to the decline of the Church and predicted its future growth. Theologians shared this optimism. They were confident that their judgements were important and that the world ought to take them seriously. By the early 1960s, however, this optimism had faded. In both numbers and influence the Church was continuing to decline. Commentators were describing the era as 'post-Christian'. Nietzsche's remark that 'God is dead' and the churches are his 'sepulchre' was no longer the cry of a madman before his time: it announced what had happened and could be seen to have happened. At the same time theologians had become introspective. Increasingly they were concerned with discerning the complexities of their task and the difficulties in establishing significant theological understanding in the present age. Thus, by the end of our period, while few theologians would agree that it was a time 'when Christian theology, if it is to be true to itself, must be silent'—the volume of their writings showed in practice how much they disagreed!—there was widespread agreement that it was 'a time for ploughing, not reaping; . . . for making soundings, not charts or maps', a time when 'the cause of truth and of the Church' was best served by theologians 'candidly confessing' where their 'perplexities lie'.[2]

The two decades from 1945 are not for theology a self-contained period. Many of its important figures had made their mark before 1945, while in 1965 theology was in the midst of a radical re-examination of its matter and methods from which, in 1972, it has not yet emerged even though the panic of the mid-1960s has subsided. In this essay, I want to outline five lines of theological investigation which were pursued during the period—Biblical theology, existentialist theology, process theology, linguistic theology, and radical theology. Although this topical approach may not do justice to the work of individual theologians, it allows me to indicate the significant patterns of thought that underlie the confused and confusing theological writing of the period. I say 'significant patterns' because I will ignore the vast amount of 'safe' theology which was produced in the period—as in others—to comfort the intelligent believer by repeating familiar understandings of the faith. My interest is in attempts to develop theological understanding, not in repetitions of an 'old, old story'.

Theology, from one point of view, is not an autonomous science but an attempt to express in a rationally coherent form the beliefs implicit in a particular religious faith. As such, theology is regarded as primarily a descriptive activity, parasitic upon some faith actually held and, usually, to be judged by the community which shares that faith. Even though this understanding of theology may overlook its revisionary role—the way, that is, that the attempt to make rational sense of a religious faith may lead to changes in its beliefs—nevertheless it does make the important point that the work of the theologian will normally be essentially connected with an actual believing community. During our period, however, the official, 'institutional' Church has been unwilling to wrestle with the disturbing insights of contemporary theology. While individual pastors and preachers have joined with theologians in attempting to understand the Christian faith in a way that is both meaningful and significant for their contemporaries, the official bodies of the different denominations have increasingly tended to devote themselves to matters of survival and internal reform. At the local level, interest in the Christian faith has degenerated into interest in how to pay for repairs to the roof. At less local but equally parochial levels, much time and energy has been spent on reforming the institutions and revising the liturgies of the different denominations. At the highest level of institutional Christianity, 'ecumenical' interest has largely become a matter of setting up international bureaucracies and slowly evolving plans for the amalgamation of dying denominations. Even the self-styled renewal groups which flourished in the different denominations in the 1960s seem to have been more concerned to seize the reins of ecclesiastical power than to grapple with serious contemporary theology. As a result, while the Church contemplated its organizational belly-button and argued passionately about such unworldly issues as the meaning of ordination, those outside grew used to ignoring it. By the late 1960s the institutional Church had developed a ghetto mentality which made it incapable of presenting its faith as a serious option to a world racked with doubt, uncertainty, and despair underneath a fading veneer of affluent complacency. Consequently those theologians who did dare to offer contemporary understandings of the nature and destiny of life found themselves increasingly isolated from the organized Church. The faith they delineated challenged the ecclesiastical community as well as the secular world.

To the observer most theologians seemed to share the malaise of the Church as they increasingly concentrated their attention on the nature of theology. There is reason to hope, though, that whereas the inward-looking concern of the churches was the regular pulse-taking of a chronic invalid, the examination of their task by theologians was the necessary preparation for restorative surgery and renewed vigour. By the 1970s theology had probably reached the edge of either total collapse or a genuine reformation. All the old authorities—the Bible, the Church, the creeds, the councils, episcopacy, and religious experience—were questioned. Having no established foundations or fixed norms, the theologian, possibly for the first time in the Christian era, had the opportunity and was faced with the challenge to start again from the beginning.

## I

The first major trend in theology that we are to examine is the attempt to derive contemporary theological understanding from the Bible. This use of the Bible took various forms.

One form was the 'theology of the Word' whose dominant exponent was Karl Barth (1886–1968). Throughout our period Barth, like a far from extinct volcano, continued to pour out further volumes of his *Church Dogmatics* as well as shorter expositions of his thought. His method, as he expressed it in 1955, was to 'listen as unreservedly as possible to the witness of Scripture and as impartially as possible to that of the Church, and then consider and formulate whatever may be the result'.[3] In this activity the role of the Bible is primary. Just as in the past 'the Old and New Testament Scriptures . . . have continually become a living voice and word, and have had and exercised power as such', so they continue to do today. They are 'a chorus of very different and independent but harmonious voices' which bear witness to and make present 'God's eternal Word', which 'in the existence of the man Jesus . . . was and is spoken in human form to us men'.[4] Although Barth strenuously maintained that his later theology fundamentally followed the same lines as his earlier work,[5] there was a change in emphasis which he himself recognized in a lecture entitled 'The Humanity of God', delivered in 1956. Whereas in his earlier work, under the stimulus of Kierkegaard's affirmation of the infinite qualitative difference between time and eternity, Barth had stressed the transcendent otherness of God, in his later writings he recognizes that this God is known only as the one who relates himself to man in grace and revelation. Thus while God cannot be known except as he chooses in his absolute freedom to make himself known, in making himself known 'He exists, speaks, and acts as the *partner* of man'.[6]

Although Barth was widely respected for his learning as well as for his overwhelming output, his theology did not dominate the theological scene after 1945. He claimed that he was expounding the Word of God to which the Bible bears normative witness. To others, who failed to find the same 'Word' disclosed to them in their reading of the Bible, Barth's assertion of the autonomy of theology seemed to free theology from external domination by the checking procedures of reason at the cost of making its understanding of the 'Word of God' dependent upon the private inspiration of the individual theologian. Barth did, however, have a number of disciples during our period. Among them was the Scottish theologian T. F. Torrance (b. 1913). In various works he powerfully advocates the Barthian understanding of theology. In his *Theological Science*, for instance, Torrance argues that 'our theological statements are true in so far as they are faithful responses to the self-communication of the Truth of God in the way in which He reveals Himself in and through the witness of the Holy Scripture, in the historical life of the Church, for it is there in the Holy Scripture that we actually hear God's Word'. The task of the theologian is to be open to this 'Word' as it is given in and through the Bible, obedient to its intrinsic logic and concerned to communicate it as it is to his contemporaries. The truth of a theological statement is not established by applying to it rules for verification laid down by philosophers independent of and prior to the consideration of the experienced reality of religious faith. Theological truth is a matter of '*justification by Grace*, and *demonstration of the Spirit*, that is, verification and action by the Truth Himself'. Torrance, like Barth and Bultmann, thus extends the doctrine of justification by the grace of God in Jesus Christ to epistemology. He holds that this does not make theological knowledge irrational but recognizes its proper logical status. It means that the individual can know the truth about God to be such only as he is enabled by the grace of God to assimilate himself in faith and action 'to the life and history of the Truth of God as it is in Jesus'.[7] Discernment of theological truth is thus presented as a product of the life of obedient faith in Christ. In contrast to what he sees as the erroneous approach of traditional natural theology, Torrance holds that man must not presume to judge God and God's truth by his human reason but must submit himself and his reason to God and to the truth which God makes known to him. This, according to Torrance, is the way for theology to be genuinely 'scientific', since only by following this method will theological statements be determined by their proper object—'God'.

At first sight Torrance's view of theology has a certain attractiveness. It seems to offer a way by which the theologian can ensure that his statements about God describe God and are not corrupted by the imposition of his own human ideals and understanding. Torrance confesses that for him 'to doubt the existence of God would be an act of sheer irrationality' and that 'scientific theology is active engagement in that cognitive relation to God' which is obedient 'to the demands of His reality and self-giving'. His experience is that God 'presses unrelentingly upon me through the disorder of my mind, . . . challenging and repairing it, and requiring of me on my part to yield my thoughts to His healing and controlling revelation'.[8] Other theologians, however, do not enjoy Torrance's experience and his confident awareness of God's self-revelation through the Bible. Consequently they judge that, however attractive it may be in principle, in practice his view of theology runs into serious difficulties because it begs fundamental and inescapable questions. It fails, that is, to meet what they regard as primary needs, namely, to establish that there is a God, where he is revealed, and on what basis the revelation is to be interpreted. To put it crudely, though perhaps not unfairly, Torrance writes as if he has a private line to the Almighty by means of which he has a clear hearing of the divine Word. Others find the task of theology much more baffling and are tempted to wonder at times just what voice it is that Torrance hears. Is it the voice of God or the echo of Torrance's own convictions?

The Barthian theology of the Word, for all its claims to express the

Biblical witness,* appeared to many theologians to stray at times far from what the Bible actually said. On the whole, postwar attempts to develop a contemporary theology primarily, perhaps even solely, by expounding the Biblical text were more restrained. For most of our period the dominant theological approach in Britain was that of 'Biblical theology'. It was based upon the work of notable Biblical scholars such as C. H. Dodd, H. H. Rowley, T. W. Manson, V. Taylor, and C. K. Barrett, most of whom had made their mark by 1945. The underlying assumption of this Biblical theology, which distinguished it from fundamentalist paraphrases of the Biblical text as it stands, was that a true understanding of the Christian faith—and so a correct understanding of Christian theology—was to be found by an exegesis of the Biblical text which took advantage of the insights given by critical investigations into its materials. Even though the critical work was sometimes less radical than it might have been—British Biblical scholars in particular seem, justifiably or not, to have an inbuilt reaction against extremism—it did lead to a considerable improvement in the appreciation of the Bible in the Church. The sacred book ceased to be treated as a sacred cow. It was recognized to be a collection of documents which records the faiths of various people and which shows clear traces of the errors, confusions, and prejudices of its authors. Although the revivalist Billy Graham, who had a limited popularity in the 1950s through his evangelistic campaigns, apparently felt that any point could be clinched simply by repeating what 'the Bible says' (usually in terms of the Authorized Version translation), more sophisticated believers followed the theologians in holding that any text must be understood in terms of its context, the apparent intentions and faith of its author, and the clues given to its meaning by a study of other contemporary literature. The result in practice was that whereas Barth had found a strange new world in the Bible, the Biblical theologians of the 1950s produced versions of Christianity which harmonized with the conservatively inclined traditional faith of most believers.

Implicitly or explicitly Biblical theologians assumed that the theological task had been completed when critical study had elucidated the meaning of the Biblical material. G. Ernest Wright (b. 1909), for instance, seeing the Bible as 'the record of the acts of God', suggests that 'theology may be defined as the discipline by which the Church . . . translates Biblical faith into the non-Biblical language

* Cf. K. Barth, *The Epistle to the Romans*, trans. E. C. Hoskyns (1933), ix, for the claim that this was Barth's intention even though he recognizes that the interpreter is always in danger of adding to what he seeks to interpret.

of another age. It is an extension of the Bible into the non-Biblical world' and 'must be under the constant restraint of the Biblical presentation of the faith'. Wright deplores the division of Biblical studies into Old and New Testament compartments for, according to him, it is 'the whole Bible' which 'becomes in Christ the source of the Church's proclamation'. Other theologians, who shared Wright's awareness of the unsystematizable nature of the Biblical material as a whole,[9] concentrated upon elucidating the faith expressed in particular books or upon the supposed Biblical bases of particular doctrines by tracing specific themes through the different books, usually considering (sometimes in spite of the appearances) that their separate studies expressed different aspects of one consistent Biblical faith.

G. E. Wright was a member of the '*Heilsgeschichte*' ('Salvation-history' or 'Redemptive-history') school of Biblical theology. Since, however, the term *Heilsgeschichte* has suffered from being understood in different ways,[10] it is not easy to define precisely what this school affirmed nor what it meant by its key concept 'history'. Emil Brunner (b. 1889), whose theology is at least close to the Barthian 'theology of the Word' in spite of his conflicts with Barth, states that 'what we believe as Christians, we believe because something particular has taken place in history', namely the revelation of 'God's Nature and His Will', and that 'this "particular thing" that has happened in history' is what is called *Heilsgeschichte*. Furthermore, both 'the unity and the real meaning of the historical revelation' can only be discerned when the Old Testament is interpreted from 'the standpoint of Jesus Christ' and Jesus Christ is seen as 'the One who fulfils the Old Testament revelation through history'.[11] But although Brunner sees theology as based upon particular historical events, the revelatory understanding of those events is not the product of historical research. *Heilsgeschichte*, for him, is supra-history which is not subject to the canons of history: 'the certainty of faith lies on another plane than the secular certainty of historical facts', since it is not the historian but 'the divine Spirit' which brings the believer to understand the 'historical documents' of the Bible as 'the instrument of the Word of God'.[12]

Oscar Cullmann (b. 1902), a New Testament scholar who asserts that theology must not only express the Biblical faith but also employ its categories, is another leading exponent of *Heilsgeschichte* and one who stresses that the Christian faith is based on facts which are part of history rather than of a supra-history independent of the actual process of events in this world. Cullmann maintains that the

Christian faith and its understanding of the whole of history is founded on a narrow series of events within history which finds its 'mid-point and meaning' in Jesus Christ. The historical element in expressions of Christianity is not 'an external framework' which can be discarded without loss in supposedly sophisticated expressions of Christianity. It is essential to the Christian conception of redemption. Nevertheless, while 'individual basic facts of this Biblical [view of] history are subject to historical investigation' and confirmation, the crucial activity for theology is the 'grouping, interpretation, and joining of events' in terms of Jesus as '*absolute divine revelation* to men'. As Cullmann recognizes, this crucial activity is one in which the historian 'who seeks to be only a historian' cannot engage.[13] History such as the historian investigates is thus a *sine qua non* of genuine Biblical faith, but the historian as such is unable by his investigations to arrive at that faith. At best he can only confirm that there are no historical grounds for doubting that the events on which it is based happened.

Other exponents of *Heilsgeschichte* expected more of the historian. Alan Richardson, for instance, allows that 'historical research cannot prove that God acted in history' but goes on to claim that 'if it is honestly and fearlessly pursued', historical research 'can strengthen our confidence that it is reasonable to believe that he [God] did so act. History points to faith. . . . History cannot do more than this; but it cannot do less.'[14] It is not, however, altogether clear what Richardson means by 'history' nor whether his later Bampton Lectures support this position. In these lectures he affirms that Biblical history is 'a real history, just as real as the history of the Caesars or the Plantagenets' and that Biblical faith is 'inseparable from the historical events which called it forth'.[15] The historian's understanding of history is described as a response to certain events as 'disclosure situations'. The meanings of history which are thereby discerned are apparently not arbitrarily related to the events of history—Richardson rejects 'existentialist' interpretations of history. Unfortunately he does not show how events and the meanings perceived in them are related. He merely points out that such disclosure situations do occur and are the basis of historical interpretations. The failure to show how events point to and justify the meaning—that is, the theological meaning—perceived in them is the fatal weakness of *Heilsgeschichte* theology. It might express a Biblical view of history but it did not show why that view is to be accepted as true.

The 'official' attempts to translate the Bible into contemporary language, the American *Revised Standard Version*, the British *New*

*English Bible*, and the Roman Catholic *Jerusalem Bible*, are monuments to the interest in the Bible in this period. They may also be regarded by later generations as the memorials of a past era—an era when the ultimate authority of the Bible was generally accepted in Christian communities. By the mid-1960s attempts to justify a theological argument by reference to Biblical texts had lost a lot of the force which they had enjoyed a decade earlier. Some who still claimed to be Christian would respond with a 'So what?', questioning the authority of the Biblical authors to legislate for the beliefs and practices of Christians many centuries later. More were less explicitly hostile to the Bible. They hid their rejection of its traditional authority by pointing to the difficulties of determining its meaning and significance for the present day. If pressed about their scepticism, they could point to the multitude of interpretations that had appeared while Biblical theology flourished. How could reference to the Bible be authoritative when its meaning was so variously assessed? Its authority is a matter of faith.[16] The trouble for Biblical theology was that that faith was in practice being undermined by the work of Biblical scholars.

During this period there was growing awareness of the difficulties of establishing a 'correct' interpretation of the Bible and of presenting its message to the present day. Here some of the work of Rudolf Bultmann (b. 1884) has major importance. His seminal essay, 'New Testament and Mythology: The Mythological Element in the Message of the New Testament and the Problem of its Re-interpretation', appeared in 1941. It provoked a furious debate in Germany and, as it became more widely known after the war, was taken seriously in the U.S.A. and eventually began to stir British Biblical theology. What Bultmann means by 'myth' is not completely clear. Roughly, though, myths are for him the forms in which men of the New Testament period understood and expressed their understanding of their existence. In these myths man speaks of the powers which he considers to be 'the ground and limit of his world and of his own activity and suffering . . . in terms derived from the visible world'. Myths, that is, describe 'the other world in terms of this world, and . . . the gods in terms derived from human life'.[17] As an example of what he means, Bultmann refers to the way in which myths express 'divine transcendence' in terms of 'spatial distance'.* His

* In *Jesus Christ and Mythology* (1958), Bultmann puts it thus: 'It may be said that myths give to the transcendent reality an immanent, this-worldly objectivity. Myths give worldly objectivity to that which is unworldly. (In German one would say, "*Der Mythos objektiviert das Jenseitige zum Diesseitigen*".)' (p. 19).

thesis is that when the New Testament 'presents the event of redemption which is the subject of its preaching', it both presupposes this mythical view and uses it as the structure of its presentation. The result is that the New Testament statement of the Gospel is 'incredible to modern man, for he is convinced that the mythical view of the world is obsolete'.[18] But although Christianity cannot expect modern man to accept the mythical view of the world as literally true, neither can it remove the mythical parts of the New Testament presentation of the Gospel to leave an acceptable 'core'. This was the method of liberal Protestant theologians like Harnack. It fails because it does not recognize that the mythical view is the basic structure of understanding for all the New Testament and is not found only in those bits that readily appear unacceptable to modern man—as in its talk about demons and eschatology. Bultmann's conclusion, then, is that 'if the truth of the New Testament proclamation is to be preserved, the only way is to demythologize it'. The reason for such 'demythologizing', though, is not to make the New Testament 'relevant to the modern world at all costs' but to confront modern man with the challenge of its Gospel.[19]

Bultmann's own demythologizing programme is based on his view that 'the real purpose of myth is . . . to express man's understanding of himself in the world in which he lives'.[20] On this basis he argues that the best way to interpret myths is existentially and that this is best done by using the conceptions developed by Martin Heidegger (b. 1889) in his existentialist philosophy. Although Bultmann himself claims that his intention is to use Heidegger's conceptions so far as they are of value in expressing the Gospel and not to reduce the Gospel to Heideggerian existentialism,[21] many of his critics suggest that his practice belies this principle. In particular they have seized upon his 'existentialist' interpretation of the resurrection of Christ as the affirmation of 'faith in the saving efficacy of the cross' and not a miraculous event of the resuscitation of a dead person.[22] Such demythologization, it is argued, throws out the Gospel 'baby' with the 'bath-water' of its mythical thought-forms. A few others, on the contrary, feel that Bultmann does not go far enough. Fritz Buri and Schubert Ogden, for instance, charge him with inconsistency because while he holds that authentic existence is a possibility open to man as man, he also retains in his demythologized Gospel the claim that such authentic existence is only possible in actual practice because of a decisive act of God in Jesus Christ.[23] They suggest that a thoroughly demythologized Gospel will not include such claims. Bultmann's work thus evoked a debate in which two questions were frequently confused: the question whether in principle demythologization is a valid method of interpretation and the question whether the demythologized interpretation presented by Bultmann (and others) is a complete and valid expression of the Gospel. It is a pity that hostility to Bultmann's use of the demythologizing method has sometimes led to a failure to appreciate the possible validity of the method in principle.

Bultmann's recognition both of the influence of the early Church's faith and practice in the oral transmission of the New Testament materials and of the use of alien thought-forms in communicating that material highlighted the profound difficulty—if not impossibility—of determining the truth about the Jesus of history. A number of those who acknowledged the importance of Bultmann's work, however, began to argue that his historical scepticism was unjustified since it was possible to reconstruct a reliable historical picture of Jesus. A new quest for the historical Jesus thus appeared in the works of Gunther Bornkamm, Hans Conzelmann, Gerhard Ebeling, Ernst Fuchs, Ernst Käsemann, and, in America, James Robinson. In spite of differences among them, these 'new questers' condemn the old quest of liberal Protestantism, whose memorial was Albert Schweitzer's *Quest of the Historical Jesus* (1910), for pursuing a religiously illegitimate aim (namely, a knowledge about Jesus which would justify faith in him) and for using a historiographically false approach (namely, seeing history as the objective determination of what happened). They consider, instead, that the role of the historian is not to chronicle deeds but, as Robinson puts it, 'to lay hold of the selfhood which is therein revealed'[24] and to respond to it in their own commitment of faith. On this basis it is argued that even though we cannot reconstruct the actual events of Jesus' life, we can reconstruct his own faith, that is, the existential understanding which directed his life and which evoked a like faith in others. It is this faith of Jesus which is the basis of the Christian Gospel. As Ebeling puts it, 'the sole ground of faith is Jesus as the witness to faith in the pregnant sense of the "author and finisher of faith" ', and elsewhere, 'No understanding of the primitive Christian *kerygma* is possible without taking into account the way in which Jesus thus qualified and illumined the situation in which he spoke.'[25] But while they hold that this 'ground of faith is certainly to be brought to expression also by historical study, because it came to expression in history',[26] the 'new questers' are sceptical of the attempts to establish the events of Jesus' life made in the old quest. In particular they doubt whether it is possible to establish the chronology of his career to any significant degree. It is at this point that their critics pounce—and justifiably. Even if we allow the possibility of inferring a person's faith from his deeds (and such inferences are always dangerous), it is hard to see how we can accept the claim that a person's faith can be discerned when we lack any considerable body of agreement about what he did and in what order. After all their insights into the nature of history, the new questers fail, like the old questers, because of the nature of their evidence. The New Testament presents neither the Jesus of history nor the Christ of faith but the composite Jesus Christ. With such data it is not surprising that the old quest failed to determine the events of Jesus' career. It is, perhaps, surprising that the new questers, on the basis of the same data, thought it might yet be possible to determine the faith that lay behind Jesus' actions. Ebeling's comment on the old quest also applies to the new: 'Scholars went out to seek Jesus, and ended once again with the primitive witness to Christ as the ultimate attainable authority.'[27]

Towards the end of our period there was further important investigation of the question of the interpretation of the Bible. This investigation is often described as a study of 'hermeneutics'—a term which fashion-conscious British theologians utter with a German or an American accent! Bultmann's demythologizing method is based on a hermeneutical presupposition enunciated by Schleiermacher and developed by Dilthey, namely, that both the author of a Biblical passage and his present-day interpreter are part of a 'universal humanity'. Since they share the same basic structure of human existence, it is possible for the interpreter to grasp the existential understanding which the author expresses in the passage. This fundamental unity of the author and the interpreter, however, is questioned in recent work on hermeneutics. Hans-Georg Gadamer and Heinz Kimmerle, for instance, stress the temporal distance between the Biblical author and today's exegete, and the important differences between their worlds of experience and ways of understanding. Gadamer, who is interested in understanding as such and not simply in Biblical exegesis, regards conversation as a paradigm model for analysing the process of understanding. In 'conversation' the participants express their views, grapple with each other's failures to understand and misunderstandings, and (hopefully) eventually come to appreciate each other's positions. In this way, as Gadamer puts it, they 'fuse' their separate horizons of understanding. Applied to the Bible, however, this model of conversation suggests that it may be impossible to arrive at a 'correct' interpretation of its material if an interpretation is 'correct' because it expresses the author's understanding of the passage. The Biblical text can exercise only a limited control over our understandings of it. It cannot, like the other person in a conversation, talk back, tell us that we seem to have misunderstood, and rephrase its statements to clarify its meaning. What the Bible tells us largely depends on the way we read it and the questions we expect it to answer. Furthermore, our appreciation of the Biblical horizon of understanding will come from our reading of the Bible and other contemporary literature and yet it is only as we appreciate the Biblical horizon of understanding that we are supposed to be able to interpret this literature correctly. Kimmerle, a pupil of Gadamer, advances a slightly different position. He sees the recognition of 'the temporal distance' between text and interpreter as 'a "critical filter"'[28] which enables the interpreter to become conscious of his own cultural prejudices and so, to some extent, able to prevent them distorting his understanding of the text. Here again the fundamental problem is how we can become aware of our prejudices in contrast to those of another age before we have understood the literature of that other age. The hermeneutical methods of Gadamer and Kimmerle can probably be defended, though, on the grounds that in such processes of understanding we do not *first* fuse the horizons of the text and of the interpreter and *then* understand the text, but rather we find that there is a reciprocal interplay between the text and the interpreter's understanding of it. Even so, there is clearly considerable scope left for the interpreter to impose his own questions and answers upon the text.*

Wolfhart Pannenberg (b. 1928) criticizes Gadamer's position for not adequately recognizing that both text and interpreter do not belong to watertight cultural compartments but are connected, with their differences, within 'the horizon of the process of history itself'.[29] Ultimately, according to Pannenberg, the full meaning of an event or of a text can only be grasped when it is viewed

> in connection with the totality of history which links the past to the present, and indeed . . . also to the horizon of the future . . . because the meaning of the present becomes clear only in the light of the future

* Cf. Pannenberg's comment: 'Gadamer himself concedes that the text does *not* speak to us "as a thou", since "we, the ones who comprehend, must on our part first enable it to speak". What this last insight means, however, is precisely that talk about the "question" the text poses to us can only be metaphorical: the text becomes a question only for the one who asks questions; it does not have this character in and of itself.' (W. Pannenberg, *Basic Questions in Theology* trans. G. H. Kehm, vol. 1 (1970), 122 f.)

Only a conception of the actual course of history linking the past with the present situation and its horizon of the future can form the comprehensive horizon within which the interpreter's limited horizon of the present and the historical horizon of the text fuse together.[30]

Holding, then, with Gadamer, that the text deals with some objective matter (*Sache*), Pannenberg argues in a Hegelian manner that what this is for us today can only be fully understood in the light of its place in the total process of history. Whereas, however, Hegel was criticized for assuming that the process had come to an end in his philosophy, Pannenberg's theology is based on the claim that in Jesus we have 'the proleptic revelation of God' who is the future destiny of history.[31] Jesus, therefore, as 'a provisional and anticipatory' revelation of the totality of history, makes it possible for us to grasp the current significance of a Biblical passage. The problem with this hermeneutical method is that it seems to require us to have the perspective of universal history in order to interpret correctly the Biblical reports about Jesus when it is only through having correctly interpreted those reports that we have the revelation of the end of history. Pannenberg himself suggests that the viciousness of this circle can be partially avoided by taking into account what the process of history as we know it suggests about its destiny—by using, that is, a historical equivalent of natural theology. Even so, the meaning found in a text is determined by the questions and presuppositions which the exegete brings to the text as well as by the insights which wrestling with the text evokes in his mind.[32]

Study of hermeneutics thus raises questions about the authority of the Bible in practice. It suggests not just that a theologian, in offering a Biblically-grounded theology, might be reading his theology into the Bible but, more disturbingly, that it is unlikely that he can avoid doing this. By the end of our period, then, the principle of a Biblically-grounded theology is questioned. The Bible for some theologians has become a respected source of theological insight and inspiration, but what the theologian finds in the Bible is regarded as due as much to the theologian as, if not more than, to the text.

## II

As I have already mentioned, Bultmann considers that in his demythologization of the New Testament he is using the concepts of Heidegger's existentialist analysis 'to make clearer to modern man what the Christian faith is'. He is not seeking to reduce the Gospel to Heideggerian existentialism.[33] Nevertheless, in Bultmann's exposition of the Christian faith, we meet another of the major trends in theology during our period, namely, that of 'existentialist theology'. Existentialist theology, though, is no more a unity than the Biblically-grounded theology which we have just considered. The phrase is a blanket term for a wide range of theological positions which are significantly influenced by the categories and insights of existentialist philosophers—who themselves disagree about major points. I will, therefore, try to indicate briefly the ideas of a few existentialist theologians who were significantly influenced by existentialist philosophers rather than attempt to describe existentialist theology as if it were a single, self-consistent position.

Bultmann's indebtedness to existentialism involves much more than an adoption of its terminology. When, for instance, he speaks of 'faith' and 'salvation' in terms of 'self-understanding' and 'authentic existence', he is not simply presenting traditional theological notions in a fashionable language: he is also advancing an existentialist interpretation of Christianity. This interpretation emphasizes in particular the fundamental role of individual decision in Christian faith and extends the doctrine of justification by faith to 'the field of epistemology'. Authentic faith is a matter of decision 'in defiance of all outward appearances' in which the believer abandons every pretence to security, 'whether he seeks it in his good works or in his ascertainable knowledge', and accepts 'that he has nothing in his hand on which to base his faith'. He finds the true security of faith 'only by abandoning all security, by being ready, as Luther put it, to plunge into the inner darkness'.[34] Through such commitment he is both eed from the disintegrating forces of a life based on the false securities of human achievement and freed for an authentic life lived in radical openness to the future. This existentialist understanding of Christianity is illustrated by Bultmann's conclusion to his Gifford Lectures, *History and Eschatology*:

> We started our lectures with the question of meaning in history. . . . Man who complains: 'I cannot see meaning in history, and therefore my life, interwoven in history, is meaningless,' is to be admonished: do not look around yourself into universal history, you must look into your own personal history. Always in your present lies the meaning in history, and you cannot see it as a spectator, but only in your responsible decisions. In every moment slumbers the possibility of being the eschatological moment. You must awaken it.[35]

Bultmann, though, holds that this 'awakening' is not something that a man can achieve by himself—no more than a soundly sleeping person can consciously decide to wake himself up. Existentialist philosophers can speak of the self-commitment that leads to authentic life and arouse in man a desire for it, but they can only offer it as a 'theoretical possibility'. In practice they leave man in anxiety and despair. The Christian preacher, in contrast, proclaims the Gospel of Christ whereby such commitment has become an 'actual' possibility for man as 'a gift of God'.[36] As Bultmann puts it in some thoughts about the meaning of Christmas, 'the eternal Light', which kindles 'the light of faith' in us, is not something which we possess by nature or attain by our own efforts: 'it can only be received—and only be received again and again—as *a gift*'.[37] Nevertheless, the word of the Gospel is that it can be and is received. Authentic life is not a dream that existentialist philosophers describe. Those to whom God has given faith in Christ now have it.

For Bultmann, then, authentic existence is made possible for man through the act of God in Jesus Christ. Other theologians are less restricted in their adoption of an existentialist position. Buri and Ogden, for instance, hold that authentic existence as a gift of God is a universal human possibility. The Gospel of Jesus Christ is a symbolic way of announcing this possibility rather than, as Christian theologians—including Bultmann—have traditionally claimed, the sole and historical locus of its availability. Buri states that 'Not in a historical fact . . . but rather in the character of the givenness of the event of grace in authentic self-understanding have we to do with the real "scandal of the cross". Only in the unconditionality of the enactment of the self-understanding of faith does the ἐφ' ἅπαξ [trans. 'once for all'] of the New Testament preaching of Christ attain its symbolic character and therein its truth for existence.'[38] Similarly he regards the doctrine of justification by faith as a symbolic presentation of 'the "experience of oneself as a gift" ' and the doctrine of 'Christ as the new Adam' as 'the symbol for the possibility' of authentic existence through grace. Thus while Buri describes Christian theology as reflection on 'the decisive saving act of God in Christ', he interprets 'the symbol-world of faith' as 'an expression of the self-understanding of existence in relation to its transcendence' and claims that 'Theology has no reason to recoil from such an existentialist interpretation of its center, for the secret of grace does not thereby become diminished, but rather all the more universal.'[39] The task of Christian theology, then, is to draw out the existential significance of the Biblical myths by thoroughly demythologizing (Buri speaks of 'dekerygmatizing') its talk of historical and historic acts of God in Jesus Christ into the message that authentic existence is available to all men through the grace of God given with existence itself.

Buri is described by Barth as 'that Jasperian theologian'.[40] Karl Jaspers (1883–1969) interprets religious belief in terms of his existentialist philosophy. While he affirms 'God', he denies that 'God' can ever be an object for man's knowledge. Consequently, whereas Christianity traditionally claims that God has revealed himself in particular events to particular people at particular times, Jaspers holds that 'the contents of revelations would become more pure, more true, if their reality were discarded'.[41] Genuine faith is 'a philosophical faith' in which 'we feel the reality of the hidden Transcendence' that encompasses all things and is always beyond our grasp. Claims for 'exclusionary', final revelations and incarnations of the Transcendent are condemned as blasphemous attempts to fix 'the distant God' in specific images. While finite man cannot do without concrete myths and images,[42] they must be understood as temporary and replaceable 'ciphers' through which man may become aware of 'the nearby God' in his actual situation. Jaspers states, though, that man will 'feel the reality of God most strongly where no concretion . . . shrouds it'.[43] The 'ciphers' of salvation are thus not to be interpreted in terms of 'a factual intervention from without'* but as expressions of the universal possibility of authentic life which is grounded in man's very being. They encourage 'freedom' by evoking awareness of the givenness of being and confidence in its ultimate ground. They liberate man from comforting reliance on some external 'God' and offer him authentic existence in the present as determined by his own commitment of faith.[44] While Bultmann holds to the necessity of the saving act of God in Jesus Christ, Jaspers offers a different interpretation of the Biblical faith—that of 'the conception of man's God-created inborn nobility':

> man is determined by God, the source of everything man can be, but only in the direct relation of his own freedom to the godhead, and without the help of an external agency. Thus man is confident that he can fulfil the will of the hidden God by an effort entirely subjected to his own responsibility, and that he will be helped by God in an incomprehensible and unpredictable way.[45]

For Jaspers, then, Christian theology offers indirect and sometimes misleading expressions of this truth. Every man, simply because he

* For this reason Jaspers is critical of Bultmann's understanding of the Gospel—cf. the debate between Jaspers and Bultmann in *Kerygma and Myth*, vol. II, and in *Myth and Christianity*, by Jaspers and Bultmann (1958), which contains a further essay by Jaspers not printed in *Kerygma and Myth*.

is a man, has the possibility of authentic existence through the givenness of faith. In such faith he is linked with 'the origin of his being' and freed 'to work and live for boundless openness, authentic reason, truth and love and fidelity'.[46] Man's salvation is thus grounded, for Jaspers, in the nature of being, not in divine interventions, and the truth of theology in the philosophical theism produced by his existentialist analysis of human existence.

Since he regards existentialism as 'the expression of the fundamental meaninglessness of existence' and the Christian faith as 'the revelation of fundamental meaning', Carl Michalson (1915–65) describes the phrase 'existentialist theology' as a contradiction in terms.[47] His exposition of the Christian faith, however, may properly be classed as 'existentialist' where that term is used broadly to refer to the philosophies of existence which stress the fundamental significance of man's commitment. Michalson's theology is based on a distinction between two structures of understanding which he calls 'nature' and 'history'. 'Nature' refers to reality as it is external to man and has nothing to say about the meaning of life. It has the structure of impersonal causes and objective knowledge. 'History', in contrast, is reality when it is 'interior to and vocal about man'. It consists of both impersonal objects and personal actions so far as they confront man as a 'Thou' which questions him about the significance of his existence. Michalson claims that his use of the term 'history' is approximately that of Dilthey. It is a special use of the term, however, and care must be taken in reading Michalson to understand the term according to his use of it. It is in terms of 'history', then, that the question of meaning arises and religious faith provides the answer. Each individual finds the meaning of his own existence through an understanding of and response to particular historical events. In this process he is subjectively involved, not a disinterested spectator. He accepts the risk of decision 'joyfully . . . but with courage', since here there can be no objective assurance of what is right or true. Each individual must choose for himself. The Christian faith is that answer to the question of meaning whose 'pivotal event' is found in 'the presence of Jesus of Nazareth in history'. Through the witness of the Church, 'the historical community which lives by its memory of him', Jesus is presented to men as the clue to the meaning of their existence.[48] Christians are those who hazard themselves by accepting it as their clue. This meaning, though, is not found in the acceptance of metaphysical claims about the ultimate nature of reality revealed by Jesus but in the challenge to share the faith of Jesus by 'assuming the responsibility for shaping a world'. The Christian Gospel is the message that 'God through the faithful ministry of Jesus of Nazareth has turned the world over to man. . . . In this event the intention of creation is radically fulfilled: henceforth man is to subdue the earth.'[49] Man is thus summoned by the 'word of God', according to Michalson, 'to create history in the face of the nothingness of historicity'. He does this by a commitment of faith in which he not only makes his own life meaningful but also makes his world meaningful. In the Christian's experience, however, the activity of God's grace may remove the terrifying aspect of the risk of faith. Believers may commit themselves to Christian faith almost as if they had not decided—'as one laughs without reflecting, yet never being surprised or sorry that he has reacted so' is how Michalson illustrates it.[50] Christian faith is thus presented in terms of acts of commitment by which existence becomes meaningful for individuals. In this interpretation, the meaning of existence is not given by Christ as a set of propositions to be accepted in faith as true. The meaning of existence is made by each individual for himself as he shares in the faith of Christ, committing himself to be open to the future and accepting responsibility for shaping it.

Paul Tillich (1886–1965) illustrates another type of existentialist theology. A refugee from Nazism, he settled in America but was never completely at home in its language. Friends and colleagues struggled 'to English' his works but they did not always succeed. Although some of his writings were admirably clear, others remained obscure because of the elusiveness of their language as well as because of the profundity of their thought. Tillich was, however, the most famous theologian of our period in the Anglo-Saxon world and, especially in America, was widely read even if not equally widely understood. I remember a stetsoned rancher arriving at a Texan seminary and offering $200—in green-backs—to any 'prawfuss'rrr' who could help him appreciate this 'Teeleesch'. Such is the value of fame!

Tillich describes the method of systematic theology in terms of 'correlation'. The task of the systematic theologian is to correlate the answers of religion with the questions of human existence exposed by philosophy, science, and culture. This does not mean, as he is careful to point out, that the answers are contained in the questions. Man's existence poses the questions but no analyses of the human situation, including those found in natural theology's traditional arguments for the existence of God, can give the answers. The answers are found in revelatory experience of God. On the other hand, the answers do not pose the questions. The significance of religious claims can only be appreciated when they are related to the actual condition of man. Theologians thus work within the theological circle determined by a particular faith's identification of God's revelation, but expound that revelation as answers to questions determined by a universally available understanding of the human situation.

Tillich uses the term 'existentialist' broadly to describe those philosophies which are concerned with 'the question of human existence in time and space and of man's predicament in unity with the predicament of everything existing'.[51] He finds 'strong existentialist elements' in various ancient and modern philosophers, including Schelling, the philosopher who predominantly influenced him, as well as in Heraclitus, Socrates, Plato, Cusanus, Pascal, Schopenhauer, Nietzsche, and Heidegger. Tillich also held that each theologian should have a competent grasp of a science and allow its insights to deepen his theological understanding. For his science he chose that of psychoanalysis and in one of his papers he stresses the close connection of existentialist analyses of the human situation with the findings of depth psychology. These 'two movements' are said to have 'infinite value for theology' because of the searching way they pose for theology the question of man's existence by revealing his 'universal, tragic estrangement' from his 'essential being'. Tillich's understanding of the question is also informed by a deep appreciation of culture, in particular of modern art. In Picasso's 'Guernica', for example, he finds 'the radicalism of the Protestant question', though not its answer.[52]

Having identified man's basic predicament as existential estrangement from his essential being, estrangement which is expressed in anxiety about meaninglessness, guilt, and death, Tillich expounds the Christian faith as answering that predicament in terms of God as 'Being-Itself' and Christ as the source of 'new being'. What Tillich, here strongly influenced by Schelling, means by 'God' is not wholly clear. Certain characteristics, though, stand out. God, first, is described as the 'power of being'. He is the 'infinite and inexhaustible depth and ground of all being' and all history.[53] As such he offers the only ultimate answer to man's fear of non-being. Secondly, as the ground of all being, God cannot be an object for man. He stands beyond the division of subject and object as that which makes the division possible. Thirdly, therefore, God must not be said to 'exist' since, for Tillich rather than for normal English usage, this is to place him in the created order of subjects and objects whereas 'he is being-itself beyond essence and existence'.[54]

Fourthly, the true 'God' stands behind or above the gods of man's religious conceptions. When applied to him, all adjectives, even superlatives, class him among other beings even while making him superior to them. Talk about his nature is thus to be understood as symbolic expression which points beyond itself. Fifthly, while no argument can demonstrate his existence—for that would be to treat him wrongly as a possible object among others—his reality cannot be denied since he is 'the power of resisting non-being' which is 'the power inherent in everything' that exists. Both atheism and literal interpretations of theism must therefore be rejected. God is known only through ecstatic encounter in which the subject transcends ordinary modes of experience and is grasped by the mystery of God as the ground of being and meaning.[55]

Christ is the one through whom the existential estrangement of man is overcome as, under the conditions of estrangement, he 'represents God to man' and 'shows what God wants man to be'. He thus both exemplifies the 'New Being' in himself and makes it possible for others as they accept in faith 'the eternal relation of God to men which is manifest in the Christ'. The identifying claim of Christianity is 'the affirmation that Jesus of Nazareth . . . is actually the Christ, namely, he who brings the new state of things'. Tillich, though, is acutely aware of the problems of establishing the Jesus of history. Consequently he does not rest the Christian Gospel on any demonstrable 'empirical factuality' of the Biblical portrait of Jesus but on its 'transforming power'. Whatever the facts of Jesus of Nazareth might be, the picture of him given in the Bible is known to present the Christ because it possesses the creative power of the New Being. This picture, furthermore, is not a gnostic redemptive myth which happens to be effective, for it is indissolubly linked to the 'concrete reality' of the life of an individual person even though the events of that life now belong, for us, to the uncertainties of history.[56]

Faith, for Tillich, is 'ultimate concern'. The description is ambivalent for it denotes both whatever concern is in fact ultimate for a believer and concern for what is truly ultimate. Tillich describes it as 'not a theoretical affirmation of something uncertain' but as 'the existential acceptance of something transcending ordinary experience. . . . It is the state of being grasped by the power of being which transcends everything that is and in which everything that is participates. He who is grasped by this power is able to affirm himself because he knows that he is affirmed by the power of being-itself.'[57] Faith is thus 'the courage to be' in face of the threat of non-being.

By it existential estrangement from the essence of being is overcome as the individual is aware of himself as grasped by the ground of being. Christian faith is the affirmation of Jesus as the Christ, the 'daring courage' to take him, the symbol of whose life is a cross, as the symbol of ultimate concern.[58] Such faith is not a theoretical but an existential affirmation. The believer does not merely risk intellectual error but commits his whole being to that which confronts him as the ground of being and the source of new being.

## III

Tillich's theology, then, is existentialist in that existentialist analyses of the human situation largely pose its questions and, consequently, to some extent give the form for its affirmations. The content of those affirmations, however, comes from revelatory experience of God apprehended in terms of an ontological structure which is greatly indebted to Schelling. Another major movement in theology during our period used a very different ontological structure. This is the movement which is called 'process theology'. As its name implies, it is based on the metaphysical position which Alfred North Whitehead propounded in the 1920s and 1930s. Starting with *Man's Vision of God and the Logic of Theism*, published in 1941, Charles Hartshorne (b. 1897) has been the leading exponent of the 'process' view of God and may fairly be called the father of 'process theology'.* Other important process theologians, such as Schubert Ogden, Daniel Day Williams, and, especially as a popularizer, Norman Pittenger, have largely started from the fundamental insights of Hartshorne's work although John Cobb has preferred to derive his process theology from the fountainhead of Whitehead's own works. The large amount of basic agreement among the different exponents allows us to discuss process theology as such without the need continually to refer to the positions of individual members of the movement. Since, however, process theology is mainly known in Britain through the writings and addresses of Pittenger, it is perhaps necessary to point out that his rather florid style of presentation is quite unlike the hard and close metaphysical reasoning of a Hartshorne or an Ogden or a Cobb.

Process philosophy starts from the insight that what is real and

* Whitehead is the father of process thought but his views on God are not greatly developed and are open to different interpretations. It is Hartshorne who has significantly developed the theistic implications of this metaphysic.

concrete is essentially in process of change from what it was to what it will become. Even apparently static entities like tables, which philosophers have frequently analysed as paradigm examples of what exists, are only *apparently* stable because they are viewed over a short period of their existence and in isolation from their relations to their environment. Considered more comprehensively their existence is found to involve identity through change just as, even if less dramatically than, is the case with persons. What is unchanging, then, is what is either dead and past or what is an abstraction from the processes of concrete reality. But if every concrete reality is in process, it follows that it must belong to some kind of temporal order. Time, therefore, is part of the essential structure of reality. Changes in individual entities, furthermore, are not wholly due to intrinsic forces. They always involve responses to forces and situations brought about by other entities. Consequently there are no discrete individuals. Each actual entity is essentially part of the 'social' order in which it is related to every other actual entity, even though its interactions with some entities are vastly more important for it than its interactions with others. My awareness of one of the editors of this volume as he presses me for this chapter is, for example, far more influential on my conduct at this moment than the thoughts of Mao or the memory of Cromwell, even though these latter are, to some extent, also part of the environment to which I am responding just because they are actual. In this 'social' structure of reality, the most effective power is not the rude compulsion of physical force but the tenderness and persuasion which 'lures' other entities into harmony with its purposes. For process thinkers it seems that it ultimately is 'love that makes the world go round'—and not only go round but also stick together! This understanding of reality is presented by Hartshorne in terms of a panpsychism which sees every actual entity as a responding and creating subject. The validity of process thought, however, probably does not depend on the acceptability of some kind of panpsychism, even though it may be easier to express its social concept of reality, including the relation of God to the world, in these terms. Finally, process theology accepts as a basic presupposition Whitehead's remark that 'God is not to be treated as an exception to all metaphysical principles' but as 'their chief exemplification'.[59] It is on the basis of these metaphysical insights that Hartshorne and others have developed their process view of God.

Hartshorne is primarily a philosopher. His importance for theology—which I regard as great as that of any theologian in our period and probably in this century *—lies in his concern as a philosopher to find a rationally consistent concept of the God of theistic religious belief, to determine the logical status of claims about God, and to show the existence of God. His concern starts from his awareness that the concepts of God traditionally employed in theology are apparently and possibly actually self-contradictory. For example, if God is absolute, *actus purus* without any potentiality at all, how can he be said, without contradiction, to be 'Creator' where 'creativity' involves the deliberate execution of intentions? Or, if God is eternal in the sense of utterly outside time, how can he be said without contradiction also to know, guide, and govern this temporal world? Or, if God is unchanging in all respects, how can he be said without contradiction also to love men where 'love' involves different responses according to the situation of its object? These, and many more, are familiar problems in theology. Hartshorne refuses either to ignore them or to pretend to have overcome them by calling them 'paradoxes' or to use them as examples of reason's inadequacy in theological matters. He argues, instead, that it is possible to speak systematically and appropriately of God as necessary, absolute, unchanging, cause, infinite and eternal in certain respects and, without contradiction, as contingent, relative, changing, effect, finite and temporal in other respects. He does this by distinguishing not only between the essence of a thing and its existence but also between its existence and its actuality.

Hartshorne outlines this distinction in the statement ' "existence" is merely a relation of exemplification which actuality (any suitable actuality) has to essence.'[60] Talk about the *existence* of a particular essence, that is, means that that essence is *actualized* in some appropriate way, but a way which is not completely determined by the essence alone. This is not an easy distinction to grasp and perhaps an illustration may help. Take the essence of being 'my wife'. This essence denotes a human being, female, over fifteen years old, neither married to anyone else nor unmarried, and subject to a legally recognized contractual relationship with me. The statement 'my wife exists' is true, then, if someone exists which has these qualities. Nothing, though, exists just as a married female human being over fifteen years old. Anyone with these qualities instantiates them as an *actual* individual in a particular way which is only generally specified

* I dare to venture this claim even though the century has included Barth. Barth, it seems to me, belongs to and is perhaps the end of a long tradition in Christian theology whereas Hartshorne offers new fundamental insights of great importance.

by the essence itself. For example, as a being described as 'over fifteen years old', my wife could be sixteen, twenty-six, thirty-six, seventy-two, or ninety-five years old: as an existing being, however, she will exist as a person with a specific birthday and so a specific age. Again, in so far as her essence denotes her as a human being, she could be red-haired or black-haired, slim or stout, a brilliant cook or a culinary disaster, and so on! As existing, however, she exists as an actual person who has a particular shade of hair, a particular shape, a particular skill in the kitchen, and so on. The actuality of 'my wife', then, is the way this essence is precisely instantiated in a particular individual out of the various possibilities open to the existence of this essence.

On the basis of this distinction Hartshorne presents what he calls a 'dipolar' view of God—'dipolar' because polar opposite categories give the formal structure of two distinct aspects of God's nature. God is uniquely supreme because in his case alone is *existence* necessary, absolute, unchanging, and so on. His *actuality*, though, is contingent, relative, changing, and so on. In terms of God's attributes, for example, this means that God's being is described as necessary in that whatever else may be the case, God will always exist, but as contingent in that the actual state of his reality depends upon what God chooses out of non-compossible possibilities to be. His knowledge of the world is absolute in that he is invariably and without loss aware of all that is the case in the world, but relative in that the actual content of that knowledge depends on what in fact is actually the case in the world. God's love may properly be described as unchanging in that whatever happens, God responds in a totally loving fashion but as changing in that its actual concrete expression is what is the appropriate expression of love for this particular situation. In spite of its initial strangeness and the difficulty of the basic distinction between existence and actuality, Hartshorne's conceptuality is an important attempt to find a way for theologians to talk consistently about God as a loving, personal reality in a way that also recognizes his unique status.

Hartshorne also describes his understanding of God as 'panentheist'. This term refers particularly to his understanding of the relation between God and the world. Whereas traditional theism so emphasizes the distinction between God and the world that it suggests the impossibility of any positive relationship between them, and whereas pantheism makes God a cipher for the real world, Hartshorne's panentheism suggests that God embraces the world within his own reality but is not wholly identified by the sum total of the states of the world. On this view God is influenced by every actual event in the world. Everything that man feels, thinks, and does is also, with unrestricted clarity, experienced by God. At the same time, God responds to every actual event. He seeks to 'lure' each entity to seek that state that will produce its greatest fulfilment that is compatible with the greatest fulfilment of all other entities. God's relation to the world is thus presented in terms of a total, immediate awareness of each entity and an influence upon each entity which is governed by care for its freedom and individuality.

It is on the basis of God's total, immediate awareness of each entity that Hartshorne develops his doctrine of 'objective' immortality. He rejects the doctrine of 'subjective' immortality, namely, the doctrine that each person continues as a subject to have experiences and to respond to them in a new mode of being after death, partly on the grounds that such an endless process is inconceivable for a finite being who has only limited potentialities. His doctrine is that God for ever preserves in his memory without any loss of immediacy each moment of each person's life. Thus death does not mark the end of their influence upon God—and so of their reality for future events—but only the end of their possibility of creative development. Some process theologians follow Hartshorne here but others have pointed out that subjective immortality is not necessarily denied by the process view of God but may even be regarded as an implication of its stress on God's concern for individuals.

His understanding of God's nature and relation to the world leads Hartshorne to a reconsideration of the notion of God's perfection. Traditionally Christian theology has understood God's perfection in terms of a static absolute, actualizing all possible values—i.e. as *ens realissimum* and *actus purus*. As such, God is held to be totally unchanging since, where no improvement is possible, any change must produce imperfections in the previously unchanging being. Hartshorne rejects such a view of God's perfection on three grounds. First, not all values are compossible. For example, one can either feel compassion for those that suffer or one can enjoy untrammelled bliss but one cannot enjoy both states absolutely and simultaneously. Not even God, therefore, can embody all possible values, since the actualization of certain values must rule out the actualization of others. Secondly, the notion of an absolute maximum of value, if reality is in process, is as untenable as the notion of a maximum finite number. Each future event adds its value to reality. As a perfect being whose value is partly constituted by his total inclusion of all the actualized values of reality, God cannot be thought of as having absolute maximum of value except by denying the process character of reality, including that of God's own being. Such a denial would, for Hartshorne, not only be wrong but would also destroy the meaningfulness of life. Thirdly, the view that God's perfection requires him to be unchanging implies that God cannot be credited with those values which involve reciprocal relationships. These, though, are the values which we prize most highly in personal relationships and which underlie believers' trust in God as one who understands and cares for them as individuals. Hartshorne attempts to overcome these criticisms with a notion of God's perfection as 'dual transcendence'. According to this understanding God is, on the one hand, unsurpassable by others: no other entity could, even theoretically, ever equal, let alone surpass, God. He embodies at every moment the maximum of value then possible. At every moment, therefore, he is never less than perfect. His perfection is thus a unique state. On the other hand, God's perfect state at any moment is surpassable and surpassed by his later states since those later states embody values that have come into being since his earlier one. For example, at a certain time, God will know all that is and has been up to that time, but at a later time God will know not only all that was and had been up to the former time but also all that comes to be between the two times. This view of God's perfection is a theologically important attempt to escape from intrinsic difficulties in the traditional view and to provide a conceptuality which is appropriate to the nature of a personal being with constant character and perfect responses to a changing reality. It means, though, as Hartshorne makes clear, that God's state cannot be thought of in terms of eternal bliss. As one who is totally aware and totally loving, God experiences the suffering as well as the joy actualized in the world. It also means that God's 'eternity' cannot be regarded as a state outside time—the state of total simultaneity of traditional theology—but as a state of 'eminent temporality' in which God is necessarily present in every moment of time.[61] Temporal sequence, therefore, is real for God as for us but, in the case of God alone, poses no threat to him. Since, though, it is real for him, it is possible to conceive of him as having reciprocal relations with our temporally-ordered world.

As well as developing a process concept of God, Hartshorne has also made many vigorous attempts to re-establish the ontological argument for the existence of God. This argument, classically given by Anselm in the eleventh century, holds that from the definition of God as 'that than which a greater cannot be conceived' it is possible to prove *a priori* that such a being exists. This argument has continually fascinated philosophers and theologians but since the time of Kant has generally been regarded as invalid. Hartshorne, though, does not agree. He holds that while Kant and others may successfully have shown the flaws in one form of the argument, they have not noticed that another and valid form of the argument is to be found in Anselm. I cannot go into the details of Hartshorne's case here.[62] It rests on the claim—also made independently by Norman Malcolm[63]—that the definition of God as the 'greatest conceivable' implies that God's mode of existence must be thought of as 'necessary existence'. Rejecting philosophical arguments that 'necessity' can only be a quality of propositions and cannot be applied to existence, Hartshorne holds that 'necessary existence' is a self-consistent concept, expressing a mode of existence which is omnitolerant, underived, indestructible, and so on, in contrast to the qualities of contingent existence. He then argues that a being which must be thought of as having necessary existence must also be held necessarily to exist. This, in spite of his many attempts to show its validity, including an expression of the argument in the symbols of modal logic, still seems to me to be fallacious. It confuses a valid description of the *mode* of God's existence (as necessary existence) with a factual assertion about the necessity of his existence. The conclusion of the ontological argument from God's necessary existence should not be 'God therefore exists' (which makes a claim about what is included in reality) but 'If God exists, then his mode of existence must be that of "necessary existence" ' (which makes a claim about how we are properly to think of God's nature). This, though, is a far more significant conclusion than yet seems to have been widely recognized, for it indicates the peculiar logical status of claims about God. If this assessment is correct, critics of theism who argue that its claims cannot be accepted as factual because they are empirically non-falsifiable have failed to appreciate the fundamental nature of claims about God. The existence of God cannot be empirically falsified (nor empirically demonstrated) because that existence is either true of any possible actual reality or true of none at all. The ontological argument, that is, presents us with the alternative that the whole of reality is either through and through and inescapably theistic or utterly non-theistic, an alternative which Hartshorne interprets as implying that the universe is ultimately rational or ultimately non-rational and so meaningless. Although Hartshorne himself may have underestimated the significance of empirical references for theistic verification and overestimated the role of *a priori* arguments,[64] his work at this point makes an important and wrongly neglected contribution to current attempts to understand the nature and logic of statements about God.

Hartshorne, as we have said, is primarily a philosopher. His views on theism are the product of reflection on reason, reality, the nature of God, and the implications of religious worship. He does not concern himself with the revelatory and Christological claims of Christian theology. Indeed, the comments of his father, a clergyman interested in canon law, seem to have persuaded him that no Christological doctrine can both make sense and not be heretical! It is, however, at least arguable that process theism cannot deal adequately with the nature of God's actuality and of his active response to the world without using some revelatory and—for Christian theology—Christological elements.[65] Other theologians, therefore, have applied process thought to Christological questions and made useful contributions to current Christological understanding. Cobb, Ogden, Pittenger, and Williams suggest in different ways how the relation of Jesus to God may be understood in terms of the man Jesus being in total empathy with the nature of God. Obeying perhaps a unique vocation, Jesus, a man with all the freedom and restrictions of a man of his day, completely accepted for his own life God's lordship, love, and supreme value. Consequently, as Cobb puts it, since his 'I' was 'constituted by his prehension of God', his life expressed 'the reality of God and his will'.[66] Similarly, according to Ogden, we meet in Jesus' life and ministry the expression and demand of 'God's trancendent love as the sole basis of our authentic existence'.[67] Some process theologians thus use the categories and insights of process thought to develop a Christology which accepts the fundamental humanity of Jesus and seeks to show how, without destroying that humanity, it is possible to maintain coherently that that life also manifested the nature of God. As with other attempts to make sense of Christology, these attempts find that the price of rationality is suspicion from the hyper-orthodox! They suggest, though, that process theologians who want to talk sense and are not intimidated by ancient credal formulae may have important things to say about the central doctrines of Christianity.

Pierre Teilhard de Chardin (1881–1955) was an independent thinker whose understanding of God and the world, in spite of its very different sources and terminology, has interesting similarities with that advanced by process philosophers and theologians. It achieved considerable popular attention during our period. When Teilhard died in 1955, he was hardly known outside certain scientific circles. As a loyal Jesuit, he faithfully obeyed during his lifetime the orders of his superiors and did not publish his writings. He made arrangements, however, for them to be published after his death. As they appeared in the following decade, interest in Teilhard grew rapidly. His thought became, for a time, both the basis of what amounted to an intellectual cult and the cause of fierce controversy. Associations for the propagation and development of his thought, with the literary trappings typical of such movements, were established. Sir Julian Huxley asserts the importance of Teilhard's thought: 'Through his combination of wide scientific knowledge with deep religious feeling and a rigorous sense of value, he has forced theologians to view their ideas in the new perspective of evolution, and scientists to see the spiritual implications of their knowledge. He has both clarified and unified our vision of reality.'[68] Sir Peter Medawar attacks his work as 'tipsy, euphoric, prose-poetry' and declares that Teilhard 'was in no sense a serious thinker'.[69] At least, then, he deserves fame for evoking such powerful and contradictory responses!

According to Huxley, Teilhard was 'keenly aware of the importance of vivid and arresting terminology'.[70] It is a pity that he was apparently not equally conscious of the need to make his terminology comprehensible. The meanings of some of his concepts are hard to grasp although, in fairness to him, the novelty of some of his ideas may perhaps require expression in new and puzzling language. What Teilhard presents is a fascinating creative synthesis of scientific views on evolution, Christian doctrine, and mystical vision. His own particular expertise in geology, palaeontology, and biology made him acutely aware of the age, size, complexity, and development of the world. What he wanted to discern is the meaning and goal of the cosmic evolutionary process and, in particular, the place of man in that process. His conclusion is that as the process of evolution has led through stages of increasing complexity to the higher states of conscious individuality now found in man, so it is destined to continue until it reaches the 'omega-point' where individual separation is overcome in unifying and universal consciousness. In this process, God is 'the Prime Mover, Gatherer and Consolidator, ahead of us, of evolution'.[71] He is '*the ultimate point* upon which all realities converge' and in which 'qualities which appear to us to be contradictory' are harmonized.[72] Christ is similarly understood on a cosmic scale. Teilhard seeks to show how the Jesus of 'the dimensions of a Mediterranean world' is capable of 'embracing and still forming the centre of our prodigiously expanded universe'.[73] The incarnation, death, and resurrection of Christ are thus presented as cosmic events. 'The Incarnation means the renewal, the restoration, of all the energies and powers of the universe; Christ is the instrument, the Centre and the End of all creation, animate *and* material; through him everything is created, hallowed, quickened.' This work of Christ happens 'with the *exactitude and the harmony of a natural process of evolution*'.[74] Through it 'not a single atom, however lowly or imperfect, but must co-operate—at least by way of repulsion or reflection—in the fulfillings of Christ'.[75] Nevertheless, this cosmic Christ is essentially linked to and an expansion of 'the historical reality of Christ'. According to Teilhard, it is the 'tangible and verifiable truth of the Gospel event' which prevents his concept of Christ being a vague and uncertain metaphysical dream.[76] With his deep optimism about cosmic development and his faith in the eventual fulfilment of all things in Christ, it was right that he died on an Easter Day. Although his thought was suspected of being heterodox and for much of his life his superiors kept him in semi-exile doing scientific work in China, when his writings were published they were widely received as an important attempt to relate belief in God and Christ to the world of modern scientific discovery. Criticism by theological and scientific experts and the perplexity of his writing seemed to make Teilhard more rather than less attractive.

## IV

Perplexing language is not restricted to Teilhard's theology. The proper meaning and logical status of any religious or theological statement is far from easy to define. Another important movement in theology during our period—and one which was particularly conducted by British theologians facing the challenge of linguistic philosophy—was the investigation of religious language. A. J. Ayer's famous exposition of logical positivism, *Language, Truth and Logic*, used the verification principle to show that religious statements are neither valid nor invalid claims but simply nonsense. There is, therefore, no significant difference between theists, agnostics, and atheists since none of them can produce empirical evidence to give meaning to their position. People who make claims about religious truths are thus, according to Ayer, 'merely providing material for the psychoanalyst'.[77] They need to be cured by a strong application of the verification principle! Logical positivism, however, fell victim to its own analyses. It was followed by a less dogmatic form of linguistic philosophy, that of linguistic analysis, which developed under the personal influence of Ludwig Wittgenstein. The verification principle was replaced by the slogan 'Don't ask for meaning, ask for use.' As a result, when linguistic philosophers investigate religious statements, they do not intend to demonstrate their meaninglessness but, accepting that these statements are used and so presumably mean something to some people, try to determine what that meaning is.*

An early example of the application of linguistic analysis to religious claims is found in John Wisdom's 'Gods'. In this paper he explores the difference between the theist and the atheist in terms of their disagreement about the recognition of a pattern—that of a divine mind—which makes sense of their common world and which results in a particular attitude to that world. He illustrates his point by a story about a garden: 'two people return to a long-neglected garden and find among the weeds a few of the old plants surprisingly vigorous.' No one can be found who has ever seen or heard a gardener at work there and careful examination of the garden produces apparently conflicting evidence: 'sometimes they come on new things suggesting a gardener comes and sometimes they come on new things suggesting the contrary.' One of them concludes that a gardener comes, even though unseen and unheard, and the other denies it. While, then, they disagree about the pattern which makes sense of the facts, their agreement about what they find and expect to find in the garden shows that the difference between them is not a matter of conflicting experimental hypotheses. Nevertheless, the difference between them is important for with it 'goes a difference in how they feel towards the garden'.[78] Disputes about the existence of God, similarly, are disputes in the first instance about which pattern, the theistic or the atheistic, is the model of understanding which best fits the accepted features of the world and, consequently, about which is the right attitude to adopt towards that world. The meaning and logic of religious statements are to be appreciated accordingly. They make claims about what is so but not at the level of straightforward empirical propositions. Statements about God are statements of non-empirical 'facts' which tell us how to regard and respond to the familiar, empirical facts of our world.[79]

In 1951 I. T. Ramsey (b. 1915) made another early attempt to indicate the logical status of religious statements in his inaugural lecture at Oxford, 'Miracles, An Exercise in Logical Mapwork'. Treating different subjects as attempts to map out the common world

* For further information on the philosophical background to this theology, see pp. 69–81, and the chapters on philosophy in vols. I and II of *The Twentieth-Century Mind.*

in terms of different ways of understanding it (as one may have geological, population, rainfall, and contour maps of a certain area), he considers on which map talk about 'miracles'—and so talk about the activity of God—is properly to be located. After examining the logics of scientific and historical 'maps', he turns to metaphysics. The function of metaphysical language is to delimit and co-ordinate the different 'maps'. Terms such as 'God' and 'activity' and 'I' are to be regarded as metaphysical terms. They do not belong to any one map but are terms by which all the maps are organized into an integrated whole. The term 'God' in particular is described as 'the metaphysical apex of our language system' since the unity of 'all discursive knowledge . . . relates to the activity of God himself'. Ramsey admits that he may have given the impression that 'this Chair was founded to enable simple questions to be so complicated as to ensure that the occupant should never be out of a job'![80] We shall return to Ramsey's other work later but his inaugural lecture not only offered some insight into talk about God but also hinted at the complexity of any satisfactory analysis of it. The problem in fact has kept a number of people in work ever since—though Ramsey himself has been translated to other service as Bishop of Durham.

Widespread recognition of the significance of linguistic analyses of religious language came, however, with the publication of *New Essays in Philosophical Theology* (edited by Antony Flew and Alasdair MacIntyre) in 1955. Nearly all its papers had already been published, though some only recently, but it was their collection together which showed the disturbing challenge that is offered by the prevalent fashion in British philosophy during our period. J. J. C. Smart, for example, suggests that the question 'Does God exist?' is a meaningless one since it has 'no clear meaning for the unconverted' who stand 'outside religion' and so cannot understand its language while 'for the converted the question no longer arises' since God's existence is presupposed by their thought and activity as believers.[81] J. N. Findlay goes further. He cunningly argues that the way a believer must think of God demonstrates that God cannot exist. His case is that 'a religiously satisfactory' concept of God's existence must conceive it as 'something inescapable and necessary'. It is an accepted dogma of modern philosophy, though, that 'necessity' cannot be a quality of existence but of propositions. Therefore 'the Divine Existence is either senseless or impossible'.[82] Findlay, in response to some of Hartshorne's work, has since abandoned this argument. When he presented it, however, it further highlighted the oddity of talk about God. C. B. Martin examines the notion of 'the perfect good' and concludes that the doctrine of the incarnation of God in Christ faces 'the choice between self-contradiction and vacuity'.[83] The most famous and disturbing papers, however, are those dealing with 'theology and falsification'. Flew opens this debate with a version of Wisdom's tale of the gardener and asks 'how does . . . an invisible, intangible, eternally elusive gardener differ from an imaginary gardener or even from no gardener at all?' It thus seems that 'a fine brash hypothesis', which at first appears to provide a factual explanation but is not open to any conceivable empirical falsification, suffers 'the death by a thousand qualifications'. Flew now suggests that this is the peculiar fate of claims about God. Believers who assert that 'God is love', for example, apparently allow no conceivable event to show that their assertion is false. They evade objections such as that of 'a child dying of inoperable cancer' by holding that God's love is 'not a merely human love' or is 'inscrutable'. Such qualifications can so erode an assertion that it finally becomes 'no longer an assertion at all'.[84] Flew thus challenges those who hold that their claims about God are factual to state what would constitute a disproof of these claims. If they cannot conceivably be falsified, they cannot be regarded as factual.

Both in *New Essays in Philosophical Theology* and, less directly, in *Faith and Logic* (a collection of essays by Oxford and Anglican philosophers and theologians which was an indirect reply to some of the problems aired in the former volume), R. M. Hare, Basil Mitchell, and I. M. Crombie offer different interpretations of religious language in reply to Flew. Hare suggests that religious statements are not empirical (and so falsifiable) assertions but report the structures of understanding in which we believe and by which we make sense of our experiences. Hare calls these structures 'bliks' and, probably unfortunately, describes them in terms of a lunatic's conviction that 'all dons want to murder him'. The difference, for example, between Saul at the beginning and Paul at the end of the road to Damascus was not an increased knowledge of empirical facts about Jesus but a different attitude to the same facts.[85] Even in sophisticated religions, though, statements of faith are said to have also some (unspecified) factual implications because facts and attitudes towards those facts can never be totally separated. Mitchell's reply is less alarming since his parable is not about a lunatic but about a partisan's trust that a stranger is on his side. Here the trust has grounds—the partisan comes to it after a night in conversation with the stranger—and certain behaviour by the stranger is recognized to be evidence against it. As trust, however, it is tested but not destroyed by contrary evidence. Religious belief is thus interpreted as a trust that certain things are the case—a trust which arises from considering various complex features in the light of the belief and which continues to be held in spite of evidence to the contrary. Religious statements, then, make factual claims whose continued acceptance is not simply determined by the available empirical evidence. The unresolved problem is how to decide when the contrary evidence makes it silly to continue in the belief.[86] Crombie takes up the notion of parable, instead of giving one, and argues that the *predicates* of statements about God are to be regarded as parables which give us authoritative disclosures concerning our right relationships with God. We can never know what the parabolic predicates are about—'God'—but, through natural theology, we do know 'that we are to refer them . . . out of our experience in a certain direction'. In this life, we can never conclusively verify or falsify a statement about God: we have to remain 'within the parable', not knowing how it actually applies but believing that 'it does apply, and that we shall one day see how'.[87]

This last point about verification 'one day' is taken up by John Hick, who argues that statements about God are factual because they could conceivably be experientially verified in post-mortem experience. His notion of eschatological verification further suggests that statements about God are logically unusual in that they may be verified but can never be falsified—since if there is no life after death, no one is going to discover it after they have died! Verification of this order, though, is hardly significant for those who look to verification to show here and now whether religious claims are factual or only bogusly claim to be such.[88] E. L. Mascall, who has sometimes been suspected of being more Thomist than Thomas himself, first denies in his *Words and Images* that the verification principle is the criterion of meaning and then argues that in any case mystical experience is genuinely empirical experience even though it is not an experience of the bodily senses. Moving into the attack, Mascall suggests that 'their assertions about the immediacy and compulsiveness of their awareness of the divine reality' even suggests that 'the mystics might almost be described as the strictest verificationists that there are'.[89] If the relation of the mystic's claims about God to his experience is somewhat problematic, so too is that between the physicist's claims about mesons and his experience. If mystical knowledge of God is restricted to a few people who have attained certain techniques through long training and devotion, the case of atomic physics is not all that different. John Baillie similarly replies to verificationist doubts about the factual significance of talk about God by referring, in his *Sense of the Presence of God*, to religious experience. He claims that religious faith is a 'primary mode of apprehension' and so 'cannot be tested by reference to anything outside itself'. What is revealed to the believer's 'eye of faith' is as self-authenticating to him as 'what is "revealed" to ordinary sense perception' is to the natural scientist.[90]

Attempts such as these to meet the challenge of the verification or falsification principle directly and thereby to show that religious statements are factual also show the oddity of their kind of 'fact'. Facts which are matters of trust in the face of empirical evidence to the contrary or which can be verified only after death or are apprehended only by a special kind of experience are, to say the least, not ordinary facts. Other investigators, however, were not convinced that religious expressions are to be regarded as some peculiar kind of factual utterance. They interpreted their apparently factual form as a misleading way of conveying utterances of a quite different nature.

The most famous attempt to interpret quasi-factual talk about God as talk about something else is probably R. B. Braithwaite's (b. 1900) 'An Empiricist's View of the Nature of Religious Belief'. In this Eddington Memorial Lecture he argues, on the basis of an examination of their use, that statements of religious belief are fundamentally statements of the believer's behaviour policy. They declare the believer's 'allegiance to a set of moral principles'. Moral behaviour is not the consequence of a believer's faith in and about God but constitutes that faith. The confession that 'God is love', then, is not a factual report about the nature of a transcendent being but declares an 'intention to follow an agapeistic* way of life'. We discover the meaning of religious assertions, therefore, by discovering, through questioning and observation, 'what principles of conduct the asserter takes the assertions to involve'. The difference between different religions which advocate the same behaviour-policy lies in the different 'sets of stories' which are associated with the policy. These stories, however, are not to be regarded as significant empirical claims. Their value lies in the encouragement they give to the believer in the pursuit of the policy. Empirical reports about Jesus, then, 'may psychologically support' the Christian believer in his resolution to follow an agapeistic way of life but they do not 'logically justify' that resolution. Braithwaite thus openly asserts

* The word 'agapeistic' is coined from the Greek word used in the New Testament for Christian love—*agape*.

that 'a religious belief is an intention to behave in a certain way (a moral belief) together with the entertainment of certain stories'. This interpretation aroused some fierce criticisms, particularly on the grounds that it confused the consequences of belief with its substance and so 'reduced' religious belief to something essentially different.[91]

A number of attempts have been made to interpret religious statements as expressions of the attitude, perspective, or stance by which the believer understands his world and responds to it. We have already met this view of religious statements, at least partially, in Wisdom, Hare, and Mitchell. In his *Languages, Standpoints and Attitudes* (1953) H. A. Hodges reminds us how our understanding of life is determined by our basic standpoints and fundamental attitudes, for it is these that determine both what we regard as facts and how we evaluate them. Our choice between rival standpoints and attitudes is not and cannot be the result of 'logical' tests but only of existential experience and expectation. Statements of faith thus express, at least in part, the standpoint and attitude of the believer. Paul van Buren expresses a similar point of view in terms of a 'perspective'. His *Secular Meaning of the Gospel* attempts to interpret Christianity in a way which can be appreciated by contemporary 'secular' men. Since such men are said to have no understanding of the transcendent and the supernatural, all such ideas are excluded from this interpretation. Statements of faith are held to 'express, describe, or commend a particular way of seeing the world, other men, and oneself, and the way of life appropriate to such a perspective'. For the Christian the norm of this perspective is the historical event of Jesus. The doctrine of the incarnation of God in Jesus is interpreted as claiming ultimate value or truth for the perspective found in Jesus. While, then, there are empirical elements in statements of belief, their significance is to describe and gain conviction for a particular way of looking at life.[92] D. D. Evans makes use of J. L. Austin's philosophical analyses of language, particularly of his ideas about 'performative language', in his detailed examination of religious language as expressions of self-involving on-looks. An 'on-look' is described by Evans as 'a *fusion* of a decision-*that* $x$ is like $y$ with a decision-*to* treat $x$ like $y$'.[93] These two elements belong together in an on-look: neither is prior to and the ground of the other. In stating an on-look, I thus both declare what I hold to be the case and commit myself to an appropriate behaviour policy with regard to it. Faith-statements express on-looks which are parabolic in form since they refer to transcendent entities that can only be described ndirectly in terms of human attitudes. They claim to be finally authoritative on-looks on the grounds that they correspond to the divine on-look. Talk about God is thus not to be interpreted simply as a quasi-factual claim but as the presentation of a fundamentally self-involving on-look which properly orientates all our understanding. W. F. Zuurdeeg and W. Hordern use the notion of 'conviction' rather than those of standpoint, attitude, and on-look in their basically similar analyses of religious language. Hordern, for example, states that 'Religious language . . . deals with the ultimate convictions of a man's life' which determine what in life for him 'is supremely worth-while, . . . truly good and real, what we can ultimately depend upon'.[94] Religious statements are thus held to combine facts, commitments, and fundamental structures of understanding and of valuing.

Other analysts of religious language consider that it ought to be understood in terms of the language and logic we use for personal encounters. God is not an object to be talked about but the 'Thou' who speaks to us and to whom we speak. The influence of Buber's *I and Thou* and of Barthian theology of the 'Word' is often very noticeable here. Hordern, who criticizes Buber for too narrow a view of the I–Thou relationship, suggests that the meaning and truth of theological statements are appreciated only by entering 'into the give-and-take of I–thou dialogue' with God.[95] Tillich, who speaks of faith as a state of being 'grasped' by ultimate concern, is troubled by the role of symbol in religious language—I say 'troubled' because his numerous remarks on the subject betray a fundamental uncertainty about how such language can be orientated by reference to a literal statement. He distinguishes between signs and symbols on the ground that a symbol alone necessarily 'participates in the reality of that for which it stands'. By symbols we are able to use finite realities 'to express our relation to the infinite' and so make statements about the object of faith.[96] The symbolic character of religious language has been variously explored by others, some of whom find important insights in pre-war philosophical works by Whitehead, Urban, and Cassirer. Aesthetic activity in art and poetry has also been explored to see what insight it may provide into the nature of religious language. H. D. Lewis, for example, has compared art and religion while R. Hepburn has questioned the value of a comparison of religion and poetry.[97] Finally, in this brief survey, we must mention I. T. Ramsey's important understanding of religious statements as models which seek to evoke unifying disclosures. In such an event the believer penetrates 'beyond' or 'behind' the ordinary empirical world to a 'depth' of reality which was previously unrecognized and which gives meaning to that world. Ramsey refers to the situations in which we speak of 'the light dawning', 'the penny dropping', or 'the ice breaking' to describe the kind of event he has in mind. Whereas Flew accuses theologians of killing the meaning of religious language through 'death by a thousand qualifications' Ramsey holds that this language receives 'life by a thousand enrichments'.[98] The qualifiers do not erode the content of the religious statement but direct those who consider it towards the situation in which a disclosure-event can occur. Such statements, then, present us with parables or models taken from this world but intended to evoke a cosmic disclosure in which we 'see' the fundamental meaning of reality and our duty in response to it.[99]

During our period, then, various interpretations of the meaning and logical nature of religious statements were produced, largely in response to the challenge of linguistic philosophy but also reflecting widespread theological puzzlement about the significance of such statements. A basic methodological error in many of the proffered interpretations is a failure to allow for the possibly great complexity of religious language. Because, for instance, an ethical element can be isolated in a religious statement, it does not follow that this is all that the statement contains. Similarly, the isolation of a perspectival element does not mean that this is the sole essence of a religious statement. Religious language, rather, is probably to be understood as a complex structure, composed of perspectival, attitudinal, ethical, factual, historical, convictional, experiential, unifying, and other elements, using both direct and indirect forms of expression. To use an analogy from natural science, the structure of religious language is to be thought of as molecular, since it contains various elements interrelated in complex ways, rather than as atomic, essentially consisting of only one element. Many of the analyses of religious language have mistakenly considered that they have identified the structure of that language when, in fact, they have only identified one or two of the atoms which belong to it. A complete exposition of religious language has not yet appeared. While some of its atoms have been recognized, there may be others yet to be discerned. Their interrelationships and the logical status of religious language is even less well understood, though there have been attempts to probe the problem.[100]

## V

There is, though, little point in trying to understand talk about God if there is no God to be talked about. The 1960s saw the development of radical theologies. Some of them went so far as to report that God is dead. Having announced the death of the old monarch, they disagreed strongly over who could be proclaimed as the new!

The first rumblings of radical theology in Britain came with collections of essays such as *Soundings* and *Objections to Christian Belief*. We have already mentioned A. R. Vidler's Introduction to *Soundings*. In the opening paragraph he writes that

> The Authors of this volume cannot persuade themselves that the time is ripe for major works of theological construction or reconstruction. It is a time . . . for making soundings, not charts or maps. . . . We can best serve the cause of truth and of the Church by candidly confessing where our perplexities lie, and not by making claims which, so far as we can see, theologians are not at present in a position to justify.[101]

In this spirit the essayists attempt to diagnose the various ills that have made contemporary Christian theology an invalid and to hint at possible restoratives. The atmosphere, on the whole, is that of the calm confidence of a well-run hospital. There may be problems but the essayists, all but one of them from Cambridge, give the impression that the prognosis is firmly hopeful. There is little hint of the drastic and risky surgery which other radical theologians were to hold to be necessary only a year or two later. The volume, *Objections to Christian Belief*, though intended to be disturbing and actually more searching than the parallel volume about humanism, is another example of healthy self-criticism by those who are not really worried by the fact that the foundations of Christianity are being called into question since they are sure that somehow or other it will triumph over its critics. It is symptomatic that the 'objections' end by reminding us that while religion is not 'an escape from conflict', Christianity, as it has done in the past, 'will survive present difficulties, objections and uncertainties, though perhaps in a different form'. Hence 'he who shall *endure* to the end . . . shall be saved.'[102]

Two explosions did shake the theological scene in Britain. The first was set off by Harry Williams's essay in *Soundings* which used Freudian insights to expose the real evil that may be hidden behind the practice of conventional Christian morality. He points, for example, to the 'enormous amount of double-think' which surrounds

Christian sexual ethics and outlines two stories about sexual encounters (they greatly enlivened a church ladies' meeting to which I repeated them in 1963 but would hardly be regarded now as lurid) to make the point that the self-giving love required of a Christian may demand actions that are contrary to the rules of chastity. Williams's comment on the stories is 'where there is healing, there is Christ, whatever the Church may say about fornication. And the appropriate response is—Glory to God in the Highest.'[103] Praise for adulterous behaviour, even in exceptional circumstances, was heady stuff for the Church in 1962 but probably would have gone unnoticed if it had not been taken up in the press under the slogan 'Charity, not chastity'. The interpretation of Christian ethics found in Williams's essay was worked out further by various writers as 'the new morality' or 'situation ethics'. The most famous exposition of its position is Joseph Fletcher's *Situation Ethics.*[104] He uses provocative stories to make the point that Christian morality is love in action. While the rules of Christian morality may provide rough-and-ready guides to what 'love' may generally involve, individual circumstances may require in the name of love actions that break those rules. Furthermore, those rules do not free the Christian from the responsibility of deciding for himself what love requires of him. Fletcher's position seems so obvious that we may wonder why there was so much fuss about the 'new morality'. It came, I suspect, because many people, believers and unbelievers, wanted to shelter from the risks, demands, and responsibilities of love behind a wall of established legalism. It is more comfortable to obey rules than to make decisions, especially when those decisions are to be orientated by self-giving love.

The other explosion occurred when the Bishop of Woolwich tried 'to be utterly honest about the terms in which the Faith can truthfully be presented today'.[105] John A. T. Robinson's *Honest to God* is important because its popularity made people at large aware of what some theologians had been saying for several years. Concepts of God as 'up there' and 'out there' are criticized and replaced by a God 'down there' as the depth and ground of our being. (This is not a deification of Australia but a use of Tillich's notions.) The doctrine of the incarnation is interpreted in terms of Jesus as 'the Man for Others' being transparent to the ultimate reality of God as love. The problems of prayer, the unsatisfactoriness of worship, the emptiness of devotional aids, and the principles of Christian ethics are honestly discussed. John Robinson does not offer any original theological insights. He largely reports the views of others. His honesty, though, cleared the ecclesiastical air in 1963 and forced complacent churchmen to recognize that the contemporary credibility of the Gospel might require a radical reappraisal of its fundamental ideas. To a large degree the success of *Honest to God* was due to the press. The Sunday before its publication the *Observer* published an article in which Robinson summed up his views under the heading 'Our Image of God Must Go'. Popular—and frequently uninformed—controversy rapidly spread. Twelve days after publication the Archbishop of Canterbury felt the need to criticize Robinson on television in order to comfort the faithful. There was a lively few months. Some established cobwebs and even dry rot in ecclesiastical timbers were noticed and threatened with removal. The controversy eventually died down and traditional doctrines widely continued to be traditionally presented. Robinson's later writings indicate that he is far from the revolutionary that was hoped or feared. Nevertheless, theological honesty had appeared. People were aware that there might be a chance for significant Christian belief and action in the present age. Encouragement was given to the groups of radicals that had been appearing in the churches and to their attempts to find new and significant interpretations of the faith.

In America a far more disturbing slogan than honesty was heard. Some radical theologians there took up Nietzsche's proclamation that 'God is dead'. Like a good slogan, this one was open to various interpretations. Confusion was rife as those who debated for and against the 'death' of God failed to recognize that by his 'death' they meant several quite different things. The confusion increased as the press took up the debate. Although the importance of the debate was established when it entered the pages of *Playboy*, the blaze of publicity tempted theologians into too rapid and ill-digested expressions of their views. In particular they generally failed to appreciate the history of antecedent expressions of their views. At least six distinct, though partially overlapping, claims can be detected in the 'death of God' literature.

The first is the claim that talk about God is 'dead'. Paul van Buren, for instance, announces that 'the *word* "God" is dead'[106] since its theistic meaning depends upon a metaphysical understanding of reality which allows us to talk about supernatural entities that transcend the empirical world. Such a metaphysical understanding is no longer possible for contemporary men. They live in an empirical, secular age which rejects all metaphysical utterances as either confused statements about the empirical world or simply meaningless. They cannot, therefore, even understand Nietzsche's madman when he proclaims that 'God is dead' because the subject-word,

'God', no longer has any significance for them. Van Buren does not recognize that this restriction of the real to what is open to empirical investigation is probably itself a metaphysical claim and so open to question on his terms.

Secondly, the 'death of God' is used as a slogan for the claim that God is no longer culturally significant in the western world. For centuries western culture has been 'Christian'. Christian symbols dominated the expression of its understandings. Even its deism, agnosticism, and atheism were reactions to the Christian concept of God. Gabriel Vahanian, in two studies of contemporary culture, points out that this is no longer the case. We live in 'a post-Christian era' where the God of Christian tradition is 'culturally irrelevant: God is *de trop*, as Sartre would say'.[107] Today man bases his culture on values which he self-consciously fashions for himself and expresses that culture in terms which have no reference to Christian belief. Vahanian regards this godlessness as a positive benefit to Christian faith. A good Barthian, he condemns the 'God' who is part of culture as a false idol. The eradication of 'God' from so-called Christian culture opens the way for men to recognize the advent of the true God who is sovereignly free and can never be objectified. Here, then, the 'death of God' presents the disappearance from culture of concepts of a false God—and affirms the living reality of the true God!

A third form of the 'death of God' theology holds that God is not experienced by man. God may exist but he does not reveal himself in any way. Man feels himself to be alone. Martin Buber affirmed in his seminal study *I and Thou* that God could only be known as he speaks to man. After the war he describes the modern age as one of divine silence. The 'death of God' announces the current 'eclipse' of God. Buber seems uncertain whether the 'eclipse' is due to God's deliberate self-concealment or to man's obsession with 'I–it' relationships preventing him having genuine 'I–thou' relationships. He is certain, though, that the 'eclipse' is temporary. One day it will pass. Men will then find themselves again in person-to-person encounter with God.[108]

William Hamilton, in contrast, holds that God is experienced by man as a 'wounding' and unavoidable 'pressure'. He confronts us as one 'whom we struggle to elude' in vain.[109] Gregor Smith similarly affirms that God encounters man today in judgement and grace. In these authors, though, we find a fourth version of 'death of God' theology—the view that God is to be thought of as one who refuses to dominate life so that men may come to maturity as free, responsible persons. An important source and enigmatic expression of this understanding of the 'death' of God is Bonhoeffer's *Letters and Papers from Prison*—especially the letters written from April to August 1944. Dietrich Bonhoeffer (1906–1945) was a theologian who doubled as a secret agent, a former pacifist who became involved in a plot to kill Hitler. After his arrest, in a Nazi prison in the middle of the war, he came to see God's non-intervention in human affairs as an example of God's grace. God becomes 'weak and powerless' and 'allows himself to be edged out of the world' so that 'he can be with us' as one who makes it possible for us to live a life of mature love.[110] God is not the nanny who protects us from the consequences of our actions but the father who summons us to take responsibility for history. William Hamilton, in *The New Essence of Christianity*, sees the suffering of Christ as a symbol of God's respect for man's freedom and of his will that man should fulfil himself through the exercise of that freedom. The 'death' of God here specifically describes both the 'withdrawal' or 'absence' of God from the world and our inability 'to affirm any of the traditional images of God'.[111] Gregor Smith similarly presents the 'death' of God as the death of a false understanding of his activity in the world but affirms his presence as a living God who calls men to the faith and obedience in which they fulfil the possibilities of their future. The most famous version of this 'death of God' theology, however, is Harvey Cox's *Secular City*. Inspired by a naïve sociological optimism, Cox interprets modern urban society with its secular attitudes as a realization of the will of God. Made in the image of God and given dominion over the world, man is intended by God to be his 'partner, . . . charged with the task of bestowing meaning and order in human history'.[112] God absents himself in order to give his partner an opportunity to exercise his powers and thereby show how he can run the set-up! At the same time, since God is apparently also quietly at work wherever life is becoming integrated, man's duty is to co-operate where he sees God at work. Furthermore, even as a *deus absconditus*, God has an eschatological relevance: one day he will return to call his partner to account. In this fourth version of the 'death of God' theology, 'death' reports the absence of God needed to give significance to man's freedom. God is not 'dead and done with'. Man is responsible to him, even though at present he is largely or wholly absent from affairs.

A fifth view of the 'death' of God is presented by Thomas J. J. Altizer. Apparently on the basis of a crude phenomenology which regards whatever appears to us as the case as in fact being the case,

Altizer holds that God once existed as a transcendent, ultimate power, threatening all life with nothingness. As such he reflected man's alienation, insecurity, and fear. This God—whom Altizer, following Blake, identifies with Satan—annihilated himself in the incarnation of Christ. God is now to be understood as a creative spirit present within life, co-operating with man's own creative activities and seeking to bring them to fulfilment. God is thus present in life today as 'a totally incarnate love', immanent within the processes of life.[113] Altizer's position is not easy to make sense of. He declares that the 'death' of God was 'an event' in which God irrevocably stopped being God, and yet also speaks of God as supremely involved in events. In the end he seems to be stating that the God who is (or was) the alienating negation of life is dead but the God who is the creative affirmation of life is 'alive'.[114] The difficulty with Altizer is that he seems to be talking about ontological realities when his position makes more sense as a discussion of man's concepts of God.

Finally, a genuinely atheistic version of the 'death of God' seems to be presented in the later papers of William Hamilton. Here he puts forward a 'hard radicalism' which declares an absolute loss of God. Hamilton distinguishes himself from atheists on the ground that they hold that God never has existed whereas he accepts that God was once a proper object of worship. God has, however, now disappeared for ever. He will not return. The universe is completely 'godless' and 'transcendentless'. The role that Jesus once played in life as the point of forgiveness and grace must now be provided by the community. God is dead, long live mankind!

These six different interpretations of the 'death of God' indicate what a mixed collection of ideas adopted the same slogan. Most of these radical theologians were strongly influenced by the optimism of American society in the late 1950s and early 1960s. They could happily shout that 'God is dead' because they felt that they lived in a benevolent world—and most of them were, in addition, citizens of 'God's own country'. Sin, evil, injustice, catastrophe would soon be eradicated by human research. Life was good and getting better. Within a few years, economic problems, student revolt, race riots and the cancer of the Vietnamese war destroyed this optimism. Those who continue to affirm the 'death of God' in one form or another do so in a much more subdued manner. The important contribution of this radical theology was in its attempts to understand contemporary society and culture in terms of God's will and vice versa. Here it produced some important insights in spite of a sometimes off-putting manner. The greatest defect of this theology was perhaps the narrowness of its appreciation of the contemporary world and its failure to criticize as well as consider the views of so-called 'contemporary' man.

With the proclamation of the 'death of God', I finish this brief survey of theology between 1945 and 1965. As the writer of the letter to the Hebrews had to recognize, 'time is too short for me to tell the stories' of many other interesting theological works that were produced. What I hope that I have done—with apologies to those who did not get in—is to indicate five major movements in theology during this period which seem to offer important insights for future exploration and possible reconstruction of Christian theology. I began by quoting William Temple saying in 1939 that future theologians 'must dig the foundations deeper'. We have noted some of the ways in which this has been done. In spite of the decline in the Church, theology has been vigorously alive in a few places. Theologians are now more aware of their problems and perhaps even of their possibilities than before. Certainly they are less hampered by traditional shibboleths. Where does theology go from here? I don't know! The past quarter-century has been an exciting period in theology. As one who is interested in the subject, I hope the next quarter will be no duller.

## NOTES

[1] W. Temple, 'Theology Today', *Theology*, XXXIX, Nov. 1939, 333.

[2] H. W. Montefiore, 'Towards a Christology for Today', in *Soundings*, ed. A. R. Vidler (1962), 162; Introduction by A. R. Vidler, ix; cf. 172.

[3] K. Barth, *Church Dogmatics*, vol. IV, pt. 2, trans. G. W. Bromiley (1958), xi.

[4] Ibid. 673 f., 409.

[5] Cf. ibid. xi.

[6] K. Barth, *The Humanity of God*, trans. J. N. Thomas (1961), 42. This lecture was first delivered in September 1956.

[7] T. F. Torrance, *Theological Science* (1969), 191, 198, 200.

[8] Ibid. ix.

[9] G. E. Wright, *God Who Acts* (1952), 108 f., 111; cf. 116.

[10] O. Cullmann, *Christ and Time*, trans. F. V. Filson (1962), xxiv.

[11] E. Brunner, *Dogmatics*, vol. II, trans. O. Wyon (1952), 193, 208; cf. E. Brunner, *The Scandal of Christianity* (1951), 14 f.

[12] Brunner, *Scandal of Christianity*, 25; cf. 15.

[13] Cullmann, *Christ and Time*, 20, 27, 22 f., 21.

[14] A. Richardson, *The Bible in the Age of Science* (1961), 140 f.

[15] A. Richardson, *History Sacred and Profane* (1964), 218; cf. 223 ff. On p.

224 Richardson writes 'All the biblical theology is . . . the theological interpretation of history.'

[16] Cf. J. N. Sanders in *Soundings*, ed. Vidler, e.g. 134.

[17] R. Bultmann, 'New Testament and Mythology', in *Kerygma and Myth*, ed. H. W. Bartsch, trans. R. H. Fuller, vol. I (2nd ed., 1964), 10.

[18] Bultmann, 'New Testament and Mythology', 2 f.

[19] Ibid. 10.

[20] Ibid.

[21] Cf. R. Bultmann, 'The Case for Demythologizing' in *Kerygma and Myth*, vol. II (1962), 181 ff.; Bultmann, *Jesus Christ and Mythology* (1958), 54–9.

[22] Bultmann, 'New Testament and Mythology', 41; cf. 39.

[23] Cf. S. M. Ogden, *Christ without Myth* (1962), 76 ff., 111 ff., 136 ff.

[24] J. M. Robinson, *A New Quest of the Historical Jesus* (1959), 68.

[25] G. Ebeling, *Word and Faith*, trans. J. W. Leitch (1963), 304; cf. 204 also; G. Ebeling, *Theology and Proclamation*, trans. J. Riches (1966), 74 f.

[26] Ebeling, *Word and Faith*, 304.

[27] G. Ebeling, *The Nature of Faith*, trans. R. Gregor Smith (1961), 49.

[28] H. Kimmerle, 'Hermeneutical Theory or Ontological Hermeneutics', trans. F. Seifert, in *History and Hermeneutic*, ed. R. W. Funk, *Journal for Theology and the Church*, IV (1967), 115.

[29] W. Pannenberg, *Basic Questions in Theology*, trans. G. H. Kehm, vol. I (1970), 11.

[30] Ibid. 129.

[31] Pannenberg, *Basic Questions in Theology*, vol. II (1971), 26.

[32] Cf. Pannenberg, *Basic Questions*, vol. I, 122 f. and 132 ff.

[33] Bultmann, 'The Case for Demythologizing', 183; cf. 181 ff.

[34] R. Bultmann, 'Bultmann Replies to his Critics', in *Kerygma and Myth*, I. 210 f.; cf. Bultmann, *Jesus Christ and Mythology*, 84 f.

[35] R. Bultmann, *History and Eschatology* (1957), 155.

[36] Bultmann, 'New Testament and Mythology', 29.

[37] R. Bultmann, *Existence and Faith*, ed. and trans. S. M. Ogden (1961), 281.

[38] F. Buri, 'The Problem of Non-objectifying Thinking and Speaking in Contemporary Theology', trans. H. H. Oliver, in *Distinctive Protestant and Catholic Themes Reconsidered*, ed. R. W. Funk, *Journal for Theology and the Church*, III (1967), 151. For Ogden's views on this question see *Christ without Myth, passim*. Ogden's work is an excellent study of Bultmann which has been much neglected in Britain.

[39] Buri, 'Non-objectifying Thinking and Speaking', 138, 147, 149.

[40] K. Barth, 'Rudolf Bultmann—An Attempt to Understand Him', in *Kerygma and Myth*, II. 102.

[41] K. Jaspers, *Philosophical Faith and Revelation*, trans. E. B. Ashton (1967), 340.

[42] Cf. K. Jaspers, 'Myth and Religion', in *Kerygma and Myth*, II. 144 ff.

[43] Jaspers, *Philosophical Faith and Revelation*, 325; cf. 278, 357.

[44] Jaspers, *Philosophical Faith and Revelation*, 242, 340 f.; 'Myth and Religion', 146.

[45] Jaspers, 'Myth and Religion', 175. Here Jaspers is giving an interpretation of the Biblical faith in contrast to that of Bultmann but thereby seems to be expressing his own position also; cf. also *Myth and Christianity*, 74 f.

[46] K. Jaspers, *The Origin and Goal of History*, trans. M. Bullock (1953), 215, 228; cf. 214 f., 218 f., 223.

[47] C. Michalson, *The Rationality of Faith* (1964), 18.

[48] Ibid. 27, 15, 101, 14, 130; cf. 74.

[49] Ibid. 131; cf. 146.

[50] Ibid. 143, 149.

[51] P. Tillich, *Systematic Theology*, vol. III (1964), 216.

[52] P. Tillich, *Theology of Culture* (1964), 118, 123, 68.

[53] P. Tillich, *The Shaking of the Foundations* (1949), 57; cf. 59.

[54] Tillich, *Systematic Theology*, vol. I (1953), 227.

[55] Ibid. 261; cf. 124 ff. and P. Tillich, *Systematic Theology*, vol. II (1957), 8 f.

[56] *Systematic Theology*, II. 108, 110, 112; cf. 132 f., 174 f.

[57] P. Tillich, *The Courage to Be* (1962), 168.

[58] Tillich, *Systematic Theology*, II. 134.

[59] A. N. Whitehead, *Process and Reality* (1960), 521.

[60] C. Hartshorne, *Anselm's Discovery* (1965), 131.

[61] Cf. S. M. Ogden, 'The Temporality of God', *The Reality of God* (1967).

[62] Cf. D. A. Pailin, 'Some Comments on Hartshorne's Presentation of the Ontological Argument', *Religious Studies*, IV. 103–22, and 'An Introductory Survey of Charles Hartshorne's Work on the Ontological Argument', *Analecta Anselmiana*, Band I, 195–221.

[63] Cf. N. Malcolm, 'Anselm's Ontological Arguments', *The Philosophical Review*, LXIX. 41–62.

[64] Cf. C. Hartshorne, *A Natural Theology for Our Time* (1967) and my comments in 'Theistic Verification', *The Living God*, ed. D. Kirkpatrick (1971).

[65] Cf. D. A. Pailin, 'The Incarnation as a Continuing Reality', *Religious Studies*, VI. 303–27.

[66] J. B. Cobb, 'A Whiteheadian Christology', *Process Philosophy and Christian Thought*, ed. D. Brown, R. E. James, and G. Reeves (1971), 393, 395.

[67] S. M. Ogden, 'What Sense Does It Make to Say "God Acts in History"?', *Reality of God*, 187; cf. 'What Does It Mean to Affirm "Jesus Christ Is Lord"?', ibid. 202 ff.

[68] P. Teilhard de Chardin, *The Phenomenon of Man* (1959), 26.

[69] Quoted in R. Speaight, *Teilhard de Chardin: A Biography* (1967), 273 f.

[70] Teilhard, *Phenomenon of Man*, 13.

[71] P. Teilhard de Chardin, *Man's Place in Nature* (1971), 121.

[72] P. Teilhard de Chardin, *Le Milieu Divin* (1960), 100 f.

[73] Ibid. 14.

[74] P. Teilhard de Chardin, *Hymn of the Universe* (1965), 144.

[75] Ibid. 152 f.

[76] Teilhard, *Le Milieu Divin*, 105.

[77] A. J. Ayer, *Language, Truth and Logic* (ed. 1952), 120.

[78] J. Wisdom, 'Gods', *Proceedings of the Aristotelian Society* for 1944–5, reprinted in *Logic and Language*, 1st Ser., ed. A. G. N. Flew (1955), 192 f.

[79] Cf. also J. Wisdom, *The 'Logic of "God"'*, a paper broadcast in 1950 and printed in *The Existence of God*, ed. J. Hick (1964), 275–98.

[80] I. T. Ramsey, 'Miracles, An Exercise in Logical Mapwork', reprinted in I. T. Ramsey *et al.*, *The Miracles and the Resurrection* (1964), 22, 29.

[81] J. J. C. Smart, 'The Existence of God', reprinted in *New Essays in Philosophical Theology*, ed. A. Flew and A. MacIntyre (1955), 41.

[82] J. N. Findlay, 'Can God's Existence be Disproved?', reprinted in *New Essays in Philosophical Theology*, 48, 54.

[83] C. B. Martin, 'The Perfect Good', reprinted in *New Essays in Philosophical Theology*, 226.

[84] A. Flew, 'Theology and Falsification', reprinted in *New Essays in Philosophical Theology*, 96 ff.

[85] R. M. Hare, 'Theology and Falsification', reprinted in *New Essays in Philosophical Theology*, 99–103; R. M. Hare, 'Religion and Morals', in *Faith and Logic*, ed. B. Mitchell (1957), 184, cf. 176–93.

[86] B. Mitchell, 'Theology and Falsification', reprinted in *New Essays in Philosophical Theology*, 103 ff.; B. Mitchell, 'The Grace of God', in *Faith and Logic*, 149–75, esp. 169 ff.

[87] I. M. Crombie, 'Theology and Falsification', in *New Essays in Philosophical Theology*, 124, 127.

[88] Cf. J. Hick, 'Theology and Verification', reprinted in *The Existence of God*, 253–74.

[89] E. L. Mascall, *Words and Images* (1957), 43.

[90] J. Baillie, *The Sense of the Presence of God* (1962), 73, 68.

[91] R. B. Braithwaite, 'An Empiricist's View of the Nature of Religious Belief,' reprinted in *The Existence of God*, 240 f., 244, 250.

[92] P. M. van Buren, *The Secular Meaning of the Gospel* (1963), 156; cf. 147, 68 ff.; cf., also, C. Michalson's *Rationality of Faith* for a similar and perhaps more convincing exposition of this view of the Christian faith.

[93] D. D. Evans, *The Logic of Self-Involvement* (1963), 137.

[94] W. Hordern, *Speaking of God* (1964), 105; cf. W. F. Zuurdeeg, *An Analytical Philosophy of Religion* (1959).

[95] Hordern, *Speaking of God*, 175 f.; cf. 155 ff.; cf. also the criticism of this type of theological understanding in R. W. Hepburn, *Christianity and Paradox* (1958), esp. chs. 3 and 4.

[96] Tillich, *Systematic Theology*, I.265; P. Tillich, *The Protestant Era* (abridged ed., 1957), 61.

[97] H. D. Lewis, *Morals and Revelation* (1951), chs. 9 and 10; R. W. Hepburn, 'Poetry and Religious Belief' in Hepburn *et al.*, *Metaphysical Beliefs* (1957).

[98] I. T. Ramsey, *Models and Mystery* (1964), 60.

[99] Cf. also *Religion and Understanding*, ed. D. Z. Phillips (1967), for a collection of papers which see 'understanding' as central to the concept of religion—cf. p. 6.

[100] Cf. D. A. Pailin, 'Theistic Verification'; D. A. Pailin, ' "Credo ut Intelligam"—A Study of Theological Method', in *Analecta Anselmiana* (1972).

[101] A. R. Vidler, Introduction to *Soundings*, ix.

[102] J. S. Bezzant, 'Intellectual Objections', in Bezzant *et al.*, *Objections to Christian Belief* (1963), 110 f.

[103] H. A. Williams, 'Theology and Self-Awareness' in *Soundings*, 81 f.

[104] Cf. J. Fletcher, *Situation Ethics: The New Morality* (1966).

[105] J. A. T. Robinson, *Honest to God* (1963)—the quotation is from the publisher's blurb on the back cover.

[106] Van Buren, *Secular Meaning of the Gospel*, 103.

[107] G. Vahanian, *Wait without Idols* (1964), 31 f.; cf. also G. Vahanian, *The Death of God: The Culture of Our Post-Christian Era* (1961).

[108] Cf. M. Buber, *The Eclipse of God* (1952).

[109] W. Hamilton, *The New Essence of Christianity* (1966), 61 ff.; cf. also the Scots theologian, R. Gregor Smith, *Secular Christianity* (1966).

[110] D. Bonhoeffer, *Letters and Papers from Prison* (1959), 122.

[111] Hamilton, *The New Essence of Christianity*, 53 f., 56 f.
[112] H. Cox, *The Secular City* (1966), 256.
[113] T. J. J. Altizer, *The Gospel of Christian Atheism* (1966), 157.
[114] Cf. also L. Dewart, *The Future of Belief* (1967), 211 f. for a similar view.

## FOR FURTHER READING

Valuable general studies which include material on theology from 1945 include John Macquarrie's *Twentieth-Century Religious Thought* (1963), Horton Davies's *Worship and Theology in England, V: The Ecumenical Century, 1900–1965* (Princeton, N.J., 1966—an extensive description of Church life during this period). David L. Edwards's *Religion and Change* (1969) considers religious developments in this century from their sociological and psychological situation. John B. Cobb, Jr., provides a valuable study of some theological methods during our period in his *Living Options in Protestant Theology: A Survey of Methods* (Philadelphia, 1962). The best way, though, to learn about the theology of this period is to read the works of its theologians. Karl Barth's *Church Dogmatics* (Edinburgh, many volumes from 1936) is a weighty series of tomes; the beginner is not advised to start with these, but those acquainted with theology find rich controversial material there. A good place to start on Barth's postwar theology is *The Humanity of God* (1961). Thomas F. Torrance's re-presentation of the earlier Barthian position is best (though rather repetitively) found in his *Theological Science* (1969). The SCM Press's *Studies in Biblical Theology* (from 1952) is a series of monographs which make known recent work in this field. One of the early ones is G. Ernest Wright's *God Who Acts: Biblical Theology as Recital* (1952). Oscar Cullmann's *Christ and Time* is a good introduction to his form of Biblical theology and should be read in the revised edition (1962) which includes a short introductory chapter replying to some of his critics. Rudolf Bultmann's seminal essay 'New Testament and Mythology' is to be found in H. W. Bartsch's *Kerygma and Myth* (vol. I, 1953; vol. II, 1962) together with other essays critical of Bultmann and replies by Bultmann. Bultmannian scholars, though, often argue about how the master should be translated into English (or American) and it is fortunate that Bultmann has published in English a short study of his position, *Jesus Christ and Mythology* (New York, 1958). A good but neglected study of Bultmann is Schubert M. Ogden's *Christ without Myth* (1962). Appreciation of recent work on hermeneutics was not helped in England by the appearance of *The New Hermeneutic* (edited by James M. Robinson and John B. Cobb, New York, 1964) since it was felt that it was harder to understand its contents than to interpret the Bible! It is, though, an important study. More apprehensible introductions to the hermeneutical problem are Heinz Kimmerle's essay 'Hermeneutical Theory or Ontological Hermeneutics' and Wolfhart Pannenberg's 'Hermeneutics and Universal History', both of which are printed in *History and Hermeneutic*, edited by Robert W. Funk (New York, 1967). Pannenberg's essay is also contained (in a noticeably different translation—illustrating thereby some problems of Biblical hermeneutics) in his *Basic Questions in Theology* (vol. I, 1970) together with other essays on this theme. The background to current existentialist theology is well introduced by David E. Roberts in his *Existentialism and Religious Belief* (New York, 1957). Carl Michalson's position is indicated in his *Rationality of Faith* (1964) but his death in an air crash prevented him from developing his thought fully. Those who want an introduction to Karl Jaspers's thought before they tackle his massive *Philosophical Faith and Revelation* (1967) could find help in his *Way to Wisdom: An Introduction to Philosophy* (1951). Paul Tillich is another whom it is best to read first in his shorter works. His *Dynamics of Faith* (New York, 1957) and *The Courage to Be* (1952) provide good starting-points for the journey to his *Systematic Theology* (3 vols., 1953, 1957, 1964). A most valuable collection of pieces on process philosophy and theology has appeared in *Process Philosophy and Christian Thought*, edited by Delwin Brown, Ralph E. James, Jr., and Gene Reeves (New York, 1971). This volume reprints material by a number of leading exponents of this thought. Another introduction is Peter Hamilton's *The Living God and the Modern World* (1967). Charles Hartshorne's contributions to theology can be appreciated initially by reading his *Man's Vision of God and the Logic of Theism* (New York, 1941), *A Natural Theology for Our Time* (La Salle, Ill., 1967) and *Anselm's Discovery* (La Salle, Ill., 1965). This should prepare students for other of his works such as *The Logic of Perfection* (La Salle, Ill., 1962) and *Creative Synthesis and Philosophic Method* (1970). Readers should be warned that this last volume shows that theology may not be suitable reading for those who are not prepared to think hard. One famous English 'theologian' was heard to remark after hearing read one of the papers in this collection that if theology was that difficult he was going to do something else! A provocative collection by a process theologian is Schubert Ogden's *The Reality of God and Other Essays* (1967). It includes an ingenious argument that Sartre's professed atheistic position in fact only makes sense if theism is true. John Cobb's *A Christian Natural Theology* (Philadelphia, 1965) is also well worth study. Pierre Teilhard de Chardin's thought is more than most bound up with his life. A good study of him is Robert Speaight's *Teilhard de Chardin: A Biography* (1967). Consideration of Teilhard de Chardin's own works should begin with *The Phenomenon of Man* (1959) and *Le Milieu Divin* (1960—in English but with the French title, as translation proved impossible). The classical start for theology influenced by linguistic philosophy is *New Essays in Philosophical Theology*, edited by Antony Flew and Alasdair MacIntyre (1955). Good introductory surveys which indicate much of the relevant literature are William Hordern's *Speaking of God* (1965), Frederick Ferré's *Language, Logic and God* (1962), Stuart C. Brown's *Do Religious Claims Make Sense?* (1969), and the collection edited by Basil Mitchell, *The Philosophy of Religion* (1971—with useful bibliography). The controversy aroused by John A. T. Robinson's *Honest to God* (1963) led to the publication of *The Honest to God Debate*, edited by J. A. T. Robinson and David L. Edwards (1963). *Soundings*, edited by Alec R. Vidler, appeared in 1962 from Cambridge and Joseph Fletcher's *Situation Ethics: The New Morality* in 1966 from Philadelphia (very suitably). The death-of-God movement produced a flood of writing. A useful introduction is the collection of papers edited by Bernard Murchland, *The Meaning of the Death of God: Protestant, Jewish and Catholic Scholars Explore Atheistic Theology* (New York, 1967). A short and incomplete survey is Thomas W. Ogletree's *The 'Death of God' Controversy* (1966). Two of the radicals, Thomas J. J. Altizer and William Hamilton, produced a collection of their papers with (in the British edition) a bibliography of radical theology as *Radical Theology and the Death of God* (1968). Many of the theologians named above have had books written about them. Generally I have not mentioned these studies as I firmly believe that the best way to understand a theologian's thought is to read him in his own words.

# 5

# Sociology

STEPHEN MENNELL

> Enfin, dans l'état positif, l'esprit humain reconnaîssant l'impossibilité d'obtenir des notions absolues, renonce à chercher l'origine et la destination de l'univers, et à connaître les causes intimes des phénomènes, pour s'attacher uniquement a découvrir, par l'usage bien combiné du raisonnement et de l'observation, leurs lois effectives, c'est-à-dire leurs relations invariables de succession et de similitude.
>
> Auguste Comte: *Cours de philosophie positive*

Though more than a century has passed since Comte proclaimed the advent of the scientific study of society, it was during the decades after the Second World War that sociology became well established as a distinct discipline within universities. In America, it had been taught in several centres before the war but there, as in most other countries, it has grown rapidly since. In Britain, sociology was in 1945 taught in few universities, the only important departments being at the London School of Economics and at Liverpool. Now it is taught in almost all of the 42 universities, at the new polytechnics, and is even becoming a widespread choice in the sixth form.[1] At times, its popularity among undergraduates has put it in danger of seeming no less than a cult.

Yet as it has grown, sociology has changed in ways which might not entirely have been predicted from its popularity. On the one hand, sociologists have increasingly refrained from wild speculation about great laws of history. And on the other hand, they have striven to acquire for their empirical research a degree of detachment from the narrow needs of policy-making and social reform, though it is open to question how far they have succeeded. Calls are still made from time to time for more 'problem-orientated' research, but sociologists widely recognize the systematic ambiguity of this phrase. For the 'problem' to which orientation is urged may be one which is regarded as a problem to and by society at large; or it may exist purely in relation to theories and the current state of knowledge. The two meanings may coincide but it is more likely, as in natural science, that though 'pure' research may be a prerequisite to solving a practical problem, its outcome and utility can rarely be discerned in advance. While such sociological research has not been policy-orientated, at the same time research techniques, statistical analysis, and mathematical formulations have become more sophisticated.[2] Thus in recent years, what have been called the 'speculative' and 'reformist' traditions in sociology[3] have both declined as distinct activities, and there has emerged a closer integration of theory and method, of hypothesis and observation. Sociology has thereby come a little closer to Comte's original vision.

## I. Philosophical Assumptions

It is difficult to attribute sociology's recent scientific self-consciousness to any one source, but I believe that Sir Karl Popper's (b. 1902) writings, especially *The Poverty of Historicism* (1957)[4] and *The Open Society and its Enemies* (1945), deserve special mention. Both books were written during the war, and in them Popper uses his own speciality, the philosophy of science, to mount an onslaught against the totalitarian implications of certain intellectual activities and beliefs. In so doing, Popper made a major contribution to that older tradition of evaluative social philosophy. *The Poverty of Historicism* is dedicated to the 'memory of the countless men and women . . . who fell victims to fascist or communist belief in Inexorable Laws of Historical Destiny'. Popper argues that certain kinds of events are, in principle, beyond the powers of prediction, and he attacks the ideological uses of 'predictions' of the 'inevitable'. Too many people have been exterminated for being on the wrong side of such inevitable laws.

In detail, Popper's arguments are complex, but he states them most succinctly as follows:

(1) The course of human history is strongly influenced by the growth of human knowledge. (The truth of this premise must be admitted even by those who see in our ideas, even our scientific ideas, merely the by-products of *material* developments of some kind or another.)

(2) We cannot predict, by rational or scientific methods, the future growth of our scientific knowledge. . . .

(3) We cannot, therefore, predict the future course of human history.

(4) This means that we must reject the possibility of a *theoretical history*; that is to say, of a historical social science that would correspond to *theoretical physics*. There can be no scientific theory of historical development serving as a basis for historical prediction.

(5) The fundamental aim of historicist methods . . . is therefore misconceived; and historicism collapses.[5]

The point is illustrated by Humphrey Lyttleton's reported reply when asked where he thought jazz was going: 'If I knew where jazz were going, I'd be there already.'

Of course, not all social processes are unpredictable, but only those which may be influenced by the growth of our knowledge. Popper argues that while 'historical prophecy' is impossible, 'piecemeal social engineering' (and research) is quite feasible. The influence of such views on postwar sociologists has been immense; historical interpretation on the grand scale, so popular in the nineteenth century and lingering well into the twentieth, has virtually disappeared as a sociological activity. Even Talcott Parsons, usually regarded as the grandest of postwar grand theorists, is classed by Pitirim Sorokin as a theorist merely of 'social systems', not venturing on to the even more grandiose level of the dynamics of cultures and civilizations.[6] Yet, on the other hand, a 'social engineering' conception of sociology has not made the subject totally subservient to the needs of policy-making. A safeguard against such slavery has been the immense influence of Max Weber's methodological views. In two famous lectures, 'Politics as a Vocation' and 'Science as a Vocation',[7] Weber drew many contrasts between the politician and the social scientist. The politician's job *is* to make value judgements, but the sociologist must strive to maintain *Wertfreiheit*. He must attempt to keep his own values out of his scientific work, because there is no scientific way of deciding which values are the correct ones. On the other hand, values play a legitimate part in the selection of problems to be studied. We cannot study everything at once, but to believe that something is worth *knowing* does not imply any judgement as to what is worth *doing*. The two considerations should be kept apart.

The reader may now be wondering at such a preoccupation with issues in the philosophy of science in a chapter on sociology. But this preoccupation is itself typical of recent sociology. While philosophy of science is peripheral to natural scientists, it has been central to sociologists, indicating their lack of confidence and a search for scientific respectability. Most sociological textbooks seem inevitably to open with chapters on these issues. Famous sociologists have echoed the philosophers of science. Robert Merton (b. 1910), for instance, writes:

> The recent history of sociological theory can in large measure be written in terms of an alternation between two contrasting emphases. On the one hand, we observe those sociologists who seek above all to generalize, to find their way as rapidly as possible to the formulation of sociological

laws. Tending to assess the significance of sociological work in terms of scope rather than the demonstrability of generalizations, they eschew the 'triviality' of detailed, small-scale observation and seek the grandeur of global summaries. At the other extreme stands a hardy band who do not hunt too closely the implications of their research but who remain confident and assured that what they report is so. To be sure, their reports of facts are verifiable and often verified, but they are somewhat at a loss to relate these facts to one another or even to explain why these, rather than others, have been made. For the first group the identifying motto would at times seem to be: 'We do not know whether what we say is true, but it is at least significant.' And for the radical empiricist the motto may read: 'This is demonstrably so, but we cannot indicate its significance.'[8]

Similar pathologies of contemporary sociology have been advanced by C. Wright Mills and Pitirim Sorokin. Mills savages the proponents of 'abstracted empiricism' and 'grand theory'; Sorokin inveighs with even more gusto against such fell diseases as 'testomania' and 'quantifrenia'.[9]

Yet it would be mistaken not to recognize that in sociology, as in other disciplines, there must be some intellectual division of labour. Sociological theorizing may take place at any of the three levels of abstraction which are commonly distinguished. There is the level of 'grand theory' associated since the war particularly with Talcott Parsons and his adherents; next the level of 'middle-range theory', a term originated and activity practised by Robert Merton; and then of course the level of all the particular empirical sociologies: sociology of religion, political sociology, urban sociology, industrial sociology, and so forth. The boundaries of the three levels are hard to define in practice, for there is considerable overlap between them. This is as it should be. There is nothing objectionable in specialization at any of these three levels; what is objectionable is a sterile situation where they have little connection with each other. We shall not have space to survey the progress of all the special sociologies since the war; they are in any case adequately surveyed in many textbooks. We shall instead look at the two 'higher' levels, involving ideas which have been the common concern of most sociologists irrespective of their own specialities.

## II. Grand Theory

Those sociologists who have indulged themselves with excursions into the realm of 'grand theory' have been concerned with very general problems: the relationship between the individual and society; the problem of social integration, conflict, consensus, co-operation, and exchange; and the problem of system integration and 'functionalism'.[10] At this level, the most prominent writer has been Talcott Parsons (b. 1902); thanks both to his own ideas and to the vigorous reaction they have provoked, Parsons has dominated post-war sociology. The book which is generally considered his greatest was his first, *The Structure of Social Action*, which though published in 1937 had its greatest impact after the war. It has a dual importance. First, more than any other single book, it introduced the work of Pareto, Durkheim, and Max Weber to the English-speaking world. An almost unbelievable amount of attention has been paid by sociologists since then to working out the implications of the thought of these writers, especially the latter two. Though they had begun their work in different countries and intellectual traditions, Parsons interpreted their thought, as well as that of the English economist Alfred Marshall, as converging towards a similar 'voluntaristic theory of action'. Parsons's substantive concern was to advance this voluntaristic theory as a general perspective on the individual's relationship to society; and in this rests his book's second source of great influence.

### *Social Action*

Social action theory, of which Parsons's is one variant, constitutes a rejection of the stimulus–response, 'operant conditioning' learning theories of behaviourism—which has been defined as 'the belief that Man is descended not from the apes but from the white rat'. Human action is for the behaviourist merely a complex set of learned responses, the individual reacting to external stimuli. In contrast, for the voluntarist, the explanation of human action must acknowledge that Man is a self-reflective animal, consciously orientating himself to his social and physical situation. His behaviour cannot be entirely understood as a reaction to externally-defined stimuli, for the stimuli themselves have to be accorded meaning by the actor. The point is made most vividly by Noam Chomsky in his famous review of behaviourist B. F. Skinner's *Verbal Behaviour*:

> A typical example of 'stimulus control' for Skinner would be a response to a piece of music with the utterance *Mozart* or to a painting with the response *Dutch*. These responses are asserted to be 'under the control of extremely subtle properties' of the object or event. Suppose instead of saying *Dutch* we had said *Clashes with the wallpaper, I thought you liked abstract work, Never saw it before, Tilted, Hanging too low, Beautiful, Hideous, Remember our camping trip last summer?* or whatever else might

come into our minds when looking at the picture (in Skinnerian translation, whatever other responses exist in sufficient strength). Skinner could only say that each of these responses is under the control of some other stimulus property of the physical object. If we look at a red chair and say *red*, the response is under the control of the stimulus 'redness'; if we say *chair*, it is under the control of the collection of properties . . . 'chairness', and similarly for any other response. The device is as simple as it is empty. Since properties are free for the asking . . . we can account for a wide class of responses . . . by identifying the 'controlling stimuli'. But the word 'stimulus' has lost all objectivity in this usage. Stimuli are no longer part of the outside physical world; they are driven back into the organism. We identify the stimulus when we hear the response.[11]

Accepting these criticisms, social action theorists share the following tenets: Men act in such a way as to achieve goals, intentions, purposes, aims, ends, or objects. They select appropriate means, techniques, methods to attain these goals. Implicit here is the assumption that social activities arise from their consciousness of themselves as subjects and of others and external situations as objects. More controversially, it is assumed that men's actions are deeply influenced by their adherence to values (shared conceptions of the desirable) and by norms of social behaviour. Their courses of action are limited by situations, conditions, and circumstances, the 'givens' of the social and physical environment. Yet the situation is not something of which the meaning is externally given. Its influence on action is mediated by the actor's knowledge of the situation and by his assumptions about it. Tolstoy's account of the battle of Austerlitz convinces us that the Russians might well have won had they not made a false assumption about the French positions. The point is summarized in W. I. Thomas's dictum that 'if men define situations as real, they are real in their consequences'.

Parsons devoted the bulk of his book to demonstrating how his chosen writers had converged towards a similar 'voluntaristic' theoretical stance. Durkheim had, in his early work *The Division of Labour in Society* (1893), conceived of social forces as impinging on the individual as external pressures. However, his subsequent works show a gradual evolution towards a realization that collective sentiments affect behaviour only to the extent that they are embedded in people's mental processes. Pareto's theory of logical and non-logical action was not so much voluntaristic as not incompatible with voluntarism. Alfred Marshall's importance to sociology lies simply in that he emphasized, as other economists did not, that society not only provides the means by which men seek to satisfy their desires;

it also strongly influences what they choose to desire. But the closest approach to voluntarism is contained in the writings of Max Weber, especially in his discussion of the nature of rational action and its manifestation in rational law, rational-legal bureaucracy, rationalized theology (especially in *The Protestant Ethic and the Spirit of Capitalism*, trans. 1930) and other distinctive features of western civilization. It is really thanks to his exegesis of the substantive work of these writers that Parsons's book has continued to be a living influence on postwar sociologists, while similar theoretical statements have not.

Parsons did, however, subsequently make a major innovation in social action theory, in the exposition of his 'Pattern Variables'. These are said to have their origins in Ferdinand Toennies's conceptualization of pre-modern and modern societies as *Gemeinschaft* and *Gesellschaft*.[12] Parsons realized that many supposedly *gemeinschaftlich* characteristics persist into a fully modern society. Relationships within the family remain intimate. The doctor combines the 'modern' characteristic of professional detachment with a 'pre-modern' rejection of the cash nexus as a basis for his service. This insight led Parsons to break down the Toennies dichotomy into five independently variable dimensions.[13] The Affectivity/Affective Neutrality choice is concerned with whether the emotions are involved in a relationship or whether detachment is the pattern. Diffuseness/Specificity involves asking whether a relationship involves the whole personality (as between husband and wife) or only a limited segment (as between passenger and bus conductor). Particularism/Universalism poses the question: is a person's performance of a role judged by special criteria (again the wife—'beauty is in the eye of the beholder') or generally accepted standards (a secretary's shorthand speed)? The Quality/Performance variable, borrowed from Ralph Linton, is more familiar as Ascription/Achievement: is a person considered suitable for a position by virtue of some quality, such as being the eldest son of the monarch, or because of some achievement like the acquisition of a degree or diploma? And finally, Collectivity-Orientation/Self-Orientation is self-explanatory, and closely related to the supposedly modern trend to individualism and instrumental relationships. Whether or not the Pattern Variables can be said to be exhaustive, they have certainly been widely employed by postwar sociologists. Originating in Parsons's study of the professions, they have proved invaluable for characterizing the innumerable specialized but identifiable roles produced by the advanced division of labour in modern societies.

Another kind of social action theory has also been influential, especially in the last decade. It is usually known as 'symbolic interactionism', and has deep roots in American sociology. Originating in the pragmatist philosophy and psychology of William James and John Dewey, it was decisively developed in the University of Chicago between the wars. George Herbert Mead (1863–1931) gave it a secure theoretical base in social psychology, and in sociology it was applied by W. I. Thomas, Robert Park, Ernest Burgess, Louis Wirth, and others to the social structure of the city, to crime and many other fields. In the forties and fifties it was somewhat under the shadow of Parsons, but has since re-emerged with new vigour.

Mead's significance is that, while rejecting conventional behaviourism, he also realized that it was not good enough to take an extreme idealist position in assuming that self-conceptions and meanings existed in the mind before the individual entered society. 'We want to approach language not from the standpoint of inner meanings to be expressed, but in its larger context of co-operation in the group taking place by means of signals and gestures. Meaning appears within that process. Our behaviourism is a social behaviourism.'[14] Mead's contribution was to give an account of how meanings and self-conceptions were generated within social interaction. Certainly meaning was learned, but the cumulative process produced such complex behaviour patterns that they could not be understood simply in terms of stimulus-response; a degree of autonomy and unpredictability appeared in human behaviour. Mead traced various stages in human development: how *gestures* become transformed into significant *symbols* which have the same meaning for people interacting with each other; how in order to co-operate, for example in children's games, we have to *take the role of the other*; and how moral judgements appear by our eventually learning to take the role of *the generalized other*, to anticipate the attitude to our actions which would be taken by the community at large.

> It is in the form of the generalized other that the social process influences the behaviour of the individuals involved in it . . . that is, the community exercises *control* over the activities of its members; for it is in this form that the social process or community enters as a determining factor into the individual's thinking.[15]

This perspective proved extremely fruitful in generating empirical research, both in sociology and social psychology. Mead's views at once resemble and have in turn influenced those of the great Genevan child psychologist Jean Piaget (b. 1896), whose research into socialization has had an immense impact since the war on social psychologists and especially educationalists. In sociology proper, the 'Chicago school' realized that socialization took place not only in the culture of the wider society, but behaviour was also learnt within the innumerable subcultures found in complex modern societies. As Rose observed, it is inadequate to think of the Chicago tradition as concerned only with urban sociology;[16] none the less the city abounds in subcultures for the sociologist to study, within which men acquire their manifold varieties of humanity. The great pre-war tradition of subcultural studies—Wirth's *The Ghetto* (1938), Thrasher's *The Gang* (1926), Thomas's and Znaniecki's *The Polish Peasant* (5 vols., 1918–20)—has been continued by such studies as W. F. Whyte's classic *Street Corner Society* (1943), and Herbert Gans's *The Urban Villagers* (1963) and *The Levittowners* (1967). Crime too was studied in subcultural context; deviant and criminal behaviour can be learnt in the appropriate setting like any other human activity. The major criminological theory of 'differential association', associated with the names of C. R. Shaw and E. H. Sutherland among others, also traces its origins to pre-war Chicago, and is a continuing influence on such writers as H. S. Becker.[17] The continuing strength of the symbolic interactionist tradition is attested by the variety of essays by many famous contributors collected by Arnold Rose in *Human Behaviour and Social Processes* (1962).

More recently still, certain authors have fused symbolic interactionism with the phenomenological approach of Edmund Husserl. The theoretically significant figure here is Alfred Schütz (1899–1959), who concerned himself with the reality of everyday life, that which we take for granted.[18] He focused on the *intersubjectivity* which underpins our mutal understanding and similar perceptions of the world. In our everyday *life-world* we suspend doubt that things might be otherwise; most of our knowledge is handed down to us, so we perceive it as being detached from us, having objective truth and being 'the same' for everyone. Yet in fact we organize our perceptions of reality according to patterns (or *typifications*) we have learned. People from different cultures organize reality in sometimes dramatically different ways; their vocabulary may for instance 'cut' the rainbow spectrum of colours at different points from ourselves. Differences between subcultures are only less marked. Even individuals do not see things in precisely identical ways; for each of us has a unique biographically determined situation, consisting of a 'stock of knowledge'. But we get by, we understand each other, because of what Schütz calls *reciprocity of perspectives*—we assume in interaction that if we changed places, we should perceive as the other does now. We simply make the assumption that for everyday purposes, different points of view do not matter, and that we are interpreting the situation in a similar manner.

Sociologists who have taken up the challenge of Schütz's work have sought to demonstrate that for the sociologist, different points of view are not irrelevant. Harold Garfinkel has frequently adopted the research strategy of purposely disrupting the 'definition of the situation' in order to expose its phenomenological structure—or in other words the unconscious assumptions made about it by participants in everyday situations.[19] For instance, students who were instructed to act as lodgers in their own homes soon found it impossible to carry on normal interaction; their parents were driven to distraction by excessive politeness. Parties to the situation defined it in different ways, and made incompatible assumptions about it. This is a trivial example of Garfinkel's work, but it illustrates his general method. A similar (if not specifically phenomenological) perspective is taken by Erving Goffman, who has become justifiably famous for his quite exceptional ability to observe and describe everyday interaction with the detachment of a Martian visitor. He calls his point of view 'a dramaturgical perspective', and portrays the process of 'the presentation of self'[20] as if it took place between actors on a stage. Or: 'To study face-saving is to study the traffic rules of social interaction; one learns about the code the person adheres to in his movement across the paths and designs of others, but not where he is going or where he wants to go.'[21]

The real value of this approach appears when generalizations about behaviour are attempted. Goffman has sought to classify the strategies which people may adopt in 'the management of spoiled identity', whether the problems arise from physical disfigurement or from social stigma such as imprisonment.[22] Both Goffman and Garfinkel have attempted to reveal the special assumptions, patterns, and rituals which develop within particular organizations, notably within mental hospitals. Goffman has sought common characteristics of all total institutions, be they prisons, armies, monasteries, boarding schools, or mental hospitals.

> The total institution is a social hybrid, part residential community, part formal organization; therein lies their sociological interest. There are other reasons for being interested too. In our society, they are forcing houses for changing persons; each is a natural experiment on what can be done to the self.[23]

*Social Integration*

Talcott Parsons has frequently said that the central task of sociological theory is to offer a solution to the 'Hobbesian problem of order'. Why do societies cohere? Why if men are free to pursue their own interests, is there not a perpetual war of all against all? What in short are the sources of social order and integration? Most postwar sociologists have agreed with Parsons's estimate of the question's importance, though it poses the dilemma in an unrealistic way. Man never has existed in a non-social condition, nor has any society ever achieved perfect harmony and integration. Certainly many have disagreed with Parsons's own solution in terms of value consensus; they have instead interpreted the coercive power of some people over others as the central feature of all societies, stressing the ubiquity of social conflict. Others again have advanced the hybrid theory of 'social exchange'.

What is not always very clearly recognized by participants in this debate is that social action theory, sketched in broad outline above, is consistent with an emphasis on the pervasiveness either of consensus or of conflict. Sometimes it is identified with the former, sometimes with the latter. In fact, while Parsons has used it as an element in a consensus theory of social integration, the Chicago school, starting from not dissimilar premises, made conflict prominent in their work. And Max Weber cannot sensibly be claimed as a member of either camp. Though Parsons believed he had contributed to the Hobbesian debate in *Structure of Social Action*, it is really only in his postwar books[24] that his intentions become clear. Voluntarism in itself does not solve the problem of social order, but Parsons emphasizes one element in it more and more: social norms and values (standards of behaviour, and conceptions of the desirable) become ever more prominent. Instead of norms and values being one element in the actor's definition of the situation, to which he feels degrees of moral commitment varying from negative through indifference to positive, they become rules *internalized* within the personality during socialization or upbringing. The actor feels moral commitment to them and guilt if he transgresses them.

Parsons needed to make one further assumption, that of value consensus. Not only are people committed to internalized values, but everyone is committed to the same values. Though the division of labour creates many roles within society, each of them with norms particular to itself, these particular norms are sanctioned by more general values, forming an apparently seamless hierarchy of values of greater generality right up to a rather abstract *central* or *core value system*. The influence of Freud is apparent in Parsons's internalization assumption, and that of Durkheim's *conscience collective* in the consensus assumption. Needless to say, both have generated considerable dispute between, on the one hand, consensus theorists and on the other conflict or coercion theorists.

Evidently the debate represents a precipitate within supposedly value-free, empirically-based modern sociology of the old traditions of evaluative social philosophy from Hobbes, Locke, and Bentham. It has generated considerable heat but little light. The issue at stake in large part concerns the relative balance in society between 'internal social control', the extent to which individuals feel morally committed and experience internal psychological pressures to conform to accepted ways of behaving, and 'external control', the extent to which they are coerced by other more powerful people. Any realist would recognize that both elements are present. Certainly the relative balance is extremely difficult to determine by means of empirical research.[25] Merely to observe people's behaviour, and still more to question them directly, is unlikely to produce decisive evidence of the proportion of coercion to willing conformity. Yet essentially this is an empirically contingent question, the answer to which varies between societies, within societies, and from time to time.

Concerning the role of internalization, it must be recognized that earlier in the century the work of sociologists such as Durkheim was hindered by a failure to appreciate the ways in which social norms may become part of the personality during socialization. Yet Parsons was not on very sure ground in making this the central tenet of his postwar theorizing. He failed even to assimilate the simple point that it is quite possible for an individual to feel moral commitment to two values which in a given situation may point his action in contradictory directions. By making the internalization process a mechanistic one of 'introjection' of and conformity to cultural norms, he appeared to abandon voluntarism in all but name and become in effect a normative determinist. By advancing an 'oversocialized conception of Man', Parsons did not so much solve the Hobbesian problem as deny its reality. Conformity became automatic, and this was far from Freud's view. As Dennis Wrong commented: 'Sociologists have appropriated the superego concept, but have separated it from any equivalent of the Freudian id. . . . Deviant behaviour is accounted for by special circumstances, ambiguous norms, *anomie*, role conflict, or greater cultural stress on valued norms than on the approved means of attaining them.'[26] Freud indeed thought many people failed to acquire superegos—'they are afraid only of being found out'.[27]

Concerning the postulate of consensus, there are still graver difficulties, both logical and methodological. As Edward Shils commented:

> The empirical analysis of consensus confronts the same difficulties as the empirical analysis of beliefs actually held by individuals. Because of the vagueness, ambiguity, unsystematic character and variations in level of abstraction, actually held beliefs are difficult to describe, and there is a tendency on the part of the sociological and anthropological analysts to systematize, clarify and specify actually held beliefs to a point which makes the holder of such beliefs appear to be a systematic philosopher. Premises are rendered explicit and particular judgements are generalized; as a result of this process, beliefs which are not knowingly held are imputed by the analysts, who thus distort the nature of consensus and the mechanisms through which it operates.[28]

Few sociologists have therefore been convinced by Parsons's and Shils's own joint effort to extrapolate from the simple level of co-operative interaction between two people to the existence of a 'central value system' in society.[29] Almond and Verba, in an international survey, identified some very general popular attitudes in Britain and America which they labelled 'the civic culture', and to which by a somewhat Panglossian inference they attributed these countries' democratic stability.[30] The central value system has sometimes appeared to amount to little more than a sense of common membership in society, as in Shils's and Young's remarks on the significance of the Coronation ritual.[31] Even Shils later emphasized that societies also contain 'peripheral' groups indifferent to or even alienated from the central values, if such exist.[32]

Besides, as Lewis Lipsitz pointed out:

> There is no direct relation between consensus and political equilibrium or integration. Consensus can retard political and social adaptation as well as facilitate it. For example . . . consensus on such norms as extreme competition, individualistic *laissez-faire*, treachery and witchcraft does not necessarily aid social solidarity. Moreover, consensus *within* groups can hinder consensus among groups.[33]

One and the same value can even legitimate two or more groups or individuals to behave in such a way as to bring them directly into conflict. Probably as important as any other kind is 'negative consensus', or agreement on means which will *not* be employed in pursuing conflict—the Geneva agreements of social life. Some of these difficulties might have been more readily apparent had the consensus theorists, who placed such emphasis on shared values, developed a detailed sociology of values. But as Alvin Gouldner noted, they did not.[34]

Among sociologists who have placed positive emphasis on the ubiquity of social conflict, there is some agreement that conflict can in different circumstances either promote or undermine social cohesion. Lewis Coser, taking his inspiration very directly from the earlier work of Georg Simmel,[35] perceives that consensual elements are present even within situations of conflict. The objective bases of conflict—often the distribution of scarce resources such as income, wealth, status, power, or territory—must be studied separately from the subjective experience of it. Conflict need not always be accompanied by hostility, aggressiveness, jealousy, or hatred. 'Here, as elsewhere, the way men define a situation, rather than the objective features of the situation must be the unit of analysis.'[36] Within loosely structured groups and in open, pluralistic societies, conflict may function to resolve both issues and tensions between antagonists, and will thus be likely to have a stabilizing effect. For in such situations, individuals have 'multiple group affiliations' and participate in a variety of group conflicts. So those who are antagonists in one conflict are allies in another; moreover, they are less likely to be involved with their whole personality in a single conflict, so passions are less aroused. On the other hand, in closed groups and rigid social structures, people are more completely involved in fewer groups, and in such circumstances conflict will be more disruptive and bitter.

A similar point is made by Ralf Dahrendorf in *Class and Class Conflict in Industrial Society* (1959).[37] His analysis is however at a grander level; he seeks to describe the major bases of conflict in modern industrial societies. Starting from a critique of Marx, Dahrendorf shows why Marx's predictions of a single deepening rift between the two great classes in society has not been fulfilled. Ownership of capital has been divorced from control; labour, far from becoming homogeneous and pauperized, now contains many heterogeneous skilled occupations; the salaried middle class has grown enormously; social mobility is possible; the Welfare State has led to greater equality in certain vital respects; and conflict has become institutionalized in Parliaments and collective bargaining. All these trends have meant that society, rather than being polarized, has become more diversified. 'Linked cleavages' (or lines of conflict) have given way to cross-cutting cleavages.

For Dahrendorf, the significant fact about society is the coercion of some members by others. Within every 'imperatively co-ordinated association' there is a 'command class' and an 'obey class'; some people have authority and others do not. Yet authority, which is so central a concept in Dahrendorf's conflict theory, is in fact distinguished from naked power by the element of consent accorded to its exercise by the obey class. Thus he admits consensual factors to his theory. Why then place such emphasis on his differences with consensus theorists? 'For purposes of exposition, it seems useful to reduce each of the two facets (consensual and coercive) to a small number of tenets, even if this involves some degree of oversimplification as well as overstatement.' Such a strategy seems to me to be a form of theoretical anarchism. On close reading, Dahrendorf's definition of authority does not differ so radically from Parsons's idiosyncratic definition of 'power'.[38] The significant difference is simply that in Dahrendorf's conception, authority is a zero-sum resource: the more one group has the less there is for others. For Parsons, power is generated within social systems in proportion to the trust placed in the leaders by the led, and everyone can have more; the mechanism is analogous to the creation of money by banks through the credit multiplier beloved of economists until recent years.

Exchange theory made its appearance relatively recently, and was intended to cut across the consensus–conflict impasse, making possible more rigorous sociological theories at the same time.[39] Not that there is anything really new about the general approach; social exchange theory represents a new evanescence of utilitarian social thought. The basic insight, that men seek many rewards which can be obtained only in social interaction with other people, is common both to Spencer, with his emphasis on the place of contract in industrial societies, and to the whole of economic theory. Much of the appeal of social exchange theory lay in its attempt to apply the seemingly rigorous paraphernalia of economic analysis to the processes of social interaction. As developed by George Homans and P. M. Blau, an elaborate analogy was drawn between economic trading and social transactions. The theory was repeatedly illustrated by reference to a situation in an office, where we find an expert at the job and a novice who needs the expert's assistance. To render assistance, the expert must pay the price of taking time off his own work. In compensation he receives deference, or 'status', from the novice. The value both of deference to the expert and assistance to the novice are subject to declining marginal utility, and a stable 'price' for the exchange of assistance and deference may be established. (It is a paradox that in such a stable exchange situation, commitment to a moral value—such as the expert's conviction that it is now time the novice stood on his own two feet—may actually be disruptive.) If the exchange is unbalanced, when for instance the novice cannot adequately 'repay' the expert, the expert acquires power over the other—the power of the bank over the man with an overdraft. In this way, a neat economic analogy develops. Blau even tries to take the analysis beyond face-to-face interaction to the level of relations between groups and organizations; at this stage, there are distinct parallels between his theory and Parsons's views on power.

On closer examination, however, the analogy is not so neat. Power, deference, and perhaps even assistance are not so easily measured as money, and under careful scrutiny the neat economic diagrams are found to be invalid.[40] Moreover, as Blau recognizes, unlike Homans, the theory becomes tautologous if it is seriously contended that *all* human behaviour is hedonistically motivated towards 'payoff'. Blau admitted that exchange theory could not explain behaviour of all kinds, especially not behaviour induced by physical coercion or motivated by irrational desires. Later he also excluded behaviour in conformity with internalized norms.[41] He was not the first to spot the limitations of utilitarian theories. Macaulay, writing in the *Edinburgh Review* in 1829 on James Mill's theory of government, remarked:

> It is idle to attribute any importance to a proposition which, when interpreted, means only that a man had rather do what a man had rather do. . . . Nothing can possibly be inferred from a maxim of this kind. When we see a man take something, we shall know that it was the object of his desire. But till then we have no means of judging with certainty what he desires or what he will take.[42]

Exchange theory began with ambition to revolutionize sociological thinking. Blau having now excluded large parts of human behaviour, such as those particularly discussed by Freudian, by conflict, and by consensus theorists, one wonders what it does explain, other than the expert and novice in an office. It is apparent that values and norms play as large a part in Blau's theory as in Parsons's: we have to know what people want before we can predict how they will get it.

### *System Integration*

Reference must finally be made to one more theoretical controversy to which postwar sociologists have paid an excessive degree of attention: 'functionalism'. The basic idea of functionalism is that of a *system*. A system, according to the dictionary, is no more than 'a complex whole, set of connected things or parts, organized body of material or immaterial things'. In short, the kernel of functionalism is the notion of a social system consisting of interdependent constituent parts. At its simplest, this involves the idea that the presence or the value of one variable in a system imposes a degree of constraint on the range of possible variation in other components of the system. For instance, sociologists have suggested that if a society has an industrial economy, it is unlikely that it will also have, or long retain, an elaborate pattern of extended kinship relations; among the reasons for this belief is that an industrial economy demands social and geographical mobility of labour, and an extended family would be incompatible with this. It is a short step from this hypothesis of interdependence between the institutions of society to suggesting that a particular institution (such as the nuclear family unit consisting of husband, wife, and offspring) fulfils certain 'functions' (such as socialization of infants) for the wider system. And it can be seen that a change in one institution of society (such as the economy) may precipitate changes in others (such as the family, the political, and the educational systems). These simple ideas have in the past often been dramatized by a 'biological analogy' between the institutions of society and the parts of the body.

In this elementary form, 'functionalism' can be traced back to Aristotle, and certainly to Montesquieu. But its more recent ancestry runs through Spencer and Durkheim to Bronislaw Malinowski and A. R. Radcliffe-Brown, the leaders of British social anthropology between the wars. From anthropology it entered postwar sociology, where its arrival provoked riotous dispute. Unfortunately, functionalism came to be identified with the consensus theory of social order; many writers have used 'functionalism' as virtually a synonym for consensus theory. Analytically, they are separate issues, though there are good practical reasons for this confusion. For one thing, Talcott Parsons and his influential followers such as Kingsley Davis, Wilbert Moore, Marion Levy, and Neil Smelser combined the functionalist approach with an emphasis on consensus, normative integration, shared values, and so on. At a somewhat deeper level, the association is a natural one; sociologists who adhere to consensus theories and stress the importance of shared values for social stability will find appeal in the functionalist view of social structures composed of interrelated units interacting harmoniously.

Yet this association is not a necessary one, as we have already seen. For all his attention to coercion and conflict, Marx himself was essentially a systems theorist. What could be more systemic than the idea that economic structures ultimately determine the form of other social institutions, or his discussion of the relationship between infrastructure and superstructure? More recently, as we noted, Coser discussed conflict within a basically functional framework; so did Max Gluckman in his *Custom and Conflict in Africa* (1959). Furthermore, George Homans, who was later to formulate exchange theory, used a functional systems approach in *The Human Group* (1950).

The faults of functionalism stem not from the basic hypothesis of interdependence, but from the slipshod logic of many functionalists. Of that, Robert Merton provided the best-known critique.[43] Radcliffe-Brown's 'postulate of functional unity' is indefensible; it is not true that 'everything influences everything else'. Indeed, another famous anthropologist, Robert Lowie, once went to the other extreme and spoke of culture as a 'thing of shreds and patches'. As Sorokin, and more recently Gouldner, have emphasized,[44] the actual degree of integration of institutions and their repercussions on each other are a matter for empirical investigation. Marx believed, as do many modern sociologists, that economic change is likely to have widespread influence on other parts of society. Other institutions have greater autonomy; we do not now look to religious institutions as a source of major social change, though it would have been reasonable to do so in the Middle Ages or Reformation.

Similarly, Malinowski's 'postulate of universal functionalism' is weak. Not all customs and institutions promote social stability. Some, like prostitution, may be *dysfunctional* with respect to (or in other words, undermine) another aspect of social structure, such as the family. Or they may not have any function at all. If we do not recognize this, we may find ourselves in the position of the famous anthropologist who sought to explain the functions of the redundant buttons on jacket sleeves. They help to maintain the sense of tradition, he said. Why, then, are we no longer wearing top hats?

This brings us to a third functionalist fallacy: indispensability. Functionalists have tended to argue that social systems have certain needs or 'prerequisites', and that certain customs or institutions are essential to meet these needs.[45] But that a need exists does not guarantee that it will be met. As P. S. Cohen neatly remarks: 'it could be argued that men need a way of settling all disputes without violence; but they do not have one'.[46] One of the worst examples of the dangers of such teleological reasoning in functionalism was Kingsley Davis's and Wilbert Moore's notorious article, 'Some Principles of Stratification'[47], the essential argument of which can be captured in a single quotation: 'Social inequality is thus an unconsciously evolved device by which societies insure [*sic*] that the most important positions are conscientiously filled by the most qualified persons.'[48] In so far as their theory has any valid content, it seems to amount to little more than the Ricardian marginal-product theory of wages. It certainly does not explain the origins of distinct social strata, but does go a long way to explain why functionalism should so frequently have been considered a mere rationalization of the social *status quo*.

To avoid such pitfalls, Merton advanced the concept of *functional alternatives* or *equivalents*, which 'unfreeze the identity of the existent and the inevitable'. Before we judge anything to be inevitable, we should consider alternative ways in which the function might have been fulfilled. This leads sociologists to see parallels between religious ritual and a drunken orgy, or to see state intervention in a mixed economy and the free market in a *laissez-faire* era as functionally equivalent forms of economic discipline.

Another of Merton's innovations is the distinction between *manifest* and *latent* functions. Manifest functions are those consequences of an action or custom which are consciously recognized and intended by the participants; latent functions are unrecognized by the people involved. There is no difficulty in explaining why a custom came into being or is continued, if it can be shown that the need was consciously recognized and the institution purposely created. In the late nineteenth century, there was a growing 'need' for various kinds of welfare and educational provision; eventually it was recognized—it became manifest—and legislation was enacted.[49] But in this case we have recourse in effect to social action theory. Latent functions are a more intractable problem, yet also the true domain of functional explanation.

Since Merton wrote, Ernest Nagel has shown that valid functional explanations in terms of the structure of systems are possible, though they require tighter logic than that displayed by immediately postwar functionalists.[50] Francesca Cancian has built on his work to demonstrate that, in spite of the repeated charge that functionalism is an inherently static approach, functional explanations of social change are possible.[51] She employs a more abstract notion of 'system', which owes much to the contemporary movement in the philosophy of science known as general systems theory and the related new science of cybernetics. Both have recently appealed to sociologists; Walter Buckley has tried to spell out their implications for sociology, though often seeming only to exchange one set of jargon for another.[52] General systems theory also seems to be the essence of 'structuralism', at least as it is interpreted by Jean Piaget.[53] Whether other structuralists like Lévi-Strauss would agree with him is a moot point; but as these developments belong largely to anthropologists, I excuse myself from further exploration.

The major criticism which is often made of postwar 'grand theory' is that it has not led to contingent hypotheses which can be tested in research. A rare instance of an attempt to do so is N. J. Smelser's use of Parsons's functional scheme in his work on *Social Change in the Industrial Revolution* (1959); yet Homans has argued that the grand theoretical paraphernalia is redundant to the substantive theory.[54] As Merton wrote:

> a large part of what is now described as sociological theory consists of general orientations toward data, suggesting types of variables which theories must somehow take into account, rather than clearly formulated, verifiable statements of relationships between specified variables. We have many concepts but fewer confirmed theories; many points of view, but few theorems; many 'approaches' but few arrivals.[55]

Or, as Homans put it, we have written 'the dictionary of a language that possesses no sentences'.[56]

## III. Middle-Range Theories

Dissensus and dispute among grand theorists should, however, not obscure the fact that in intention, even grand theory in the postwar years conformed both to Comte's predictions and to Popper's strictures. It was intended to be some guide to research. Much of its value has been lost, however, in the tendency of grand-theory specialists to concentrate only on the differences between the 'approaches', rather than on synthesizing them on the basis of their common elements, many of which have been suggested above.

Yet in practice most sociologists have achieved a working synthesis in their research by using 'sociological theories of the middle range'. They have engaged in theoretically relevant empirical research—theoretically relevant in the sense that both the theories which guided their research and those which emerged from it were not of all-encompassing scope, but interpreted and explained particular ranges of phenomena. Furthermore, these theories intelligibly related findings in one project to another, and thus gave rise to some cumulative growth in sociological knowledge. The appeal for 'stepping stones in the middle distance' was originally made by T. H

Marshall and echoed by R. K. Merton.[57] The significance of middle-range theory, as Merton noted, was that:

They are frequently consistent with a variety of so-called systems of sociological theory. . . . Marxist theory, functional analysis, social behaviourism, Sorokin's integral sociology, or Parsons's theory of action. . . . Comprehensive sociological theories are sufficiently loose-knit, internally diversified, and mutually overlapping that *a given theory of the middle range*, which has a measure of empirical confirmation, can often be subsumed under comprehensive theories which are themselves discrepant in certain respects.[58]

Thus can the inspiration of the 'founding fathers' of sociology often be expressed in modest, far from monomaniac, but cumulative research to generate theories of wide application. For instance, none of the several varieties of social action theory is incompatible with the great bulk of the findings of social psychology which has burgeoned since the war. The related theories of cognitive balance, congruity, and dissonance are capable of widespread application whenever we are interested in people's definitions of the situation.[59] Consider Leon Festinger's test of his own theory in *When Prophecy Fails* (1956): what happens when members of a millenarian sect face the bitter disappointment of the world not coming to an end when they predicted? Do they revise their beliefs, update their predictions, or leave the sect? Do they feel greater or less enthusiasm? These are empirical questions to test a middle-range theory; 'grand theory' cannot provide the answers. On the other hand, it does suggest probing questions about research findings. *The Authoritarian Personality*, by T. W. Adorno and his associates (1950), sparked off extensive research, but little of it directly faced the basic problem of whether authoritarianism was to be understood as a phenomenon of individual psychology or as the product of certain kinds of usually lower-class environment.[60]

Though the subtler aspects of their thought may have given several decades of grand theorists grist for their mills, the real significance of Weber and Durkheim was that they were in essence middle-range theorists. Even Weber's codification of his ideas in *Wirtschaft und Gesellschaft* is not an all-embracing system in the nineteenth-century tradition. Durkheim's insight into religion's part in promoting social cohesion[61] has continued to influence recent work in the sociology of religion, as can be seen most clearly in Guy Swanson's *The Birth of the Gods* (1960). The influence is even greater of Weber's *The Protestant Ethic*. Authors such as Lenski, Demerath, Glock, and Stark have thought it worthwhile to continue to look for the effects of religious belief and affiliation on behaviour in contemporary America, to ask, among other questions, does 'inner-worldly asceticism' persist and is it still associated with entrepreneurial vigour?[62] R. N. Bellah examined the history of Japan for parallels to the modernizing impulses of the Protestant sects,[63] giving the lead for many extensions of the Weber thesis to the contemporary developing world.[64] And Weber's work directly inspired David McClelland to look for a more general psychological element in economic growth, namely 'need for achievement', and to test his bold hypothesis by an even bolder (because expensive) international and historical comparative survey.[65]

Weber's discussion of rational-legal bureaucracy[66] has been no less influential. It has been a major inspiration of the sociology of organizations, a most active field since the war. Weber provided an essentially functional analysis of bureaucracy, emphasizing its internal efficiency and the stability it contributed to the wider society; but he was also aware of the threat it posed, speaking of a 'disenchanted world'. As a principle of organization it has pervaded many aspects of modern life—not only governmental administration, but armies, political parties, schools and universities, prisons and factories, all of them studied by sociologists. Theoretical issues which they have raised include dysfunctions, such as the danger of the individual bureaucrat becoming a ritualistic over-conformer[67]; the diversity of organizational structures and their adaptation to different technical environments[68]; and their internal tensions and dynamics.[69]

Another rich complex of middle-range theory took its departure from the Durkheimian concept of *anomie*. Durkheim implied that human wants have no natural limit; such limits as there are stem from social norms, which define for each class of people to what they are legitimately entitled. The breakdown of these rules leads to the deregulation of their aspirations, and a situation of *anomie* prevails. This situation, which is common during rapid social change, is personally disruptive. Merton seized on this insight to advance what became an influential theory of deviant behaviour. He referred to three aspects of social structure. First,

> culturally defined goals held out as legitimate objectives for all or for diversely located members of the society. The goals are more or less integrated—the degree is a question of empirical fact—and roughly ordered in some hierarchy of value. Involving various degrees of sentiment and significance, the prevailing goals comprise a frame of aspirational reference. They are the things 'worth striving for'.[70]

Wealth is one such common goal. However, there are also norms governing the approved or tolerated means of attaining these goals. Furthermore, the opportunities for attaining these aspirations are unequally distributed in society. To cut a long story short, a man in a situation where the desirability of being well-to-do is emphasized with no corresponding emphasis on the legitimate means of becoming so, and moreover where there are few opportunities to do so legitimately, is more likely to turn to crime. This is to oversimplify; Merton's theory casts much light on the varying patterns of deviance found in different strata of society. It has initiated a fruitful tradition of research, even more fruitful when integrated with the Chicago 'differential association' theory which draws attention also to the unequally distributed opportunities for learning deviant behaviour.[71]

From *anomie* theory it is but a short step to the ideas of *reference groups* and *relative deprivation*. A reference group is one from which standards of aspiration are taken by other groups or individuals. For example, for marginal, white-collar workers, the established professional middle class is a reference group which may be imitated or in which future membership may be sought. For that matter, the manual working class may be a negative reference group for the same clerical class. The basic idea is now familiar to all of us in the shape of the 'customary differentials' which so bedevil attempts at national incomes policies. Sociology received it from the work of Herbert Hyman, and more famously from S. A. Stouffer's *The American Soldier* (1949), in which study it was used to explain a number of seeming paradoxes, such as the comparative contentment of soldiers in units with poorer promotion chances. It has since been widely used to explain such phenomena as conflicts within firms between professionals (lawyers and accountants—reference group the profession with its ethical standards) and ordinary managers (reference group the firm, with its overriding goal of commercial success). The related notion of relative deprivation has been widely used too. Deprivation is usually not experienced in absolute terms but rather relatively to some appropriate standard. Thus J. C. Davis and T. R. Gurr have used the idea to explain why revolutions usually occur when things are improving; discontent is at its highest when aspirations begin to soar.[72] W. G. Runciman carried out a survey to investigate why the British were not more dissatisfied with social inequalities; his answer too lay in the comfortable, accustomed relativity of their deprivation.[73]

*Mass society* has been another popular middle-range theme in research. The idea has its origins in several earlier writers—Karl Mannheim, Ortega y Gasset, even Karl Marx's *The 18th*

*Brumaire*—and is dialectically related to the investigation of the social bases of stable democracy. The chief argument is that dramatic social change, whether industrialization, urbanization, slump, or military defeat, can so disrupt social structure that people no longer belong to stable associations (like trade unions and so forth) which contain and express their aspirations. In this atomized state, the theory of mass society suggests, people are more easily manipulated and mobilized into extremist political movements. There is considerable controversy as to whether such movements are best explained by the 'mass society' theory or in terms of their class base, and the origins of numerous movements such as Nazism, Poujadism, Perónism, and American populism have been examined in a so far unsuccessful attempt finally to settle the matter.[74]

Mass communications clearly are a key feature of a mass society, being the means by which demagogues can appeal to atomized followers. Communications have therefore received a good deal of attention from sociologists, who have also been concerned with the slightly less dramatic issue of whether their effect has been to create cultural homogeneity and conformity. The quality of mass communications has received impressionistic but highly illuminating analysis by writers such as David Riesman and Richard Hoggart, who have attributed to them a decline in the variety of local and minority cultures, and a greater uniformity of mass concerns.[75] More rigorous sociological research has cast doubt on the 'hypodermic' theory of influence; the mass media do not have a direct brainwashing effect on all who see or hear them, but rather influence a minority of opinion-leaders who carry the information to associates through the structure of face-to-face groups.[76] This does not necessarily mean that in the long term the media may not have a considerable effect on the quality of mass culture and opinion; it does leave open the issue of whether the media serve to atomize people and involve them vicariously in remote events (as the mass society theorists suggest) or rather to make possible their responsible participation in national and civic affairs (as the Chicago sociologist Robert Park tended to believe).

If mass society theorists have looked for diminishing social differences within industrial societies, others have tried to discern convergence between societies, though usually in a more limited way than the grand speculators did. As originally advanced by American writers strongly influenced by functionalism, the convergence thesis resembled an anti-Soviet Marxism—a belief that as Russia and the communist states achieved industrial maturity, their political and social institutions too must eventually come to resemble those of the west.[77] In this crude form, the theory has little merit. It is far too early to be sure that a more complex economy, creating more specialized skills and skilled groups, will necessarily lead to a similarly pluralistic polity. Concerning stratification and inequality east and west of the Iron Curtain, opinions differ. J. H. Goldthorpe has argued that the pattern of Soviet inequality, being the creation of the political regime, will not necessarily change in response to economic change. Parkin on the other hand seems to believe that for this very reason the political system will become a focus of powerful discontent.[78] When applied to such broad aspects of social structure, the convergence thesis becomes inconclusive and speculative, yet it is a healthy sign of continuing international comparative research. Similar ideas have initiated research into international rates of social mobility and family structures. Lipset and Bendix found that similar economies were associated with similar rates of movement from manual to non-manual occupations. Using more comprehensive data, however, S. M. Miller cast doubt on the uniformity of mobility rates; there were significant differences between nations, especially in terms of longer-range mobility, as from manual to professional occupations.[79] W. J. Goode in comparison examined emerging family structures in many industrializing nations, and found considerable evidence for the growing dominance of the nuclear family (husband, wife, and offspring) as the typical household unit.[80]

No claim is made to have more than sampled a few current middle-range theories. These examples nevertheless illustrate some of the bridges which have been built between 'grand theory' and empirical research. No doubt it remains true that sociology's theoretical reach exceeds its grasp, but this is a healthy state for any science to be in.

## IV. Conclusion: The Sociology of Sociology

In the late 1950s, 'the end of ideology in the west' was widely proclaimed both by sociologists and laymen.[81] Political conflicts seemed to have declined both in bitterness and in scope. During the Cold War, as the West stood united against the perceived Communist threat, internal political differences seemed less significant, as witness so-called 'Butskellism' in Great Britain. During the 1960s, the story was very different. Great political conflicts broke out in America over the Vietnam war and race; partly in consequence, the student protest movement arose and added further to the cacophony. These conflicts found echoes throughout the world—a world now containing many newly independent nations often in turmoil themselves. It would have been surprising had sociology not reflected these events. One consequence was a spate of studies of student protest movements. Another was a renewed interest in the hitherto dormant field of the sociology of knowledge, the study of ideologies and beliefs and their rooting in social groups and situations. The Marxist mould was finally broken, and ideologies were no longer seen as the exclusive property of such leviathans as 'the working class' and 'the bourgeoisie'.[82]

More significantly, however, the turn of events caused some sociological introspection. It seemed somewhat incongruous in the face of endemic violence, upheaval, and conflict, that the dominant Parsonian *Weltanschauung* should so emphasize consensus, stability, and harmony. Dissatisfaction with the sociological *status quo* had issue in three recent books of protest, by A. W. Gouldner, R. W. Friedrichs, and D. Atkinson.[83] There are important differences between the three, but the resemblances are more striking. Their common theme is the breaking up of the sociological consensus. Our survey so far may scarcely have suggested that such agreement existed, bu in the sense that Talcott Parsons and his followers were dominant, overwhelmingly so in American sociology, and that even dissenter had to pick away at the great edifice of their work, there was a degre of consensus. As a variety of sociological 'approaches' have onc more appeared, no longer necessarily in conscious response t Parsons, the consensus has declined. All three authors reject th hitherto dominant model of man as largely moulded and enmeshe by the social system, and call for a greater recognition of his innova- tive and creative potential; they are therefore markedly more sympa- thetic to the early Parsons of *The Structure of Social Action* than t the later, systemic, Parsons. All three authors further note a curiou convergence between Parsonian functionalism and more orthodo Marxist sociology. For all that Parsons has been seen as an ideologis of capitalist society, Marxist sociology especially in Eastern Europ has come to emphasize similar concerns: systemic interdependence social harmony, and man as dominated by his environment. Ye Marxism too is facing fragmentation; the publication of Marx' early writings[84] and the assimilation of the work of Marxists such a Gramsci and Lukàcs have stimulated a plurality of Marxisms.

Gouldner, Friedrichs, and Atkinson furthermore call in differen ways for the greater involvement of the sociologist, and attack th 'pretence' of value-neutrality. It is paradoxical that while sociologist in Britain are usually thought of as radically inclined, and in Americ have often been accused of conservatism, both groups have overwhelmingly adhered to the belief that their research should not be tinged with their own values. As George Homans is fond of asking: 'Never mind whether it's good politics—is it a good theory?' However, the increasingly influential Frankfurt school of 'critical sociology' has prominently attempted to combine sociological research with social evaluation.[85]

Yet sociological research, like any other kind of social activity, is liable to have unintended consequences. Gouldner in particular probes the relationship between the sociologist and the 'Welfare State'. As the functions of governments have expanded in a predominantly empirically minded age, politicians have increasingly demanded the facts on which to base policies; even seeking to defy David Hume by deriving 'ought' from 'is'. The general public too have seemed to share this empirical mood.[86] Gouldner and Friedrichs argue that in this situation, the sociologists' stance of value-neutrality has very conveniently enabled them to do the politicians' bidding—to play, in Friedrichs's term, a 'priestly' role. Or, as Gouldner sees it, they adopt 'ameliorism', discovering how to repair the minor deficiencies of the system, without considering the need for or possibility of major change. Ameliorism might in Britain be identified with the work on poverty and the problems of the welfare services by Richard Titmuss and his associates, who have nevertheless retained a radical image. More sinister issues are raised, especially in the U.S.A., by the funding of social science research on a vast scale by government and private industry. Robert Nisbet has detailed the corrupting influence of 'the higher capitalism' on the integrity of American universities; L. Baritz has illustrated how American academics in the field of industrial relations have adopted as their own the perspectives of industrial management.[87] The danger was most dramatically illustrated in 'Project Camelot', the vast research programme financed by the American military into the social sources of guerrilla insurrections. Camelot collapsed, leaving American social scientists greatly chastened.[88]

Such turbulence as sociology is now experiencing should not be allowed to veil the very great progress the discipline has made in the last three decades, theoretically, empirically, and in acceptance as a distinctive subject. No doubt a greater self-consciousness will be required—a 'reflexive sociology' which considers the social consequences of its own activities. Most sociologists, nevertheless, are too modest to accept blandishments to become the prophetic critics of society.

## NOTES

[1] *Report of the Committee of Social Studies* (Heyworth Committee), Cmnd. 2660 (1965).

[2] See for example H. M. Blalock, *Social Statistics* (1960); J. S. Coleman, *Introduction to Mathematical Sociology* (1964).

[3] G. D. Mitchell, *A Hundred Years of Sociology* (1968).

[4] Popper's *The Poverty of Historicism* was originally published in three parts in *Economica*, n.s., XI–XII (1944–5).

[5] K. R. Popper, *The Poverty of Historicism* (1957), v–vi.

[6] P. A. Sorokin, *Sociological Theories of Today* (1966), ch. 12. Sorokin's own *Social and Cultural Dynamics* (4 vols., 1937–41) represents one of the last and most sophisticated fruits of the tradition of grand historical interpretation.

[7] *From Max Weber*, ed. H. H. Gerth and C. W. Mills (1946).

[8] R. K. Merton, *Social Theory and Social Structure* (enlarged ed., 1968), 139.

[9] C. Wright Mills, *The Sociological Imagination* (1959); P. A. Sorokin, *Sociological Theories of Today* and *Fads and Foibles in Modern Sociology* (1956).

[10] The useful distinction between social integration and system integration was drawn by David Lockwood in his 'System Integration and Social Integration', in *Explorations in Social Change*, ed. G. K. Zollschan and W. Hirsch (1964).

[11] N. Chomsky, in *Language*, XXXV, No. 1 (1959), 21–32.

[12] F. Toennies, *Fundamental Concepts of Sociology* (trans. 1940).

[13] T. Parsons, *The Social System* (1951), ch. 2.

[14] G. H. Mead, *Mind, Self and Society* (1934), 6.

[15] Ibid. 155.

[16] *Human Behaviour and Social Processes*, ed. A. M. Rose (1962), vii.

[17] C. R. Shaw *et al.*, *Delinquency Areas* (1929); E. H. Sutherland, *Criminology* (1924); H. S. Becker, *Outsiders* (1963).

[18] Alfred Schütz, *Collected Papers* (3 vols., The Hague, 1964–7). Schütz's ideas have been popularized by Peter Berger and Thomas Luckmann in their well-known book *The Social Construction of Reality* (1966). The influence of Schütz, indirectly at least, also seems apparent in T. S. Kuhn's controversial work, *The Structure of Scientific Revolutions* (1962). Kuhn shows that scientific knowledge, like any other, can only be understood in social context; physical reality is typified in ways socially acceptable within the scientific community to generate scientific 'paradigms'. Paradigms are moulds which are shattered only with difficulty when major 'anomalies' arise which are inconsistent with them. Phenomenology has also been a key influence on the clinical psychologist R. D. Laing; see his *The Divided Self* (1960) and *The Self and Others* (2nd ed., 1969). On the other hand, E. A. Tiryakian has argued that a not dissimilar perspective was the common property of many of the classical sociologists ('Existential Phenomenology and the Sociological Tradition', *American Sociological Review*, XXX, no. 5 (1965), 674–88).

[19] H. Garfinkel, *Studies in Ethnomethodology* (1967). See also N. K. Denzin, 'Symbolic Interactionism and Ethnomethodology, A proposed Synthesis', *American Sociological Review*, XXXIV, no. 6 (1969), 932–4.

[20] E. Goffman, *The Presentation of Self in Everyday Life* (1959).

[21] E. Goffman, 'On Face Work' (1955) in *Where the Action Is* (1969).

[22] E. Goffman, *Stigma* (1963).

[23] E. Goffman, *Asylums* (1961).

[24] Especially *The Social System*, and *Toward a General Theory of Action*, ed. T. Parsons and E. A. Shils (1951). For a critique of the transition in Parsons's thought, see J. Finley Scott, 'The Changing Foundations of the Parsonian Action Scheme', *American Sociological Review*, XXVIII, no. 5 (1963), 716–35.

[25] See P. M. Blau, 'Structural Effects', *American Sociological Review*, XXV, no. 2 (1960), 178–93.

[26] D. H. Wrong, 'The Oversocialized Conception of Man in Modern Sociology', *American Sociological Review*, XXVI, no. 2 (1961), 183–93.

[27] S. Freud, *Civilisation and its Discontents* (ed. 1962), 72.

[28] E. A. Shils, 'Consensus: I. The Concept of Consensus', in *International Encyclopaedia of the Social Sciences* (1968).

[29] Parsons and Shils, *Toward a General Theory of Action.*

[30] G. Almond and S. Verba, *The Civic Culture* (1963).

[31] E. A. Shils and M. Young, 'The Meaning of the Coronation', *Sociological Review*, n.s., I, no. 2 (1953), 63–81.

[32] E. A. Shils, 'Centre and Periphery', in *The Logic of Personal Knowledge: Essays Presented to Michael Polanyi* (1961), 117–30.

[33] L. Lipsitz, 'Consensus: II. The Study of Consensus', *International Encyclopaedia.*

[34] A. W. Gouldner, *The Coming Crisis of Western Sociology* (1971), 140.

[35] L. A. Coser, *The Functions of Social Conflict* (1956); G. Simmel, '*Conflict*' and '*The Web of Group Affiliations*' (1955).

[36] L. A. Coser, 'Conflict: III. Social Aspects', *International Encyclopaedia*, III. 233.

[37] But also see his later qualifications: R. Dahrendorf, *Conflict after Class: New Perspectives on the Theory of Social and Political Conflict* (1967).

[38] T. Parsons, 'On the Concept of Political Power', *Proceedings of the American Philosophical Society*, CVII, no. 3 (1963).

[39] The vogue was initiated by George Homans's paper 'Social Behaviour as Exchange', *American Journal of Sociology*, LXIII, no. 6 (1958), 597–606. The other key references are Homans's *Social Behaviour: Its Elementary Forms* (1961); P. M. Blau, *Exchange and Power in Social Life* (1964); J. W. Thibault and H. H. Kelley, *The Social Psychology of Groups* (1959).

[40] A. A. Heath, 'Economic Theory and Sociology', *Sociology*, II, no. 3 (1968), 273–92.

[41] P. M. Blau, 'Interaction: IV. Social Exchange,' *International Encyclopaedia.*

[42] Cf. Chomsky, quoted above.

[43] R. K. Merton, 'Manifest and Latent Functions', *Social Theory and Social Structure*, ch. 3.

[44] P. A. Sorokin, *Social and Cultural Dynamics*, vol. I, ch. 1; A. W. Gouldner, 'Reciprocity and Autonomy in Functional Theory', in *Symposium on Sociological Theory*, ed. L. Gross (1959).

[45] D. F. Alberle *et al.*, 'The Functional Prerequisites of a Society', *Ethics*, LX, no. 2 (1950), 100–11. Cf. Parsons's system of four functional exigencies, first outlined in T. Parsons, R. F. Bales, and E. A. Shils, *Working Papers in the Theory of Action* (1953). See also L. Sklair: *The Sociology of Progress* (1970).

[46] P. S. Cohen, *Modern Social Theory* (1968), 41.

[47] K. Davis and W. E. Moore, 'Some Principles of Stratification', *American Sociological Review*, X, no. 2 (1945), 242–9.

[48] K. Davis, *Human Society* (1949), 367.

[49] J. H. Goldthorpe, 'The Development of Social Policy in England, 1800–1914', *Transactions of the 5th World Congress of Sociology* (1964), IV. 41–6.

[50] E. Nagel, 'A Formalization of Functionalism', in *Logic without Metaphysics* (1956).

[51] F. Cancian, 'Functional Analysis of Change', *American Sociological Review*, XXV, no. 6 (1960), 818–27; and 'Functional Analysis: II. Varieties of Functional Analysis', *International Encyclopaedia.*

[52] W. Buckley, *Sociology and Modern Systems Theory* (1967).

[53] J. Piaget, *Structuralism* (1971). Cf. R. Boudon, *The Uses of Structuralism* (1971), and also W. G. Runciman, 'What is Structuralism?', *Sociology in its Place* (1970), ch. 2.

[54] G. C. Homans, 'Bringing Men Back In', *American Sociological Review*, XXIX, no. 6 (1964), 809–18.

[55] Merton, *Social Theory and Social Structure*, 52.

[56] G. C. Homans, 'Contemporary Theory in Sociology', in *Handbook of Modern Sociology*, ed. R. E. L. Faris (1964), 957.

[57] T. H. Marshall, Inaugural Lecture 1946, reprinted in *Sociology at the Crossroads* (1963); R. K. Merton, 'Sociological Theories of the Middle Range', ch. 2 of *Social Theory and Social Structure.*

[58] Ibid. 43.

[59] L. Festinger, *A Theory of Cognitive Dissonance* (1957); R. B. Zajonc, 'The Concepts of Balance, Congruity and Dissonance', *Public Opinion Quarterly*, XXIV, no. 2 (1960), 280–96.

[60] Cf. S. M. Lipset, *Political Man* (1960).

[61] E. Durkheim, *The Elementary Forms of the Religious Life* (1915).

[62] G. Lenski, *The Religious Factor* (1963); N. J. Demerath III, *Social Class in American Protestantism* (1965).

[63] R. N. Bellah, *Tokugawa Religion* (1957).

[64] See the essays in Part III of *The Protestant Ethic and Modernization*, ed. S. N. Eisenstadt (1968).

[65] D. C. McClelland, *The Achieving Society* (1961).

[66] M. Weber, 'Bureaucracy', ch. 8 of *From Max Weber*, ed. Gerth and Mills.

[67] Merton, *Social Theory and Social Structure*, ch. 8.

[68] J. Woodward, *Management and Technology* (1958); A. Etzioni, *A Comparative Analysis of Complex Organizations* (1961); T. Burns and G. M. Stalker, *The Management of Innovation* (1964).

[69] P. M. Blau, *The Dynamics of Bureaucracy* (1955); M. Crozier, *The Bureaucratic Phenomenon* (1964).

[70] Merton, *Social Theory and Social Structure*, ch. 6.

[71] R. A. Cloward, 'Illegitimate Means, *Anomie* and Deviant Behaviour', *American Sociological Review*, XXIV, no. 2 (1959), 164–76.

[72] J. C. Davis, 'Toward a Theory of Revolution', *American Sociological Review*, XXVII, no. 1 (1962), 5–19; T. R. Gurr: 'Psychological Factors in Civil Violence', *World Politics*, XX, no. 2 (1968), 245–78.

[73] W. G. Runciman, *Relative Deprivation and Social Justice* (1966).

[74] Compare W. Kornhauser, *The Politics of Mass Society* (1960) with Lipset, *Political Man*, ch. 5.

[75] D. Riesman *et al.*, *The Lonely Crowd* (1950); R. Hoggart, *The Uses of Literacy* (1957).

[76] The theory of the 'two-step flow of communication' was one outcome of P. F. Lazarsfeld *et al.*'s pioneering *The People's Choice* (1944), since when much

research has been carried out. For a survey, see E. Rogers, *The Diffusion of Innovations* (1962).

[77] C. Kerr, *Industrialism and Industrial Man* (1962); W. W. Rostow, *The Stages of Economic Growth* (1960).

[78] J. H. Goldthorpe, 'Social Stratification in Industrial Society', *Sociological Review Monograph 8* (1964); F. Parkin, *Class, Inequality and Political Order* (1971).

[79] S. M. Lipset and R. Bendix, *Social Mobility in Industrial Society* (1959); S. M. Miller, 'Comparative Social Mobility', *Current Sociology*, IX, no. 1 (1960), 1–89.

[80] W. J. Goode, *World Revolution and Family Patterns* (1963).

[81] D. Bell, *The End of Ideology* (1960); Lipset, *Political Man.*

[82] See Berger and Luckmann, *The Social Construction of Reality*; *The Sociology of Knowledge*, ed. J. Curtis and J. W. Petras (1970); *Ideology and Discontent*, ed. D. E. Apter (1964).

[83] Gouldner, *The Coming Crisis of Western Sociology*; R. W. Friedrichs, *A Sociology of Sociology* (1970): D. Atkinson, *Orthodox Consensus and Radical Alternative* (1971).

[84] K. Marx, *Economic and Philosophic Manuscripts of 1844* (Moscow, 1959).

[85] See especially J. Habermas, *Toward a Rational Society* (1971) and *Knowledge and Human Interests* (1972).

[86] R. E. Lane, 'The Decline of Politics and Ideology in a Knowledgeable Society', *American Sociological Review*, XXI, no. 5 (1966), 649–62.

[87] R. A. Nisbet, *The Degradation of the Academic Dogma* (1971); L. Baritz, *The Servants of Power* (1967).

[88] I. L. Horowitz, *The Rise and Fall of Project Camelot* (1967).

## FOR FURTHER READING

There are available literally hundreds of general introductory sociological textbooks, most of which, after preliminary remarks about 'sociology as a science' and such concepts as roles and interaction, move on to discuss various institutional areas of society—the family, religion, and so on. Choice between them is invidious. The newcomer is probably as well served by a compendium of significant recent contributions; *Modern Sociology—Introductory Readings* (1970), edited by Peter Worsley *et al.*, is excellent. Of the more theoretically organized texts, Marvin Olsen, *The Process of Social Organization* (New York, 1968) is a model of clear-headedness. The *International Encyclopaedia of the Social Sciences* (17 vols., New York, 1968) is authoritative, exhaustive, and always worth consulting for further reading.

On the higher reaches of sociological theory, Percy Cohen, *Modern Social Theory* (1968) is reliable and balanced. Parsons's impenetrable prose is most nearly penetrable in his General Introduction to *Theories of Society*, ed. T. Parsons, E. A. Shils, K. D. Nagaele, and J. R. Pitts (New York, 1961); this book is a collection of extracts from many major writers of the past century, and emphasizes the links between their work and contemporary theory. *Human Behaviour and Social Processes*, edited by A. M. Rose (Boston, 1962) is the best guide to the symbolic interactionist perspective. The links between this and

Schütz's work are evident in Peter Berger's and Thomas Luckmann's influential renovation of the sociology of knowledge, *The Social Construction of Reality* (New York, 1966). P. M. Blau, *Exchange and Power in Social Life* (New York, 1964) is representative of exchange theory, as is Ralf Dahrendorf, *Class and Class Conflict in Industrial Society* (1959) of the conflict school of thought.

Robert Merton, *Social Theory and Social Structure* (enlarged ed., New York, 1968) contains some of the most influential essays written since the war, both advocating and exemplifying the value of 'theories of the middle range'. Alvin Gouldner, *The Coming Crisis of Western Sociology* (1971) is the most powerful critique of the present state of sociology, but some familiarity with the subject is assumed—and is necessary in order to detect Gouldner's prejudices.

Finally, Richard Rudner, *Philosophy of Social Sciences* (Englewood Cliffs, N.J., 1966) can be recommended as a guide to the complexities of sociology's philosophical assumptions.

# 6

# Structural Anthropology

ERIC J. SHARPE

'Structuralism' is a term widely (albeit somewhat vaguely) used at present to denote a general type of approach to, and analysis of, areas of human communication.* Originating in the field of linguistics, its methods and insights have come to be applied to a variety of hitherto separate disciplines, not least in the social sciences. This essay is concerned with its impact upon one such discipline, the study of anthropology, or ethnology, and in particular with the contribution to structural anthropology of one man, Claude Lévi-Strauss (b. 1908), the influential Professor of Social Anthropology at the College de France.† To write about the work of Lévi-Strauss in any smaller format than that of an entire book is a hazardous undertaking. Where his arguments cannot be recapitulated in detail, it is perhaps better not to attempt to recapitulate them at all; and so we have chosen to attempt to relate his work to the broad stream of twentieth-century anthropological thought and practice. Although the risk of misrepresentation is considerable, it is hoped that by this means this extraordinarily gifted and provocative scholar can be viewed in some kind of perspective.

Lévi-Strauss has described anthropology as 'a restless and fervent study which plagues the investigator with moral as well as scientific questions'.[1] Elsewhere he has spoken of the anthropologist's goal as being 'to grasp, beyond the conscious and always shifting images

* There is no concise definition of structuralism, but Jean Piaget has suggested that it rests on two pillars: '. . . first, an ideal (perhaps a hope) of intrinsic intelligibility supported by the postulate that structures are self-sufficient . . .; second, certain insights—to the extent that one has succeeded in actually making out certain structures, their theoretical employment has shown that structures in general have, despite their diversity, certain common and perhaps necessary properties' (*Structuralism* (1971), 4 f.). To this we might add the following, from Lévi-Strauss's inaugural lecture *The Scope of Anthropology* (1967), 31: 'That arrangement alone is structured which meets two conditions: that it be a system, ruled by an internal cohesiveness, and that this cohesiveness, inaccessible to observation in an isolated system, be revealed in the study of transformations, through which the similar properties in apparently different systems are brought to light.'

† Nevertheless it is sometimes pointed out that his experience of fieldwork is not very extensive: cf. E. R. Leach, *Lévi-Strauss* (1970), 18 f.

which men hold, the complete range of unconscious possibilities'.[2] Beginning with an investigation into the conscious mind of man, the anthropologist should attempt to penetrate more and more deeply—by means of structural analysis—into the unconscious levels of social life and collective phenomena, there to examine the 'unconscious foundations' on which social life rests. In so doing, he accomplishes a transition from the particular to the universal in the life of mankind. He may well use historical data, but he passes beyond the limits of history as commonly conceived. His work should be dominated, not by the desire to establish simple chronological and cause-and-effect sequences, but by the desire to enter into the innermost recesses of the mind of man, there to understand its motives—and above all its structures:

> If, as we believe to be the case, the unconscious activity of the mind consists in imposing forms upon content, and if these forms are fundamentally the same for all minds—ancient and modern, primitive and civilized (as the study of symbolic function, expressed in language, so strikingly indicates)—it is necessary and sufficient to grasp the unconscious structure underlying each institution and each custom, in order to obtain a principle of interpretation valid for other institutions and other customs, provided of course that the analysis is carried far enough.[3]

Such, then, is the potential scope and task of structural anthropology: an interpretative enterprise of a high order.

There is a world of difference between this type of anthropology and the anthropology (or perhaps one should say anthropologies) of the earlier part of the present century, concerned as they were either with the elaboration of evolutionary patterns or with purely descriptive studies of 'primitive' peoples, their physical features and social institutions. As we shall see, Lévi-Strauss and his followers are convinced that the presuppositions and methods of the earlier phases of anthropology are no longer adequate, if indeed they ever were. A radical change of perspective has taken place. This is not to say, however, that structural anthropology owes nothing whatever to the pioneers of anthropological science. Significantly, Lévi-Strauss himself was once regarded as a disciple of Émile Durkheim, and dedicated his book *Structural Anthropology* (trans. 1963) to the memory of Durkheim, founder of the journal *L'Année Sociologique*, '. . . that famed workshop where modern anthropology fashioned part of its tools and which we have abandoned, not so much out of disloyalty as out of the sad conviction that the task would prove too much for us'. There is in fact both continuity and discontinuity with the past in structural anthropology; and our first task will therefore be to sketch briefly something of the history of anthropological thought and practice in the twentieth century, with a view to deciding where the boundaries go. Against this background we may then consider whatever is distinctive in the structural approach to the science of man.

## I

By the turn of the century, post-Darwinian evolutionism had come to enjoy almost axiomatic status as a method of inquiry into social phenomena. The theory of progress, development, or evolution had begun life as a somewhat indeterminate philosophy of history; Darwin and Wallace had suggested practical ways in which evolution might conceivably have taken place on the biological level; and between 1859 (the year of *The Origin of Species*) and the end of the century the idea of evolution had been seized upon by a host of synthesizers and popularizers of varying attainments, and pressed into service as the one comprehensive method, the key which would unlock every door. At first a theory, by the end of the nineteenth century evolution had become an atmosphere.[4]

The most influential of the synthesizers was probably Herbert Spencer, who had attempted to show, in his *System of Synthetic Philosophy*, that

> . . . the law of organic evolution is the law of all evolution. Whether it be in the development of the Earth, in the development of Life upon its surface, in the development of Society, of Government, of Manufactures, of Commerce, of Language, Literature, Science, Art, this same advance from the single to the complex through successive differentiations, holds uniformly.[5]

To those who accepted such statements as these (and there were few who did not), it seemed that the whole of human history and experience had been brought within the scope of a single all-embracing law, and it seemed entirely feasible to speak of a single unitary science—anthropology—in which man could be studied *in evolution*. In the writings of the period one occasionally senses something of the intoxication of this new approach: witness, for instance, the writer in Hastings's *Encyclopaedia of Religion and Ethics* who affirmed that 'From the standpoint of evolution, the entire organic world, not excluding man, reveals a unity, a harmony, and a grandeur never before disclosed under any system of speculative philosophy.'[6] More soberly, it was possible for the anthropologist R. R. Marett to write in 1912 that 'Anthropology is the whole history of man as fired and pervaded by the idea of evolution. . . . Anthropology is the child of Darwin. Darwinism makes it possible. Reject the Darwinian point of view and you reject Anthropology also.'[7]

The same popular textbook in which this statement appeared shows just how comprehensive the anthropological field was: its chapter headings were Antiquity of Man (this chapter was on physical anthropology), Race, Environment, Language, Social Organization, Law, Religion, Morality, and—significantly—Man the Individual. Throughout, the approach was evolutionary and genetic; the most typical questions asked of each phenomenon or group of phenomena were 'How did it begin?' and 'Through what stages has it passed since?'*

There were, of course, points of controversy within the anthropological area. While some anthropologists held to a theory of unilinear evolution, maintaining that all else being equal, the process of development must have been more or less identical in all areas, others held to a theory of diffusion, or the spread of culture from one or two well-defined areas. Again, while on the whole the pioneer British anthropologists (among whom the names of E. B. Tylor, R. R. Marett, J. G. Frazer, and Andrew Lang are worthy of particular mention) tended to view culture in individualistic terms, their German and French counterparts (Wilhelm Wundt, Émile Durkheim, Marcel Mauss, *et al.*) were far more concerned with its social manifestations.

Throughout its history, anthropology has been peculiarly interested in the problems of religion and mythology—an interest maintained by the structuralists. In the first period, theological theories of revelation having been ruled out of court *a priori*, the anthropologists' task was taken to be that of outlining the stages through which religion had passed on its way to Liberal Protestantism, secularism, or whatever happened to be regarded as its highest point thus far. The investigator-anthropologist would collect from those sources which happened to be available to him, instances of 'primitive belief', i.e. beliefs (and to a lesser extent, practices) observed among peoples at a low level of material culture. He would then compare and contrast these with parallel material from the ancient and modern

* An important corollary was the theory of survivals, on which view there are various pockets of culture in various corners of the world (and in the mind of man) which have failed to evolve, and which can be studied *in situ* for the light they are able to throw on past stages of evolution.

civilizations, and on this basis formulate a theory of development, paying particular attention to its 'earliest' forms. Sir John Lubbock (Lord Avebury, 1834–1913) was perhaps the first to erect an entire evolutionary ladder, beginning with absolute atheism and culminating in ethical monotheism.[8] But of more significance were the animistic theories of E. B. Tylor (1832–1917), according to which religion began with a belief in spiritual beings, discerned in dream and trance.[9] R. R. Marett (1866–1943) went one step beyond this, holding that the original form of religion was a vague belief in impersonal supernatural power, which, borrowing a word from Melanesia, he called *mana*.[10] And perhaps the greatest theorist of them all, J. G. Frazer (1854–1941), author of the magisterial *The Golden Bough*, accepted the Comtean thesis of the three stages of culture, and urged that an age of magic everywhere preceded an age of religion, and that an age of science will inevitably succeed both.[11] On the social level, particular interest was paid to that phenomenon, which, following J. F. M'Lennan and W. Robertson Smith, came to be called 'totemism'—belief in the corporate affinity of a tribe or group with some animal, bird, or natural object.* The 'stage' of totemism was almost universally accepted as a necessary stage in the development of religion and of primitive society, and since it was so obviously a social, rather than a purely individual phenomenon, totemism as a theory proved highly attractive to those anthropologists who were less than completely convinced that the British individualists were on the right lines. Durkheim in particular constructed an entire theory of the origin and function of religion on the basis of totemism in his celebrated book *Les Formes élémentaires de la vie religieuse* (1912).

What all these anthropologists had in common, apart from their reliance on one or another form of the evolutionary theory, was the fact that none had had any extensive first-hand acquaintance with any 'primitive' (i.e. pre-literate) people. Their information they had perforce to find where they could—from the accounts of explorers, colonial officers, missionaries, and others. Perhaps one might argue that there was really no alternative. Engaged as they were in the heady task of sketching out the entire evolutionary history of mankind, they needed security, leisure, and opportunity to grasp the synoptic vision as it presented itself. But they had begun by assuming that the synoptic vision was in fact there to be grasped, and although

* The theory was first launched by M'Lennan in a series of articles in the *Fortnightly Review* for 1869–70, on the subject of 'The Worship of Animals and Plants'.

they were as a class by no means unaware of the dangers of undue reliance on second or third-hand material, they did tend to use their material to prove a case—a case which rested in the last resort on a philosophy of history. It was simply axiomatic that the only way to understand a phenomenon was to understand it in its historical development—not in the first instance for the light which such a study was able to throw on the mind of primitive man as such, but for the sake of the light which it was believed to throw on the developing mind of modern man. This is not to say that early anthropology was incapable of detailed descriptive work within a limited area. Such was in fact very far from being the case. But the pressures of the dominant theory ensured, first, that the final result would for the most part be expressed in given categories, determined by the kind of question which was being asked of the material, and secondly, that primitive cultures, whatever their virtues, were inevitably weighed in the balances of civilization and found wanting (though conceivably growing).

A further point which is at least worth bearing in mind is that in these same years, sociology and anthropology were not easily distinguishable.* Particularly in France, where the positivist tradition was so strong and the habits of mind fostered by the Revolution were so deeply entrenched, the identical data which served the British anthropologists so well formed the foundation of sociological theory—though with this difference, that whereas the British tendency was to seek for the emergence of 'Man the Individual', the writers of *L'Année sociologique* (Durkheim's influential periodical, founded in 1898) were far more concerned with their new-found abstraction 'society'. Again to take the example of religion, the French sociologists (anthropologists with an alternative label), led by Durkheim, were convinced that religion was, and is, a 'social fact', and that 'The forces before which the believer bows are not simple physical energies, such as are presented to the senses and the imagination; they are social forces.'[12] It was of little moment that the objection was advanced that the individual acting under the pressures of other individuals was still an individual, and that the sociologists had not broken free from individual psychology so completely as they had

* Thus we find in 1908 L. T. Hobhouse saying that 'The comparative study of religion goes together with that of jurisprudence, of ethics, of politics, and of economics, to make up the whole body of truth which forms the subject-matter of Sociology' (*Transactions of the Third Congress of the History of Religions* (1908), II. 433). The same claim might well have been made at this time of anthropology.

imagined; characteristic emphasis continued to be placed on the evolution of man in society, and anthropological data continued to be used to this end.

We have considered the original basis of anthropology at some length purely as a basis for comparison. On developments between the wars we may be more brief. In the inter-war period anthropology was dominated by an empirical method, associated above all with the names of Bronislaw Malinowski (1884–1942) and A. R. Radcliffe-Brown (1881–1945) in Britain, and by Franz Boas (1858–1942) and his disciples in America. Perhaps the most important new departure (apart, that is, from the abandonment of the evolutionary synthesis as a goal) was the recognition that the days of the 'armchair anthropologist' were over, and that it was necessary at all costs to 'come down off the verandah' and actually live among the people who were being studied. Perhaps the Victorian intellectuals were treated harshly; at all events, some found a certain pleasure in complacently trampling on the fallen colossi. But a new (and highly desirable) precision entered anthropology; the grand synthesis was succeeded by the field-work report, the scientific monograph, and the intensive cultivation of a limited area. The long historical perspectives of the post-Darwinian era were replaced by an approach in which history was very largely discounted: by a strictly empirical method in which the anthropologist had simply to deal with what confronted him, without undue regard to its ultimate provenance. By 1951 E. E. Evans-Pritchard was thus able to record that

> The viewpoint in social anthropology today may be summed up by saying that we now think we can learn more about the nature of human society by really intensive and observational studies, conducted in a series of a few selected societies with the aim of solving limited problems, than by attempting generalizations on a wider scale from literature.[13]

Most working anthropologists would certainly still agree with this judgement.

## II

It is now high time to return to Lévi-Strauss.

Developments between the wars having obliterated the last vestiges of the evolutionary synthesis in anthropology (and in other sciences), it seemed that what was being said was that no synthesis of any kind was possible—indeed, that the attempt to generalize on any grounds whatever was a faintly (or thoroughly) disreputable exercise. Lévi-Strauss, like some of the pioneers in the field, had been trained, not in anthropology, but in philosophy; and he has borne witness to his own profound interest in such diverse areas of study as geology, psychoanalysis, Marxism, and music; one might add that his own use of words suggests that there is also a good deal of the poet in his makeup.* 'Today I sometimes wonder', he wrote in his autobiographical book *Tristes Tropiques* (1955; trans. *A World on the Wane*, 1961), 'if I was not attracted to anthropology, however unwittingly, by a structural affinity between the civilizations which are its subject and my own thought-processes.'[14] Probably he was: in addition there appears a certain *tristesse* in Lévi-Strauss, a certain rejection of the values of western civilization, which has driven him to seek his own self-identity far away from its pressures, and which has ensured that he could never have been content to worship at the shrine of empirical scientific method, producing the occasional report to prove himself. In seeking for the structure of the primitive mind, and through it the structure of the mind of man, he appears to have been seeking his own mind. Again to quote from *Tristes Tropiques*:

> Anthropology affords me intellectual satisfaction: it rejoins at one extreme the history of the world, and at the other the history of myself, and it unveils the shared motivation of one and the other at the same moment. In suggesting Man as the object of my studies, anthropology dispelled all my doubts: for the differences and changes which we ethnographers deal in are those which matter to all mankind. . . .[15]

The implication is that he had set his face against evolutionism, and here we may be a little more explicit.

In his little UNESCO pamphlet *Race and History* (1958) he criticizes sharply what he calls 'false evolutionism' as being 'an attempt to wipe out the diversity of cultures while pretending to accord it full recognition'.[16] In other words, it is illegitimate to treat the varieties of human culture as being merely '*phases* or *stages* in a single line of development, starting from the same point and leading to the same end'.[17] The very idea of social or cultural evolution he holds to be a tempting, but 'suspiciously convenient' way in which otherwise intractable facts may be given some semblance of order. He

* Cf. Leach, *Lévi-Strauss*, p. 20: 'Lévi-Strauss has not actually published poetry, but his whole attitude to the sounds and meanings and permutations of language elements betrays his nature.'

suggests, further, that although it is possible to speak of some cultures as 'stationary' and others as 'moving', everything depends upon the point of view from which such observations are made. If we in the west, for instance, characterize primitive societies as being stagnant, may this not be due purely to the fact that these societies are not moving in precisely our direction, and that their values do not happen to be those which we can appreciate in an intelligent way? This he certainly believes to be the case; and he believes, further, that societies are infinitely diverse, not because of the elements of culture which each possesses (which may be more or less similar in a number of instances), but because of the different things that can be done with them, and the different combinations and permutations which are possible. To understand a remote, exotic, or primitive society, then, requires above all an understanding of the structure of its constituent parts.

In approaching this task, Lévi-Strauss derived his model from the area of linguistics, and from the structural theories of de Saussure, Jakobson, and Troubetzkoy. It was in 1945 that his first significant publication, the essay 'Structural Analysis in Linguistics and Anthropology', appeared.[18] From linguistics he derived, for instance, the ideas of infrastructure, the relations between terms, phonemic systems, and the possibility of establishing general laws of relationship. His first area of investigation was kinship systems (long an important area of anthropological investigation): 'Although they belong to another order of reality,' he noted, 'kinship phenomena are of the same type as linguistic phenomena'—since both have to do with human communication.[19] From this initial observation he proceeded to a more and more intricate analysis of kinship elements. Subsequently he published the books *La Vie familiale et sociale des Indiens Nambikwara* (1948)—based on field studies carried out in the late 1930s—and *Les Structures élémentaires de la parenté* (1949). Having been appointed in 1958 to the Chair of Social Anthropology at the Collège de France, in 1962 he published what is perhaps his most accessible work (after *Tristes Tropiques*), the two-part study *Le Totémisme aujourd'hui* and *La Pensée sauvage*.

Once more we observe here the extent to which Lévi-Strauss has taken leave of the evolutionary tradition, particularly in its long concentration on the phenomenon of 'totemism'. The elements making up totemism he holds to have been 'arbitrarily grouped and ill analysed',[20] and to have given rise to what he calls 'the totemic illusion'; nevertheless when approached afresh by way of structural analysis (as opposed to the genetic approach) they are both interesting and revealing. We cannot here recapitulate his argument, which depends on close and detailed analysis, and defies brief summary; but it is noteworthy that although he dismisses the efforts of many anthropologists in the field, he allows that two philosophers, Rousseau and Bergson, had come close to the heart of the matter, to the psychological foundations of exotic institutions,

> . . . by a process of internalization, that is, by trying on themselves modes of thought taken from elsewhere or simply imagined. They thus demonstrate that every human mind is a locus of virtual experience where what goes on in the minds of men, however remote they may be, can be investigated.[21]

Is, then, Lévi-Strauss's structural anthropology no more than an intricate game, played for the sake of the intellectual exercise it affords, but which serves merely to reinforce an unconscious process based not on analysis, but on private intuition? There are certainly those who think so. His arguments are of an indescribable intricacy; his language is allusive and often cryptic; but within this, some consider that in the last resort what he is doing is to set up before the primitive mind not a window or a prism, but a mirror. This is not a question which can be answered satisfactorily, although the critical question is if anything reinforced by his later production, such as his multi-volume *Mythologiques* (1964 ff.). However, it is the problem raised here of the nature of myth which has aroused the widest (and most respectful) attention. We may consider it briefly.

In an earlier part of this essay we pointed to the role of religion in anthropological theories of the earlier part of the century. Lévi-Strauss is not particularly interested in religion (at least not as the comparative religionist or the theologian would understand the word), but he is profoundly interested in myth—that extended verbal image in which relations between man and the supernatural order are dynamically depicted. The place of myth as one of the main modes in which religious traditions have been transmitted has been recognized for long enough. But more interest has been shown in the content of specific myths than in the form or structure of myth as a category (which, incidentally, may prove to be a dangerous abstraction; the reification of abstractions is seldom guarded against in critical discussion).

In Lévi-Strauss's view, the various elements which go to make up a myth are, like the elements which make up a society or culture, less interesting in themselves than in the way or ways in which they are combined, or structured. Working once more on the linguistic model, he identifies those elements (which are, of course, themselves linguistic) as 'gross constituent units' or 'mythemes'. These are significant, not in total isolation—Lévi-Strauss tells us that he began by separating out every single sentence of a myth, with unsatisfactory results—but in groups, complexes, or bundles. He uses the telling analogy of the full orchestral score, which has to be read diachronically from left to right, and synchronically (i.e. vertically) at one and the same time, to emphasize his point; the meaningful units are not simply the notes in each separate instrumental part, but the vertical combinations, in which a variety of instruments 'sound' simultaneously.

The actual application of this scheme to a specific myth is, however, fraught with difficulties, and reference must be made to his seminal essay 'The Structural Study of Myth',[22] in which he uses the myth of Oedipus as a test case. He sets out in vertical columns (irrespective of chronological sequence) those elements in the myth which have reference to the same type of idea or the same type of phenomenon. Reading of the columns as columns then discloses a pattern which is certainly not evident in a straightforward reading:

> The myth has to do with the inability, for a culture which holds the belief that mankind is autochthonous. . . . , to find a satisfactory transition between this theory and the knowledge that human beings are actually born from the union of man and woman. Although the problem obviously cannot be solved, the Oedipus myth provides a kind of logical tool which relates the original problem—born of one or born of two?—to the derivative problem: born from different or born from same?[23]

It is interesting, further, to note that for Lévi-Strauss, a myth is for structural purposes made up of all its variants, and not merely of its most original or purest version. He analyses an American Indian myth, the 'emergence myth' of the Zuni, with an eye to *all* its reported variants—a procedure which would have seemed suspect to earlier generations of anthropologists and comparative religionists alike.[24]

This method of dealing with myth is certainly systematic, but it remains a moot point whether it can be successfully applied in every instance. Lévi-Strauss has no doubts on that score. He claims that it brings order out of chaos, and 'it also enables us to perceive some basic logical processes which are at the heart of mythical thought'.[25] However, these 'logical processes', which were presumably operative in the mind of the myth-maker, must reflect a collective, rather than an individual mind. Hence they provide an insight, not into the mind of a man, but into the mind of Man, which, Lévi-Strauss holds, has always been basically logical.* In studying myth structurally, he concludes, '. . . we may be able to show that the same logical processes operate in myth as in science, and that man has always been thinking equally well; the improvement lies, not in alleged progress of man's mind, but in the discovery of new areas to which it may apply its unchanged and unchanging powers'.[26]

Once more we have been brought back to the same point: if the method is applied rigorously and systematically, it provides an understanding of the mind of man, always and everywhere unchanged and unchanging, cultural varieties notwithstanding. Small wonder, then, that Lévi-Strauss is at times too ethnological for the philosopher, and at other times too philosophical for the ethnologist. G. S. Kirk has written, somewhat wryly, that 'It would really be more helpful if Lévi-Strauss would announce when he was going to change roles, rather than bundle together two quite distinct approaches',[27] and even comes close to calling him a mystic—though the label is hardly appropriate. But it might not be out of place to compare the role of Lévi-Strauss at the present time with that of, say, J. G. Frazer at the turn of the century. To be sure, their actual methods could hardly be more different: but so much is the same—the patience, the industry, the ascesis, and the attempt to reach results which are not merely descriptive of particular cultures, but valid in all contexts as expressive of something inalienably human. And there are anthropologists today who, disillusioned with the extreme fragmentation of studies under the 'field-work epoch', are suggesting that it will be necessary to rediscover the lost synthesis, either by going back to Frazer, or by moving on into whatever territory Lévi-Strauss is able to open up.[28] Actually, it would be surprising if these were to prove to be the only alternatives; but the choice is a serious one, and one the implications of which would stretch far beyond the bounds of technical anthropology.

We may add one final brief word. There are few who can claim to have followed Lévi-Strauss into the dark hinterland of his thought; he makes few concessions to lesser mortals and (no doubt partly as a

* One feels that there is a more or less deliberate polemical edge here, aimed at Lucien Lévy-Bruhl and his theory of 'primitive mentality' as 'pre-logical'. Actually there is a great deal in favour of Lévy-Bruhl's theories, despite the unfortunate terms which he sometimes used. See, e.g. *Les Fonctions mentales dans les sociétés inferieures* (1910), *La Mentalité primitive* (1922), etc.

result) he has few uncritical followers.* But he has the rare gift of always suggesting more than he communicates. '*On ne revient pas indemne de la lecture des œuvres de Lévi-Strauss.*'[29]

## NOTES

[1] C. Lévi-Strauss, *The Scope of Anthropology* (1967), 51.
[2] Idem, *Structural Anthropology* (1963), 23.
[3] Ibid. 21.
[4] On this subject generally, see, e.g. J. B. Bury, *The Idea of Progress* (1932), J. Baillie, *The Belief in Progress* (1950), J. W. Burrow, *Evolution and Society* (1966).
[5] H. Spencer, *First Principles* (1860), 148.
[6] *Encyclopaedia of Religion and Ethics*, I (1909), 572.
[7] R. R. Marett, *Anthropology* (1912), 8.
[8] J. Lubbock, *The Origin of Civilisation* (1870).
[9] E. B. Tylor, *Primitive Culture* (1871).
[10] R. R. Marett, *The Threshold of Religion* (1909).
[11] J. G. Frazer, *The Magic Art*, I (1932).
[12] E. Durkheim, *De la Définition des phenomènes religieux* (1899), 24.
[13] E. E. Evans-Pritchard, *Social Anthropology* (1951), 91 f.
[14] C. Lévi-Strauss, *A World on the Wane* (1961), 56.
[15] Ibid. 62.
[16] Idem, *Race and History* (5th imp. 1968), 14.
[17] Ibid., loc. cit.
[18] This essay is reprinted in *Structural Anthropology* (1963), 31 ff.
[19] Ibid. 34.
[20] C. Lévi-Strauss, *Totemism* (Pelican ed., 1969), 83.
[21] Ibid. 176.
[22] Also reprinted in *Structural Anthropology*, 206 ff.
[23] Ibid. 216.
[24] Ibid. 219 ff.
[25] Ibid. 224.
[26] Lévi-Strauss, *Structural Anthropology*, 230.
[27] G. S. Kirk, *Myth: its Meaning and Functions in Ancient and other Cultures* (1970), 48.
[28] This point is made by I. C. Jarvie, in his book *The Revolution in Anthropology* (1964).
[29] Y. Simonis, *Claude Lévi-Strauss ou la 'passion de l'inceste'* (1968), 9.

---

* At one point even a fundamentally sympathetic commentator like Kirk loses patience with him altogether, and writes (*Myth*, p. 59) that '. . . if Lévi-Strauss wants to be taken with the seriousness that his brilliance and industry warrant, then he must abjure this Sybilline tone and make certain concessions to the rules of ordinary discourse.'

## FOR FURTHER READING

There is no modern history of anthropology which covers al the developments hinted at in this essay. Among the older histories, R. H. Lowie, *The History of Ethnological Theory* (1937) is to be recommended for background; T. K. Penniman, *A Hundred Years of Anthropology* (1935) is concerned almost entirely with physical anthropology. The pioneer anthropologists have been poorly served by biographers, though Marett wrote an illuminating biography of his distinguished predecessor *E. B. Tylor* (1936), and Marett's autobiography *A Jerseyman at Oxford* (1941) is well worth reading. Also valuable for the history of ideas of this period is Margaret Hodgen, *The Doctrine of Survivals* (1936). A general study in which anthropology is given a large place is J. W. Burrow, *Evolution and Society* (1966), one chapter of which is devoted to Tylor. Modern anthropologists are not always interested in the pioneers; an outstanding exception is E. E. Evans-Pritchard, who dissects early anthropological theories on religion in *Theories of Primitive Religion* (1965). His *Essays in Social Anthropology* (1962) contain historical material, as well as a series of essays on the Azande, and his *Social Anthropology* (1951) provides a concentrated statement of aims and methods, together with a first reading list for the apprentice anthropologist.

It is not easy to recommend elementary (as opposed to superficial) works on structuralism, and a fair knowledge of French is almost indispensable for anyone who would pass beyond the elementary stage. The veteran psychologist Jean Piaget has attempted in his *Structuralism* (1971) to lay foundations, but not altogether successfully, and the literature of specific structural methods is often of a daunting technicality. W. G. Runciman's article 'What is Structuralism?' in the *British Journal of Sociology* (1969), pp. 235 ff., is critical, but clears away much of the undergrowth. Y. Simonis, *Claude Lévi-Strauss ou la 'passion de l'inceste': Introduction au structuralisme* (1968) approaches the problem via the works of Lévi-Strauss himself, and incidentally also provides the student with a first-rate bibliography.

There are two readily accessible introductions in English to the work of Lévi-Strauss. E. R. Leach, *Lévi-Strauss* (1970) in the 'Fontana Modern Masters' series is clear and concise, and is to be highly recommended. Roger C. Poole's introduction to the Pelican edition of Lévi-Strauss's *Totemism* (1969) is also valuable, though it does not offer quite the same degree of practical guidance as does Leach's book.

Opinions differ as to the best order in which to approach the published works of Lévi-Strauss. Presumably the reader with linguistic ability and insight could start anywhere, though scarcely with *Mythologiques* (1964 ff.). Simonis's book could usefully be taken as a guide. For the reader who only has English (and giving details of only the English translations) it is undoubtedly best to begin with *A World on the Wane* (1961); as well as being autobiographical, it offers valuable clues to much which might otherwise be obscure. Next should be read his inaugural lecture *The Scope of Anthropology* (1967) and the pamphlet *Race and History* (1958), both of which show that Lévi-Strauss can be a model of lucidity when he so chooses. The next stage would be to turn to the volume *Structural Anthropology* (1963) and particularly to the essays 'Linguistics and Anthropology', 'Structural Analysis in Linguistics and in Anthropology', and 'The Structural Study of Myth'. It is at about this stage that close attention should begin to be paid to introductions and critical essays, since the going gets progressively harder from this point. *Totemism* might well come next (preceded or accompanied by a short course of reading in Victorian anthropology for balance and perspective), and then *The Savage Mind* (1966). By now the reader will either have become an addict, or be totally lost. In neither case is further guidance necessary.

It will be useful, however, to observe Lévi-Strauss's method being used by someone else. E. R. Leach, *Genesis as Myth and other Essays* (1970) and G. S. Kirk, *Myth: Its Meaning and Functions in Ancient and Other Cultures* (1970) are both good examples, one by an anthropologist, the other by a classicist. Finally, a useful symposium, edited by E. R. Leach, is *The Structural Study of Myth and Totemism* (1967).

# 7

# Linguistics

ROGER FOWLER

Language is a universal, and instantly recognizable, branch of human knowledge and behaviour: as natural as breathing, and as essential. We take it for granted, scarcely reflecting on its character or on its value to us—its many values, rather. It is our most efficient and powerful medium of communication, if we define 'communication' in its basic sense of the transmission of information between organisms, getting meaning from my brain to yours and yours to mine. It also has great personal and social significance beyond this information-channelling function. For the individual, grasp of language is closely tied up with cognitive processes, with the quality of his conceptual engagement with the world. The words he possesses, and their interrelationships, make available to him an ordering of experiences, a way of structuring the flux of percepts to which he is exposed. The semantic structure of language symbolizes 'the way things are', partly through the necessities of human thought and partly as a result of a particular society's arrangement of its knowledge and values. Language also permits and controls some more 'external' aspects of social organization. In its 'instrumental' function it helps to get things done: through language we give orders, make requests, seek information, do all kinds of things which contribute to division of labour in a complex society. We also use it to ensure the continuity of knowledge, since it is available to store information and to pass experience on from one generation to the next. It creates, reinforces, and modifies traditions, binding communities through the passage of time. It serves as a badge of solidarity, togetherness: it defines communities—cultural patterns are reflected in varieties of language use, and speakers of the same language, dialect, or variety feel that they belong together; outsiders are betrayed by their speech.

Since speakers have such profound investment in their faculty of language, it's not surprising that language is the focus for heated controversy, protectiveness, prejudice, rage, delight. The letters columns of the more conservative dailies and weeklies testify to the strength of feelings provoked by language. At a more serious level, language attracts potent myths: Adam's naming of the beasts, Babel, *Logos*. When a society recognizes the values assigned to its language, professional curiosity is aroused and we have the beginnings of academic study. Around 600 B.C. the Indian grammarian Pāṇini wrote a remarkable grammar of Sanskrit, the language of Vedic religious texts. This was the act of a conservationist intent on preserving a 'sacred' tongue, but simultaneously it was a great achievement of linguistic science. Almost continuously throughout recorded history civilized communities have had their own Pāṇinis, philosophical and descriptive grammarians. My account of linguistics is going to concentrate on language studies of the present century—and particularly, of the last fifteen years—but I want to stress that linguistics is not a new, trendy movement invented in America and popularized by middlebrow journalism. The modern science of linguistics owes its existence and vitality as much to the long and massive heritage of the past as to the (undoubtedly creative) ideas of twentieth-century linguistic thinkers.

## I

Perhaps I should say what linguistics is *not*. A 'linguist' is not a 'polyglot', a speaker of many languages; one can be very gifted at learning languages and yet remain quite innocent of the nature of what it is one has learnt. Nor is the linguist a Henry Higgins, a manipulator of other people's speech. Nor is he an academician, a legislator in linguistic matters: linguistics is a *descriptive*, not *prescriptive*, undertaking. Linguists are not concerned to set people right, to lay down the law about phonetic and grammatical etiquette, but to discover facts about what language is and how speakers actually use language. A final misunderstanding needs dispersing: it is sometimes falsely assumed (e.g. by educationists) that if linguistics is not prescriptive, it must be permissive—that linguists subscribe to a doctrine of 'anything goes'. Certainly, linguists respect actual usage above people's prejudices about usage, but at the same time they recognize that language is strictly 'rule-governed' and that mature speakers usually have fairly reliable intuitions about what is grammatical and what is not. 'Rule' for a linguist—as for any scientist—is a *constitutive* rather than *regulatory* notion. (Constitutive rules report patterns of organization in some activity or system, patterns which define the phenomenon concerned: chess, football, and language have no existence apart from the rules which define them. Regulatory rules are extrinsic, super-added: it is quite possible to eat even if one does not possess rules prescribing which hand to use to hold the fork.)

Linguistics is, then, a descriptive science with ideals parallel to those of better-known social and humane sciences: sociology, economics, psychology. Its primary motivation is quest for knowledge: linguists aim to find out whatever can be found out about particular languages and about the nature of language in general, its formal characteristics as a symbolic code, its implications for individual thought and action and for societal structure. In linguistics, the interaction of theory, analysis, and application is much the same as it is in other social sciences. Any linguistic description ('grammar') may have practical uses, and may indeed be inaugurated for some practical design: a grammar of an unlettered language which needs to be provided with an alphabet, for instance. A sociological survey of housing estates might be commissioned by a city council wishing to learn from its findings before planning new developments. Regardless of the *practical* usefulness of the results (we may emerge still not knowing whether to use a syllabic or a phonetic alphabet, whether to build tower blocks or maisonettes), the research will always have theoretical interest: an hypothesis has been checked against empirical evidence, and a bit more insight into the workings of language or society has been gained.

## II

Linguistics flourished in the nineteenth century as 'comparative-historical philology'. Hundreds of scholars in Europe collected and systematized massive quantities of information about the histories of, and relationships between, the members of the great linguistic family Indo-European. Culturally prominent tongues such as Sanskrit, Greek, English, German, French, were very thoroughly investigated, their shared characteristics and their regular divergences one from another were exhaustively documented. Apart from the sheer scale of the enterprise—reconstruction of the unrecorded ancestor primitive Indo-European and patient building up of the whole network of its offspring—there was considerable advance in the techniques and the conceptual apparatus of the subject. On the technical side one could instance growing precision in the observation and description of phonetic facts: many comparativist hypotheses about inter-language relationships could be stated only in terms of the sound-structure of language, so an adequate phonetics had to be developed. On the conceptual side, the main achievement of the nineteenth century was undoubtedly a consciousness of the essential regularity and systematicity of linguistic forms, processes, and relationships: realization of the centrality of the notion 'linguistic rule', and refinement of the procedures for arguing and stating rules ('Grimm's Law' and 'Verner's Law' are famous nineteenth-century examples).

I cannot chart the successes of the century of philology here (the history is available in Pedersen's book cited on p. 223 below); nor do I wish to seem to belittle the linguists of that time by mentioning their efforts so briefly. One deficiency has to be mentioned, though: comparative-historical linguistics was a synthesizing rather than exploratory discipline. Its theoretical framework was drawn from the Graeco-Roman 'school grammar' tradition, and to this framework were assimilated many diverse, though genetically related, languages. Since the various branches of Indo-European naturally fit this framework well enough, the model is found to work well for Indo-European, and *assumed* to work well for unrelated languages. At the turn of the century, however, American linguists and anthropologists began to encounter 'exotic' tongues which would not fit at all easily into the Latin–Sanskrit mould: the indigenous languages of North America. The challenge of these languages stimulated the building of a new linguistics, designed to be flexible enough to cope with heterogeneity of linguistic form, to avoid subjecting all tongues to the strait-jacket of Latin grammar.

Pioneers in the study of Amerindian languages, and thus in the development of modern linguistics, were Franz Boas (1858–1942) and Edward Sapir (1884–1939). They and their students amassed valuable information about these extremely varied languages, providing a convincing demonstration of the great range of structural types with which linguistic analysis must be ready to cope. At the same time, there was a tendency to begin to *use* these scattered facts in reflections on the general character of language and the obligations of linguistic science: Sapir's very readable book *Language* (1921) illustrates well the growing concern of his times for a general conception of the nature of linguistic studies, and is also a model for the connection of particular structural observations with general statements about language as a whole. 'General'—inevitably occurring three times in the previous sentence—is the key to a difference of objective between the nineteenth and twentieth centuries: the search, in our period, for a science of language transcending the given facts of the actual utterances under current analysis. The philologists had neglected the speculative, philosophical qualities of earlier discussions of language (particularly, the insights of seventeenth-century grammarians and epistemologists), so that, while comparativism was undoubtedly an impressive and instructive scholarly industry, it was hardly a *discipline*: it was not sufficiently self-conscious, did not scrutinize its own aims and methods. The new tone, the striving for a true science of general linguistics, appears in two books which contributed more than any others to the establishment of an identity for modern linguistics. One is the *Cours de linguistique générale* of the Swiss Ferdinand de Saussure (1857–1913), compiled from students' notes on his lectures and published posthumously in 1916. Equally famous is *Language* (1933) by the American Leonard Bloomfield (1887–1948). Saussure and Bloomfield bestowed very different gifts on linguistics (and two quite independent traditions, French and American structuralism, issued from their work) but they share a concern for the foundations of linguistic theory and for the identity of linguistics as a science. For Saussure, general linguistics is a branch of an overall science of signs, *semiology*. His book begins with a statement of the aims of linguistics, the culminating one being 'to define and delimit itself'—an objective which did not much occupy the philologists' attention. Definition is to be achieved through a theory of the general nature of the sign (including non-linguistic signs) and of its uses in human society. Language is a system—a structured network, not just a list—of signs; there are other sign-systems functioning in human society (fashion, architecture, gesture are among examples mentioned by Saussure's disciples), but language is the prime system. According to Saussure, a sign is an intimate union of *signifiant* and *signifié*, a two-sided coin linking on one face the object or concept symbolized and on the other the physical instrument (sounds or letters) of its symbolization. The relation between the two parts of the sign, though integral, is arbitrary, e.g. the word *tree* does not necessarily or essentially signify 'tree', but does so by convention. Saussure goes on to explore further aspects of the sign. For instance, he distinguishes between *signification* (as outlined above) and *value*, value being the meaning of a word as partly given by reference, perhaps more importantly by association with other words: 'association' captures the central structuralist principle, that the sense of a sign is a product of its place in the whole formal network of signs constituting a structured vocabulary. (This notion connects with Frege's conception of 'sense' (*Sinn*) as the key to meaning, contrasted with 'reference' (*Bedeutung*), and with Wittgenstein's analogy of language as 'game'.)

Even from this fragmentary sample of Saussure's ideas, it can be seen that he strove to characterize linguistics as an abstract, theoretical—*principled*, above all—science. I might add that he was willing to grant *psychological* status to the theoretical entities of language: for instance, he speaks of *signifiant* and *signifié* as 'acoustic image' and 'concept' respectively. In this respect Bloomfield parts company with him. Bloomfield belonged to a more pragmatic linguistic tradition than Saussure; like Saussure, he had experience of the philological process, but he was practised in the new Amerindian linguistics too. The study of Amerindian was anthropological as well as linguistic: encouraging detailed work 'in the field', it fostered practical habits of mind, an interest in the observable rather than the abstract. Bloomfield's book asserts a strict opposition of 'mechanist' and 'mentalist' styles of scientific investigation, and comes down strongly for the former. He takes the emerging physical sciences as his model, and argues for a linguistics which sticks close to *data*, to the observable facts of verbal behaviour. He denounces mentalism, believing it to be misleading and mystifying to postulate unobservable entities such as 'mind' or 'thought'. Language is to be explained only in terms of what one can see, and therefore the technique of 'seeing' becomes exceptionally important. Hence, in Bloomfield's work, an insistence on methods of observation and analysis: theory becomes the theory of *analysis*, not the theory of *language*. At least this is true of his followers, who took his advice in a very literal-minded way. For instance, Bloomfield observed that the study of meaning is bound to be the weak point in linguistics, since to state the meanings a speaker knows would entail a complete scientific description of all the objects in his universe. (This is an extremely questionable attitude to 'meaning'.) Taking this declaration very seriously, Bloomfield's followers chose to concentrate on phonetics and syntax, and devised techniques for analysis at those two more superficial levels which allegedly did not require the analyst to have recourse to semantic considerations. The stress was on field-work procedure, on the mechanics of syntactic and phonetic observation and notation; in applied linguistics, there was investment in language-learning programmes, on practical grammar-writing for underdeveloped or disappearing communities, and, after the Second World War, on machine translation and the instrumental analysis of speech. Such emphases dominated American linguistics for a good quarter-century, down to the mid-fifties. It was a practical rather than conceptual linguistics, a far cry from the style of Saussure and his descendants. However, neo-Bloomfieldian linguistics, like Saussurean, held dear the notions of system and structure. Language was thought of as a regular, formal device, capable of rational exploration and explication; and linguistics was thought of as an exact empirical science, with its own object and its own principles.

## III

Much of the effort of American structural linguistics was devoted to syntactic analysis, and it was in relation to syntax that Noam Chomsky (b. 1928), the most famous of contemporary linguists, first began to expound his controversial ideas. Ever since the appearance of his book *Syntactic Structures* in 1957, Chomsky's conception of syntactic analysis and of the nature of linguistic theory has been at the centre of argument in the discipline. Even his bitterest opponents would concede that his work has been the principal, and enduring, stimulus to a renaissance of linguistics.

Chomsky begins by careful examination of the American structuralists' (his teachers') model of syntactic analysis. They knew it as *immediate constituent analysis*, and it consists of a formalization of the traditional grammatical technique of *parsing*. Texts are divided into sentences, and each sentence is progressively broken down into its constituent parts until the smallest constituents are reached. For example, *The dogs chased the cat* is first analysed into *The dogs* (Noun Phrase, Subject) and *chased the cat* (Verb Phrase, Predicate); the Predicate consists of a Verb *chased* and an Object Noun Phrase, *the cat*. The two Noun Phrases (*the dogs*, *the cat*) resolve into combinations of Article plus Noun. Finally each word is divided into *morphemes*: *dog* + *s*, *chase* + *ed*, and (because the absence of a suffix on *cat* indicates 'singular') *cat* + $\phi$ ($\phi$ = 'zero'). There is a hierarchical relationship between the constituents as they progressively build up to the whole sentence, and this hierarchy can be shown visually in a tree-diagram, thus:

(1)

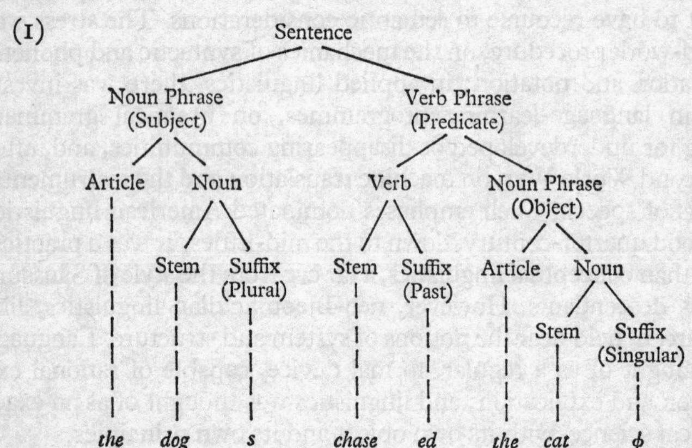

I think any reader will agree that this analysis checks with his intuitions about the structure of a simple English sentence of this type. Now Chomsky takes issue with the structuralists at this point. Although their analyses, at this level of sophistication (which is rather crude), are basically correct, they rely too much on readers' linguistic intuitions: they do not seek to *explain* linguistic structure, but simply *present* it. We need, says Chomsky, a 'generative' grammar. A generative grammar is, first, *formal* in the sense of giving a principled, step-by-step explanation of the facts of linguistic structure. 'Generative' means, secondly, 'descriptive' in a rather special sense of that word: a grammar must 'generate' or 'describe' the sentences of a language by specifying the structure of 'all and only the grammatical sentences' of that language. 'All' means what it says: a grammar must not be merely tied to the sentences the linguist has chanced to observe, but must also predict unobserved sentences —i.e. it must allow the linguist to describe every new sentence he encounters. 'Only the grammatical . . .' means that the grammar must show that sentences like *chased the dogs the cat*, *the the dogs cat edchase*, etc., are deviant. Modern structuralist grammars of the kind produced by Chomsky's immediate predecessors fail by both of these criteria. Only a grammar comprising explicit, formal, and predictive rules will do.

In *Syntactic Structures* Chomsky attempts a formalization of immediate constituent analysis by constructing the beginnings of what he calls a *phrase structure grammar*. This is a set of formal rules expressed in such terms as S → NP + VP, VP → V + NP, etc. (cf. the labels in the diagram above). His phrase structure grammar ('PSG') is very clearly expounded in several of the books recommended below, so I will not explain it here.

Chomsky is known as the inventor of 'TG' (this is not entirely accurate—he built on some ideas of his teacher Zellig Harris and he himself has repeatedly asserted that his grammar is 'traditional'). The 'G' stands for generative, 'T' for *transformational*. When he had examined the possibilities of formalizing PSG, he moved on to assess its potentialities and deficiencies. He concluded that, if a PSG *can* describe the syntactic structure of a natural language (which is doubtful) it can do so only very clumsily: many complicated and *ad hoc* rules are necessary. In *Syntactic Structures* and in his more recent writings Chomsky has argued that there are many important constructions which PSG rules cannot explain, or can explain only with great difficulty. PSG analysis works by dividing a construction into its constituent parts, noting the linear order of the parts which occur. For instance, there is a Noun Phrase *the cat* in (1) above, and its structure is generated by a rule NP → Art + N, 'a Noun Phrase consists of an Article followed by a Noun'. But often linear word-order is not a good guide to structure. Consider the italicized elements in the sentences below:

(2) He *took* his hat *off*.
(3) John *has* just eat*en* his supper.

Despite the interruption in the ordering, *took . . . off* is a single, unitary constituent, with one whole meaning (cf. *remove*); similarly with *has . . . en*, which is one of the complex ways, in English, of marking Perfect Aspect. *Take . . . off* is one unit of meaning, one constituent; but it is 'discontinuous', and discontinuous constituents cannot easily be incorporated in PSG—to test this, the reader may try drawing a tree diagram like (1) for (2) or (3): an extremely awkward enterprise.

Now compare (4):

(4) He took off his hat.

Suppose, for a moment, that we could assign an immediate-constituent analysis to (2). It is clearly easy enough to do so for (4): *took* and *off* are side by side and can be treated as one single verb. However, (2) and (4) would seem to have different structures, since they display different word-orders. Yet they have the same meaning. Chomsky points out that PSG is obviously deficient if it cannot assign the same analysis to sentences which are synonymous. Similarly, it fails by being incapable of showing certain other sentence-relationships. For instance, the active-passive relationship does not emerge from a PSG analysis; because active and passive variants have rather different constituents, and very different arrangements, they must in PSG receive quite different descriptions:

(5) Peter upset the sugar.
(6) The sugar was upset by Peter.

If we analyse these sentences according to the constituents which occur, and the orders in which they occur, we emerge with the impression that they are quite unrelated; but, given the closeness of their meanings, that cannot be so.

In many cases, PSG cannot show when one utterance has two

separate meanings (is ambiguous). Chomsky's famous example is *Flying planes can be dangerous*; two more are

(7) The chicken is ready to eat.
(8) He's a plausible actor.

'He's plausible as an actor', 'He's a plausible man who's an actor'. From the point of view of PSG, (8) is just one string of constituents, despite its double meaning:

(9) Pronoun + Copula + Article + Adjective + Noun

The analysis fails to reveal the different semantic roles played by both *plausible* and *actor* in the two interpretations.

To remedy the inherent deficiencies of PSG, Chomsky proposed that it should be supplemented by a set of *transformational* rules, rules of a quite different format from PS rules. A PS rule says simply 'an A consists of a B followed by a C'; in an alternative wording, 'the constituent A has as its constituents B followed by C'; e.g. 'S → NP + VP'. A transformational rule, transformation, or T-rule *changes* constituent-structure. For instance, if we have a string of constituents (10), we may effect the structural change indicated by the T-rule (11) to generate the new string (12):

(10) NP + *take* + *off* + NP
(11) NP + Verb + Particle + NP
⇒ NP + Verb + NP + Particle
(12) NP + *take* + NP + *off*

So we need not go through the contortions of describing (2) by PSG; (11) applied to (10) will provide (12), which is a representation of (2), among many other sentences of the same type.

Notice a very significant consequence of having the T-rule (11) in our grammar: because it takes (10) as its basis, the T-rule allows us to relate the synonymous (2) and (4)—they both have the same underlying representation (10), but (2) has undergone the transformation, (4) not. Thus transformational grammar permits us to give synonymous sentences the same analysis; PSG does not have this facility. Looking back on (5) and (6) (which are not synonymous, but are at any rate alternative descriptions of the same state of affairs), it should be clear that a similar treatment is possible here: (6) can be derived transformationally from a structure identical with, or very much like, that which underlies (5) also.

I have had to dwell on the technicalities of PSG and transformational grammar, because without this introduction it would be difficult to give an accurate picture of the *general* significance of Chomsky's work. Though the system of transformational grammar itself is the supreme and continuing interest of linguists—it has now received fifteen years of intensive study, not to mention extensive revision—Chomsky has a much wider public for his political views and for the philosophical and psychological ramifications of (or extrapolations from) his linguistic theories. (Chomsky now devotes most of his effort to radical political activities. I mention his political views—for which see his *American Power and the New Mandarins* (1969)—because they are interestingly in total harmony with his conception of the philosophy of science and of linguistics.)

On p. 1 of his 1968 book *Language and Mind*—the title itself is an indication of a broadening scope of interest since 1957—Chomsky casually refers to the 'branch of cognitive psychology known as linguistics'. This remark is both playfully provocative and literally serious. The truth of the 'institutional' content of the assertion—whether the subject linguistics is or is not part of the subject cognitive psychology—need not concern us. What is important is Chomsky's assumption that an extreme mentalist position is natural to linguistics. For some years before *Language and Mind*, in the face of opposition from the surviving unconverted Bloomfieldians, he had been arguing that the subject-matter of linguistics is not the observable characteristics of sentences and texts, but rather, psychological properties of language-users. He revived and refurbished one of Saussure's 'abstracting' distinctions, long neglected or misinterpreted outside Europe: that between *langue*, 'language', and *parole*, 'speech'. *Parole* is the concrete act of speech, utterance on a particular occasion: this Chomsky calls *linguistic performance*. For him Saussure's *langue* is *linguistic competence*, the abstract underlying system which constitutes speakers' linguistic knowledge—the tacit knowledge which speakers have internalized and which enables them to use language. The object of linguistics is competence, not performance; not performance, because performance reflects not only the basic communicative ability of speakers, but also linguistically irrelevant factors—hesitations, slips of the tongue, distractions causing sentences to remain uncompleted or to change structure in mid-course, and so on. A grammar should be a representation of linguistic competence, with all these unfortunate performance factors 'idealized' away. Thus a grammar is an hypothesis about unobservables in the minds of speakers, not a mere organized rehearsing of the observed facts of linguistic behaviour. Most linguists nowadays would accept this statement of the aims of linguistics, although (as I shall argue below) it is now clear that Chomsky's view of linguistic performance is unnecessarily impoverished and negative: competences additional to his 'linguistic competence' must be proposed to explain fully the richness of the act of speaking.

Chomsky's redefinition of the goals of linguistics has had many consequences for the progress of the discipline and the attitudes of its followers. I want to mention two implications which are particularly important for the character and the activities of linguistics. First, transformational-generative grammar, in its general formulation as given by Chomsky, provides a new way of looking at sentences, at actual language samples. Second, it offers a way of making linguistics more than a routine charting of the structures of languages: it leads to the possibility of connecting the nature of language and the nature of man. In the period of Bloomfieldian linguistics, justifications for the subject tended to be offered in mundanely utilitarian terms—accurate grammars would help with language-teaching, translation, and so forth. Since the 'Chomskyan revolution', there has been a revival of the traditional emphasis on the interrelations between linguistic, psychological, and philosophical studies: we want to know about language and about languages because this knowledge may help us understand some very crucial characteristics of man the symbol-user. (From the standpoint of contemporary linguistics, 'naked ape' is an impertinent and inaccurate characterization!)

We may approach the second, more ambitious, aspect of the new linguistics by way of the first—the new way of looking at sentences. For Chomsky, sentences are only *data*, not *subject-matter*: since we are primarily interested in *langue*, observed utterances are interesting chiefly in so far as they provide insight into the linguistic competence which they (indirectly) reflect. This attitude leads to, frankly but not destructively, a rather sceptical focus on sentences, a suspicious vision, unwillingness to take them at their face value. For instance, the sentence *He took his hat off*, with its discontinuous structure, is viewed as an unstraightforward realization of a more abstract entity in which there is semantic unity, no discontinuity between the meanings of *take* and *off*. The difference with (4), *He took off his hat*, is that it reveals its underlying structure more directly. An analogous —though not entirely the same—commentary would be relevant to (5) and (6) above (the active/passive pair): they are very different on the surface, but at some more abstract level they must be rather similar—not identical in meaning, but presumably having the same cognitive content with the reader invited to focus on the event in different ways. Transformational grammar deals with such cases by positing a distinction between *surface structure* and *deep structure*: (2) and (4) have the same deep structure, different surface structures; (5) and (6) have different surface structures, almost the same deep structure. Conversely, each of the ambiguous utterances (7) and (8) is one surface structure underlain by two deep structures. Every sentence may be regarded as a union of two levels of structure. At the more superficial level, there is all the information relevant to its existence as a string of words and morphemes, and ultimately much of the information which governs its physical form as pronounced or written down. The abstract, underlying level of structure contains all information relevant to the meaning of a sentence. A structural description of a sentence must therefore show (*a*) its analysis at the level of sound; (*b*) its analysis at the level of meaning; (*c*) its transformational structure. Even though the details of (*a*) and (*b*) are controversial in present-day linguistics, it is obvious that the two levels themselves are rationalizations of essentially traditional concepts. The innovation is (*c*)—the proposal that sound and meaning are related by the device of transformation.

In the most recent version of transformational grammar (which seems not to have Chomsky's blessing), sentences are described in approximately the following way. The basis is a very abstract set of semantic components conveying the objects, concepts, and processes being communicated, with these semantic materials in certain primitive relationships such as 'actor-action', 'process-object', etc. Presumably, this complex of elements of meaning answers to the immediate communicative intentions of the speaker; but also, the speaker is not absolutely free to structure his linguistic intentions as he wills. The themes and objects of discourse must be in some way restricted by factors outside his choice: first, by the cognitive dispositions he enjoys simply through being a human organism; second, by that particular adaptation of his human world-view which is enforced by his belonging to one rather than another society. I shall have more to say in a moment about these 'unwilled' semantic constraints. The point to be observed here is that the basis of an act of communication is something totally abstract (but certainly not ineffable: semantic structure is describable); the theory of transformations explains its 'concretization'—the way a message gets expressed in the form of a physical signal. Linguists describe sentences by showing how an ordered sequence of applications of transformational rules, forming and reforming transitional structures, eventuates in a 'pronounceable' surface structure. For the details of this mode of description, see any of the textbooks cited below, p. 223.

Through the device of transformation, the linguist is able to show, in a systematic way, how observed linguistic surface is underlain by unobservable structures of meaning. He is able also to demonstrate that language is a good deal more orderly than appears on the surface. If we look only at the superficial structure of language, without pushing back to its underlying form through the transformational process, we are likely to assume that sentences are more random and haphazard, languages more diverse one from another, than they actually are. European linguists have generally assumed the homogeneity and systematicity of language as a general phenomenon, and after the coming of TG contemporary American linguistics began to provide a means for demonstrating this coherence. But American linguistics before Chomsky, linguistics in the Bloomfield tradition, was committed to the opposite attitude: as one of its exponents (Martin Joos) put it, 'languages could differ from each other without limit and in unpredictable ways'. Nowadays, it is obvious that this view must be incorrect: if language structure were literally unpredictable, there could be no restriction on the sort of thing which might count as a language; but we know that Russian and French and English are languages, that *Finnegans Wake* and *Lessness* are made out of language, that the word 'language' in such expressions as 'the language of flowers', '. . . of chess', '. . . of dancing', '. . . of music' is used metaphorically. Though, as Roland Barthes has reminded us, we must be watchful for semiological systems (like those just cited) which are somewhat modelled on language, we know that there is a dividing line and that some phenomena are recognizably on one side of it, some on the other. We now see that the American structuralists' refusal to put limits on possible language forms was a result of being over-impressed by variety of surface structures, of emphasizing *observation* rather than *explanation*, of failing to see surface structures as partially misleading transforms of more abstract, regular, and language-invariant deep structures.

The mistake of the structuralists is now so obvious to us that it is difficult to believe a simplistic 'observationalist' view could have been held only fifteen years ago; but if we listen to Joos again, editing a reader in American linguistics in 1958, we find him speaking like the inhabitant of a topsy-turvy world. He takes Troubetzkoy to task for 'offering too much of a phonological *explanation* where a sober *taxonomy* would serve as well', and continues: 'Children want explanations, and there is a child in each of us; descriptivism makes a virtue of not pampering that child.' Surely the values of the world of American linguistics on which Joos was reporting had become unnaturally—and unscientifically—inverted? Surely we (like creatively imaginative children) ought to want to understand, not simply to perceive the appearances of things? And what is to be more desired, if the linguist requires a valuable goal, than an explanation of the general nature of language?

The separation of semantic from phonetic structure, or deep from surface structure, or meaning from sound, and the proposal that the members of these oppositions are linked by transformations, is a procedure very much compatible with a search for linguistic universals. Sapir and Saussure participated in this search; Chomsky now announces it as the primary goal of linguistics; before Chomsky a model for a 'universalist' generative linguistics had been provided by Roman Jakobson. Jakobson was born in Russia in 1896 and received his linguistic education not in the Boas/Bloomfield American school but in cosmopolitan, modernist Europe between the wars. He was a founder of the Linguistic Circle of Prague and a friend of the great phonologist Prince Nicholas Troubetzkoy (1890–1938). Jakobson has lived in America since 1941. His learning, command of languages, and range of interests are of Nabokovian proportions, but, following the influence of Troubetzkoy, his enduring interest has been the universal principles of sound-structure in natural languages. In a succession of short, imaginative monographs published from the forties onwards, he has argued that the *distinctive* sounds of language—the 'phonemes' which are employed significantly to mark oppositions of meaning (*pin* from *bin*, *thigh* from *thy*, etc.)—are built by selecting sound-elements from a small, finite inventory of available phonetic oppositions. For example, there is the opposition between consonants that are 'voiced' (articulated with vibrating vocal cords) and those that are 'voiceless' (the vocal cords open and passive): *b* versus *p*, *g* versus *k*, the two contrasting *th* sounds, etc. Or there is the contrast between nasal and non-nasal vowels—in the first case the sound issues from the nose as well as the lips. Such contrasts are universally available, and each language makes its own distinctive selection: French employs the opposition between nasal and non-nasal vowels, English does not. Jakobson's hypothesis allows us to account for the overt dissimilarities among individual languages (at the level of sound) by reference to universal principles which ensure the covert homogeneity of language as a general institution: phonetic heterogeneity is explained by appeal to universals of sound-structure.

Jakobson's theory of universal sound-structure is conceived and expressed in quite abstract terms—it is a schematization of the facts of raw sound. Yet it also makes perfect sense transposed into *biological* terms. The sound-producing apparatus of human beings does not vary substantially from individual to individual or from race to race. Thus there is every reason to suppose that the potentialities for phonation will be the same for all (biologically normal) speakers of any language. Physical restrictions upon sound-production must be constant for all speakers, hence some such basic universal repertoire of phonetic distinctions as that sketched in Jakobson's hypothesis is naturally to be expected. But since human societies shape their behaviour according to idiosyncratic cultural conventions, culture-specific arrangements of elements from a species-wide stock, we would also expect distinctive linguistic selections from the universal range; and this is what happens with sounds. The importance of Jakobson's theory is that it presents distinct languages as not randomly divergent (as the American structuralists would have had us believe) but regularly related to a common linguistic core.

Jakobson's linguistic universals are discovered at the level of sound. Can the principles which govern the theory be extended to the other, more abstract, levels of linguistic form? It would seem so. Phonetic universals exist not only because the peripheral organs of articulation—lips, tongue-shape, etc.—are more or less uniform throughout the species; probably the most important biological factor determining linguistic universals is the constant nature of man's central nervous system. If the characteristics of brain structure which control language are shared by all human beings, we must predict that every language is built on the same semantic and syntactic, as well as phonetic, principles. (The anatomical and physiological evidence relevant to this argument is summarized in Lenneberg's book cited on p. 223 below.) Note that this prediction (like Chomsky's straight-faced quip about linguistics and cognitive psychology) once more commits us to an extreme mentalist position: the essential characteristics of language are assumed to be explicable as a product of the 'nature of man' rather than as an almost accidental outcome of individual man's interaction with his environment. Chomsky proclaims this commitment in his book *Cartesian Linguistics* (1966), in which he aligns modern generative linguistics with the ideas of the rationalist philosophers of the seventeenth and eighteenth centuries. In this and a number of other publications he condemns the empiricist bent of American structural linguistics, most particularly empiricist theories of language-learning (where it is held that language is a set of habits picked up from external sources, for instance by imitating the speech of others because one is rewarded if one behaves in that way). Chomsky maintains that this explanation (which is Bloomfield's, B. F. Skinner's, etc.) at the very best imputes an extraordinarily inefficient learning process to the child—how would he have the *time* to learn all the sentences of a natural language, if he had to copy them one by one?—and at the worst is totally wrong-headed. He counters with the 'innatist' thesis, claiming that language-structure is largely inborn, a natural faculty of man which depends only on maturation, and minimal example from the speech of others, for its release.

There is a great deal of circumstantial evidence, and some experimental evidence, for the basic rightness of the innatist thesis as applied to language—and very little good support for the stronger versions of the empiricist argument (e.g. the 'blank slate' metaphor traditionally applied to the newborn infant's competence). Nowadays, many psycho-linguists would admit that Chomsky underplayed the function of environment in language-learning: that his innatist theory is somewhat exaggerated. However, this is no place to argue the exact balance of nature and nurture in language-learning; I want simply to draw attention to the consequences for general linguistic theory of allowing nature a substantial part. It means that we may devise certain hypotheses about the necessary form of language, for testing in our investigations of particular tongues. For instance, we might make a number of (testable) assumptions about syntactic universals: that all languages have transformations, that transformations fall into a limited set of structural types—permutation rules, deletion rules, amalgamation rules—that some operations are prohibited. (E.g. Chomsky has predicted that there are no 'structure-independent' transformations: no rules for turning, say, A: *John is easy to please* into B: *Please to easy is John*, where A becomes B by mere reversal of physical sequence. The only operations one may perform on A are ones which take into account its *structure* rather than the crude linear order of its words.) Armed with a body of hypotheses about the syntactic privileges generally open in language, the linguist can examine how these privileges are exploited differentially in particular tongues. For example, he will discover that in Indo-European languages certain types of reordering rule govern the modification of nouns by adjectives and relative clauses. He will notice that, within this shared matrix of rule-types, differences emerge: in most styles of English the adjective precedes the noun, whereas in French most adjectives follow their head nouns. The syntactic rule-types controlling adjective–noun concatenations are just the same, but English happens to be more complicated, since an extra rule-application is needed (in the usual analysis) to get the adjective in front of the noun.

I hope the analogy with Jakobsonian phonetics is clear: differential selection from common resources. The advanced mentalism of Chomsky's argument is significant—he proposes that the 'algebraic' possibilities of language are dictated by the species-uniform structure of the mind.

This deterministic mentalism once granted, we can proceed to more ambitious speculations about linguistic universals. Some of the most exciting research in recent years has been the investigation of semantic structure: aspects of language deep below the observable surface of utterances. Although the vocabularies of languages differ enormously as a result of cultural and technological discrepancies, these are only superficial differences in the range of the word-stock: if one language has fifty words for kinds of parrot, another a large vocabulary concerned with air travel, another a proliferation of words having to do with ice and snow, we are entitled to assume no more than that the objects named figure prominently in the environments of the speakers of these languages.

The once-fashionable 'linguistic relativity hypothesis' of Benjamin Lee Whorf (1897–1941) argued (on the basis of just such data as that referred to in the previous sentence, plus syntactic evidence) that differences of language-structure reflected, or correlated with, or in the strongest interpretation *caused* differences of 'world-view' as between speakers of distinct languages. Contemporary semantic theory disputes Whorf's thesis (which is based on observation of very superficial aspects of structure). We now assume that since speakers the world over exhibit no significant differences in cerebral make-up, and since, despite technological discrepancies, all societies inhabit the same space–time universe, our cognitive and thus semantic dispositions must be uniform. Intended messages can only be shaped in accordance with our natural world-view, and for all speakers there must be shared notions such as the separateness of objects, the similarity of some and the disparateness of others, persistence of objects in time, convergence, contact, and divergence, causation, change, agency, passivity, and so on. I can do no more than mention two facets in the recent many-sided progress towards constructing a semantic theory based on such assumptions. There is *componential analysis*, a technique devised by anthropological linguists in the 1950s: working on highly structured sections of vocabulary such as kinship terminology, or systems of nomenclature for families of plants and animals, they determined that the most economical way of presenting their analyses was to represent each word as an individual set of primitive semantic components. The components recur in different words, so each word can be displayed as a particular selection of elements drawn from a basic stock. The economy of this system (as, *mutatis mutandis*, with Jakobsonian phonetics) is that a large number of word-meanings can be constructed from a small number of elementary semantic 'atoms'. There is the added advantage that, because the same semantic components are found in different words, the meanings of words can be related to one another through possession of the same, or contrasted, or otherwise linked components. For instance, we can see that the words *man*, *woman*, *child*, *boy*, *girl* all belong to the same semantic system if we represent them thus:

| | | |
|---|---|---|
| (13) | man: | [+ HUMAN, + ADULT, + MALE] |
| | woman: | [+ HUMAN, + ADULT, − MALE] |
| | child: | [+ HUMAN, − ADULT, ± MALE] |
| | boy: | [+ HUMAN, − ADULT, + MALE] |
| | girl: | [+ HUMAN, − ADULT, − MALE] |

(The terms in small capitals are not *words*, of course, but the names of semantic features.) Actually, other components are needed to complete the definitions, but since they are implied by the components I have mentioned in (13), they need not be given explicitly. Any word-meaning which contains the component [+HUMAN] must contain [+ANIMATE] (and contrast *stone*, *sincerity*, which are [−ANIMATE]); also [+HUMAN] implies [+ORGANIC] (*daisy* and *cabbage* are also [+ORGANIC] but they are [−HUMAN] and [−ANIMATE]); finally, [+CONCRETE] is a component in the meanings of all the words in (13)—and *stone*, *daisy*, *cabbage*, but not *sincerity*. Notice that the semantic features mentioned in (13) (and the ones necessary to complete the definitions of the words therein) are very abstract and general; it is easy to think up examples of other words into whose meanings they enter, in English and in other languages. We would expect such features to be universal: they code cognitive contrasts which are surely indispensable to the human being's intellectual engagement with the world, and if so they will recur in all languages. Superficial heterogeneity of word-stock conceals basic similarity of semantic structure; the recurrent semantic 'atoms' reflecting universal conceptual categories which in turn reflect the structure of mind.

The second major enterprise in 'universal semantics' which deserves mention is *case grammar* or *role grammar*. If componential analysis concerns the relationships between word-meanings in abstract, outside sentences, case grammar is a way of looking at semantic structure within propositions. The former is the 'vertical' axis of structure, Saussure's 'associative' or 'paradigmatic' dimension; the latter, the 'horizontal' or 'syntagmatic'. It has been pointed out in the last few years that functional notions such as 'subject' and 'object', which are fundamental to traditional as well as Chomskyan grammar, are actually too crude to capture distinctions in structure found in the propositions of natural language. For instance, (14) below is ambiguous:

(14) William crushed the box.

This may mean (*a*) that he took a sledgehammer to it; (*b*) that he (accidentally) sat on it. In interpretation (*a*) William is *agent*—we think of him as a person actively, deliberately, performing an action; but in (*b*) we think of William as a body, a physical thing not *acting* but simply the immediate tangible cause of the crushing. In (*b*) William is *instrument* (like the sledgehammer or whatever other instrument is involved in (*a*)). Under both (*a*) and (*b*) interpretations, the box is *patient*. *Agent*, *instrument*, and *patient* are 'cases' or 'roles'. As a second example, consider (15) and (16):

(15) I was singing a song.
(16) I was rewriting a song.

In traditional grammar, as in Chomskyan generative grammar, the noun phrase *a song* performs the same function—object—in both sentences. But the semantic role is different. The state of the object *a song* in (15) is not changed; the phrase merely 'completes' the meaning of the verb; so we say that *a song* in (15) is the *complement* of the verb. But in (16) *a song* has the same semantic role as *the box* in (14): it is *patient*, that which is affected by the process designated by the verb. There is a song which antedates the action of (16), and it is changed by the action of (16); but in the case of (15), *a song* is mentioned only to contrast with *a madrigal*, *an aria*, etc.: it specifies what is being sung (and singing it does not change it).

We see from the above examples that the syntactic concepts 'subject' and 'object' indiscriminately gather together types of noun phrase which actually perform very different semantic roles. The new 'case grammar' is an attempt to enumerate the range of such semantic functions. 'Cases' had been neglected in English grammatical studies because they are not signalled in English surface-structure as they (or many of them) are in highly inflected languages such as Finnish, Greek, Latin. The leading proponent of case grammar, Charles J. Fillmore (b. 1929), has argued that the absence of morphological markers of case (inflectional endings such as Latin *-a*, *-am*, *-ae*, etc.) should not deter us from positing different cases for apparently identical noun phrases—which is what I did for *William* and *a song* in the examples above. This argument of Fillmore's is within the spirit of contemporary linguistics by its refusal to take surface-structure at its face value (but a Fillmorean grammar would be very different from a Chomskyan grammar, since the former would not put the 'deep structure/surface structure' distinction in anything like the terms of the latter). Also, the mistrust of surface structure, the hypothesizing of covert, abstract forms of linguistic organization predictably goes with a search for universals. Fillmore suggests that there is a set of cases or roles common to all languages, and that this set corresponds to the basic cognitive dispositions of mankind—the natural necessity that we should regard objects, concepts, events, etc., as existing in certain kinds of relationships: so, for instance, a human being mentioned in a sentence may figure as an agent, a patient, an instrument, a beneficiary, an experiencer, and so on. Fillmore suggests, very plausibly, that language has these categories because of the nature of the conceptual universe to which language (indisputably, most intimately) relates.

## IV

It would have been impossible, in one chapter, to offer a categorized survey of the activities of contemporary linguistics, and so my contribution to this volume has had to be brutally selective—some will say, selective to the point of misrepresentation. Some of the modern linguistic traditions I have omitted are: the Copenhagen School of 'glossematics' presided over by Louis Hjelmslev (b. 1899); the Prague School; the various European traditions descending from Saussure (the 'Geneva School', modern French semiology, etc.); the 'Firthian' tradition of London and (for a time) Edinburgh, a distinctive style of linguistics stimulated by the insightful and generous writings of J. R. Firth (1890–1960), holder of the first professorship of linguistics to be established in England; the British tradition of descriptive phonetics and its most distinguished exponent Daniel

Jones (1881–1967); and no doubt I have oversimplified the story of modern American linguistics. Among the topics not mentioned are: the whole field of applied linguistics—computational linguistics including information retrieval, mechanical translation, and concordance-making, applications of linguistics to communications engineering, to language-teaching (particularly, programmed courses in books or on tapes), to literary analysis, etc.; experimental phonetics, which has been revolutionized by the invention and development of precise measuring and synthesizing instruments since the Second World War; the more pragmatic side of psycholinguistics, involving experimental investigation into such matters as the relationship between linguistic structure and learning, memory, perception, understanding and misunderstanding; studies in the breakdown of language (*aphasia*) and its causes; inquiries into the anatomical, physiological, and neurological correlates of language; and many more linguistic and semi-linguistic areas of research.

I particularly regret having to omit description of modern work in sociolinguistics, anthropological linguistics, or ethnography of communication. The gravest (and most obvious) defect of the generative models of grammar, Chomsky's and related grammars, is their total neglect of language in its social context. Generative grammar is concerned with the explanation of patterns within sentences; it takes the phenomenon language as an isolatable system and pushes deeper and deeper inside the system. From the point of view of generative linguistics, there are aspects of verbal behaviour which are not relatable to the system of grammar, and thus appear random and uninteresting: for instance, all facts about style, about appropriacy of language to cultural context, all facts about the relative frequency of linguistic units and structures. These are aspects of linguistic *performance*, and Chomsky's version of linguistic performance (see above, p. 210) sometimes suggests a kind of convenient waste-bin into which any difficult or inexplicable linguistic facts can be dumped. Sociolinguistics may be thought of as taking over where linguistics leaves off: the linguist has to 'idealize' language-data in order that grammars may be written at all, and the sociolinguist takes responsibility for many of the facts which are too coarse to pass through the linguist's purifying sieve. What is random, variable, deviant, to the linguist, assumes pattern, regularity, and meaning under the sociolinguist's eye: the latter sees linguistic performance as obeying meaningful cultural conventions, adding the social dimension to the linguist's informational dimension. (Further reading on sociolinguistics is recommended on pp. 223–4 below.) This new emphasis has important *psycholinguistic*, as well as sociolinguistic, implications. The 'branch of cognitive psychology known as linguistics' explains only one part of speakers' communicative competence, the ability to associate sounds and meanings in sentences; sociolinguistic theory adds to this necessarily limited model a concern to explain why and how speakers are able to select sentences appropriate to the context of utterance. This study of speakers' linguistic interaction with and response to patterns of social organization should be seen as complementary to and integratable with the study of language in the narrower sense found in generative linguistics. Linguistics and sociolinguistics are not, as some have alleged, antagonistic; together they interrelate as the major components of a general theory of the language faculties of man.

A final word on the notion of 'theory'. In this chapter I have chosen not to present a list of the more practical branches of the linguistic sciences, and I have specifically ignored concrete applications of linguistics—demonstrable, beneficial technological by-products of the sort which generally make a science attractive to non-specialists. Moreover, I have narrated, with approval, the movement of linguistics in the last fifteen years away from an empiricist, pragmatic style to a speculative, abstract mode of inquiry. Linguistics has become 'theoretical' to an unprecedented degree. But though linguists are undeniably searching for an understanding of abstract entities, the enterprise is not 'metaphysical' in the pejorative sense of that word—inaccessible, uncommunicable, unreal, not useful, and therefore irresponsible. We can tell, by comparing the superficial structures of utterances with what we know them to mean, that there is more to language than meets the eye. Therefore, a scientific understanding of language is not to be achieved by mere observation and mechanical analysis of the surface properties of discourse; we need instead to form hypotheses about the underlying nature of the subject under investigation, hypotheses which can be tested empirically and rejected or adopted. A body of validated hypotheses is a theory, an explanation of *how* something (e.g. language) works; it is not necessarily 'unreal' for being expressed in abstract terms. This is the way reputable sciences proceed. Finally, once a theory has been built, once the phenomenon has been explained, 'consumers' of a science can benefit by its application in social engineering. The theory of generative grammar is by no means stable yet, nor does it approach comprehensiveness (as I have just pointed out, it needs to be complemented by a powerful sociolinguistic theory). But its hypotheses are already far richer than the generalizations of postwar American structuralism, and we can expect the eventual practical benefits of the new linguistics to be richer in proportion.

## FOR FURTHER READING

Histories of linguistics: Holger Pedersen, trans. J. W. Spargo, *Linguistic Science in the Nineteenth Century* (Cambridge, Mass., 1931; reissued 1962 as *The Discovery of Language*); R. H. Robins, *A Short History of Linguistics* (1967); John T. Waterman, *Perspectives in Linguistics* (Chicago, 1963). Useful surveys, partly bibliographical, are Christine Mohrmann *et al.*, *Trends in European and American Linguistics, 1930–1960* (Utrecht and Antwerp, 1961); Mohrmann *et al.*, *Trends in Modern Linguistics* (Utrecht and Antwerp, 1963); and Bertil Malmberg, trans. Edward Carney, *New Trends in Linguistics* (Stockholm, 1964).

Introductory books on linguistics: Dwight Bolinger, *Aspects of Language* (New York, 1968); David Crystal, *Linguistics* (Harmondsworth, 1971); Roger Fowler, *Understanding Language* (1973); H. A. Gleason, Jr., *An Introduction to Descriptive Linguistics* (2nd ed., New York, 1961); Charles F. Hockett, *A Course in Modern Linguistics* (New York, 1958); R. W. Langacker, *Language and its Structure* (New York, 1967); John Lyons, *Introduction to Theoretical Linguistics* (1968). *New Horizons in Linguistics*, ed. John Lyons (Harmondsworth, 1970) collects a number of excellent papers on most branches of the linguistic sciences, but is not as easy as some of the other books listed above.

Some primary texts which are relatively accessible: Leonard Bloomfield, *Language* (New York, 1933); Roman Jakobson, *Child Language, Aphasia and Phonological Universals* (The Hague, 1969); Edward Sapir, *Language* (New York, 1921); Ferdinand de Saussure, *Course in General Linguistics*, ed. Charles Bally and Albert Sechehaye; trans. Wade Baskin (New York, 1959).

The major works of Chomsky are *Syntactic Structures* (The Hague, 1957) and *Aspects of the Theory of Syntax* (Cambridge, Mass., 1965), but non-specialists will find these books hard going. More readable are *Language and Mind* (New York, 1968) and 'The Formal Nature of Language', Appendix A in E. H. Lenneberg, *Biological Foundations of Language* (New York, 1967). (Lenneberg's book is also to be read in its own right; see p. 215 above.) Perhaps the best place to begin is *Chomsky: Selected Readings*, conveniently edited by J. P. B. Allen and Paul Van Buren (1971). See also John Lyons, *Chomsky* (1970).

Textbooks on transformational grammar include Emmon Bach, *An Introduction to Transformational Grammars* (New York, 1964); Roger Fowler, *An Introduction to Transformational Syntax* (1971); Roderick A. Jacobs and Peter S. Rosenbaum, *English Transformational Grammar* (Waltham, Mass., 1968); Andreas Koutsoudas, *Writing Transformational Grammars* (New York, 1966); D. Terence Langendoen, *The Study of Syntax* (New York, 1969); Langendoen, *Essentials of English Grammar* (New York, 1970). Langendoen's second book incorporates material on 'case grammar' (see above, p. 220).

Some writings in sociolinguistics: introductory textbooks: Joshua Fishman, *Sociolinguistics* (Rowley, Mass., 1970); J. B. Pride, *The Social Meaning of Language* (1971). David Crystal and Derek Davy, *Investigating English Style*

(1969) contains much practical exemplification, and is based on the distinctively British concept of 'register' (though the authors eschew the term). Perhaps the best introduction to sociolinguistics is provided by the many collections of essays and field studies: e.g. J. Fishman, *Readings in the Sociology of Language* (The Hague, 1968); J. J. Gumperz and Dell Hymes, *The Ethnography of Communication* (Special Volume of *American Anthropologist*, 1964); Hymes, *Language in Culture and Society* (New York, 1964).

An example of applied linguistics: linguistics and literature: *Literary Style: A Symposium*, ed. Seymour Chatman (New York, 1971); *Essays on the Language of Literature*, ed. S. Chatman and Samuel R. Levin (Boston, 1967); *Essays on Style and Language*, ed. Roger Fowler (1966); Roger Fowler, *The Languages of Literature* (1971); *Linguistics and Literary Style*, ed. Donald C. Freeman (New York, 1970); Geoffrey N. Leech, *A Linguistic Guide to English Poetry* (1969); Samuel R. Levin, *Linguistic Structures in Poetry* (The Hague, 1962); *Style in Language*, ed. Thomas A. Sebeok (Cambridge, Mass., 1960).

# 8

# Psychology

IAN M. L. HUNTER

Psychology is traditionally defined as the systematic study of mind, and the purpose of this chapter is to outline ideas which enriched British psychology between 1945 and 1965. However, it must be stressed that these ideas were part of an international scene embracing all economically developed countries and so it would be misleading to pay too close attention to national boundaries. Let us begin with two broad questions. What were the dominant features of psychological developments in this period? And, why did these developments take place?

### *Intensified Empirical Inquiry*

Perhaps the best answer to our first question is: an intensification and diversification of empirically oriented inquiries. The twenty years saw rapid increases in the amount of effort devoted to psychological studies, the variety of contexts within which these studies were pursued, the number of specialized branches of psychology, and the collaboration of psychologists with workers in other disciplines. Furthermore, these studies were predominantly and increasingly empirical: they sought to answer questions by assembling observations of an objective kind; they emphasized careful gathering of data and rigorous testing of hypotheses by statistical and experimental means; they distinguished factual issues from speculation, and were prone to avoid debates about grand theories which did not lend themselves to factual verification and prediction. This intensification and diversification occurred in other countries besides Britain, notably the U.S.A., which retained its firm pre-eminence in psychology, and the result might be described as an explosion of empirical inquiry. Let us consider manifestations of this explosion.

Within Britain, the explosion was seen in the number and size of psychology departments at universities and other institutions of advanced study, in the number of people employed as professional psychologists, and in the variety of learned societies devoted wholly or partly to psychological studies. Within universities, there were, in 1945, six professorial chairs of psychology (at Cambridge, Edinburgh, Birkbeck College in London, University College in London,

Manchester, and Reading). In 1965, there were forty chairs. During these years it became increasingly possible for undergraduates to specialize in psychology and, further, to make graduate careers as psychologists in education, industry, hospitals, the Civil Service, and Government establishments. New societies arose to cater for specialized and inter-disciplinary interests in, for example, animal behaviour, human work and efficiency, child development, programmed instruction, clinical psychology, and social psychology. Of these new societies, the Experimental Psychology Society was noteworthy. It was founded in 1946 to enable a small group of psychologists to discuss experimental work of a rigorous and quantitative kind. In 1948, it began to publish the *Quarterly Journal of Experimental Psychology* and, although its membership was deliberately kept small, the Society grew to include active contributions from physicists, neurologists, pharmacologists, and computer scientists. The activities of this Society reflected growing contacts between psychology and other disciplines (in this case, biological and physical sciences), greater availability of new techniques of investigation, and increasing needs for experimental laboratory studies. The growing professional responsibilities of psychologists were also reflected in the British Psychological Society (founded 1901) to which most British psychologists belonged. In 1945, this Society had a British membership of just over one thousand and could be joined by anyone interested. By 1966, it had two-and-a-half thousand members and could be joined only by people with graduate qualifications in psychology; it had just blessed the formation, by its Australian branch, of an independent Australian Psychological Society with a thousand members; it had just received a Royal Charter which, among other things, acknowledged its scientific and social usefulness; and it was publishing, apart from its quarterly house bulletin, five research journals—in general, educational, medical, mathematical and statistical, and social and clinical psychology.

Perhaps the most tangible evidence of explosion was the increase in new psychological literature. The professional psychologist, whatever his special interest, faced a mounting spate of research journals, books reporting recent work, and series giving periodic surveys of advances. Much of this literature was home produced, but most of it came from the U.S.A. while a significant proportion came from the Soviet, European countries, Commonwealth countries, and Japan. For undergraduates, there were more, and larger, introductory textbooks. For example, Munn's *Psychology* (1946) aimed to provide a comprehensive, unbiased, up-to-date, and empirically oriented introduction to the entire field of psychology. By 1965, it had undergone four extensive revisions and had been joined by more than a dozen worthy competitors which, with minor variations, conformed to the same overall pattern. By 1965, growing undergraduate needs had also created a host of texts which pursued restricted topics in greater depth. This output of student-oriented publication was a boon to university teachers: it was also a historically important contribution to the internationalization of knowledge about, and attitudes to, psychology. Students in Oslo, Oxford, Otago, and Ohio were familiar with many of the same texts: a student in Edinburgh would be as likely to know of recent work at Cambridge, Massachusetts, as at Cambridge, England. To an unprecedented extent, students in widely separated places were exposed to the same empirical attitudes and ideas concerning the study of mind.

Popular (in the best sense) literature contrasted with professional and undergraduate literature because its growth came later and, predominantly, in this country. In 1950, the first book appeared in the Pelican Psychology Series, under the general editorship of Professor C. A. Mace (b. 1894). This series was important in informing educated laymen about what psychologists were doing, and helped to dispel some erroneous stereotypes about psychology, for example, that it was exclusively preoccupied with rats running through mazes, or with pestering people with questionnaires, or with acrimonious doctrinaire disputes, or with the abnormal, bizarre, and even occult. Certainly many a school-leaver who decided to study psychology at university was first stimulated to do so by reading some of this series. By 1965, the series, now under the general editorship of Professor Brian M. Foss (b. 1921), still held pride of place in the good-quality popular market, even though there were now many competitors and an increasing number of psychology articles in such periodicals as *Scientific American*.

### *Causes*

Why this explosion in empirical psychological inquiry? The root cause almost certainly lay in the growing extent to which, in economically developed countries, people's daily lives were influenced by scientific and technological developments. New techniques in engineering, computers, communication, and medicine impinged on everyone in a growing population and had three broad consequences for psychological studies. One consequence was that new scientific knowledge provided psychologists with fresh analogies and ways of thinking about their subject-matter; and also with improved tools of study which enhanced their ability to make accurate observations and better enabled them to draw valid conclusions from the data they gathered. A second consequence was a reinforced belief in the power of scientific inquiry and, at the same time, a highlighting of lack of knowledge about man himself. Success had come from scientific scrutiny of the properties of inanimate matter and of living tissues. Such scrutiny had increased man's control over his physical universe and over disease, and demonstrated that empirical inquiry was a potent means of understanding and solving many problems. This induced a readiness to adopt the same approach towards the properties of human beings as people. Furthermore, the spectacular growth of knowledge about the physical world made it all the more evident how little was understood about man himself and how great a challenge it was to extend the methods of science to the complexities of man and how he functions. A greater understanding of people also took on urgency as it became more evident that the human factor was the weakest link in man's world, that catastrophes of destruction and hunger and accident increasingly emanated from man himself more than from a hostile uncontrollable environment. A third consequence of technological innovations was that they highlighted the practical importance of various specific psychological problems. This consequence can best be indicated by citing three examples from the spheres of industry, education, and medicine.

Industry made increasing use of mechanical instruments and automatic devices. So, as in the case of an aeroplane pilot, a person might need to read dials and other visual displays, select from this sensory information, interpret its implications, decide what actions to take, and express these actions by adjusting levers, pressing buttons, or whatever. These interactions between man and machine made minimal demands on muscle-power but heavy demands on ability to deal with information. They raised practical questions. Was the relevant information best presented to eye or ear, and what was the optimal form of presentation? How much information could be presented in rapid succession without overloading his capacities or risking lapse of attention? Could his decisions best be expressed by pressing buttons, moving levers, or giving vocal commands? Such questions needed answers from experimental research rather than guesswork, and were sufficiently pressing to create a special field of inquiry called engineering psychology and sometimes, less happily, human engineering.

It was through education, formal and informal, that new generations mastered the accumulated knowledge, attitudes, skills, and ideals of older generations, and so maintained the community and modified it. What should be taught? How should it be taught? To whom, and by whom, should it be taught? These perennial questions required fresh answers according to the changing needs and resources of the community. In postwar years, communities became larger, more complex, and more rapidly changing. So these questions became more urgent, not only in relation to the rearing and schooling of children but also in relation to the altering attitudes and knowledge of adults and to the readjustments of older people facing novel occupations and ways of life. These problems inescapably involved psychological questions about how people acquire and use new knowledge, abilities, attitudes. There was, then, need to find out more about the physical, emotional, and intellectual development of children and adults. Under what conditions did learning take place? How could learning be accelerated without loss in the quality of eventual mastery? How was learning affected by differing relationships between teacher and pupil, and by different means of communication between them? How far, and in what ways, could the functions of a teacher be delegated to a machine? The study of such issues was promoted by urgent educational needs.

Medicine continued to increased its effectiveness in diagnosing and treating human ailments, especially those which might be called, by historical hindsight, the more straightforward physical diseases. This meant that a larger proportion of the less easily managed illnesses were of a kind which involved emotional or intellectual disturbance or deficit. The study of such indispositions involved psychological issues such as accurate description, classification, and prediction of abnormal behaviour, and the devising of effective techniques for their prevention and for the rehabilitation of patients. The need to study these issues was intensified by the development of new drugs with selective and specific action on the nervous system, and by the development of more refined techniques in brain surgery; for the more ingenious and powerful the means of treatment, the more pressing the need to assess their precise effects on human functioning.

### *Psychology as a Unified Body of Knowledge*

In relation to psychology as a unified body of knowledge, developments between 1945 and 1965 had two broad effects which worked in opposing directions. Divisions created by so-called schools of psychology became weaker while new divisions arose between areas of specialism.

Earlier in the century, many psychologists were partisan to some distinctive school of thought about the essential nature of psychological man, and they debated the correctness of one school against another. But as empirical attitudes grew, so these literary and philosophical debates waned. Theoretical issues continued to play as important a part as ever, but their nature shifted from doctrinal disputes towards those clashes which could be resolved by empirical inquiries. Psychologists increasingly accepted that theoretical assertions should be grounded in, and have implications for, observable facts. The merits of rival theories were to be settled on factual grounds and, indeed, the very value of a theory lay importantly in the extent to which it could be verified or refuted by facts. Many of the issues which divided the schools turned out to be non-factual, and so their interest waned. As evidence of this weakened interest, consider the book *Contemporary Schools of Psychology* by one of America's most widely informed and perceptive psychologists, Robert S. Woodworth (1869–1962). When this book was published in 1931, it could, without much violation, survey current ideas by describing a succession of schools, i.e. Functionalism, Structuralism, Associationism, Behaviourism, Gestalt, Psychoanalysis, and Purposivism. When the second edition appeared in 1949, Woodworth observed that, while these schools were still contemporary, they lacked their former distinctiveness, had not been joined by new schools, and that *rapprochements* were becoming evident among them. With the third edition, published posthumously in 1964, he noted that this *rapprochement* had markedly accelerated and that these schools were perhaps of more historical than contemporary interest.

While the decline of schools promised to unify psychology, the growth of detailed knowledge and techniques made it difficult, not in principle but in practice, for individuals to encompass psychology as a whole. The mid-century years were busy ones. In the forties and fifties, for example, there were ambitious developments in learning theories including the notable attempts by Clark L. Hull (1884–1952) of Yale to devise and test rigorously deductive theorems about learning processes. Such theories, although they turned out to be premature, left behind an increased knowledge about learning and more sophisticated methods for its study. Part of the legacy of the 'learning theory epoch' was the pioneering work of B. F. Skinner (b. 1904) of Harvard. He studied what came to be called operant conditioning and made various discoveries which gave impetus to practical advances in training, and, particularly, in programmed instruction ('teaching machines'). There were significant advances in understanding the complex functioning of the central nervous system. There was the impact of studies on how animals behaved in their natural environments; a body of studies known as ethology and pioneered by the Austrian Konrad Lorenz (b. 1903). There were developments in studying human social behaviour, and groups, and the organization of managements in business and industry. As a consequence of such diverse inquiries, specialisms thrived and, notably in America, whole research institutions were devoted to those specialisms. For example, to cite but a few, the Institute of Personality Assessment and Research at the University of California, which grew out of wartime work on personnel selection, concentrated on intensive studies of adults who were highly accomplished in various professions and on discovering the characteristics of such persons as compared with people who were less accomplished. In Wisconsin, Harry F. Harlow (b. 1905) and his colleagues concentrated on their remarkable long-term studies of how infant monkeys developed when reared under various conditions of maternal, social, or sensory deprivation. J. P. Guilford (b. 1897) and his California associates concentrated on refining techniques for assessing and measuring intellectual, personality, and attitudinal characteristics, and stimulated work on what came to be called creativity. The Harvard Center for Cognitive Studies concentrated interdisciplinary resources on studies of learning, thinking, and language.

Thus sophisticated techniques of investigation, different areas of practical application, and the sheer increase of empirical knowledge all fostered specialization and weakened contacts between specialists. The differences between areas of specialism were not of the kind which had separated the schools, but they were divisive nevertheless and raised increasingly difficult questions about the feasibility of regarding psychology as a distinctive discipline. By 1965 it still remained for the future to show whether, and in what ways, psychology could continue its many-sided growth and also retain its identity as a unified body of knowledge.

### *A Distinctive Theme*

It is impossible here to deal with all important lines of inquiry, much less to mention the many individuals, even in this country, who contributed advances by teaching, research, administration, the organization of professional services, writing, and editorial work. So let us select by asking the following question. Is it likely that future historians of psychology will look back on this period and see any single large theme of work which not only distinguished it from what had gone before but also left a secure heritage for the future? Presumptuous though it is for a participant observer to answer this question, historians might see such a theme in the study of what could be called human control and communication. At the heart of this theme was a concern for *function*, an interest in how people actually carry through their activities in terms of bodily and neurological processes and in terms of social interactions, an interest in the functioning of complexly organized and regulated activities. Skilled performances were studied to reveal much about how the person controlled and co-ordinated many activities into smooth overall performance; and how, in acquiring skill, component activities were progressively organized together to produce eventual flexible mastery. Fruitful studies were made of sense organs as systems for selecting and transmitting environmental information to the brain, and of perception as a continual reformulation of such information so as to control and guide adaptive action. There were ingenious experimental analyses of selective attention and concentration. New micro-electrode techniques explored the physiological functioning of precisely located regions within the nervous systems of animals and discovered several hitherto unknown properties of nervous systems, such as the important role of various lower sub-cortical regions in controlling degrees of general alertness and in initiating and terminating specific emotional states. Thinking, decision-making, and the acquisition of knowledge were scrutinized as strategic central control processes and, around 1951, the term psycholinguistics became current to describe the growing volume of work on the functioning of language. Social skills were examined to show something of how people formed impressions of each other and interacted by means of gestures, facial expressions, and verbal messages. So future historians might well see, as the outstanding contribution of this period, an increasing understanding of control and communication processes. Historians could see this as redressing the earlier neglect by psychologists of on-going central processes; and also as echoing wider interests of the times because, during this period, there was greater preoccupation than ever before with control and communication.

This was the age which felt the revolutionary impact of computers and telecommunications, that is, the development by electronic engineers of elaborate automatic information-processing systems. Television systems were designed to receive pictures, transform (or encode) them into patterns of impulses, transmit these impulses through relay stations to distant destinations, and then transform them back (decode them) into a semblance of the original picture. Calculating machines encoded numbers into messages, carried out operations on these messages, such as multiplying, and then decoded the outcome into numbers which could be read from the machine. High-speed computers dealt with coded information in even more elaborate ways, transforming it and augmenting it from stored information, to generate an eventual set of data or instructions. All such systems functioned to transmit, store, combine, transform information in accordance with sets of rules; they comprised subsystems, and sub-sub-systems, organized together to carry through the multi-stage information-handling tasks for which the whole system was designed. These systems revolutionized many aspects of living. They spanned geographical distance with world-wide radio and television linkages. They made possible the merging of economic and political organizations into yet larger organizations with correspondingly enlarged problems of co-ordination, communication, and management. They made feasible complexly planned projects of the kind most dramatically evident in space research.

Such developments, and the impressiveness of the systems themselves, heightened general awareness of ideas about information control and communication. By the late forties, these ideas were being given distinct mathematical formulations, variously called Information Theory or Communication Theory. In 1947, the word 'cybernetics' was invented by the American Norbert Wiener (1894–1964) to describe general ideas about control and communication in all self-governing systems, whether mechanical or biological. These ideas were seen to have relevance for the study, not only of physical systems, but also economic, political, and biological systems, e.g. geneticists talked of genes carrying coded instructions for governing embryonic growth, and the genetic code was cracked. These ideas were also relevant for psychology since, in important respects, people functioned as systems for handling and controlling information. Some of these ideas were already important in psychology, but the computer revolution gave them greater currency and more precise formulation. A case in point was the idea of hierarchical organization of levels of functioning. As will be seen later, this idea was fundamental to much work on the psychology of control and communication.

The idea of hierarchical organization was familiar in the organization chart of a business concern, with the director at the top level, then deputy directors, department managers, supervisors, and individual operatives. Each level performed distinctive functions which constrained the functioning of lower levels and were constrained by the functioning of higher levels. In describing the business, the work done at each level required description in its own terms; and an exhaustive description of the whole required description of all these levels and how they inter-related with each other. Large electronic computers also worked in terms of hierarchical organization, but one which had precise physical embodiment and correspondingly precise detailed specifications. There was an executive programme which provided the overall sequence of instructions. Some of these instructions were to bring into play some sub-programme which ran its course to a predetermined point at which the executive programme picked up once more. There were various sub-programmes, and each might bring in a sub-sub-programme if circumstances required. So, there were many different levels of operation which were organized, either simultaneously or successively, to accomplish the flexibly adaptive task of the system as a whole. Computers were the most complex and elegant physical embodiments of hierarchical organization which had so far been devised by man. And the powerful properties of these embodiments gave psychologists a renewed appreciation of this form of organization in the functioning of man himself.

It has been suggested that work on processes of control and communication was the outstandingly productive theme between 1945 and 1965. Let us now elaborate this theme under the respective headings of skilled performance, thinking, and language.

### *Skilled Performance*

The study of skilled performance was the most distinctive British contribution to psychology during these twenty years. These studies were largely pioneered in this country in response to the needs of the Second World War and, although they were taken up on a larger scale by North America, British work remained important through the fifties and sixties. The early work dealt mostly with complex sensory-motor skills, for example, the performance of aeroplane pilots in detecting and interpreting signals from display panels and earphones and in taking appropriate actions on the basis of these signals (these particular studies were carried out in a simulated cockpit). Later work dealt increasingly with linguistic skills, the handling of symbolic material (such as words and numbers), attention and thinking. But, throughout, the interest led away from previous fashions of examining isolated responses to isolated stimuli and of considering the person merely as a passive recipient of sensory stimuli who responded in reflex-arc fashion. Rather, the emphasis was on goal-directed activities, on performances comprising component activities being carried through in co-ordinated sequence towards furthering some objective, such as bringing a plane safely to ground on a landing strip. The person was a decision-maker continually engaged in selecting from environmental information and implementing appropriate actions. In short, what was being studied were the properties of the person as an active control system imposing order on his own varied activities and also on the relationships of these activities to his changing environmental circumstances.

The bulk of British work on skilled performance originated in Cambridge and must always be associated with Professor Sir Frederic Bartlett, F.R.S. (1886–1969). By 1945, Bartlett already had an international reputation, had contributed notably to psychology, and had built up, at Cambridge, a flourishing centre for teaching and research. His approach involved concrete laboratory studies of real-life problems with as few artificial simplifications as the laboratory situation allowed, and with little recourse to elaborate theory but constant alertness for general implications of particular findings. He also had the quality of encouraging younger investigators in the pursuit of interesting problems. It was these younger men who carried out and published work on skill but, as they would be the first to acknowledge, it was Bartlett's interest and support which made this possible. The first of these younger men was Kenneth J. W. Craik (1914–45). He was an Edinburgh graduate, with talents in music, philosophy, and engineering, as well as in psychology. He went to Cambridge in 1936 and there pursued a brilliant career until his accidental death in 1945. When war broke out, he put his talents at the service of committees concerned with manpower and, particularly, with man–machine interaction. He worked, for example, on dark adaptation and the use of night photometers, on basic principles of radar display, on efficient combinations of movement responses in the control of instruments, on effects of fatigue in aeroplane pilots. In 1944, the Medical Research Council established, at Cambridge, its Applied Psychology Research Unit for further studies of such issues, and Craik was appointed Director. This Unit continued after Craik's death, first under Norman H. Mackworth (b. 1917) and then Donald E. Broadbent (b. 1926). The Unit was a highly productive centre for applied and theoretical research in human performance and, by 1965, had twenty full-time scientific staff plus technical and secretarial staff and some visiting psychologists from abroad. Throughout these years, the Unit expanded and diversified the pioneering work of Craik, and enjoyed the continued interest of Bartlett.

The early work on sensory-motor skill exemplified what might be called a control-systems approach in psychology. This approach became increasingly dominant, not only in skills research, but also in the study of perceiving, learning, and thinking, and of both physiological and social psychology. So it is worth trying to catch the flavour of this approach by citing an early statement of it and then considering just two of the characteristic notions which it made prominent. Here is Craik's own statement of the approach. In reading this, it helps to think of a person in process of aiming a gun at a target.

As an element in a control system a man may be regarded as a chain consisting of the following items. (1) Sensory devices, which transform a misalinement between sight and target into suitable physiological counterparts, such as patterns of nerve impulses, just as a radar receiver transforms misalinement into an error-voltage. (2) A computing system which responds to the misalinement-input by giving a neural response calculated, on the basis of previous experience, to be appropriate to reduce the misalinement; this process seems to occur in the cortex of the brain. (3) An amplifying system—the motor-nerve endings and the muscles—in which a minute amount of energy (the impulses in the motor nerves) controls the liberation of much greater amounts of energy in the muscles, which thus perform mechanical work. (4) Mechanical linkages (the pivot and lever systems of the limbs) whereby the muscular work produces externally observable effects, such as laying a gun. Such considerations serve to bridge the gap between the physiological statement of man as an animal giving reflex and learned responses to sensory stimuli, and the engineering statement in terms of the type of mechanism which would be designed to fulfil the same function in a wholly automatic system. The problem is to discover in detail the characteristics of this human chain . . . with a view to showing the various advantages and disadvantages of the human operator as compared with the automatic system.*

This quotation might almost be a statement of the programme of work which was to engage many psychologists in different countries for the next twenty years and lead, as perhaps its most ambitious outcome, to attempted simulations of human thinking by means of computers. The approach was to study the functional organization of performance by detailed examination of its component activities and of the ways in which these were inter-related in pursuit of some

* K. J. W. Craik, 'Theory of the Human Operator in Control Systems, Part II', *British Journal of Psychology*, XXXVIII (1948), 142.

goal. Apart from the idea of hierarchically organized levels of functions, two of the notions given prominence by this approach were goal-directedness, and utilization of feedback.

Goal-directedness meant that component functions were affected by, and subservient to, the purpose of the task. A simple illustration was provided by visual search.* On a sheet of paper were printed letters of the alphabet in haphazard sequence: there were, say, five letters in each line and forty lines in all. A person was to locate, as quickly as possible, that one line in which a particular target letter occurred, say K. With practice people improved until they were spending only about one-tenth of a second in examining each line of five letters. It could be shown, at such speeds, that even the apparently simple component of identifying a letter of the alphabet was not an all-or-none activity but one which involved a succession of stages. The searcher examined each letter in terms of various characteristics, such as presence or absence of curves, and developed proficiency in terminating his examination as soon as he decided that this was not the target letter, e.g. whether it was O or S or R was left undetermined, it was not K, so he passed on. Only when he came to a K, or something like it, did he deepen his examination to identify the letter fully. Such deeper examination took longer and meant, among other things, that the task became much more time-consuming if it was altered so that, now, there was only one line without a K, and this line was the target to be found. Other changes occurred with practice, such as the fact that the searcher, like an experienced worker in a news-clipping agency, became able to search for a multiplicity of targets in the same time as he needed to search for just one target. However, the main point was that the person's goal importantly influenced the detailed ways in which he dealt with the visual material available to him.

Utilization of feedback was another pervasive phenomenon. In skilled performance, much relevant information was in the form of stimuli arising from immediately previous responses or their consequences. Such information was called feedback and was important whenever performance lasted for more than about one second. People were often unaware of feedback, but interference with it had dramatic results as could be illustrated by delayed auditory feedback of speech. Ask a person to talk. Place a microphone in front of his mouth and record what he said on magnetic tape; then play the record back, delayed by a fifth of a second, into earphones which muffled other bone-conducted and air-borne sounds. Under these

* For details see U. Neisser, 'Visual Search', *Scientific American*, June 1964.

conditions, the speaker heard only his own voice delayed by a fifth of a second, and he began to lose control of speech. He raised the pitch and volume of his voice, began to stutter, and might well find himself unable to speak at all. He became vividly aware of the extent to which his normally effortless speaking was guided by auditory feedback, that is, by his hearing what he had just said. The importance of feedback was further demonstrated in some neurological diseases where its loss, from ears or eyes or muscles, seriously impaired activity. It was also demonstrated in much of skills research where it was found that artificial augmentation of feedback was a powerful technique for increasing the precision of skilled performance and the rapidity of its acquisition.

The control-systems approach to skilled performance was, in its origins and subsequently, aimed chiefly at solving practical problems concerning man–machine systems. It aimed to design machines which better fitted the capacities of men, and to train men so that they were better able to control their machines; broadly, to link men and machines in such ways as to use man's capacities to his maximum benefit. These applied researches, however, generated findings and ideas with much wider implications. They showed man as the user and creator of countless skills, varying from the near-universal skills of walking and grasping objects, to the rarefied skills of symbolic logic and the judgement of experienced experts. They showed man as having some severe, and surprising, limitations of capacity. They showed some of the ways in which, despite these unalterable limitations, man widened the scope of his control by developing higher-order skills. Man increased his abilities by linking himself with physical devices, for example, telescopes to augment limited senses, power-tools to augment limited musculature, and computers to augment limited ability in reasoning about large amounts of data. So too, and more fundamentally, man increased his control by organizing and reorganizing his own central processes so as to streamline old skills and create new syntheses of old skills into yet higher-order skills.

Over the years, and in many centres throughout the world, these studies of skilled performance brought in new concepts, cast old issues in new light, raised new questions, and generated new knowledge about processes which had very different time-scales and levels of complexity. Concerning time-scales, for example, processes of selective attention, short-term memory, and signal detection spanned seconds or milliseconds, while processes of skill acquisition and changes of skill with ageing spanned weeks or years. Concerning levels of complexity, there were qualitative differences between the small-scale, hunt-and-peck components which made up the typing performance of a novice, and the more complexly integrated performance of the expert with its larger functional units and its greater involvement of anticipation and central co-ordination. Furthermore, these studies helped to establish a broad framework for considering all manner of on-going organizational processes in humans—and in machines and animals. For example, knowledge about bodily, and linguistic, and symbolic skill was co-ordinated in ways which harmonized with developing knowledge about, on the one hand, the structures and functions of the nervous system and, on the other, inter-personal communication, work-sharing, and social interaction. This did not mean that psychology now had a rigidly all-embracing theory, much less that psychologists regarded people merely as information-processing machines. What it meant was that many apparently different areas of psychology shared a common frame of reference which was perhaps comparable, in both its flavour and effects, to the framework which biologists had earlier gained from the theory of evolution by natural selection.

*Thinking*

Psychologists had always been sensitive to the importance of thinking but, by 1945, had made slender progress in its empirical study. Apart from the undoubted complexities of thinking, there had been perhaps three main obstacles. One was the tendency to regard thinking as disembodied; as set apart from, even opposed to, bodily actions and sense organs; as an intruding ghost in a machine. A related obstacle was lack of specificity in questions asked; psychologists were often unclear about what they wanted to know. Some questions were unmanageably broad, e.g. what is thinking? Others narrowly concerned fragments of thinking, e.g. what happened when a person prepared himself to multiply rather than add numbers which would shortly be presented? A third obstacle was preoccupation with introspection as the main source of information about thinking. An extreme hope was that the thinker might be a privileged and fully informed spectator on his own private thinking, and that he might describe it, rather as a radio commentator watches a football game and describes it to a listening, but unseeing, audience. This extreme hope was not justified for reasons which, by the fifties, could be understood in terms of what was known about attending, remembering, language, and man's limited capacity to do several things at once. It became evident that a person was only a partial observer of his own thinking who was liable to distort his selective observations in recalling them, and distort further in putting them into words. So, introspective reporting could not provide an exhaustive account of all that thinking involved. Some psychologists reacted to this inadequacy by assuming, erroneously, that introspection gave no information whatever, and by further assuming, again erroneously, that since introspection must be the main source of information about thinking, then thinking could not be studied empirically.

After 1945, the study of thinking progressed markedly because of two changes of emphasis. The first was that many instances of goal-directed thinking were regarded as high-level skilled performances in their own right, comparable to sensory-motor skills except for their more complex organization and their greater involvement of the 'computer element' mentioned by Craik. Consider someone trying to locate a fault in a motor engine. Guided by past experience, he made successive tests, drew conclusions from these tests about the possible location of the fault and about what further tests to make. He engaged in a co-ordinated sequence of activities which might be carried through smoothly or clumsily, in that he failed to do the tests in optimal order or failed to utilize all the information which they could have given to him. Fault-finding was an important skill. It improved with practice. It could be studied in control-system fashion. It was also a performance which, in any meaningful sense, involved thinking among its many components. So also were the performances of drawing conclusions from lists of verbal statements, and solving mathematical problems. Such performances could be, and were, subjected to profitable experimental study.

The second change of emphasis was to regard thinking as the operation of higher-order skills which had been evolved out of lower-order bodily skills. The development of these more complex, centrally organized skills had great adaptive utility because they enabled the person to escape from exclusive dependence on immediately present circumstances: to build up, within himself, a progressively veridical small-scale model of external reality and of his own possible actions; to anticipate future situations before they arose, try out possible alternative actions and, before the event, decide which was the best of them; to co-ordinate more lengthy sequences of planned activity; in many ways, to control his activities in fuller and more competent fashion. An emergent view of thinking was not new. What was new was the detailed evidence in its favour and, more important, evidence indicating ways in which these emergent developments took place, and the circumstances on which they depended. Such evidence came from several lines of inquiry. There were studies of how people adjusted to wearing distorting spectacles, and to other forms of distorted sensory information: these studies showed how, depending on the nature of the distortion and of the person's movement activities, the person might successively modify his sensory-motor co-ordinations until his visual world looked normal once more.* There were studies of skill acquisition, in dealing with industrial operations and various data-processing tasks. There were studies of the disintegration of performances under the influence of drugs, fatigue, emotional disturbance, and, particularly, brain injury. Not least important, there were the far-reaching studies of child development by Professor Jean Piaget (b. 1896) and his colleagues at Geneva.

Since the twenties, Piaget had been known for his studies of children's notions about everyday events. But it was not until the fifties that he was recognized as a major figure in psychology. This recognition followed his later, and more sophisticated, studies of children's thinking; these aroused increasing interest and, by the sixties, had stimulated much follow-up work. Even a provisional assessment of Piaget's, still active, contribution was not yet possible, but its objective was the construction of a comprehensive theory of genetic epistemology, that is, of knowledge and its development from birth, into adolescence, and beyond. This theory was to be worked out in logical-mathematical terms which were, necessarily, complex; it was also to be empirically based. Over the years, this objective led Piaget into directing ingenious experimental inquiries concerning the ways in which children, from early infancy upwards, dealt with problems involving movement, space, time, measurement, logical relations, and scientific inferences. Piaget was also led to interpret his findings in theoretical terms which became increasingly complex. Reports of all this work gave rise to a literature which was vast, stimulating, and often obscure. Few psychologists claimed to understand the full range of Piaget's theorizing, but many appreciated the originality, and repeatability, of his experimental findings, and their implications for educational practice. There was also recognition of the support given by these findings for regarding thinking as the progressive emergence of higher-order control processes which were synthesized out of the child's on-going interactions with the world around him. Some flavour of Piaget's work

* For details see R. Held, 'Plasticity in Sensory-Motor Systems', *Scientific American*, November 1965.

may be caught by briefly considering the child's developing appreciation of conservation of quantity.

Conservation of quantity was familiar to adult experience, namely, the amount of a substance remained constant provided nothing was taken away from it or added. A dozen bars of chocolate remained a dozen whether they were stacked in a heap, spread out in a row, or arranged in a circle: a pound of flour remained a pound whether it was in a bag, tipped into a bowl, or strewn over the floor. In brief, changes in spatial arrangement, and consequently in appearances, were irrelevant to quantity. To be sure, adults were sometimes misled by appearances, e.g. one cup might look as though it held more than another cup of different shape. But if the adult found that he could exactly fill one cup with water poured from the other, he readily concluded that, despite appearances, they held equal volumes. In such situations the adult implicitly appreciated conservation of quantity; but not so the child who had still to acquire this appreciation by experience. Consider the following task involving twelve wooden beads, two identical glass beakers which were short and wide, and a third beaker which was tall and narrow. The two short beakers were placed in front of a six-year-old who was asked to count six beads into each. This done, the child agreed that there was now the same number of beads in each. While he watched, the beads were poured from one of the beakers into the tall beaker. Then he was asked: was there the same number of beads in the tall beaker and in the untouched short beaker? If the child appreciated conservation of quantity, he would, adult-like, reply that the number was still the same in each. But if he did not appreciate conservation, he would judge by the appearances of what was in front of him at the moment: he would look at the tall beaker with its column of beads, at the short beaker with its layer of beads, and conclude that one contained more than the other: as the beads were poured back and forth into differently shaped beakers, so his judgements of equality would shift in ways which were inconsistent by adult standards but consistent with altered appearances at different times. In fact, when this beads-and-beakers task was given to a large cross-section of normal school children, it was found that, at $5\frac{1}{2}$ years, nine out of ten children consistently judged by appearances, while, by $7\frac{1}{2}$ years, only one in ten was still doing so.

Experiments were done to answer questions about this developing appreciation because, trivial though it might seem, it was basic to the development of much mathematical and scientific thinking. Consider just three of these questions. First, did appreciation develop in all-or-none fashion? Did the child suddenly 'get the idea' and then generalize it to various situations? No. The child might conserve in one task but not in another, and his appreciation of conservation turned out to vary systematically with various features of particular task situations. However, as he grew older, this appreciation was shown in a progressively widening range of situations. Secondly, why should almost all children develop this widening appreciation, and do so without formal instruction? Why did they not continue to judge simply on immediate appearances? The answer seemed to lie in the greater self-consistency which this development brought to the child's judgements. In more general terms, Piaget called this the attainment of a more stable equilibrium of action, a shift from relatively exclusive dependence on the vagaries of simple, superficial appearance towards the consistencies of more complex, deeper 'realities'. Notice that this developmental trend did not involve an ignoring of appearances but rather an increasing ability to distinguish appearances from 'realities' and to base judgement selectively on either, as the situation required. Thirdly, could conservation be taught? More precisely, given a young child or a mentally retarded older child with only very narrow appreciation of conservation, could he be led through experiences which would accelerate widening of this appreciation? Early attempts to do this met with little success. Neither demonstrations nor verbal explanations had clear effect. For a time, it seemed as though acceleration was impossible. However, later attempts, based on more detailed knowledge of just what such appreciation involved, were more successful.

*Language*

One of the most striking developments between 1945 and 1965 was the intensified study of language by psychologists working, not only on their own, but also in collaboration with linguists, phoneticians, neurologists, computer engineers, and teachers. Language was studied in its various uses; e.g. as a means by which people, effectively or ineffectively, communicated with one another by speech and writing, or thought about events by representing them in words and then drawing conclusions by verbal reasoning, or organized emotionally tinged attitudes around verbal slogans and generalizations. Language was studied in relation to underlying brain processes, and casualties from the Second World War tragically provided both the need and the opportunity to discover more about language disorders resulting from brain injuries. Language was studied as a system of skilled activities which showed remarkable properties in relation to the basic limitations of human capability; and there were searches for more efficient ways of fostering these skills in children and adults. Language was studied in comparison with growing knowledge about communication processes used by animals, and it became increasingly likely that animal communication, despite its complexities, failed to meet the criteria of language, that language was a uniquely human accomplishment.

Much of this work was a continued elaboration of earlier pioneer work, yet certain circumstances gave it additional impetus and some new directions. During this period, many developments heightened general awareness of the importance of language, and posed problems for investigation. For example, there were more frequent contacts between people from differing regional and language backgrounds, more mass media with effects in shaping opinion and spreading knowledge, more filling in of forms and data returns, more specialized fields of knowledge held apart by semi-private languages, more children to be educated, larger economic organizations with complex problems of communication among their participant members. All such developments emphasized problems of language and the need to know more about them. Also during this period, engineering developments in telecommunications and computers raised both practical problems about language and also general questions about the properties of communication processes. For example, the design of more efficient telephone systems required detailed knowledge about those properties of purposive speech which made it intelligible to a listener. How far did the intelligibility of a single word depend on its being heard in the context of the message as a whole? In what ways could reproduced speech be reduced in quality without its becoming unintelligible? What were the advantages and disadvantages of vision-based as opposed to hearing-based systems of communication? Computers, too, stimulated interest in language by bringing people into contact with, literally, a new and important group of languages. A computer operated according to a system of rules which was, by any criteria, a language. These artificial languages, with names like Algol and Fortran, had their own vocabularies and grammars, and the systems of rules by which they worked were precisely known. These computer languages raised far-reaching problems of how best to translate, to and fro, between them and such natural languages as English. They also prompted questions about the ways in which they were comparable to, and different from, natural languages; and so provided new kinds of questions to ask about natural language.

By 1965, these many-sided studies were still gathering momentum. But already, they had established so much of lasting value, and raised so many new questions, that it was difficult to say which studies were most outstanding. Let us, arbitrarily, consider that line of work which, from about 1951, was called psycholinguistics. In detail, this work had many technical features, and involved much ingenious experimental inquiry, but its rationale and its broad implications could perhaps be outlined briefly.

Speech comprised various kinds of elements, ranging from vocal sound, through phoneme, word, clause, and sentence, to coherent argument. The larger elements comprised sequences of smaller elements, and at all levels, sequential arrangement (or syntax) was important: the same phonemes in different arrangements could produce different words, and accidental inversions of words in a sentence could produce grotesque alterations in the meaning of the sentence, or render it meaningless. Linguists, in describing speech, had long recognized regularities in syntax. A simple example was that a singular noun, ending in a voiceless consonant, usually took a voiceless sibilant in the plural (cats, lips) whereas, when it ended in a voiced consonant, it usually took a voiced sibilant (dogs, ribs). Other, more complex, regularities concerned relations between words belonging to different parts-of-speech (such as nouns, verbs, adjectives), and their arrangements in a sentence. Linguists had discovered many such regularities, and continued to discover more. Now, were these regularities merely a fortunate convenience for the purposes of linguistic description? Or did they reflect something fundamental about people as users of language? It turned out (as language teachers had long suspected) that these regularities reflected rules which were actually used by the speaker to control his moment-by-moment language activities, rather as a computer used the rules of computer language to control successive changes in electric circuits. In short, the language user engaged in a rule-governed system of activities. He used these rules, even though he could rarely describe them, or might be unaware of their very existence, and even though linguists had not yet identified all of them.

The recognition of this rule-governed feature of language was a far cry from older views of language in terms of associations, and it had four broad consequences for language studies. First, it helped to make sense of many puzzling findings concerning people's activities in formulating and articulating purposive speech, and also in listening to and comprehending the speech of others. Secondly, it helped in understanding something of the familiar, but remarkable, fact that a speaker could produce meaningful novel speech, that is, say things which were meaningful to himself and others but which had never been said by anyone before, and so could not have arisen by any simple kind of imitation. Thirdly, it helped in understanding how the developing child accomplished the enormous task of acquiring his native language, and also some of the stages through which he progressed during acquisition. An important aspect of acquisition was that he behaved, so to say, like an intuitive linguist. Experiments showed that he somehow extracted regularities out of the speech he heard, and then used these as rules to construct his own speech (hence errors like saying 'two mouses'). This extraction and use of rules required much experience and learning, but vastly less than would be required if he were mainly dependent on verbatim memorizing of the speech he heard. As he enlarged his experience of hearing and producing speech, he continued to extract progressively more refined rules. In this way, he built up, within himself, increasingly complex systems of rules which enabled him, not to repeat literally what he had heard in the past, but to synthesize afresh what he wanted to say when he wanted to say it. Fourthly, it prompted basic questions concerning the nature of language in relation to man's biological endowments, and in relation to the social world which he created and by which, in turn, he was shaped. For example, why should language have this rule-governed organization, a kind of organization so powerful that man had created computers in its likeness? It seemed that this organization was not fortuitous but arose from the properties, and the limitations, of his nervous system, and that, in a real sense, the groundplan of language rules was inherent in the genetically controlled properties of the human nervous system.

In attempting to outline the ideas which dominated British psychology between 1945 and 1965, this chapter began by emphasizing three general points. Firstly there was an enormous acceleration and diversification in psychological studies of a predominantly empirical kind. Secondly these heightened empirical inquiries were associated, directly and indirectly, with the growth of science-based technology in economically developed countries. Thirdly these inquiries freely crossed frontiers between countries and between traditional subject-matters. Turning to more specific issues, the chapter then sought to find a single broad theme which future historians might see as distinguishing these twenty years. The theme chosen was the interest in functional processes of control and communication. To illustrate this theme with a minimum of technicality, commentaries were then given on skilled performance, thinking, and language. In conclusion, it cannot be certain that future historians will see these twenty years as dominated by the exploration of human control and communication. But it is certain that these years will be seen as an exciting and productive period in the long story of how men have sought to find out more about themselves.

## FOR FURTHER READING

This guide to further reading falls into two distinct sections. Section 1 considers how a reader might find what he wants amid the proliferating literature of psychology. Rather than present a bibliography, this section suggests how a reader might compose a bibliography shaped to his own requirements. Section 2 names twenty-one books which relate to this chapter's selective treatment of developments between 1945 and 1965. Each book is chosen either because it played an important part in these developments or because it reflects the impact of these developments on the treatment of long-standing issues. Furthermore, each book will be worth reading in its own right for a long time to come.

### 1

How might a reader approach the task of finding what he wants? The best approach, used by psychologists themselves, is to ask a specialist to name a reference which is both authoritative and written at the level of detail required. However, since this approach is not always possible, there are four other approaches which can guide readers to references at increasing levels of specialism.

A first approach for the general reader is to use Penguin Books as orientation. Their Psychology Series, begun in 1950, contains some well-written volumes, and their Modern Psychology Readings Series, begun in 1966, provide competently edited collections of readings on varied topics.

A second approach is to use one of the comprehensive introductory texts as a guidebook. These texts are clearly written and, although they do not treat any particular topic in depth, they provide valuable orientation and references for further reading. They are American in origin and are usually up-dated every few years. The following three texts are representative (the date of each refers to the first edition, but there are later editions): F. A. Geldard, *Fundamentals of Psychology* (1962); E. R. Hilgard, *Introduction to Psychology* (1953); N. L. Munn, *Psychology* (1946).

A third approach, at a more penetrating level, makes use of *Psychology: A Study of a Science*, ed. S. Koch (1959–63). This six-volume work is a co-ordinated attempt by many authors to consider trends and ideas in psychology as a whole. The very titles indicate the wide scope. The first three volumes carry the collective title *Conceptual and Systematic*. Vol. I is *Sensory, Perceptual, and Physiological Formulations*, vol. II, *General Systematic Formulations, Learning and Special Processes*, vol. III, *Formulations of the Person and the Social Context*.

The second three volumes carry the title *Empirical Substructure and Relations with Other Sciences*. Vol. IV is *Biologically Oriented Fields: Their Place in Psychology and Biological Science*, vol. V, *The Process Areas, the Person, and some Applied Fields: Their Place in Psychology and in Science*, vol. VI, *Investigations of Man as Socius: Their Place in Psychology and the Social Sciences*.

A fourth approach is provided by the *Annual Review of Psychology*, begun in 1950 and published by Annual Reviews Inc., Palo Alto, California. Each volume contains some 17 chapters, each devoted to reviewing recent literature on a particular topic. Topics change from year to year but the chapter headings of the 1965 volume indicate the scope: 'Developmental Psychology'; 'Human Abilities'; 'Operant Conditioning'; 'Comparative Psychology of Learning'; 'Personality Structure'; 'Hypnosis'; 'Psychotherapeutic Processes'; 'Physiological Correlates of Mental Disease'; 'Consumer Psychology'; 'Personnel Selection'; 'Audition, Visual Acuity'; 'The Chemical Senses'; 'Psychological Aspects of Ageing in Man'; 'Scaling'; 'Mass Communication and Educational Media'.

Other approaches are available, depending on the contacts and library resources of the reader. But these four approaches should allow most readers to find their way to what interests them.

2

*Control Systems:* K. J. W. Craik, ed. S. L. Sherwood, *The Nature of Psychology* (Cambridge, 1966), a posthumous book, collects writings of a man who was at the forefront of influential cybernetic ideas. The editor remarks that Craik's first question about psychological function was 'What is the *go* of it?' and his second question 'What is the *particular go* of it?' A statement of important, sometimes difficult, ideas. N. Wiener, *Cybernetics, or Control and Communication in the Animal and the Machine* (1948) is a classic statement of cybernetic views applied to the functioning of animals, machines, individual persons, and social systems.

*Organization of Psychological Functioning:* D. O. Hebb, *The Organization of Behavior* (1949), a well-written book by a leading Canadian, synthesized much psychological and neurological evidence. It helped bridge the old distinction between trial-and-error and insight learning, and stimulated new lines of research into perception and the effects of childhood experiences on later, adult functioning. D. E. Broadbent, *Perception and Communication* (1958) is an influential account of human perception, attention, and information processing. It stimulated further work in these areas and demonstrated the contribution of laboratory experimentation to more detailed understanding of human functions. G. A. Miller, E. Galanter, and K. H. Pribram, *Plans and the Structure of Behavior* (New York, 1960), an important work by three distinguished American psychologists, further enriched ideas about organization by considering analogies with electronic computers. This book is informative, and written in a delightful style. A. R. Luria, *Higher Cortical Functions in Man* (1966), a large book by a distinguished Soviet psychologist, summarizes the history of ideas about the organization of psychological functioning in relation to brain functioning. It also summarizes much work on the effects of brain injury in a way which was harmonious with other references here mentioned. *Amnesia*, ed. C. W. M. Whitty and O. L. Zangwill (1966) surveys the organization of memory functions in humans. It exemplifies the use made of recent ideas about organization and recent techniques for psychological investigation.

*Skilled Performance:* A. T. Welford, *Ageing and Human Skill* (1958) is a report of experimental work on skilled performance and its changes with age. It not only stimulated studies of problems of ageing but also gave one of the earliest general accounts of skilled human performance. F. C. Bartlett, *Thinking: An Experimental and Social Study* (1958) applies to the study of thinking some ideas derived from the study of perceptual-motor skills. Written in a readable but deceptively simple style, it considers varieties of thinking, ranging from anagram-solving to the adventurous creative thinking of scientists and artists.

*Thinking:* M. Wertheimer, *Productive Thinking* (1945), a posthumous work by one of the leaders of Gestalt psychology, attempts to answer the question 'What happens when, now and then, thinking really works productively, forges ahead?' It did not answer the question satisfactorily but stimulated interest in important characteristics of thinking which had been neglected. G. Humphrey, *Thinking: An Introduction to its Experimental Psychology* (1951), by Oxford's first Professor of Psychology, surveys pre-1945 attempts to study thinking by experimental methods. A scholarly history of these attempts, it stimulated new work on thinking and supplied that new work with a historical context. J. S. Bruner, J. J. Goodnow, and G. A. Austin, *A Study of Thinking* (1956), by a group of Harvard psychologists, was the first relatively systematic account of newer approaches to thinking. Its subtitle gives its flavour: 'An Analysis of Strategies in the Utilization of Information for Thinking and Problem Solving'. J. P. Guilford, *The Nature of Human Intelligence* (1967), an advanced textbook by a distinguished American, attempts to relate recent work on thinking to earlier work on intelligence testing. It indicates that interest in the functional analyses of ongoing activities had built upon and modified older static descriptions of abilities.

*Children's Thinking:* B. Inhelder and J. Piaget, *The Growth of Logical Thinking: From Childhood to Adolescence* (1958). Piaget's works are not notable for their readability but this book is perhaps among his easiest. Still conceptually difficult, it gives an overall impression of his approach and the kinds of ideas to which it leads. Readers not already familiar with the work of Piaget are advised to begin with one of the references mentioned below. J. McV. Hunt, *Intelligence and Experience* (New York, 1961) provides an admirably readable account of the work of Piaget, and Hebb, and more recent developments in the field of intelligence testing. It gives perhaps the best up-to-date overview of ideas about the development of thinking and intelligence. J. H. Flavell, *The Developmental Psychology of Jean Piaget* (1963) is an American's systematic and scholarly account of the work of Piaget which assumed the status of a standard advanced text on Piaget's ideas and findings.

*Language:* G. A. Miller, *Language and Communication* (1951), a readable textbook, gathers together much diverse work on language and communication. It continues to be a valuable survey, although it includes nothing of the later, more sophisticated work on language. *Psycholinguistics*, ed. C. E. Osgood and T. A. Sebeok (Bloomington, Ind., 1965), a collection of rather technical papers, was first published in 1954 and was the first book dealing with psycholinguistics. The 1965 edition is a reprint containing an additional survey of developments between 1954 and 1964, and a stimulating paper by G. A. Miller entitled 'The Psycholinguists: On the New Scientists of Language'. C. Cherry, *On Human Communication* (Cambridge, Mass., 1957), considers human language and communication from the viewpoint of a telecommunications engineer. Although oversimplified in places, it provides a readable and stimulating introduction to some new ideas about language. F. Smith and G. A. Miller, *The Genesis of Language: A Psycholinguistic Approach* (Boston, 1966) contains the proceedings of a conference on language development in children. Although not easy reading, it gave the flavour of the kinds of question currently being asked about language, its development, organization, and functions. R. Brown, *Social Psychology* (1965), a large book, has the merit of being highly readable. Much of it concerns an overview of recent work on personality, motivation, and attitudes, but its Part Three gives a valuable general account of some of Piaget's work and of recent work on children's acquisition of linguistic rules.

# 9

# Physics

G. H. A. COLE

> To agree with everything or nothing are two equally simple solutions . . . they both avoid the necessity of making up your own mind.
>
> H. Poincaré

In 1945 physicists were able to return from the harrowing tasks of war to the more agreeable and constructive problems of peace. Like almost every other activity, developments in physics since 1945 can be seen in retrospect to have been affected by the war in characteristic ways. Not only did mere technological aspects develop at a much enhanced pace during the war but their nature was such as to change our basic attitudes to physics. Pre-war physics was fun for those lucky enough to be involved with it, but it scarcely affected anyone else; postwar physics was still fun for those lucky enough to be involved with it, but the general world community now could not stand back uncaring. Physics was now inextricably involved with the technologies of both war and peace, and the work that most people accepted as necessary (or indeed inevitable) but also feared, consumed more and more money and included more people professionally. The application of science to war was not new in itself (Leonardo da Vinci, Galileo, and many others had made this long ago) but the scale and importance of the application were new. Again, the application of science to problems of peace was undertaken on a scale unknown before. The result was a technological expansion, involving a world in the shadow of Hiroshima and Nagasaki, of wide scope and of irreversible consequences.

A few examples will suffice to indicate what I mean. The use of electromagnetic waves in the short wave-length region (a few tens of centimetres), initially for the detection of enemy bombers, has developed into the wide complex we now call radar. As a by-product it was discovered in the early 1940s that the sun emits electromagnetic waves in this wave-length also, and this was the first step to the new area of radio astronomy. Parallel with this, the development of infra-red devices for detecting the approach of an enemy by land in the dark has had important consequences in medical physics and quite separately in astronomy. The development of rocket vehicles for the delivery of explosive warheads began, after the war, the great age of space exploration. In a different connection, the properties of atomic nuclei were exploited in the construction of the atomic bomb, and this work has been applied to peaceful uses in the development of the nuclear power station. The development of the submarine in special forms led to the first steps in undersea exploration, and this is expanding into a major enterprise.

Thus it can be seen that the domain of physics has widened as the importance of the implications of the physical bases of related subjects has been recognized. The result has been the realization that physics is important for the wider study of related subjects, and the blurring of the boundaries of the subject continues. The technical skills that must be developed to bring the various and often vast projects to satisfactory conclusions provide a reservoir of know-how for experimental science. This has also led to the increased acceptance of scientists as valued colleagues with non-scientists in the board rooms and corridors of public decision-making. Physics, therefore, entered 1939 as a largely isolated academic activity, and emerged in 1945 as a major growing influence on our lives.

It is the pure developments in physics since 1945 that will concern us in what follows, rather than the technological and allied aspects. But even our discussion of the modern aspects of pure physics must appear cavalier within the space available here. I can do no more than touch briefly on a few aspects that interest me particularly, and the picture will inevitably become distorted. Much must be left unsaid and many significant experimental developments (such as the field of laser physics, based very largely on the early theoretical work of Einstein, and holography, exploiting the full classical optical wave field) must unfortunately be overlooked altogether. Such topics could well find a place in a further volume of this series, perhaps in 1985! From this chapter it may appear that the present-day position in physics is not one abounding with new discoveries of principle, and that a further chapter written twenty years from now would be thin if development and technology were excluded. But might this not have been the prediction for the future made by someone writing in the year 1870?

### *The Nucleus and Nuclear Particles*

Our understanding of the extra-nuclear structure of the atom reached such a level of completeness in the late 1930s that the prediction of atomic spectral features was a matter of computation and not dependent on matters of principle. The computational difficulties increased with the addition of each electron in the atom. The application of the theory then was severely restricted because of the practical difficulties of carrying through the necessary numerical calculations, but there was no doubt that all the matters of principle had been established to sufficient approximation. The essential mathematical problem was that of solving a partial differential equation (the Schrödinger equation) or equivalently a matrix equation (the Heisenberg representation) for the motion of the electrons around the nucleus. Each electron could be treated as interacting separately with the nucleus, but in addition the interactions between electrons needed to be accounted for and this effect is not always a small perturbation of the electron-nucleus interaction. The problems of war brought about great advances in the techniques of numerical computation, and led to the development of the electronic computer which began to become available generally in the late 1940s. Thus began the wide exploitation of the theories developed in the decade before the war.

During the 1930s it was found that the nucleus itself is a complex structure of protons and neutrons (collectively called nucleons), and many nuclear properties began to be recognized. Of particular importance later was the discovery that the nucleus can be split by neutrons (nuclear fission), and especially significant was the discovery (in 1939 by Hahn and Frisch) first that the uranium isotope U235 is split by neutrons of thermal energy, and second that several products result, including on the average two neutrons with thermal energy. The fission process provided a large excess of free energy which could be available for use. The thermal neutrons would be available to cause the fission of other uranium nuclei that might be near by and a continuous process of energy production could be provided by making a suitable concentration of the 235 isotope. The discovery of the chain reaction in uranium 235 was one of the most momentous discoveries ever made by man. On the one side it led to the construction of the atomic bombs dropped over Japan in 1945. On the other side, the nuclear power station became a reality in the late 1940s, once the methods of controlling the energy release had been mastered. The technological derivatives have been wide indeed. One has been the production at will of artificially radioactive materials for medical use; another has been the production of atoms heavier than those occurring naturally, of great interest for the study of nuclear stability as well as providing alternative sources of power.

We cannot explore these matters here, but we can notice that one important by-product of these experimental developments was the need to have a model of the heavy nuclei to act as a guide for technological purposes. Application of experimental data to daily affairs can take place only when the data can be adequately described, and such a description must involve at least a minimum of theoretical understanding. The direct result of experiments of nuclear fission were efforts to provide models of the nucleus able to account for at least a restricted set of known nuclear properties. The construction of models of the nucleus has been a constant activity since 1945 and the work still continues. This theoretical work is of substantial mathematical complexity and we need only mention certain of the broad principles here.

To begin with we must suppose that the theoretical methods already found of value in treating the extra-nuclear electrons will also allow the nucleus to be described: modification may be recognized as the work proceeds but we must start by using that which is already available. In fact many nuclear features can be described in these terms although it soon became apparent that no single model was able to account adequately for all the known nuclear properties. And again, the nature of the forces between nucleons was different in principle from the two basic forces already known, viz. the gravitational and electromagnetic forces. The extreme stability of the nuclei required forces enormously stronger than the gravitational force (in fact some $10^{39}$ times as strong!), and the small size of the nuclei (measured in units of $10^{-13}$ centimetres, i.e. 100,000 times smaller than the characteristic size of an atom) meant that the nuclear forces must be of extremely short range (small in comparison to the nuclear size). Again, the roughly equal proton and neutron numbers in stable nuclei showed that the force could not be electromagnetic. We were here meeting a new fundamental force of nature, to take its place as an equal partner alongside the gravitational and electromagnetic forms. The nature of the nuclear force is still only partially understood.

The density of matter in the nucleus is essentially the same for all nuclei; if the fission process is likened to the instability of a vibrating liquid drop, the constant liquid density has a counterpart in the constant density of nuclear matter. The representation of the nucleus as a liquid drop provided a very useful semi-empirical model of the nucleus able to account for many properties of nuclear fission, and particularly of uranium. The analogy with a liquid can be carried further and refined models constructed. The atoms in a liquid are in continuous interaction with their neighbours and this suggests that account might be taken of the continuous interaction of the nucleons. Collective models of motion must be explored, and the notorious unsolved difficulties of such N-body systems must be circumvented. Excitation features of the nucleus can be treated this way. At the simplest level we can explore the motion of individual nucleons in the same way that the individual electron orbits outside the nucleus had been explored. The picture of electron energy levels comes to mind and this can be transferred to the nuclear case by representing the nucleus as a potential well with quantized energy levels inside. This picture has considerable support from the observed range of particularly stable nuclei with specific nucleon numbers. Thus, nuclei with 8, 16, 20, 28, 38, 50, 82, and 126 neutrons or protons were found experimentally to be spherical and particularly stable, and the interpretation of these numbers as characteristic of nuclear closed shells is irresistible. Unfortunately the concept, while useful in accounting for observed stability, has not yet been notably useful in a wider context.

Although nuclear matter has on the average constant density, local deviations can be expected to occur. More than this, the nucleons can have wave properties ascribed to them according to the notions of quantum physics. The treatment of nuclear reactions in wave terms has given rise to the optical model which attempts to exploit the features of 'black-box' theory so well exemplified by thermodynamics. Such arguments are attractive because the complicated structure of the system is represented by a few general parameters, and physical processes are described in semi-phenomenological terms. For the nuclear case, consider the scattering of a moving particle (a neutron or proton) by a nucleus. The incoming particle is represented by an advancing plane wave; the nucleus is represented as a suitably refracting medium, which acts as a secondary (Huygen's) source, emitting a spherical wave as a result of the interaction with the incoming particle. The nuclear properties are inferred through the process of getting the correct refractive properties as judged by the measured diffracted secondary spherical wave. This model is being actively developed, along with the other model approaches to the nucleus, and substantial progress can be expected in the future.

One of the most remarkable outcomes of the study of nuclear matter has been the discovery of a range of particles which throw new light on the nature of the long-known electron, proton, and neutron. The new particles have been discovered through the study of the high-energy interactions between nuclear particles. We have already seen (volume II, p. 231)* that the concept of particle spin was given a firm theoretical interpretation by Dirac in 1928 by an application of the theory of special relativity. As a result of this work, it was predicted that the electron should have a 'mate', identical in all respects except that of the electric charge which should be positive and not negative. This particle, the positron, was discovered in 1932. The 'mate' is more properly called an anti-particle, and Dirac's arguments had sufficient generality to apply to other particles as well, e.g. to the proton. The anti-proton (with negative instead of positive charge) was discovered experimentally in 1955. A characteristic feature of matter and anti-matter is a strong propensity for interaction with each other: electrons and positrons combine (under appropriate conditions of conservation of energy *and* momentum) to form a photon (see II. 232); the proton and anti-proton also react to produce particles of smaller mass that are not electrons or positrons. (Actually they are pions and kaons: the pion can have a mass of either 273 or 264 times that of an electron and a positive or negative electron charge, although some may be electrically neutral; kaons are heavier, either 967 or 974 electron masses, and can be similarly charged to pions.) This is no doubt confusing to the reader, and the physicist often feels in the same state.

Generally speaking three groups of particles are now recognized: the leptons (electron and positron, neutrino and anti-neutrino—of which two distinct types were recognized in 1962 from a study of certain decay processes) and muon; with 207 electron masses and either a positive or negative charge, the mesons (pion and kaon); and the baryons (proton, anti-proton, neutron, anti-neutron, lambda particle, discovered 1947, sigma particle, with about 2330 electron masses, omega minus, discovered in 1964, with 3270 electron masses, and others).

It has become clear from detailed study that the pions are intimately connected with nuclear forces (the idea of such particles was earlier predicted by Yukawa, but his calculated mass was different) and could be viewed as the quantized particle of the nuclear force. The vast array of particles now known, with lifetimes often measured in units of $10^{-10}$ seconds, have the appearance of excited states of more basic particle entities. New and novel conservation laws may need to be enunciated to supplement those already accepted (the conservation of parity and of strangeness are two that must already be added to those of energy, momentum, and electric charge). Much remains to be learned, and radioactivity must in the end be

* Page references to the chapters on Physics in volumes I and II of *The Twentieth-Century Mind* will be given hereafter as follows: II. 231.

involved (at a deeper level than that of the weak-interaction processes so far developed). The situation has certain similarities with that met with in gravitation long ago when Kepler had propounded his laws (I. 255–6) but before Newton had elucidated the form of the gravitational force. This is one area where fundamental discoveries can be confidently expected in the near future, but the prosecution of this work shows an interesting side-effect. The energies involved are so high that enormous apparatus is required and the financial cost is prodigious. Against the claims by workers in space research, astronomy, and plasma physics—to mention but three other areas of research within physics—it is necessary to balance the money and resources to be allocated to nuclear work. International co-operation is part of science, so these problems of financial administration become international problems. We are used to allocating restricted resources, but these new problems bring us face to face with basic truths. The acquisition of knowledge and understanding is one of the aims of culture and culture costs money; we may be approaching the limit of the knowledge that we can afford. Here is a possible restriction on scientific activity that was not generally foreseen in 1945.

*Applications of General Relativity: Cosmology*

In the non-quantum world, general relativity stood as an isolated tower of intellectual achievement not fully integrated with the other branches of the subject. Its history was curious and broke many of the rules by which new developments were to be expected. It arose as an attempt to generalize the special theory (see I. 275) but the arguments depended more on intellectual beauty than hard experimental fact. The mathematical formulation was based on simplicity, and amounted to evolving the simplest set of mathematical equations consistent with the requirements of the relativity of all events (whether the frame of reference is inertial or not) and of the conservation statements of energy (and so also mass according to relativity results) and momentum. These equations are still of very considerable mathematical complexity; attempts have been made to find solutions for cases other than those of empty space, but without any marked success so far, despite the considerable effort expended by many people in this work. These frustrations have led to efforts to rethink the mathematical formulation of the theory by means of a more penetrating analysis of geometry itself and Erwin Schrödinger (b. 1887) has played a leading role in this work* which is still very

* These matters are too technical to pursue here in detail, but the concept of affine connection was central to much of the work.

much in progress. It forms an academic pocket which might have the greatest importance in the future, but which might, alternatively, prove in the end abortive.

Early on, Einstein attempted to develop a unified theory combining the gravitational and electromagnetic forces—the two fundamental interactions known until the very late 1930s—into a single geometrical formulation. These attempts continue, but have met a fundamental difficulty which still bars the way. The geometrical representation of gravitational particle trajectories in terms of a geodesic (shortest path) of an appropriate geometry is possible because of the unusual property of the gravitational interaction in producing a constant acceleration for all particles independent of their mass. (Remember the experiment of Galileo, who dropped weights of different magnitude from the Leaning Tower of Pisa: the experiment was recently repeated on the moon where a mass of moon material and a feather were found to reach the surface of the moon simultaneously when dropped together from the same height.) But for charged particles in an electric field, the acceleration depends upon the ratio of charge to mass of the particle. For the interaction between charged particles and electromagnetic forces it would appear that each type of particle needs to be assigned its own four-dimensional geometry, and the concept of unification is not sympathetic to such an assignment. Attempts to treat such a multiplicity of four-dimensional worlds as sub-spaces of a single five-dimensional manifold have not been successful and the future of even the concept of the unified field theory is obscure. The complication has been increased by the recognition of the nuclear force as a third fundamental force (see p. 254). It could well be that the idea of a unified representation of all natural forces is an illusion arising out of the particular restrictions which result from the ideas of general relativity, which must themselves be generalized to give a truer picture of more general observations. What is aesthetically possible when nuclear forces are not included becomes unattainable when they are: this is another example of the way our fundamental appreciation of the universe may need to change when new knowledge becomes available.

The status of the three crucial tests (I. 276) needs reassessment in the light of these later views. We have seen already that the reddening of light as it escapes from a gravitating region and the bending of light by a massive body may be observed in practice but that the numerical agreement between observation and theory is far from close. The remaining effect, viz. the advance of the perihelion of the planet Mercury, is also under a cloud even though at first (i.e. in the 1920s) it seemed perhaps the safest of the three effects. The recognition of the effect (see I. 276) follows when all the perturbing effects of the other members of the solar system have been accounted for, and its interpretation as offending Newtonian gravitation theory depends upon the internal properties of Mercury having a simple symmetry about the rotation axis. The closeness of the planet to the sun can be a reason for doubting the correctness of this assumption of symmetry and the matter can be explored further only when information is available about the figure of the planet. Methods of space exploration using space vehicles can be of great value here in the future. Until then the possibility remains that Newtonian theory may be adequate for this effect after all; but the other two tests remain outside its competence.

In spite of doubts about the fine details of the theory of general relativity, its broad structure remains available for the description of the behaviour of matter in the large; this has allowed a new independent field of study, cosmology, to emerge as a branch of physics in its own right.

The early applications of general relativity by Einstein were to the study of the universe as a single entity, but there is not much more than historical interest in this work now because it was undertaken before the new knowledge of the universe became available as a consequence of the advent of the large optical telescopes. The universe was regarded then as static and probably young; the expanding universe which characterizes the 1930s (see II. 249) was yet to be discovered. The emergence of cosmology as a self-contained discipline probably came about as a result of new attempts to understand the history of the universe as a dynamic unit. The expansion of the universe leads to the difficulty that energy conservation (so vital an aspect of other parts of physics) is possible for the universe treated as a whole but not locally, because the whole universe is expanding presumably at constant energy. As the galaxies move apart, space-time becomes continually 'flatter' so that strain energy associated with geometrical curvature must manifest itself in other forms as the curvature becomes less severe. It is true that any change of energy locally would be too small to measure, but the basic principle might be at stake. We know now that the situation is considerably more complicated than this, but the difficulty is important.

The discussion of the universe as a whole must be based on the premise that we are now able to view a representative sample of the whole. There is the complication, of course, that in viewing the galaxies now we are necessarily looking back in time—in fact back through perhaps half or more of the time since the galaxies were very close together. But remembering this, we enunciate the cosmological principle that the universe looks everywhere the same to all observers. The observed expansion, which is to be accepted as genuine on several grounds including thermodynamic, as well as through the interpretation of the Doppler shift, could mean that each observer would see the universe melt away around him if he were able to view it for a sufficient length of time (measured in thousands of millions of years). Later observers of this picture would not see other galaxies since all would have moved too far apart for the light to pass between them. It is indeed lucky that we are able to build telescopes now and that our evolutionary saga did not occur thousands of millions of years later. (We might notice in passing that had we been in this position long ago when the galaxies were close together we would have seen less than now because there could have been too much light!) Physicists are always suspicious of lucky circumstances, and it is worth exploring the possibility that in this case luck has played no part at all. This viewpoint is the starting point of the steady-state theory of cosmology, originated by Bondi and Gold, and by Hoyle, which caused great discussion during the 1950s.

Besides supposing that the universe everywhere gives the same overall appearance, it is also supposed that this has always been so. The expansion of the galaxies observed today has always been present and always will be; the universe is in a steady state although it is a dynamic body. Because the expansion of the galaxies implies a thinning out of material locally, the steady-state condition is possible only if matter is continually being created to replace it. This continuous creation of matter was perhaps the most revolutionary hypothesis of the theory, even though the rate of creation to counterbalance exactly the loss of material by galactic expansion is necessarily too small to observe—the mass of one hydrogen atom in each litre of space every one thousand million years. More explicitly, the rate of creation of matter must be, on the average, three times the mean density of matter in the universe multiplied by the Hubble constant (see II. 248), viz. $10^{-43}$ gm per $cm^3$ per sec. The details of the creation process were never explored beyond the initial stages, but the suggestion was certainly provocative; instead of one mighty creation process at the beginning of time, a continual, imperceptible trickle over all time. It appeared that the question of the origin of the universe itself was about to be discussed quantitatively, but this soon proved not to be so. Observational data, of galactic distributions principally but including other data as well, would be interpreted differently on the basis of the steady-state theory than on the simple expansion theory. Both optical and radio astronomical techniques began to show that the steady-state theory required more hypotheses to sustain it; apparently the universe was different in the past from what it is now. The steady-state idea has now lost favour, but the excitement it once engendered provided a great stimulus to theoretical analysis and observation alike.

But general relativity had other interests in store. It is a field theory (see I. 275) and in consequence gravitational energy will be transmitted with finite speed—the speed of light locally. Two concepts follow: one is the quantization of the energy through the existence of gravitons, as yet unknown other than formally; the second is the existence of gravitational waves in matter which is dilated or is rearranged appropriately. The existence of such waves would seem an unavoidable consequence of continuity of energy and many efforts were made to detect them. Very recently (1970) it has been claimed that such waves have been detected, with an apparent source in the central nucleus of our galaxy. Efforts are being made to extend the observations and assess the rate of emission of energy more accurately, but the waves seem to be there. Indeed there is some embarrassment because, although the measured effect is minute (it involves resonances of density variations in a large laboratory mass of simple geometry), the energy flux implied for the source is enormous, and would suggest that most energy in the galaxy is gravitational. From having nothing we have too much—physics is a very human subject. The study of gravitational waves, now beginning, could well provide surprises in the future.

*Continuum Mechanics*

It was seen earlier (I. 263) that the mechanical properties of matter can be described fully by the appeal to the laws of particle mechanics provided the basic 'particle' is defined appropriately. For non-relativistic fluids, we introduce the concept of the fluid particle (I. 264) and derive the conservation statements of mass, momentum, and energy in characteristic forms involving the dissipative mechanisms of viscosity and thermal conduction. Before 1942 the fluid was supposed to be an insulator and the behaviour of the fluid had been fully investigated by many workers. Wave modes had been recognized, and within the confines of the theory only longitudinal wave modes were possible if the fluid was in any way compressible. If the fluid behaved exactly incompressibly no wave modes were possible, for the carriage of energy; and in any event, the rigidity of the fluid was insufficient to allow transverse modes to propagate. The situation was clear and quite unambiguous. But new ideas arise from the joining of different ideas together and such was the case in 1942 when the Swedish physicist Alfvén (b. 1908) began a new branch of fluid mechanics, for which he was recently awarded the Nobel Prize. This is called magnetohydrodynamics or more simply hydromagnetics.

The idea is simple, as all good ideas are. Suppose the fluid is a conductor of electricity and suppose further that the fluid is moving differentially relative to a magnetic field of external origin. The passage of an electrically conducting fluid is equivalent to an electric current and the passage of an electric current is affected by the presence of the magnetic field (through the Lorentz force). But the effect is a mutual one, for an electric field has an associated magnetic field which is superimposed on that externally maintained. Looking again at the fluid, the motion of the fluid is affected by the magnetic field but the fluid itself affects the magnetic field. Remembering the experiments of Faraday in the early 1800s (see I. 265), a magnetic field can be regarded as equivalent to a set of elastic strings in tension, and a small disturbance in the fluid will propagate in a way analogous to the twanging of an elastic string. The result is a *transverse* wave, even though the fluid may be strictly incompressible. The wave speed will, according to the usual wave theory, be given by the square root of the magnetic stress per unit fluid mass: the transverse magnetohydrodynamic waves, often called Alfvén waves, will have a speed proportional to the strength of the undisturbed magnetic field of external origin and inversely proportional to the square root of the undisturbed fluid density. For the ideal case where the electrical conductivity is indefinitely large, the wave will move along the lines of magnetic field and will not show dispersion. The Alfvén wave speed is typically a few hundred centimetres per second and so is substantially less than the local speed of sound. Finite electrical conductivity will allow deviations of path from the ideal ('slippage') and will cause the waves to be damped as they travel: damping also results from the effects of fluid viscosity.

The general equations for the flow of a fluid under magnetohydrodynamic conditions, expressing continuity of mass, momentum, and energy, and accounting for thermodynamic effects, were available for use in the late 1940s. These equations are mathematically more complicated than the corresponding expressions for an insulating fluid to which they reduce when the electrical conductivity is equated to zero (insulating fluid). The essential feature of the theoretical basis is that any changes of the fluid condition must be slow and in terms of Maxwell's equations of electromagnetism (see I. 265) refer to vibration frequencies orders of magnitude lower than those for electromagnetic disturbances. Because Maxwell's work had the special feature of accounting for high frequencies (through the displacement current), it will be realized that magnetohydrodynamics is in essence pre-Maxwellian. This pocket of work had escaped discovery for a hundred years and arose in the 1940s much like a coelacanth from the past.

The theory has many ramifications which are still under active investigation, particularly for thermal flows involving the transfer of heat. There are technological implications to this work as well as those of pure science, and experimental data can be most helpful. In this connection there is one very important feature of the hydromagnetic interaction. It turns out that the strength of the coupling between the electrically conducting fluid and the magnetic field is proportional to the product of the electrical conductivity and the square of the characteristic length over which the field acts. For laboratory situations the length is small, so a strong coupling can arise only if the electrical conductivity is very large. For cosmic physics the situation is quite different; here the characteristic length is so large (often measured in light years) that the value of the electrical conductivity is almost irrelevant providing it is not actually zero. Scale is often very important in physics and it is not easy to pass from laboratory to cosmic measurements.

The increasing speed of aeroplanes, and other considerations, have added interest to the properties of discontinuous shock flows, including those involving magnetohydrodynamic couplings. But no new fundamental aspects of physics have been involved in this work.

In concluding this section we might mention the particular study of turbulent flows which we shall need to mention again later. We might also note efforts to extend the arguments to elastic liquids, where the linear relation between internal stress and rate of strain (see I. 264) must be replaced by a more complicated relation. Such studies, which are as yet only in the beginning stages, are still proceeding.

*Statistical Physics*

The principles of statistical mechanics (see I. 280) were applied to the detailed study of solid crystals and simple dense fluids and the theory of matter not in equilibrium was developed. The central feature has been the accounting for the simultaneous interaction of many atoms and molecules.

For solids, perhaps the central feature has been the detailed study of the consequences of the properties of the crystal lattice. This is, of course, a problem in quantum physics and the equivalence of energy modes in wave and particulate forms is central. An especial achievement of this work has been the elucidation of the property of superconductivity, where a range of elements lose their electrical conductivity when cooled below a characteristic temperature (usually at most a few degrees on the absolute temperature scale). The explanation of this effect by Cooper, Bardeen, and Schrieffer, an effect first noted by Kammerlingh Onnes some sixty years previously, relied on subtle considerations of statistical theory and was a minor triumph for the so-called N-body theory of the interaction between many particles simultaneously.

A new experimental tool became available as a result of the atomic bomb work of the Second World War, namely the atomic pile which is a prolific source of neutrons of controllable energy. Neutrons from this source can be formed into a beam and used to explore the atomic motions within a specimen much as X-rays had been used before (see I. 287). But neutrons have the advantage of travelling much more slowly and can be used to highlight the actual motion of the atoms in the specimen, whereas X-rays provide only a smeared-out average picture. This aspect of technology has developed rapidly in recent years.

As for solids, so for dense gases and liquids, neutron studies have added important information about the motion of the molecules. Thermodynamic variables for simple fluids (such as pressure, internal energy, entropy, chemical potential, and so on) have been calculated for various assumed laws of force between the molecules (some, like the hard sphere form, highly idealized, while others, like the van der Waals form, are more realistic) and successful comparisons made with experimental measurements. Virial coefficients for dilute gases have been calculated up to the seventh or eighth and considerable activity of technological importance has been reported by many workers. No new matters of principle are involved here, the theoretical basis for the work having been laid long ago (see I. 280), but no theoretical development is complete without the most rigorous comparison with experiment. This has proved possible now because of the availability of electronic computation facilities without which the heavy algebra would be intractable. Of course, computers are moronic entities that do no more than they are told to do: our present inability to treat theoretically the simultaneous interaction of many molecules (up to 25 may be involved in real matter) other than approximately is shown up in the numerical work through certain inconsistencies. By so arranging the theories as to reduce these inconsistencies as far as possible, the numerical work plays a part in the further development of the underlying theories.

The problem of accounting for the simultaneous motion of many particles, where each continuously affects the trajectories of the others, is a major outstanding deficiency of our work. Of course, the problem is not new and was met long ago in connection with the detailed calculation of planetary orbits (see I. 256), and quite separately in connection with the study of dilute gases (I. 278). There we saw that solutions are possible if the full interaction can be simplified by being separated into two parts: the first is the essential controlling factor for the trajectory of a representative particle arising from one other particle; the second is a small perturbing part which is the sum of the small contribution of each remaining particle taken separately. In this way the full interaction involving many particles can be dealt with as a succession of pair interactions. Progress in the study of condensed matter was closely bound up with the successful representation of molecular interactions in the same way. The theory of the dilute gas was extended to encompass higher densities, and alternative methods were developed for treating very dense fluids, including liquid densities.

Of especial interest has been the development of the possibility, originally detailed by Prigogine, of applying the mathematical techniques of quantum physics to problems in classical fluid theory. This work appears to offer interesting possibilities for the future, particularly in connection with dense fluids not in equilibrium, an area of statistical physics still not finally understood and one that could have important implications in other branches of science and also in technology. Of especial significance has been the evolution of expressions for the transport coefficients of a simple liquid (coefficients such as shear viscosity, bulk viscosity, thermal conductivity, and electrical conductivity) in terms of the properties of the molecules and of the interaction forces between them. Such expressions bridge the gap finally between theories of micro- and macro-matter and pave the way for generalization to include more complicated fluids. Ideas of irreversibility (I. 285) first developed in the early years of the century have been adapted to apply to these cases and have proved generally correct. Irreversibility does indeed appear to be a reversible phenomenon but with an inordinately long recurrence time, so long that we cannot wait for the initial state to return. Von Smoluchowski took this view in 1915 and seems to have been correct; but this could only be made clear by much more detailed work than was possible then.

All these arguments rely to a greater or lesser extent on the forces between the molecules having a short range, effectively no greater than two molecular diameters or so. This is clearly a restriction that is undesirable in principle, and the practical need to remove it arose with the study of the plasma, which was an important post-1945 activity closely linked with the arts of both war and peace. A plasma is a collection of particles of opposite charge, some positive (usually ions, but protons are the simplest case) and others negative (almost always electrons). The essential point about a plasma is that the two types of charge are present in equal numbers in a macroscopic volume, so that the total volume is electrically neutral: of course, local deviations from neutrality occur and these regions give the whole plasma properties that are characteristically different from those of the other phases of matter. Indeed, the plasma state has been named the fourth state of matter, although this title is misleading and wrong.

The interest in a plasma from a fundamental point of view is that the forces between the charges are the Coulomb forces between charges and so have a long range (the force decreasing at large distances as the inverse square of the distance rather than as the inverse seventh power, as for neutral atoms). The charge imbalance locally in a plasma leads to a macroscopic electrical conductivity so that a plasma is affected by the presence of an external magnetic field as a magnetohydrodynamical fluid (see p. 262). The problems of statistical physics posed by a plasma are immense and many remain unresolved; of especial importance are those relating to the calculation of transport coefficients with magnitudes in accord with experimentally determined values. The wave modes available to plasmas are both complicated and interesting, and have been extensively investigated. Thermal conditions within a plasma can be highly interesting if only because they are not yet fully understood theoretically. It is unlikely that the theoretical study of plasmas will provide new problems of fundamental importance, but the study is absorbing and is being actively pursued by many physicists and mathematicians.

The practical interest in plasmas is many-sided, and two aspects can be mentioned here. Because it is necessary to break a neutral atom up into a positively and a negatively charged part, the production of a plasma generally involves the expenditure of energy. This separation is accomplished in gases by the expenditure of electrical energy, and gaseous plasmas are very hot; the highest temperatures yet achieved in the laboratory—perhaps as high as $10^8$K over a very small volume for a very short time ($\sim 10^{-6}$ sec)—have used plasmas. Such high temperatures are known to exist in the central regions of stars where fusion reactions involving the conversion of hydrogen into helium occur. This conversion releases large quantities of energy over a short time period and is attractive technologically as a cheap and simple source of energy. This is the essential mechanism of the hydrogen bomb, but the harnessing of the thermonuclear process to peaceful uses has proved difficult. One difficulty is the inherent instability of the configuration of a plasma, and another is the problem of containing so hot a gas for any period of time. Large sums of money have been spent by many nations on solving these problems, along with others that would present themselves if the method were to be applied commercially, but all the answers have not yet been found. This work has not been viewed in isolation from the future world needs for energy and is one region where science and living overlap.

Another practical interest in plasma physics arises from the recognition that much of the universe is a plasma: indeed, those regions (like the earth and planets) which are not, form an insignificant part of the whole.

Although we have spoken of plasma physics in terms of gases, the concept of a plasma arises in the solid state as well. The ions of a crystal form a lattice, and the electrons are shared as if they were a gas of negative particles. Fundamental studies of plasmas as well as technological applications can be expected to follow from this branch of physics.

### *Astronomy and Space*

Progress in astronomy during the present period has been so enormous that we cannot attempt anything other than the briefest of comments here. The spectacular advances have been the result of several facts: partly the increased optical power available to observers; partly the development of radio astronomy as a powerful observational tool; and partly a deeper theoretical understanding of the physical processes occurring in stars. Space probes have made only a small contribution so far.

One of the earliest developments soon after the war was the recognition that the distribution of hydrogen gas can be inferred from a study of the 21 cm. wave-length radiation that it emits. This radiation arises from the difference of the energy of the hydrogen atom when the nuclear and electron spins are parallel and in the same direction and when the spins are parallel but pointing in opposite directions (anti-parallel). Observations of this radiation gave the first information about the structure of our own galaxy, confirming it to have a spiral form. It was further found that the sun is some 27,000 light years from the galactic centre, the total system rotating with the sun taking 230 million years to complete one revolution. The sun will have made some 25 revolutions during the life-span of the earth. Further theoretical analysis leads us to believe that the mass of the galaxy contained within the orbit of the sun is some $6 \times 10^{11}$ solar masses. This information was of particular interest because it followed close on the recognition (by Baade in 1944) of the division of stars into two separate populations. This was suggested by the observation that elliptic galaxies are apparently composed of stars that are quite different from those comprising irregular galaxies; spiral galaxies contain both types. The 'elliptic' type stars were called by Baade Population II stars; we now know that these are old stars of high heavy element abundance. The 'irregular' type stars were called Population I stars, now known to be young stars of low heavy element abundance. These terms are not much used now, but the possibility of recognizing stars of different ages was exciting when first discovered.

Since then, however, the evolution of stellar objects has begun to be understood in detail, particularly using electronic computational techniques. The picture emerges of a dilute gas cloud with stellar mass, which contracts under its own gravitation. The temperature inside increases with the density until the temperature is sufficiently high for thermonuclear processes to begin, the overwhelmingly predominant hydrogen content beginning to be converted into helium. Heat is produced, so enhancing the further development of the heat source, but eventually the process is halted by the helium 'ash'. The star is then unstable and will rearrange itself, perhaps not to burn more or perhaps to allow more burning either of hydrogen outside the immediate centre or of helium which is converted into beryllium. The arrangement of stars in the Hertzsprung–Russell diagram (see II. 259) is now understood in these terms, the evolution of a single star forming a single trajectory over the diagram. The rate at which the processes will occur will vary from one star to another, the empty spaces in the diagram not being forbidden in any sense but rather reflecting the short time interval required for the completion of this evolutionary sequence.

This gives a grossly oversimplified picture but shows the broad features. Other aspects are known. There appears now to be a multiplicity of types of star, each radiating principally in one wave-length region of the electromagnetic spectrum. X-ray stars were soon discovered when photographs were taken from rockets outside the earth's atmosphere (which is opaque to X-rays): infra-red sources were similarly found. Perhaps the most far-reaching results have come from radio sources. One early discovery was strong radio sources which could be identified optically as two galaxies in collision. Galaxies are now known to occur in clusters, which may include many tens of component members, and even clusters may be clustered. The initial rules such as Hubble's law (see II. 248) can apparently still be applied but now in a special way, e.g. by considering the brightest member of a cluster. But many radio sources, closely defined in angular terms in space, were known which did not have an obvious optical association. One extraordinary feature was a phenomenally high wave-length shift which, if interpreted in terms of a Doppler shift, would imply a high speed of recession. Invoking the Hubble law, such high shifts would need to be associated with sources at enormous distances—far greater very often than those seen optically. In these terms the radio sources would refer to an early period of the history of the universe, interpreting the expansion as a unique event. The steady-state theory would need to supply a special interpretation of these data. The problem arose once again of locating these radio sources. If the sources were nearby objects, they would be very small and very weak but the wave-length shift would not be a Doppler effect; if the sources were as distant as the wave-length shift might imply, then the intensity would be enormous. Much controversy arose on this point and was resolved as more sources were found: each interpretation could be applied to different sources. There were indeed immensely strong sources at enormous distances, but at the same time others nearer (such as the Crab nebula) are more modest sources of radio power. The distribution of optical and radio sources could be used to distinguish between the predictions of the steady-state and other theories. It is now generally agreed that the steady-state concept is not able to account for the observed galactic distribution and that the universe does indeed change in time. This being so, the strong distant radio sources, now called quasars, represent a source of energy far more powerful than any other known, and these must be associated with the far distant past. The study of such sources offers many interests for the future.

But nearer objects are also posing interesting problems of physics. Some radio sources have been found to pulsate regularly, perhaps over a period of a few seconds or even less—one example is the central object in the Crab nebula—and optical wave-lengths are involved as well. The period of vibration can be interpreted as the time of passage of a disturbance through the object and in these terms the object would be very small—much smaller than the sun. Some objects of stellar mass appear to have a diameter of only a few kilometres, and if this is so the density of matter in them must approach that of nuclear matter. Such stars, as much more dense than a white-dwarf star as the white dwarf is more dense than a normal star such as the sun, must be composed of nucleons—the neutron stars theory predicted long ago.

Very dense matter has implications on space curvature from the viewpoint of general relativity, and a fully inverted region cut off from the rest of the universe could result from the presence of mass of sufficient density. Since no radiation could leave such a region it would appear 'black' to measuring devices and such 'black holes' have already been tentatively identified. Astronomy has always produced interesting new phenomena for physics (nuclear reactions would have needed to be postulated to account for the strength of stellar energy sources even if they had not been discovered in the laboratory), and the process is clearly continuing still. The next generation of change in physics could well arise from astronomical data, but meanwhile much remains to be done in traditional astronomy. For instance, the evolutionary processes of galaxies such as our own are still mysterious, and the origin of magnetic fields has so far defied analysis.

### *Planetary Studies*

The first attempts at understanding the physical basis of planetary bodies dates from the nineteenth century. Perhaps the first clear statement of the problem in quantitative terms was made by Darwin who, in 1886, sought the radius of a condensed rotating mass of matter of prescribed mechanical properties. Later, Weichert (1898) considered the same problem but in restricted application to the earth, when he sought to discover the nature of the terrestrial interior from a knowledge of the observed mass, radius, and mean moment of inertia of the earth. This work was pursued between the World Wars, particularly by Jeffreys and by Bullen, and has emerged again since 1945.

A planet is a cold body in contrast to a normal star such as the sun, which is a hot body. The terms hot and cold in this context do not refer directly to temperature: a hot body is one where the gravitational inward acting force is opposed by a radiation pressure acting outwards, the stable configuration occurring when these two forces balance exactly. For this to happen the internal temperature of the object must be high and the material will usually be gaseous. But the balance will break down when the pressure is still appreciable. Radiation pressure makes no contribution to the equilibrium of a cold body, the balance now being one between gravitational force and the compression forces characteristic of the material. A planet is a cold body in these terms, and although its internal temperature may be several thousand degrees it can be treated as of uniform internal temperature (isothermal) to good approximation.

The observed figures of the planets follow very closely the form they would be expected to have if they were fluids of the same mass and density. This fact was early used in the study of planetary interiors where it was envisaged that conditions were those of hydrostatic (fluid) equilibrium. This is not as odd as it might seem at first sight. The pressure within the planet will increase quite rapidly with depth (due to the weight of material above) and a depth will soon be reached at which the local pressure exceeds the rigidity strength of the constituent material (this will occur at a depth of about 30 to 40 kilometres for the earth). Below this depth the material will behave as a plastic material and its equilibrium form (reached after many thousands of millions of years perhaps) would be expected to be indistinguishable from that of a corresponding normal fluid material. The essential feature here is the behaviour of rock material under pressure, within the range from essentially zero (objects such as the moon have no atmosphere) up to several million million atmospheres (which will be the order of the pressure at the centre of Jupiter).

The members of the solar system can be viewed as a single entity in these terms, even though the major planets (Jupiter, Saturn, Uranus, and Neptune) differ very radically in their properties from the terrestrial group (Mercury, Venus, Earth, and Mars). The outermost planet Pluto is neglected here because its properties are even yet not well enough known, but it has the appearance of being broadly similar to terrestrial planets rather than similar to the major ones. The essential difference between the two planetary groupings appears to be the proportional content of hydrogen and other light elements. For Jupiter and Saturn this content is very high, and the lighter elements are well represented in Uranus and Neptune. The terrestrial planets by comparison are very deficient, relatively speaking, in these elements.

Surprisingly enough, the availability of space vehicles has not so far been of much importance in these studies. The reason is easy to see: space vehicles can at best touch the surface of the planet but this is not of itself very useful in assessing the conditions inside. Other techniques must also be used, such as the propagation of elastic energy (by earthquakes for the earth, and corresponding processes will be useful for other planets as well—indeed, seismic techniques have already been applied to the moon with success), but even then considerable interpretation of data must still be made on the basis of laboratory and theoretical experience. But we know enough already to realize that the established principles of physics will be adequate for a quantitative account of planetary interiors to be developed in the future.

The magnetism of the planets is of interest because earth and Jupiter are known to possess permanent magnetic fields, whereas the remaining planets appear not to. The origin of such fields is obscure, except that it is now generally accepted as being a magneto-hydrodynamic effect (see p. 262) analogous to that of the self-acting dynamo. For the earth the origin of the field is now accepted as being in the core region, but for Jupiter the location of the source is still a matter of conjecture. There is recent evidence that the Jovian field has a strength comparable to that of the earth, making an angle of some 9° with the rotation axis (for the earth the corresponding angle is 4°) but with the polarity oppositely directed to that of the earth's field. The known polarity reversals of the terrestrial field robs the polarity direction of any essential significance. Again the future should be interesting but no new fundamental problems of physics are likely to be involved in this work.

The same seems true of the interplanetary conditions even though the details remain to be elucidated. This is one region where space probes and satellites have proved of the greatest importance. It had been conjectured since the beginning of the century that the sun emits particles as well as radiation (see II. 261) but the form of this emission was difficult to deduce from measurements at the terrestrial surface. There was, of course, the evidence to be deduced from the measured features of magnetic storms, but the effects were very small and of very complicated structure. Only with the use of satellites could more useful data be collected.

But independently of measurement, Biermann in Germany realized, in the late 1940s, that any emission from the sun must be essentially continuous, although its intensity could fluctuate from time to time. Space-probe measurements have confirmed this effect, now called the solar wind, and have led to the recognition of a complex magnetic field-plasma structure acting as an extended 'tail' downwind of the earth. Because the speed of the solar wind in the vicinity of the earth is greater than the local Alfvén speed in the plasma (see p. 262) a bow shock-wave structure exists on the noon-side of the earth, facing the sun. The elucidation of these magnetic features is interesting, and we can look forward to further developments.

We have come to the end of our story, and it is perhaps worth summarizing not only the period under discussion now, but also, briefly, the two previous periods, treated in detail in earlier volumes.

The face of physics has changed beyond all recognition since 1900. New areas of discovery have led to the recognition of new underlying processes, but also the few cracks discernible in 1900 have proved to have their origins in the very foundations of the subject. Instead of an absolutist viewpoint in a more or less closed world, physics now is fundamentally relativist, and covers an enormous range. The new discoveries and changes of attitude up to 1939 were breathtaking in both their depth and beauty, and have not been equalled since. Perhaps this is not surprising. A period of such change and trauma must be followed by a period of stock-taking and relative quiet, and the period since 1945 can be looked at in these terms. The full recognition of the nuclear force as a third basic interaction of nature is a new achievement, but much else has been in the nature of exploring ideas already available. But the nature of the nuclear force is still a mystery and although much that is new is now coming from astronomical observation there is, so far, no fundamentally new understanding as a result. New recognitions are abroad. No one, be he scientist or not, can remain unaffected in his attitude by the advent of the atomic and hydrogen bombs, nor can he remain unaffected by the changing social conditions. This is particularly so of the physicist because his subject over the last fifty years or so has helped to bring these very things about. Knowledge costs money and this fact has affected the development of physics more and more in recent years. Already the exploitation of the international nature of science by collaborative ventures involving international finance is failing to provide the ever-increasing cost of modern research in physics—and in science generally. It might be argued that physics has become too tightly enmeshed with a technology which is increasingly neglecting the longer-term effects of its development. The pace of technology increases steadily and the adage 'if it works it is obsolete' can be argued as leading to an unstable and wasteful spiral of only loosely controlled development. These comments contain more than a grain of truth and should lead us to reflect the more carefully on the future role of science and especially of physics.

So much information is now available that physics stands as a gigantic structure with specialisms within specialisms that in many ways act against a deep understanding of the data themselves. It could be that physics as a subject now awaits a period of synthesis and inward digestion. This will be a lengthy and hard, but an immensely rewarding undertaking. Looking to the future, the remaining years of this century could well be a period of reassessment of physics as a fundamental discipline, although the recent tendency for it to link more closely with other subjects (such as the geological or the biological sciences) will surely continue. In some ways, the situation in physics now bears some resemblance to that existing in the 1870s, before our present story began. If this be so who can predict what the next century will produce except that problems will still remain to be solved as we approach ever nearer to the penumbra that we expect to be reality?

## FOR FURTHER READING

See the bibliography following Chapter 11, at p. 317.

10

# Chemistry

JARLATH RONAYNE

In the previous chapters on chemistry in this series, particular emphasis has been laid on the materialist aspect of the subject. The synthetic dyestuffs, polymers, and chemotherapeutic agents which emerged in the first half of this century have had such a profound effect on our everyday lives that it is obvious that of all the intellectual pursuits chosen in the series as representative of the twentieth-century mind, chemistry is by far the most practical. Equally obvious is the realization that these practical advances have usually preceded the advances in theoretical knowledge which explain the nature of the processes involved. This phenomenon is not unique to chemistry, of course, but it does mean that discussions on the development of chemistry tend to focus on the materialist rather than the cognitive aspect of the subject. The reader should, by now, be aware of the profound effect which chemistry has had on our material existence and that the major changes wrought have occurred largely as a result of either serendipity or sheer empiricism. In considering the postwar development of chemistry it is appropriate that we should now consider the ways in which chemistry, as an idea system, has been an intellectual as well as a material force in the twentieth century.

In the hierarchy of the scientific disciplines, chemistry stands midway between physics and biology and contributes to the conceptual framework and practical applications of both. The various hybrid disciplines, biochemistry, molecular biology, physical chemistry, chemical physics, astrochemistry, and geochemistry all testify to the importance of the principles of chemistry to other disciplines within the scientific community, but it is to its close relationship with physics that we must first look in order to explain the developments which have transformed the theory of chemistry in the first half of the century, and the practice of chemistry since 1945.

## *The Nature of Scientific Advance*

In order to place the intellectual development of chemistry in perspective it is instructive to examine the scientific enterprise as a whole to see if we can identify those characteristics which distinguish it from other areas of knowledge and which contribute to its unique success in fostering its aims. Traditionally, the scientist is viewed as an objective seeker of truth, a man who by the application of 'scientific method' uncovers the secrets of nature, proposes general laws, and makes valid predictions based on a logical interpretation of the facts. Asked to describe the way in which they work, scientists themselves usually reveal their belief in this orthodox view. But in the 1920s, the logical positivists, chastened by the crisis in physics engendered by Heisenberg's uncertainty principle, removed from science the ability to uncover absolute truth, substituting instead the ability to describe objectively the veil of appearance which covers reality. Michael Polanyi (b. 1891), the Manchester chemist and philosopher, restored to science the ability to discover reality, but for him the scientists' contact with absolute truth is intuitive rather than logical. This was, perhaps, the first renunciation of the 'principle' of objectivity in scientific investigation; an element of faith was introduced into the psychology of the scientist.

A more systematic refutation of the positivist approach is due to Sir Karl Popper (b. 1902), philosopher of science at the London School of Economics. In Popper's view science progresses towards absolute truth and the methodological imperative is a process of falsification. The logic behind this assertion is that whereas we can never know that a given hypothesis is true, we can at least be sure if it is false. The initial hypothesis is arrived at by an imaginative process, not a logical one; again an element of subjectivity is introduced into the scientists' work.

But neither Polanyi nor Popper concern themselves with the structure of the scientific community nor with the sociological pressures acting on scientists. For an analysis of scientific methodology which takes into account these factors we must turn to the influential *Structure of Scientific Revolutions*, published in 1962 by T. S. Kuhn, philosopher of science at Princeton. Kuhn has identified a number of phases in the development of a scientific discipline. In the first phase, which for the moment we can regard as pre-scientific, investigations are conducted in a random fashion and tend to circle back upon one another; new facts are rapidly discovered, lost, and rediscovered, there is little consensus about fundamental principles, and each investigator tends to verify the basic facts for himself before embarking upon his main research theme. There are many competing schools of thought with the proponents of each school endeavouring to disprove the theories of their rivals. This situation is resolved in the second phase of development by the emergence of a first *paradigm*, a procedural model which now guides the investigations into fruitful areas; chemistry after Lavoisier or electricity after Franklin may be regarded in this way. The guidance which the paradigm gives to theoretical and experimental activity engenders in the disciplinary community a deep loyalty to it and this loyalty or commitment which Kuhn perceives in all branches of mature science is the most extraordinary facet of his work. This commitment gives rise to *normal* science, the third phase in the development of a mature science; normal science is what all scientists do most of the time and most scientists do all of the time. It is essentially a puzzle-solving activity; the scientist attempts to fit nature into the 'boxes' provided by the paradigm and if the attempt should fail it is upon the scientist or his instruments that suspicion falls, not upon the paradigm. Normal science does not aim at real novelty. The outcome of the various investigations can be anticipated, often in detail so great that what remains to be known is itself quite uninteresting. But the solution of instrumental, conceptual, and mathematical puzzles has its own rewards, both institutional and personal, for the scientist, and the challenge of the puzzle is an important part of what drives him on. In practice, a great deal of useful data are accumulated in this phase of research. The predictions of the paradigm are fulfilled—a new planet is discovered as predicted, or a new element is found; quantitative measurements are made to greater and greater degrees of accuracy and relationships between various parameters are evaluated.

But if the acquisition of a paradigm heralds the emergence of a mature science, the continuing vitality of that science depends upon progress from paradigm to paradigm. In the period of normal science following the emergence of the first paradigm, there is usually full agreement on fundamental principles with a consequent increase in specialization. In view of this consensus, serious anomaly is not readily perceived as such; results which do not conform to expectations or to the predictions of the paradigm are often seen as human or instrumental errors. But it is also true that because of the consensus anomaly is rapidly seen even though it is not perceived as such. It is only when anomalous results begin to mount up that the research tradition enters a period of crisis which is usually resolved by a paradigm change; this change is called a *scientific revolution* and happens at relatively infrequent periods in the history of science. The conversion of the individual scientists to the new paradigm has been likened by Kuhn to the 'Gestalt switch' of modern psychology.

The scientists' way of looking at the world is changed and this change owes nothing to formal logic. The conversion is never total, however, as is clearly evident from the resistance which is invariably offered by the scientific community to revolutionary ideas, a resistance which is symptomatic of the commitment which the community owes to the old paradigm. Nor is the conversion total. Max Planck, the physicist who introduced the revolutionary quantum theory, has remarked that a new scientific truth does not triumph by convincing its opponents and making them see the light. The opposition dies only with the death of the opponents.

Kuhn's analysis has, of course, been sharply criticized; the rational image of the scientist is threatened and his objectivity is in question. But there is little doubt that there are many scientists who are acutely aware of the accuracy with which he has described the scientific community. And it is partly within the Kuhnian framework that we shall be examining the intellectual development of chemistry in the period under review.

If a branch of science is to be evaluated in terms of its revolutionary episodes then there is little doubt that in the twentieth century chemistry has fared relatively badly, since many of the conceptual novelties which have borne fruit in chemistry belong to other disciplines, physics in particular. We will direct our attention, therefore, to the role of physics in the development of chemical theory and experimentation, and in order to do this properly, developments in the earlier part of the century will have to be discussed in some detail.

### *Chemistry and the Electron*

If the nineteenth century was, for chemistry, the century of the atom, the twentieth is, without doubt, the century of the electron. As the nineteenth century was drawing to a close the Daltonian atom became less and less adequate to explain the facts of physics and chemistry. The solution to the problem was to come, not from chemistry, but from physics where the interpretation of spectral lines, radioactivity, and gas-discharge phenomena demanded that the atom no longer be regarded as indivisible but as composed of subatomic particles. Thomson's proof, in 1897, of the existence of a particle considerably less massive than hydrogen was received with characteristic scepticism by the scientific community of the time, but its revolutionary implications for physics and chemistry soon became abundantly clear. It was proved to be a part of every atom and a prominent feature in the theoretical problems of physics and chemistry, problems associated with chemical binding and reactivity, spectroscopy and electrical phenomena.

At first it was not clear how the new particle might be used in chemistry, but Thomson steadfastly insisted that the origins of chemical attraction must lie in the electronic structure of matter; indeed, before Rutherford proposed a nuclear atom, the chemist Ramsay, co-discoverer of the noble gases, was thinking of chemical combination in terms of electronic interaction. But there was no further elaboration of this until after 1913. In 1902 G. N. Lewis, the American physical chemist, proposed that the electrons were arranged around the nucleus at the corners of a cube, but he was hampered in his work by the fact that he did not know how many electrons there were in an atom. This information was made available by the physicists Bohr, Sommerfeld, and Moseley, and in 1916 Lewis and Walther Kossel, Professor of Physics at Danzig, arrived at a scheme for dealing with chemical bonding; this was refined in 1919 by Irving Langmuir, a physical chemist working with the General Electric Company. Lewis and Kossel developed a static model of the atom based on eight outer electrons. Kossel placed these electrons around a ring; Lewis placed them at the corners of a cube. While all the corners of the cube should be occupied, this ideal condition was achieved only by neon and subsequent rare gases. These gases were predicted to be, and were, exceptionally stable, undergoing no chemical reactions. Chemical reactivity was thus explainable in terms of donation or sharing of electrons in order to achieve the full octet of outer electrons.

This model was, of course, doomed to a short life since it was a static model and the physicists could not contemplate an atom with stationary electrons; but it was a triumph for chemistry nevertheless, since it drew attention to two very useful working rules—the importance of the number eight in chemistry and the idea of electron pairing as a basis for chemical bonding. An important paradigm for chemical theory, which gave rise to an enormous amount of normal science, was born in this work. The closed-shell paradigm was, as we shall see, overthrown in the sixties but the electron-pair concept remains as a heuristic model in much of the chemistry practised at the present time.

### *The Idea of Mechanism*

A major problem confronting the student of chemistry is the immense volume of factual material with which he must be familiar. Organic chemistry in particular has had an unenviable reputation in this respect; organic compounds can be grouped into particular types—aldehydes, ketones, amines, and so on—but the number and variety of reactions undergone by these various types have presented the chemist with a formidable array. From the work of Lewis and his successors has come the sophistication and refinement needed to impose a semblance of order upon this fact-laden discipline. The idea of *mechanism*, one of the most significant developments in teaching and research in organic and inorganic chemistry, owes much to the work of what is now known as the English school of electronic theory, under the leadership of Sir Robert Robinson (b. 1886) and Sir Christopher Ingold (1893–1970). Lewis recognized that the electron pair forming a bond between two atoms (or radicals) is quite responsive to a variety of inter- and intra-molecular forces. For example, he pointed out that in symmetrical molecules such as ethane ($H_3C{-}CH_3$), hydrazine ($H_2N{-}NH_2$), and chlorine ($Cl{-}Cl$) there is obviously an equal sharing of the electron pair, but in many molecules such as methylamine ($H_3C{-}NH_2$), methanol ($H_3C{-}OH$), and methyl chloride ($H_3C{-}Cl$) there is a permanent polarization of the electrons leading to a detectable dipole moment. In other words the electrons are not shared equally between the two 'halves' of the unsymmetrical molecule, and it behaves like a tiny bar magnet, one end having a slight positive charge and the other a slight negative charge.

In the 1930s, Robinson and Ingold undertook the examination of the probable role played by electrons in organic reactions and out of this work emerged concepts of permanent relevance to the theory of organic chemistry. Ingold introduced such concepts as inductive effect, which reflects the contribution to reactivity of the type of permanent polarization discussed above, and tautomeric effect, which explains in a qualitative manner changes in reactivity due to the drift of electrons from their normal positions in unsaturated systems. Ingold also discovered that these polarization effects, in addition to creating permanent differences in electron density in chemical bonds, were responsive in a dynamic way to environmental influences; thus it was realized that reaction rates and pathways could be influenced by the effect of reagent, solvent, or catalyst on the polarization of electrons. This work, and his work on the classification of reagents into nucleophilic (seeking centres of positive charge) and electrophilic (seeking centres of negative charge), was of immense importance in the establishment of reaction mechanism as a powerful new tool in research and teaching of organic chemistry. The general theories which emerged as a result of the painstaking measurement of reaction rates by the English school, research based upon the electron-pair paradigm, has provided indispensable guidance in the complex problems associated with the synthesis of the natural products. The synthesis of morphine, accomplished in eighteen steps by Gates and Tschudi in 1952, illustrates the complexity of the molecules with which the organic chemists are now concerned; the synthesis of compounds such as morphine would have been considered out of reach prior to the introduction of the principles of reaction mechanism.

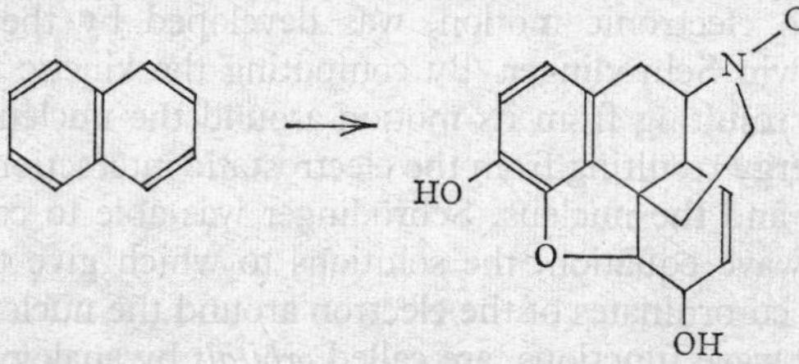

HO O OH N $CH_3$

naphthalene → morphine

The most successful exponent of synthetic sequences programmed in theoretical terms has been the Harvard Nobel Prize-winner, R. B. Woodward (b. 1917), whose syntheses in the fifties and early sixties include quinine, reserpine, cortisone, and chlorophyll. A major problem in the synthesis of biologically active natural products is concerned with stereospecificity. Molecules that consist of identical atoms attached to each other in the same order may, nevertheless, have different properties unless their three-dimensional configuration is also identical. Reserpine, for example, has 64 stereoisomers, all different in three-dimensional space. *One* of these stereoisomers has remarkable physiological properties which have led to its extensive use in treatment of hypertensive nervous and mental disorders. Woodward's 30-step high-yield synthesis in 1958 was stereospecific only because of an understanding of reaction mechanism which permitted the effective control of the geometry of almost every step of the reaction sequence.

*Orbital Theory*

So far in what has been said there has been little to suggest that a model of the atom more sophisticated than the simple planetary model of Niels Bohr is needed to understand the elementary principles of chemical bonding and reaction mechanism. But, despite the fruitfulness of this model, many details of physics and chemistry remained inexplicable and a more sophisticated version was rapidly developed by the theoretical physicists. The revolution leading to the new quantum mechanical description of the atom was initiated by Louis de Broglie, who treated the electron, not as a particle orbiting in Newtonian fashion, but as a standing wave. The work of Werner Heisenberg, who enunciated his principle of uncertainty in 1925, signalled the end of the planetary model of the atom; and in 1926 de Broglie's method of wave mechanics, proposed by him as an answer to the problems encountered in the application of classical mechanics to electronic motion, was developed by the German physicist Erwin Schrödinger. By computing the kinetic energy of the electron resulting from its motion around the nucleus, and its potential energy resulting from the electrostatic interaction between the electron and the nucleus, Schrödinger was able to construct a differential wave equation, the solutions to which give the three-dimensional co-ordinates of the electron around the nucleus. These solutions, or wave functions, are called *orbitals* by analogy with the solutions to equations of planetary motion which define the *orbits* of planets. The probability of finding the electron within a given volume of space around the nucleus can be specified using the solutions to the wave equation, and the orbitals define this space. Orbitals have been described as a housing arrangement for electrons and some very strict rules apply to every orbital; it can be empty, or it can hold one electron, or it can hold two electrons. Every electron has a spin, rather like the earth's spin on its axis, and if there are two electrons in an orbital their spins are opposed. A prominent feature of Bohr's model of the atom was the *Aufbauprinzip* (building-up principle), according to which if electrons are fed one by one into an atomic nucleus and the atom is allowed to subside to its normal energy state, the first electrons fall into the lowest energy orbits, the next into those next lowest in energy, and so on.

Some of the three-dimensional shapes which emerged from the wave mechanical description of the electron at various energy levels are illustrated. At the lowest energy level, commonly called the first quantum level, the orbital shape is spherically symmetrical about the nucleus. This is designated the 1s orbital. At the second quantum level, a new shape emerges at a higher energy level than the spherical 1s and 2s orbitals. The new type of orbital is called the 2p, and there are three of these of equivalent energy mutually perpendicular to one another in three-dimensional space. An important feature of these orbitals is that they are directed in space. As we proceed to higher quantum levels further eccentric orbital shapes emerge which are designated d and f orbitals, but it would be inappropriate to deal with these in detail at this stage. Suffice it to say that the periodicity observed by Mendeleeff and implemented in his periodic table of the elements is readily explicable in terms of the *Aufbauprinzip*.

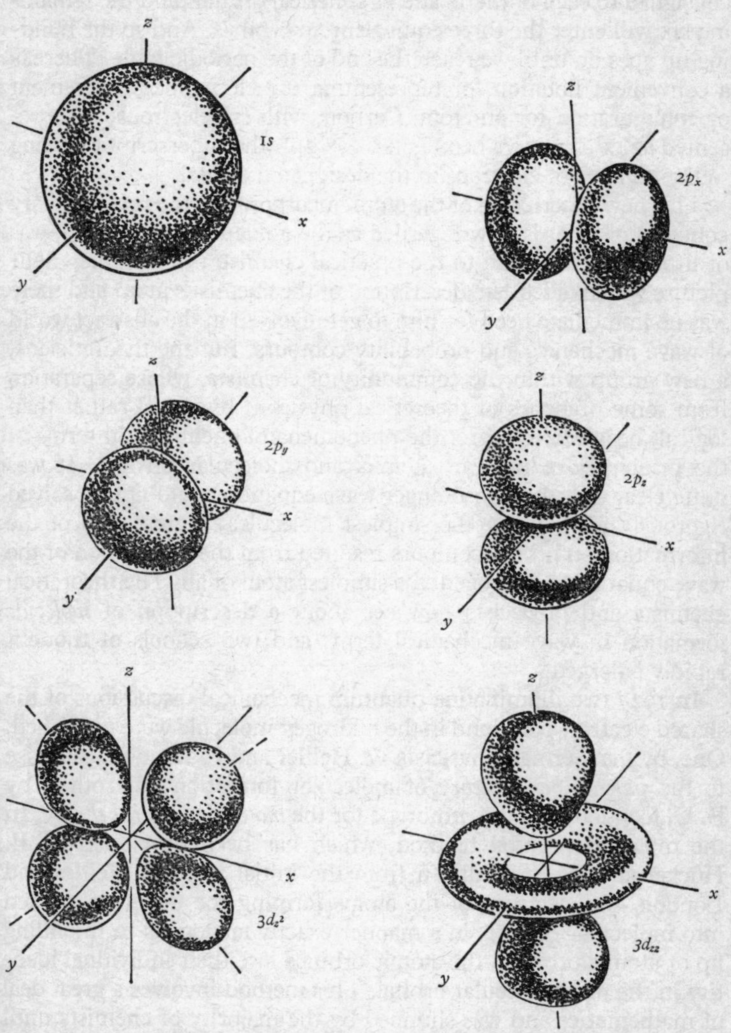


Probability contours for electrons in s, p, and d orbitals

Starting with hydrogen, the very first element in the periodic table,* its lone electron will enter the 1s orbital; the two electrons of helium will also be consigned to a 1s orbital. Moving now to the end of the second period or quantum level in the periodic table, neon, with ten electrons, will house them as follows: two will be consigned to each of the 1s and 2s spherical orbitals and the remaining six will enter the three equivalent 2p orbitals. And so the building up goes on until we reach the end of the periodic table. There is a convenient notation for representing the electronic arrangement or configuration for an atom. Carbon, with six electrons, is represented as $1s^2$, $2s^2$, $2p^2$; neon is $1s^2$, $2s^2$, $2p^6$, the superscript referring to the number of electrons in the designated orbital.

This new description of the atom, incorporating the revolutionary concepts of what is now regarded as the golden age of physics, was of little immediate use to the practical chemists; the simpler Bohr picture was an adequate description of the chemist's atom and there was no immediate need for him to get involved in the abstract world of wave mechanics and probability contours. But the theoreticians, a new group within the community of chemists, whose separation from some branches of theoretical physics is historical rather than logical, began to interpret the phenomena of chemistry in terms of the principles of nuclear, atomic, and molecular physics. It was quite clear that the Schrödinger wave equation could not be solved rigorously for any but the simplest molecules; a great deal of the information on orbital contours resulted from the application of the wave equation to hydrogen, the simplest atom of all. The theoretical chemists and physicists now set about a description of *molecule* formation in wave mechanical terms and two schools of thought rapidly emerged.

In 1927 two illuminating quantum mechanical discussions of the shared electron-pair bond in the hydrogen molecule were published. One, by the German physicists W. Heitler and F. London, gave rise to the *valence bond theory* of molecular formation; the other, by E. U. Condon, was the prototype for the *molecular orbital theory*. In the molecular orbital method, which has been developed by E. Hückel and R. S. Mulliken from the initial ideas of Heitler and London, the electrons of the atoms forming the molecule are fed into molecular orbitals in a manner exactly analogous to the filling up of atomic orbitals; the atomic orbitals lose their individual identity in the new molecular orbital. This method involves a great deal of mathematics and was shunned by the majority of chemists until

* See *The Twentieth-Century Mind*, vol. I, p. 339.

the 1950s when the availability of high-speed digital computers made the calculations more manageable. The valence bond method which was developed by Linus Pauling (b. 1901) and J. C. Slater regards the molecule as composed of atoms and the electronic structure is described using atomic orbitals of these atoms; in this method the atoms, though interacting with one another by orbital overlap, retain a large part of their individual character. The valence bond theory was very popular with chemists until the early 1950s in spite of the fact that there were a great many problems with which it was unable to cope. The molecular orbital theory was conceptually simpler and, although approximate, rendered answers which were more accurate and explained more facts than the valence bond method. The main advantage to the chemist in adherence to the valence bond theory was the relative ease with which it could be understood, since in the construction of the wave equations to describe the molecule, various chemical structures were used which were compatible with the chemists' customary ways of thinking. Molecular orbital theory has now emerged as the dominant paradigm in the calculation of molecular parameters and has given rise to a great deal of typical normal science. *Ab initio* calculations, as they are called, of the shapes of molecules, of their bond energies and lengths, and of the special properties of molecules such as aromaticity (benzene-like behaviour) are characteristic of an extremely fashionable area of modern research in theoretical chemistry.

The ultimate aim of all this work is prediction. It is claimed that laboratory investigation may well be rendered obsolete by the predictions of the theoretical chemists; properties of molecules, products and pathways of reactions will all be known prior to experimentation. But not yet, and experience tells us that it will be a long time indeed before properties and reaction products become predictable in this way. Some success has been achieved, however; the existence of aromatic monocyclic hydrocarbons with ring systems ranging from three to nine carbons was successfully predicted when the only aromatic hydrocarbon ring system known was the benzene ring. In 1965, R. B. Woodward and Roald Hoffmann developed some rules based on molecular orbital theory which successfully predict the stereochemical course of electrocyclic reactions (reactions involving ring formation).

But the Woodward–Hoffmann rules have been heavily criticized by M. J. S. Dewar, a well-known English theoretical chemist, for the unsound mathematical base upon which they rest. Correct predictions made by the molecular orbital theory have been attributed by Dewar to pure chance and he maintains that a great deal of work has been wasted in the synthesis of uninteresting compounds because the molecular orbital predictions were wrong. This need not have been the case since the measure of approximation in the molecular orbital theory used by Woodward, Hoffmann, and others can be significantly reduced by the application of more sophisticated mathematics. This would all seem to indicate that much needs to be accomplished before the theoretical concepts discussed here can be applied with confidence to the practical situation in the laboratory.

*Dogma in Chemistry*

Before we conclude this discussion on the development of chemical theory we will refer to a discovery of the early 1960s which ranks as one of the most visible demonstrations of the failure of a ruling paradigm to explain critical anomaly and of the extraordinary commitment of a scientific community to dogma.

The academic community had assured the students of three generations that the gases in group eight of the periodic table were totally inert; their confidence in this assertion rested not so much upon experimental evidence as upon an undue reliance on the prevailing 'closed-shell' dogma that if an element had an outer shell (quantum level) which was completely filled with electrons then the element would not engage in chemical combination. The reader may recall that this particular dogma or paradigm had its origins in the work of G. N. Lewis at the beginning of the century.

Argon, the first of these gases to be discovered, was chemically inert and therefore assigned a valence of zero. By 1900 the other four gases, neon, krypton, xenon, and radon, were discovered; they also were quite inert, were assigned a valence of zero, and placed, with argon, in a new group in the periodic table. The noble gases, as they were called as a mark of respect for their aloofness, were inert because each atom had an outer shell which was completely filled with electrons. There was no reason whatever why they should engage in chemical combination. This was the ruling paradigm which lasted nearly fifty years and in 1962 was shown to be wrong. It is true that, occasionally, a chemist would try his hand with the noble gases; there was a minor stir in the 1930s when Linus Pauling calculated from his valence bond theory that the noble gases could conceivably combine with fluorine, but the few who tried to confirm his prediction failed to do so and, lacking confidence in the prediction, returned to more fruitful lines of work.

Then in 1962, Neil Bartlett (b. 1932), a British chemist working at the University of British Columbia, noticed that oxygen, which is normally quite greedy for electrons, lost them easily when mixed with a very reactive gas called platinum hexafluoride. This indicated, of course, that the hexafluoride attracted electrons very strongly, and in order to find out how strongly, Bartlett looked up the tables of first ionization potentials for the elements (first ionization potentials are a measurement of the energy required to remove an electron from a neutral atom or molecule) and was immediately struck by the fact that the ionization potential of oxygen was almost the same as that of the noble gas xenon. Could xenon, he wondered, be persuaded to give up an electron to platinum hexafluoride in the same way? The oxygen experiment had been quite simple; no high temperatures or pressures, no electric discharges or catalysts were needed. It seemed inconceivable that the ruling dogma of 46 years could be overthrown by a simple experiment at room temperature. But Bartlett tried. A glass diaphragm separated the two gases in his experiment, and when the glass was broken and the gases allowed to mix, the colourless xenon and deep red hexafluoride combined to give a yellow powder, the first genuine compound of the noble gases. Bartlett's revolutionary discovery was quickly verified and a new area of chemistry was born. The first international symposium on the new chemistry of the noble gases was held in April 1963 only ten months after the original discovery. Soon the chemists were making simple compounds by just heating xenon and fluorine and soon too they were reporting compounds of radon and krypton. The old paradigm was overthrown and the new one was defining for normal science the puzzles which would guarantee results. The repercussions of the discovery were widespread. At a time when chemistry was seeking large sums for fundamental research it seemed as if the chemists had not been doing their homework. The influential American physical chemist Philip H. Abelson commented that for fifteen years or more a million chemists had been blind; all they required to overthrow an entrenched dogma was a few hours of effort and a grain of scepticism. Although further development of Pauling's valence bond theory allowed for valence shell expansion to take place, and Pauling had predicted that the inert gases could form chemical compounds, there was little confidence placed in his predictions and it is certain that he did not give primary emphasis to this aspect of his theory. It was also a fact that neither the valence bond theory nor the molecular orbital theory predicted the screening effect of the inner electrons of the heavier atoms, which shielded the outer electrons from the attractive influence of the nucleus, a factor which is important in the removal of electrons from closed shells.

### *New Tools*

We turn now from the conceptual development of chemistry, an area in which the influence of the theoretical physicist has been profound, to another aspect of the subject which has been revolutionized by discoveries in theoretical and experimental physics. Before 1945 the laboratory practice of chemistry, and organic chemistry in particular, was little different from that of 1900. But certain techniques, which originated in the physical laboratories, have found such widespread application in chemistry and have so transformed its cope that they are now generally considered to belong primarily to the subject. Of course the boundaries between the disciplines are manmade and are not necessarily rational nor recognized by nature. When the physicist and the chemist contemplate the electron the difference between them is in reality a divergence of interest only. The physicist concentrates mainly on the energy of the electron and its interactions with other subatomic particles; the chemist, although interested in this, has as his main focus the manipulation of outermost electrons as agents of chemical combination. But there is always an interplay between disciplines as conceptually close as physics and chemistry, and there is an inevitable mobility of research personnel between the two. Irving Langmuir, whose chemistry was pure enough to gain him the Nobel Prize, was equally competent in physics, where he made notable contributions; R. S. Mulliken, another Nobel Prize-winner, was trained as a chemist but has always regarded himself as a physicist, and his molecular orbital theory, now being applied with such zeal in chemistry, emerged as a result of his work in theoretical physics. The chemist's crystal has become the physicist's transistor, and the physicist's spectroscopy and X-ray crystallography have transformed the practice of chemistry. It is to this transformation that we shall now turn.

It would be impractical to deal with all forms of spectroscopy in this chapter so it is inevitable that the discussion will be selective. The spectroscopic techniques which have had the greatest impact upon chemistry since 1945 have all been concerned in one way or another with the absorption of energy by the molecules under investigation. Ultraviolet, visible, and infra-red absorption spectroscopy have been known and used since the last century, but it is only in the last two decades that advances in instrumentation and commercial development have made the techniques available for routine use. The electromagnetic spectrum stretches from the extremely short wave-lengths of cosmic radiation ($10^{-4}$ Angstroms) to the very long waves of electric current ($10^{15}$ Angstroms). When we wish to scan the ultraviolet, visible, or infra-red spectra of a compound, radiation of appropriate wave-length is passed through the compound in solution or in the solid state. The wave-lengths of resulting absorptions are detected and recorded and the information contained in the spectrum is interpreted by the chemist in terms of molecular structure. Long and laborious methods of functional group analysis have been eliminated by the use of this branch of spectroscopy; information on unknown compounds which can now be obtained in a matter of minutes would have taken weeks or even months prior to its introduction. The absorption of radiation in the ultraviolet and visible regions of the electromagnetic spectrum is a consequence of the promotion of valence electrons in the molecule under investigation to a higher energy level. Infra-red radiation, on the other hand, promotes the molecule as a whole to a higher energy level.

Our discussion of the development of chemistry has until now been concerned with the important role of one subatomic particle, the electron. The chemists' picture of the atom remains a relatively simple one, in spite of the efforts of the theoretical physicists to confuse him with fundamental subatomic particles of ever-increasing number. The electron has served the chemist well and will continue to do so, but a new branch of spectroscopy has, in recent years, brought to prominence another part of the chemists' atom. *Nuclear magnetic resonance* spectroscopy was discovered in 1945 by two American physicists, E. M. Purcell of Harvard and F. Bloch of Stanford, and, within ten years, the technique was established as an indispensable tool in the chemists' armamentarium. It is hardly an exaggeration to say that no modern laboratory undertaking serious chemical research is without a nuclear magnetic resonance spectrometer.

The magnetic resonance phenomenon owes its existence to the fact that the nuclei of certain atoms possess a mechanical spin and, because there is an electric charge associated with an atomic nucleus, their spins cause these nuclei to act as tiny bar magnets. Hydrogen is one of the atoms whose nucleus possesses a spin, and when a small sample of a compound containing hydrogen atoms is placed between the poles of a powerful magnet the nuclei of all the hydrogen atoms align themselves either with the field (a low energy state) or against the field (a high energy state). The reason for the two modes of alignment need not concern us here nor need we concern ourselves with the fact that there is always a slight excess of nuclei in the low energy state. But when electromagnetic radiation in the radio-frequency range is applied to the sample while it is still between the poles of the magnet, the nuclei in the low energy state will, at a certain frequency value, be promoted to the higher state and an absorption signal will be detected and recorded. The frequency value at which a nucleus will absorb energy is dependent upon its molecular environment and, since the absorption signal intensity is quantitative, the nuclear magnetic resonance spectrum gives valuable information concerning the number of hydrogens in each molecular environment. The spectrum of ethyl alcohol ($CH_3 \cdot CH_2 \cdot OH$)

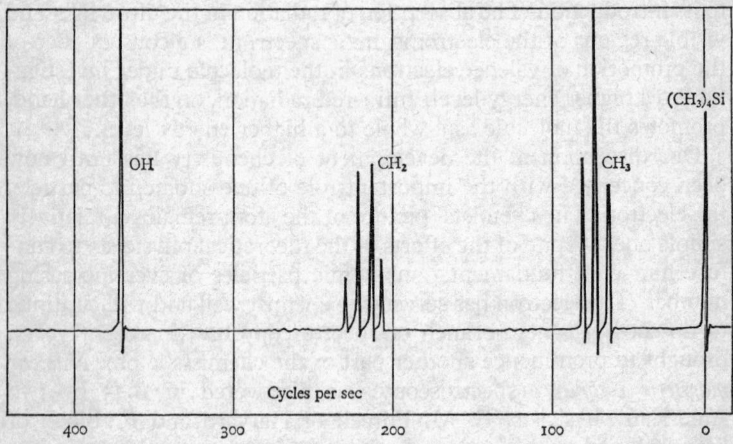


60 MHz. Nuclear magnetic resonance spectrum of ethyl alcohol using tetramethylsilane as standard

illustrates some of the important information which nuclear resonance can provide. The hydrogens in ethyl alcohol are obviously in three different molecular environments and this is clearly shown in the n.m.r. spectrum. The multiplicity (or fine structure) of each of the signals for the methyl ($CH_3$) and methylene ($CH_2$) groups is also quite informative since there is an empirical rule in magnetic resonance spectroscopy which states that in simple (or first order) spectra the multiplicity of the signal for any hydrogen attached to carbon is numerically equivalent to the number of hydrogens on the adjacent carbon atom plus one. Since the methyl group has a neighbouring carbon with two hydrogens attached the multiplicity of its signal is three; likewise the multiplicity of the methylene hydrogens is four in accordance with the empirical rule.

This simple example gives us some indication of the wealth of information which may be gained by a technique which utilizes minute samples and is non-destructive. Organic chemistry has been the main beneficiary, since the majority of organic compounds contain carbon and hydrogen; the former does not display a nuclear resonance phenomenon, a factor which is most important in the interpretation of the spectra. Chemistry, before the Second World War, used to be what has come to be known as 'little science'. It required little in the way of equipment and could be carried out on a shoestring budget. But the introduction of the new machines like nuclear magnetic resonance spectrometers, costing up to £75,000, and mass spectrometers (£40,000) has changed all this. Chemistry is now 'big science'. As a further example of the influence of big machines on the practice of chemistry we will consider X-ray crystallography, a technique which also originated in physics and which has had an extraordinary impact in chemistry and its associated discipline, molecular biology.

In 1912, in an attempt to explain the nature of von Röntgen's X-rays, discovered seventeen years previously, Max von Laue, Professor of Physics at Zürich, suggested that the distance between the atom layers in crystals might be of the proper order of magnitude for use as a diffraction grating for these mysterious rays. Previous attempts to characterize the rays as a form of ordinary light failed because, unlike ordinary light, they could not be diffracted even with the most closely ruled diffraction gratings. By passing a thin beam of X-rays through a zinc sulphide crystal, von Laue and his collaborators obtained a symmetrical pattern of spots on a photographic plate; this diffraction pattern showed that the nature of X-radiation was similar to ordinary light. But the von Laue experiment suggested something else to the Cambridge physicists W. H. Bragg and W. L. Bragg. To them it suggested a means whereby the atoms and groups in crystals might be located in space giving the three-dimensional space co-ordinates of the crystal unit (or space lattice). Subsequent developments in the new field of X-ray crystallography testified to the wisdom of this remarkable suggestion. Without discussing the details of the measurements, which one carries out using an X-ray diffractometer, it may be said that it has now become possible to determine, with a high degree of accuracy, the mutual disposition of the atoms in a crystal lattice. The method has verified structural formulae which have, hitherto, been accepted on purely empirical grounds and has lent to these formulae a degree of reality which they did not formerly possess. The introduction of high-speed digital computers in the late 1950s had a profound effect upon the development of the X-ray diffractometer as a research instrument. A large organic molecule with, perhaps, thirty major atoms currently requires about one month of diffraction-pattern recording and up to nine hours of computer time. Twenty years ago the total time required would have been of the order of three years.

But it is in the field of molecular biology, a new sub-discipline which came into existence in the early 1950s to explain the processes of life in chemical terms, that X-ray crystallography has made its greatest contribution. The X-ray analysis of crystalline proteins and viruses was begun at the Cavendish Laboratory in the middle 1930s by J. D. Bernal. In 1937 Bernal moved to the Chair of Crystallography at Birkbeck College, London, leaving his student, M. F. Perutz (b. 1914) in Cambridge with a formidable problem—the determination of the three-dimensional structure of haemoglobin, the main component of the red blood corpuscles. From 1939 Perutz worked with (Sir) Lawrence Bragg, who was able to convince the Medical Research Council of the value of his work. The outcome of this was the foundation of an M.R.C. Research Unit with two members, Perutz and another chemist, J. C. Kendrew (b. 1917); this unit was to become the internationally renowned M.R.C. Laboratory of Molecular Biology. From the M.R.C. Unit have emerged the three-dimensional structures of haemoglobin and myoglobin and the spectacular success of F. H. C. Crick (b. 1916) and J. D. Watson (b. 1928) in unravelling the double-helical structure of deoxyribose nucleic acid (DNA). The structure of myoglobin, the protein molecule which carries oxygen in muscle, was solved in 1957 by Kendrew and in 1959, twenty-two years after he had taken his first X-ray picture of the molecule, Perutz solved the structure of haemoglobin. The structure which emerged was of great complexity; ten thousand atoms were assembled into four chains, each chain twisted into the form of a helix with several folds. The molecule was found to have one shape when ferrying oxygen to the tissues and a slightly different one when carrying carbon dioxide back to the lungs.

The work with X-ray crystallography brings into sharp focus the unique position of chemistry with respect to its adjacent disciplines. The twentieth-century relationship between physics and chemistry could be described as parasitic rather than symbiotic; the theory and practice of chemistry has been changed dramatically by revolutionary advances in physics but physics has had little in return. On the other hand the wealth of knowledge which chemistry has bestowed upon the biomedical sciences goes some way towards redressing the balance, although due recognition is not always given to this contribution. Sometimes it is difficult to apportion credit for the major advances which have distinguished the biomedical sciences in the past three decades. The first major successes in the use of X-ray diffraction were achieved by the chemists Perutz and Kendrew. The second generation of X-ray crystallographers like Wilkins and Crick were mainly physicists and would describe themselves as molecular biologists or molecular biophysicists; and their successes were of even greater magnitude. But these successes could never have occurred without the vital information on chemical composition which the natural-products chemists had supplied.

The term molecular biology has been coined to identify that segment of biochemistry which seeks to explain life processes at the molecular level. Biochemistry, a hybrid of chemistry and physiology, came into existence at the beginning of the twentieth century, a period when the organic chemists were necessarily developing their knowledge of structural chemistry and synthesis and were not prepared to spend time on the biologically attractive but chemically repellent molecules whose function was of extreme importance in medicine and physiology. The characteristics of any living organism are determined by the properties of its individual cells and the characteristics of these are, in the last analysis, imposed by the molecules from which they are built up. The ideas of biochemistry and molecular biology are, therefore, largely derived from chemistry, and current advances in these fashionable areas rely heavily upon the knowledge generated by the organic and physical chemists. But the glamour has gone out of chemistry; its sparkle has been dulled by a lack of excitement and the credit for the spectacular discoveries has gone to others. Its usefulness has not yet declined, however, and we shall now consider some of the practical benefits which chemistry has continued to bestow since 1945.

### *The Antibiotic Era*

The discovery of penicillin and its subsequent success in the treatment of bacterial disease ushered in a new era in the traditionally close collaboration of chemistry and medicine. The search for new chemotherapeutic agents following Ehrlich's discovery of Salvarsan was echoed in the 1950s and 1960s in the search for new antibiotics in the soils of the world. If the methods by which these new antibiotics were found are reminiscent of Kuhn's description of normal science, this does not detract from the usefulness of the results. The contributions of the chemists to the practice of medicine may owe a great deal more to pure chance than to revolutionary insight or programmed research based on theoretical predictions; but this does not make the contributions any the less valuable to the stricken patient who benefits from them.

The first major antibiotic to emerge after the penicillin breakthrough was streptomycin, isolated from twisted fungus-like organisms called actinomycetes by Selman Waksman (b. 1888), a microbiologist working at Rutgers University, in New Jersey. Waksman, who, incidentally, coined the word antibiotic, had been studying soil micro-organisms since 1915. During his studies he noted how rarely he found pathological organisms in the soil and attributed this to the fact that they were destroyed by other soil organisms. But the necessary impetus to examine this hypothesis in detail was missing and he did little work on it until penicillin showed that it might be true. His first product, isolated in 1940 at the laboratories of the Merck Company, who provided funds and facilities for the work, was actinomycin, a metabolic product of a strain of *actinomyces*. This compound had a bactericidal effect but was highly toxic to animals; in 1943, however, in another strain of *actinomyces* which he found growing in a heavily manured field, Waksman isolated streptomycin, which clinical trials soon showed to be harmless to animals but deadly to the tubercle bacillus, the scourge of man since the beginning of recorded history.

The success of penicillin and streptomycin immediately led to what has since been called a rather undignified scramble amid the refuse of the earth for more wonder drugs and hundreds of thousands of soil samples were screened for antibiotic activity. The search may have been undignified, but not the results. In 1947 chloramphenicol was isolated from a variety of the fungus *streptomyces* and found to be a powerful antibiotic active against typhoid and dysentery. Its chemical structure was established in the laboratories of Parke-Davis Pharmaceutical Company in 1949 and a commercial synthesis was developed in the same year. Further studies on *streptomyces* yielded the tetracyclines, a closely related group of antibiotics discovered in 1948 by Benjamin Duggar, a plant physiologist working for the Lederle Company. Aureomycin (from *Streptomyces aureofaciens*) and terramycin (from *Streptomyces rimosus*) were shown by R. B. Woodward to have the structures (1) and

(2) respectively. Catalytic removal of the chlorine atom from aureomycin gives tetracycline (3), which has now replaced its naturally occurring precursor as the antibiotic of choice in the treatment of pneumonia and other bacterial infections.

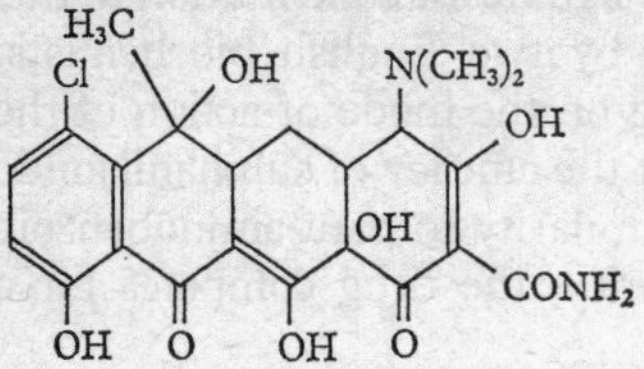

Aureomycin (1)

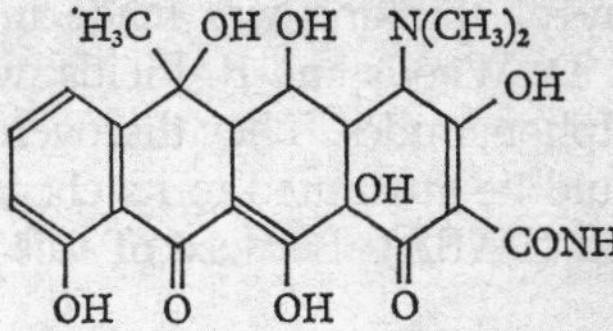

Terramycin (2)

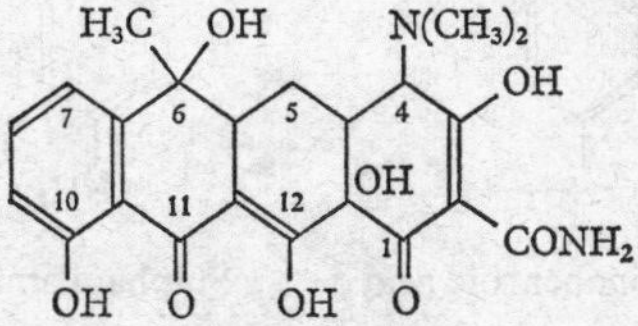

Tetracycline (3)

The synthesis of tetracycline, an antibiotic which is not found in nature but which surpasses the natural product in its antibacterial activity, illustrates the important role of the chemist in pharmaceutical research. The alteration of naturally occurring compounds to enhance their chemotherapeutic properties is sometimes referred to as 'molecular roulette', a disparaging term which is meant to convey its intellectual sterility.

But the focus of interest in antibiotic research has gradually shifted from the screening of samples for the elusive wonder drug to an attempt to understand the mechanism of action of the drugs we already possess. It is true that the search is still being carried on by some pharmaceutical companies, but the lustre has gone out of this field of activity. Many years have now passed since the discovery of the tetracyclines and few antibiotics of real value have emerged except, perhaps, the cephalosporins. Millions of soil samples from all over the world have, by now, passed through the laboratories of the pharmaceutical houses but it seems that, against all mathematical probability, the first few antibiotics have proved to be the best. Advances in the understanding of the mode of action of most drugs, including the antibiotics, have, typically, failed to keep up with the practical advances. It is true to say that we do not yet know how the simplest drugs operate in the body. But within the scientific community there is a well-known article of faith which states that if the mechanisms by which the various drugs alleviate pathological conditions are unravelled then the way is clear for the design of drugs to relieve these conditions. The most significant contribution to this way of thinking was made in 1940 by two English biochemists, D. D. Woods and P. Fields, working on the mode of action of the sulphonamides. They discovered that the efficacy of sulphanilamide could be attributed to its chemical similarity to para-aminobenzoic acid (PABA). Because of this similarity, the drug competes for a

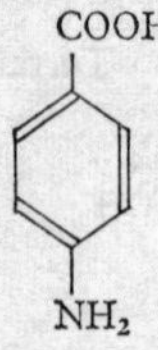

| COOH | $SO_2NH_2$ |
|---|---|
| $NH_2$ | $NH_2$ |
| Para-aminobenzoic acid | Sulphanilamide |

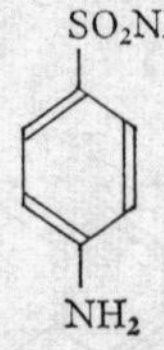

bacterial enzyme which uses PABA as its substrate. The bacterial cell, unable to cope with the 'foreign' molecule, is destroyed. Hundreds of analogues to PABA have since been made but none has succeeded in the same way as the sulphonamides. So the problem of mechanism still remains and is being increasingly studied by the biochemists and molecular biologists.

But other problems of chemotherapy remain which are, in many respects, manmade and demand the synthetic skills of the chemists. The antibiotics are effective against specific bacteria but not always against their mutants. With the extermination of the normal bacteria, the mutants are able to flourish and a new antibiotic must be used to destroy them. This is why, despite Waksman's pride in his streptomycin, tuberculosis is not yet eradicated even in the developed countries. The problem is aggravated by the use of minute quantities of antibiotics such as penicillin and aureomycin as growth stimulants in animal feeds, and by indiscriminate use of antibiotic therapy in the medical profession; the mutant bacteria are allowed to multiply and our only recourse is to 'molecular roulette' to change the antibiotic molecule in such a way as to deal with the mutant strains. Apart from mutant proliferation there is also the problem of exposure to the residual antibiotics in meat which can, in some people, cause sensitization, a reaction which precludes any future use of the antibiotic in the large doses necessary for therapy because of the danger of severe anaphylactic shock. The danger of the total collapse of antibiotic therapy arising out of this misuse is averted only by the provision of alternative drugs by the skilful chemical manipulation of nature's molecules.

*The Chemical Messengers*

When chemistry knew much less about the mechanisms of the body it concerned itself mainly with the three major foodstuffs—fats, carbohydrates, and proteins. Then the chemists and the biochemists became interested in the subtle control mechanisms in the body and the vital importance of three groups of organic chemicals in the maintenance of normal bodily function was soon established. The *enzymes* are biological catalysts of extraordinary specificity and efficiency which promote the complex chemical reactions in the body; the *vitamins*, whose structures are now known in complete detail, are accessory factors essential for the utilization of foodstuffs by the body; and the *hormones* are the chemical messengers of the body without which it loses its ability to maintain a sense of chemical balance.

The term hormone was introduced by the English physiologists William Bayliss and E. H. Starling in 1902 when they isolated from the duodenal mucosa a substance which stimulated the secretion of pancreatic juice. Unlike the vitamins, most of which are obtained from food, the hormones are synthesized in the body and are secreted directly to the bloodstream by ductless glands such as the adrenals, which are situated above the kidneys, and the pituitary, a small gland which rests at the base of the skull. Of all the ductless glands, the pituitary is, perhaps, the most important; its hormones, circulating in the blood, stimulate the other glands to produce their characteristic secretions in the correct quantities. A delicate balance of hormone activity is essential, since overproduction can be as damaging as deficiency; human growth hormone, for example, causes gigantism in excess and dwarfism in deficiency, and, unless a delicate balance is maintained in the production of insulin, the pancreatic hormone, the inevitable result is coma followed by death.

The pharmaceutical industry entered the hormone field at an early stage when Friedrich Stotz, a chemist working at the Hoescht Dyeworks in Germany, synthesized adrenaline, one of the hormones of the adrenal medulla. This hormone constricts the blood vessels and its primitive function is to prepare the body for fight or flight. It is now used extensively in dentistry, in combination with a local anaesthetic, to prevent the anaesthetic from being carried away too quickly from the operating site and as an anti-haemorrhagic. Insulin, discovered in 1921 by Frederick Banting (1891–1941) and Charles Best (b. 1899), is perhaps the most famous of all the hormones. It is secreted in the Islets of Langerhans, strange cell clusters found in the pancreas, and regulates the utilization of sugars by the body. The chemistry of insulin has been extensively investigated and it is now known to be composed of two peptide chains of 30 and 21 amino-acids respectively, joined together by sulphur 'bridges'. Frederick Sanger (b. 1918), the Cambridge biochemist, received the 1958 Nobel Prize in chemistry for his painstaking analysis of the insulin structure, a task which he successfully completed in 1954 after ten years' work. Insulin has now been synthesized by Helmuth Zahn at Aachen but his synthesis is hardly commercially viable; it involves no less than 223 steps and has a yield of only 2 per cent. Commercially, insulin is still obtained by extraction from animal pancreas.

The adrenal medulla produces just two hormones, adrenaline and the closely related noradrenaline. The adrenal cortex, on the other hand, is quite prolific; extraction of the secretions from the adrenal cortex produces about 30 different substances, called corticosteroids, and it is with these secretions that the collaboration between the chemist and the physiologist has been extraordinarily fruitful. The first major triumph was the discovery in 1949 of the beneficial effects of cortisone on rheumatoid arthritis, a crippling and painful affliction. The two names most commonly associated with the isolation and characterization of cortisone are Edward Kendall, of the Mayo Clinic, Rochester, and Tadeus Reichstein, Professor of Chemistry at the University of Basle. Kendall's work had been directed towards the alleviation of Addison's disease, a severe disturbance of the mineral and water balance in the body resulting from the degeneration of the adrenal cortex. It was known that treatment with an extract of the cortex alleviated the condition, but Kendall hoped to isolate, and possibly synthesize, the hormone responsible for the alleviation. He separated six steroids from cortical extract and sent his most promising one for clinical trial in 1948. Dr. Philip Hench, a specialist in rheumatic disorders at the Mayo Clinic, received a sample and tried it on his arthritic patients. The extraordinary results received world-wide acclaim and Kendall, Reichstein, and Hench were almost immediately awarded the Nobel Prize for Medicine.

Cortisone has now been replaced by synthetic derivatives of much greater potency; indeed the problems of large-scale production of cortisone were only just overcome in the early 1950s when 'molecular roulette' synthetics replaced it as the treatment of choice in rheumatoid arthritis. These synthetics, prednisone, prednisolone, and dexamethasone, are used nowadays in conjunction with ACTH (adrenocorticotrophic hormone), an important non-steroidal hormone isolated from the pituitary in 1948. ACTH has the important function of minimizing the risks of acute anaphylactic shock which accompany the use of the steroidal corticoids. Hormone-replacement therapy, although effective, is nevertheless an unsatisfactory type of medication, since it offers a palliative not a cure. Because of its relative unspecificity, side-effect problems will continue to be a hazard unless an understanding of the mechanism of action of the hormones is gained. But the long-term aspect of this sort of research makes it an unattractive commercial proposition; the pharmaceutical companies prefer to play 'molecular roulette' in an effort to synthesize alternatives with fewer side-effects rather than tackle basic problems such as the reason why nature's ACTH molecule contains 39 amino-acids whereas the synthetic product, marketed under the name Synacthin, contains only 24. Eventually, fundamental problems like this will be solved and a more rational approach to hormone therapy will surely follow. Until then the empirical methods of former decades will continue to be used to practical advantage; to the intellectual development of chemistry and physiology it adds very little. It is the practical value of endocrinology, the sub-discipline which encompasses the chemistry and physiological function of the hormones, that has assured its place in our records of great achievements. The relief which hormones like insulin, the corticoids, thyroxin, and oxytocin, have brought to millions of sufferers makes this one of the most worthwhile and rewarding areas of chemical science.

*Chemistry and World Population*

The world population, now 3,600 millions, would increase to 7,000 millions by the end of the century if the present rate of growth continues. It is obvious to all thinking people that the planet cannot sustain such growth indefinitely. Equally obvious is the fact that the chemist has played a significant role in creating the environment in which such an increase is inevitable. Insecticides, herbicides, and antibiotics have increased dramatically the level of our food production, and chemical additives have ensured that wastage need only be minimal. The grim horsemen of a few decades ago—the bacterial and deficiency diseases—no longer claim the victims they once did.

But even though chemistry can claim some of the responsibility for the creation of the world population problem it can also claim that it has placed the solution to the problem at our disposal. The development of the oral progestins as effective and safe contraceptives represents the first success in man's efforts to interfere with the secretions of the body for purposes other than the relief of a deficiency or infective state. Interest in fertility control by contraceptive techniques can be observed as far back as 1850 B.C. where one finds in the gynaecological papyrus of Kahun, in the reign of Amenhat III of Egypt, various prescriptions for contraception ranging from pessaries of crocodile dung and draughts of quicksilver (mercury) to incantations, superstitious rites, and physical mutilation. But it was not until the main features of the physiology of reproduction, and the role of the sex hormones in the reproductive process, were well understood that effective oral contraception could be envisaged.

The sex hormones are steroids which are generated by the gonads (testes or ovaries) when stimulated by peptide hormones released into the bloodstream by the pituitary gland. The obvious effects of male castration were first attributed to a lack of an internal secretion in 1833, and in 1849 A. A. Berthold at Göttingen demonstrated the existence of male sex hormones when he restored secondary male characteristics to previously caponized roosters by transplanting into them the testes of cockerels. In the 1920s, F. C. Koch at the University of Chicago reported a similar effect on injection of an extract from bulls' testes. Meanwhile, in the 1920s, organic chemistry had progressed to the point where leaders in the field such as Adolf Windaus (1876–1959) and Adolf Butenandt (b. 1903) at Göttingen and Leopold Ruzicka (b. 1887) at Zürich were able to attack problems as complex as the structure of cholesterol,* a steroid which has widespread occurrence in the bile and in animal tissues. In 1931, Butenandt reported the isolation and characterization of androsterone, a crystalline male steroidal hormone, from 15,000 litres of urine; subsequently a small quantity of a much more powerful male hormone, testosterone, was isolated from a ton of bulls' testes.

Studies on female sex hormones proceeded at a vigorous pace in the 1920s and 1930s. This work culminated in 1934 in the discovery of progesterone by Butenandt and others. Physiological studies being carried out concurrently in the United States were to show that progesterone was the key to the oral contraceptive. A detailed discussion of this work would be out of place in this chapter, but the main conclusions can be simply stated.

* See *The Twentieth Century Mind*, vol. II, p. 300.

The female reproductive cycle is controlled by the hypothalamus, a region of the brain where neurohormonal secretions control the pituitary gland by means of releasing factors. Two of these, the follicle stimulating hormone-releasing factor (FSH.RF) and the luteinizing hormone-releasing factor (LH.RF), induce the pituitary to secrete the follicle stimulating (FSH) and luteinizing hormones (LH) respectively. During the first half of a 28-day menstrual cycle, increasing amounts of FSH are released into the bloodstream by the pituitary gland, causing the development of a primordial follicle in the ovary. Near day 12 of the cycle LH is suddenly secreted by the pituitary, the ovarian follicle ruptures under its influence, an ovum is released and passes to the Fallopian tube where fertilization can occur. Should the ovum be fertilized it travels to the womb (uterus) where it becomes embedded in the uterine wall. But before that happens the remains of the ruptured follicle, under the continuing influence of LH, rapidly changes its appearance, becoming what is known as the *corpus luteum* or yellow body. Its function also changes to that of a prolific producer of progesterone and estradiol, two female hormones which are of vital importance in the completion of the preparation of the uterus for implantation of the fertilized ovum. But these hormones have another vital function; it is obviously quite important that there should be no further ova released through FSH activity in the pituitary, and this is ensured by a negative feedback system. The high levels of progesterone and estradiol in the blood block the hypothalamic production of releasing factors thereby inhibiting ovulation. If fertilization does not occur the *corpus luteum* degenerates rapidly, the levels of progesterone and estradiol fall, and there is no negative feedback to the hypothalamus. The lining of the uterus suffers disintegration and the cycle starts all over again.

The crucial role of progesterone and estradiol in contraception should now be quite clear. If the body could be 'persuaded' that it is pregnant by the artificial maintenance of progesterone and estradiol in the blood, then no ovulation could occur and conception would be impossible. Unfortunately, progesterone and estradiol are both destroyed by the gastric juices, so that oral administration is not feasible.

In 1937, A. W. Makepeace at the University of Pennsylvania published what must have been the most definitive research on the role of progesterone in the reproductive cycle. A great deal of interest was aroused by this paper in the possible uses of the sex hormones in the alleviation of hormonal imbalances in the female, with particular reference to the problem of infertility. Later the contraceptive implications were realized by Gregory Pincus and M. C. Chang at the Worcester Foundation for Experimental Biology, and in 1952 the first clinical trials began. By 1960 the first oral contraceptive had been approved for general use.

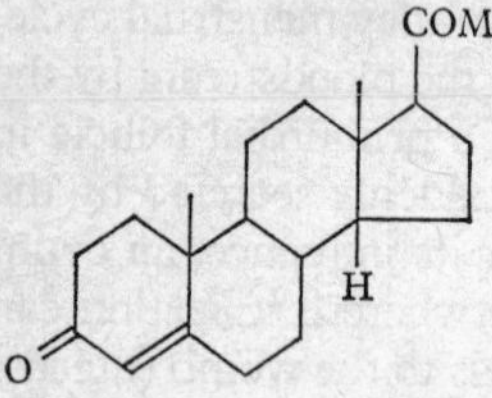

Progesterone (Me = $CH_3$)

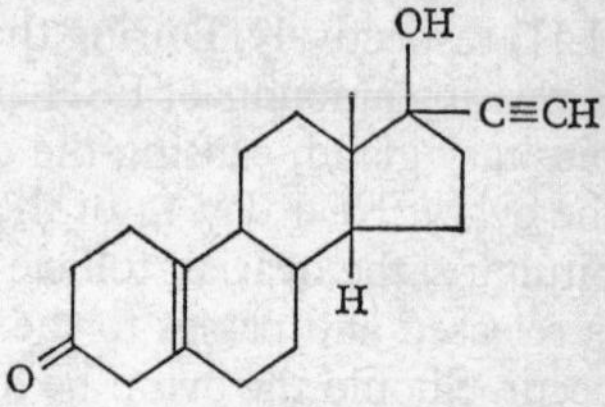

Norethynodrel

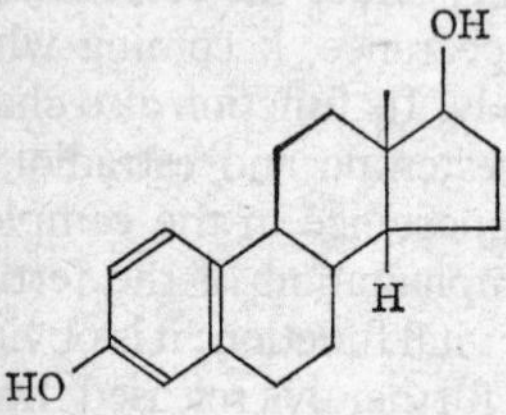

Estradiol

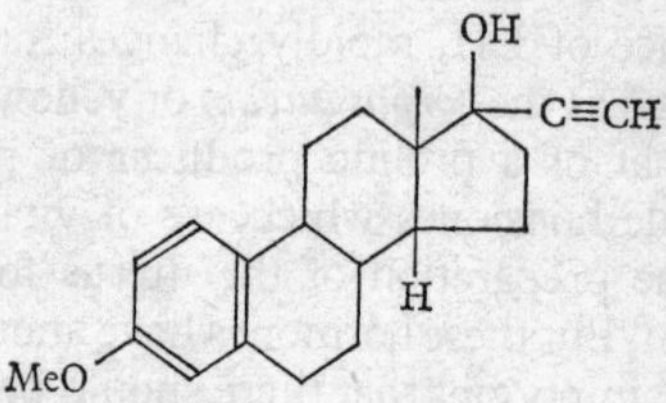

Mestranol (Me = $CH_3$)

The experience gained by the steroid chemists in the earlier part of the century was of vital importance in the development of *acid-resistant* steroidal analogues of the female hormones. The breakthrough which made these available on a massive scale was made by Russell Marker, an unknown and rather eccentric organic chemist, working at the University of Pennsylvania. In 1940 the market price of progesterone was about £70 a gram because of the vast numbers of animal glands needed for processing. Marker discovered that the roots of certain plants of the lily family contain a hormone-like substance called sapogenin which could be converted to progesterone in an efficient five-step process. He was able to synthesize a sufficient quantity of the hormone to enable him to purchase Syntex, a small pharmaceutical company in Mexico City. This company is now one of the world's major pharmaceutical firms. The efficient and cheap method of production of progesterone left only one chemical problem to be solved, the incorporation of functional groups in the molecule which would render it acid-resistant. This was accomplished in 1952 by Carl Djerassi, at Syntex, and the first clinical trials were carried out using his norethynodrel. An analogue of estradiol (mestranol) was later added to the formulation and the first oral contraceptive pill to be passed for general use was marketed in 1960 under the name Enovid. Population control as a socially attainable goal, made possible by the fruitful collaboration of physiology and chemistry, dates from that time.

*The Origin of Life*

In concluding this chapter we shall refer to some current work in chemistry which contains little of the pragmatism with which the subject has become associated. Unlike the physicists and the biologists, the chemists have never been troubled very much by the philosophical implications of their work. Except for the unique Polanyi, there is little evidence to suggest that the chemist in reflective mood ponders the problems associated with uncertainty and reality, mind and body, or life and non-life. But the work of a new group of chemists in probing the origin of life and the important conclusions such work holds for philosophy and theology may change all this.

The astonishing success of the molecular biologists in unravelling the secrets of the genetic replicating system has shown that the life process is as susceptible to 'rational' scientific investigation as the other phenomena of nature. And the evidence being accumulated in the laboratories of the new 'primordial' chemists lends some support to the view that life processes, incredibly complex though they may be, do not have a mystical origin. Among the leaders of this new group is Melvin Calvin, of the University of California, who won the 1961 Nobel Prize in Chemistry for his work on photosynthesis, by which plants assimilate carbon dioxide, water, and sunlight into sugars and other energy-rich compounds that maintain our planetary existence.

In 1871, Charles Darwin in a letter to Sir Charles Hooker wrote:

> It is often said that all the conditions for the first production of a living organism are now present, which could ever have been present. But if we could conceive in some warm little pond, with all sorts of ammonia and phosphoric acid salts, light, heat, electricity, etc., present, that a protein compound was chemically formed, ready to undergo still more complex changes, at the present day such matter would be instantly devoured or absorbed; this would not have been the case before living creatures were formed.

Speculating on whether animal or plant life evolved first, Calvin decided to construct Darwin's 'warm little pond' to see how the simplest life could have evolved. After the natural changes in the earth's first environment of some 5,000 million years ago it is probable that although there was no free oxygen in the atmosphere there were, nevertheless, some simple molecules such as hydrogen, water vapour, methane, ammonia, and carbon dioxide. Calvin reasoned that for the development of more complex molecules than these energy, in the form of ultraviolet light, cosmic rays, or lightning flashes, would be needed. In his first attempt to reproduce the primordial conditions, he bombarded mixtures of carbon dioxide, ammonia, and water vapour with α-particles (high velocity helium nuclei) and obtained an interesting mixture of formaldehyde and formic acid. Others now joined the quest for the origin of life and in 1953 the first simple amino-acids were isolated by Harold Urey, of the University of Chicago, when he subjected a mixture of simple gases to an electric discharge. In 1961, Calvin produced one of the constituent bases of DNA, the molecule of heredity, by bombarding Urey's mixture of hydrogen, methane, carbon dioxide, and ammonia with a stream of electrons. From this extraordinary achievement Calvin and his group have gone on to synthesize the three other bases of DNA and, in addition, adenosine triphosphate (ATP), from primordial mixtures. For all its activities, the cell must use ATP, which stores and transfers energy obtained from food. Of course the synthesis of the molecules of life does not mean that anything living has yet appeared, but the speculative chemistry of Calvin and his colleagues has presented us with a plausible explanation for the evolution of life on this planet. No one supposes, however, that primordial chemistry or, indeed, molecular biology will yield all the answers to the problem of the origin and nature of life; but in an area in which the philosophers have for a long time been in something of an impasse, there is the possibility that from the dispassionate methods of science some insight may be gained.

## FOR FURTHER READING

See the bibliography following chapter II, at p. 317.

11

# Biology

C. H. WADDINGTON

In a review of the first volume of this work Cyril Connolly claimed that 'there is nothing Edwardian about scientific thought. Physics, chemistry and biology went ruthlessly forward towards the atom bomb and the DNA.' Actually the progress of biology was much more tentative and halting than this suggests, and in the period we are now to consider, from the 1920s to the present, the story is not that of a ruthless and uninterrupted march, crowned with the successful achievement of a final resting place. It is rather that of a convergence from many sides on to a problem which gradually became recognized as one of fundamental importance; when success in solving it was achieved, the success at first turned out to be more illuminating than anyone had a right to expect; but then it gradually became clear that the problem, though certainly of the utmost importance, still left very many of the basic issues of biology out of account. The drama might in fact be called 'The Rise and Fall of the City of Molecular Biology'—although, of course, the 'Fall' is very far indeed from being a collapse.

In more concrete terms, the second quarter of this century saw a steadily increasing recognition among biologists that the science of genetics occupies a key position in the study of living processes, and that one of the most fundamental of all the biological problems must be that of the nature and actions of the hereditary factors or genes. This outlook had only just about become generally accepted by the time when, almost exactly at the mid-century, the chemical nature of the gene was triumphantly and quite suddenly discovered. This discovery ushered in a new period, one devoted first of all to exploring the many ramifications which the chemical constitution of the gene opened up, and then later to the more sobering question of whether an understanding of the gene and its actions really does solve all the major problems of the life sciences.

As the first of the lines of thought that converged on the nature of the gene, one may mention the development of the theory of evolution. The geneticists of the beginning of the century, such as Bateson and Morgan, had urged that the new knowledge that heredity is transmitted by separate discrete hereditary factors which maintain their identity for many generations, changing only rarely by the random process of mutation, supplied an essential missing component in Darwin's theory, namely a plausible theory of heredity. Little advance beyond this general point, which was discussed in the earlier account,* was made until the mid-'20s. At that time J. B. S. Haldane began to formulate a mathematical theory of evolution, based on natural selection operating to favour the differential multiplication of one or another of the various forms (alleles) in which a particular gene may occur. Similar and independent efforts were soon made by R. A. Fisher and Sewall Wright. In the very early '30s all three of these men produced books or extended treatments of their developments of mathematical evolutionary theory.

These works were soon adopted as the basis of a new type of evolution theory, which came to be known as neo-Darwinism. Although Haldane, Fisher, and Wright differed in the precise mathematical methods they employed, the intellectual content of their theories was essentially the same, on two basic points. It accepted that genes change only by a process of mutation, which is 'random' in the sense that the nature of the change is not related in any way to the environmental circumstances which influence the direction in which the evolutionary process is proceeding. Secondly, it was agreed that evolutionary direction is dependent wholly on a process of natural selection, which in itself amounts to the differential multiplication of the different forms of the gene, i.e. of the unmutated or the mutated gene. Evolution, the neo-Darwinists argued, essentially depends solely on these two processes of random gene mutation and natural selection of the genes: other influences which may operate, such as migration of a population from place to place, or the appearance of geographical barriers which they cannot cross, are essentially secondary in nature. Clearly this theory focuses its main attention on the genes and their nature.

Another major current of biological thought which found itself becoming more and more focused on the nature of the gene arose from the study of the development of biological organisms. There were two main strands. Some geneticists began to ask themselves what lies behind the bald statement that a hereditary factor or gene determines a 'character' of the adult organism? One of the first concrete suggestions was made by the English physician Garrod. In his book *Inborn Errors of Metabolism* (1909), he pointed out that certain mutant forms of genes bring about an interruption of one of the

* See *The Twentieth-Century Mind*, vol. I, p. 343.

normal pathways of biochemical change by which particular substances are dealt with in the normal metabolism of the body. This suggestion lay dormant for some years, but by the mid-'20s a few authors were beginning to urge that the action of genes is to bring about changes in the activities of the enzymes which control biochemical processes. At first the most prominent exponent of such views was the German biologist Richard Goldschmidt. His great service was to direct the attention of biologists to the problem of the relation between genes and enzymes, but he advocated the mistaken view that what genes do is primarily to produce a quantitative change in enzyme activity, either by causing a smaller quantity of the enzyme to be produced, or by restricting in some way the activity of the enzyme.

During the '30s it gradually became clear that this was too limited a point of view. H. J. Muller made a classification of gene activities in which most of the categories could be interpreted in terms of quantitative changes in biochemical activities, but at least one of his classes involved the production by a mutated gene of quite novel effects which must demand new types of biochemical process. J. B. S. Haldane and some of his associates, studying the genetic control of flower pigments, also described many effects which seem to demand qualitative rather than merely quantitative changes, although they could not point at all definitely to the enzymatic mechanisms involved. By the early '40s G. W. Beadle and B. Ephrussi had developed a biological system in a very simple organism (the bread mould *Neurospora*), which allowed them to induce new mutations in an organism where it was relatively easy to test the nature of the enzymatic reactions of which it was capable. They were able to demonstrate conclusively that a change in a gene (a mutation) produces as its prime effect, not a change in the quantity of an existing enzyme, but a qualitative alteration in the nature of an enzyme. On this basis they formulated a theory, which became famous for some years, known as the 'one gene, one enzyme' hypothesis: namely that each gene is in control of the production of one particular enzyme, and an alteration in the gene by mutation causes an alteration in the nature of the enzyme.

The other strand of developmental thought stemmed from the work by experimental embryologists who were concerned to make a causal analysis of the processes by which an egg develops into the more complicated structures of an adult. The foundations of modern approach to this had been laid by Spemann, whose work was considered in volume I. To Spemann himself, and his co-workers in the first quarter of the century, the problem of embryological development was phrased in terms of rather ill-defined concepts, such as 'potency', 'competence', and the phenomena they described were changes in the appearance or properties of complex cells or groups of cells. It was not until the late '30s that a few authors, mainly in Britain, began to argue that the 'potencies' of a cell are to be looked for in the genes contained in its nucleus. They did not suppose that there is any single gene which has various mutant forms which can control the difference between, say, a muscle cell and a nerve cell; rather they supposed that these differences must result from the differential activity of large numbers of genes contained in the nuclei of the two different cell types. The essential point of their thesis was that it was to the genes and their differential activity that we must eventually look for an explanation of the phenomena of cellular differentiation. This point of view won acceptance only rather slowly, particularly in the United States, where there was for some years, in the 1930s and '40s, a rather surprising disassociation between geneticists and embryologists.

A third current of thought converging on the gene arose from at first sight a rather unlikely source. During the '20s one or two of the more inventive biologists began to offer serious hypotheses about possible processes by which life might have originated from non-living matter. The first speculations were perhaps those of the Russian biologist Oparin in 1924. He was followed a few years later, and quite independently, by J. B. S. Haldane in Britain. They both argued that the conditions on the earth's surface in the very early periods of geological history, before any living things had appeared, must have been quite different from what they are at present, and they put forward more or less plausible hypotheses how under these early conditions complex molecules might arise of the kind which we now know to support living systems. They soon realized that an essential condition for the appearance of any living system is that it should have the ability not only to reproduce itself, but to undergo changes in its hereditary properties, so that it could be subject to the processes of natural selection and evolution. This led to the suggestion that the first things worthy of being called living must have been of the nature of 'the naked gene', to use a phrase employed a few years later by H. J. Muller.

All the authors who took part in the early stages of these developments tended to think of the genes which they were discussing as essentially proteins. The students of the effects of mutations in single genes detected these effects as alterations in enzymes, and enzymes are proteins. The study of cellular differentiation is concerned with changes in the character of cells, or differences between cell types, and these again are expressed mainly as alterations in the protein content of the cells, as for instance in the content of contractile proteins, such as myosin and actin in muscle cells, of haemoglobin in blood cells, etc. Finally, the speculations about the origin of complex molecules in the early earth's surface were concerned mainly with the conditions under which protein-like molecules could have been expected to arise. The early convergence of biological interest on to the problem of the nature of the gene occurred, therefore, in an atmosphere in which it was considered most probable that the genes were proteins.

During the '30s and '40s the direct study of the biochemistry of genes was confined for technical reasons to investigations of the hereditary material of higher organisms, both plants and animals, but not including the very simplest plants or bacteria or viruses. As we saw in volume I, Morgan and his school had demonstrated conclusively that the genes are carried in the chromosomes contained in the cell nucleus. Now it could be shown that these chromosomes contain proteins, but they also contain another type of molecule, nucleic acid. At that time very little was known about the nature of nucleic acids. It had been discovered that they contained certain organic bases, sugars and phosphate groups, but the relation of these constituents to each other was not at all understood. The general impression was that the molecules of nucleic acid were not very highly organized, and that the substance served as some sort of packing or skeleton material, which played a relatively unimportant role in comparison with the proteins, which were thought likely to represent the active genes themselves. This belief was reinforced by the fact that geneticists, particularly those studying the processes of mutation under the influence of ionizing radiations, such as X-rays, had come to the conclusion that the gene must be a particle about the same size as, or a little larger than, the largest known protein molecules.

It was particularly this work on induced mutation, using the physical tool of X-rays, begun and carried forward largely under the influence of H. J. Muller, that brought into the picture a new type of thinking that was to prove of great importance. Several of the leaders of the latest developments in physics, particularly in Germany, found their imagination greatly stirred by the discussions that were going on in biology about the nature of the gene. Niels Bohr, and later Schrödinger, were particularly intrigued by the philosophical point that genes, which may be reproduced through many generations, seem to have much greater stability than was easily accounted for on the general principles of physics. It seemed not impossible to them that the gene might exemplify principles of construction which had not yet been incorporated into physical theory. Bohr, in fact, discussed the possibility that biology, and in particular its foundation-stone the gene, might involve a 'complementarity' with the notions appropriate to the non-living physical world, requiring for its interpretation a point of view as different from that of physics as the particle formulation of physical laws is from the wave formulation.

A few younger physicists, particularly Max Delbrück, were sufficiently intrigued by this possibility to delve deeply into the experimental study of genes, their stability and their reproduction. They brought to the design of their experiments a notion which had proved of basic importance in the study of physics, namely to search out the simplest possible system which exemplifies the process in which you are interested, and to devise experiments from which it would be possible to deduce by very strict, though perhaps refined logic, clear-cut answers to definite questions.

Delbrück soon found that the contemporary state of biology was just opening up an experimental system which seemed perfectly adapted to this purpose. It had recently been found possible to make experiments on the genetics of such simple life forms as bacteria, and shortly thereafter ways were discovered for studying still simpler forms, the viruses or bacteriophages which may live on bacteria. Delbrück had to move from Germany to the United States at the beginning of the Second World War. Once there he took up the study of bacterial viruses, or bacteriophages, with great energy and soon attracted around him a small group of extremely clever experimenters, many of them originally trained as physicists. During the war years and immediately thereafter this group formed the spearhead of the attack on the nature of the gene. For most of this period it was still generally assumed that the gene would turn out to be essentially a protein. However, in 1952 it was definitely demonstrated by Hershey and Chase that genetic information could be conveyed by particles which did not contain any protein but which were constituted by one of the types of nucleic acid, namely DNA. Evidence for this had in fact been obtained some eight years earlier, by Avery, MacLeod, and McCarty in experiments with bacteria, but, perhaps because of the general climate of opinion at that time, they were rather surprisingly diffident in emphasizing the importance of their result and it had, in practice, very little influence on the majority of the biologists concerned with studying the gene. The results of Hershey and Chase, however, could not be neglected or avoided. It led several people who had been studying the structure of protein molecules to switch their interest to the study of the DNA molecule.

The most important group concerned with the study of complex molecules was at this time in Britain. It had been started by two physicists, the father and son W. H. and W. L. Bragg, who invented and developed the technique of X-ray crystallography from 1912 onwards. This method was first applied to relatively simple chemical molecules, but by the '30s workers such as Astbury and J. D. Bernal were starting to tackle such complicated subjects as protein molecules and virus particles. It was a young pupil of this school, Francis Crick (b. 1916), who joined with a still younger American product of the virus group, J. D. Watson (b. 1928), to propose a revolutionary but totally convincing structure for the DNA molecule, only a year or two after biologists' attention had been focused on nucleic acids.

The discovery of the double helical structure of DNA is almost certainly the most important single discovery ever made in relation to biological systems. Its importance was much more widespread than merely giving us an understanding of the structure of a particularly important molecule. The structure of some molecules when elucidated often turns out to be rather uninformative and unsuggestive of anything further. The structure of DNA was quite different in that it immediately suggested a way in which the DNA might be reproduced and how the DNA gene might embody the detailed information necessary to specify the production of a particular protein. Thus, far from appearing uninformative or enigmatic, it immediately stimulated a large number of lines of future research. Relatively soon thereafter, another major discovery was made, namely that the DNA may be copied into a so-called messenger RNA, which is the agent immediately in control of the production of the protein. After that new discoveries followed thick and fast. The story of the development of molecular biology has frequently been told; it is far too full and complex even to be summarized here. What we need to consider in this context is not the content of molecular biology, but rather what effect it has had on the twentieth-century outlook on the nature of living systems.

Its main effect for the first ten or fifteen years of its existence was undoubtedly to reinforce a rather simple mechanistic, or 'reductionist' philosophy of biology. The rather romantic notion of Bohr, that the gene might depend on principles complementary to those of physics, receded into the background; indeed most biologists probably felt that it had disappeared entirely, although there are a few who feel that it still requires further exploration in connection with some of the still unsolved problems of quantum physics, such as the transition from micro to macro states (the so-called 'measurement problem'). Then the torrent of successes stemming from the use of the simplest experimental systems, such as bacteria and viruses, seemed to show that the physicists had been right in insisting that one must always look for the simplest possible examples of phenomena in order to understand them. All the phenomena of biology seemed to be reducible to the actions and interactions of molecules, and the general opinion was that we already know or can suggest with considerable plausibility, mechanisms of molecular interaction which can account for nearly if not quite everything which goes on in the biological world. A not untypical expression of this point of view is that of Gunther Stent (1968): 'There now seems to remain only one major frontier of biological inquiry for which reasonable molecular mechanisms still cannot be even imagined: the higher nervous system'.

However, such moods of euphoric optimism never last very long. By the late '60s many leading biologists were beginning to feel less completely satisfied with the undoubtedly enormous advances in understanding which molecular biology had brought about. Not only does the functioning of the central nervous system remain a mystery whose surface has only been scratched, but several of the molecular mechanisms which had been postulated to explain other phenomena, such as embryonic development and cellular differentiation, which had originally looked quite plausible and as if they must be on the right lines even if not correct in detail, began to seem less satisfactory as evidence accumulated that there might be considerably more complexities than had been previously thought.

One of the discoveries most disturbing to previous complacency was the demonstration that the genetic systems in many higher organisms may contain multiple copies of genes, and not only one or two as had been supposed. This was first demonstrated for a particular class of genes, those concerned with the production of the small bodies within cells, known as ribosomes, at which proteins are actually synthesized. One could perhaps argue that this may be a special case; but, not long after, it was shown that the phenomenon of reiteration of genes is much more widespread and affects many genes which had previously been supposed to exist only in one copy in each chromosome. This introduces the possibility of a new type of variation within genetic systems, a variation not in the qualitative nature of the genes, but a quantitative variation in the number of a particular gene which is present. Many new phenomena would be theoretically possible if we have to deal with quantitative variation as well as qualitative, and some of these are already being demonstrated. They are, however, still phenomena depending on molecular interactions, and in that sense they are still part of molecular biology, though a more flexible molecular biology than what was accepted as orthodox a few years ago.

Moreover, it turned out that there are hereditary particles of a gene-like nature, carried not in the nucleus of the cell as are conventional genes, but in some of the particles located in the body of the cell outside the nucleus, such as the mitochondria, chloroplasts, etc.

Perhaps the main challenge to the complete adequacy of molecular biology arises from a consideration of evolution. Many of the most profound thinkers, even among those whose own research is in the field of molecular biology, recognize that one of the most fundamental characteristics of a living system is the way in which it carries out its activities in relation to its environment. For instance in a recent discussion of the philosophy of biology (*Chance and Necessity*, 1971), the great French molecular biologist Jacques Monod describes 'the more general properties that characterize living beings and distinguish them from the rest of the universe [as] . . .: teleonomy, autonomous morphogenesis, and reproductive invariance'. Of these three the last, reproductive invariance, is of course dependent on the molecular properties of DNA. Autonomous morphogenesis Monod would also attribute, to my mind not wholly convincingly, entirely to molecular interactions; but the first, teleonomy, is in a different position. By teleonomy, Monod refers to the fact that living things carry out their lives in a particular way, characteristic of the species to which they belong. As Monod puts it, each living thing carries out a particular 'project'. It acts in such a way as to attain a goal, that goal being 'the transmission from generation to generation of the invariance content (i.e. genetic material) characteristic of the species. All the structures, all the performances, all the activities contributing to the success of the eventual project will hence be called "teleonomic".'

Now these teleonomic projects, which are seen by Monod and many other biologists as among the most fundamental characteristics of living things, are moulded by the forces of natural selection during evolution. The actions of natural selection, acting for instance to increase the efficiency with which horses can run away from their enemies by developing longer legs, cannot without great artificiality be reduced to molecular interactions. They require another category of explanation, and a rethinking of the subject suggests that the evolutionary geneticists, who were mentioned at the beginning of this essay, were unduly optimistic in thinking that they had satisfactorily solved the problems involved.

Their formulation, as we have seen, was in terms of random mutations of genes, and of a natural selection which favoured the differential multiplication of some genes over that of others. Neither of these points seems nowadays to be wholly satisfactory. In the first place, now that we understand the chemical nature of genes, we can no longer be content to regard their mutations as random in any complete sense. One of the most flourishing branches of genetics at the present time is in fact the study of mutagenesis, that is to say, the processes by which gene mutations occur. A mutation is not just a change from one stable state of a molecule to another stable state of the same molecule. Definite chemical changes are involved. We already know a great deal about the end-results of a mutational change, and quite a lot about the conditions that bring it about. There is no reason to suppose that we shall not eventually have a complete chemical theory of the process. However, this might not make so much difference from the point of view of evolution, since the chemical processes inducing changes in genes are, in general, in no way connected with the factors in the organism's environment which are exerting natural selection by determining the number of its offspring. There would therefore still be some sense in regarding the mutational process as random insofar as evolution is concerned.

However, there are at least two other criticisms to be made of that part of the neo-Darwinist theory which referred to random gene mutations as a basic element in the evolutionary process. In the first place, the study of evolution as it occurs in plants and animals, living in nature, has made biologists realize that the basic entity which undergoes evolution is not an individual—which of course merely dies—but a population of individuals. This has forced biologists to adopt a whole new set of concepts, a new 'paradigm' to use the phrase popularized by Kuhn. The leader in the development of 'population genetics' was Theodosius Dobzhansky (b. 1900), who was born in Russia, but spent most of his working life in the United States. From the late '30s onwards he has been insisting that when thinking about evolution, we must think not so much about the genes in individuals, but rather about the 'gene pool' which comprises all the genes carried by all the individuals in a population. The individuals in a population are, of course, genetically distinct individuals. The gene pool therefore must contain several versions (alleles) of any particular gene. These versions have, of course, originated through the process of mutation, but they are being shuffled about into different combinations as members of the population breed with one another and give rise to offspring. If there is a change in the environment, so that natural selection would favour a type of organism rather different to the previous average, this new type is likely to be produced by a new shuffling of old genes, rather than by the mutation to new genes. This is particularly important in higher organisms, where the characters important for natural selection are likely to be complicated ones involving the actions of many genes during their development. Advantage and disadvantage at the demands of natural selection will then depend on combinations of genes rather than on single ones. Moreover theory, assisted by simulations of evolutionary processes on computers, has suggested that satisfactory combinations of genes, once built up by natural selection, may, through the complicated processes going on in populations, effectively be maintained as combinations, rather than being continually broken down again and having to be resynthesized. Thus we find one of the leaders of the most recent school of evolutionary geneticists, R. C. Lewontin (b. 1929), writing a paper entitled 'On the Irrelevance of Genes'.

Further, the evidence which we mentioned above, that genes occur outside the nucleus, in bodies such as mitochondria, of which the egg cell contains very many and the sperm sometimes contributes several more during fertilization, and that even within the nucleus genes may be reiterated into multiple copies, provides a whole new range of variations for evolutionary forces to act on, which were quite unthought of in the simple formulation of random gene mutation. There is, in fact, the possibility of a type of selection acting within single cells of higher organisms. The rates of multiplication of mitochondria and other cell particles certainly differ in different cell types, and it is by no means unlikely that they are responsive to the metabolic conditions in the cell, which in turn would reflect the conditions in the external environment. We have here a possible mechanism—not yet demonstrated, but theoretically conceivable—for the direct 'inheritance of acquired characters', the topic which above all the neo-Darwinists had declared anathema and impossible. The mere fact that we cannot now confidently rule out such a possibility on theoretical grounds shows how far we have moved since the apparent certainties of the '30s.

There is also a basic flaw in the other half of the neo-Darwinist position, that which referred to natural selection controlling the rates of reproduction of particular genes. Natural selection does not act directly on genes; it is the name given to the differential reproduction of organisms. Now the development of an organism from the time of the fertilized egg till it reaches the stage of reproducing itself and making a contribution to the next generation, is of course guided by its genes, but it is also affected by the environmental circumstances in which the development occurs. Natural selection operates not on genes alone, but on things which are the product of gene and environment acting together. One may easily have two organisms which have the same value as far as natural selection is concerned—for instance horses which can run equally fast—but which differ in their genes, one perhaps having 'good genes' but bad environment, and the other 'bad genes' and good environment. Natural selection, one might say rather fancifully, can never know quite what genes it is favouring. There is a basic indeterminacy built into the principle of natural selection insofar as its action on genes is concerned. Now it may well be that over a long enough period, of a sufficient number of generations, in a large enough population evolving in an environment which is not too variable, this uncertainty would be swamped out by the sheer weight of statistics, just as the quantum indeterminacy in physics is swamped out in large-scale phenomena; but it is by no means certain that we can always take that for granted in evolution as it actually goes on in nature.

These last few paragraphs will, I think, have made clear that the grand central topic of biology—evolution—still poses very challenging problems. Certainly the very rapid advances which molecular biology has made in our understanding of the nature of genes and of how they operate, have shown us the character of the basic units out of which evolutionary phenomena are constructed. They do not, however, suffice to explain those phenomena, any more than the knowledge that an internal combustion engine is made of atoms of iron, carbon, oxygen, and so on, explains the operations of the machine. Twentieth-century biology went through—in fact is still going through—a wonderful period of flowering after the invention of the DNA double helix and the development of molecular biology, but it is now realizing that these flowers are not the whole tree.

## FOR FURTHER READING: SCIENCE

For a descriptive bibliography in physics, chemistry, and biology from 1900 forward, see *The Twentieth-Century Mind*, vol. I, pp. 357–9. Following are some titles with special relevance to the period covered by the present volume.

GENERAL: *The Origins and Growth of Physical Science*, ed. D. L. Hurd and J. J. Kipling (1964), biographical essays on scientists in physics and chemistry.

PHYSICS: In addition to titles listed in *The Twentieth-Century Mind*, vol. II, pp. 305–6, three important general studies are: W. Heisenberg, *Physics and Philosophy: The Revolution in Modern Science* (1959; new ed. 1971); K. R. Popper, *The Logic of Scientific Discovery* (1968); and R. Carnap, *The Philosophical Foundations of Physics: An Introduction to the Philosophy of Science*, ed. M. Gardner (1966). For detailed reading in physics, see vol. I, p. 357.

CHEMISTRY: *Chemistry and Man* (The Chemical Council, 1953) is a collection of essays by well-known chemists on the impact of chemistry on society. Some of the contributions are remarkable for their insight into our contemporary environmental pollution problems. *Scientific Thought, 1900–1960*, ed. R. Harré (1960) is a collection of articles on the main currents of scientific thought since the beginning of the twentieth century. Of particular note are the chapters on biochemistry and molecular biology. A. J. Ihde, *The Development of Modern Chemistry* (1964) is a useful reference book on the history of chemistry since 1750. Except for the post-1945 period, which receives scant attention, the twentieth century is dealt with in a comprehensive and readable fashion. The book contains an invaluable bibliography. P. J. Farago, *Introduction to Chemistry* (1965) is an entertaining and informative account of the development of modern chemistry. *Chemistry: Opportunities and Needs* (1965), published as the Westheimer Report by the National Academy of Sciences, describes some of the exciting discoveries in the main branches of chemistry since 1945. *The Mystery of Matter*, ed. L. B. Young (1965), is a remarkable collection of essays by distinguished scientists and scholars. Through their original writings the book traces the development of physical concepts which led to the discovery of atomic energy and the structure of living matter, and the social implications of the discoveries are placed in perspective.

BIOLOGY: Important, and somewhat contrasting, accounts of the rise and intellectual impact of molecular biology will be found in F. Crick, *On Molecules and Men* (1966); J. Monod, *Chance and Necessity* (New York, 1971); J. D. Watson, *The Double Helix* (1968). On the *Origin of Life* (1967), the book with that title by J. D. Bernal is perhaps the best study. For evolution, see E. Mayr, *Populations, Species and Evolution* (Cambridge, Mass., 1970); T. Dobzhansky, 'On Some Fundamental Concepts of Darwinian Biology', in *Evolutionary Biology*, II (1968), 1–34; and *Mathematical Challenges to the Neo-Darwinian Interpretation of Evolution*, ed. P. S. Moorhead and M. M. Kaplan, Wistar Institute Symposium Monograph No. 5 (1967). A short and simple account of modern views on biology is C. H. Waddington, *The Nature of Life* (1961); a longer discussion from a different point of view is *La Logique du vivant*, ed. F. Jacob (Paris, 1970). There are a number of essays from rather philosophical points of view by many leading biologists and other scientists in the series of volumes (three, shortly to become four) *Towards a Theoretical Biology*, ed. C. H. Waddington (Edinburgh, 1968, 1969, 1970, 1972).

12

# The Novel

MALCOLM BRADBURY

In nearly all the literatures of the west, the World War of 1939 to 1945 marks a watershed, a transition into a new aesthetic as well as a new historical phase. It is not hard to see why the postwar arts have a new flavour, why the tradition seems now to shift. The war was not only a shock to western culture and society, but also to western cultural values; it created not only a new political, social, and ideological environment, but inevitably a new intellectual and artistic environment as well. If it led to new forms of society, and new doubt about old forms of society, new balances of power and new patterns of politics, it also brought new functions, new difficulties, new species of exploration for the arts. The immediate effects of the war were succeeded and continued by the more complex but equally radical consequences of the twenty-odd years of uneasy peace that followed it—a peace which has itself changed our cultural and intellectual boundaries, questioned many of our familiar assumptions. It is a period in which we have seen the rise, socially, of new forms of mass society, liberal-capitalist and communist; and in which we have seen a type of economic growth and expansion that has suggested that we live in a universe of constant materialistic modernization, of one-directional change. It is a period in which we have also become exposed in new ways to the breadth of the world, an exposure brought about by new forms of access, communication, and worldwide politics which have threatened nationalism and indeed considerably undermined western cultural confidence. What is more, our map of the universe has been changed by other things too—by the radical developments in science and technology, for instance, which have made the moon accessible, the apocalypse of the nuclear bomb at hand, and the human heart a property transferrable from one body to another. Altogether we have come in many ways to see the world differently; less locally, less patriotically, less morally, with a greater degree of neo-scientific rationalism and impersonality. We have shifted in our notions of ethical responsibility, social obligation, personal identity; shifted finely or greatly, with resentment or with willingness. And such changes inevitably affect the arts, and perhaps the novel above all.

So the years since 1945 have been tumultuous ones in literature, and given the contemporary mood of mental ferment they are likely to go on being so. The problem is that, since the writing of these twenty-odd years is very much *our* literature, a literature directly immersed in our own recognizable experience, placed in our culture, not to be viewed with any real historical distance, this means that the full significance of the literary activity of these years is not, in critical terms, entirely apparent. The writing of the period is still engaged in our lives as an immediately contemporary writing, and we judge it in part for the way it illuminates and instructs us, even in the way it agrees with us, certainly for the way it conducts us through and enacts our kind of world. We hence tend to separate it off, for that reason, from the writing of the earlier part of the century; that we *can* view with more detachment. And if certain figures stand out for us as self-evidently important—Beckett, Camus, Sartre, say—most others seem too deeply embroiled in their careers and affairs to stand out with absolute distinction. We sometimes like to suggest that ours is a lesser period of literary production, an age without giants, though when the time comes the critics of the future will surely find some. It may be, though, that they will not find in the contemporary scene the kind of clarity and importance that has already been acquired by certain kinds of writing, and certain writers, in the earlier part of the century. The postwar generation of writers is in effect the third literary generation of the century, and it seems to exist in a kind of mid-century limbo.* What came before it must seem in many ways more radical. There was, first of all, modernism, with its eminently aesthetic and symbolist emphasis, a new literature for the new era. After that came what seemed like a revolt—social realism in the thirties, with its tendency towards a radical political emphasis—but was only half a revolt; modernism's victories still applied. With the forties, fifties, and sixties, no very clear movement or tendency seemed to appear, but at the same time literature shifted farther away from the real centres of modernism while holding on to many of modernism's ways. Ours has not been a period of marked aesthetic statement from writers themselves, except, perhaps predictably, in France; it has not been a period of clear movements (again France is an exception); and the critics have not been any more able than the writers themselves to name what has been happening, except perhaps in drama, where we speak of the theatre of the absurd. Otherwise, most of the definitions have been

* Hence the apt title of the Italian literary magazine of 1953–7, *La Terza Generazione* ('the third generation').

negative rather than positive. An age of No Style, A. Alvarez has called the period; the period of the Post-Modern, Frank Kermode has said; while the appropriate novel for the era for the French writer-aestheticians has been the *anti-roman*. And one is indeed struck by the highly multiple and heterodox nature of contemporary literary enterprise, the wide variety of modes and voices, even the radical confusions of artistic level which make it harder than ever to distinguish the serious from the non-serious, the highbrow from the lowbrow, the non-pop from the pop.

And in fiction in particular it has been hard to discern a central tendency. That may be natural enough to the nature of fiction, for the novel is a highly various species that can live by particularization and can spare itself an abstract aesthetics. But since the war the variety of this various species seems to have increased, while the self-conscious formalistic argument seems on the whole to have declined. It will hardly do to argue that the novel has grown less important and less sure, since it has held on hard to its traditional fascination, the fascination possessed by the power that narrative and prose re-creation of the environment we live in always has. In any case, the postwar novel has done much more. It has, as we shall see, carried many of the central fascinations of the time—from the philosophical crises of existentialism and the metaphysical worries we have about loss of meaning and identity in modernized society, to the specific exploring and mythologizing of new foci in the culture, like youth, changing sexual mores, changing moral standards. It has sought in many directions for a new character and new forms. But from the point of view of the critics the contemporary novel has existed in the shadow of modernism; and it is still frequently judged (or for that matter frequently neglected) by critics obsessed by modernism as the norm of modern art. Yet, even if its character isn't easy to discern, the contemporary western novel has altered vastly in theme, emphasis, mode over the postwar years. It has produced a wealth of considerable, and some major, writers whose work has illuminated not only contemporary society and our contemporary selves but the resources of the novel-form itself. The important thing criticism can do is to try to illuminate all this not only by comparing our present writers with Joyce and Proust, but by seeing the way they are responding to new and different conditions, are imagining and creating in a world subtly but considerably different from that of the early modernists, or the writers of the thirties, a world in which art has been, sometimes quietly, sometimes with fanfares, becoming something other than it used to be.

Postwar literature therefore stands at least a generation on from that basic tendency of the twentieth-century arts: the 'modernist' revolution. What one means by modernism is not of course one movement, but a complex of them through which run several discernible threads, the main ones being a basically symbolist aesthetic, another a basically *avant-garde* and experimental posture. Modernism has different phases, waves, and variations, and the term includes attitudes as various as Eliot's Neo-Classicism and the nihilism of Dada. But the tendency comes out of an international revolutionary fervour in all the arts that was associated with the new century, the new modern environment of man, the new pressures on literary language; and it is the most visible mark of literature's passing beyond the enviroment of Romanticism and Victorianism. Modernism reached its peak at different times in different countries—fairly early in France, Germany, and Russia, rather later in England, and later still in the United States—and in some of these countries, particularly France and America, it found more hospitable environments than in others. Often it existed along with a native tradition less obviously radical, more clearly evolved from the past. Even so, it inescapably transformed the arts of the west, and in different ways penetrated into the modern comprehension of and use of the arts. It gradually moved into the lore of literary criticism; and though much more *outré* and more specialized than romanticism it acquired even a considerable acceptance in popular taste. In fiction the tendency began early; even before the First World War had transformed and modernized the human environment, many of the important novels and the aesthetic statements about the novel that we associate with a modernist art had appeared. Many of the names in the novel we particularly associate with the modernist, experimental sensibility fall quite early on in the century, though they reach through into the thirties and forties. Different critics would produce different lists, but there are certain obvious names: Flaubert, James, and Dostoevsky as forerunners, and then Proust, Conrad, Joyce, Gertrude Stein, Svevo, Mann, and Faulkner. Then, moving in various directions from that centre, there are other novelists who also fed the tendency: Lawrence and Hemingway, Gide and Virginia Woolf, Forster, Kafka, Musil, and Fitzgerald. Obviously these are not the only important novelists of our century, and experimentalism of a self-conscious sort is not the only way the novel in our century changes. But these are the names that suggest the revolution in technique that modernism accomplished in the novel, and the change of social function and location it achieved; they suggest an essential temper in if not the total temper of modern fiction.

Modernism in the novel meant, generally, a revolution in form, technique, and perception, the making of the novel into a much more self-conscious and a much more oblique genre. It meant a stress on the novel as structured according to its internal artistic life rather than according to those objective structures a writer might 'copy' from the world; it meant a novel that was, in a phrase of Ortega y Gasset's, an art of figures rather than an art of adventures. These writers took the novel through into a new aesthetic environment, and in doing so they gave the form one of the most marked attributes of modernist art: a sense of strain, a certain terminal quality, an air of the form's exhausting itself in each new work. The common currency of language, the common understanding of history, the common sense of order and structure in society—all were thrown into question; modernism is an apocalyptic view of art. Novels tended to move 'inward' towards the mythography of consciousness, psychic states, fleeting sensations, or concealed emotions; or else they tended to become ironic social epics dealing in modern history as—to quote Eliot's phrase about Joyce—'an immense panorama of futility and anarchy'. To a point this stage represents the end of the novel as the 'burgher epic'—the novel of bourgeois empiricism which sceptically tests the distortions of social hypocrisy or sentimental romanticism in society, for in fact these works forewent many of the traditional appeals to the day-to-day contingencies and details of life, the familiar realities of society. Yet no works are more epical than the great works of modernism; and the best of the novels retain the traditional appeal of the form towards fullness and range, inclusiveness and structural scale. In both dimensions—in the experimentalism that suggested that each work was a kind of terminus, the next succeeding logical act being silence; and in the epical inclusiveness which made their novels a conspectus of modern history—they made succession difficult. In some ways modernism more or less exhausted experiment; or at least gave much subsequent experiment the status of a footnote.

The implications and complications of the modernist view of the novel are still with us, and modernism still remains something of an inescapable environment for the modern arts. Yet in an odd way it was those early works of the century which seem the most modern literature we still have; much of the subsequent production has the air of being a footnote to that dominant change. A good many modern critics have been disappointed by this, and felt that we are no longer producing an important and relevant art. But this is somewhat to misunderstand the situation. Modernism is indeed still significant for us, and many aspects of what it saw—loss of meaning in a context of accelerating change; the discontinuity of culture; the failure of communal meanings and languages—we ourselves have had to face, simply because one of the things that lies behind modernism is modernity, the modern as a world environment of change in a recognizable, post-industrial direction. But change has caught up with modernism's view of change, in many important respects. Certain other aspects of the movement or tendency no longer seem very pressing (the aesthetic revolt against environmental realism or Victorian sentimentality, for instance) and the need for literary revolutionism is in many ways less sharp, with so much of the war won already. We have moved away from the immediate historical context in which modernism was formed, and the modernist needs are less inexorable. And because we have moved on, and because we are successors to a movement which said in effect that no succession was really possible, the contemporary writer has found it hard to establish the *next* aesthetic environment.

We can hardly doubt that the Second World War and the long uneasy peace that followed it do represent a kind of transition out of modernism. This is partly because of the gradual disappearance of the major figures who stood for the tendency, since most of the important modernists had either died or were coming towards the end of their life's work by the beginnings of the postwar period. It is also, of course, because history was moving us through into a new kind of world, in which a different order of human experience was present and different ideas and ideologies were becoming active: in which, above all, the progressivist disposition suffered the double shock of what Camus called Hitler's 'nihilist revolution' *and* of Russian cold-war imperialism. The moods of post-modernism began to crystallize after the war. 'Periods end when we are not looking . . . ,' said Cyril Connolly in his literary magazine *Horizon*, which ran from 1940 to 1950, in the issue for August 1941. 'The last two years have been a turning point; an epidemic of dying has ended many movements.' He was talking particularly about the recent deaths of Virginia Woolf, Freud, Hugh Walpole, and Sir James Frazer, all great figures of the previous two decades. By the issue for December 1947, he was even more doubtful of the modernist revival for which he had been hoping: 'such a thing as *avant-garde* in literature has ceased to exist,' he said. This may seem a piece of English parochialism but in fact it reflects an international mood. In some cultures the continuity was less broken than in others—in France, for instance, there were major semi-modernist figures like Camus and Sartre, in Italy Silone, Pavese, and Moravia, and in America Faulkner and Hemingway, who straddled the war. Even so there is a certain bleakness in the literary scene in most countries—in England, Germany, Italy in particular—in the late forties and early fifties, a sense of a difficult transition. So Malcolm Cowley, writing on the American postwar scene in *The Literary Situation* (1954), was claiming that the form that was really developing wasn't fiction, poetry, or drama, but literary criticism. And John Aldridge, in *After the Lost Generation* (1951), made a similar point about American writing, suggesting that writers were in a sterile situation, too bereft of moral or mythological community to allow the existence of good art. This sort of view seemed to run across the cultures in this time, and even the interesting writers who did emerge seemed themselves to express the problem. They came, after all, from a generation for whom the works of the great modernists were not stimulating cultural shocks but required reading for class, and for whom the techniques that once seemed amazing violations were part of the traditional grammar of writing. Sometimes they simply assimilated modernism; sometimes they saw no particular reason for literary radicalism of this kind, any more than for that most outdated and discredited of all the literary attitudes—the left-wing political radicalism of the thirties. None the less, writers were emerging in considerable numbers, perhaps inevitably enough as in most western countries education boomed and meritocracies expanded, a situation which often gave writers and intellectuals a distinct sense of satisfaction with their cultures. Generally the environment was one productive of art, but not directly productive of any distinct artistic species. The social order was becoming increasingly inchoate and—as Irving Howe once pointed out—mass society itself made modernism less viable: for behind modernism lay a sense of the solidity of society, of the eternal values of culture, of a specialized higher understanding which art must be committed to. In postwar literature the cultural fabric was less secure; and the postwar scene was one that encouraged a high rate of literary production, a full and extensive use of the media, a proliferation of art through an extending audience for it—but also a less clear view of what art was, a greater stress on professional skills rather than cultural values, and powerful competition for the novel from newer media—notably television and the cinema.

It is not hard to see why many writers at this time should feel their age to be one of the artistic melting-pot, or why one of the recurrent images of the period should be one given by André Malraux: that of the 'imaginary museum without walls'. Malraux is speaking of a stylistic situation in which all the art of the past can be laid out, by modern techniques of reproduction and transmission, so that the whole history of style can seem to exist synchronically. All manners therefore can become available, and also, particularly if the culture has no other basis for acquiring a cultural centre, equally valid. A knowledge of the cultural melting-pot was certainly present in modernism, which rewrote the traditional idea of a literary 'tradition'; but it acquired full force only when the McLuhanite era of proliferating media, increased availability of art, increasing exposure of class to class, nation to nation, and present to past coincided with a phase of the questioning of the traditional idea of culture itself. This came with the growing disappearance of classes, a growing inflation, and a widening of the social sources from which art was derived and in which it was consumed—in short, with the rise of something like mass-society. And these are substantially postwar phenomena.

Hence postwar literature has come in a jostling variety of modes and styles, has emerged from a wide variety of cultural centres, and it has gone out to a wide variety of audiences. Modern fiction has grown out of numerous communities and locales and has been presented in every possible mode—naturalist and symbolist, socially realistic and wildly grotesque, highly physical and highly metaphysical. The absence of any marked norms is part of a similar absence—in England and America, though less in France or Germany—of any real movements or even of any coherent artistic groupings, like that of Bloomsbury in pre-war England, or the expatriate communities of Paris in the 1920s, both highly productive centres for an *avant-garde* and self-conscious art. The lack of any marked cultural positivism has been accompanied by a general unease about the status of the literary and artistic imagination in contemporary society, and the place of the artistic vision in it. This, surely, is part of the reason why the contemporary arts have not on the whole created those summative, epical images of modern man or the modern world that we associate with the highest powers of modernism. Modernism's tendency towards an epical conclusiveness is associated with its conviction that art could hold time and history still, and that the artist's was a priestly vocation. But contemporary literature has felt itself a good deal more exposed to time, history, and society, has claimed a lesser separateness and independence, has seen art less as an eternal species or a timeless court of appeal. It has retained a disposition towards a radical view of art, an interest in new experience, in stylistic change and the claims of the future; and in some literary traditions more than others has pursued a sense of the need for literary radicalism, innovative curiosity. To this extent it has extended modernism and altered it. At the same time it has tended towards a greater social realism, a concern with the nature of immediate life and immediate history, a documentary interest in mores, a sense of the powers of historical process and force. And to this extent it has brought back into the novel many attributes of the realist novel of the past.

The postwar style and temper in the novel may, then, be hard to characterize, but one can suggest a general stylistic range in which it seems to exist. It has retained some of the *avant-garde* disposition of modernism—in some literatures more than others, and at some points in postwar development more than others. In American, French, and German writing, for instance, the bias towards a radical inventiveness and towards stylistic self-consciousness seems to have been stronger than in the English novel, or the Italian and Russian novel, a difference for which there are probably good contextual reasons—radical and innovative stances in literature do have to do with the nature of the society in which it is written, and with the status and function of the writer and the intellectual in the society. At the same time this radicalism seems more often to have been presented as a matter of 'content' rather than 'form': the urgency has derived from a sense of the strange and distorted nature of modern society or modern experience rather than from an inquisitive exploration of the nature of language, structure, and myth per se, or else from dwelling on the loss of structure and myth. On the whole, the modernist conviction about the power and universality of symbol and myth has not so securely survived, though the modernist sense of extremism and apocalypse has returned in some writers, like Burroughs and Beckett, who have given their art a futurist dimension, a dimension of openness to the next phase of experience which in part, as in modernism, appears to threaten the writer's own place and position. On the other hand, contemporary fiction has also tended to question this radical and formal bias from the standpoint of literary realism, that social realism which is concerned with the exploration of social experience and social detail, the documentation of mores and manners, the recognition of the working of social and historical process. So, as Iris Murdoch has said, it has tended to find itself strangely placed between the 'journalistic' novel, which is documentary and open to experience, and the 'crystalline' novel, which moves from contingency towards patterning, towards the highly composed artefact. The result is, she has suggested, that writing has lost something of its traditional centre in an awareness of the relation between individual and public experience; it has tended to dichotomize the universe into separate inner and outer worlds. 'We no longer see man against a background of values, of realities, which transcend him. We picture man as a brave naked will surrounded by an easily comprehended empirical world. For the hard idea of truth we have substituted a facile idea of sincerity.'[1] The writer no longer *grapples* with reality; and one consequence of this has been that the modern novel is inclined to retreat into the self, finding the world large, strange, and phantasmagoric, and the self a lonely and imprisoned place; it has tended in short to see the human situation as farcical or absurd.

So if contemporary writing has lost something of its sense of a meaningful mythology, it has also lost something of its sense of a meaningful reality; it has questioned the two main traditional sources of fiction, in myth and in reality. Hence it has often found its centre in idiosyncracy, in the individual vision of the self. Often this self is antinomian; or else he is the centre of a reality composed only around him and relevant only to his individual use. As Alfred Kazin has said, this leads to the loss of the traditional breadth and dimension we associate with fiction: 'What many writers feel today is that reality is not much more than what *they* say it is. This is a happy discovery only for genius. For most writers today, the moral order is created, step by step, only through the clarifications achieved by art and, step by step, they refuse to trust beyond the compass of the created work.'[2] Its mythical novels are therefore often novels about the loss of mythical meaning; its social novels are often about anti-social people and the inaccessibility of public meanings. All this has corrugated the surface of modern fiction and lies behind its ways and modes, yet neither modernism nor realism seems to have provided a conclusive voice for mapping out and re-creating the contemporary sense of the universe, for the making of a satisfying fictive structure. The difficulties of creating a modern hero and a modern literary language to encompass the complexity of the contemporary world has obviously been great. Even so, a period which has given us Camus, Sartre, and Robbe-Grillet, Vladimir Nabokov and Samuel Beckett, Alberto Moravia and Max Frisch, Günter Grass and Heinrich Böll, Angus Wilson, Iris Murdoch, and William Golding is obviously an important one. These are all considerable names, and they are followed by and surrounded by writers less securely well known yet obviously of real stature. Perhaps even more important, behind the debate about the status of fiction, fictiveness, and language, behind the sense of artistic dilemma that has marked our writing, there has also been a steady survival of that traditional business of the novel—its interest in exploring given detail, given event, individual and personal lives in particular environments. This may not provide us with that kind of greatness that criticism most values, but it does give a sustained and continuous importance to the novel as a form; it keeps it alive, busy, and read.

*The English Novel Since the War*

With the end of the war, a marked gap seemed to emerge in the continuity of the English novel. Several important writers who had made their names in the twenties and thirties—notably Aldous Huxley, Evelyn Waugh, Graham Greene, George Orwell, Christopher Isherwood, and Ivy Compton-Burnett—were still writing fiction and were yet to publish some of their best books—Orwell's *1984*, Greene's *The End of the Affair* and *The Heart of the Matter*, Waugh's *The Loved One*, Isherwood's *A Single Man*. But the climate that had sustained the novel in the 1930s—perhaps essentially the climate of Bloomsbury, which had made an effective marriage of interest in experiment and in social realism—seemed exhausted; and the new writers who should have followed seemed slow to emerge. When they started to do so, they often seemed to critics remote from all the literary energies that had gone into fiction in the first half of the century. The writer who now seems the most important figure among them, Samuel Beckett, was perhaps the only one who could be said to be reaching back to the traditions laid down by writers like Joyce or Wyndham Lewis; and he went virtually unnoticed for many years. The other important figures to emerge did not seem at first sight particularly experimental. It was as often as not their able efficiency in catching the new manners and mores of a gently but rapidly changing society that won them notice; that, and their point of access to a view of English culture, which was frequently neither upper-middle-class nor proletarian, but lower-middle-class. Their primary gifts were great competence rather than a radical novelty of vision; and even now the critical estimate of them has not become very sure. At the centre are a group of figures of great distinction and fascination, like Angus Wilson, Iris Murdoch, Lawrence Durrell, and William Golding; surrounding them are a number of considerable writers, like Kingsley Amis, Alan Sillitoe, Muriel Spark,

Doris Lessing, and John Fowles, whom one still hesitates to call major.

Yet on the whole English postwar fiction has tended to come out with the reputation of one of the less exciting of contemporary fictions, of not entirely sustaining its great tradition. It is not hard to see why. It has not produced many figures of major authority in the novel; it has not, unlike some French writing, much concerned itself with large questions of style and manner; it has not, unlike some American writing, tended to devote itself to making large myths or epical structures. No real aesthetic community has grown up in the recent English novel, and there has been little sense of a shared aesthetic development among novelists themselves. It is not therefore so very surprising that many of the critics who have commented on the postwar scene in English fiction have tended to see this as something of a Silver Age rather than a Golden. Often they have expressed a disappointment, or a conviction that ambitiousness has gone from the English novel today. The judgement seems less than accurate, but one can see why it is made. So, for instance, Frederick R. Karl, in his *A Reader's Guide to the Contemporary English Novel* (1963), puts a fairly familiar complaint; he argues that from about 1930 onwards the English novel tended to become restrictive rather than extensive and to withdraw from its earlier mode of development, to go back on its distinguished past. It has tended, he says, 'to bring back traditional character and plot rather than to speak the inexpressible; in brief, to return to more self-contained matter while retaining, however, many of the technical developments of the major moderns. The contemporary novel is clearly no longer "modern" '. And in his book *The Struggle of the Modern* (1963), Stephen Spender uses exactly the same distinction, between the 'moderns' and the 'contemporaries', and sees our time as one in which writers are 'contemporaries'—engaging rather prosaically with immediate political and social circumstances rather than with inner crises of sensibility, matters of form, or problems of language, as the 'moderns' did earlier on. And both imply that modernism was never quite as influential in England as in some countries—the twentieth-century English arts may have *had* an *avant-garde*, but they never *became avant-garde* (any more than the English intelligentsia became characteristically 'alienated')—and so the tradition lies in craft rather than art, local rather than large-scale explorations. More challengingly, Bernard Bergonzi has said that the English novel today has stopped being novel; it has tended towards pastiche, the development of minor sub-genres, the documentation of small communities from limited angles. The novelist today has inherited a form 'whose principle requirement is novelty; yet he has nothing more to be new about, either in experiences or the manner of treating them'.[3]

This sort of assumption about the contemporary novel in England has a certain truth. Yet its presumptions are sometimes a little suspect, and in any case it is hardly complete. Yes, indeed, there has been only a limited survival from modernism (though some of its modes and assumptions seem to be returning now in new ways). But the postwar English novel has had at least two main streams. One is social documentary, which seemed dominant in the 1950s, and was heavily concerned with making over into literary material the new social alterations and new social viewpoints of postwar Britain, often from a lower-middle-class or working-class perspective. This kind of social colonization and intrusion of new attitudes has long been part of the novel's nature, and hardly violates its character. The significant names here are those of Amis, John Wain, Sillitoe, John Braine, David Storey, and other similar writers, and they represent an important if somewhat limited phase in the readjustment of postwar fiction to a postwar world. The other is, however, a marked visionary or philosophical strain, concerned with an alternative reality not defined primarily in social terms. In different ways we can find that in the work of late Evelyn Waugh and Graham Greene, in Iris Murdoch, Angus Wilson, William Golding, Muriel Spark, and other writers with a bias towards the mythical, religious, or 'grotesque' novel. On the whole, this tendency seems to have become even more marked in the 1960s, when mannerism and surrealism in the novel showed signs of revival, and when the phase of social colonization seemed to fade a little even in the work of the writers who had been active in it. This suggests that the 'narrowness' of English postwar fiction, which is so often seen as a matter of social documentary, can be overstated. And we must also note that the suggestion that these 'social' writers are traditionalists is itself sometimes overstated. It is true that much of this writing has tended to draw its novelty from the life it observes rather than the techniques of presentation it employs; but it would be too easy to conclude that this produces a fiction that is not at all exploratory, a pastiche fiction. The quiet radicalism of postwar English society has made its mark on the modes as well as the matter of fiction, even if the tendency has often been for writers to concentrate on the given events, the contingent and detailed stuff, of what is happening rather than on larger epistemological inquiry—that kind of inquiry that often comes about when writers feel their own role and position has been profoundly challenged. Such inquiry does tend to produce an *avant-garde* literature; this the postwar novel in England has not really been. But that does not disable it from interest or virtue. Indeed, a free-wheeling and formally imprecise involvement with the given matter of life has been one of the most obvious sources of the richness and density of the novel form in England.

This may, however, explain why it is that the three most obviously experimental writers who came to notice in and have been active in the period should be *older* writers, whose roots lie in pre-war modernism. The three—Samuel Beckett, Lawrence Durrell, and Malcolm Lowry—are of varied statures, and draw on very different aspects of modernism. But all three were expatriate writers who subjected themselves to an international range of influence and often inherited traditions well outside the English; and all held in different ways to the ideal of the artist as the free cosmopolite, the international artist following art and form as matters of dedication. All had bohemian phases and fairly direct links with modernist writers or groups; and their modes of life, assumed audience, and self-characterization were clearly inherited from mentors like Joyce, Proust, Fitzgerald, and Henry Miller. All published novels before the war, where perhaps their literary careers and values were formed, though all made their substantial reputations after it. All really pose some problems of assessment; we can too easily take their commitment and pretensions as themselves guarantees of merit, or obversely doubt whether theirs is a worthwhile tradition in fiction. Certainly Lowry and Durrell do raise critical problems, since one senses in both cases that their claims and intentions never were properly satisfied in the work we have from them. Beckett is an exception in several ways; his modernism is less inherited than radically remade into something else, and his work is obviously full and complete. Indeed he is internationally one of the most important figures to emerge both in drama and fiction since the war; and though better known for his plays is probably at his best in the novels, which form a remarkable and continuous *œuvre* central to modern writing in at least two respects—in its technical obsession, with problems of the status and nature of language; and in its comic metaphysic of the absurd as a metaphor for the state of modern man.

It is perhaps doubtful whether Samuel Beckett (b. 1906) should properly be linked with the English novel at all. An Irish expatriate in France, once James Joyce's friend and helper, he began that *œuvre* in the 1930s with *Murphy* (1938), written in English and published in London, followed by *Watt*, written in the early war-years and published in Paris in 1953. But then follows a body of work written in the adopted language of French and later translated into English by the author—the trilogy of *Molloy* (1951), *Malone Dies* (1952), and *The Unnameable* (1953); and more lately *How It Is* (1961). The work comes then out of a bohemian expatriate context and is a brilliant progression, of purist and philosophical kind, on from modernism—intensifying the tradition of irony and comedy in it to the point of creating an absurdist universe. It proceeds by a developing *reductio* in a logical sequence—a kind of minimalization of the familiar human and social content of fiction accompanied by an intensive questioning of the fictive act itself. *Murphy*, the first, is thus the densest and most social of the fictions set in a defined place, London; with a defined central character, Murphy, and with associated neo-bohemian friends and contacts; and with something like a continuous plot, about the inconsistency of Murphy's quest for success in life and his move towards intellectual self-extinction. The novel culminates in his death but, being created by the author rather than a first-person narrator, as more commonly in late Beckett, it continues beyond; to Murphy's remains, scattered among the butts and vomit of a London pub floor, to the final kite-flying sequence where Mr. Kelly tries to determine where seen and unseen meet. It is none the less a comedy of ideas of a somewhat Sterne-like kind; it is the life of the mind that gives Murphy pleasure, and equal pleasure is apparent in the author as he parodies logic, language, form. Murphy is a 'seedy solipsist' and his split being—divided between social body and hermetically sealed mind, the abeyance of the one being needed for the life of the other—is a comic essence in Beckett's entire work. In *Watt* the parody of intellectual activity advances as characters shift further towards being abstract concepts, while the action now goes further into the problematic nature of a created fictional world. Watt wants an answer; instead he is blocked by a succession of objects and quandaries (how to feed a dog, how to name an object) in the surreal confines of the house of Mr. Knott. But Watt is humanized to the extent that he has the power to survive, to contend amid the negatives, and this comic survival is also a basic theme in Beckett's work.

With the trilogy, written in French in the late forties, Beckett's manner becomes more abstract and his vision more purgatorial; the mood and mode change into a more total image of the absurd. In *Molloy* the central character is poor, old, impotent, hung in a hardly defined landscape with a minimum of objects—the bicycle, the few stones he has in his pocket, and so on. He is hunting for his mother, while apparently hunting in turn for Molloy is a second character, Moran, a private detective. Both are parody quests and in general the circularity and meaninglessness of the Beckett universe is intensified; with progression possible in no real sense, the reader's attention is shifted off development on to the interpretation of objects along the line of sequence, only to doubt if they *are* in sequence. To a point there is progression: Molloy loses his bicycle and crutches and is left to crawl on, remarking: 'But I am human, I fancy, and my progress suffered, from this state of affairs, and from the slow and painful progress it had always been, whatever may have been said to the contrary, was changed, saving your presence, to a veritable calvary, with no limit to its stations and no hope of crucifixion.' This doubtful progress in the fiction is complicated by a circularity around the fiction; Moran's narrative returns at the end to its first sentence, save with the addition of negatives, so that narrative truth is in question. The quandaries of the narrative act are the main theme of *Malone Dies*, where the act of writing itself begins to fulfil a function similar to that of the objects such as the stones which Molloy has put through all the permutations that theory of numbers can offer; Malone, dying, fills time with fictive time which disposes fact and space differently. With *The Unnameable* language moves close to silence—as the hero, always minimal, disappears entirely, and only words make him. So the gradual taking away of all that seems to make an identity which has been going on throughout the novels comes to the point where possession of a name is in question and only the physical body is left; yet, equally, because the mind *can* claim a species of independent activity, it is associated with the fictive power to make bodies by words. *How It Is* goes one step further; at its centre is a naked being crawling forward through mud in a world of minimal names and objects (mud, sack, can-opener, cans) and so the book depends on the permutations of a limitedly variable set of linguistic signs which can turn into gabble ('quaqua') and are then finally questioned. The story is proposed as untrue; but not quite, for in the *reductio* is a stable centre that permits both life and fiction to exist: 'something happened yes'.

Beckett has a superb and ironic comic talent, which to me seems at best in the middle work, before the language-game fully sets in, and we are concerned most with images of man; in these books we attend not to the inexorable logicality of the next stage but to the element of play and game that sustains an essential part of Beckett's comic meaning. Here the vision is clearly an absurdist one—sustained at a level of tragic comedy comparable to Laurence Sterne, and depending on a narrative tone which parodies philosophical quandaries and intellectual procedures to the point of making human consciousness a comic manifestation. The body too, particularly in sexual activity, is comic; the irony is in the division. Beckett's world here is one of social and intellectual decline, an absolute split in orderly existence, but his own logic is not so exacting as to limit his talents. Later on, it surely is. Nonetheless, the whole sequence is a fully consistent vision, intellectually dense and aware and at the same time genuinely contemporary. One cannot quite say the same of Durrell and Lowry, who exist in a rather more timeless world of modern art. Both have a sense of tragedy and decadence; but both still have the romantic will to redeem it, Durrell through sexuality and Lowry through art.

Lawrence Durrell (b. 1912) showed something of the same capacities as early Beckett in his first, best book, *The Black Book* (Paris, 1938), though the essential influence was Henry Miller. It contains a vision of decadence and a mixture of sexual realism and social surrealism similar to Miller's, as well as a similar psychosexual occultism, an obsession with the evolution of consciousness from regression back to the infantile womb towards a more independent condition, the second womb of rebirth. The context is a grotesque and cancered England which has lost the essential centres of life, a theme coming through in part from Huxley and Lawrence; the tone and treatment are surrealist. Durrell attempted a complicated extension of the theme in *The Alexandria Quartet* (*Justine*, 1957, *Balthazar*, 1958, *Mountolive*, 1958, and *Clea*, 1960) but his crossing of an obsession with fictiveness and a theme of romantic renewal seems too patterned and schematic, while his decadence turns to an uncomfortable exoticism. The complex technique—a mixture of a Freudian space-time continuum concerned with the renewal of personality, and a fictive analysis depending on the use of multiple narrators and internal novelists—remains as a technique rather than as a vision. A similar quandary comes up in the work of Malcolm Lowry (1909–57), where the problems of limiting the author's overt romanticism by modernist ironies seem to have prevailed to such a degree as virtually to prevent him completing any given work. Basically all Lowry's books are romantic tragedies focused on the need for quest into and immersion in experience. The most positive is the first, *Ultramarine* (1933; reissued in revised form 1963), very much a book of its period. A young man of middle-class background ships for an Asian voyage, is taunted by the crew, finally accepted by them, so producing in him a sense of the complex interdependence of men, ship, and universe. Lowry is good on the agonies of the quest and its uneasy end in a kind of ironized romantic vision. In his best-known book, *Under the Volcano* (1947), the order is reversed as his fictional universe becomes one of chaos and damnation, in sympathy with the Faustian damnation of the hero, an alcoholic who by abuse of his 'magical powers' brings about his own death in a Mexican barranca. *Lunar Caustic* (1968, posthumous), basically set in New York City, was to have become a Purgatorio to this Inferno, and Lowry planned to relate the novels to one another in a sequence of six or seven books showing different versions of the creative imagination working in a world which is assimilated to it. At the same time various distancings and relations between the books were planned; and in the short stories in *Hear Us O Lord from Heaven Thy Dwelling Place* (1962) we can see some of the pattern. Here Lowry begins to place some of his own novels into the career of a surrogate writer, Sigbjørn Wilderness, so as to distance and interrelate his various versions of himself. This introduces the 'modernist' theme of the violation of fiction by reality and of the need for a self-critique in fiction. If life follows art in being made vigorous and living by the artist, it also leads the artist out of himself towards reality. But this may silence creativity; and Lowry, himself silenced, never completed the entire enterprise. What is important about both Durrell and Lowry is that they are concerned with the image of the creative force, and the critique out of art towards life, in their view of experience—a theme that tends to become subordinate or to disappear in their contemporaries. And insofar as they do, in their better work, sustain this seriously they are of real importance.

This markedly experimental emphasis, this critique of life by art, certainly has not been dominant in the postwar British novel. Nor has what tends to go with it—an emphasis on the wrought, distinctive nature of literary language; an emphasis on the subjective or artistic consciousness; a tendency to incorporate within the work an analysis of the creative process that has made it; above all a notion of the artist as an independent and supra-cultural visionary. Indeed postwar novelists have often been fairly explicit in rejecting this 'cosmopolitan' ideal of art and the writer—in part out of necessity, since the 'international republic of letters', that conscious European tradition of the preserved artistic community, has not been very much available to them as a social entity. Hence, perhaps, the fact that one of the movements of the postwar English novel was a return to a kind of nativism and provincialism, both as a centre of moral values and as a subject-matter—a return accompanied by a rejection of large artistic pretensions, be they elaborate perceptual techniques, a view of the specialness of the artist, or a notion that art can judge the world. So many postwar novelists have tended to stake a lot on the comparative ordinariness and accessibility of their vision, even to the extent of finding bohemian intensity morally fallacious. They have tended to make a virtue of their provinciality, their relative cultural 'ignorance', their populist viewpoint. In doing that, they have in some ways reverted to traditional practices of English fiction, which contain many of the attributes and tones of a popular form. Undoubtedly they have drawn on that fascinating mixture of social observation and moral critique that has been there in the English novel since the eighteenth century (though one can question the depth of their analysis or the adequacy of their critique, which hardly compares with that of the major figures of the past). And even where something more speculative and withdrawn, or something more self-consciously artistic, has emerged in the postwar novel, it has usually done so without benefit of assistance from those urbane centres of artistic dedication that modernism had in bohemia. Altogether, the sense of the romantic solitude of the artist or (as in Beckett) of the hero has tended to yield to a more public view of man's nature; and the sense of the singularity of the created word has tended to yield to a more social use of language. This is not completely so, but it is an important tendency in the evolution of artistic forms in England, and part of the lost centrality of the artist which seems to have been known to many contemporary writers in several countries. And in England, certainly, one of its effects has been a phase in which the referential and contingent nature of fiction has been emphasized at some cost to its other great power—the power to transcend life in time in order to create a distinctive poetry, luminosity, or completeness of vision.

This withdrawal, I have said, is most evident in the fifties, and is an explicit tendency, a deliberate development, on the part at least of some of the writers involved. For instance, Kingsley Amis's *I Like It Here* (1958) states some of the terms of an anti-romantic and anti-modernist aesthetic, a distrust of bohemianizing and word-spinning, which comes out as an explicit preference for Henry Fielding over Henry James. More polemically, a similar view was put by several writers, particularly C. P. Snow, Pamela Hansford Johnson, and William Cooper, in a number of articles around the same time. So, for example, William Cooper's 'Reflections on Some Aspects of the Experimental Novel':

During the last years of the war a literary comrade-in-arms [C. P. Snow] and I, not prepared to wait for Time's ever-rolling stream to bear Experimental Writing away, made our own private plans to run it out of town as soon as we picked up our pens again—if you look at the work of the next generation of English novelists to come up after us, you'll observe we didn't entirely lack success for our efforts. We had our reasons for being impatient. We meant to write a different kind of novel from that of the thirties and we saw that the Thirties Novel, the Experimental Novel, had got to be brushed out of the way before we could get a proper hearing. Putting it simply, to start with: the Experimental Novel was about Man-Alone; we meant to write novels about Man-in-Society as well. (Please note the 'as well'; it's important. We had no qualms about incorporating any useful discoveries that had been made in the course of Experimental Writing; we simply refused to restrict ourselves to them.)[4]

In fact, Cooper's attack—the thirties novel was hardly entirely experimental—was probably meant as an assault on Bloomsbury and its artistic dominance in the previous decade; and there is a concealed element of class war here. He is really attacking a phase of *mannered* experimentalism, and pleading for a prosier kind of novel: a debate that has long been active within the novel form. But certainly this sort of plea also involved a move towards more traditional and more *provincial* sources for literature. The effect of this, as Cooper sketchily suggests, was to produce more interest in society than sensibility, to restore a stronger sense of the public language of reference, of shared common sense and shared recognitions available to the novelist, and to encourage nativism. That could mean a variety of things—from, say, the realistic anti-utopianism of the later George Orwell, as in *1984* (1949), to the emphasis on the moral need for the loving heart in society so delicately explored by L. P. Hartley in the *Eustace and Hilda* tetralogy, which appeared between 1944 and 1949, or in *The Go-Between* (1953).

But what Cooper had in mind is undoubtedly the attempt to return to more traditionalist sources in his own work—as in *Scenes from Provincial Life* (1950)—or in the novels of C. P. Snow (b. 1905). Snow is a convenient contrast; he is not a major novelist, but he is a highly competent and powerful one, and despite some of the attacks made on him he has, it seems fair to say, done what he has done ably. He too began writing in the 1930s, but not in the thirties of bohemia or experiment; rather of social realism. An early novel,

*The Search* (1934), is a detailed, neo-Wellsian book about a young provincial entering the big world of London and science and being taken by what he finds, despite thwarted hopes and personal difficulties. This theme continues into his best-known work, the long *roman fleuve* called *Strangers and Brothers*, which starts with a novel of that title published in 1940 and has just been completed with the eleventh volume. Though it is all based on a close historical attentiveness, there is something oddly timeless and public about Snow's prose, which is workably efficient and does not markedly belong to any particular phase of modern rhetoric. At the centre of the sequence lies the first-person storyteller who 'speaks' the prose and commands the narrative; there are no modern ironies about his position. Lewis Eliot is a lawyer, don, and man of affairs with a provincial background; his life is both public and private, and draws into relationship public affairs and personal tensions, historical moments (like the discovery of the atomic bomb in *The New Men*, 1954) and familiar and familial experiences over a stretch of English history from 1914 to the present. People here lie in relation to the past and the community, live in families and do jobs, and Eliot takes as his viewpoint a lay or scientific progressivism, a social hope. His historiography is complex, though, and involves real attentiveness to psychological strain and dilemma, awareness of solitude, confrontation with emptiness, though all this is related to the public forum and often played out through it. The socio-historical web is always there, then; families, towns, societies, historical change are inescapable and crucial, as are the contingencies of humdrum, day-to-day reality. This gives a somewhat loose and contingent method of composition even for a *roman fleuve*, save that Snow normally turns his novels on dilemmas where public and private worlds meet. In *The Masters* (1951) the focus is morally textured around the appointment of a new master to a Cambridge college; in *The Sleep of Reason* (1968) the focus is the murder trial of a lesbian couple who have killed a small boy—an event calling into question many of the liberal premises about the growth of freedom and self-expression that Eliot had supported in earlier books. But both in his way of drawing on traditional practices in the novel without great disturbance, and in his fairly progressive and positivistic view of modern history, Snow obviously leads the way into a socially complicated yet not remarkably corrugated fiction which has been a mode for other writers to follow.

Hence we can find similar qualities in many of the young writers of the 1950s, though not quite in Snow's form. The conventional account of the decade in fiction is that it was dominated by a group of social realists who saw things sufficiently differently from their predecessors to be Angry, but not sufficiently differently to be revolutionary in either literary or social terms. Their theme was class and classlessness, their standpoint a lower-middle-class or working-class dissent from those who ran things, their mode involved the mixture of social documentation and the making of new heroes drawing on contemporary values. The work of Kingsley Amis (b. 1922) makes a convenient test of the accuracy of this. From *Lucky Jim* (1954) on, the centre of Amis's work has been rather variously a hero concerned with his own integrity in a social environment which, though in many ways unattractive, he comes to terms with: the terms are usually more or less his own. The separation of hero and environment gives the basis of his great gift—for a moral comedy which grants a fortunate comic justice to those who, while not always admirable, are honest with themselves. Though called an Angry Young Man, his virtue lies in a moral realism—less angry than appreciative of the pleasant, ordinary things in life, like girls, drink, and moral unpretentiousness—and a notion of the degree of moral self-analysis required to deserve such things. So in *I Want It Now* (1968) the book turns on the author's sense that the gluttonous sexual liaison begun right at the beginning of the action must acquire a greater factor of responsibility, a modest moral redemption, before it can be made fully satisfactory. In many ways one can see the link between Amis and his admired Henry Fielding; both create comic worlds in which an empirical, ordinary morality is granted the space to explore itself and then is granted the final blessing of the comic muse, through the gift of the girl, the estate: so the Tom Joneses and the Jims win and deserve their luck. His heroes are contemporaries out to explode something: Jim Dixon is the enemy of boredom, Garnet Bowen in *I Like It Here* the enemy of 'bum', all unnecessary pretensions and rules, and Patrick Standish in *Take a Girl Like You* (1960) the enemy of outmoded realities and codes, the voice for getting out of the present what it can give. The pattern here grows more complicated, for Patrick is a 'bastard' too, and Amis establishes another centre of value in Jenny Bunn, the girl whom Patrick finally rapes when she is drunk at a party. Patrick is less 'virtuous' than she; but he is historically up-to-date, so that Jenny ends the novel feeling that what has happened has a kind of historical necessity. Thus though Amis is a moralist, and rather obviously draws on the empirical decencies of a new middle-class meritocracy, coupled with a sense of the pleasures of living in the present, he also establishes a kind of hero who has a quirky and individual code of his own. Hence to some extent Amis creates a private language—a personal rhetoric which enables him to lay out his field of preferences, his moral sorting out of good from bad, not through any abstract concepts but through the effective fictional working of the old Jowett principle of 'Never apologize, never explain'. So the hero is usually hero by virtue of his identification with the system of linguistic preferences embodied in the novel, its private moral language, comically individualized and only really appropriate to this faintly stylized world.

In this respect Amis does, certainly, differ somewhat from writers who have been associated with him. John Wain (b. 1925), a more irritably ironic novelist, has in many ways a much more traditionally liberal sense of the private integrity that must be preserved against the explored social world. In *Hurry On Down* (1953), Charles Lumley reacts against the residual Christian and liberal values of his grammar school and university, and the meritocratic rat-race it points to, by drawing on a fund of other values, themselves residually Christian and liberal, to support a modestly underground existence which is a convinced misuse of his talents. The present is not *all* for the best. The topic returns in Wain's later novels, which look at middle-class marriages, the life of provincial artists, the struggles within the family, in pursuit of an answer to the same question: in *A Travelling Woman* (1959) it is posed as 'Does one person in a hundred thousand know what he really believes or what he really ought to do?' Wain's gift for evoking the moral confusion of a changing society is considerable, though his sense of moral evil is often somewhat thin and melodramatic. In John Braine's (b. 1922) *Room at the Top* (1957), the story of a latter-day Julien Sorel who exploits his own body and brain to succeed in a society whose ethic of success, competition, and self-advertising he sees clearly, moral density is much more lacking —rather the fable is presented fairly flatly to leave a moral residue in the reader. In *Saturday Night and Sunday Morning* (1958), by Alan Sillitoe (b. 1928), the story of a new affluent worker whose life is divided between slavery at work and week-end pleasures, these followed by a Sunday morning repentance, the moral centre is again thin: here what is activated is a kind of half-thought anarchism, an ideal of personal freedom, seemingly but ambiguously sacrificed at the end as marriage and respectability make their claims. In all these writers there is a stronger sense of social servitude, a feeling that modern society, with its new consumables and new pleasures, does stifle some humanity or vitality, does violate some half-glimpsed freedom. To some extent the world is seen as external and therefore hostile to the true world of the self, a dangerous reality-principle; yet its clear reality does invite a form of final adjustment to it. These are indeed social novels, but they lack those densities of relationship between individual and society we find in the great Victorian novels, even as they also lack the full force of cultural criticism we also find in the novelists of that period. Rather they suggest the difficulty of finding a right relation between self and society as a given reality, the kind of moral and philosophical confusion Iris Murdoch speaks of in the essay I have quoted from. Moreover it is as if the novelist, faced with the confusions of the Welfare State society of postwar England, cannot see it large and must therefore see it from a provincial or classbound standpoint; individualism never attains the force of a full vision, as it sometimes does in comparable American novels (say J. D. Salinger's *The Catcher in the Rye*).

But, as I have suggested, this is not the only kind of novel to emerge in postwar England, and these very difficulties may suggest why it is that there has been a strong vein of mythic or romance writing, which has grown even more marked in recent years. Indeed this is true of some of the novelists whom we have perhaps associated too readily with the *vraisemblance* tradition. Alan Sillitoe's work varies between the modes: his long short story *The Loneliness of the Long Distance Runner* (1959) is not just a social-realist portrait of a Nottingham delinquent but a deeply abstracted myth about freedom of spirit. The pattern is even clearer in David Storey (b. 1933), whose first novel, *This Sporting Life* (1960), was an effective example of that kind of north-country fiction about the brash assertive hero that came so alive in the fifties (Stan Barstow, Keith Waterhouse, Louis Battye, or more gently Stanley Middleton), but whose best book, *Radcliffe* (1963), is highly mythic. The northern setting has been transformed into a fabulous landscape and the novel is a psychological allegory about the division of spirit and flesh; the effect is rather as if Emily Brontë and the psychologist R. D. Laing had conspired together on a novel—a vast panoramic work in which landscape, social struggle, and psychic forces battle towards definition.

The clearest and most remarkable case is Iris Murdoch (b. 1919). Her first book, *Under the Net* (1954), was brought under the net of anger; in fact it was the first of a long and developing sequence of symbolist-philosophical novels dealing with the problems of language, meaning, and myth-making, and concerned with a kind of structuralist anthropological view of the root-forces that live through and behind society—love, power, totemism, force. Jake Donaghue in *Under the Net* may seem a typical fifties *picaro*; but he is a novelist, facing the problem of the possible collapse into contingency of language and the fascinations of silence, and he is set within a highly surrealized and symbolically ordered world (obviously in part derived from two of Miss Murdoch's heroes, Queneau and Sartre). Jake finally reaches a sense of the 'unutterable particularity' of things, a neo-existentialist discovery that paradoxically enables him to order and write. Her later books employ a variety of different modes, and at times fall uncomfortably close to the novel of sentiment or the love story, but in fact they normally heighten and exploit different kinds of romance-mode for the purposes of a fairly elaborate mythography. In *A Severed Head* (1961), the French farce manner moves beyond the civilized, Bloomsbury-ish world of personal relationships and fashionable affairs towards a kind of totemism that is focused in the power-centred figure of Honor Klein, an anthropologist and 'dark god' dominating the action. In *The Unicorn* (1963) it is the panoply of the nineteenth-century governness romance that is called up to take the brunt of the shimmering, intense symbolism. Her work is concerned with the specifics of relationships, but her real power is to structure the world of force lying behind. And with a number of other women novelists who have come into importance since the war—from Christine Brooke-Rose, who is explicitly experimentalist, to writers like Margaret Drabble and A. S. Byatt who retain more of the traditional surface—she has made the novel of sentiment into a more analytical form.

There are other novelists who have been still more explicit about using the forms of romance and myth for religious and metaphysical purposes, for instance, Gabriel Fielding (*The Birthday King*, 1963) or William Golding (b. 1911). Golding's capacities for the metaphysical romance are perhaps shown at fullest in *Lord of the Flies* (1954), which exploits a boys'-book fable of the *Coral Island* type to create a complex, vividly rendered questioning of a liberal or progressive view of the unfallen state of man. The book is, like all his novels, founded on the conviction of civilization as a moral paradox, a disguise for what really is, and Golding's universe is normally a-social or perhaps pre-social, primitivistic at its core and yet also conscious that it is only through *knowing* our primitivism that we will find our innocence. In short, Golding rejects the idea of progress through history, and history figures in his work as a paradox. It obscures the fundamental truth, though of course it is through the tools of history that the truth can be revealed—for there is a deeply modernistic and post-Freudian element in Golding's fictive universe.

It is indeed out of the experience of modern man, and above all out of the confusions of his sense of moral freedom, his opened capacity to do harm to himself and others, that Golding creates his vision. Hence he seeks to reinstate the factor of theology in his view of man, but theology in the form of an archetypal image or root-myth: 'I do feel fable as being an invented thing out on the surface whereas myth is something that comes out of the roots of things in the ancient sense of being the key to existence, the whole meaning of life, and experience as a whole,' he has said in claiming to be a mythic writer. There is in fact something highly *made* about his myths, at least in the way in which they are decorated with a rhetorical extravagance; but his best work comes out of a balance between the power of the mythical substance, those Ur-forms and primitive orders he appeals to, and a kind of technical inventiveness sufficiently held as to seem discovered rather than made. He is, that's to say, a kind of neo-modernist primitive, an unusual and interesting combination.

If a recurrence of the mythical or symbolist novel has been one of the postwar styles through which writers have sought to penetrate beyond or outside a social or sociological view of man, then of equal importance has been the powerful reappearance of comedy within the English tradition. As I have suggested, the comedy of Amis is Fielding-like; the comedy of adjustment to reality, a comedy working against any grand deliverances. But we have also seen the reactivation of a much more surreal comic species, a kind of macabre or black humour of which Evelyn Waugh is surely the immediate precursor. This is a kind of comedy which infuses the world of reason, order, and society with an anarchic vision, which sees it as a debased and unstable world that can be treated with great distance and unconcern. The vanities of this fallen universe are caught with a supreme bland detachment in the work of Muriel Spark (b. 1918), a delightful writer whose pleasurable tone runs blandly across a profoundly macabre vision. Mrs. Spark's real quality as a writer depends very much on sustaining the security of this comic blandness, as she brilliantly does in *Memento Mori* (1959), a farce about an older generation seeking to hold on to the manners of the young, though they are surrounded by the ominous presence of death. In *The Mandelbaum Gate* (1965), her most explicitly Catholic novel, something of this nonchalance gets lost; there is an element of too apparent suffering that strains beyond the capacity for macabre farce. But something of her primary quality—her capacity for invading social and human stability with gratuitous violence, deception, and death—is there in several other important comic writers of this period: in the brilliant work of Anthony Burgess (*A Clockwork Orange*, 1962, etc.), for instance, or John Bowen (e.g. *The Birdcage*, 1962). In a number of other recent writers, the comic vision has been directed at the principle of fictiveness itself, at the ironies inherent in the absence of a context for making moral or social dilemmas grand or meaningful; so in David Lodge (*The British Museum Is Falling Down*, 1965), the novels of B. S. Johnson, or in Nigel Dennis's splendid comedy of ideas, *Cards of Identity* (1955).

But the supreme example of the novelist of the comic grotesque is surely Angus Wilson (b. 1913), precisely because here the grotesque is profoundly caught up in a viewpoint of liberal honesty and integrity which demands a full exploration of experience. Wilson is one of those writers who seem at first sight to belong right in the tradition of the English novel—perhaps not one tradition, but two. He obviously inherits a great deal from the social-panoramic novel, notably from Dickens; he equally inherits from the line of the liberal novel, that kind of novel concerned both with the virtues and the moral self-deceptions of the liberal mind, that comes through from E. M. Forster. But it is at this intersection between the social-moral and the comic grotesque novel that he stands. He has said himself (*The Wild Garden*, 1963) that the social-documentary instinct in a novelist can tend to silence his creative energy, and that he must invest in the force of his own imagination and allow it to take over. In his own work, this usually happens through the penetration beyond social existence into a world of darker and bleaker and more radical forces of upheaval within the individual self. Wilson clearly has an intrinsic appreciation of the powers that make for sanity and control—the pluck and courage of Meg Eliot in *The Middle Age of Mrs. Eliot* (1958) or of Sylvia Calvert in *Late Call* (1964)—or the forces of liberal integrity and self-honesty, as in Bernard Sands in *Hemlock and After* (1952). These things he creates with a real pathos, though it is a pathos that contains a profound comic element of mimicry, parody, and a sense of human grotesquerie. This is complicatedly given; the grotesquerie is partly a matter of social formation and a consequence of social change, which can create disorientation of spirit, but it is also a consequence of the curious and difficult patternings of authorial involvement and distance Wilson creates. Wilson is genuinely a writer of scale; and his is a complex universe where—what Bernard Sands recognizes—the 'dual nature of all human action' is apparent, where rational order and control are in part at least a moral disguise covering darker places either of emotional dishonesty or emotional disorder.

As these energetic versions of symbolism and comedy may suggest, the social-documentary bias of the postwar English novel can be too considerably overstated. What is apparent is that behind the exploration of modern society there runs a deep sense of personal crisis, of value deprivation, of social uncertainty and aimlessness, and that the sense of cultural uncertainty which touches a good deal of postwar English writing has found a variety of modes for its expression. The withering away of past norms of manners and morals has I think observably thrust English novelists towards a rather oblique interpretation of their times. In fact, the 'social' bias of the English novel has never been quite as fundamental as many modern critics have claimed, and if it is true that there is in English writing a kind of pervasive awareness of social identity that limits the English writer from some of the more extreme forms of experience other literatures have pursued, there are signs that it is being treated from more and more oblique viewpoints. This is not only because it grows harder for the writer today to draw on an effective consensus about what society is really like or how it may be judged; it has to do also with the contemporary disposition to find meaning for life not only in the social field but in psychic recesses, in inward geography, and with the problematic status of myth and legend. The postwar novel has found no great heroes or grand myths; nor has it produced many remarkable fictional experiments. But of course these are not the only things that make novels fine or great, and to pine for the support of a metaphysics or a grand philosophical theme, as some critics have in looking at contemporary English fiction, may be to divert attention from the distinctive virtues of the writers I have discussed. In fact, however, there are signs that the deliberated modesty of the English novel is perhaps slipping away, and that a new will-to-style is emerging. The problem of making modern myth, of passing beyond contingency to coherence, has had increased attention lately in England, and it has shown up in novels themselves. Doris Lessing's *The Golden Notebook* (1962) is one remarkable instance; another important example less noticed by critics being John Fowles's *The Magus* (1966), a large and exploratory novel concerned with how myths may be made and how the ironies of fictiveness are involved in their making. The signs of the revival of aesthetic debate in the novel are themselves likely to create an environment encouraging to formalism and experiment, an environment in which accelerating change in other quarters of the culture puts an increased stylistic pressure on the novelist. In that situation the deliberated modesty of the novelist may slip away; but even if so we should not forget that modest novelists can be substantial and important.

*The American Novel Since the War*

Compared with the English novel over the same period, the post-war American novel has been much more energetically various, and has undoubtedly pre-empted much of the critical attention given to contemporary writing in the English language. To understand why this is so, and why it is that many English and European writers and readers turn readily to the American novel for sustenance, we need, I think, to look back over the different history the American novel has had in our century. It was not perhaps until the 1920s that the American novel came confidently of age, became really a separate entity surely founded in a different experience, rather than an idiosyncratic offshoot of European and particularly English traditions in fiction. Modern critics have lately shown us how very different from European writing the American novel of the *nineteenth* century was, too—focusing their case upon its much more symbolist, metaphysical, and romance bias, and their attention above all upon Nathaniel Hawthorne and Herman Melville. But both of these two conceived of themselves as very lonely and self-consciously eccentric writers, men lost from a tradition rather than writing in one; while most of the American novelists of the nineteenth century remained in some way aware of the power over them of the European and above all the English mode in the novel. This awareness was encouraged by several factors: the popularity of the English novel in America, made the more popular because American publishers could pirate the great English names without paying them royalties; the dependence of American writers on a good reception in England if they were to make their reputations in the United States; the prevalence of the habit of expatriation; and so on. So the virtues now seen by modern critics in the classic American novelists of the last century were often seen—by the writers themselves—as faults, and certainly they never represented an entirely solid tradition, but rather a sequence of brief phases of communal influence. The degree to which the American novel was disposed towards extra-social experience, and hence towards broad national myth, another aspect much praised by modern critics, was often treated as a matter for embarrassment; the absence of manners for the satirist, of solid institutions and customs for the novelist of manners, of a sure social function for the novelist himself, was remarked upon with discomfort by many American writers, including Cooper, Hawthorne, and

Henry James. The American author seemed to be trapped between staying in his own country in a state of imaginative isolation and becoming an expatriate and losing the native stimulus: a dilemma that many of them spoke of and that Van Wyck Brooks, in the 1920s, explored in a fascinating pair of books designed to show that failure lay inevitably in *both* directions: his two exemplary studies were *The Ordeal of Mark Twain* and *The Pilgrimage of Henry James.* But it was Brooks who, while maintaining that the same situation still prevailed, introduced a further proposition: American literature was by about 1915 at last 'coming of age', developing its own themes, manners, and modes under the impact of a totally un-European experience.

It was this confidence, whether justified or not, that gave so much force to the major American novelists of the earlier half of this century: notably to Hemingway, Faulkner, Fitzgerald, and Dos Passos. They were conscious of little behind them in the way of a tradition: Hemingway appealed not to a fictional heritage but to one book, Twain's *The Adventures of Huckleberry Finn,* while Fitzgerald appealed to the curious twosome of Edith Wharton and Gertrude Stein. Both Faulkner and Dos Passos were more explicitly 'experimental' novelists, in some though not all of their work, and here the debt was to European modernists and above all to Joyce. Leslie Fiedler has suggested that their experimentalism was 'the reaction of the tourist',[5] and it was certainly a very nativized variant of modern internationalist techniques, which they drew on with a sense of the need for working out a new national species. But what was important about these major figures is that they did appeal to a novelty of experience that seemed somehow manifested in American life. The spare, tough heroes of Hemingway encountering their nihilistic universe; the lost heroes and heroines of Fitzgerald, beautiful but damned in an economic boom that lacked a moral philosophy; the central figures of Faulkner with their profound burdens of cultural transition; the multiple characters of Dos Passos individually experiencing the transition of their nation into a climactic emptiness of purpose—all were touched with a raw, nervous newness of knowledge that seemed to belong to the nation and the age. And all of these writers clearly felt that American experience was new and particular, but also universally representative. In the 1920s, when they started to write, 'something subtle passed to America, the style of man', Scott Fitzgerald said. Clearly, the cultural confidence of this generation of American novelists depended on the way they had acquired certain essential assumptions about their form from the European arts; indeed, it is perhaps finally because of that that we are able to grant them their considerable place in world literature. But what has obviously been important for the writers who followed them—the writers of the last three decades in the United States—has been the native acquisition of this mood of cultural confidence. These newer, postwar writers have, to some considerable extent, retained many of the characteristics of this classic age, however different the temper one feels is in them; they have retained some of its propensity towards epicality and scale, its tendency towards heroes of large representativeness, its recurrent obsession with the mental and psychological dispositions of cultural transformation and the rapid transition of human fortunes.

In brief: we might say that, if we were to look back over the history of the English novel, what it has achieved in the twentieth century has been only a small part of the totality, and the work of the postwar writers is likely to be seen by critics and indeed by the writers themselves as a late and not notably vast contribution to that totality. In American fiction, though, the twentieth-century novel constitutes not only about half of the total tradition, but in many ways the more confidently energetic half. The task of making the form is still alive, and the dominant themes of the American novel, the themes laid down in its past, tend to be relatively modern and often highly usable ones. The novelists of the 1920s wrote as if the world began anew in that decade, as if human experience had been transformed, almost, indeed, as if little about either had been noticed before. Their broad technical originality, their mixture of nihilism and despair, their concern with making moral life in a world growing more and more disoriented and in a society in radical change, was thus picked up in new ways by postwar American writers who have gone much further into the idea of a transformed world. Like those writers, they have tended to make their fiction between two poles: the search for a large redeeming myth, and the desire to show the pressures in modern society which make the heroic purpose questionable or invalid. More and more they have done so in a society that is centred in the city, has lost its Anglo-Saxon culture, has taken on a vast cultural amorphousness. In some ways, therefore, the postwar novel has tended to become more naturalistic; to this extent, it has also drawn on the tradition set up by the late-nineteenth-century and early-twentieth-century American realist writers like Dreiser, London, Norris, and Crane. But it has also tended to retain those themes of national epical hopefulness and of cosmic depression, those themes in which the entire universe is implicated in the fortunes of the individual hero (or anti-hero), that we recognize as part of the quality of the best writers of the twenties.

This, indeed, contributes to a paradox that has often been recognized in the contemporary American novel: it has been both a fiction of alienation and solitude, *anomie* and human plight, and a fiction of social expansiveness and fullness. In some ways it has been a much more conspicuously 'alienated' fiction than the British novel of the same period (a fact that, despite the emphasis of some modern critics, should *not* be regarded as an automatic guarantee of quality); it has also at its best given a morally full and exacting exploration of the fabric of its time and society. Its heroes have often been 'philosophical' heroes, desiring to make sense of their individual lives in relation to a complex and fully experienced world outside themselves. In the writing of the 1950s, these themes often came through as a serious moral ferment, and part at least of the concern can be caught in a sentence from Saul Bellow's first novel, *Dangling Man*: 'He asked himself a question I still would like answered, namely, "How should a good man live; what ought he to do?"' More recently, in a darker and bleaker period in American society, the note has grown a good deal more desperate and nihilistic. But on the whole the postwar American novel has been deeply conscious of the obligation to reach forward into new experience, into futures, dreams, frontiers of sensation; and it has done so in a clear awareness that it comes out of a growing, expanding, technologized and post-industrial society that is bringing about new versions of man. As Saul Bellow once observed, much of the interest present-day American writers have had for their European counterparts is the fact that they have seemed to validate, with minds freed from theories or intellectual preconceptions, many of the new physical, psychological, and philosophical ideas that have suggested the dilemmas and difficulties of modern life, the violence and aggressiveness of modern man, his uneasy sense of identity and anxiety.[6] In some ways this has given the American novel a kind of automatic modernity; it has also, however, been, in the case of the best of American contemporaries, a matter for full and serious exploration, and hence involved moral and technical discovery.

If one were to look for a temper in the postwar American novel, it would surely lie in its interesting mixture of naturalism and aesthetic finesse. When the Second World War ended, the signs seemed to be that the new writers were devoting themselves to a naturalistic mode. There was a spate of war novels—some of considerable quality, like

Norman Mailer's *The Naked and the Dead* (1948), Irwin Shaw's *The Young Lions* (1948), and James Jones's *From Here to Eternity* (1951)—most of them concerned with showing the belittlement of man by the complex military machine. And there was also a spate of naturalistic urban fiction—novels like Nelson Algren's Chicago stories (*The Man With the Golden Arm*, 1949, etc.), or Chandler Brossard's *Who Walk in Darkness* (1952), or the fiction of Herbert Gold. In many cases there was an implied political dimension to this writing, though it was rarely an explicit party-line, more commonly a sense of unease and dissent. There was often a sensational extremism, too, frequently in the form of a psychological analysis pressed to the point of psychic distortion, of violent acts and extreme imaginings. As Harvey Swados, a writer of naturalist bias, once put it: 'Obviously the novelist has now to deal with the human heart pushed to such extremities as would have been beyond the most horrid imaginings of a Jane Austen or an Anthony Trollope, or even a Henry James.'[7] And at times—one might take as fairly extreme examples the work of novelists like John Hawkes or Truman Capote—this took the form of a conscious grotesque, a deliberate evocation of the landscapes of horror and nightmare. But as frequently as not the tendency of such fiction was to see society as a large impersonal complex, as an army or a city, and to find man lost and lonely within it, or else himself violent and distorted. The tradition behind this kind of writing was, moreover, potentially a 'raw' one—what Philip Rahv once called a 'redskin' as opposed to a 'paleface' tradition.[8] Many of these novels took their essential force from the material over which they ranged, the scenes of violence and sexuality they encompassed, their documentary report on horrors and disorders. Their central figures are often victims of the society or, when dealt with more positivistically, conscious violators of its values, like heroes of the 'Beat' novels such as Dean Moriarty, the 'burning shuddering frightful Angel' who travels wildly through Jack Kerouac's *On the Road* (1957), or the more comically conceived Sebastian Dangerfield of J. P. Donleavy's *The Ginger Man* (1955). And often, with such heroes, there is an attempt to validate them as philosophically or religiously serious men, making honest sense out of a crazily misshapen world. Indeed this kind of victim–hero becomes a familiar figure of the American novel of the 1950s; and in his famous brief essay 'The White Negro' Norman Mailer distilled many of his lineaments.

But at its best this general tendency reached out well beyond any simple naturalistic confines, any simple fictional primitivism. It tended to establish the sense of an American society vast, anonymous, and distorted, to the point of making it an accepted fictional convention for the postwar American novelist. But it was capable of considerable fictional sophistication, and in this respect it links with another important tendency of the postwar American novel: its tendency towards decorum and formal sensitivity. This, perhaps, is best seen among the body of Southern writers that also began to come to notice shortly after the war had ended, though it is by no means confined to the South (nor to women writers). But one can see in works like, say, Eudora Welty's *Delta Wedding* (1946), Carson McCullers's *The Member of the Wedding* (1946), Truman Capote's *Other Voices, Other Rooms* (1948), and Flannery O'Connor's *A Good Man Is Hard to Find* (short stories, 1955), a much greater degree of formalism and of fictional 'cultivation'. Theirs is a literature much less concerned with the urban, inchoate, and masculine matrix of American society, much more with particular communities *as* communities, with their own mores, ethics, and involvements. But their heroes, though more characteristically sensitive and concerned, and often adolescent, commonly meet an element of violence and disorder in the world, which is itself made up often of grotesque people living out their own personal existences and needs in a solitude rarely redeemed. Virtue again finds no easy counterparts, and the element of distortion in the extant universe is once again apparent. But what one is aware of in the work of such writers (and a few others—Peter Taylor, Jean Stafford, and Katherine Anne Porter—might here be mentioned) is the degree of conscious craft that has gone into their writing, their deep deliberation of technique. It is a high finesse rather than a willed experiment; and this finesse has marked a good deal of postwar American fiction (naturally enough surely in the country of the creative-writing class and the Guggenheim Fellowship). Perhaps the writers who most thoroughly manifest it in a major way are three writers closely associated with the *New Yorker* magazine, itself a centre for highly finished writing—J. D. Salinger, John Updike, and Mary McCarthy. The mode is also apparent in the highly social and mannered writing of John Cheever, Louis Auchincloss, or John O'Hara, or in its comic variant in Peter De Vries; here it is a literature of social conduct in a much more European sense. However, the finesse I am talking of is by no means necessarily a social finesse, and it does not manifest itself only in a social fiction. Rather it is an emphasis on the language, coherence, and structure of the finished work, an aesthetic exactitude, a basic concern with fictional craft.

The American novel since the war has not, then, been notably *avant-garde* either; but it has shown a greater formal curiosity and concern, and this has been true even of many writers whose primary disposition seems at first realistic or naturalistic. Indeed, in the post-war American scene the distinction between naturalism and formalism has grown much harder to make. Whereas earlier in the century naturalism grew out of a strongly determinist view of society and man, and formalism was often a reaction against this, a move towards elaborating both the inner consciousness of the individual and the inner coherence of the work of art, the two tendencies have tended to draw together. Writers of strongly formalist or even symbolist bent are often less concerned with radical experiment than with giving a qualitative density and precision of technique to the novel, while the writers of naturalist disposition are frequently formally and technically exploratory as well. Perhaps it was above all Hemingway who showed that naturalism could consort with a subdued symbolism and an absolute authority on the writer's part to make entire his own fictive world—and who therefore showed, too, that it was possible to draw dense connotative out of ostensibly denotative meanings. Or, to express the point differently, he seems to have shown many subsequent American novelists that it was not necessary to use what D. H. Lawrence called 'art-speech' in a novel in order for it to gain further dimensions of significance; the personal vernacular of the author or of the broader society could be drawn on for such purposes. The results are apparent in an author like Norman Mailer, who has said very explicitly that a concern with craft can be disabling to a writer, and that his first obligation is to keep his consciousness alive to the tendencies of history—yet whose best work is clearly heavily composed and controlled.

It is in a group of writers who came to conspicuous notice in the 1950s that this fusion is most apparent. At their centre are a number of Jewish-American writers—Saul Bellow, Bernard Malamud, Norman Mailer, Philip Roth—who succeeded in giving the urban novel a remarkable moral and intellectual density. To a large extent, the force of most of them resides in their gift for expanding and universalizing a theme traditional in Jewish-American fiction: that of seeing America as a promised land in which a man must find a place and define his nature. The titles of some of their novels—*The Victim* (Saul Bellow), *A New Life* (Bernard Malamud), *Goodbye, Columbus* (Philip Roth)—suggest the oscillation between the ultimate hope of renewal and the ultimate fear of belittlement which these novelists draw from that tradition. At the same time, the theme of the true immigrant seeking the promised land touches the heart of American mythology itself. And as the essential Jewishness becomes a mixture of hope and exile in the urban environment, rather than a religious or a racial matter, it also takes the form of a representatively modern mythical situation. As Leslie Fiedler has put it, the Jewish writer becomes for all readers 'the metropolitan at home, though expert in the indignities, rather than the amenities, of urban life'.[9] To know the world yet not to possess it has been a sufficiently common experience to make a writing shot through with such awarenesses representative; and the representativeness has been further intensified by the fact that most of these writers are themselves cast in the mould of the writer as intellectual, knowing the forces that have made things thus. Moreover they have tended to draw on their multiple heritage, American and European, for their fictional modes: the Russian psychological novel as well as the American realist novel lies behind them. And then, too, their inherited Jewishness has given them a moral concern and, to support it, a moral terminology for writing of it. In the work of Bellow and Malamud, particularly, a sense of moral law, religious obligation, and even of the supernatural stalks through the pages, corrugating the surface of generous liberalism.

Of these writers, the best seems to me Saul Bellow (b. 1915); indeed he is probably the most important writer to emerge in the States over this period. Bellow is very explicitly an urban novelist, and one very conscious of the realist tradition of Dreiser: the city he writes of, whether it be New York or Chicago, is a melting-pot of races, a dense agglomeration of misery and competition. Survival is a Darwinian struggle, but the direction of survival, in Bellow's work, is essentially moral—it turns towards understanding and the acceptance of others. His heroes are frequently at odds with the society they inhabit, searching for the freedom of self; but it is as much the self as the world that must undergo a proper adaptation. This being so, his novels have a dense moral and psychological dimension which owes a good deal to Dostoevsky and similar European novelists; and his urban landscape is not simply anonymous, but a landscape of the spirit which must be realized as reality and turned into a condition for growth and self-renewal. There is an explicit resistance in his novels, in particular in *Herzog*, to those who would instruct us in the bleak absurdity of reality, who say that man is necessarily alienated, who tell us that the age of the moralized and personal self is finished. It is in conducting his quarrel with such views that Bellow gets much of his energy as a writer; and his standpoint is not, as many critics have suggested, one simply of adaptation to the 'system', but one that liberally seeks to restore a true sense of fullness of selfhood, that demands that the world be made for men. There is a core of deeply realized humanity in his clear conviction that the essential task is to discover the basis of individuality and brotherhood in a world of singularly complex reality. Most of his heroes bear the burden of working out, in the most difficult circumstances, a satisfactory relationship to other men and to the moral demands of the self in a universe intensely complicated philosophically and socially—a world in which, as one of these heroes, Henderson, puts it, no man has a place any longer. Through his six novels—*Dangling Man* (1944), *The Victim* (1947), *The Adventures of Augie March* (1953), *Henderson the Rain King* (1959), *Herzog* (1964), and *Mr. Sammler's Planet* (1970)—and the novella *Seize the Day* (1956), he works these themes with an exuberant imaginative zest. In part this comes from the richness of a prose that can effectively allude to moral matters because it has all the force of Jewish soul-searching rhetoric behind it, which can reach from the comedy of suffering to the ideal of aspiration towards human grandeur, which can sustain appeal to the transcendental and eternal as a consistent and fundamental element of his style. In the earlier novels the essential theme of inquiry is man's obligations towards others; in the later ones it becomes an often euphoric exploration of the grandeur of self—Henderson's claim that '. . . the universe itself being put into us, it calls out for scope'. The euphoria is sustained, often, as a relieving comedy that carries this sense of grandeur without at all diminishing the nature or significance of human suffering and pain. *Herzog*, though not Bellow's best book, draws all these themes and qualities together in its portrait of Moses Herzog, the disturbed Jewish intellectual moving through New York and Chicago and quarrelling, in letters addressed to the great living and the great dead, with their pessimistic answers to the problems of the world, with their abstract historicism and fading humanism.

Bernard Malamud (b. 1914) is much more explicitly a Jewish writer than Bellow; his fictional world is closer to the ghetto and to Jewish lore and mores, his themes are much closer to those basic themes of suffering and ethnic identity that lie in the tradition of Jewish fiction, and his manner is clearly indebted to older Jewish writers of mythical and sometimes mystical bias like Isaac Bashevis Singer. There is something more distinctly private and something more surreal about his world than Bellow's, though he shows the same intensity of awareness of the strains and stresses of the modern urban world, and the same concern with moral conduct and duty. His first novel, *The Natural* (1952), is a reworking of the Grail legend in terms of a baseball hero, and it establishes his basic theme of renewal and discovery of new life in a dead world. In *The Assistant* (1957), a brilliant novel, he makes his theme the story of a Gentile hoodlum who becomes an honorary Jew after robbing the store of a Jewish grocer; it is in evoking the saintly suffering of the storekeeper, eternally on the edge of failure, that Malamud most fully realizes his ideal of human decency in a world of misery. In *A New Life* (1961), a comic novel set in a West Coast college, he comes closer to the idea of a full human redemption in exploring the ironic fortunes of S. Levin, the former New York drunkard and failure, who finds a new life in the West; a life smaller and more ordinary than the one he hoped for, but a new life, a mild human promise, after all. With *The Fixer* (1966), he takes his most ambitious theme in his story of Yakov Bok, the Jew who comes to Kiev in the Russia of the Tsars and is accused of a ritual child-murder. The novel has all Malamud's virtues—an intense moral and psychological rendering, a complexity of interpretative tone, a deep human sympathy—and yet a somewhat narrowing conclusion, as Bok, after long imprisonment, acquires not the deeper humanism that has been the ideal of the earlier novels, but a politicalized, revolutionary Jewishness. But it is, throughout, Malamud's moral intensity and seriousness coupled with an extraordinary power and range of social creation that makes his work so important, so central—as compared, say, with the novels of Edward Lewis Wallant (1926–62), another significant but finally less profound and universal writer (*The Tenants of Moonbloom*, 1963, etc.). Philip Roth (b. 1933), on the other hand, concentrates on a more sophisticated Jewish world, further away from the ghetto and the immigrant past: a world of suburbia, rich Jewry, and graduate students. He works too with a sophistication of social observation greater than Bellow's or Malamud's, and so with a much more socially realistic register, a deeper fascination with manners and specifics. In a sense it is the triumph of the domain of the ordinary, and the problems about human hope and moral duty it raises, that are Roth's theme. Behind his world hovers the Hassidic Jewishness of a former generation, ahead the ideal America; but here in the middle are those ordinary inadequacies of ordinary life that, in *Goodbye, Columbus* (1959), *Letting Go* (1962), and *When She Was Good* (1967), he catches with such precise perfection.

Norman Mailer (b. 1923), too, makes his claims on us by informing a realistic, indeed a journalistic, bias with a radical moral energy, but in a way much more difficult to assess. High claims have been made for him as a novelist, and from time to time he has deserved them. Yet he has been—almost boastfully—frank (in *Advertisements for Myself*, 1959) about his sense of not having fully succeeded in fiction, which he has seen as a search for a new order of passionate consciousness in a history that seems to be destructive of feeling, genitality, and fullness of being. At the centre of the Mailer dream is the noble savage who is at once sexually harmonious *and* the historical consciousness, the evolving human and political species. Mailer is superbly good at conveying what we might call the politics of sexuality and the sexuality of politics, two orders of being that we have often made abstractly separate and hard to fuse. From *The Naked and the Dead* (1948), a good, fairly realistic war novel, perhaps the best of the post-Second-World-War batch, through *Barbary Shore* (1951) to *The Deer Park* (1955), he made a considerable transition from a reformatory liberalism to a neo-sexual anarchism—the last-mentioned book really beginning a sequence of explorations into the need for an existential self-discovery, primarily won in the field of sexuality and violence, that will drag the body politic with it into vigour. The theme is intensely romantic and in many respects naïvely given; it is also sketched with an overweening and often fashion-conscious arrogance, in an attempt to universalize and validate the rebellious demands of the self. Its most explicit expression comes in *An American Dream* (1965)—hastily written, often disturbingly vulgar, an unself-conscious, obscene, in some ways diabolic, semi-autobiographical novel. In essence its theme is that murder is better than suicide, diabolic self-assertion better than the deathliness that surrounds man. But it, too, is a political fable: an attempted outrage on bourgeois society, conveyed through wild and surrealistic images and an extravagantly wild prose. It none the less emerges as a work of singularly inventive force. The symbolic and the real interfuse in curious and perhaps finally undirected ways, and the moral centre it seems to work from can seem often only perverse. But it does have the energy of a deeply-dredged cultural dream and, read against some of Mailer's recent brilliant journalism and against his genuine capacity for self-irony, it comes out as a strikingly significant work.

Reading through the works of these writers, one is deeply struck by the degree to which a moral fervour, and almost a religiosity of standpoint, suffuses their writing and gives it a measure of mythological significance, derived as much from an exuberant sense of possibility and of obligation to the nature of one's experience, one's formed personal reality, as from any inherited beliefs. Hence it would of course, be a mistake to identify this with Jewish writers alone. The same qualities are present in J. F. Powers's brilliantly comic novel about a commercially inclined Catholic priest, *Morte D'Urban* (1962), a superb critique of the fate of American religiosity; or in the novels and stories of John Updike, another magnificent and devastating inquirer into the ordinary and detailed world of suburban middle-class American life (in particular his *Rabbit, Run* (1960) is a technical *tour de force* about instantaneous consciousness, written in the present tense); or in many of the Southern writers already referred to. And J. D. Salinger (b. 1919), though part Jewish, hardly draws on the Jewish tradition. *The Catcher in the Rye* (1951), now an adolescent classic, achieves its remarkable force by bringing alive as a moral universe the world, linguistic as well as social, of a middle-class adolescent boy caught at the point of pre-social and pre-sexual innocence. Holden Caulfield is adult and sophisticated enough to know the world, the world of adult 'phoneys', of New York pick-ups, of bars, hotels, and show business; and when he is expelled from his prep school he makes his way picaresquely through it. But, caught on the edge of the cliff over which one falls into adulthood, his preference is for innocence: for his younger sister Phoebe, for the ducks on the lake in Central Park, for the Museum of Natural History, for the things that look too 'damn nice' to damage. And this is the basis for an almost religious view of the world, a respectfulness and concern. In *The Catcher in the Rye* this religiosity is mutedly given, in such ambiguities as the last sentence of the penultimate chapter, when Holden, watching his sister Phoebe turning on the carousel, says: 'It was just that she looked so damn *nice*, the way she kept going round and round, in her blue coat and all. God, I wish you could've been there.' In Salinger's later work—the group of long stories collected as *Franny and Zooey* (1961) and *Raise High the Roofbeam, Carpenters* and *Seymour: An Introduction* (1963), the religious dimension becomes highly explicit and not a little cloying, though the complexity of his art also increases in proportion. The stories, centred on a family of youthful intellectuals, the Glasses (some of whom Salinger had established in earlier stories), turn on a sequence of semi-Buddhist revelations deriving largely from Seymour Glass, the oldest and wisest of the whiz-kids, who committed suicide in an early Salinger story called 'A Perfect Day for Bananafish'. The aspiration of the stories is towards a philosophy of total inclusion of the stuff and persons of the universe; so Zooey Glass's revelation to Franny Glass is that the world is the ugly Fat Lady out there and that the cancered Fat Lady is 'Christ Himself, buddy'. But this, part of the total acquired wisdom of the Glasses, gained at the cost of widespread neurosis throughout the family and Seymour's suicide, is oddly reductive, since the Glasses are a withdrawn, self-congratulating tribe guilty of a certain spiritual vanity. The Glasses are in fact presented as a kind of Elect, living outside the world, who in practice have acquired a philosophy of almost total exclusion, a vision of a vulgarized universe. In addition, the building up of Seymour as a saint and a guru involves a process of artistic inflation so considerable that Salinger seems to develop a coy if fascinating artistry in order to deal with it. His real and prime virtue as a novelist is, in fact, less in his revelation than in his detailing: that superb and precise documentation of manners, mores, even the contents of an American medicine cabinet, that exact registering of the world of squalor and ordinariness, against which the desire to establish the ideal of love is sustained.

Almost all the novelists so far mentioned have evoked something bleak and menacing at the centre of American or modern life; Salinger's 'squalor', Mailer's 'death', Bellow's depersonalized world of the 'less than human'. As the fifties shifted into the sixties, there were signs that this bleakness was souring the moral centre to which the novelists I have discussed appealed; and we have already seen a coarse, outrageous reaction in one work, Mailer's *An American Dream.* The tendency towards violence and emotional extremism seemed, in fiction, to sharpen; if the appeal of writers like Bellow and Malamud is essentially to reason and humanity, the appeal of many subsequent writers has been to madness and anarchy, or to some messianic hope beyond the world of the real which does not so much belittle its ordinariness as condemn its reality outright. One place where we can see the tendency emerging is in the black novel, which perhaps bears a relation to the sixties similar to that of Jewish writing to the fifties. American writing, with its dissident heroes and its hipsters, was already drifting in the direction of outrage before this, and it would be wrong to suggest that the black novel invokes a new tradition; rather it extends what had gone before in writers like Kerouac and Mailer. In any case, the important black novels of the fifties—Ralph Ellison's *Invisible Man* (1952), James Baldwin's *Go Tell It on the Mountain* (1953) and *Giovanni's Room* (1956)—are really classically liberal novels, though wrought with deep internal strain. *Invisible Man*, a finely controlled book with a deep surrealistic inventiveness, sees the plight of its black hero, denied an individual identity by society, as a classic instance of the human need to become visible. It raises, too, a classic dilemma: 'When one is invisible', says the unnamed narrator, 'he finds such problems as good and evil, honesty and dishonesty, of such shifting shapes that he confuses one with the other, depending upon who happens to be looking through him at the time.' The book, in fact, makes the black situation a superb existential or absurdist instance. Baldwin's novels, equally, are done with a sustaining intelligence. *Go Tell It on the Mountain* catches in its evocation of a Negro family the messianic passions and the religiosity in which, once again, the theme of personal rebirth is focused in a universe of hope and damnation; and similar strains touch the otherwise rather different *Giovanni's Room*, a sophisticated expatriate novel about a homosexual love relationship in Paris. But with *Another Country* (1962) Baldwin produced a different kind of book. It has much less obvious finesse; the prose is more extravagant, its black hero, Rufus, the jazz drummer, is tough and unyielding, and the complex of black and white relationships that the book follows out is a savage sexual battlefield. It is very much an urban, New York novel; but the city is a poisoned climate. And there is a clear sense of an ineradicable gangrene at the centre of everything; forces that cannot be gainsaid, wrongs that cannot be resolved. Baldwin seems to suggest that through the homosexual relationship of white and black the reconciliation of races *might* come, but he is obviously savage at the expense both of whites and normal heterosexuality; even as he conveys the strains of the kind of primitivistic homosexuality that seems to come out of the tribal norm of his other country. But such themes are not confined to the black novel, and in works like, say, Ken Kesey's *One Flew Over the Cuckoo's Nest* (1962), Thomas Pynchon's *V.* (1963), John Rechy's *City of Night* (1963), or Hubert Selby's *Last Exit to Brooklyn* (1964) one can see the same desire either to press beyond the world of rationality to madness or to move beyond the world of normal human relationships to manifestly grotesque and distorted ones.

Often behind such writing one finds a vision of nihilism or absurdity so disposed towards the grotesque that one is in the presence of 'black humour'. Grotesque and apocalyptic writing is not, of course, a novelty in the American fictional tradition; it reaches back certainly to Melville, is manifest in Nathanael West, and it is part of the strain of the 1950s in many of the Southern writers or in important and so far unmentioned voices such as James Purdy, Paul Bowles, or William Styron. But the mode has undergone a conspicuous renewal in the works of, for instance, Terry Southern, one of the most brilliant performers. In *Flash and Filigree* (1958) and

*The Magic Christian* (1960) he produces superbly and sinisterly comic novels of socio-psychic distortion, and in *Candy* (1964), the comic-pornographic novel he wrote with Mason Hoffenberg, he makes high farce out of a sequence of sexual outrages conducted on the body of a representative American innocent, both mocking and celebrating the perversities of the clinical distortion America has practised upon itself. American society becomes a grotesque and bleak farce, without a meaning or value. There are no virtues to save, only an absurd apocalypse to come. And in a number of novels—John Cheever's *The Wapshot Scandal* (1964), which fascinatingly transforms a much more stabilized community Cheever had created in an earlier novel into a sequence of farce-situations set in a technological nightmare; Alfred Grossman's *Acrobat Admits* (1959); the novels and stories of Bruce Jay Friedman and Donald Barthelme—the theme of the utter and manifest absurdity of society and its human contents is treated with comic grotesquerie. The best-known instance is probably Joseph Heller's *Catch-22* (1961), about a group of American airmen in Italy during World War II. It turns on a sequence of delicious absurdities like the catch of the title—you have to be certified crazy to get out of combat duty, but anyone who wants to get out of combat duty can't be crazy—and on an entire culture of almost automatic dissent. As one character puts it: 'There are now fifty or sixty countries fighting in this war. Surely so many countries can't *all* be worth dying for.' In fact, for Yossarian and his fellows, none are. The war and the army are anonymous technological machines operated by freaks and bearing no relation to any cause whatever; and it is only technology and minds programmed in relation to it, rather than culture or values or morals, that surrounds man in his world, unless he stands aside to survey it absurdly. The novel, though it goes on too long, is a farcical success because it is a distinctive creation: a total and convincing vision made out of the macabre and horrifying that is also a real contribution to the fortunes of the comic novel.

One other writer who has not particularly been associated with this tendency surely belongs in it: this is William Burroughs (b. 1914), a writer who has been extravagantly praised both for his devastatingly satirical view of American society and for his technical innovation. Burroughs certainly belongs to the tendency at the point where it becomes *avant-garde*, though his novelty of method is hardly as radical as it is sometimes made to sound. Basically it is a method of presentation, the 'cut-up' or 'fold-in' method, which increases the possibilities of artistic serendipity—it is a mode of chance construction. In fact, the material contained within his work is fairly consistent and fairly rigorously controlled. 'Old word lines keep you in old word slots,' Burroughs has explained; but in fact the essential structure of his best-known novels, *The Naked Lunch* (1959), *The Soft Machine* (1961), and *Nova Express* (1964), derives from science-fiction pastiche; while the escape from the old-word vision comes out as a species of indulgent nausea. Burroughs certainly excoriates contemporary American society, though it is hard to see whether he is or is not also excoriating himself; his disgust, which some critics have called Swiftian, is often close to a scatological revelling in the horrors of human society, the human body, human life, that he explores. His vision has some allure as a radical standpoint, since it is supported by a fascination with drugs and hallucination and with states of changed consciousness; but the consequent revelations, though momentarily funny, are often naïve and even dreary. Only where the comic grotesque manages, for a few moments, to fuse into an illuminating observation does the apocalyptic vision of his work come alive. The trouble is that his undoubted will to radicalism both in vision and technique never seems quite fully secured; and one can't help feeling that it is his strategic representativeness—the desire of readers to have what he seems to have the wish to give—that has won him so much esteem.

Much more successful, to me, seems the work of John Barth (b. 1930), a writer who has, through four fascinating novels, conducted a complex exploration both of technique and absurdist philosophical comedy. Barth is obsessed by the comicalities and ironies of a meaningless world and with the consequent meaninglessness of fiction and language; and he has followed his themes through with a logical consistency far in excess of Burroughs's. His first novel, *The Floating Opera* (1956), traces a suicidal hero from the point at which he decides, the world being meaningless, to commit suicide, to the point at which he decides, the world being meaningless, to stay alive; a semi-philosopher, he establishes as his final proposition: '*There is, then, no "reason" for living (or for suicide).*' There is still life as a showboat, as a fair equivalent to Adam's Original and Unparalleled Floating Opera, 'chock-full of curiosities, melodrama, spectacle, instruction, and entertainment' and still the joys of fiction, even if these are essentially the joys of pastiche. Barth has characteristically emphasized the patent fictiveness of the book by providing for the English edition a new ending (1968)—less, one feels, to improve an old one than to create a sense that all endings are variable. *The End of the Road* (1958) takes a somewhat similar, first-person hero (he begins his tale: 'In a sense, I am Jacob Horner'), also without feeling or a sense of meaning, who starts the novel virtually incapable of action but is guided by a doctor who advises him to teach grammar in a college as part of a 'mytho-therapeutic' cure. There he is drawn into adultery with the wife of a colleague, a philosophical pragmatist who is a kind of theoretic obverse to Horner, for whom actions have no meaning whatsoever. The book concludes in tragedy for the wife, but Barth sustains a comic bravura to the end. *The Sot-Weed Factor* (1960), a superb exercise in pastiche of eighteenth-century fiction, is pseudo-history, a piece of Barth's own mytho-therapy, drawing in half a dozen of the essential dramas of the great American novel, from the Pocahontas story to the Newtonian discovery of gravity; and *Giles Goat-Boy* (1966) is a wild global allegory which sets Barth's persistent fascination with the split between the thinking and the animal self in a fable about the university as cosmos. The later novels, despite their scope, vitality, and cleverness, and their persistence in the themes established, lack the distillation and precision of the earlier books, and are, I think, finally inferior to them. But all have, in addition to a superb comic invention, the philosophical consistency of a genuine *œuvre*.

Barth's philosophical irony and artistic self-awareness are qualities he shares with another writer of the postwar American scene who is of even greater importance. That is Vladimir Nabokov (b. 1899), contemporary America's most direct link with modernism. It is perhaps as imprecise to claim Nabokov as an American novelist as to claim Beckett as an English one. His early novels were written in Europe in the 1920s and are only lately translated from Russian to English; but after becoming an exile to America in 1940 he began a 'love affair with the English language' which resulted in a new sequence of major novels, including *Lolita* (1955), *Pnin* (1957), and *Pale Fire* (1962). Nabokov clearly inherits from the Russian comic novel of Gogol and others; he also, quite clearly, inherits from the modernist disquiets of the European novel in the 1920s. Like Barth, he sees the work of fiction as a comic game of knowledge, a fictive acrostic which must manifest its fictional nature; his work therefore abounds in subtle dispersions of the illusion (by, for instance, the sudden intervention of the narrator), in verbal puns and linguistic tricks, in the ultimate fascination of the word as symbol and cipher. His heroes themselves are obsessive game-players, chasing butterflies with linguistic nets, seeking in some illusion or fleeting reality to hold on to an image from which they are persistently exiled. Around the lost image lies a disordered reality, illuminated by linguistic serendipities; Humbert Humbert's pursuit of Quilty ('Guilty of killing Quilty') in *Lolita* is not only one of the most superb and devastating evocations of contemporary American detail we have had in fiction, but a magnificent punning sequence of clues laid and tracked down through the common link of language that binds murderer and victim together. Nabokov's standpoint throughout remains that of the tragic ironist; in most of his novels there is a centre for compassion and a complex shield around it, a perpetual mode of parody. He is one of the most flamboyant and successful of all modern comic novelists, and his urbanity extends beyond that of any of his American contemporaries. Yet at the same time the American climate seems aptly appropriate for him, and the later American novels in fact constitute his best work.

Nabokov is a convenient reminder that the *avant-garde* as such has not played a central part in the emergence of the postwar American novel either; even though there has been, perhaps, a greater disposition in that direction, and even though—in the work, for instance, of such neo-surrealistic writers as John Hawkes and Susan Sontag—there has been an active *avant-garde* fringe. This is partly, I think, because the postwar American novel has been sufficiently obsessed with the realistic mode, sufficiently fascinated with the forces and fantasies at work in its own society, to the point at times of associating the novel with factuality or history (as with Truman Capote's *In Cold Blood* or, more remarkably, in Norman Mailer's obverse strategy, in *The Armies of the Night*, of presenting history as a novel). The American novelist has been obsessed with history and society, even in his grotesquerie and surrealism; for these things too, *are* constitutents of modern history. In varied ways then, a realism of sorts—an interest in the power of social forces and processes, a sense of man as a victim, a fascination with disaster—has still managed to produce a fiction of mythical proportions. And perhaps what has most kept postwar American fiction alive is its fascination with experience, so that its drift towards despair could be aligned with the sense of hope, or at least of that willingness to respond to experience with a creative euphoria that would allow the novel and its characters a certain field for expansion and growth. We have heard much about the sense of alienation and despair in American writing, and it is clearly there. But it has frequently co-existed, in the best American fiction, with a sense that even within the limitation of option, or the sense of absurdity, some human space can still be found and enjoyed. And it has been that conviction that has tended to give the American novel postwar a largeness of theme and a creative energy and fullness, a human and a technical curiosity which has been rather different from the general mood of the European or the English novel. Its fortunes over the past twenty years have in some ways paralleled that of English fiction, as the liberal concerns of the fifties gave way to a greater sense of disorder or absurdity; but they have been experienced through a rather fuller spectrum consonant with the strange, often apparently unhappy, but intellectually and emotionally exposed place that America bears in the modern world.

*The French Novel Since the War*

In the postwar period there has been, throughout the western nations, a considerable similarity of flavour or temper in the novel, and yet at the same time marked differences of national emphasis. We have seen, in looking at English and American fiction, how certain marked tendencies seem to inhabit both. In both there has been a certain retreat from modernism, a certain return to realism; in both there has been a tendency towards a concern with a liberally moralized view of life in the fifties, and then a bias towards absurdist surrealism or grotesquerie in the sixties. Yet the essential portraits of society and the condition of man, while they bear some resemblances, are remarkably different in detail, and the difference has produced serious differences of style and tone. Some of the same intellectual forces that we have already seen at work run through the French novel as well, but once again they have been expressed in different ways and in markedly different tonalities. There can be no doubt, for instance, that the postwar novel in France has been heavily influenced by American fiction; and Henri Peyre, in emphasizing this, has pointed out that three out of four translations from the English language into French are of American works.[10] In 1945 André Malraux said: 'To my mind the essential characteristic of contemporary American writing is that it is the only literature whose creators are not intellectuals,' and no doubt this was part of the reason for the intense popularity of Dos Passos, Caldwell, Steinbeck, Hemingway, and perhaps above all Faulkner at his more experimental. As Saul Bellow has pointed out, these writers and their successors have shown a 'brutal or violent acceptance of a new universal truth [about the inauthenticity of the individual life] by minds free from intellectual preconceptions', and he stresses that this theme is very close to that of those French and European writers 'whose novels and plays are derived from definite theories which make a historical reckoning of the human condition and are peculiarly responsive to new physical, psychological, and philosophical theories'.[11] If the French novel has touched similar themes, it has indeed frequently touched them with a philosophical bias, in the vein of the *roman d'analyse*. And many readers, and many writers too, surely do go to the French novel for this sort of radiating intellectual centrality, and at this level the influence of French writing has been very considerable indeed, its penetration into other literatures considerable.

At the same time, the contemporary French novel can sometimes be intensely fascinating without being intensely enjoyable. If the English novel risks itself in contingency, in following the free run of events, then the French novel risks itself in abstractness, even in that kind of existential and post-existential fiction where the theme is, precisely, the contingency and disorder of experience, its absence of meaning. One cannot make this complaint of the really classic instances in the French fiction of the last thirty years—Sartre's *Nausea* (1938), Camus's *The Outsider* (1942) and *The Plague* (1947), Malraux's *Man's Fate* (1933)—for these novels are sufficiently humanized and humane to concern us realistically even as they engage us abstractly as well. But if, as many critics believe, the writers of the *nouveau roman* in France are the closest case we have today of the making of a genuinely contemporary aesthetic, then the absence in many of these works of the liberal and humanized centre raises severe problems for the reader. The development from the liberal or neo-liberal novel of Camus and Sartre to this newer fiction does indeed parallel, to some extent, the movement in other fictions towards fictiveness or absurdity; and we have already seen it at work in Beckett (certainly a virtual Frenchman) or in Americans like Heller and Barth, or in Nabokov (we shall also see it in Günter Grass). But the mood of the French developments is somewhat different and in some ways finally divergent; and it seems to have taken the recent French novel, or a main tendency in it, into a place where few others have followed. There are, I think, two very obvious differences between this activity and that of the American and English novel. The first is that, though the English-language novelists have often explored the theme of absurdity or the overwhelming contingency of things in the modern world, they have often done so not only, as Bellow says, untheoretically but also comically—as an ironic–tragic situation which none the less leaves the disarranged universe open to the writer's comic surveillance, as in Waugh, Barth, Nabokov, Heller, or Muriel Spark. And where the view is solemnly given, it is usually in the form of a tragedy of experience rather than a tragedy of thought, of ideas (except in the case of obviously French-influenced writers like Christine Brooke-Rose and Susan Sontag). The overwhelmingly solemn tradition is very French, and when comedy comes into it it is usually clearly signalled, as in Raymond Queneau or Robert Pinget. Part of Beckett's absolute attraction as a writer is surely his capacity for levity; and it is that which detaches him from, often elevates him over, other writers with whom he is otherwise linked. The second is that, whereas the English-language novel has done little to elaborate an explicit contemporary *aesthetic* or technical theory, several French novelists have sought to do so. The theory is neither monolithic nor totally consistent; it draws on a broad community of highly various aesthetic assumptions. But, closely allied as it is to a number of important developments in linguistic and semiological theory and in philosophy, it has already acquired in some quarters that inexorable historical validity that ideological minds like aesthetics to have; it is the representative, necessary, and logical art of our time. Obviously there are the strongest grounds for quibbling with the view that the French *nouveau roman* writers have found the only genuinely modern way to write. In some ways their theories are very traditional, and in many respects less radical than those implied by the work of writers like Nabokov, Barth, or even Burroughs. But there has indeed been a real and lively debate about the novel in postwar France which has hardly been matched elsewhere among novel-practitioners as such (though similar debates have been alive in England and the States among critics and scholars).

But one further factor making for difference needs noting; the postwar French novel has been created in a very different political and social climate. The strong stress on commitment and moral rebellion that touches French writing in the forties and fifties obviously has a lot to do with the climate of the Occupation and the Resistance, in which most of the important writers were involved. The movement away from committed action, and even from action in fiction at all, that has taken place since also surely has something to do with the climate of the Gaullist Republic, where nationalist politics replaced, at least in theory, liberal politics. So John Fletcher has seen a link to be made between this and the *nouveau roman*; he quotes Jean Bloch-Michel's study of the new novel, *Le Present de l'indicatif* (1963), which argues that this species of novel is the product of a climate in which genuine choice cannot be exercised. 'It can be convincingly argued', says Fletcher, 'that the stagnant nature of French political life has led the leading writers of the present generation to forsake the paths mapped out for them by Sartre and other militant authors on the left, and seek to advance their art, rather than some illusory political cause.'[12] Certainly the intellectual climate in France did alter remarkably in the 1950s—when the dominance of Sartre and Camus declined and existentialism passed both as a serious philosophy and as a fashion, and when the era of the absurd in the theatre, the anti-novel in fiction, and the new wave in the cinema set the climate. Yet, of course, the continuity between the phases is very considerable, and the very idea of 'absurdity' and the philosophical emphasis on the phenomenological practised by more recent writers has very clear roots in Sartrean existentialism. In many respects the line of progression is unbroken and the evidence is perhaps plain to see in the fact that Sartre has praised such successors as Nathalie Sarraute and Jean Genet in expansive terms. Altogether the atmosphere of postwar France has generally continued to encourage the special significance awarded in that country to the intellectual as philosopher and novelist—a role that has long taken writers into politics and out again, yet left them conscious of a kind of unbroken aesthetic line of literary obligation running through, despite whatever social upheavals, from Flaubert or Mallarmé.

In fact it is striking that, despite the radical change brought to France by war and occupation, then by the political upheaval that has followed it, the French novel has still come through with a considerable intellectual and artistic continuity, a situation very different from that in Germany in 1945, where the intellectual continuum was obviously broken by Nazism and then by defeat. Many important French novelists who had made their reputation before it went on writing during the war—Mauriac, Malraux, Bernanos, Montherlant, Aragon, Céline, Green—while others of the succeeding generation made their names during it. The two major instances here are of course Sartre and Camus, whose reputations blossomed forth once the war was over—to the point, virtually, of making them charismatic leaders of their intellectual generation. Jean-Paul Sartre (b. 1905) made his essential reputation as much as a philosopher, critic, and committed intellectual as a novelist; but none the less his fiction is central to his work, as indeed it is to the thought and art of the century. As Iris Murdoch has pointed out, this is surely in part because the novel, like Sartre's philosophy, tends to be by nature phenomenological, to describe as well as to explain.[13] Sartre's novels do not do that alone, of course; but they do allow him to explore the contingencies of experience, and also the terms of his own instinct towards moralism. For, in part, Sartre has always been a philosopher concerned with human conduct and human choices, which is to say with making meaning out of life. It is surely this as much as anything that leads him, in *What Is Literature?* (1950), to his famous judgement that prose literature, as opposed to poetry, must necessarily be 'committed'. His argument is based on the view that language in the modern world is divorced from things—a view, expressed by the hero of his first novel, *Nausea* ('The word remains on my lips; it refuses to go and rest upon the thing'), which has dominated much of the French *avant-garde* obsession since Flaubert—but that in fiction this situation is redeemable, since the language of prose can become transparent in use. Sartre's tendency is therefore to see it as analogous to propaganda, journalism, or speech; the force of a novel is the force of a kind of action. Hence it can be judged morally, and hence in turn the prose writer has 'only one subject—freedom'. In fact, *Nausea* (1938), probably Sartre's best novel, does not lead us quite to this conclusion. His lonely hero, Antoine Roquentin, becomes progressively more aware of a self-alienation which is also an alienation from the stuff of the world; all is existence, a universe separated from the past, from meaning. But, as he becomes aware of what existence is, it takes on its own meaning: 'Existence had lost the offensive air of an abstract category: it was the very stuff of things.' By the end of the novel he has accepted his nausea, his sense of his own superfluity. 'I too wanted to be. I wanted nothing else,' he reflects of his past self; but now he is willing to suffer in tune with things. And, beyond the radical and complete boredom which the novel has so brilliantly created, he too plans a novel which will create a rhythm or radiance that will let him 'remember my life without disgust'. The theme of *deserving* existence rather than only living it, essentially a moral theme, runs through the stories in *The Wall* (1939; collected in England as *Intimacy*) and through the three volumes of the sequence *The Roads to Freedom*: *The Age of Reason* (1945), *The Reprieve* (1945), and *Iron in the Soul* (1949). This sequence, with one volume yet to come, takes its characters through from 1938 to the fall of France and involves much larger political dimensions than does *Nausea*. It involves a perplexed search for an essence that is more than existence, for meaningful action and identity, on the part of all its central figures—Mathieu, the intellectual seeking to cultivate an inner independence; Daniel, who has willed his homosexuality; Brunet, the communist; and others whose fortunes are less precisely followed. But it is a search through history and a broad, dense, social and intellectual panorama as well as through the relation of men and things. Indeed, although Sartre stressed that his novels are anti-determinist ('Every one of my characters, after having done anything, may still do anything else'), the world he makes is seriously conditioned by history and by that radical release of evil that Sartre sees as an essential part of the contemporary situation. Mathieu's failure, in some sense the failure of liberalism, is historically as well as personally determined; and a knowledge of history as well as of personal obligation is involved in the instruction he receives about his own *mauvaise foi*. If the novel reaches towards freedom, towards Mathieu's moment on the tower when he fires his gun against, among other things, his former scruples, then freedom is not freedom from anxiety but a full acquaintance with it: 'Freedom is exile and I am condemned to be free.'

In this sequence, Sartre does not show himself as a contained or aesthetically precise writer; that, indeed, is part of his work's force, just as it is part of his philosophy for prose. The novel is part of the world of history and ideas, and there is a necessary pressure upon the individuals in it to pass beyond their individualism into some form of moral community. In this respect Sartre, if hardly liberal, is humanist; and this is what links him with Camus. Albert Camus (1913–60) also made of his first novel, *The Outsider* (1942), a philosophical fable, a statement on man's condition consonant with his philosophical statements in *The Myth of Sisyphus*, published in the same year. Both works are explicitly concerned with the 'absurdity' of man's state, as in Sartre, though Camus's assumptions involve certain considerable differences, even if equally they involve the attempt to transcend nihilism. *The Outsider* is a classic of the century by any measure: the classic story of the man without affect or feeling who both is formed by and manifests the world's indifference. But unlike *Nausea* this novel is not concerned with an intellectual odyssey but with the registration of the conditions—the social and natural forces, the instincts and psychic pulls—that precede, produce, and follow one crucial act: Meursault's killing of an Arab for no precise or directly recognizable reason. (As Sartre pointed out, even the causal connections of syntax are withdrawn from the prose.) It is an estranged act in an estranged world; yet the estrangement or sense of absurdity is not total. For, as is clear from Camus's earlier stories and his writings in *Noces* (1938), the universe also involves and binds us in its pagan and amoral livingness, which though it is undifferentiated is also involving; it is the sun, blurring the focus, cracking into Meursault's head, which helps kill the Arab. By the end of the book, when Meursault is about to be executed in the face of general social incomprehension, the indifference of the universe has become 'benign'—which is apparently to say without outright malevolence. But what is central about the book is the way in which Camus manages to transform, through a first-person narration taken forward in diary-like stages, his man of indifference, Meursault, into a representative figure, a man whose 'intentions' are the sum of every action, every factor in the context which he describes. The novel is a tight sequence of immediacies, of living moment by moment; and this gives the livingness not only to Meursault's almost allegorical dilemma but to all the stuff of the novel itself—it gives it a deep intensity of artistic success.

In *The Plague* (1947), where Camus, like later Sartre, strives to see human fortunes in a much more collective frame, the notion of liberal solidarity and potential human community emerges much more strongly, though, again as with Sartre, the movement beyond nihilism is by no means complete. The essential theme, of bubonic plague in Oran, obviously takes some of its imaginative stamina from its allegorical relationship to the German occupation of France, though it is also clearly intended to suggest the 'present sickness' of mankind and the human condition itself. Camus explores the horror through a wide range of characters, some of whom despair, some revel, some accept the situation as a scourge of God. Camus's views, though imaginatively responsive, increasingly became associated with those of the concealed narrator of the book, Dr. Rieux, who exemplifies a notion of service and secular humanism, and of human solidarity: a solidarity that does not redeem solitude, but is still a moral imperative. If there is exile, there is also a kingdom that might be possessed. This increasingly humanist view is also clearly accompanied in Camus's development by an uneasy sense that it leaves behind the polymorphous paganism with which his work began. It involves, in fact, a puritan and conscience-laden development which in turn becomes the theme of Camus's third novel, *The Fall* (1956), a self-analytical and semi-philosophical confession by a modern ordinary man which is, appropriately, set among the northern fogs of Amsterdam (rather than in the Algeria of most of Camus's fictional struggles between exile and the kingdom, where they can be played out in the light of the at once ominous *and* beneficent sun). Taken altogether, Camus's *œuvre* is a remarkable one; it has something of the philosophical authority of Sartre's (despite growing differences of attitude between them over political and moral matters), but it has the greater imaginative authority, the greater generosity of the responsive novelist towards his characters. It also leads the way more directly into the technical explorations of the next generation of writers.

Among these developments, one, perhaps, is closer to Sartre and to the climate of real disgust that touches his work. This is the work of Jean Genet (b. 1910), the pervert and former thief whom Sartre welcomes as 'Saint Genet'. It is essentially Genet's mixture of gross realism and lyric imagination, and the material over and through which it works (often homosexual and masturbatory hallucinations), that has fascinated critics. But, in the novel at least, Genet is surely finally a contemporary footnote to the nineteenth-century romanticism of Baudelaire and Rimbaud, or even to Villon; and like many contemporaries who have sought to transcend realism, he ends up with the lyricism of the traditional poetic stock, which provides the superstructure over a highly primitivistic vision. Genet's is a subversive imagination, and the heroes of his universe are the perverts, assassins, and traitors. But the effusions of his imagination are lyrical; they have a brooding lushness and make a claim for the transformation of reality by luxurious imaginings, by rebellious beauty. *Our Lady of the Flowers* (1943) consists of a homosexual prisoner's acts of 'metamorphosis' whereby 'nobilities' of language and dream intersect with gross and violent acts; the autobiographical *Thief's Journal* (1948) similarly consists of moments whereby the real and realized world is transformed into an imaginative landscape. But the imaginatively surrealistic landscape is much more fully and significantly explored by other writers: above all, of course, by Beckett, who has already been discussed, but whose profound influence on French writing must here be recognized; and by other writers like Raymond Queneau and Robert Pinget (*The Inquisitory* (1962), etc.), who do in fact belong much closer to the climate of the *nouveau roman*.

Whatever its merits (and to my mind they are often merits of abstract aesthetics and theory-game rather than the merits of imaginative expansiveness), the *nouveau roman* has certainly been the most remarkable force for new theory to appear in recent fiction; and like any new theoretical force it has involved a considerable critical revision. In many ways it is a logical development out of modernism and the symbolist theory implicit in much of it; that is to say, the idea that a work of art is primarily a formal structure. It has, in some of its manifestations at least, involved not only a withdrawal from the Sartrean notion of the commitment of prose but also from the idea of fiction as a humanist activity. The *nouveau roman* is perhaps really a fiction of extreme classical restraint, severely limiting on the grounds of a logician's aesthetics the matter appropriate to the novel. At the same time *Nausea* and *The Outsider* are explicit predecessors, and so are Sartre's theories of the alienation of man from environmental objects which he seeks to humanize, and his theories of the modern crisis of language, which likewise suffers alienation. It is perhaps only Sartre's special dispensation for prose that the *nouveau roman* disagrees with; that, and the humanist persuasions of both his and Camus's work—which, in Alain Robbe-Grillet's view, lead them to present as a tragedy a normal state of affairs: that of man's living with the 'smooth, meaningless, mindless, amoral surface of the world'. To assume any differently therefore becomes a form of the pathetic fallacy (and what surely comes to haunt the new novel is the *apathetic* fallacy, the belief that ours is a world of things). This means for certain of this group of writers—and here perhaps the best spokesman is Roland Barthes, the critic closest to them intellectually—an analogous problem for language itself, which (as Sartre had already suggested for poetry) loses its objective frame of reference. In fact, in looking at the new novel, a certain justice in Sartre's argument about the difference between poetry and prose becomes apparent—since diminishing the referential quality of language in fiction clearly becomes a good deal more difficult than doing the same in poetry. This is a crux which has given the new novel the quality of a persistent scientific experiment in which no writer has quite emerged with the right or perfect answer. Or, one might say alternatively, the perfect answers to the main question have already been given by earlier experimentalists like Joyce, Proust, Virginia Woolf, and Faulkner. Despite the strongly historicist slant of several of the aesthetic statements we have about the new novel from practitioners like Robbe-Grillet (*Towards a New Novel*, 1963), Nathalie Sarraute (*The Age of Suspicion*, 1956), and Michel Butor (*Répertoire*, 1960, 1964), one has the sense that the cycle is being turned back towards modernism, that the onward movement is not great. In some at least of the works in the genre one finds that the essential devices (violation of chronological sequence; use of multiple point of view; disappearance of named narrator or characters; sequence by topic or recurrent motif) are directly from the post-Flaubertian or post-Jamesian stock; while the recurrent proposition that the novel must not mean but be (or, to quote Robbe-Grillet: 'No true creator starts off with an idea of his "meaning"; the writer's project is always more or less a project of form. A novel must *be* something, before it can begin to *mean* anything') is familiar modernist lore. The true imaginative originality of the tendency seems to lie, in fact, in the attempt to establish a new hinterland between the realms of the subjective and the objective—which formally means the attempt to denature character in the traditional sense, both as the individualism of agents and as the equivalents of real people caught up in a story-sequence, *and* to dehumanize the objective world as a symbolic referent. This leaves a narrow space for fictional action. So much of the aesthetic activity is determined by convention and tradition, as the Ur-forms of the novel of sentiment or the quest-myth show through; or, alternatively, the novel becomes the field for a contingent triviality, putting a frame of art around a content of gossip. Only, in short, where the new novel does establish something profoundly rooted in the content of consciousness and behaviour does it seen properly to succeed.

There are, however, obvious dangers in linking too tightly together a loose band of novelists of several kinds, several degrees of seriousness, and several generations. Many names have been associated with the new novel, among them Nathalie Sarraute (b. 1902), Marguerite Duras (b. 1914), Claude Simon (b. 1913), Alain Robbe-Grillet (b. 1922), Michel Butor (b. 1926), and writers younger still like Phillippe Sollers and J. M. Le Clezio. Nathalie Sarraute once commented in an interview: 'I am interested—as are some other modern writers—in taking that development [the twentieth-century revolutionizing of the novel] up again. We are trying to go if only a few steps farther *each in his own direction.*' It is important to stress the wide differences of direction. Nathalie Sarraute, for instance, has a very explicit concern with the development of the psychological novel, frequently seeking to catch psychological force at the moment of interaction with other people. 'I am not interested in certain characters but in creating certain movements of mind which best develop when people are in contact with one another. . . . [These are] the movements and feelings common to all of us. . . . ,' she has said. Her first novel, *Tropisms* (1939), is concerned with the neo-biological response to external stimuli of her female bourgeois characters; but there is a gradual development through her subsequent work—coming to fruition in her fourth novel *The Planetarium* (1959) and in *The Golden Fruits* (1963)—of a technique of conversation and sub-conversation which manifests the force of the world below intimacy. It is a technique, conducted with skill and subtlety, seeking to bring alive the fringes of consciousness which make every mind its own place, while also seeking to track the forces which make too clear a notion of independent character redundant. There are clear resemblances here to Virginia Woolf, and a similarly fairly full degree of 'made' reality in the form of characters' locales; and the essential difference is that whereas Mrs. Woolf trembles persistently on the edge of making a revelation, of bringing her atoms into unity, Mme Sarraute does not, preferring a tone of neo-scientific detachment. Marguerite Duras, though not dissimilar, is much closer to the novel of sensibility: above all to that world of the tragic passions of love which links her with many French women novelists, including Françoise Sagan. *A Sea of Troubles* (1950) is set in Indo-China and concerns the attempt of a poor French woman to protect her lands against the sea, but in later novels like *The Little Horses of Tarquinia*, *The Square*, and *The Afternoon of Monsieur Andesmas*, as in screen plays like *Hiroshima, Mon Amour*, she has narrowed and refined her world to one in which subtleties of communication and feeling lie at the centre. Her technical awareness is much more consumed into the content of her art, and above all into the creation of a lyrical-elegaic tone of feeling. Her objectivity is rather a matter of concern with immediacy; with a given present into which the past infuses, delicately, from the remote distances of, perhaps, yesterday.

But for a much more radical questioning of reality, character, time, and fictional structure one would have to turn to the novels of Alain Robbe-Grillet. Mme Sarraute's 'age of suspicion', in which all realities must be subject to fictive questioning, tended, she stresses, to produce a behaviourist novel in which only sense-impressions count. Robbe-Grillet's earlier novels are *chosiste* and phenomenological in this way; they are concerned with, as Roland Barthes suggests, a realism that is new because the thing registered has no transcendence, and 'claims to survive enclosed within itself'. It so denies patterns and meanings, and inhibits any sense of structure at all; it seeks to de-universalize the novel. But as Bruce Morrissette stressed in his study of Robbe-Grillet, structure does inevitably come in again through the back door as something inherent in fiction, for novels are patterned in systems of syntax and artistic choice. By making realism a matter of the particularity of things, Robbe-Grillet tended to attribute the problems of structure to some vague force in the creative process, to a sense of 'discovered' form—which itself must be transferred to the imagination of the *reader*, since the novel can no longer be 'complete, finished, and closed in upon itself'.[14] Increasingly, he has drawn on the 'collective' images of popular culture to this end—on the matter of the detective-story in earlier books, on the staple images of the popular cinema in more recent 'ciné-novels'. *The Erasers* (1953), his first work of fiction, about an investigator who murders the man whose death he is investigating, elaborates its detective-novel content by multiplicity of viewpoint, a-chronological telling, and a systematic pattern of allusion to *Oedipus the King*, which gives its basic pattern and its choric devices. *The Voyeur* (1955) and *Jealousy* (1957) both accrue round an emotion or passion to do with the psychological states suggested by their titles and round a technical perspective, one which Bruce Morrissette has called the method of the 'absent-I' or suppressed first-person narrator.[15] With *In the Labyrinth* (1959) the technical concern becomes even more explicit, making the creation of the novel the essential theme. And in his more recent screen plays (*Last Year at Marienbad*, *Trans-Europ Express*, etc.) the essential technique of proliferating images a-chronologically undergoes further massive exploration; and John Fletcher has valuably explored the way in which this synthesis of new novel and cinema has seemed to give new life to both by uniting the power of copying reality with the processes of subjective ordering.[16] Like Nathalie Sarraute or Marguerite Duras, Robbe-Grillet has not forsaken reality altogether, and the complexities of his structure still leave a centre of psychological fascination intact. In Robbe-Grillet it is an emotional obsession, as in Sarraute it is a 'tropism'; in Michel Butor, a finely intelligent novelist, it is a sense of place—Manchester ('Bleston') in *Passing Time* (1956) or Rome in *Second Thoughts* (1957). Butor, though technically oblique, actually seems somewhat less bound by his methods—perhaps partly because of a willingness to allow experience markedly to change his characters' consciousness (as in *Second Thoughts*) and perhaps because one feels, as with Claude Simon, that his technical development is consonant with an increasing exploration of the fictive world he is making available to himself. What is apparent in all of these works, however, is that the notion of their authors as 'objectivist' novelists is something of an illusion; in fact it is an intense technical subjectivity that is their main theme. The fictive crisis in which they deal gives a neo-scientific face to the matter they deal with, and the complex structural logics involve one almost theoretically in proceeding through the work. But there is a marked difference between their work and that of a latter-day new novelist like Phillippe Sollers—who describes his novel *Drame* as dealing in grammatical heroes. ('If there is a story', he says, 'it tells fundamentally how a language (a syntax) tries to discover itself, brings itself into being, and is at once a transmitting and a receiving agent—an experience of the living violence of speaking and being spoken.') In their work and that of Claude Simon (*The Grass*, 1958; *Flanders Road*, 1960, etc.) the desire to find a structure analogous to myth through certain semi-universal experiences still subsists.

One needs to add that, of course, not all the important French writers of the last fifteen years have taken the path of the new novel, even though it has been a remarkable and vigorous part of the French aesthetic environment. This discussion has rather scanted many writers who are on the extreme edges of the tendency (like Roger Vailland), or who have radically varied it (like Robert Pinget, who has said that 'Objects are no use when one aims at the soul'), or who have found the force of the novel-form in totally other places (like Romain Gary, who has said: 'The modern novel will be picaresque or it will not exist'). The self-analytical quality of the new novel, and the case that it has made for itself as the necessary and logical evolution of the novel form, has not silenced narrative, as the fiction of writers like Simone de Beauvoir, Françoise Mallet-Joris, or André Schwartz-Bart well shows.

*The Postwar Novel in Other European Countries*

Unlike France, Germany emerged from the war, and the years of book-burning and intellectual emigration that had preceded it, almost without a literature; and the remaking of a fictional climate was a difficult and anguished process. The famous Group 47, which sought to produce social reform and intellectual renewal, was the first obvious force to work on the task; and the climate of artistic engagement in social matters they sought has still not entirely disappeared. Of the four or five German novelists of international importance to emerge since then, one, Heinrich Böll, derives directly from the Group, while others were obviously influenced by it. After some early short stories about the social problems of the postwar period, Böll came to general notice with *Billiards at Half-past Nine* (1959), a complex distillation of the social experience of Germany in this century. Something like the manners and techniques of the anti-novel touch the book, but like much of the best postwar German writing it is touched with a social surrealism and a deep undercurrent of social indignation. In *The Clown* (1963) this surrealism is further intensified around the complex identity of the clown figure at the novel's centre; he bears a certain obvious relationship to the Oskar of Günter Grass's *The Tin Drum* in that his ambiguous identity is itself anarchistic, but Böll emphasizes the reality of the anguish at the centre of this man pulled and pressed in all directions, and above all his insecure liberalism. *The Tin Drum* (1959), on the other hand, is overtly unmoral, a monument of anarchistic literature; Oskar, the thirty-year-old dwarf storyteller, is a creature without any moral centre at all, who can effectively be used both to symbolize and to mock the distortions of the pre-war and postwar German environments through which he has, simply, survived. The supreme comic fertility of the novel, which develops not only through a series of real and significant historical situations but also through a series of surreal and grotesquely inventive images, is the force by which it overcomes any problems of form, the force being located in Oskar, battering his tin drum of nonsense when faced by any imperative or cause. *Cat and Mouse* (1961) shifts from the profusion of *The Tin Drum* to a tighter and more symbolist model; but in *Dog Years* (1963) Grass reverts to his freer expressionist grotesque by tracking the fortunes of Hitler's missing dog. In all three books there is the spectacle of a wildly idiosyncratic imagination creating not only an extension of the novel form for the treatment of an almost unimaginable phase in German history, but also attempting to recognize the meaning of that history in the psychology of man.

In the works of Uwe Johnson there is a much more explicit, though no more bold, will to technical experimentalism. As with many of the French novelists, one senses the influences of Faulkner and Virginia Woolf behind the technical obsessions, and of the new novel itself in the concern with the labyrinthine world of objects. *Speculations about Jacob* (1959) is a novel which attempts to cross through the powers of the imagination the line between East and West Germany. That line of itself, Johnson has stressed, involves a complexity of viewpoint and a crisis for language. The German mind has lived in an ethos of multiple ideologies and ideological changes; and it is this that Johnson's work, his speculations, seek to catch. The theme of the intelligent man caught between these two worlds and so seen inevitably from many different viewpoints recurs in Johnson's second novel, *The Third Book about Achim* (1961). Achim T. is an East German champion cyclist; and the third book about him is to be written by Karsch, a West German writer visiting East Germany. It is never written, as Karsch discovers the difficulties of all the ideological truths that can be applied to the situation. His paralysis as a commissioned writer is precisely what Johnson himself seeks to overcome through a language of detail and of free-run sentences. In some ways one might say that here is a fiction in which the new-novel techniques have their sharpest justification—a justification deriving from the confessed complexity of the material to be dealt with and the absolute difficulty of making a novel a vehicle of any ideology. German writing too, then, has gone through a surrealist and speculative revival, though the work of important writers like Jakov Lind has shown that simpler and more luminous forms can thrive in writers of serious imagination.

Switzerland, too, has produced two important novelists with somewhat similar themes and emphases: Max Frisch and Friedrich Dürrenmatt, both also playwrights. And here again one can see how deeply the themes of lost identity and lost values, of modern society lapsing from its bourgeois moral confidence and so making difficult the novelist's possibility of taking an effective moral stand, have penetrated through the literature of contemporary Europe, as of contemporary America. Dürrenmatt's is a sinister fiction, usually in the form of the detective story; Frisch's two fine novels, *I'm Not Stiller* (1954) and *Homo Faber* (1957), are brilliant explorations of the severance of the present from the past. *I'm Not Stiller* is a somewhat Kafkaesque work about a man who returns to his country under another name, and whose return therefore raises the profoundest problems of identity. But he is not only the victim of officialdom but of his own desire to be a new man. *Homo Faber*, written with a similar superb control, involves again the problem of identity, but here what is also explored is the question of the kind of manufacturing, scientific spirit man is creating for himself.

Like Germany, Italy had the pressures which Fascism had put on the liberal imagination to overcome before it could produce a full postwar literature—though it had a much greater continuity with its own past in that novelists like Silone, Pavese, and Moravia continued to write and could hand on the torch. In some respects the best work of these writers was associated with the wartime or postwar period—when Silone, for instance, undertook a fascinating rewriting of some of his earlier novels, and Moravia extended some of his studies of modern boredom, particularly sexual boredom, which had begun with *The Time of Indifference* (1928). On the whole, the continuity has taken the form of a social realism concerned with poverty, urban or rural, and often with oppression, or else with the analysis of luxury and boredom; and the novels of Elio Vittorini, Ottiero Ottieri, and Vasco Pratolini are all broadly of this tendency, though writers like Italo Calvino and Nathalia Ginzburg have somewhat diverged from it. But, within it, the most remarkable postwar work is surely Giuseppe di Lampedusa's *The Leopard* (1960), a panoramic historical novel written in the last year of the author's life. It has something of the same grand force as Pasternak's *Dr. Zhivago*, a novel of profound historical transitions, engaging us with the 'immense ash-heap' of life and history in which one seeks the brief moment of happiness or stability. In evoking the fortunes of the house of Prince Fabrizio di Salina in the 1860s and the period of Garibaldian revolution, Lampedusa evokes a sequence of images of the breaking of a feudal world in which the exposure of man to misfortune, death, and nothingness is seen both as a complex human and a complex social cycle. The book is, in short, more than the sentimental period piece it has sometimes been taken to be, a fable that touches hard on our own times.

Predictably enough, the postwar Russian novel, too, has been dominated by social realism, or rather socialist realism of usually a sharply doctrinaire kind. The Russian revolution soon ceased to be kind to modernism and symbolism; and even as eminent a Marxist critic as Georg Lukàcs has seen modernism as a dying fall of the bourgeois conscience and a manifestation of the artist's flight from reality. But in recent years Soviet literature has undergone a decided sophistication, and the manifest vulgarity of many of its products has begun to drop away. In writers like Alexander Solzhenitsyn (*One Day in the Life of Ivan Denisovich*, *Cancer Ward*) and some of the writers like Dudintsev and Tarsis who have won acclaim in the west for reasons often less than primarily literary, one can see deeper acts of imagination, real complexities of realist technique. And latterly we have seen a signal of something else, particularly in the work and critical writing of 'Abram Tertz', who has appealed—in an essay called 'On Socialist Realism'—for a 'phantasmagoric art', while his own writing (in *Fantastic Stories*, 1967) has a strong surrealist constituent. If the Russian novel is generally disappointing, it is not of course because it is realist, even socialist realist, but because it is so frequently the product of the unexpansive imagination; it is, simply, dehumanized in the way in which so many Marxist critics have claimed that western society and the western imagination is. There are exceptions, and the classic one is the one Russian novel we all know, Boris Pasternak's *Dr. Zhivago* (1958). It is, finally, a novel about the ideal revolution, the ideal cultural redemption, and in its theme and the scope with which it is treated it best compares with the great works of the earlier part of this century—with Joyce's *Portrait of the Artist as a Young Man* or the novels of Lawrence. For though in many ways it is a traditional novel in the nineteenth-century mode—neo-realistic, panoramic, with an omniscient narrator, following the fortunes of a hero and a love-relationship over an extended society and span of time—it does not quite flow with that undogmatic naturalness that we respect in Tolstoy, or work at the same level of realism. It catches its action up in spots of time, surprising moments of coincidence when the threads are tightened; and this in its turn is linked with a notion of life as an evolution of action and consciousness in which different people move on parallel paths but at different speeds through history. The idea of life as a process and an energy is essential to the linked vision of Yuri Zhivago as at once doctor and poet; that is, to the basis of the humanism of the novel. It is not a humanism that is set *against* the Marxist view of history as an impersonal and evolutionary process; it seeks rather to link history and individual living and if the Russian revolution is seen to fail in the novel it is surely on this account. The complex ideal of organic existence in the novel —Yuri reflects that 'form' is the key to it in art—reminds us of one of the essential modernist passions; and, as John Wain has pointed out, Pasternak, who grew to artistic maturity in the context of Russian symbolist poetry, works the novel with all the 'mythopoetic density' of symbolist writing.[17] *Dr. Zhivago* is also, of course, a novel of failure, of submission to something less than the ideal which informs it; but it is one of the great contemporary versions we have of the idea of art not as linguistic play or procedural inquiry but as discovery. Pasternak—with Nabokov the greatest of modern Russian writers—suggests its force in a comment in his own *Essay in Autobiography*, when he says, 'I believe the most astonishing discoveries of all have been made at moments when the sense of his work so possessed the artist that it left him no time to think and he was driven by his urgency to speak new words in the old language, without stopping to know if it was old or new.'

*Postscript*

Obviously, the novel today is not dead. Television and the cinema have not killed it; nor has that supposed disquiet many people—indeed, many novelists—have told us we have with the idea of an objective reality; nor has that passage behind the bourgeois stage of society that many social critics—and, again, many writers—believe we have taken. In many writers, in several countries, it has gone about its business with a marked strain and tension, a tension we should not perhaps take too finally as evidence of our own social and cultural unhappiness, for part of it comes, surely, from the need of art to keep evolving beyond the point it has reached into its own obsessional inquiries. Looking across the literatures of the west, we can see—more in other literatures than English—the emergence of a new kind of realism which is almost surrealist, or often becomes surrealist, because it distrusts the constituents of reality so much, or the orders in which they can be placed in the conventional progressions of fictional creation. We can see, along with that, a new passion for the grotesque, a new commitment to the subjective, a new disquiet about the novelist's omniscience or wisdom, a will towards a new artistic consciousness. There is a contemporary temper in the arts, hard though it may be to define. And though it does not do to see literature with too historicist an eye, and to see certain forms as absolutely historically inevitable (that sort of estimation has led to a too low assessment of the achievement of the recent English novel, as we have seen), we can recognize in the new forms and obsessions an imaginative truth about the times. Michel Butor once observed in making the case for the new novel, that in his works man gropes, as in modern life, 'with the old conventions and principles crumbling under him'.[18] That has been broadly true of the postwar novel in its very various forms; and not only formally but experientially the modern novel has tended towards an area of existential suffering, or of seeking vision at those extremes of life where reality seems to be most real. In French fiction this has tended to lead to the disappearance of a sympathetic reality; in German, to a view of the grotesqueness of the social order; in American, to an exploration of extreme states of consciousness; in English, to a fiction about anti-social heroes seeking social credence. These are not visions of an absolute truth about the age; they are ways that the novelist, exploring both his form and his world, may know it through the performance of his powers and skills.

This survey has sought to suggest something of the width and range of the modern performance in the novel. It cannot pretend to be complete, and there are many important absences—within the literatures discussed, and outside them (we must not overlook the importance of the emergence of the novel in Africa and the West Indies, or of Patrick White in Australia, Mishima in Japan, Borges, one of the most remarkable writers of our time, in Argentina). There is a tendency in modern criticism, which has itself become a sophisticated formal art, to be fascinated by writers who manifest a conspicuous consumption of their form, and to overlook the importance in fiction of the diachronic, narrative level of the novel, its immersion in the detail of life as it is lived, and of those writers who serve that dimension of fiction; it is often novelists of this kind who win international reputations though not always the interest of general readers. In the postwar period many writers have been critics or teachers, and they have shown the same passion towards an abstractly formal view. Yet the novel lives with and through experience in its vividness and its particular feel, and even as traditional notions of reality, character, and event become uneasy it tends to be pressed back, in one way or another, towards these things. The novelists who finally seem to us greatest are, I think, those whose formal explorations have to do with finding ways of giving us that livingness and feel of life. And there have been enough of these in the postwar period for us to believe the novel survives as a vigorous and thriving form.

## NOTES

[1] I. Murdoch, 'Against Dryness', *Encounter*, Jan. 1961, 16–20.

[2] A. Kazin, 'The Alone Generation', *Harper's Magazine*, Oct. 1959, 127–31.

[3] B. Bergonzi, 'The Novel No Longer Novel', *The Listener*, 19 Sept. 1963, 415–16. He extends this argument in *The Situation of the Novel* (1970).

[4] *International Literary Annual*: No. 2, ed. John Wain (1959).

[5] L. A. Fiedler, *Waiting for the End: The American Literary Scene from Hemingway to Baldwin* (1965), 21.

[6] S. Bellow, 'Some Notes on Recent American Fiction', *Encounter*, Nov. 1963, 23–9.

[7] H. Swados, 'The Image in the Mirror', in *The Living Novel*, ed. Granville Hicks (New York, 1957).

[8] P. Rahv, 'Paleface and Redskin', in *Literature and the Sixth Sense* (1970).

[9] Fiedler, *Waiting for the End*, 84.

[10] H. Peyre, *The Contemporary French Novel* (New York, 1955), 263–78.

[11] Bellow, 'Some Notes on Recent American Fiction', 23.

[12] J. Fletcher, *New Directions in Literature: A Critical Approach to a Contemporary Phenomenon* (1968), 14.

[13] I. Murdoch, *Sartre: Romantic Rationalist* (Cambridge, 1953).

[14] B. Morrissette, *Les Romans de Robbe-Grillet* (Paris, 1963); see also the preface by Roland Barthes.

[15] Ibid.; and cf. B. Morrissette, 'The Evolution of Narrative Viewpoint in Robbe-Grillet', *Novel*, Fall 1967, 24–33.

[16] Fletcher, *New Directions in Literature*, chs. I and III.

[17] J. Wain, 'The Meaning of *Dr. Zhivago*', *Critical Quarterly*, Spring and Summer 1968, 113–37.

[18] M. Butor, 'The Case for the New Novel', *New Statesman*, 17 Feb. 1961.

## FOR FURTHER READING

Although it is expanding all the time, discussion of postwar fiction—especially British—is not noticeably advanced. There are a number of basic books worth exploring, however, as well as some interesting comment by writers themselves.

Useful general surveys, most setting postwar fiction in the context of the modern novel, include Walter Allen, *Tradition and Dream* (1964), G. S. Fraser, *The Modern Writer and His World* (rev. ed., 1964), and Anthony Burgess's introductory *The Novel Now* (rev. ed., 1971), which concentrate on English fiction; and Leslie A. Fiedler, *Waiting for the End* (1965) and Maxwell Geismar, *American Moderns* (1958), on the American. Also see such essay collections as Alfred Kazin, *Contemporaries* (1963), Norman Podhoretz, *Doings and Undoings* (1964), and Frank Kermode, *Modern Essays* (1971), the last drawing on two earlier collections by Kermode, one of the best critics now writing on the contemporary novel. The most effective anthology of essays covering postwar fiction generally is *On Contemporary Literature*, ed. Richard Kostelanetz (1964). To sense the general and ongoing debate about the novel today, see also Frank Kermode, *The Sense of an Ending* (1967), Robert Scholes, *The Fabulators* (1967), Bernard Bergonzi, *The Situation of the Novel* (1970), David Lodge, *The Novelist at the Crossroads* (1971), and William H. Gass, *Fiction and the Figures of Life* (1971).

Discussion on the postwar English novel has, unfortunately, concentrated on the topic of social reportage, to the exclusion of most other matters. The best detailed studies are Frederick R. Karl, *A Reader's Guide to the Contemporary English Novel* (1963), James Gindin, *Postwar British Fiction: New Accents and Attitudes* (1962), and Rubin Rubinovitz, *The Reaction Against Experiment in the English Novel: 1950–1960* (1967), best read alongside the broader illuminations of the books by Kermode, Scholes, Bergonzi, and Lodge mentioned above. A convenient selection of books on individual authors might be Richard N. Coe, *Beckett* (1964) and John Fletcher, *The Novels of Samuel Beckett* (1964); *The World of Lawrence Durrell*, ed. Harry T. Moore (1962) and G. S. Fraser, *Lawrence Durrell: A Study* (1968); William Cooper, *C. P. Snow* (1959) and Frederick R. Karl, *C. P. Snow: The Politics of Conscience* (1963); A. S. Byatt, *Degrees of Freedom: The Novels of Iris Murdoch* (1965); Jay Halio, *Angus Wilson* (1964); and Mark Kinkead-Weekes and Ian Gregor, *William Golding: A Critical Study* (1967). Also see the Columbia Essays on Modern Writers series.

The American novel has received vastly more attention. Among overall studies are Frederick J. Hoffman, *The Modern Novel in America* (1951), Ihab Hassan, *Radical Innocence: The Contemporary American Novel* (1961), Chester E. Eisinger, *Fiction of the Forties* (1963), Harry T. Moore, *Contemporary American Novelists* (1964), and Tony Tanner's very good *City of Words: American Fiction, 1950–1970* (1971). There are several good anthologies collecting criticism on the modern American novel, notably *The American Novel Since World War II*, ed. Marcus Klein (1969), *Fiction of the Fifties*, ed. Herbert Gold (1959), and *Recent American Fiction: Some Critical Views*, ed. J. J. Waldmeir (1963). Among the many works on individual authors are Henry A. Grunwald, *Salinger: A Critical and Personal Portrait* (1964), Charles T. Samuels, *John Updike* (1969), *The Added Dimension: The Art and Mind of Flannery O'Connor*, ed. Melvin J. Friedman and Lewis A. Lawson (1966), Tony Tanner, *Saul Bellow* (1965), K. M. Opdahl, *The Novels of Saul Bellow* (1968), Oliver Evans, *Carson McCullers: Her Life and Work* (1965), Barry H. Leeds, *The Unstructured Vision of Norman Mailer* (1969), Eric Mottram, *William Burroughs* (1970), L. S. Dembo, *Nabokov: The Man and His Work* (1967), and Gerhard Joseph, *John Barth* (1970). Also see the University of Minnesota Pamphlets on American Writers series.

On the postwar European novel, useful references are John Fletcher, *New Directions in Literature* (1968), John Sturrock, *The French New Novel* (1969), Maurice Nadeau, *The French Novel Since the War* (1967), Vivian Mercier, *The New Novel* (1971), H. M. Waidson, *The Modern German Novel* (1960, rev. ed., 1971), and Michael Hamburger, *From Prophecy to Exorcism* (1965). Also important, of course, are statements by the novelists themselves, including Alain Robbe-Grillet, *Snapshots* and *Towards a New Novel* (1965), Nathalie Sarraute, *Essays on the Age of Suspicion* (1963), and Michael Butor, *Inventory* (1970).

13

# English Poetry

PATRICK SWINDEN

In 1950, an Oxford scholar and critic of English literature, F. W. Bateson (b. 1901), closed a survey of English poetry with a chapter called 'Towards a Poetry-Reading Élite'. In it, he noted that the most favourable circumstances in which poetry can be written are those where three classes of readers can be distinguished, and be seen to be in a proper equilibrium. These are, in Dr. Bateson's own words, '(i) the poet's own immediate friends, (ii) the enthusiastic strangers who often tend to turn the poet into a cult, (iii) the general poetry-reading public'. The second group is in many ways the most important, insofar as the enthusiastic strangers who comprise it are responsible for establishing channels of communication between the poet and his circle and the audience beyond. This is Dr. Bateson's 'élite', 'missionaries of poetry in a world of prose', who alone can create and consolidate a class of common readers of a kind which, most satisfactorily, existed in the Augustan period of English letters—the period, that is, that we associate with the names of Pope, Swift, and Dryden.

These views, and views like them, have been influential in the period between the end of the Second World War and the middle 1960s. During this time a poetry grew up in this country which seemed to have been made to fit just such a prescription. In its most doctrinaire form it was called 'The Movement' and made itself known to Dr. Bateson's common reader in a slim anthology, *New Lines*, published in 1956—which can be taken as the peak year for the production of this kind of poetry. *New Lines* was edited by Robert Conquest (b. 1917), himself a contributor, and a poet and reader after Dr. Bateson's heart. Not only is Mr. Conquest a poet, he is also a celebrated commentator on Soviet affairs; in other words an intelligent and cultivated man whose liberal, élitist temperament is well suited to that ambience of taste and reasonableness which is held to be the proper domain of poetry writer and poetry reader alike. Conquest agrees. In a polemical introduction to his anthology he too is preoccupied with 'serious authority' and with discriminating and undiscriminating atmospheres; with the way art has been let down by its public which, consequently, needs to be corrected by a general tendency of what he is prepared to admit may be 'lesser talents'.

Let us aspire to membership of the third class, of common readers. Or rather, you are the common reader, having picked up this book and chosen to read this chapter in it. I am of the second group, the enthusiastic stranger who is drawing your attention to the poetry that members of the first group, the poet's immediate friends, have pressed upon me. In the first poem I quote the poet is his own friend, I am afraid, since this is Bateson himself, prefacing his little book with a poem called 'The Anti-Romantics':

> So we are the music-unmakers it seems—
> Against pastoral pipings disinfecting your dreams;
> At La Belle Sauvage, sir, the sardonic 'irregulars',
> Of skylarks, etc., the scarers, the nobblers of Pegasus . . .
>
> Treeless in their towns that acquisitive age
> Filched the last foxglove from the prefigured ledge.
> Unhappy those hunters! their hybridization
> Grew a Goliath for a neurotic nation.
>
> I have heard them hallooing in the guilty wood,
> Papa and Grandpapa by the poltergeist pursued;
> Green were the grasses-O under the weeping ashes,
> But combine, crawler and mole-drain have settled the hashes
>
> Of the Shires and their squires, the peaches in the pleasance:
> Lucy and Lycidas, you must re-learn your lessons.
> See, Pope, 'tis Science holds the Muse's hand
> 'As laughing Ceres re-assumes the land.'
>
> Man makes the country. And money made the town;
> But devaluation will melt Sir Midas down.
> In Whitehall meanwhile, much-waistcoated, wandering,
> The poemless persons—what are *they* pondering?[1]

Robert Conquest is Kingsley Amis's (b. 1922) friend. The Amis poem that follows is included by Conquest in *New Lines*. It is called 'Against Romanticism', and I can afford the space to quote only the second of its two long stanzas. It is quite self-contained, I think, and comprehensible without benefit of its predecessor:

> Better, of course, if images were plain,
>     Warnings clearly said, shapes put down quite still
> Within the fingers' reach, or else nowhere;
>     But complexities crowd the simplest thing,

And flaw the surface that they cannot break.
  Let us make at least visions that we need:
Let mine be pallid, so that it cannot
  Force a single glance, form a single word;
An afternoon long-drawn and silent, with
  Buildings free from all grime of history,
The people total strangers, the grass cut,
  Not long, voluble swooning wilderness,
And green, not parched or soured by frantic suns
  Doubling the commands of a rout of gods,
Nor trampled by the havering unicorn;
  Let the sky be clean of officious birds
Punctiliously flying on the left;
  Let there be a path leading out of sight,
And at its other end a temperate zone:
  Woods devoid of beasts, roads that please the foot.[2]

Both poems are about the need to unlearn something, and in each case that something is called 'romanticism'. What is romanticism? That is an inoffensive-sounding question, but to answer it at length would probably offend many people. Here, however, the word seems to mean the same thing in each poem. At least the imagery used to refer to it is very similar—skylarks, officious birds, Pegasus, the unicorn. We might say, something at once elevated and immodest (the birds, Shelley's enraptured skylark pouring forth its 'profuse strains of unpremeditated art') and mythical, absurd (a winged horse, a fabled beast). It is this combination of pretension and absurdity, the claim to mysterious knowledge and the inability (so it is claimed) to produce the evidence for it, that both Bateson and Amis are mocking in their poems. The 'we' of Bateson's poem are 'nobblers of Pegasus'; 'Papa and Grandpapa by the poltergeist pursued' are embarrassingly silly ancestors—a fact that the excessive alliteration on the *p*s makes clear. The question is, what is to replace the poltergeist and Pegasus, and what, in us, is to replace the part these fictions played in the emotional life of papa and grandpapa?

Amis's poem is a poem of answers, not questions. 'Let us make at least visions that we need'; in his case—and remember he is a representative man, common poet is talking to common reader, so the assumption is they (we?) have all this in common—'pallid' visions. They are literally pallid: the removal of grime from public buildings reveals a paler colour beneath it. They are also metaphorically pallid: life itself is to be made 'temperate'. Perhaps these are the visions that the 'poemless persons' of Bateson's poem *should* be pondering if they were given the right poems to read—'The Anti-Romantics' or 'Against Romanticism' for instance. If so, it is important to note that in Amis's view they will have achieved, as Swift put it in one of his satirical pieces, 'the sublime and refined point of felicity, called, the possession of being well deceived; the serene peaceful state, of being a fool among knaves'. Amis is a self-confessed and self-satisfied fool because he admits to closing his eyes to what he doesn't want to see: namely the 'complexities' that 'crowd the simplest thing, / And flaw the surface that they cannot break'. Another contributor to *New Lines*, John Holloway (b. 1920), critic and philosopher, closes one of his most successful poems, 'Warning to a Guest', in a similar vein:

> I have watched you, as you have visited at this house,
> And know, from knowing myself, that you will be
> Quick to people the shore, the fog, the sea,
> With all the fabulous
> Things of the moon's dark side. No, stay with us.
> Do not demand a walk tonight
> Down to the sea. It makes no place for those
> Like you and me who, to sustain our pose,
> Need wine and conversation, colour and light.[3]

Drink up the Château Rothschild (Amis prefers beer) and forget about the monsters. Significantly, though the things of the moon's dark side are 'fabulous', the poets who have made them up need to sustain a 'pose' in order to ignore them. We poets are both imaginative and sensible, is the gist of this poem, as it was of Amis's. Look, we can invent these ghastly chimeras and then—hey presto!—beer, talk, poems, and four walls around us—and they're all gone. This is not just fiddling while Rome burns. It is lighting a cigar with the flames—providing it is one of the *best* cigars. This the poet can do with impunity because Rome is only really burning in the grate. It has been domesticated and made safe. The surface cannot break, for Amis. For Holloway, maybe it can—but not in 'this house'.

We have looked at three poems all of which, in one way or another, are about romanticism, and how to deal with it. Do away with it (Bateson), replace it (Amis), ignore it (Holloway). I have emphasized the dangerous aspect of the romantic vision, the poltergeists, frantic suns, and whatever it is that is wriggling down on the beach out of sight of John Holloway's drawing-room. But of course these terrors are what the romantic poet knows he has to face to pay for the more invigorating substance of his vision: Pegasus could take you to fabulous countries unexplored by any aeroplane, and the romantic scene in Amis's first stanza is filled with a 'grand meaning'. On the other hand, Pegasus doesn't exist, and a 'grand' meaning isn't necessarily a true one. That is to say, Amis and Conquest certainly, Bateson possibly (difficult to be sure because in spite of one or two clever lines, 'The Anti-Romantics' isn't a very good poem), are just a little bit ambivalent about the status and value of what they are excluding. Certainly it is 'safer' to exclude them. But is it a poet's job to be 'safe'? Probably they would answer, yes. In this country, at any rate. Because 'safe' is a loaded word. They would prefer the word 'responsible' or 'civilized'. It is a poet's job to be these things, and in England especially poets have operated close to the centre of national life. They have taken upon themselves the duty of interpreting and understanding the forces at work in the society they live in from a position close to the centre of that society. As far as we know, the Russian czars and their politicians were not poets. Neither was Bismarck or Napoleon III. But Canning, Palmerston, and Disraeli were. Russell and Gladstone read a great deal of poetry. So did civil servants, public-school masters, and members of the other professions, until the rot set in during and after the First World War. What we must do is get back to before the flood—and the monsters. Bateson says this directly. The way Amis and other *New Lines* poets write their poetry strongly suggests it. If poetry is a way of communicating values, indeed the very best way of doing so—as has been proved in the past—then it is right and proper that the audience that should be the recipient of such a communication must be reconstituted. Since poetry has been let down by its audience (again Conquest, in his introduction) then the poets must take up the challenge of creating a worthy audience which will *not* let them down again; and since that audience is to be found principally where it has been found in this country for the two or three centuries before the holocaust—namely among the administrators and members of the professions—it must be encouraged by being given poetry that, in its heart of hearts, confirms its values, its confidence in itself.

So, basically these poems are conservative and responsible, because civil servants, doctors, and teachers are conservative and responsible. These are the visions that we need, though Amis is intelligently dubious about their status as 'visions'—which is why the deflating 'at least' precedes them. They are indeed 'lesser' things than the 'grand meanings', the real visions of unreal things in the first stanza of his poem. This is why contemporary English poetry has been so often self-deprecating, mocking, and ambivalent. There is a ubiquitous feeling among poets that their social and their personal duties—their duty to their audience and their duty to their craft/integrity—might not be entirely identical. What if the real visions were of real things all the time? What if there really are monsters at the water's edge, not just the products of the poet's fevered imagination: 'Here be monsters', instead of a temperate zone at the end of the garden path? The creature from the sea has its claw down the chimney. In a more recent poem by an English poet who did not contribute to *New Lines*, this is just what does happen. The poem is called 'Ghost Crabs', by Ted Hughes (b. 1930):

At nightfall, as the sea darkens,
A depth darkness thickens, mustering from the gulfs and the
  submarine badlands,
To the sea's edge. To begin with
It looks like rocks uncovering, mangling their pallor.
Gradually the labouring of the tide
Falls back from its productions,
Its power slips back from glistening nacelles, and they are
  crabs.
Giant crabs, under flat skulls, staring inland
Like a packed trench of helmets.
Ghosts, they are ghost-crabs.
They emerge
An invisible disgorging of the sea's cold
Over the man who strolls along the sands.
They spill inland, into the smoking purple
Of our woods and towns—a bristling surge
Of tall and staggering spectres
Gliding like shocks through water.
Our walls, our bodies, are no problem to them.
Their hungers are homing elsewhere.
We cannot see them or turn our minds from them.
Their bubbling mouths, their eyes
In a slow mineral fury
Press through our nothingness where we sprawl on our beds,
Or sit in our rooms. Our dreams are ruffled maybe.
Or we jerk awake to the world of our possessions
With a gasp, in a sweat burst, brains jamming blind
Into the bulb-light. Sometimes, for minutes, a sliding
Staring
Thickness of silence
Presses between us. These crabs own this world.
All night, around us or through us,
They stalk each other, they fasten on to each other,
They mount each other, they tear each other to pieces,

They utterly exhaust each other.
They are the powers of this world.
We are their bacteria,
Dying their lives and living their deaths.
At dawn, they sidle back under the sea's edge.
They are the turmoil of history, the convulsion
In the roots of blood, in the cycles of concurrence.
To them, our cluttered countries are empty battlegrounds.
All day they recuperate under the sea.
Their singing is like a thin sea-wind flexing in the rocks of a
  headland,
Where only crabs listen.

They are God's only toys.[4]

'Ghost Crabs' was written ten years after the poems from *New Lines* that have engrossed our attention so far. It appeared in Hughes's third book of poems (for adults—he has written several other excellent books of poems for children), called *Wodwo* (1967). The two previous collections, *The Hawk in the Rain* and *Lupercal*, were published in 1957 and 1960, and one other, *Crow* (1970), has appeared subsequently. The poems in all these books, especially the two most recent, are of a totally different kind to those recommended by Bateson and Conquest, as 'Ghost Crabs' graphically demonstrates. The extent of the difference can be assessed by looking at the use to which personal pronouns and possessive adjective are put. I mean all those words which establish the relationship that exists between the poet and the reader. The identity of the 'we' and the 'you' to whom 'your' dreams apply in Bateson's poem is clarified by the apostrophe 'sir' in the third line. 'We' poets have a duty to 'you' readers (we shall disinfect your dreams for you). We are separate, sir (for the moment I am performing a service and you are receiving it), but equal. When Lucy and Lycidas are admonished to re-learn their lessons (stanza 4), both poet and reader are presumed to stand in a certain traditional and amicable relationship to each other which includes the assumption that both are perfectly well aware of who Lucy (Wordsworth's) and Lycidas (Milton's) are. They also both cleverly spot the quotation from Pope's 'Epistle to Burlington' that follows.

Amis's audience isn't so literary, except that it is expected to identify the birds, beasts, and unicorns as standard poetical properties. But they are again assimilated without effort to the poet's way of looking at things. 'Let us make at least visions that we need.' 'We' is English for the French '*on*'. This is held to be generally true, and the reader is expected to agree. Then the the poet can go on to express a less categorical personal bias, strictly within the terms of a larger, impersonal truth—which is a social, pragmatic, convenient truth: it depends on leaving things out, and then forgetting that you left them out. Poet and reader conspire to deceive each other. That is to a large extent what a highly evolved social system contrives to do. Some things don't bear looking into. The obvious solution is not to look into them. Unfortunately eyes have corners that such arrangements cannot do away with; and whether they will or no, poets see out of them. What Ted Hughes has done in 'Ghost Crabs' is to twist the corner into the centre. Having done so he has found that what he sees is what a great many other poets outside of this country, especially in East Europe, have also seen—without having had to undergo the ocular operation that Hughes has performed on himself. He looks out on a world in which pronominal accommodations between poet and reader, of the kind we have been looking at, are inadequate because they lack urgency. They insist upon a two-way communications system between the two parties, when what is of more pressing importance is the eruption of a third party which throws poet and reader into a common posture of fear and desperation. So the 'pull' of the poem, the focus of its energies, is the space, or lack of it, between us (human beings) and them (the ghost crabs). Polite accommodation is not in order. What is in order is an urgent warning and the acknowledgement of a common danger.

With aims so different, Hughes's use of language is not at all like that of Amis and Bateson. Quite apart from the urgency of the rhythms and the insistence on what I have called 'warning' words (those words that are used to address us as fellow victims), the poetry is much more densely encrusted with metaphor. Relationships between the images the poem is packed with are felt to be mysterious, uncertain, and a source of great imaginative power. No reader sees much of the beasts that the woods are devoid of, or the roads that please the foot, in Amis's poem. This is not in itself a bad thing. It is a fallacy that all the best poetry is metaphorical. But it may constitute evidence that the threshold of the reader's expectations has been artificially lowered in the service of a culture that is socially vivacious and cohesive, but is psychically enervated and weak. It all depends on the level at which 'agreements' are made—literary ones, and the social ones on which they depend. Hughes obviously feels that the level in this country at the time he is writing is very low, and that because it is very low he is not prepared to enter into agreements on conventional terms, as far as his poetry is concerned. The reason Amis can get away with his insubstantial unicorns and officious birds is that he and his readers have agreed upon the area in which they are prepared to meet each other—as givers and receivers. No bird is really 'officious'. The word simply consolidates a tone of voice that poet and reader are prepared to adopt in respect of what the birds stand for—inquisitive frenzy, which, in Amis's scheme of things, is undesirable and gets in the way. Hence they are officious.

I shall return to Hughes and 'Ghost Crabs'. In the meantime this matter of establishing agreements is very important, and I must add an historical note to make clear what I mean by it. Probably the most influential English poet of the fifties and sixties has been W. H. Auden (b. 1907). He is now an American citizen, and has been one throughout our period—but that has not prevented him from remaining very English, or at least Anglo-American in his preoccupations. One of the most important of these has been the establishment of a working relationship between himself as a poet and his audience as a suitable cultural milieu. In other words he has tried to do from the poet's end of the stick what Bateson tried to do from the audience's (which might be why 'The Anti-Romantics' sounds so much like an indifferent Audenesque exercise). The way Auden has made his attempt strikingly anticipates the general ambience and method of the *New Lines* poets, a fact which explains Conquest's deferential attitude towards him in his introduction to that book. Here is a poem Auden published just after the war, in 1947. It is called 'Our Bias':

> The hour-glass whispers to the lion's roar,
> The clock-towers tell the gardens day and night
> How many errors Time has patience for,
> How wrong they are in being always right.
>
> Yet Time, however loud its chimes or deep,
> However fast its falling torrent flows,
> Has never put one lion off his leap
> Nor shaken the assurance of a rose.
>
> For they, it seems, care only for success:
> While we choose words according to their sound
> And judge a problem by its awkwardness;
>
> And Time with us was always popular.
> When have we not preferred some going round
> To going straight to where we are? [5]

Like Amis's unicorn, the lion and the rose have no substantial existence. They are pegs on which to hang arguments, rather like the tigers and giraffes of the linguistic analysts in the philosophy schools.

The personal pronouns are again drained of their personality: 'we' and 'us' are the *a*s and *x*s of a human algebra, defining general qualities and relations between unidiosyncratic units. Also you will notice that, as in the poems written by Bateson and Amis and Holloway, the metrical and rhyme schemes are regular. 'Our Bias' is a sonnet with a couple of syllables left off the end—for an intriguingly witty reason, the discovery of which is calculated to elicit the sort of smile that ratifies a basic agreement between the poet and his reader. The fact of agreement, together with the willing delimitation of the total linguistic field which makes it practically viable in poetry, can be a great strength. It was so for the Augustans, whom Dr. Bateson and most other *New Lines* poets admire, and it is obviously intended to be so again by both Auden and many of the *New Lines* poets themselves.

One of them, Donald Davie (b. 1922), wrote a whole book on the subject of diction which he called *Purity of Diction in English Verse* (new ed., 1967), and diction is what, on the linguistic side of the social-literary equation, we are concerned with. A poet who is not in agreement with his readers over fundamentals—which can be 'understood' in the selection of syntactical forms and individual words and phrases poet and reader agree to use and accept—eschews the diction of poetry that prevails at the time of writing, and goes on to do one of two things. Either he tries to establish a different diction, and hence to shift the terms of the agreement from his end of the process of communication (Wordsworth in *Lyrical Ballads*). Or he evolves a wholly personal language which he expects his audience to adjust to, helped by the fact that he is after all writing from within the habits and arrangements of a common *language*, if not a common *diction*, and also by the fact that no such personal language can be created out of nothing, i.e. the poet is likely to forge his style out of what he observes of the practice of other poets who wrote before him; and since we have access to the same poets, we can get something of the measure of his achievement.

Ted Hughes belongs to the second type of what we might reasonably call 'romantic' poets. He has ransacked the language for materials to construct his poems out of, and he has made use of some of his literary ancestors—Hopkins, D. H. Lawrence, Dylan Thomas, and, I believe, the American poet John Crowe Ransom—to feel his way towards what has now become a confidently grasped poetic method. Typically, his innovations have been mainly in respect of rhythm and image. Rhythmic peculiarities are always difficult to discuss, especially where they are not subjected to the discipline of a pre-established verse form. In *Wodwo* and *Crow*, they are rarely subjected to such a discipline and, as in Lawrence's poems, the pauses and turns within phrase and sentence are deeply personal. In 'Ghost Crabs' the positioning of the lines has much to do with Hughes's sense of where units of sound or of meaning, either alone or in alliance with each other, are completed; and, especially in the last half of the poem, where the system of repetition—of opening words and grammatical pattern—reinforces the more personal 'timing'. The ante-penultimate line—'Their singing is like a thin sea-wind flexing in the rocks of a headland'—is as good an example as I can find of a rhythmic unit which is a unit both in consequence of its completed sense, *and* of the sound pattern it forms. The eerie sibilance of the first half of the line turns at 'flexing' to a more open rush of sound, which would be ruined if it were split in two with the 'turn'-word opening the second line. This would set up a rocking motion quite at odds with the more secretive, insidious power we sense in the opening and gradually in the full line. The fact of a long line also gives additional force to the last two lines, which are menacingly abrupt and final. Excellent short poems in the same volume which communicate a similar sense of rhythmic subtlety and wholeness are 'Thistles', 'Fern', and 'Sugar Loaf'.

The imagery a poet uses is less difficult to talk about than his manipulation of sound and 'timing'. In 'Ghost Crabs' it is clearly both more substantial and more of a piece than it is in either 'Against Romanticism' or 'Our Bias'. Hughes does not use imagery to embellish an argument or add to an idea. We have the impression that the ghost crabs are themselves the idea in the sense that we can talk of the idea of Hughes's crabs as we cannot of the idea of Amis's unicorn or the idea of Auden's lion. The unicorn and the lion are properties used in the expression of an idea that could have been expressed otherwise: that we must subdue our vision to the needs of the time; or that we should think ourselves lucky we have a sense of time which is different from the one animals have and which is a precondition of whatever is creative in our achievement. But what is the idea 'behind' Hughes's crabs? That there are forces operating in and upon human life which are powerful themselves and that are the more powerful on account of the energy they drain from us? That we are a condition of their existence in that we are used by them to perform functions that are not our own but that we are entangled and compromised with? That these forces are both outside of us, in history, and inside us, 'In the roots of blood', etc.? These are hardly ideas, and they are not consecutive, as I have had to make them appear. They 'mount each other', like the crabs, and acquire meaning only through their incarnation in the image of the crabs. The crabs are far more real than anything we can 'say' they represent. Bacteria, a 'trench of helmets' from the First World War, 'the smoking purple of our woods and towns', and the crabs are all parts of a continuum of imagery that is far more organically conceived than are the links between clock-tower, rose, lion, etc., in Auden's poem. The crabs look like helmets from above, and they may be murderous like a soldier in a trench. Then the idea of a war in Western Europe displaced on to the English coast and inland issues out of the simile quite naturally: 'Giant crabs . . . staring inland / Like a packed trench of helmets . . . They spill inland', etc. But the comparison of one physical horror with another gives way to more peculiar comparisons in which the physical crabs dematerialize into 'shocks' gliding through water—thus combining frightening corporeal attributes (though 'straight' physical description is very sparse) with immaterial powers that easily get entangled with such grand abstractions as history, convulsion, and concurrence. We know them more by what they do—staring, spilling, sliding, stalking, etc.—than by what they are. And the centre from which they do what they do is strangely malleable and untraceable. '*It* looks like rock*s*'; '*Its* power . . . and *they* are crabs.' 'Their *hungers* [not their bodies] are homing elsewhere.' No wonder they can fasten *on to* each other at the same time as they stalk *around* and *through* us.

When so much weight can be thrown on to the insignificant little prepositions and pronouns and the metaphorical substance is still so much there, as well as in the more obvious nouns and verbs, we are convinced that the language is being made to work hard, that the deliberate avoidance of a diction, with all the allowances and accommodations which issue from it, has forced the poet to compensate in terms of sheer imaginative energy and conviction. 'Ghost Crabs' and other poems in *Wodwo* represent a culmination of Hughes's search for an appropriate language to embody his intuitions on the nature of existence which began in the 1950s with less ambitious, but still very beautiful poems like 'The Thought Fox' and 'A Modest Proposal' and continued through the many fine 'animal poems' of *Lupercal*. In his next volume, *Crow*, he was found to be evolving a language to 'cope with', to 'engage' what so far he had succeeded only in describing and embodying. But the late fifties and early sixties were dominated by other poets who were trying to maintain the Movement consensus of the previous decade, while creating a more personal diction which, it was hoped, would enable them to range more widely over the permitted territory.

We can take John Wain (b. 1925) as a good example of the 'Movement' school. Like Amis, he is probably better known as a novelist than as a poet: he was writing novels like *Hurry on Down* and *The Contenders* at about the same time as he was writing the poems he contributed to *New Lines*. This is a poem he wrote during the fifties and included in his first volume, *A Word Carved on a Sill* (1956). It is called 'The Last Time':

> 'The last time' are the hardest words to say.
> The last time is the wrong time all along,
> The morning when we pack and go away.
>
> It must be true. The angel beats the gong.
> The heart floods over when we thought it dry.
> Sums that work out too easily are wrong.
>
> It is not only for escape we fly.
> We fly because the world is turning round
> And permanence lives only in the sky.
>
> The Red Queen's canter over shifty ground
> Is the best logic, though we learn it late;
> Hoping each day to balance Lost with Found;
>
> And if, as we suspect, it is our fate
> To find that what we lost was always more,
> So that the ledger never works out straight
>
> And each day finds us poorer than before;
> Still it is searching makes us seem sublime,
> Hoping each night to gain the happy shore,
>
> To say there for the last time 'the last time'.[6]

This is a better poem altogether than Kingsley Amis's, and in important respects it is better than Auden's too. It is 'clever', like theirs. The way the poem turns on the play on words of the title is clever; so is the easy movement within what might have proved to be a damagingly restrictive verse form—a traditional metre, rarely used in English, called *terza rima*. But as well as that, it *feels* more serious than 'Against Romanticism' or 'Our Bias'. The direct indicative sentences (as in the first two lines) have an air of gravity that testifies to a lived experience we sense exists behind them. The frequent 'we's' are again impersonal—not 'the poet and us' but 'everybody'. The imagery is again strictly utilitarian—promoting the greatest sense for the greatest number. The difference lies in what the poem is about, rather than in the brisk way it communicates what it is about. Wain admires Dr. Johnson. One of the poems in this first volume has a passage from Boswell's *Life* as its preface. And Johnson's example is widespread in many of the poems, not in respect of particular opinions, but in the general air of good sense, empirical temper, and a certain unruffled pessimism. Rasselas also, in Johnson's short novel of that name, seemed sublime on account of his searching, and what he found was usually less than what he lost in faith, hope, and the ability to remain self-deceived. The difference lies in the ages of the two men and in the fact that Johnson had, after all, written *Rasselas*, 'The Vanity of Human Wishes', and the *Rambler* essays a hundred and fifty years before Wain was born. Having acquired that sort of good sense at such an early age, and displayed it fully in a first book of poems, how was Wain to write his *Life of Savage*, so to speak? Like many another Movement poet, Wain has been condemned to a maturity that is part real and part literary. In later volumes (*Weep before God*, 1962, *Wildtrack*, 1965, and *Letters to Five Artists*, 1969) he has either repeated himself (often very beautifully: 'Poem', 'Poem without a Main Verb', 'Distances to Go', 'Au Jardin des Plantes') or he has indulged in an unnecessary and spurious experimentalism ('A Boisterous Poem about Poetry' and *Wildtrack* itself). His long poems have been short poems added together. His poems on public themes have been little more than verse-journalism ('A Song about Major Eatherly', which was first published in the *Bulletin of Atomic Scientists*).

Wain, then, is representative of many poets of the fifties and early sixties, who could write good poems within the terms set by the 'agreement' I defined above, but who have discovered that the agreement, as they understand it, doesn't permit the writing of poems that are *more* than good. Their 'contract' stipulates that they shall go on producing the same kind of poem at about the same high level of technical expertise and good sense. All one can say is that, on the evidence, it was a good contract, but that there is a case for not signing contracts at all, if you are the kind of poet that Wain has occasionally produced evidence he would like to become.

The three most celebrated poets to make their reputations in the fifties (all of them contributed to *New Lines*) were Philip Larkin (b. 1922), Thom Gunn (b. 1929), and Donald Davie (b. 1922). Philip Larkin has been by far the most popular; possibly the most popular living English poet after John Betjeman (b. 1906), whom he greatly admires. The award to him of the Queen's Gold Medal for poetry in 1965 is probably to be accounted for by this, as well as by the fact that he is a most accomplished poet of a traditional kind. He loves Thomas Hardy's poems, and his own verse, though much less profuse than that of his master, has the same combination of wistful sadness, amusement, respect for the commonplace, and a deep compassion. This is a poem from his second collection, *The Less Deceived* (1955), called 'Next, Please':

Always too eager for the future, we
Pick up bad habits of expectancy.
Something is always approaching; every day
*Till then* we say,

Watching from a bluff the tiny, clear,
Sparkling armada of promises draw near.
How slow they are! And how much time they waste,
Refusing to make haste!

Yet still they leave us holding wretched stalks
Of disappointment, for, though nothing balks
Each big approach, leaning with brasswork prinked,
Each rope distinct,

Flagged, and the figurehead with golden tits
Arching our way, it never anchors; it's
No sooner present than it turns to past.
Right to the last

We think each one will heave to and unload
All good into our lives, all we are owed
For waiting so devoutly and so long.
But we are wrong:

Only one ship is seeking us, a black-
Sailed unfamiliar, towing at her back
A huge and birdless silence. In her wake
No waters breed or break.[7]

A deeply moving poem, and one that depends on a sense of what, both linguistically and substantially, is to be expected. I have associated this with respect for an accepted diction and acknowledgement of an agreement drawn up in invisible ink and arrived at within a social consensus that is both provincial and well rooted in the society that constitutes the province. The diction is both precise and relaxed: how else could the common reader stomach the vulgar/

clever rhyme on 'tits' and 'it's' at the opening of stanza four? And what an accurate image is that of a hand holding those 'wretched stalks / Of 'disappointment' on a bluff overlooking the empty sea. What are they? Dandelion clocks blown bare, time passing, promises fading? The abstraction of 'disappointment' renders them at once spectral and hard to the touch. Or the superbly rhetorical black sails at the end, with their desolating sense of the futility of death poised against the futility of the life that sluggishly, hopefully, awaits it. Larkin's poems are replete with such felicities of image and phrasing. They do what Pope said all poetry should do—describe what oft was thought, but ne'er so well expressed. Except, usually, by Pope. Others in the same volume are the by now famous 'Church Going', 'Maiden Name', and 'At Grass'; and in his most recent collection, *The Whitsun Weddings* (1964), the title poem, 'Love Songs in Age', and 'An Arundel Tomb'. There are many more, in both volumes.

Thom Gunn and Donald Davie are more adventurous poets, less easily satisfied with the linguistic conditions under which Larkin has been happy to work—perhaps because they achieved less under them. In other respects, too, they have been unable to take for granted what Larkin has taken for granted. This has most often been a matter of their relationship to the physical world around them. Gunn's early poems, in two collections, *Fighting Terms* (1954) and *The Sense of Movement* (1957), were, on the whole, simple-mindedly philosophical. They asserted their creator's identity by describing his struggle with a recalcitrant environment which provided a sort of testing ground for the will. The motorcycle hoodlums and tough guys ('Lofty in the Palais de Danse', 'On the Move') who populate his early poems were stand-ins for Gunn's own adolescent personality. They dramatized and brutalized his preoccupation with what he took to be the distinctive human attributes of power exerted with deliberation and foresight, planned control of the natural world, the making of choices, and the exercise of free will. This poem, 'Human Condition', is one of the more successful of his forays into the territory of the isolated consciousness imposing itself on the external world and, in doing so, defining its own powers and limits:

Now it is fog, I walk
Contained within my coat;
No castle more cut off
By reason of its moat:
Only the sentry's cough,
The mercenaries' talk.

The street lamps, visible,
Drop no light on the ground,
But press beams painfully
In a yard of fog around.
I am condemned to be
An individual.

In the established border
There balances a mere
Pinpoint of consciousness.
I stay, or start from, here:
No fog makes more or less
The neighbouring disorder.

Particular, I must
Find out the limitation
Of mind and universe,
To pick thought and sensation
And turn to my own use
Disordered hate or lust.

I seek, to break, my span.
I am my one touchstone.
This is a test more hard
Than any ever known.
And thus I keep my guard
On that which makes me man.

Much is unknowable.
No problem shall be faced
Until the problem is;
I, born to fog, to waste,
Walk through hypothesis,
An individual.[8]

The rhyme scheme is as regular as we found it in Amis, Wain, Auden, and Larkin; but after the first stanza it ceases to be as obtrusive because the metrical arrangement within the line, though regular in the strictest sense (six syllables to the line), shifts the rhythmical emphases to unexpected words, which are often not the rhyme words (see stanzas two, three, and four). The result is that the poem gives the impression of being more exploratory than did those of the other fifties poets we have been looking at. In terms of the linguistic procedures of the poem, the 'guard' of the penultimate stanza is the strict rhyme scheme and rigid stanzaic form. But the 'staying' and 'starting' of stanza three are reflected in the metrical uncertainty of what happens within and across those superficial regularities. So 'Human Condition' looks towards the more secret and tentative movements in Gunn's subsequent collections.

Donald Davie, was, from the first, a less obviously ambitious poet than Gunn. The poems in his first volume, *Brides of Reason* (1955), were very much what the title would lead one to expect: chaste of diction and sparkling with intellect. Their stanzaic patterns were strictly constructed and agilely negotiated. Indeed, there was something almost too finickily eighteenth-century about them: and Davie was forced to concede that there might be something in the accusation that he was 'a *pasticheur* of late Augustan styles'. The poems were preoccupied with nature, and the history of man's often wary, sometimes arrogant relationship with nature in a way that Gunn's were not. Where for Gunn nature was a testing ground for the more important human attributes that were his sole subject, for Davie it was never so much a usable object, a commodity, and man's relationship with nature was never so one-sidedly simplistic. The following poem from his second collection, *A Winter Talent* (1957), shows the many-sidedness of his idea of 'virtue', the three types of personality and awareness that he feels he has to come to terms with in himself. It is called 'Dream Forest':

These have I set up,
Types of ideal virtue,
To be authenticated
By no one's Life and Times,
But by a sculptor's logic

Of whom I have commanded,
To dignify my groves,
Busts in the antique manner,
Each in the space mown down
Under its own sway:

First, or to break the circle,
Brutus, imperious, curbed
Not much by the general will,
But by a will to be curbed,
A preference for limits;

Pushkin next, protean
Who recognised no checks
Yet brooked them all—a mind
Molten and thereby fluent,
Unforced, easily strict;

The next, less fortunate,
Went honourably mad,
The angry annalist
Of hearth and marriage bed,
Strindberg—a staring head.

Classic, romantic, realist,
These have I set up.
These have I set, and a few trees.
When will a grove grow over
This mile upon mile of moor?[9]

In subsequent collections by Gunn and Davie, the Pushkin 'type' of this poem has been dominant. Both have come to value the ideal of a mind that is 'Molten and thereby fluent, / Unforced, easily strict'. Fluency and fluidity—of thought, of language, and of the transactions each of these makes with a world that exists apart from what are strictly and necessarily human concerns—become almost the same thing. The result has been what can be best, though rather pedestrianly, described as a recognition of the otherness of nature. Davie expressed this view in a published conversation with A. Alvarez, the poet and critic, in 1963, when he commented sarcastically that 'It's only when what seems to be a nature-poem can be converted into a human-nature-poem that we begin to take it seriously.' As long ago as 1955, before *New Lines* was published, he had implied much the same thing in the introduction he wrote to a slim volume by Charles Tomlinson (b. 1927), called *The Necklace* (1955).

Tomlinson's role in freeing Davie certainly and Gunn perhaps (the influence need not be a matter of direct engagement with the work that is believed to be influential) has been very great, both on its own account and on account of the alternative tradition of writing poetry to which it beckons. That tradition is, fundamentally, American. It is represented by such diverse individuals as Ezra Pound (b. 1885), Wallace Stevens (1879–1955), and William Carlos Williams (1883–1963), all active before the Second World War, and all very different poets, but with certain basic preoccupations in common. They are the preoccupations brought to mind by Pound's statement that the poet must 'make it new' (the title of one of his books of critical polemic), by Stevens's belief that the poet must 'become an innocent man again / And see the sun again with an innocent eye', and Williams's that 'However hopeless it may seem, we have no other choice; we must go back to the beginning.' These were the views upon which the great Anglo-American experimentalist writing of the early years of this century was based, but which—by and large—the English side of the partnership rapidly discarded. The greatest of these poets, T. S. Eliot (1888–1965), was an American intellectual who became a naturalized British subject in 1927. At the time he changed nationalities, he was moving towards a theory of poetry that, while similar in many respects to that of his fellow American experimentalists, placed a greater stress than they did on the unbroken tradition—the unbroken national, within the international, tradition—of a culture, and the poetry which was its highest expression. Where Eliot came more and more to emphasize the actuality of a poetic continuum extending in time, Pound and Williams insisted upon the immediate contemporaneity of the past. Since 1944, the date of the publication of Eliot's last and most remarkable long poem, *Four Quartets*, the traditions of writing that Eliot and Pound/Williams represented have diverged radically. American poetry has been, at its best, a provincial poetry extending laterally, in love with space and the enormous continental land mass that makes space possible, together with a variety of contour, climate, racial and geographical differences. English poetry has also been provincial, but it has extended temporally, reaching out into the national past for verse forms, traditional subject-matter, and, most important, that sense of a homogeneous and 'tactful' audience that is the unsubmerged apex of a common culture. It is a culture which is expected to value the poet and produce for him the social status, the role within a given social context, that is the precondition of his making those contracts and agreements we saw were so important to Auden, Wain, Larkin, and other postwar English poets.

Apart from maverick writers like Robert Lowell (b. 1917) and Ted Hughes, much of the best poetry to come out of both the U.S.A. and the British Isles since the war has been that which has taken notice of the alternative tradition on the other side of the Atlantic. By and large, Europe has been a dead loss (with the important exception of some Russian and East European poets—a matter that is too complex to go into within the space at our disposal). Charles Tomlinson has visited the U.S.A. His first two volumes of poetry appeared there, and were favourably received there, some time before they were published in this country. (Thom Gunn has lived in California for more than ten years at the time of writing and Donald Davie has recently taken up a professorial chair at Stanford University.) This poem appeared in Tomlinson's second collection,

*Seeing is Believing* (New York, 1958), and is called 'Tramontana at Lerici':

Today, should you let fall a glass it would
  Disintegrate, played off with such keenness
Against the cold's resonance (the sounds
  Hard, separate and distinct, dropping away
In a diminishing cadence) that you might swear
  This was the imitation of glass falling.

Leaf-dapples sharpen. Emboldened by this clarity
  The minds of artificers would turn prismatic,
Running on lace perforated in crisp wafers
  That cut like steel. Constitutions,
Drafted under this fecund chill, would be annulled
  For the strictness of their equity, the moderation of
    their pity.

At evening, one is alarmed by such definition
  In as many lost greens as one will give glances to recover,
As many again which the landscape
  Absorbing into the steady dusk, condenses
From aquamarine to that slow indigo-pitch
  Where the light and twilight abandon themselves.

And the chill grows. In this air
  Unfit for politicians and romantics
Dark hardens from blue, effacing the windows:
  A tangible block, it will be no accessory
To that which does not concern it. One is ignored
  By so much cold suspended in so much night.[10]

Does that sound very original? At first it may not seem so. There is not the immediate impact of novelty we receive in Hughes's free-verse 'Ghost Crabs', for instance. But put it beside a piece of descriptive verse by a highly proficient exponent of what I have called 'Movement' poetry—a couple of stanzas from James Kirkup's (b. 1923) 'A House in Summer', which is about the sense of heat and fatigue in a midsummer English domestic scene:

At an open window, a tree rustles, curiously close, its wood
Full of exhausted patience, patient still.
The window seems to take in much more than it should—
An entire garden, the lake beyond, a dog over a hill:
They are all inside the open house, like the air
Moved in from the afternoon, left hanging round the stair.

In the bedrooms, twilight cannot quite extinguish
The blank abandon of beds unmade by heat.
The morning's thrown-back coverings bloom and languish
Like knocked-out lovers under the ceiling's even sheet.
The attics throb like ovens and their stone tiles tick.
Baked books are warm still, their floury pages thick.[11]

The description strikes me as being accurate, and indeed the whole poem is delightful. But description, impressions, are all there is. The sense of a mind as well as a body experiencing the scene is absent. In Tomlinson's poem, on the contrary, the cold, the stillness, and the indefinable sense of clarity imperceptibly merge with what one can only call (loosely) their mental and emotional counterparts: definition, conviction, 'strictness'—though never at the expense of the non-human discreteness of the glass, the dusk, the shadows of the leaves. (We expect dapples to be adjectival—'dappled'—and we expect things that are dappled to be 'soft', not 'sharp', in respect of colour and outline.) The alternation of engagement and disengagement at several different levels between the poet and the landscape (which may be a city-scape, with people in it: Tomlinson's third book (1963) is called *A Peopled Landscape*) is what Gunn and Davie have also moved towards in their more recent collections—Gunn in three books: *My Sad Captains* (1961), *Touch* (1967), and *Moly* (1971); Davie in two: *Events and Wisdoms* (1964) and *Essex Poems* (1969). This poem, by Gunn, appeared in *Touch*, and is called 'Snowfall':

It is no wonder
People look circumspect against the white:
Sharp-edged, darkly filled-in; the creature's heat
Being closely hoarded under
Layers of wool, long coats, and scarves pulled tight.
The element is dazzling and complete:
The floor they tread is bright.

Unseen below
Stir brooks that, under hard panes withdrawn deep,
Still work a secret network through the land
With iced and darkened flow.
Joining, dividing, through black earth, they creep
And honeycomb the country where I stand
With galleries of their sleep.

And here, the floor
Is founded on them: I can see or guess

It follows subterranean bay and fall,
Like them in each contour.
Yet unlike—what the ice-packed heel must press
Not quite resistant, not quite palpable,
I find an edgelessness.[12]

This one, by Davie, is called 'The Hill Field', from *Events and Wisdoms*:

Look there! What a wheaten
Half-loaf, halfway to bread,
A cornfield is, that is eaten
Away, and harvested:

How like a loaf, where the knife
Has cut and come again,
Jagged where the farmer's wife
Has served the farmer's men,

That steep field is, where the reaping
Has only just begun
On a wedge-shaped front, and the creeping
Steel edges glint in the sun.

See the cheese-like shape it is taking,
The sliced-off walls of the wheat
And the cheese-mite reapers making
Inroads there, in the heat?

It is Breughel or Samuel Palmer
Some painter, coming between
My eye and the truth of a farmer,
So massively sculpts the scene

The sickles of poets dazzle
These eyes that were filmed from birth;
And the miller comes with an easel
To grind the fruits of earth.[13]

In both poems nature is strange. It accommodates itself partially and uncertainly to our ways of knowing it. 'Secret networks' of water flow beneath the ice that Gunn's heel digs into. The ice itself is 'Not quite resistant, not quite palpable'. Davie's cornfield is a rich and colourful natural scene which half accepts, half resists the human activities that try to make it into something other than what it is. The farmers see it as a potential loaf that the miller will grind into being; the poet sees it as part of a painting by Breughel or Palmer; and in the last stanza the aesthetic and the utilitarian uses of the cornfield come together with the miller and his easel. But some time before, the 'truth of the scene' is compromised the other way round: the human reapers have become cheese-mites slicing into the metaphorical cheese. Nature exists simultaneously as something for us to use, an object for contemplation, and an entity with its own powers and claims upon us. Gunn, Davie, and Tomlinson have reverted to the old, but still very much alive, romantic preoccupation with the relationship between man and nature, the relationship adumbrated in Coleridge's 'Dejection: an Ode' and Wordsworth's 'Tintern Abbey'. How far, in Coleridge's words, do we 'receive but what we give'? Within what limits do we dominate nature and how does nature deal with those who transgress those limits? What is the relationship between nature and art—such as the poem I am now writing? Old questions, but continually in need of a new answer. These three poets have discovered in American poets like William Carlos Williams, Gary Snyder (b. 1930), and James Wright (b. 1927) a way of re-approaching these questions. In doing so, they have moved further away from the 'area of agreement' they had occupied fairly comfortably in the 1950s.*

In 1970, Ted Hughes brought out a new volume of poems called *Crow*. Crow is a comical, repellant, and heroic 'persona' whose adventures are described, and often in a sense re-created, in most of

* There are many more poets than I have space to deal with here, who have written successfully both within and to some degree apart from this 'area of agreement'. Good examples of poets who have been basically satisfied to work within the limits are Roy Fuller (b. 1912), Thomas Kinsella (b. 1924), and Seamus Heaney (b. 1939). R. S. Thomas (b. 1913), Jon Silkin (b. 1930), Geoffrey Hill (b. 1932), and the late Burns Singer (1928–64) are less 'conformist' poets who, nevertheless, have been able to work within traditionally acceptable forms of poetic discourse.

Stevie Smith (1902–71) was writing fine poetry before she died. Dylan Thomas's (1914–53) later poems were written in the early years of our period. So was some of F. T. Prince's (b. 1912) best work. Louis MacNeice (1907–63) produced his best volume of lyric poetry since the 1930s, *The Burning Perch*, in 1963, shortly before he died. The same can be said of Edwin Muir (1887–1959), whose *One Foot in Eden* appeared in 1956. Robert Graves (b. 1895) is still producing his exquisitely chiselled lyrics. Notable American poets of the period are Marianne Moore (1887–1972), Elizabeth Bishop (b. 1911), Theodore Roethke (1908–63), Robert Lowell, Charles Olson (b. 1910), Louis Simpson (b. 1923), Sylvia Plath (1932–63), William Stafford (b. 1914), and Robert Creeley (b. 1926). See the list of Further Reading (p. 412) for books describing the achievement of these writers.

the poems. Almost all the others—about ten in all—take the form of perverse creation myths in which Adam and Eve and God treat one another abominably. Crow sometimes participates—as a gloating or horrified spectator. In the rest of the poems he is the central character, drawing imaginative life and vigour from his origins in beast fable, primitive myth, strip cartoons (he survives the most appalling disasters, like Donald Duck and Felix the cat), and, of course, the savage natural world that Hughes had already exploited in his earlier collections. Here, 'Crow Goes Hunting':

Crow
Decided to try words.

He imagined some words for the job, a lovely pack—
Clear-eyed, resounding, well-trained,
With strong teeth.
You could not find a better bred lot.

He pointed out the hare and away went the words
Resounding.
Crow was Crow without fail, but what is a hare?

It converted itself to a concrete bunker.
The words circled protesting, resounding.

Crow turned the words into bombs—they blasted the bunker.
The bits of bunker flew up—a flock of starlings.

Crow turned the words into shotguns, they shot down the starlings.
The starlings turned to a cloudburst.

Crow turned the words into a reservoir, collecting the water.
The water turned into an earthquake, swallowing the reservoir.

The earthquake turned into a hare and leaped for the hill
Having eaten Crow's words.

Crow gazed after the bounding hare
Speechless with admiration.[14]

What does it mean? Before we can answer that question, *how* does it mean? It is clever, but not in the way Wain or Auden are clever. Cleverness isn't the first thing we notice. In fact we don't 'notice', as if the poem were spread out to be looked over and enjoyed like a painting, or extended in time with recurrent motifs and themes that make it 'of a piece' like a musical composition. It bounds forward as a tale bounds forward, one of the Scandinavian myths about Odin and Loki, for example. Or, again, like a strip cartoon—moving from picture to picture. It is a poem to be spoken, and Hughes has produced a spoken version of great power. So 'Crow Goes Hunting' is a little gnomic myth about the nature of words, which means the way we try to manipulate reality. Words, like reality, get out of control—but at what point do they get out of control, whose fault is it—the words' or the things'? 'Crow was Crow without fail, but what is a hare? / It converted itself to a concrete bunker. / The words circled protesting, resounding.' Crow's grasp on himself, from inside, is not subject to contradiction or confusion. But his grasp on the hare is rudimentary. He cannot encompass it. Words fail him, can't cope with the rapid change of subject as the hare disappears and is replaced by the concrete bunker. So Crow turns the words from being hounds into being bombs—he adapts their nature to their function—usually predatory and destructive, though not always: Crow turns them into a reservoir to collect the water from the cloudburst. Then at the end the hare returns, having completely eluded capture by the words, which he has eaten. What exists, is the master not the slave of our paltry efforts to subdue it to our own requirements; it leaps free of the myths we use to explain it, even inside the myth itself, which it eats. The myth feeds upon itself, returns back into itself (it has swallowed its own tale) like the narrative of Hughes's own later 'Song for a Phallus' in which Oedipus begins and ends in his mother's womb.

Hughes is fascinated by myth. He is also fascinated by those East European poets who make use of, indeed *make*, myths in their own poems. Introducing a collection of Vasko Popa's poems in 1969 (Popa is a contemporary Yugoslavian poet), he said of them: 'There is a primitive pre-creation atmosphere about his work, as if he were present where all the dynamisms and formulae were ready and charged, but nothing created—or only a few fragments.' The *Crow* poems are recognizably created out of the same circumstances. They are poems exposed to a world of violence and catastrophe that is alien to most English experience—at the public level—during the last half-century, and much further back than that. Whether they are alien to our more personal traumas and neuroses each reader will have to determine for himself. Hughes is a strange, but not altogether eccentric poet with whom to close this survey of recent English poetry.

## NOTES

[1] F. W. Bateson, *English Poetry* (1950; reissued 1966), vii. Quoted by permission of the author and Longman Group Ltd.

[2] K. Amis, *A Case of Samples* (1956), 31. Quoted by permission of the author and Victor Gollancz Ltd.

[3] J. Holloway, *The Minute and Longer Poems* (1956), 46.

[4] T. Hughes, *Wodwo* (1967), 21–2. Quoted by permission of the author and Faber & Faber Ltd.

[5] W. H. Auden, *Collected Shorter Poems, 1927–1957* (1966), 171. Quoted by permission of the author and Faber & Faber Ltd.

[6] J. Wain, *A Word Carved on a Sill* (1956). Quoted by permission of the author and Routledge & Kegan Paul Ltd.

[7] P. Larkin, *The Less Deceived* (1955), 18. Quoted by permission of the author and The Marvell Press.

[8] T. Gunn, *The Sense of Movement* (1957), 18–19. Quoted by permission of the author and Faber & Faber Ltd.

[9] D. Davie, *A Winter Talent* (1957), 3–4. Quoted by permission of the author and Routledge & Kegan Paul Ltd.

[10] C. Tomlinson, *Seeing is Believing* (1960), 18.

[11] J. Kirkup, *The Prodigal Son* (1959), 10.

[12] T. Gunn, *Touch* (1967), 50. Quoted by permission of the author and Faber & Faber Ltd.

[13] D. Davie, *Events and Wisdoms* (1964). Quoted by permission of the author and Routledge & Kegan Paul Ltd.

[14] T. Hughes, *Crow* (1970), 45. Quoted by permission of the author and Faber & Faber Ltd.

## FOR FURTHER READING

For obvious reasons, it is difficult to write dispassionately about recent poetry. The line between criticism and propaganda is a fine one. Much of the best comment on English poets who have emerged since the war balances precariously on that line, and is to be found in small magazines which offer a platform to some of the poets they comment on. The dangers of excessive self-regard and inflated mutual esteem are not always avoided. Fortunately some of the best essays in one of the best of these magazines, *The Review*, are collected together by one of its editors, Ian Hamilton, in *The Modern Poet* (1968). This includes an important 'conversation' between A. Alvarez and Donald Davie on 'A New Aestheticism'. Alvarez's views are more clearly set out in his introduction to *The New Poetry* (Penguin, 1962), which he calls 'Beyond the Gentility Principle'. Davie has more to say about his view of modern poetry in his 'Postscript' to the reissue of his book, *Purity of Diction in English Verse* (1967). Another contributor to *The Review*, Martin Dodsworth, has edited a symposium on contemporary poetry in *The Survival of Poetry: a Contemporary Survey* (1970).

Robert Conquest's *New Lines* has been referred to in the text. It was published in 1956, and was followed by *New Lines 2* in 1963, which also contains a polemical introduction. There are many other collections of contemporary poetry. Often they contain introductory and biographical material. The Penguin Modern Poets series is useful, though the volumes contain nothing but the poetry itself—a selection from the work of three poets in each. In the U.S. two paperback volumes have been published of *The New Poets of England and America*, edited by D. Hall, R. Pack, and L. Simpson (New York, 1957, 1962). In this country Corgi have begun a series of Modern Poets in Focus, edited by D. Abse and J. Robson (three volumes in 1971).

The later sections of J. Press, *A Map of Modern English Verse* (1969), are useful for the reader interested in comments of living poets on their poetry.

Two books devote themselves to the 'history' of poetry in England since 1945. One, J. Press, *Rule and Energy* (1963), restricts itself to British poets. The other, M. L. Rosenthal, *The New Poets: American and British Poetry since World War II* (1967), is, as its title suggests, more catholic. Neither is enormously invigorating, but both are sound introductions to the subject.

G. S. Fraser, *Vision and Rhetoric* (1959) smells less of the lamp. Unfortunately, only its last two chapters, 'Experiment in Verse' and 'Contemporary Poetry and the Anti-Romantic Idea', are about the postwar poets, but they make interesting and, I think, somewhat chastening reading.

# 14

# Drama

ARNOLD P. HINCHLIFFE

## I

Although the Government closed every theatre (except the Windmill) when war was declared in 1939, by 1941 London was once more the centre of British theatre, and after the war there were many actors and theatres, some producers, and sufficient old plays to suggest an exciting future. No one could have foreseen, however, how exciting the next two decades were to be. British theatre became intimately aware of what was happening in Europe, particularly of the work of two dramatists, Beckett and Brecht, and this awareness was a significant factor in the exploration of ways of creating 'poetry of the theatre'. This phrase occurred in Cocteau's preface to *Les Mariés de la Tour Eiffel* (1921). It is part of theatricalism, the anti-literary movement which insists that language is only one element of a whole, which is the performance, and rejects dramatic literature in favour of the fullest exploitation of theatrical resources. Cocteau insisted that verse could not be part of this plastic beauty since verse was like delicate lace, invisible in the theatre which required coarse rope. Obviously, poetry of the theatre can be created in more than one way, but the implied subordination of the dramatist to the producer points to another important strand in recent theatrical history: the struggle for first place in that assembly of talents we call a performance.

In 1950 Kenneth Tynan published a collection of essays called *He That Plays the King*, a title which indicates who had first place in postwar theatre and what kind of theatre it was. Geared to the needs of a tired world, it was an age of heroic acting, which enjoyed the special talents of actors such as Olivier, Richardson, Gielgud, Redgrave, Edith Evans, and Sybil Thorndike in roles written to show off their abilities. These abilities were a fine stage presence and magnificent speaking voices. Going to the theatre was an occasion, giving an elegant and memorable impression, escapist or at least largely devoid of social and political content, but relevant to the mood of the time. As Peter Brook reminds us in his book, *the empty space* (1968), the theatre of the forties was 'a theatre of colour and movement, of fine fabrics, of shadows, of eccentric, cascading words, of leaps of thought and of cunning machines, of lightness and of all forms of mystery and surprise—it was the theatre of a battered Europe that seemed to share one aim—a reaching back towards the memory of lost grace'.

Shaw had returned to the theatre with two plays in 1948 and 1950 but neither was worthy of him. 1951 was Festival of Britain Year and musicals like *Kiss Me, Kate* and *South Pacific* followed the success of *Carousel*. In 1952 audiences attended the first performances of a new thriller called *The Mousetrap*. A list of serious dramatists would include names like J. B. Priestley, R. C. Sherriff, veterans like Noël Coward and Terence Rattigan, and a surprise newcomer in 1953, Graham Greene. In 1954 Rattigan invented Aunt Edna, that staunch playgoer whose tolerance, or lack of it, was the major criterion of what could be said or done on the stage. The quality of social comment could be judged from Coward's *Relative Values*, which portrayed the confusion in a stately home when the son decides to marry a film star who turns out to be the sister of his mother's personal maid. By any standards the theatre of the forties and early fifties looks conservative, but there were harbingers of change. 1949 saw the London productions of two American plays: Arthur Miller's *Death of a Salesman* and Tennessee Williams's *A Streetcar Named Desire*.

Arthur Miller (b. 1915) showed the moral earnestness, social responsibility, and inquiry into the insecurity of man in modern industrial civilization one could expect from a writer who had grown up facing the complex fate of being American (and Jewish) during the depression. Miller had joined the Federal Theatre Project on leaving university in 1938, and had been, with reason, described as a well-made playwright indebted to Ibsen.* The dialogue, tone, and situations of his plays also show considerable indebtedness to Chekhov. In *Death of a Salesman* Miller produced an unheroic hero out of the conflict between Willy Loman and the American Dream. Conceived as a monodrama (called *The Inside of His Head*), the play anticipated Osborne's technique as well as his suffering hero, but, unlike Osborne, Miller did not forge a style to carry this theme. T. C. Worsley, reviewing the play as 'Poetry Without Words', suggested that Miller had attempted to make a poetic approach to everyday life without using poetry or even heightened speech. The 'poetry' was to be supplied by symbols, lighting, time-switches—in short, the production, and this created an atmosphere 'heavily scented with self-importance'. Worsley concluded that words are

* His version of Ibsen's *An Enemy of the People* was produced in New York in 1950.

necessary for poetry. But the novel skeletal set by Jo Mielziner was entirely appropriate, for the house is as much a character in the play as anyone else. Noticeably, too, Miller kept Loman ethnically neutral, making the play an examination of the American Dream rather than anti-Semitism in the American business world. As Miller himself pointed out, Willy could not be seen as an average American since he kills himself; nevertheless, Willy Loman seemed to represent a modern American. In *The Crucible* (1953), Miller tackled a hero outside his society, and returned to chronological narrative, a larger cast, and more scene changes. Marion L. Starkey had published her study *The Devil in Massachusetts* in 1949 and *The Crucible* was the third play in 1953 on the subject. It was actually written before Miller became a victim of McCarthyism but it showed an understanding of the way hysteria builds up among decent people, and the impotence of common sense against evil. The seventeenth-century setting gave the play perspective in which to ask the question: should the rights of minorities be set aside in times of national crisis? This questioning was not continued. Miller's next two plays were social—the first originally written in verse but finally printed in prose in an enlarged version as *A View From the Bridge* (1956). Miller's use of hot-blooded immigrants was possibly an answer to criticism that he did not write plays like Tennessee Williams's *The Rose Tattoo*, but his theme is, once again, the idea that no man can prosper unless his *polis* prospers. After a gap of seven years, Miller wrote *After The Fall* (1964), another look at a man trying to be a separate person, but also a play that began to explore the theme of man as a passive being, an accomplice of his own destruction. Miller continued to examine this idea in his play *Incident at Vichy* (1966), which is again about people caught up in witch-hunts. With *The Price* (1968), he returned to a family conversation-piece, with four characters (including a comic Jew called Solomon). Accused of ignoring the events of the time, Miller replied that the qualities of the two brothers in this play were necessary to our present world, and that their conflict was at the heart of the social (i.e. political) dilemma. Miller is still asking what can save us. In 1949 he was a lonely voice.

The idea of a tradition of American drama is wishful thinking, but Miller had a rival in Tennessee Williams (b. 1914). Like Miller, Williams is the dramatist of trapped people, but where Miller asks what should be done, Williams observes how pitiful it is; where Miller is a moralist, Williams is a sensationalist—in its best and worst sense. *Battle of Angels*, based on a short story by D. H. Lawrence, was a failure in Boston in 1940, but Williams had arrived in the

American theatre and given audiences a first taste of his style. *The Glass Menagerie* (1944) received critical acclaim and after its New York opening in 1945 Williams was an overnight success. It is called a Memory Play, and is Williams's most consciously autobiographical—its hero is called Tom. Its expressionistic technique was offered by Williams as part of the new plastic theatre which he felt must 'take the place of the exhausted theatre of realistic conventions' if theatre was to remain a vital part of culture. Thus he was offering illusion as theme and illusion as technique in 1944, in a play which captures the illuminating moment in four lives which the world will destroy. For, although a non-violent play, the universe of *The Glass Menagerie* is destructive, and against its forces human beings need to cherish illusion if they are to survive at all, a theme continued in *A Streetcar Named Desire* (1947). Blanche Dubois was a composite of previous heroines. She has no illusions about her illusions, and these she puts on like her glass necklace, as a defence against life which produces flowers only for the dead. But her antagonist, Stanley, too, has his illusion—that of muscle-man—and it is that illusion which must be preserved at the expense of Blanche, though clearly by the end of the play life will never be the same again. This play established Williams as the poet of the inadequate. It is interesting—from 1971, the year of Andy Warhol's *Pork*—to remember that when the play was produced in London in 1949 (with Vivien Leigh as Blanche directed by Laurence Olivier) it was attacked as obscene, and first aid had to be rendered to members of the audience overwhelmed by Stanley's pyjama-clad rape of Blanche, behind a curtain.

Obscene or not, Williams's portrayal of the damned in sexual terms continued unbroken, except for *The Rose Tattoo* (1950). This play, written with Anna Magnani in mind, and in gratitude for the healing powers of the Sicilian sun, was carefully devised (and re-written at least four times), but its optimism rests finally on the hope that the cruelties of the universe can be settled in a big bed. *Camino Real* (1948), a parable of the human condition, was more characteristic. Unfortunately Williams seemed to have left the human out altogether from his poetic definition and the poetry itself often seemed little more than decoration. That these people were trapped in a cruel universe, and usually with curious sexual dilemmas, intensified their situation but removed the possibility of tragedy and opened the way to sensationalism. *Cat on a Hot Tin Roof* (1955) continued to explore this view of life, but created two vital characters in Big Daddy and the Cat herself, which give theatrical importance to an otherwise muddled play. In 1958 Williams wrote *Suddenly Last*

*Summer*, which many consider his most perfectly realized play. Here the organization is so economical that the play resembles a narrative poem, and this overall poetic quality justifies the significant objects and symbols for which Williams has always shown a fondness. Here the universe is palpably voracious, destroying the weak without mercy. Williams has written nothing as powerful since this statement of what happens to the sensitive nonconformist. If his heroes are Don Quixotes, the mills they tilt at are very real. Opposing this implacable view of life is Williams's lyricism, which produces exciting illusions about illusion on the stage. Many of his plays have become well known through their carefully-edited film versions which ironically destroy the quality for which he should be remembered in the theatre: the poetic treatment of naturalism. But frequently Williams loses sight of poetry of the theatre because he writes poetry and expects it to work in the theatre. That it does not necessarily work can be seen in the revival of verse drama. For before 1956 the liveliest debate in British theatre concerned the relative merits of two verse dramatists: T. S. Eliot (1888–1965) and Christopher Fry (b. 1907).

That verse drama—poetry *in* the theatre rather than poetry *of* the theatre—proved a red herring comes now as no surprise. John Russell Taylor dismisses it as modish and parochial, and even Denis Donoghue, in *The Third Voice* (1959), a book about verse drama, concedes that the poetry is not necessarily or solely a verbal construct: it inheres in the structure of the play as a whole. The battle between dramatist and producer is a constant one but when the dramatist is a poet the conflict seems to be intensified. Gordon Craig, for example, allowed the poet no right to be in the theatre at all, while others, like Arthur Symons, insist that prose cannot possibly portray the obscure imageries of the inner life. But neither can verse fulfil domestic tasks. Most exponents of verse drama were, like Eliot, poets first and dramatists later, and few were able to follow Lady Gregory's advice and make the poetry serve the theatre. Rather theatre was to serve the poet and the result was minority drama, like Yeats's, or religious drama. Thus *Murder in the Cathedral* (1935) could be successful because it was a Festival play watched by a congregation. Eliot wanted to avoid the more obvious effects of writing in verse: poetry was a medium to look through not at. But as a poet he naturally assumed that poetry of the theatre would be gained through the use of verse. He also seems to have persuaded himself that the problem could be solved if only the right verse form could be found. Eliot was more fortunate than many poets, since his poetry was exceptionally dramatic and made use of domestic words, but his use of myth as a means of giving echoes to his plays was only moderately successful. Often audiences must have felt tricked rather than surprised into an awareness of Christianity, and many missed the point altogether. Eliot's verse grows more and more prosaic, and his plays less theatrical.

Fry, on the other hand, came to verse drama as an actor and producer. He chose verse for his celebration of life. Donoghue dismisses him as the writer of precious comedies which say very little, and, certainly, the celebration of life is not a theme capable of much development. Fry unashamedly made poetry the reason for his plays and the delight soon palls. But delight there was and *The Lady's Not for Burning* (1948) was as relevant to its time as *Look Back in Anger* was to 1956. Fry intended to produce a comedy of seasons—each play matching scene, character, and mood to a season—a project only completed in 1970 with his summer comedy. As this is a limited source of drama, it is not perhaps surprising that Fry turned to writing film scripts. But it is equally true that, as he says, the appeal of the inarticulate and the pleasure of hearing the speech of the streets is not the whole duty of man as far as language is concerned. The colour and richness of his verse were, unfortunately, obviously decorative and not married to strong situations. Even had Fry managed this, the restoration of verse to a central place as the medium of drama is far from being possible or even desirable. When Eliot noted effects gained by Ibsen and Chekhov in prose he put them down to luck or momentary success and overlooked the amazing and far from fully-tried possibilities of prose. Nevertheless, the verse dramatists not only served the heroic actors well, but also invited people to think about the way plays were written; and Eliot at least also suggested that the theatre could be used to say something important. The absence of new dramatists whose plays were relevant to the situation in postwar Britain rather than continuing to portray the memory of pre-war Britain was beginning to be felt. An audience was growing up for whom beauty and nostalgia were inappropriate, who found a cocktail party an inadequate catalyst for drama in a world that had come to terms with a new social structure, and faced the problems of the Cold War and the Atom Bomb.

There was one important new British dramatist: John Whiting (1915–63). It is difficult to believe that *Saint's Day* was written in 1947, two years after Hiroshima, when audiences were flocking to see *Bless the Bride* and *Annie Get Your Gun*. *Saint's Day* asks questions about destruction, self-destruction, the place of the artist in society, and the uses of compassion and wisdom that comes too late. *Saint's Day*, then, is a play of ideas, but it started in Whiting's imagination with the recollection of a mural painted in a derelict house, and this image is the strongest impression of the play, aided by witty language, symbolic objects, and suggestive proper names. These give the play what Whiting called a 'density of texture'. In *Marching Song* (1954) Whiting produced his own austere version of the form which Shaw took from Chekhov in *Heartbreak House* (and which reappears in Osborne's *West of Suez*), but Whiting's play takes place in a timeless world where what a man does makes him what he is. Thus *Marching Song* is one of the finest existentialist plays in English, without, of course, the political direction Sartre would have included.

Apart from starting to write almost a decade too soon, Whiting was unfortunate in his relations with the theatre. Although *Saint's Day* won a prize, it was hardly Festival of Britain material; all his plays were dogged with ill-luck, including his very funny comedy, *A Penny for a Song* (1949). He was persuaded to return to the theatre in 1960 and wrote *The Devils*, in which the hero, Grandier, provided another example of self-destruction, but the result was not entirely satisfactory. Like Miller, Whiting concentrated on private suffering. Soon the New Wave would be tackling these very themes of doubt, despair, and failure, but in terms of personal relationships. Whiting's central character is always a man who cannot or will not respond to emotional or social commitment. He gains in honesty thereby, but he also reminds us of Meursault in Camus's *L'Étranger*: he is distant from us. Moreover the New Wave could not accept Whiting's absolutes. For Whiting life is tragic and the only response is heroic nihilism. But he produced remarkably articulate characters who were required to handle long speeches and complex imagery, making great demands on the audience. British audiences had not yet been trained to listen to something difficult and important. Thus Whiting illustrated the need for a theatre where new dramatists could develop unrestricted by box-office pressures; he also suggested that intensity could be achieved in prose rather than verse.

## II

Looking back at the theatre before 1956 Kenneth Tynan remarked that to be worthy of serious dramatic treatment a character had to have an income of £3,000 net or be murdered in the house of someone who had. With few exceptions this was true. But during the summer of 1955 Peter Hall produced a play by an Irishman exiled in France. *Waiting for Godot* (1953) puzzled everyone (including the actors) but fortunately struck a chord, became a fashion, and was followed by plays from Ionesco and Genet. In 1956 the Berliner Ensemble visited England to confirm rumours that a Marxist poet called Brecht was doing exciting things in East Germany. With the arrival of Beckett and Brecht things began to change and two labels gained currency: Theatre of the Absurd and Committed Theatre. Later Committed Theatre was rather loosely called Angry Theatre, but in fact both kinds of theatre were angry, not least with the state of theatre. The influences worked slowly but surely. Fortunately new dramatists had at their disposal a new institution called the English Stage Society, resident at the Royal Court Theatre. Under George Devine the idea was to run a writers' theatre in opposition to the commercial theatre—with the right to fail. The Court opened on 2 April 1956—the year of Hungary and Suez—with Angus Wilson's play *The Mulberry Bush*; but it was the third production, a new play called *Look Back in Anger*, which caught the mood of the moment and ushered in the new breed of actor suited to this kind of theatre. Subsequently the Royal Court supported three major dramatists, all thought of as committed: Osborne, Wesker, and Arden.

*Look Back in Anger* was not the first play by John Osborne (b. 1929) but it was his first success. Its initial impact was probably more a matter for the sociologist than the drama critic, but its permanence is assured because it is more than a topical play. It is the first example of Osborne's intention to give people 'lessons in feeling', letting them think afterwards. Osborne is not a reformer like Shaw, using argument, but he is like Shaw in that he requires operatic-type actors with strong voices and stamina—even if the accents were to be less posh. The size of these roles is heroic, since the plays are virtually monologues. But *Look Back in Anger* is not a committed play in a political sense. The lament about causes is there to concentrate our attention on Jimmy, the suffering hero. The only person he is not allowed to meet is Alison's father, the Colonel, who is presented sympathetically. Thus, although the national failure required a political solution (socialism), the play is primarily about personal failure, and in sexual terms. This incapacity is supposed to expand into a general national incapacity, but this does not always work, here or in later plays. This is because the hero keeps our interest and from Jimmy Porter onwards Osborne seems unable to make up his mind about his heroes. Is Jimmy the product of his times or naturally mediocre? Very early, A. E. Dyson reminded admirers of Jimmy that he is not just a warm-hearted idealist. He is also a monster, a morbid, cruel misfit let loose on a group of kindly, well-disposed people. He is Hamlet in a domestic setting and therefore complex, interesting, but not necessarily likeable. The ending of the play captures this ambiguity well: is it happy or does the retreat into nursery games suggest a final failure to grow up into adulthood?

This ambivalence, emphasized by the sympathetic portrayal of the Colonel, sets the pattern for most of Osborne's plays. *The Entertainer* (1957) may solve the formal problem, since Archie's work is talking to audiences, and the theatre is useful as an emblem of the national condition. In Archie's father, a genuine entertainer, we see the nostalgia for those confident Edwardian times when, if mistakes were made (and the present mess suggests they were), they were made with panache: at least, then, people were not dead behind the eyes. The failure of *The World of Paul Slickey* (1959) showed that Osborne's strength was less in topical satire and more in the creation of unhappy monsters. He turned to history, for example, in *Luther* (1961), but it is the private rebel who is convincing, not the international consequences. Osborne followed Luther with Maitland, Redl, and a hero borrowed from Lope de Vega, all ambiguously presented in plays that are, again, very nearly monologues. His most recent plays—for a mean time—show a shift. *Time Present* (1968) has a heroine rather than a hero, which led many critics to confuse anger with bitchiness, but this may have been because Pamela attacks things still fashionable at the Court. She opposes the mindlessness of the young with the memory of her father and a passion for drinking champagne, so that it seemed as if the angry young man had indeed turned into a middle-aged Tory. But this work is still a play of feeling, and Pamela reminds us several times to listen to the way a thing is said as much as what is said. The same rule applies in *Hotel in Amsterdam*. Both plays concentrate on talk at the expense of action, a direction confirmed in *West of Suez* (1971). It is the literary quality of this talk which counts in the theatre. In Shaw the argument is important, in Osborne the spell of the talker, and this probably explains the attractiveness of Osborne's plays to actors and producers. True, his usual hero is contemporary, shabby, and a failure, but he is immensely articulate. And no one listens to him, making Osborne's plays personal tragedies, not ideological documents.

It would be over-simple, too, to describe Arnold Wesker (b. 1932) as a man who writes political plays. The didacticism is obvious, but his plays are personal in the sense that they resemble their author intimately. As with Osborne, we are apt to confuse the dramatist with his heroes. Wesker has a clear-cut political point of view, a reputation for naturalistic detail, and has put a great deal of working-class material on the stage. When this has been said, qualifications have to be made. His Jewishness, for example, is a matter of recognizing the brutishness of life and asking how the masses can be made more human. His answer is socialism not because it will solve problems but because it will clear away difficulties (for example, economic), leaving people free to face the complex problem of being fully human. Wesker's answer, finally, is educational rather than political. *The Kitchen* (1956) shows the working world in the metaphor of a kitchen, suggesting that people go berserk if cooped up. Wesker intended to work in films, but *Look Back in Anger* convinced him that serious things could now be said in the theatre, and he began a trilogy on three kinds of socialism. *Chicken Soup with Barley* (1958) is a sprawling epic-type play documenting the ups and downs of a Communist Jewish London family whose personal disillusionments reflect problems on the national level. At the end only the mother, Sarah, manages to preserve her revolutionary ideals, but not her family. Against the problem of Hungary she can only offer a personal warning on the dangers of apathy. *Roots* (1959) tackled the problem of mass culture through the education of Beatie Bryant, but, again, it is only when Beatie *suffers* that she becomes articulate. The third play, *I'm Talking About Jerusalem* (1960), by its title, suggested parable and at least shifted the discussion from those confusions about naturalism which had preoccupied critics and audiences. But Jerusalem is not built, and the play ends once more on a personal cry from Ronnie that anyone who cares must be a bloody fool. *Chips with Everything* (1962) took the training of recruits in the R.A.F. as a metaphor of society and, as in *The Kitchen*, the metaphor does not quite work. The play showed a movement on Wesker's part from words to actions but suffered from the implication that chips must be replaced by sautée potatoes. But, as Wesker pointed out, he was attacking a state of mind not an institution. He wanted people educated into choosing—chips if they wanted them—rather than accepting.

While in prison in 1961 Wesker decided to commit himself wholeheartedly to the cultural experiment of Centre 42. It was not a successful venture and Wesker's disappointment, particularly with the lack of response from the trade unions, produced three plays:

*Their Very Own and Golden City* (1965), *Four Seasons* (1965), and *The Friends* (1970). The first carried on the theme of *Chips*, the relationship of the rebel to society, and, although Andy is not as completely corrupted as Pip and does get one city built, the savour of compromise is bitter. *Four Seasons* was an interlude, concentrating on the male–female relationships which have always been central to Wesker's plays, if secondary to the ideas. It is a play to remind us that art essentially should show people that they are part of humanity and, even in private pain, share an experience common to us all. Although the most interestings things in the play are non-verbal (e.g. the making of the strudel), Wesker is clearly striving for verbal music. It is a pity that he frequently shows up as poetaster rather than poet. This exploration of a human relationship following the explorations of a rebel and society leads to *The Friends*, produced at the Roundhouse in 1970. Wesker said that he wanted to write it like a symphony and insisted on producing it himself. In fact, chamber music would probably be a better description for this revaluation forced upon a group of people by the untimely death of their leader. In this discussion, all the themes that have preoccupied Wesker are brought together: rebellion, revolution, art, the past, tradition, human relationships, and the value of words themselves in discussing such things.

No one has been better able to show what is and what ought to be simultaneously than Wesker. He does so through unusual people who are made to suffer. Wesker believes that optimism is not happy endings, but facing the truth even when that truth is sad. Facing the truth has meant compromise and ambivalence in his plays; it has also made them plays of feeling rather than didacticism, which brings him close to Osborne. It also sets Wesker in marked contrast with Arden where ambivalence strikes a note of coldness. John Arden (b. 1930) makes no secret of his personal angers but he writes plays that are austerely impersonal. His characters are representative, and his plots create conflict between groups in society. He reflects the national condition in a particular situation—an isolated town—observed with an accurate eye but written with a strong historical sense, 'to translate', as he says, 'the concrete life of today into terms of poetry that shall at one time illustrate that life and set it within the historical and legendary tradition of our culture'.

The Court has supported Arden loyally although his plays have met with apathy and hostility from critics and audiences. In view of his neutrality this is not hard to understand. His plays suggest as many moral values as there are individuals, and the audience that is forbidden to participate and then guided into neither agreement or disagreement will be puzzled and probably bored. Arden of all British dramatists resembles Brecht, and more intimately than just using devices borrowed from Brecht. Yet it is Brecht the technician and not Brecht the Marxist that Arden resembles. He invites us to watch and judge a play, but that play is not worked out on an ideological level. Arden sees politics as the art of living together and therefore everything about life is political and must concern us, even if the actual business of politics is for professionals. His second play, *Live Like Pigs*, staged at the Court in 1958, concerns the introduction of a gypsy family on to a northern housing estate. For Arden, the gypsies represent vitality, but are an anachronism while their antagonists, the Jacksons, are decent but dead. This kind of opposition—lively anarchy versus decent deadness—is the mainspring of much of his subsequent writing.

In his most popular play, *Serjeant Musgrave's Dance* (1959), Arden abandoned naturalism in favour of epic poetry. Here the theme of violence and how it should be met is treated in the form of a political ballad. Arden, an admirer of Fry, has taken over the ballad as a popular art form suitable for the kind of treatment he wants: it historicizes and universalizes but leaves the situation particular. In *Serjeant Musgrave's Dance*, the clash between violence and pacifism (his own choice), between principle and expediency, which fascinated Wesker, is examined in detail. During 1959–60 Arden, as playwrighting Fellow at Bristol, wrote *The Happy Haven*, a play probably conditioned by the special circumstances which produced it, but he returned to his basic theme of good government in a Nativity play which looked at matters from the point of view of Herod. He later, in *Left-Handed Liberty* (1965), turned King John into the lively hero of a play about the signing of Magna Carta. But he was also working on a translation of Goethe which reminded him of the epic scope of some plays, another echo of Brecht. This epic scope is first seen in his comedy of local government *The Workhouse Donkey* (1963). Here the conflict is, once more, between an unscrupulous anachronism Butterthwaite and a moral, upright man, Feng. In the end both lose, leaving the system to lesser men, a conclusion that anticipated Arden's most ambitious ballad play, *Armstrong's Last Goodnight* (1964). Arden fused a contemporary situation in the Congo with an incident in Scottish history, opposing the robber baron Armstrong (anarchy) to the civilized but devious Lindsay (order): at the end both men are guilty of treachery to their own codes and it is the little king who wins. This seems to be an end to Arden's work, and it is pessimistic. He has written no major work since, but collaborated with his wife, happily, on community drama.

The final impression of his work is that whereas absolutes are wrong, compromise is a betrayal. The method of the plays confers on this moral a strangeness appropriate to a view of the world as senseless, absurd. But Arden differs from Absurd dramatists because his world is always rooted in the real and his vision is never subjective. His characters represent social groups and their failure or success is a comment on the state of society. Moreover, unlike Absurd dramatists, Arden must have a great deal of plot to produce that network of social interrelationships necessary to his aims. These remain obvious but obscure since he curtails sympathy and refuses guidance. Brilliant as a technician, compelling in his language, characterization, and use of incident, he remains unpopular. To empathy and alienation he adds ambivalence as a theatrical device; and he is the most prominent poetic dramatist of the sixties.

These were fertile years. In any period less rich in dramatic talents there would be space and reason to write about or mention the particular qualities of such dramatists as Behan, Bolt, Cannan, Campton, Delaney, Exton, Gray, Howarth, Hopkins, Helliwell, Jellicoe, Kops, Livings, Marcus, Mortimer, Owen, Orton, Rudkin, Shaffer (Peter and Anthony), Saunders, Simpson, and Wood. But there seemed to be no obvious second wave.* After Devine's retirement in 1965 the Court was run by William Gaskill, later with Anthony Page and Lindsay Anderson, and it once more supported dramatists with talents such as Bond and Storey. Edward Bond (b. 1935) is popularly remembered for the controversy over *Saved* and the stoning of an invisible baby, battles with the Lord Chamberlain, and his later play *Early Morning*, which had such features as cannibalism and a Queen Victoria with a Lesbian crush on Florence Nightingale disguised as John Brown. All Bond's work illustrates his view that man is corrupted by his environment and education, through social abstractions like order, morality, and the law. These frustrate personal freedom and lead to violent reactions. He denies that there is such a thing as instinctual evil, but cannot suggest how evil originated without it, a view of human nature that seems faulty. He intends us to follow the dilemma of right action through the heroes of *Saved* (1965), *Early Morning* (1968), and *Narrow Road to the Deep North* (1969). In the last the Japanese setting is a Brechtian device to show familiar problems in a different light. The dialogue is economical to the point of being sparse, but the play ignores too

* John Russell Taylor has found it: see *The Second Wave* (1971).

many crucial points. If Basho had picked up the baby then the action of the play would probably not have taken place; but then Basho would not have been a poet. When Bond says that we should behave like animals because they have good manners he concedes that they do not write plays! He also appears to be muddled morally. When he writes that the stoning of a baby is as nothing compared with the atrocities of our time we can agree, but the worst that Bond can find as an atrocity in our time is the strategic bombing of German towns. *Lear* (1971)—Bond's version of *King Lear*—confirms his over-simple view of life and politics; the presentation of consistent evil becomes monotonous and, since no lessons are learned, an audience has the right to feel that the artist is not fulfilling his responsibility.

By comparison David Storey (b. 1933) seems old-fashioned in every sense. His plays began to be known after he worked with Lindsay Anderson on the film version of *This Sporting Life* (1960), and Anderson has since directed these plays at the Court. If *The Restoration of Arnold Middleton* (1966) leaves the impression of not fully justifying itself, *In Celebration* (1969) was accused of explaining itself too fully. This play examines love and hate in a family gathered to celebrate a fortieth wedding anniversary. The same technique of gathering people together occurred in the next play, *The Contractor* (1970), during which a tent is put up and taken down. They are good theatrical plays with a nice blend of action and dialogue, and in two —in the characters of Arnold and Steven—madness picks up the theme of Storey's novel *Radcliffe* (1963) as the high price to be paid for detachment. *Home* (1970) continued this theme. Four characters sit and talk at a little white table. Gaping silences, non-communicating dialogue, little action—such methods collect together the themes of roots, home, and insanity: for these losers in life home is an asylum. Storey also shows how a good dramatist needs brilliant production and brilliant acting, and all three come together once more in *The Changing Room* (1971), which again exhibits Storey's gift for blending a little dialogue and mundane action into something highly evocative and poetic.

## III

Such writers have, in their own ways, exhibited the power of language as part of the theatrical occasion. They are committed in the British sense because they are concerned with social anguish, personal failure, and the possibility of an alternative. A dramatic alternative is metaphysical anguish, or the Theatre of the Absurd. This is defined by John Russell Taylor as a group of dramatists who share an attitude to man's predicament, who explore an awareness of the purposelessness of life and the anguish such awareness brings. It is now generally agreed that this kind of theatre enjoyed a brief vogue and that its force was spent by 1963. If it passed quickly it nevertheless caught the mood of its moment as much as *Look Back in Anger*. Martin Esslin has traced its distinguished antecedents flamboyantly in *The Theatre of the Absurd* (1961), where he remarks that it has never before enjoyed so wide a reception. The plays are blatantly theatrical, but the principles of writing are self-limiting: the absence of character and plot and a mistrust of language leave such a dramatist with limited means. Trapped in his own philosophy, he ultimately has to succumb to the irresistible conclusion that writing plays is absurd. Precursors are *Ubu Roi* (1896), the Diaghilev ballet, Apollinaire's *Les Mamelles de Tirésias* (1917), and Cocteau's *Les Mariés de la Tour Eiffel* (1921), all of which suggested anarchy but more significantly, theatricalism: the battle against Sire Le Mot. The prophet of Absurdity should be Artaud who reminded a wordy French theatre that the stage is a space to be filled, and not with yesterday's masterpieces. Artaud compared theatre to the plague (when all inhibitions vanish) and saw it as the double of life not its imitation. He wanted his audience to be surrounded by actions, lights, music, colour, gestures, and, occasionally, words. Absurd dramatists, in spite of their mistrust of language, differ from this concept of theatre by writing carefully constructed plays, using language and usually set behind a proscenium arch. It was for another kind of theatre to exploit Artaud. Although short-lived, Absurd Theatre was a lively and liberating force and if, as critics alleged, it suggested that you could be profound for the price of a theatre ticket, then this is no different from the suggestion that you can be committed for the same price.

Ionesco's *The Bald Prima Donna* (1950) was the first well-known play of this kind of theatre and Ionesco has emerged as its spokesman. For most people, however, Absurd Theatre is Beckett's *Waiting for Godot* (1953). Samuel Beckett (b. 1906) is most important as a writer of prose, following the maxim that there is nothing to express, nothing with which to express, no power to express, no desire to express, and the obligation to express. His tragi-comedy is a two-act play in which nothing happens twice. On a lonely roadside two tramps pass the time in chatter. They are visited by a man and his servant and finally by a boy who tells them that Godot will not come that evening. Act Two repeats this with differences that emphasize the sameness. The play is rich in echoes, particularly in its English version where the title contains the word God. The dialogue reminds us of music-hall clowns. And the play offers hope although this may be only a linguistic illusion or what Sartre calls Bad Faith. Since then Beckett's plays have diminished in size and scope, eliminating movement and any possibility of faith, good or bad. *Fin de Partie* (1956) contained the possible vision of a young boy seen through the window at the end of the world, but *Happy Days* (1961) has its central character buried in a mound, while *Play* (1963) puts all three characters in urns. Nameless, these three characters are denied action, movement, facial gesture, and vocal inflection, and the second act is a repeat of the first. More recently Beckett has diminished to a 25-second lighting scheme as in the prologue to *Oh! Calcutta!* Beckett has shown considerable ingenuity in using devices—such as tape-recorders and cameras—to capture lost times and contain his silences. He strives to find meaning in a world subject to incessant change, and he does this through language—a limited means of arriving at or expressing truth. Yet his heroes champion the belief that a meaningless world must have meaning. Beckett portrays, whether with admiration or disgust is not clear, not nihilism but people unable to face up to nihilism.

Beckett is part of the French theatre, and metaphysical anguish does not come easy to the British temperament. The influence of Beckett could, perhaps, be traced in the work of Pinter. Harold Pinter (b. 1930) is, like Beckett, remarkable for his use of silence, but unlike Beckett, Pinter's dialogue exploits the vernacular and his plays are rooted in very real situations. Pinter rejects the idea of purposeful dialogue while he constructs it. Silence is an evasion, and there are two kinds of silence: one when no words are used, the second when a torrent of words is used. Each is a stratagem to cover nakedness and protect the room. From his first play, *The Room* (1957), Pinter used the basic image of his early work: the intrusion into a stuffy but safe room of an outsider. His plays were rightly called Comedies of Menace: the menace was there but so also was comedy. His first full-length play, *The Birthday Party* (1958), if badly received, is an early example of the comfortable title that belies its play. Pinter's exploration of intruders ended with *The Caretaker* (1960), the play which brought him success. It also marked the end of rooms, or rather an opening out into bigger rooms and further facets of his basic question. For the use of silence and the protection of rooms are stratagems to keep the self from being known. Heroes who insist on knowing or give themselves away go mad. The question has always been: Where is home? and it is closely followed by the question: Who are you? The idea of answering such questions is now explored through husband and wife who, we should expect, would be better acquainted with one another than most. But in *The Collection* (1961) the husband is disturbed to find that in marrying a woman he has taken on a collection of women: mistress, whore, wife, and mother—a theme Pinter continues with until *The Homecoming* (1965). Pinter has done a great deal of film work, and some producing, and his writing for the theatre has grown less and less. It has also grown more like his first love, poetry, which puzzled many in plays like *A Slight Ache* (1959) and *The Dwarfs* (1960). If the careful use of language is a mark of power it now emerges as a means to lyricism, nostalgia, and a Beckett-like struggle to recapture time past. *Landscape*, *Silence*, and, finally, *Old Times* (1971) all show this, and Beckett's brevity. Pinter looks most metaphysical in his latest work, and elegiac, like Osborne and Wesker. Many find his vision of the world limited, although he has always moved on when the image has been fully explored. Opposing his sense of craft is instinct, opposing his fantasy is common sense: the balance ensures that he will not fade away into metaphysics.

Pinter has had his imitators, and probably the most popular of these is Tom Stoppard (b. 1932). But although Stoppard has borrowed the trappings of the Absurd he has no instincts. His plays are philosophical, intellectual, and derivative. His popularity seems to rest on the fact that he produces an Absurd drama in which everything has been worked out: as one critic pithily said—Beckett without tears.

If Absurd Theatre does not suit the English temperament neither is it congenial to the American spirit, although Martin Esslin has claimed the American dramatist Edward Albee (b. 1928) for Absurd Theatre. Certainly *The Zoo Story* (1960) was performed with *Krapp's Last Tape*; certainly, too, Albee is fascinated with disillusioned man in a decaying world, but he rejects pessimism. *The Zoo Story* attacked the sterility of American life but the sacrifice at the end, with its echoes of the Crucifixion, was intended to suggest meaningfulness. Moreover, unlike his European peers who think highly of being solitary, for Albee it is an escape route, not the way to reality. *The Sandbox*, *The Death of Bessie Smith*, and *The American Dream* (all 1960) probe sterility and the meaninglessness of human relationships, and in the final play Albee exposes the heartlessness beneath the comfortable family image, devoted to security and wealth.

*Who's Afraid of Virginia Woolf* (1962) is probably Albee's only popular success. Its central characters are called George and Martha, which suggests an American subject, but this Strindbergian comedy set in New England has a more universal significance and is not limited to a look at the American Dream. George and Martha 'entertain' a young couple and as the night proceeds reveal the inadequacies of their childless marriage, a mistake the young couple are beginning to make. The play moves towards an exorcism of the illusions behind which all four have sheltered so that, at the end, the young couple may have a child, and George and Martha are left to face the future, fearfully, unprotected by their illusions. Audiences in 1962 were ready for and responsive to the games, dialogue, and undercurrents, and the sheer vitality of George and Martha, but they were unprepared for *Tiny Alice* (1964). Albee has said that its meaning is clear but it seems to have escaped most people (including Gielgud who played Julian); indeed, audiences and critics have divided, regarding the play as either therapy for Albee or a confidence trick. Certainly the play is bewildering in the number of 'realities' it offers, and Albee has given way to the same tendency as Tennessee Williams and littered the stage with significant objects, including the famous model of the castle with Miss Alice inside it, inside which is, presumably, a model of the castle with Miss Alice in it *ad infinitum*. The social aspects in Albee have become metaphysically suggestive. Julian is described by the butler (who is called Butler) as walking on the edge of an abyss, but balancing, an idea that leads to Albee's next play, *A Delicate Balance* (1966). This play seemed to mark a return, at least, to ordinary life and the drawing-room, although this drawing-room was redolent of T. S. Eliot. The plot rests, too, on a nameless terror which drives two friends to invade the drawing-room and threaten the delicate balance. Once more Albee is probing middle-class security to expose greed and hypocrisy; but the play is muddled and fails to create those large, vital monsters who had made *Virginia Woolf* so successfully theatrical. Like the Absurdists, Albee is troubled with the condition of man and the condition of the art which reflects man, but unlike them he seems to see possible reforms, causes for hope, and his allegories refuse to move to complete despair. In his most recent work, *Box-Mao-Box* (1968), he moves further away from monstrous characters, trying to replace linear narrative with something abstract and musical. It offers no clue to the continuing identity of Albee the dramatist, but he has made his mark. His plays are all on the edge of an abyss, and sometimes it seems as if the balance has been maintained too delicately, if at all, for theatrical purposes.

## IV

Such dramatists, whether Committed or Absurd, write plays which indicate to the producer and actor what must be done; they give little liberty to a producer as a creative artist in his own right. Such producers turned, therefore, to Brecht rather than Beckett, for revolution has always taken place in the theatre rather than in drama. The theatre was obviously changing. The challenge of the cinema gave way to the more serious challenge of television, and such challenges are as much to writers and actors as to audiences. Any writer or actor can reach a wider audience (and earn more money) by working for television or in the cinema. We easily forget the dramatic growth of television. As late as 1953, many people watched the Coronation ceremony in bars and hotels. Television audiences are supposed to be uncritical; writers for the medium have to work within slot time and produce frequently. But television certainly helped Pinter and it has produced competent writers like Exton, Plater, Owen, Mortimer, and John Hopkins who have transferred to the theatre. The emergence of a really important dramatist from television has, however, been rarer than logically it could be. The work of David Mercer (b. 1928) straddles all media and is more than usually powerful. As a political writer he follows the British trend of moving from politics to a personal situation which reflects those politics. Mercer began with a trilogy of television plays called *The Generations*. The second play dealt with nuclear disarmament but in the third, *The Birth of a Private Man* (1963), Mercer moved from social realism and political problems to his own personal theme of alienation: characters trying to be private men—treated in a series of plays including his first stage success, *Ride a Cock Horse* (1965). These plays reflect his own experience of mental illness and his development from old-fashioned liberalism through Marxism to being a communist without a party. When he wrote his first plays he was committed, and felt strongly about things like C.N.D., but in *The Birth of a Private Man* he became interested in one character, a disillusioned idealist, Colin, who goes mad trying to escape from his social situation. Mercer has been much influenced by the work of R. D. Laing, who suggests that the definition of madness may be too finely drawn. Mercer turned to the gorilla in *A Suitable Case for Treatment* (filmed as *Morgan*) (1962) because the gorilla rarely uses its great strength in aggression. Mercer's most recent work for television is another trilogy concerning the doubts that assail a left-wing novelist, the fate of his friend tortured first by the Nazis and then by the Communists, and his mistress, left alone after the novelist's death. The bitter-sweet scent of disillusionment continues in *After Haggerty* (1970), although tempered and intensified by rich comic invention. Mercer's main theme is that neurosis may be a creative way of revealing personality and madness the consequence of a person struggling to act consistently with himself as personal and social relationships break down. As with Storey, madness seems to be the high price paid for such consistency.

In this kind of work the dramatist is dominant still but in television he is part, and a small part, of a team. The methods of film and television are seductive to producers and have crept into the theatre. Indeed, as early as 1956, producer-dominated theatre asserted itself when, two weeks after *Look Back in Anger*, Joan Littlewood and her Theatre Workshop produced *The Quare Fellow* at Stratford East. Littlewood's reputation was high on the Continent, but it was not until 1956 that the quality of her Workshop began to be appreciated here. As its name implies her company relied on collaboration. Littlewood herself insists that she does not believe in the supremacy of director, designer, actor, or writer, but noticeably she does believe in the supremacy of Littlewood; and in any multi-media performance someone must dominate. Her writers—Behan and Delaney, for example—seem not to have minded what she did to their scripts, but the best example of this collaboration was her production of *Oh, What a Lovely War* (1963). The dangers of the method can be seen in the abortive *Twang*. Littlewood staged the first *Mother Courage* in England in 1955, and her Workshop recalls Brecht's Ensemble in Berlin.

Brecht offered the theatre not only plays but ways of presenting them which could be influential with producers. A dramatist must write in his own voice, but the producer could use lighting, acting, design—all as part of his own overall concept of performance. Brecht's methods were, of course, a consequence of his alienation theory and have been rapidly absorbed as another convention. The relationship of an audience to theatrical illusion has puzzled writers from Aristotle onwards. Although Brecht forgot his theories whenever they were inconvenient, his basic idea was to remind the audience constantly that they were watching an action, and prevent them from identifying with particular characters. He believed that such an identification would prevent thought. It should be possible to sympathize with a character while at the same time judging that character a fool or victim of historical circumstances which no longer exist.

Catharsis, Brecht objected, may purge but it does not lead to questions. Brecht's theatre is not basically ideological because the audience must be left at the end asking questions not shouting slogans. He used methods which broke up the natural flow of the play—placards, film, songs—he wrote in episodes with no narrative connection or logical development, showed scenery as scenery, lights as, obviously, lights, and encouraged his actors to pretend they were not pretending. He recreated epic theatre to give distance and thus help the audience to make an objective judgement, and frequently chose historical subjects or rewrote well-known plays to suggest the differences between then and now. Thus, Mother Courage has only her own cunning to fall back on whereas now she could join the Communist Party.

There is alienation, of course, in Ionesco and Beckett, but the difference illustrates the basic opposition of these two kinds of theatre. In Ionesco and Beckett we can see no possibility of altering the world of the play, whereas even if we feel for Mother Courage we can also see how her situation could be altered. It was mainly Brecht, then, who influenced British theatre both at Stratford East and Stratford-upon-Avon.

The appointment of Peter Hall as director in 1960 not only enlarged the season at Stratford, it altered the kind of production to be seen there. A second branch of the Royal Shakespeare Company opened at the Aldwych and is still working there pending the completion of a new theatre in the Barbican. An experimental season at the Arts Theatre in 1962, the formation in 1963 by Peter Brook and Charles Marowitz of a small company to perform Theatre of Cruelty, and the World Theatre Season at the Aldwych organized in 1964 by Peter Daubeney and the *Sunday Telegraph* all suggest the same direction: an openness to European influences, European companies. They all suggest the same vision, too, of the world as an existential nightmare. *The Wars of the Roses*, *The Marat/Sade*, Middleton, Rudkin, Scofield's *Lear* move towards the social conscience collaboration *US*. Both Stratfords, in short, show the new domination of producer rather than actor or writer. But producers' theatre is a name to cover a multitude of activities and its rise coincides with two factors: the changing shape of the theatre and the end of censorship by the Lord Chamberlain.

Theatre changed in two ways: firstly because it can be subsidized by the Arts Council and the rate-payer, and secondly because the subsidy from the rates means local, civic theatre. The Arts Council report *The Theatre Today* (1970) confirmed the gloomy picture of the state of British theatre, and is largely out-of-date in its support of the large tour. The present trend is towards local reps, with educational programmes for children, and favouring whatever happens to be the director's idea of drama. Civic theatre is in every sense parochial, and it means that provincial audiences have little opportunity to see London productions; it also rules out opera and ballet. The idea that local theatres serve the community that pays for them depends largely on an optimistic interpretation of the words 'serve' and 'community', and the repeated insistence that theatre should be as freely available as libraries sounds beguiling but is ridiculous. The numbers using a theatre do not compare with the numbers using libraries, nor, for that matter, can there be the same resemblance between a production of *Hamlet* in Wigan and one in London as there would be between copies of the play. Some productions are expensively mounted in the provinces but this is a sure sign that a transfer to London is intended—very necessary if the actors and producer are to remain at least noticed.

Not only the kind of drama but the shape of the new theatre is in the hands of the producer. New theatres come in many shapes and sizes, but mainly small and mainly what is called adaptable. Dramatists are, naturally, much less preoccupied with the shape of the stage—as Wesker once remarked, an actor can get off and on a proscenium-arch stage as well as any other. Producers, however, see the shape of the stage as yet another device whereby the performance can be made relevant. Small theatres are, of course, linked with economic realities, declining audiences, anti-heroic acting, and audience participation. The trend is against the proscenium-arch stage which—it is said—isolates the action from the audience and divides the audience into social classes. Such theatres recall undemocratic, non-participating days and were built anyway for opera, melodrama, and heroic acting. Their size suggests that an actor might well have to project beyond the conventions of the play to remain audible and visible. But the new intimacy brings its own conventions, and does not always result in audibility or visibility. How far television training or the method acting system are responsible for the new mumble has not yet been shown. As for audience participation this seems to mean physical involvement. It is no longer assumed that imaginative participation is taking place. But audiences have their rights, too, one of which is certainly protection from assault, verbal or physical, unless it enjoys that sort of thing.

Stephen Joseph's arguments for the most extreme case of all—theatre-in-the-round—are that such a shape throws a greater responsibility on the actor, encouraging him to improvise and making the writer less important or totally submerged in the project. The battle once more is between theatricalism and Sire Le Mot. Improvisation—the latest weapon (if a very old one)—was of course illegal under the Lord Chamberlain. Ironically the battle against censorship was fought by the dramatists and came to a head with *Saved* by Edward Bond. The Royal Court was found guilty but conditionally discharged and in 1966 the House of Lords proposed a Select Committee. On 28 September 1968 the Lord Chamberlain ceased to function as dramatic censor. It had certainly been annoying for dramatists to have their plays censored when, apparently, anything could be danced or sung, and when many of the excisions were ludicrous. But the right to use four-letter words on the stage was granted just in time for the action itself to be simulated. The end of the Lord Chamberlain as censor was celebrated by the musical *Hair*, but its timid nude scene was a little sign of things to come. In *Oh! Calcutta!* Tynan planned an evening of elegant erotica, but the results were far from being either and the show has ended up appropriately at a theatre owned by Paul Raymond, the strip-king. By 1969 Equity was obliged to lay down six points to protect actors less from prosecutions than from abuses within the profession; blackmail has now been added to the hazards of acting, particularly while nudity remains such a box-office draw. The argument by necessity is circular since anything can be made necessary. Most significantly, simulated sex challenges the theory of mimesis. The alienation of Brecht or Beckett continued to insist that the action watched was an imitation of life not the real thing. Setting aside the suggestion that real sex ought to lead to real death and real love (not a novel idea), the sexual act in the male cannot be imitated. The failure or presence of an erection throws doubts on theatre as imitation. Moreover, sexuality is very single-minded; as one critic remarked, on being introduced to a naked lady it is difficult to think about her powers of conversation.

Producers' theatre, more than any other kind, because of its stated democratic intentions, faces the choice between mass consumption and discipline. Peter Brook cites three examples of living theatre: Cunningham, Grotowski, and Beckett. All three share rigorous discipline, small means, hard work, and limited audiences. They are élitist theatres, and élitist theatre runs contrary to the thinking which wants to get 'the people' back into the theatre, educate the working classes, and wean them away from the television set.

At its most extreme, producers' theatre almost ceases to be

theatre: it becomes a Happening. The Happening is the most paradoxical of all contemporary dramatic forms. Its charm and existence rest on impermanence, spontaneity, but if these qualities are to work they must take some form and that form must be determined. Alan Kaprow has described them as having no structure. Happenings should exist for a single performance and no more. Essentially theatrical, they will take place in the street, basements, or old lofts with no separation of audience and actors. There is no script and if words are used they may or may not make sense and can have only a 'brief, emergent, and sometimes detached quality'. The element of chance (not found in ordinary theatre as a basic principle) must not be taken to mean chaos, for Kaprow seems to claim that some organization arises from creators who work together—which may suggest that there is chance and chance. Happenings must be perishable. Their immediate source is Artaud and Schwitters whose theory of *Merz* was formulated in the 1920s as 'a stage event that would embrace all branches of art on one artistic unit'. This recalls Wagner's *Gesamtkunstwerk*. But Wagner, Artaud, Brecht, Littlewood, and Peter Brook did control and determine the form of the performance. The economics of Happenings are unsound, too. The idea of an audience is odious but then who pays? Some people act better than others and should, perhaps, be paid for this special talent.

Even so casual an event as a Happening claims to be is being replaced by the next stage: Actuals—in which life is lived rather than imitated and where art and the theatre would seem to disappear completely.

The difficulty with improvised theatre is that simple means lead to simple ends. Such theatre tends to be propagandist and falls back on its own clichés. Brecht's insistence that we keep awake and make judgements is surely wasted on this kind of theatre. It is also a strident, intolerant theatre which ends by preaching to the converted. In spite, then, of its declared intention to seek out the people and restore them to the theatre it finds a minority audience. Indeed theatre has probably never been so completely polarized and parochial as in 1970. The Royal Court venture, *Come Together*, illustrated this. Young theatre versus middle-aged theatre: the non-verbal, left-wing, participating theatre versus the verbal, non-political, non-participating theatre. Ironically the former expects and receives a subsidy from the hand that it bites. But however charming the theatre of Bali is, or *commedia dell'arte*, the tradition of western theatre is literary. Dramatists continue to write plays and instruct audiences and actors thereby. But the younger dramatists write of madness and despair, the older dramatists of nostalgia and bitterness. If drama is always in danger of turning into literature or spectacle, the productions of Littlewood and Brook and the plays of Wesker and Pinter remind us that poetry of the theatre is still achieved out of the tension between the two extremes: *montrer pur* and *parler pur*.

## FOR FURTHER READING

The two central books are, obviously, John Russell Taylor's *Anger and After* (1969) (and its sequel, *The Second Wave*, 1971) and Martin Esslin's *The Theatre of the Absurd* (New York, 1961) (and essays in *Brief Chronicles*, 1970); unfortunately *Anger and After* is not provided with a bibliography but Dr. Esslin has included a carefully arranged bibliography with *The Theatre of the Absurd*.

General works of interest on the period and the years leading up to it include Eric Bentley, *The Playwright as Thinker* (New York, 1955), *The Theatre of Commitment* (1968), and his anthology *The Theory of the Modern Stage* (1968); Herbert Blau, *The Impossible Theatre* (New York, 1965); Peter Brook, *the empty space* (1968); Robert Brustein, *The Third Theatre* (1970); John Elsom, *Theatre Outside London* (1971); J. L. Styan, *The Dark Comedy* (1968); Kenneth Tynan, *Tynan on Theatre* (1964); Raymond Williams, *Modern Tragedy* (1966) and *Drama From Ibsen to Brecht* (1968). There is a useful collection of essays edited by Travis Bogard and W. I. Oliver called *Modern Drama* (1965), and *The Encore Reader* (1965) edited by Charles Marowitz, Tom Milne, and Owen Hale recalls the events of the years 1956–63.

The drama in Europe centres mainly on French theatre which is covered in D. I. Grossvogel's *Twentieth Century French Drama* (1961), Roger Shattuck's *The Banquet Years* (1959), and L. C. Pronko's *Avant-Garde* (1962). Many of the dramatists have written about themselves as in Antonin Artaud, *The Theatre and Its Double* (New York, 1958), Bertolt Brecht, *The Messingkauf Dialogues* (1965), and Eugéne Ionesco, *Notes and Counternotes* (1964) (which includes the documents in the famous Tynan/Ionesco debate). Ronald Gray's *Brecht* (Edinburgh, 1961) still makes a useful introduction, as does R. C. Coe's *Beckett* (Edinburgh, 1964), while Coe's *Ionesco* (1971) is excellent. The two views of theatre and the consequences are now comprehensively treated in Julian H. Wulbern's *Brecht and Ionesco: Commitment in Context* (Urbana, Ill., 1971), which has a full bibliography.

Some idea of American theatre can be gathered from *The Modern American Theater*, edited by Alvin B. Kernan (Twentieth Century Views, Englewood Cliffs, N.J., 1967), and there is an excellent collection of essays on Miller in the same series edited by R. W. Corrigan and published in 1969. Dennis Welland's *Arthur Miller* (Edinburgh, 1961), written from the point of view of American Studies as much as drama, is an introduction, to which Sheila Huftel's *Arthur Miller* (1965) adds little. Signi L. Falk's *Tennessee Williams* (New York, 1961) is a useful collection of material; the only addition since is E. M. Jackson's *The Broken World of Tennessee Williams* (Madison, Wis., 1965). Two short studies of Albee have appeared: C. W. E. Bigsby has extended his work in *Confrontation and Commitment* (1967) in *Albee* (Edinburgh, 1969) and Ruby

Cohn's *Edward Albee* (Minnesota Pamphlets on American Writers, Minneapolis, Minn.) appeared in the same year.

The verse drama movement is discussed in Denis Donoghue's *The Third Voice* (Princeton, N.J., 1959) but unfortunately this book has no bibliography. D. E. Jones has written *The Plays of T. S. Eliot* (1960), but the only study of Fry is by Derek Stanford in 1951. Ronald Hayman's pamphlet, *John Whiting* (1969), is now complemented by Simon Trussler's study of this fascinating dramatist, *The Plays of John Whiting* (1972). Mr. Trussler is working on assessments of the recent major dramatists and has also published *John Osborne* (1969) and, in collaboration with Glenda Leeming, *Arnold Wesker* (1971). 1969 also saw the publication of Martin Banham's *Osborne* and Alan Carter's *John Osborne*, both published in Edinburgh. Harold U. Ribalow's *Arnold Wesker* (New York, 1965) is still useful, and Wesker himself has published a collection of essays, *Fears of Fragmentation* (1970). Pinter is covered extensively in Martin Esslin's *The Peopled Wound* (1970), but the only treatment of Arden remains Ronald Hayman's pamphlet, *John Arden* (1968).

# 15

# Literary Criticism

C. B. COX AND A. E. DYSON

## I

F. R. Leavis's journal, *Scrutiny*, died in 1953. It was replaced by F. W. Bateson's *Essays in Criticism*, from Oxford, and by *The Critical Quarterly*. *Essays in Criticism* is written by academics for academics. A major feature of literary criticism since 1945 has been the domination of university-centred writers. There are some important exceptions; major books of criticism were published by creative artists, such as T. S. Eliot or W. H. Auden. But most developments have been firmly in the control of university teachers. The effect of this on literature is difficult to assess. This is a peculiarly twentieth-century phenomenon, and has been regarded by many practising writers (such as Philip Larkin) as sinister.

*The Critical Quarterly*, edited by the authors of this chapter, was started in 1959; its avowed purpose was to counter the narrowing effect of specialist academic criticism, and to oppose certain features of the *Scrutiny* creed. In the 1930s *Scrutiny* published a series of lively, intelligent articles, in which, by and large, the critical ideas of Henry James, T. S. Eliot, and D. H. Lawrence were developed and applied, with exciting results, to the whole of English literature. After 1945 Leavis turned his attention particularly to the novel. *The Great Tradition* (1948) includes major studies of George Eliot, Henry James, and Joseph Conrad. This was followed by a full-length study of D. H. Lawrence and reassessments of Dickens. But over the years the *Scrutiny* doctrines had hardened into dogma. In the original 1932 manifesto, it was stated that *Scrutiny* 'will also publish original compositions'. In fact it published a few poems in its first issues by writers such as Ronald Bottrall, C. H. Peacock, and Selden Rodman, but soon lost heart and began to oppose, often with contempt, almost all the major creative writers of the 1930s and 1940s. A reviewer in 1940 lumped together Auden, Isherwood, Spender, Day Lewis, MacNeice, Charles Madge, and George Barker, and accused them of 'pretentiousness', 'monotonous repetition of technical tricks', and 'lack of real substance'. Contributors also attacked contemporary writers such as William Faulkner, Dylan Thomas, and

Graham Greene. The *Scrutiny* prejudice against post-1930 writing stemmed largely from a naïve conception of the history of language and the value of rural society. Leavis held that the incessant rapid changes of the Machine Age had destroyed our great cultural traditions: 'The result is breach of continuity and the uprooting of life. This last metaphor has a peculiar aptness, for what we are witnessing today is the final uprooting of the immemorial ways of life, of life rooted in the soil.' In 1933 Denys Thompson similarly argued in *Scrutiny*: 'That the power age destroyed the agricultural basis of life and thereby the best soil for a satisfactory civilization should be a generalization trite enough.' This pessimistic view of history was accompanied by the belief that words have been debased by the advertisers and the yellow press, and language has become generally devitalized. In the past, the language of peasants was supposed to have derived naturally from environment, from daily personal contact with the earth, the plants, the trees; and this vital language was seen as an essential nourishing force of great literature, in Shakespeare or in Bunyan. In our modern waste land, such contact is lost, so the chief purpose of literary criticism is to keep language alive in an admittedly alien climate by preserving the traditions of the past. In this view the vitality of language, of modern culture, depends upon contact with the great works of civilization. The evangelical purpose of the literary critic is to make his students aware of the debased quality of their own culture by revealing the riches of the past.

*The Critical Quarterly* took over the *Scrutiny* emphasis on the value of past traditions, but refused to accept its entire cultural pessimism about the present. *The Critical Quarterly* rejected the 'waste land' mentality, both in theory and in practice. From the beginning, we committed ourselves optimistically to faith in the possibility of an expanding élite, and gave an appreciable amount of space to the publication of new poets such as Philip Larkin, Ted Hughes, Thom Gunn, R. S. Thomas, and Sylvia Plath. We believe that it is worth devoting a life to presenting, teaching, and celebrating great art, both of the past and the present, and that academic criticism can be enormously beneficial to the new reading public. In contrast to *Essays in Criticism*, *The Critical Quarterly* discovered an audience among intelligent readers outside the university, particularly in the schools. The aim of our journal was to promote high standards in common educated discourse, to make literature accessible to any student with goodwill, and, in Northrop Frye's words, to prevent it from 'stagnating among groups of mutually unintelligible élites'.

## II

The philosophy of *The Critical Quarterly* has developed new emphases in recent years, but these are best discussed in relation to major conflicts in art and letters. The diversity of literary criticism since 1945 makes it difficult to fit writers into any coherent pattern of ideas. Great classics of criticism have been published, such as Erich Auerbach's *Mimesis* (1946), whose insights into western imagination and culture have profoundly influenced subsequent literary studies. The movements described by Professor Jones in Volume II of *The Twentieth-Century Mind* still attract support, and there remain active followers of F. R. Leavis and of the New Criticism. Still newer gods have arisen, particularly Northrop Frye, the Canadian critic, or the Geneva critics, whose cause has been championed by J. Hillis Miller in the States. Marxism has revived, most notably in the influence of the Hungarian Georg Lukàcs (1885–1971) and the French playwright and novelist, Jean-Paul Sartre (b. 1905). The most recent fashion is for 'structuralism', a blanket term for developments that link together anthropology, linguistics, sociology, and literary criticism.

Although too much schematization is unwise, perhaps trends from 1945 to about 1960 in Britain and America can best be summarized as a conflict between symbolism and its opponents. This debate has been conducted on the level of sophisticated theory, but its ramifications are profoundly influential on education and culture. In *Romantic Image* (1957) Frank Kermode discerns in recent criticism a quarrel between the symbolist tradition and the surviving elements of an empirical, utilitarian tradition, which depends upon common, rational discourse: 'Indeed a good deal of the best modern criticism is interesting as evidence of the oscillations and tensions in the minds of critics between the claims of the Image and the claims of ordinary discourse.' The symbolist tradition still retains great influence: 'It may be said that the strenuousness, as well as the obscurity of such modern criticism, is a direct consequence of its Symbolist inheritance. . . . What still prevails is the Symbolist conception of the work of art as aesthetic monad, as the product of a mode of cognition superior to, and different from, that of the sciences.' The 'modern' artist (and his attendant critics) believes in the autonomy of art so thoroughly indeed that he may even declare that the author's intentions and his influence on his readers are irrelevant. The 'intentional' and 'affective' fallacies have been described by W. K. Wimsatt in

*The Verbal Icon* (1954), where the case is overstated. But the symbolist arguments survive their excesses in the central insight that works of art create their own harmonies and forms of knowledge.

In the 1950s a major attack on symbolist aesthetics took place, particularly in the writings of Donald Davie, John Bayley, and Graham Hough. In Britain this critical shift accompanied a minor poetic revolution against modernism. 'Movement' poets such as Philip Larkin, Donald Davie, Anthony Thwaite, and Elizabeth Jennings reacted against the excesses of symbolism, and tried once more to employ the conventions of rational discourse. Their poetry was gathered together and edited by Robert Conquest in *New Lines* (1956).

In *Articulate Energy* (1955) Donald Davie demonstrates that language communicates in a variety of ways, but particularly through the use of orthodox syntax. He discerns two prevalent attitudes towards language. On the one hand, the writers impose order upon their material through syntax and show the way in which the conscious mind can perceive harmonious relationships between apparently disparate fields of experience. Their language is thought of as an instrument of articulation, a way of establishing relationships like the harmonies of music or the equations of algebra. The second attitude, popular among poets of the 1920s, often accompanied a loss of faith in syntax. For the symbolists and their followers, language is trustworthy only when it is broken down into units of isolated words, and abandons any attempt at large-scale, rational articulation. The poet is an isolated man, achieving sympathy with others in momentary flashes, and expressing himself in the unit of the image. In the seventeenth and eighteenth centuries, poets acted on the assumption that syntax in poetry should carry a weight of poetic meaning; in the twentieth century poets have tended to act on the opposite assumption. For them, a poem has organic form, often dependent on the structure of images, and when syntactical forms are retained they carry little weight.

Davie argues that 'systems of syntax are part of the heritable property of past civilization, and to hold firm to them is to be traditional in the best and most important sense . . . the abandonment of syntax testifies to a failure of the poet's nerve, a loss of confidence in the intelligible structure of the conscious mind, and the validity of its activity'. Eliot's theory of the objective correlative indicates a loss of faith in conceptual thought, and much subsequent analysis of poetry is grounded on the delusion that what cannot be imagined cannot be conceived. In fact, abstract language can often be more concrete, more adequate as an articulation of experience, than imagery. Coleridge himself believed that conceptual thinking outstripped thinking in images. One of Leavis's favourite examples of 'concrete' imagery is Keats's 'moss'd cottage trees'. Such imagery is by no means necessarily a more penetrating account of experience than the rational descriptive language of the philosopher.

Davie's aim is to show the inadequacy of the symbolist and post-symbolist tradition both in poetry and criticism. He makes a sharp break with critics such as Leavis, who have put great stress on the poet's need to break down 'stock responses', to get through or behind the existing conventions of the reader's mind. In contrast, Davie believes that words should be part of a sort of contract entered into tacitly by speaker and hearer, writer and reader, a *convention* which both observe. For Leavis, the poet's task is to be faithful to his unique experience, and to read his verse we must go through a period of strenuous training and rehabilitation. But Davie argues that the poet should communicate with his readers in terms of contracts to which they are accustomed: if a reader knows a poem to be an elegy or an epistle or a satire, then he is prepared to give it a certain kind of attention. Both the conventions of any particular genre and syntax itself are forms of contract which assist the poet to communicate with his reader. Words themselves are another type of contract and, if civilized communication is to be achieved, it is essential that words should keep their relation to everyday meanings, and not be transformed into a private language by the poet himself. In short, Davie requires poets to mean what they say, and to relate their poems to common experience.

Such anti-symbolist theories found a counterpart in new attitudes to drama and the novel. In the 1950s the post-symbolist criticism of Shakespeare (transforming his plays into dramatic poems dependent on patterns of imagery) was tempered by a rediscovery of A. C. Bradley and the importance of 'character'. According to this new phase, Lady Macbeth should be considered as a woman—even as a woman with children—and not just a poetic symbol of damnation. John Bayley's *The Characters of Love* (1960) and *Tolstoy and the Novel* (1966) were particularly influential: Bayley argues that a novel may properly be concerned with the real problems of living, and in 'Against a New Formalism', argues:

> Rhoda, in *The Waves*, says: 'The world is entire and I am outside of it'. The artist who is outside 'life' sees the work he is shaping, the autonomous object, as life. For Virginia Woolf, as for Henry James, a passionate

and omnivorous interest in life is laid upon them as a sacred duty. Tolstoy and Jane Austen, by contrast, are only concerned as artists with what they do as livers. As communicative or imitative artists, they are too far inside life to find it 'interesting'. In *Emma* and elsewhere, Jane Austen implied without flinching her lack of understanding of what does not concern her daily existence. In his preface to *1805*, the first unpublished version of *War and Peace*, Tolstoy said openly that he was not interested in the lives of 'merchants, peasants, theological students'. This is not a question of a writer's range: in a sense Virginia Woolf and Henry James have actually a wider range than Tolstoy and Jane Austen, as a man with binoculars can see more than a man inside his house. The art of the latter pair is not showing us something but living something for us. (*Critical Quarterly*, Spring 1968)

The most revolutionary changes in attitudes to the novel came, however, from Wayne Booth's *The Rhetoric of Fiction* (1961). This is a highly polemical book, brilliantly written, and novel criticism is never likely to be again quite as it was before. Booth's view is that fiction is not imitation, nor self-expression, but effective communication. Literature is rhetoric: 'nothing the writer does can finally be understood in isolation from his effort to make it all accessible to someone else—his peers, himself as imagined reader, his audience. The novel comes into existence *as* something communicable, and the means of communication are not shameful intrusions unless they are made with shameful ineptitude.' These views challenge the orthodoxy which derives from the critical assumptions of Henry James. James believed that 'the air of reality' is the 'supreme virtue of a novel', and that this virtue can best be obtained by suppressing the presence of an omniscient author and presenting the action as it is perceived by a created character, a 'centre of consciousness' with ordinary human limitations. The Jamesian criticism led to the view that novels have organic unity, not unlike lyric poems, each part, each character, contributing to the total vision of life, or 'image' of reality. Thus, impersonal, indirect narration was preferred to authorial intrusion: the author should not speak to readers in his own person, since this pollutes the novel's autonomous creation of a total image. The novelist must not 'tell', but 'show': everything must be dramatized at one remove or more. If Wayne Booth does not wholly dispose of these arguments, at least he makes mincemeat of naïve orthodoxies built in their name. He points out that the author *is* in control of his work, whether in overt omniscience, as by Thackeray's direct speeches to the reader, or covertly, as in James himself. Whether or not he acknowledges it, the author is revealed in all the nuances of tone, structure, and development. Since a story must be the utterance of a man speaking to men, neither audience nor author can ignore the other's existence.

In an excellent summary of Wayne Booth's arguments, David Lodge writes:

> Professor Booth demonstrates that the categories with which we are accustomed to describe narrative method—first person, third person, impersonal, omniscient—are much too crude for the job, and that it is dangerous to attribute particular aesthetic values to any of them when they are considered abstractly (i.e. dissociated from their operation in any particular work). He suggests a more delicately calibrated scale of reference, based on the axiom that all novels have an 'implied author', a creating mind to whom, ultimately, we attribute everything that we read (and who must be carefully distinguished from the actual historic man who wrote the book: the 'implied authors' of *Tom Jones* and *Amelia* are different both from each other and from the historic Henry Fielding). Sometimes this implied author narrates the story directly, either retaining his anonymity and impersonality (Hemingway's *The Killers*) or openly declaring his presence (*Tom Jones*). In the latter case, however, the implied author has dramatized his own personality—he has become a character in his own right. Sometimes the implied author appoints a narrator or narrators, who either tell their stories in the first person (*Clarissa*, *Great Expectations*) or whose stories are mediated to us in the third person (*The Ambassadors*). Narrators may be agents—participating in the events of the story—or observers; they may be self-conscious (*Tristram Shandy*) or unself-conscious (*Huckleberry Finn*). Most important of all, narrators vary infinitely in the 'distance' that separates them from the implied author, from the reader and from the other characters in the story. 'For practical criticism,' says Professor Booth, 'probably the most important of these kinds of distance is between the fallible or unreliable narrator and the implied author who carries the reader with him in judging the narrator.' (*Critical Survey*, Winter 1966)

Wayne Booth's polemic includes contentious attacks on the ambiguity of modern literature, and is not definitive, but it rescued novel criticism from the narrow confines of the more rigid forms of symbolist aesthetic.

The anti-symbolist attitudes of the 1950s are admirably represented in Graham Hough's *Image and Experience* (1960). Following Yvor Winters, the American critic, Hough attacks the experiments of Eliot, Pound, and Joyce. In his view, the poetry of Larkin and the Movement returns to the true tradition, for modernism, although it produced some great art, was moving down a *cul-de-sac*. In the twentieth century, the great tradition is represented by Hardy,

Graves, Edwin Muir, Larkin, and John Betjeman. The images used by these poets are often richly significant, but at the same time their poems offer a straightforward rational meaning. The poet no longer sees himself exclusively as an alien speaking in a special language to a few initiates. He feels himself, as the great Romantics did, as a man speaking to men.

## III

The conflict between symbolism and its opponents continues to the present day, but before proceeding to post-1960 developments we must include here three major critics, W. H. Auden (b. 1907), Frank Kermode (b. 1919), and Northrop Frye (b. 1912), whose originality is particularly difficult to fit into any general scheme. In his recent verse, Auden with gusto and wit deliberately shocks the readers who want poetry to be a substitute religion, a form of magic offering panaceas for the times. In recent years he has insisted that poetry is comparatively unimportant, only a game of knowledge. In his elegy for Louis MacNeice, he reflects sadly on the small influence his unpopular art can have in our affluent society. He does not agree with Shelley that the poet is an unacknowledged legislator; this description is more appropriate to the secret police. In his selection of prose essays, *The Dyer's Hand* (1962), he argues that in modern society the poet is 'singularly ill-equipped to understand politics or economics'; his interest is in unique individuals and personal relations, while politics and economics are concerned with the average man (with whom the poet is bored to death). He is no prophet, for as soon as he raises his voice he sounds phoney. The man of action today is a scientist: 'When I find myself in the company of scientists, I feel like a shabby curate who has strayed by mistake into a drawing-room full of dukes.'

The increased amount of light verse written by Auden in recent years, even including *graffiti*, has offered some readers further confirmation of their belief that Auden's best work was written before about 1940. According to this view, Auden's insistence on poetry as a game of knowledge is only a rational justification for his withdrawal from active engagement in post-1945 society. Many critics feel his best poems were written between 1933 and 1939, when he identified his own personal crises, the conflict between adolescent romantic heroism and fear of catastrophe, freedom and necessity, with the tensions driving Europe towards war. Such conflicts give a disturbing vitality to his verse which, after his emigration to America in

1939, he never recovered. For readers who prefer the early verse, *Another Time*, published in 1940, already marks the replacement of neurotic strain and sinister landscape by a tone of leisured, almost academic detachment.

These views seemed justified by the excessively literary poems that Auden produced in the 1940s, and although *The Sea and the Mirror* (1944) and *The Age of Anxiety* (1947) had their admirers, there was a general feeling that Auden's pilgrimage from Freud and Marx to Kierkegaard and Reinhold Niebuhr might have solved his personal problems at the cost of making him a lesser poet. The three books of short poems, *Nones* (1951), *The Shield of Achilles* (1955), and *Homage to Clio* (1960) included, however, many good poems, and *The Dyer's Hand* (1962) brought increased understanding of his new techniques—which he has continued to employ successfully in *About the House* (1966) and *City Without Walls* (1969). There is much gaiety and exuberance, even if major claims for poetry seem to have been given up.

In a postscript to the 'Elegy' for Louis MacNeice, Auden explains that serious philosophic and religious ideas underlie his light verse:

> At lucky moment we seem on the brink
> Of really saying what we think we think:
> But, even then, an honest eye should wink.

Because modern science has destroyed our faith in the naïve observations of our senses, telling us that we cannot know what the physical universe is *really* like, art can no longer be accepted in the traditional way as 'mimesis', an imitation of nature. Poetry is a series of analogies that can never be a completely adequate representation of either religious truth or 'the baffle of life'. The poet, therefore, must 'wink', must keep his readers conscious that his words are part of a game. In *The Dyer's Hand* Auden says that 'the sterility of the substitution of identity for analogy is expressed in the myth of Narcissus'. The poet must not believe that the order and beauty of his work accurately reflect himself or his world. The conversational tones in much of his later verse remind us that he is just another man talking at his ease. The poem, the game of analogies, exists between the ideal harmonies of 'that paradisal state for which we all long' and the absurdities of this poor, bare, forked creature, man.

In *Romantic Image*, Frank Kermode brilliantly analyses twentieth-century symbolism; in his subsequent writings he has developed and refined his ideas about the value of literary 'fictions'. *Romantic*

*Image* became particularly famous for its attack on T. S. Eliot's theory that a dissociation of sensibility had taken place in the seventeenth century. Kermode shows that T. E. Hulme, Yeats, and Eliot date this 'Fall' at different times, and that in fact the whole notion has no historical justification. The theory was produced by Eliot as an attempt to define what he himself was trying to achieve in verse; it should never have been used as an historical truth determining the way in which poems are analysed.

Kermode's theory of 'fictions' is elaborated in *The Sense of an Ending* (1967). It is not easy to summarize Kermode's compressed argument, with its awe-inspiring range of reference. Today, we live in a mood of end-dominated crisis, threatened by nuclear war. According to Kermode, this is not unique, but is found throughout history. He gives numerous examples. Christians expected apocalypse in A.D. 1000. When it failed to arrive, many thought the calculations were wrong, and that we should perhaps count 1,000 from the Passion rather than the Nativity. Kermode sees this pattern of crisis and apocalypse as a model that explains the nature of literary form: 'when we refuse to be dejected by disconfirmed predictions we are only asserting a permanent need to live by the pattern rather than the fact, as indeed we must.' The Victorian novel pandered to this desire by providing a last chapter, containing, as Henry James said, 'distribution at the last of prizes, pensions, husbands, wives, babies, millions, appended paragraphs, and cheerful remarks'.

Today, confronted by the vastness of the universe and by the apparent contradictions of quantum physics, how can we satisfy our hunger for significant form? Intelligent readers are sceptical of ideas of order that do not conform to their sense of reality, and so the modern experimental novels of Sartre or Robbe-Grillet break old patterns to make new adjustments to reality. But, Kermode points out, new novels have always done this, whether written by Fielding, Jane Austen, Flaubert, or Nathalie Sarraute. And even novels as revolutionary as Sartre's *La Nausée* or Burroughs's *The Naked Lunch* cannot escape from the reader's expectation of beginnings, middles, and ends, using this, through satire or irony, as they create new 'concord fictions'. Surrounded by chaos, we are 'equipped for co-existence with it only by our fictive powers'.

Kermode approves of these fictions because their form invests life with gaiety and dignity. He quotes Wallace Stevens:

> Natives of poverty, children of malheur,
> The gaiety of language is our seigneur.

In his last chapter, he describes the solitary confinement of Christopher Burney, a British agent captured in occupied France. In his deprivation, he was forced to create fictions to preserve his sanity. He invented ends convenient to himself—that he would be released by Christmas. When Christmas passed, he re-created a new end, by estimating the time needed for the Allies to accumulate the required number of tanks and landing-craft. So, in his poverty, he tried to impose his humanity on his world. Reality was transfigured by such fictions, as by an act of love. 'Down on the bedrock,' Burney writes, 'life becomes a love affair of the mind, and reality merely the eternally mysterious beloved.'

This is Kermode's image of modern man. In solitary confinement, he imposes fictions on a continually intractable reality. In Kermode's view, we need fictions to make sense of our contradictory world, but we err if we transform them into myths. In our love affair with reality, the mind may rearrange the world to suit its longing for forms, but to test its concord fictions in life may result in the Third Reich and the gas chambers. It's here that the brilliance of Kermode's argument could do with the lucidity of a Graham Hough. Can our concord fictions satisfy us as art, and not affect our behaviour? Kermode seems close to a belief in art for art's sake.

Northrop Frye's *Anatomy of Criticism* (1957) is a dazzling, irritating work, full of brilliant insights into literature, but not always satisfying in its definitions of 'myth'. His theories have been extended and developed in a number of works, but *Anatomy of Criticism* is his classic, and this has had a major influence, particularly in North America. Frye's impetus as a writer comes largely from his problems as a teacher, and the three questions about 'English' this prompts him to ask. How can a critic most usefully illuminate literature? Can what a critic knows about literature be taught coherently and rationally to others? Finally, can a study of literature also help us to understand something other than literature, and if so, is it the nature of language, or of society, or what? Michael Green has written a most useful summary of Frye's answers to these questions:

For Frye a new kind of criticism, if it *is* possible, must begin in the recognition that no discipline can try formally to reject its own subject-matter without disestablishing itself. The first requirement is a willingness to be open to the whole area of literature and to recognize its various kinds of power. For this reason, value-judgements are an unnecessary distraction: not because some writers are not felt by everyone to be greater than others, as they are, but because of what he sees (optimistically?) as the 'fact' that no amount of adverse criticism can destroy a work or prevent us finding ways of taking pleasure in it: 'literary values are not *established* by critical value-judgements. Every work of literature establishes its own value; in the past, much critical energy has been rejected or wasted in trying to reject or minimize these values. But all genuine literature, including Shakespeare, kept turning up, like the neurotic return of a ghost, to haunt and perplex the criticism that rejected it.' 'Sensible' criticism is concerned not with rejection but with 'recognition': 'it does a student little good to be told that A is better than B, especially if he prefers B at the time.' (*Critical Survey*, Summer 1968)

Many commentators, like Michael Green himself, are most unhappy about these claims. Can we really describe literature without implying a valuation? Even more contentious is Frye's rejection of the usual view that literature is an organization of an area of experience, and that therefore we must dislike certain works because we detest the author's assumptions. Frye presses to the limit Sidney's view that the poet 'nothing affirms, and therefore never lieth'. Michael Green writes:

Frye finds literature 'not a field of conflicting arguments but of interpenetrating visions' and the literary universe a place 'where no dispute can come, where everything is equally an element of a liberal education, where Bunyan and Rochester are met together and Jane Austen and the Marquis de Sade have kissed each other'. This is because 'in all literary verbal structures the final direction of meaning is inward . . . questions of fact or truth are subordinated to the primary literary aim of producing a structure of words for its own sake, and the sign-values of symbols are subordinated to their importance as a structure of interconnected motifs. Whenever we have an autonomous verbal structure of this kind, we have literature.'

Also highly controversial is Frye's concept of myth. Green writes:

This leads directly into Frye's central argument, that in literature certain themes, plots and images reappear again and again so constantly as to suggest that all books are drawing upon a limited number of fundamental 'patterns' which exist as imaginative models or 'hypotheses' to be filled out in detail by different writers in various ways. Art thus begins in a 'pure' form as a shape or structure unrelated to anything in the world 'and then works towards ordinary experience; that is, it tries to make itself as convincing and recognizable as it can'. These shapes are 'myths', and any understanding of literature must begin by recognizing how they underlie and organize all books (at school this is best done by reading thoroughly in classical and Biblical mythology). The purpose of the *Anatomy* is to show what are the 'basic' myths; what imagery is regularly associated with them; how they exist, historically, in different 'modes'; and how, ultimately, they so relate to each other as to give all literature a fundamental unity.

This concept of myth is pursued by Frye with a display of intelligence and wit which throws the reader into a bemused trance. In the end many commentators feel Frye's ideas are elusive and historically invalid; but he is a most stimulating writer to argue with, and his stress on the human value of literary myths is powerfully presented. In *The Stubborn Structure* (1970) he writes:

> But in the arts, particularly the literary arts, we become aware of many human factors relevant to them but not to science as such: emotion, value, aesthetic standards, the portrayal of objects of desire and hope and dream as realities, the explicit preference of life to death, of growth to petrifaction, of freedom to enslavement. Literature is not detached but concerned: it deals with what is there in terms of what man wants and does not want. The same sense of the relevance of concern enters into many other verbal areas, into religion (where the concern is 'ultimate', in Tillich's phrase), and a great deal of philosophy and history and political theory and psychology. . . . The humanities . . . express in their containing forms, or myths, the nature of the human involvement with the human world, which is essential to any serious man's attitude to life. As long as man lives in the world, he will need the perspective and attitude of the scientist; but to the extent that he has created the world he lives in, feels responsible for it and has a concern for its destiny, which is also his own destiny, he will need the perspective and attitude of the humanist.

## IV

Towards the end of the 1950s developments in literary criticism were profoundly affected by new styles in literature. Already before 1960 America had seen some major experiments, and these were to prove increasingly dominant. The Beats (Allen Ginsberg, Gregory Corso, Jack Kerouac, Gary Snyder, Lawrence Ferlinghetti), centred upon San Francisco, and the Black Mountain group (Charles Olson, Robert Creeley, Edward Dorn, Robert Duncan) were searching for new forms to express the American sensibility. The name 'Black Mountain' derives from Black Mountain College, in North Carolina, an institution now defunct, where several important poets came together in the early 1950s. Charles Olson (1910–70), who served as rector of the college from 1951 to 1956, published in 1950 an essay-manifesto, *Projective Verse*. Olson wanted to promote a kind of poetry which would get rid of 'the lyrical interference of the individual ego'. The Black Mountain poets were looking for a new apprehension of reality, which submits to nature, and does not indulge the subjective fantasies of the poet. Robert Duncan wrote: 'the order man may contrive or impose upon the things about him or upon his own language is trivial beside the divine order or natural order he may discover in them.' Gary Snyder has been influenced by this kind of thinking, and this explains his belief that industrial society is finished: the order of nature is to be discovered, not imposed. Places and things take great importance in this type of poetry, whose purpose is to move in the field of its recognitions, the 'open field' described in Olson's *Projective Verse.* In Britain, Charles Tomlinson's poetry is the most obviously in tune with the Black Mountain group. He too argues against the premise that the natural world is the plaything of man, and concludes that we are shaped by our surroundings. If we wish to know ourselves, then we must permit the world unobstructed entry to our senses, and we must seek to determine its 'facts'.

More sensational in its influence on British thinking was the publication of Robert Lowell's *Life Studies* (1959). In this collection of poems and prose, Lowell proclaimed the end of the 'tranquillized fifties', and showed a new determination to involve himself with the violence both of his own psyche and the outside world. Lowell had a considerable influence on the late work of Sylvia Plath, and his example started a school of 'confessional' poetry. In the poems written by Sylvia Plath just before she committed suicide, the formal patterns barely control the hysteria and terror of her private experience. For many new poets in the 1960s contemporary society seemed to reflect a kind of schizophrenia. The so-called civilized conventions still exist, the forms of reason prevail in schools and universities, but these are superficial coverings for the power of the irrational and the 'abyss'. As the Vietnam war and the Black Power movement escalated, rejection of all the accepted forms of western civilization became fashionable, and the anarchist manifestations of Dada attained a new popularity.

The sense of the inadequacy of human reason is particularly reflected in the products of neo-modern art, and this is discussed by Edward Lucie-Smith in his chapter on The Other Arts. In the 1960s, symbolist techniques were increasingly taken into new, popular areas of entertainment. In *Innovations*, a symposium on recent developments, Bernard Bergonzi tells us that what is

> most noticeable about neo-modernist art is its lack of concern with overall 'order', with goals or ends. Professor Meyer (in 'The End of the Renaissance?') describes it as 'anti-teleological'; its main function is simply to exist, to catch a perceiver's attention, and not to move in any particular direction, or manifest any ultimate purpose. 'Order', it seems, is rejected as part of an obsolescent metaphysical view of the world, and

with this rejection goes the traditional notion of the artist as someone who imposes form and order on 'life' or the raw flux of experience.

In 'The New Mutants', Leslie Fiedler particularly stresses the growing sense of the irrelevance of the past for the neo-modernist artists, and how they strive to disengage themselves from the tradition of western humanism and, in particular, from the 'cult' of reason—'that dream of Socrates, redreamed by the Renaissance and surviving all travesties down to only yesterday'. Art must be random, indeterminate, and precise communication is deemed impossible. These theories are the justification for much pop and op art, or for concrete poetry.

In a book on a similar theme, *The Truth of Poetry* (1969), Michael Hamburger examines our modern 'word scepticism', our difficulty in creating meaningful patterns of words. In his opinion, an extraordinary degree of alienation from language, even as a medium of simple communication, has become increasingly widespread in 'advanced' societies. To achieve a high level of articulation, we need a sense of confidence, order, and purpose, and these are certainly untypical today of the young.

These attitudes reflect what Martin Green has called the neo-Freudianism of many American writers in recent years. The writers he lists under this title include Norman O. Brown in *Life Against Death* (1959), Herbert Marcuse in *Eros and Civilization* (1955), Philip Rieff in *The Triumph of the Therapeutic* (1966), Susan Sontag in *Against Interpretation* (1966), and Norman Mailer in *Advertisements for Myself* (1961). Brown conducts us into that world of free associations, free speech, random thoughts, spontaneous movements, which recently has become modish in the theatre. He writes:

> The function of art is to help us find our way back to sources of pleasure that have been rendered inaccessible by the capitulation to the reality principle which we call education or maturity—in other words, to regain the lost laughter of infancy. . . . Art, if its object is to undo repressions, and if civilization is essentially repressive, is in this sense subversive of civilization.

The writers Green lumps together are different in important ways, but together they are influenced by the symbolist tradition, often preaching a withdrawal from social reality into the aesthetic aspects of behaviour, the interest in play, in the non-serious, in self-expression which is to be 'an enlargement of humanity': 'Orpheus and Narcissus, the artist figure and the figure of self-delighting, self-sufficient beauty, stand beside Dionysos, the figure of lawless, instinctual energy, in opposition to Apollo and the realm of reason and organization and morality.' Art will liberate man's sensuality, will help to produce a non-repressive civilization.

In this odd manner, post-symbolist aesthetic has been used to support the idea of a common culture and a popular art. Also of great popular influence are the eccentric writings of Marshall McLuhan (b. 1911), whose *The Gutenberg Galaxy* (1962) and *Understanding Media* (1964) argue optimistically that the triumph of electronic technology is introducing a happier state of culture, and add weight to the view that verbal forms are in decay. According to McLuhan, until the fifteenth century aural and visual models of thought continued to co-exist in relatively fruitful tension. With the invention of printing, however, a 'Fall' took place, from which western civilization has only just started to recover. As knowledge and experience came to be transmitted increasingly not by the spoken word but by its visual equivalent in inscription or manuscript, men travelled farther from the muddled, communal, and involving culture of the ear towards the sharply-defined, isolated individualism of the eye. Gradually, the linear, sequential, and segmented ordering of syllables and words on the page came to serve as a model for all thought, and western culture began to take on its characteristic individualistic, analytic, and visual form. The medium is the message.

McLuhan's optimism arises from his theory that media are extensions of some human faculty, psychic or physical—wheel extends foot, gun extends eye and teeth, radio extends mouth and ear, writing extends eye, computer extends mind, and so on. In the past, new technological development intensified only one element of the body, and so produced imbalance. During the Gutenberg era, for example, hypertrophy of the eye was the chief source of error. However, because electric technology differs from other 'media' by extending the whole nervous system rather than just one faculty, a new era of human history is about to dawn, restoring a proper, harmonious ratio to all the faculties. Instead of isolation and specialization, imposed by the printed word, we shall all become secure and contented members of a utopian global village.

These trends support those left-wing writers who wish to see the end of so-called 'divisive' high culture. In *The Society of the Poem* (1971), for example, Jonathan Raban attacks the conservative emphasis on tradition in the works of T. S. Eliot, arguing that the concept of high culture is out of touch with the living forces in art today. High culture is said to be essentially a product of aristocratic or bourgeois society. Leavis's concern for value, greatness, worth, richness, and substance reflects his meritocratic social assumptions. According to Raban, when we say an artist is great and another vulgar, we draw upon our experience as members of an economically stratified, competitive society. The value attached to originality in western culture stems from our élitist assumptions, whereas this concept is relatively unimportant in most folk art or in the culture of contemporary China. Raban is typical of left-wing sociologists in his determination to savage the 'bourgeoisie' for its old presumptions to be the repository of lofty and classless values. The implication of these arguments is that poets such as Eliot, Auden, or Larkin are no longer to be seen as superior to the 'pop' artist. The confusion of high culture with 'pop' values, so that the Beatles can be called major poets, is a characteristic of our times. In *In Bluebeard's Castle* (1971), George Steiner shows how the democratization of high culture has been brought on by a crisis of nerve in culture itself. As high culture has become increasingly the expression of despair, so the young have turned to 'pop' for life and energy. He analyses the breakdown of aristocratic and bourgeois concepts of hierarchy, and links this with a revulsion from language:

> An explicit grammar is an acceptance of order. . . . The counter-culture is perfectly aware of where to begin the job of demolition. The violent illiteracies of the graffiti, the clenched silence of the adolescent, the nonsense-cries from the stage-happening, are resolutely strategic. The insurgent and the freak-out have broken off discourse with a cultural system which they despise as a cruel, antiquated fraud.

## V

The literary tradition which is neutral and non-ideological depends on the existence of a community of good taste and reason. This obviously no longer exists. The reaction of a liberal humanist to this situation is seen in the post-1960 works of Lionel Trilling (b. 1905). He finds most academic writing devitalized: 'Of modern criticism it can be said that it has instructed us in an intelligent passivity before the beneficent aggression of literature. Attributing to literature virtually angelic powers, it has passed the word to the readers of literature that the one thing you do not do when you meet an angel is wrestle with him. . . .' In twentieth-century literature the structures of words are not intended as pyramids or triumphal arches, built only to attract admiration, but are meant to be aggressive, to transform readers' lives. 'One does not describe a quinquereme or a howitzer or a tank without estimating how much damage it can do.'

Trilling's dissatisfaction with academic traditions is brilliantly set forth in *Beyond Culture* (1966). He stands very much in the liberal tradition of Matthew Arnold, for whom a society is intellectually mature when its members are willing to judge by reason, to observe facts in a critical spirit, and to search for the law of things. These principles lie behind the traditional humanist idea of the university. Trilling describes how in the twentieth century much of our thinking has undermined this concept of civilization. Frazer's *The Golden Bough* appeared to validate the romantic absorption in the primitive imagination, and works such as Thomas Mann's *Death in Venice* or Conrad's *Heart of Darkness* acknowledged the undeniable attraction of the Savage God. The writings of Freud led, in crude popularization, to the view that civilized conventions are a form of repression, and that, in the tradition of Blake, Nietzsche, and D. H. Lawrence, the individual achieves freedom and fulfilment by liberating Dionysian energy: 'Nothing is more characteristic of modern literature than its discovery and canonization of the primal, non-ethical energies.' Like Mr. Kurtz in *Heart of Darkness*, the artist goes into the hell of the primitive soul, preferring this 'reality' to the 'bland lies' of the civilization that has 'overlaid' it.

Trilling's indictment of modern literature is that it has gravitated towards the socialization of the anti-social, the acculturation of the anti-cultural, the legitimization of the subversive. For Freud 'the pain that civilization inflicts is that of the instinctual renunciation that civilization demands, and it would seem that fewer and fewer people wish to say with Freud that the loss of instinctual gratification, emotional freedom, or love is compensated for either by the security of civilized life, or by the stern pleasures of the masculine moral character.' Norman Mailer's writings exemplify much of the new culture Trilling deplores. In *An American Dream* (1965) Rojack, the hero, chokes his wife to death in a horrifying episode. After the murder, he feels an enormous exhilaration, but nothing in the novel suggests that we should condemn him on moral grounds. *An American Dream* takes to an extreme a concept of violence implicit in much modern writing, from D. H. Lawrence to James Baldwin. For Rojack, the murder has been a kind of spiritual experience, a release of psychic energy; so, particularly in America, drug-taking, eroticism, crime, even madness itself, have become in art the forms of religious activity. In a corrupt, materialistic civilization, the artist asserts his independence by acts of violence and perversity. So, in much twentieth-century writing, the Negro or the homosexual or, more recently, the criminal or the more extreme exemplar of perversity becomes the hero, symbolizing rebellion against existing social patterns. An alarming phenomenon, in the last few years particularly, is the manner in which former liberal humanists have drifted into accepting this analysis, with only the haziest awareness—seemingly—of its total destructiveness of their own values.

In *Beyond Culture*, Trilling is particularly concerned indeed with the way this new opposing culture becomes itself a comfortable convention. He quotes Auden's saying that a real book reads us, asking us terrifying personal questions, disturbing our security. But, as he discussed modern attitudes to violence with his students, he was shocked by their self-confidence. They wallowed at ease in horrors, unruffled, unperturbed. Yeats's cries of rage and sexuality became 'a significant expression of our culture'. Lawrence's exasperation and the subversiveness of Gide became 'the alienation of modern man as exemplified by the artist'. Trilling thinks that this was not just one more example of academic pedantry, but a new characteristic in our society. In the last decade such intellectuals have increased in number and power; they are becoming a class, with imprisoning conventions of their own. This new group enjoys its alienation, accepting too uncritically, as Saul Bellow has said, its romantic estrangement from the modern world. It is now several years since Trilling wrote these essays, and in the interim this new Establishment has increasingly put its values into practice. Particularly in American universities, the subversive quality of modern thought has left behind the purlieus of art, and engaged in violent combat with its enemies. It has typically been associated with the youth cult.

In *Beyond Culture*, Trilling admits that he surprises himself when he writes that 'art does not always tell the truth or the best kind of truth and does not always point out the right way, that it can even generate falsehood and habituate us to it, and that, on frequent occasions, it might well be subject, in the interests of autonomy, to the scrutiny of the rational intellect'. Does the academic literary critic wish to prepare students to enter the area of 'alienation' prescribed by the dominating forces in contemporary art? We 'may one day have to question whether in our culture the study of literature is any longer a suitable means for developing and refining the intelligence'.

Trilling's doubts reflect a growing uncertainty among literary critics about the value of literature. The benevolent neutrality of academic writing seems an opting out from life, and the abandonment of the large claims made by Leavis has left a vacuum into which have moved disciplines such as linguistics, structural anthropology, and sociology, with their global pretensions. This process is particularly marked among some of the younger academic critics. In Malcolm Bradbury's introduction to *Contemporary Criticism* (1970), he describes a loss of confidence in literature as a social power:

> Ours is a Tocquevillean age in which the writer must be the ordinary man, and in which the individual signature on anything is in doubt; we are tempted to believe that literature must be written by societies or particular stages in the historical process, rather than by persons; and we are tempted to doubt the conviction of any species of creativity, or any discipline, that it should not be confronted on terms other than those it prescribes itself. We tend to see literature less as a force for value in society, and more as a phenomenon of it. Moreover not only do we live in an age of different values, we also live, apparently, in an age of *fewer* values; significantly held in common. As a result, literary criticism seems to have become a good deal less sure about the evaluative activity that has always been considered a part of its function, and has tended recently to proliferate description and interpretation rather than judgement.

This lack of confidence in the Arnoldian traditions has persuaded many writers to turn to Marxism for illumination concerning the relation between literature and society. Georg Lukàcs's studies of the novel examine how basic Marxist concepts can be applied in detail to past eras, how, for example, the structure of novels reveals historical forces. The most influential applications of Marxist methodology have appeared outside Britain, in Sartre's *What is Literature?* (1948), Lucien Goldmann's work on Pascal and Racine in *The Hidden God* (1955), and Roland Barthes's *Writing Degree Zero* (1963) and *Mythologies* (English trans. 1972). According to Barthes, since 1789 Western European myths have conveyed a form of thinking whereby middle-class society confirmed its prejudices, and disguised the historical phenomena of capitalist society in permanent features of nature. Barthes analyses aspects of everyday life—sport, advertising, motor-cars, the cinema—to show how the apparent surface message, whether expressed in language or images, conceals or half-conceals a secondary message tending towards the depoliticization of political reality in the interests of the *status quo*. Myth is self-delusion at all levels of society, so that the foundations of society are not questioned. The process may work in selling toothpaste or in literature or in an evangelical crusade. Barthes considers myth to be chiefly a right-wing phenomenon, for it is capitalist society which requires these deceptions. The function of the critic is to explode myth, and this programme has been eagerly adopted by many left-wing critics.

In Britain the Marxist tradition has often seemed the province of amateurs, without the serious philosophical application of a Sartre. The most important writers who have studied literature and society are Raymond Williams (b. 1921) and Richard Hoggart (b. 1918), neither of whom is a Marxist. Particularly in *Culture and Society* (1958) and *The Long Revolution* (1961), Williams makes influential reassessments of Marxism and of the difficult relation between high and common culture. Hoggart achieved fame with *The Uses of Literacy* (1957), in which he examines working-class culture and the baleful influence of the mass media. These writers stress the social sickness induced by ultra-modern big cities, and they imply, following Leavis, that older and smaller forms of social organization still maintain a style of organic life that fosters health in the individual. They are greatly influenced by sociology, and accept definitions of person, literature, and society which make any straight division between individual life and work, and the social forms within which this is available, unthinkable. They condemn the divisive society, the so-called alienation produced by bourgeois capitalism, and look forward to a reconstitution of a new community. The weakness of this neo-Marxist movement lies in its inclination towards sentimental optimism in its view of man, and, with regard to literature, its failure to produce any major British works to confirm its theories. Raymond Williams has himself written a couple of novels, but these are not very successful. His influence has depended mainly on his non-fictional writings.

These new debates in literary criticism concern the very status and continuing existence of the subject itself. The response of *The Critical Quarterly* to this new situation was the publication of the highly controversial and influential Black Papers on Education, which reasserted the value of high culture and the Arnoldian tradition. *The Critical Quarterly* began with the idea of an expanding élite, which acknowledges its duty to serve the total community. In recent years it has campaigned for the maintenance of humanist and Christian traditions. Although these are not fashionable, their influence is still considerable. The Christian faith claims T. S. Eliot, W. H. Auden, Evelyn Waugh, David Jones, Graham Greene, J. R. R. Tolkien, R. S. Thomas, and many more. T. S. Eliot's *Notes Towards a Definition of Culture* (1948) argues the case for a Christian society; *Four Quartets*, with its repeated discussions of words and poetry, has had a major influence on Christian writers such as Helen

Gardner. C. S. Lewis achieved popular fame for polemical works such as *The Screwtape Letters* (1942) and his science fiction.

Helen Gardner (b. 1908) and C. S. Lewis (1898–1963) have not only produced much valuable criticism of specific writers, but have also published works on literary theory which, if less self-consciously innovatory than much else mentioned in this chapter, are close to normal reading responses. Helen Gardner's *The Business of Criticism* (1959) remains a luminous account of the central human function of literary studies. The critic's purpose, she argues, should not be to impose canons or to create literary fashions. His function is to keep in the mind of his culture the memory of its past; for a civilization, like a person, is conscious of itself through memory, and the richer our memories, the richer we are. The voices of the past must speak to us in the present, liberating us from the narrowness of our own conventions. C. S. Lewis was a vigorous opponent of the Puritanism of the *Scrutiny* tradition, with its offer of salvation through faith in a limited number of great works of art. There was something too arrogant in the claim in the first issue of *Scrutiny* that 'there is a necessary relationship between the quality of the individual's response to art and his general fitness for a humane existence'. This was the wrong kind of élitism, insufficiently humble in its advocacy of the power of literature to civilize, and almost mechanical in its notion of cause and effect. It overlooked the obvious truth that ordinary people who are granted neither the natural gifts nor the sophisticated education required to appreciate great art often exemplify in daily living the highest moral virtues, and put to shame most of those who spend their lives in university English schools. By the same token, it overlooked the grim evidence, pointed out with such power by George Steiner, that those who appreciate art are capable of the worst villainies, often well beyond the verge of bestiality; it overlooked the reality of free will and sin.

C. S. Lewis's *An Experiment in Criticism* (1961) brilliantly argues the case for critical reading as homage to works of art which are in themselves objects of great beauty and significance; and which extend our consciousness by initiating us into the minds of other men, often greater, and certainly more articulate than we can hope to be:

> This, so far as I can see, is the specific value or good of literature considered as Logos; it admits us to experiences other than our own. They are not, any more than our personal experiences, all equally worth having. Some, as we say, 'interest' us more than others. The causes of this interest

are naturally extremely various and differ from one man to another; it may be the typical (and we say 'How true!') or the abnormal (and we say 'How strange!'); it may be the beautiful, the terrible, the awe-inspiring, the exhilarating, the pathetic, the comic, or the merely piquant. Literature gives the *entrée* to them all. Those of us who have been true readers all our life seldom fully realize the enormous extension of our being which we owe to authors. We realize it best when we talk with an unliterary friend. He may be full of goodness and good sense but he inhabits a tiny world. In it, we should be suffocated. The man who is contented to be only himself, and therefore less a self, is in prison. My own eyes are not enough for me, I will see through those of others. Reality, even seen through the eyes of many, is not enough. I will see what others have invented.

The ordered patterns created in literature have their own kinds of autonomy, but in the end they relate to reality either as a consolation for the meaninglessness of experience (Kermode) or as a pointer to divine truth (T. S. Eliot). Writers who share the latter view necessarily identify among the chief enemies of literary art those who would limit or corrupt the greatness of man by linguistic manipulation; the analyses of such techniques in Aldous Huxley's *Brave New World* (1932), George Orwell's *1984* (1949), and F. A. Hayek's *The Road to Serfdom* (1944) remind us of societies, such as Russia, where great literature cannot be freely read and discussed, and of the relationship between linguistic vitality and fullness of life. A major battle is now being waged between those who value literature for its power to extend consciousness and freedom, and those who in their hearts hate it for this same reason. Among critics in the humanist tradition, John Wain (b. 1925) has written lucidly and persuasively in support of the supreme value of literature, and we give him the last word:

. . . What we need, those of us who enjoy the art of literature, whether as readers or writers, and wish to see it continue, is a sense of the importance of what is at stake and a quiet determination to face down the opposition. If imaginative writing goes, what remains? If language is never to be used for anything but information and analysis, if poetry, from being a repository of emotions and associations that would otherwise remain undefined and unfelt, becomes a play-area for delinquent children, how is a civilization possible? (*Critical Quarterly*, Spring 1972).

## FOR FURTHER READING

Our text discusses a large number of works of literary criticism, and we feel that rather than extending this list we should prefer to recommend students to read more original literature. The state of postwar criticism is usefully discussed in a series of articles in *Contemporary Criticism* (1970), edited by Malcolm Bradbury and David Palmer, and this provides details of other books of criticism. J. Hillis Miller's description of the Geneva critics is in *Critical Quarterly*, VIII (Winter 1966).

# 16

# The Other Arts

EDWARD LUCIE-SMITH

## I

In the immediately postwar period, the situation in the visual arts was affected by a new factor: the rise of America. When France fell in 1940, the Surrealist Movement fled almost *in toto* to New York. The migration was led by André Breton, and among the exiles were many of the best-known of the surrealist painters. They included Max Ernst, Salvador Dali, André Masson, and Roberto Matta. Ernst was at that time married to Peggy Guggenheim, and it was she who opened The Art of this Century Gallery in 1942. It was here that many of the most important American painters of the next decade were to exhibit their work.

Though distinguished European exiles of an earlier wave of emigration, such as Hans Hofmann (1880–1966) and Josef Albers (b. 1888), had already begun to exercise an influence over American art, the impact of surrealism was decisive. Arshile Gorky (1904–48) was the first American artist to make the breakthrough. During the twenties and thirties Gorky had made, in his own painting, a recapitulation of the successive styles of modern European art in a fashion extremely typical of the American art-scene of the time. He progressed from Cézanne to the Picasso of the mid-thirties. His first contact among the surrealist exiles was Roberto Matta (b. 1912). He did not meet Breton himself until 1944. But first-hand experience of the group and its ideas proved almost immediately decisive. By 1947, Gorky had reached a stage of his development which was recognizably beyond the frontier of European surrealism. The principal difference was the greater degree of calligraphic improvisation. Gorky's late paintings are as much the record of a process of thinking and feeling as a final statement about either thought or feeling.

Gorky, however, remained a surrealist, while Jackson Pollock (1912–56) was recognizably something else. He owed a great deal to the encouragement provided by the Art of This Century Gallery, and by its owner. His first one-man show was staged there in 1943. By 1947, he too had achieved a personal breakthrough into the style which was afterwards to be labelled Abstract Expressionism. His innovations were technical as well as stylistic. Pollock achieved his calligraphic effects, not through the use of the brush but through free pourings, drippings, and smearings of paint. He put himself at the mercy of the promptings of the unconscious mind after a fashion which Breton had recommended to the original group of surrealist poets.

Abstract Expressionism, thanks very largely to the notoriety achieved by the 'drip paintings' of Pollock, tended to be hailed as a new triumph for abstract art. This was plainly an error, as figurative imagery played its part not only in some of Pollock's work, but in that of painters such as Willem de Kooning (b. 1904) who were closely associated with the movement. De Kooning makes us aware of the strong expressionist component in the new American manner.

The painters who are now usually grouped together as part of an Abstract Expressionist movement—besides those already mentioned, they include such men as Franz Kline (1910–62), Mark Rothko (1903–70), and Clifford Still (b. 1904)—were often very different in manner, but their art did, for all its variety of technique, have one thing in common. It symbolized the way in which Americans were turning away from the social concern of the thirties towards an introverted exploration of the individual psyche. In addition to this, they provided the spearhead for the American artistic conquest of Europe, and set a pattern of stylistic revolution in the visual arts which was to persist into the middle sixties.

In Europe, naturally enough, people expected Paris to be restored to its position of pre-eminence in the visual arts as soon as hostilities were over. This expectation was largely disappointed. True enough, the giants of modern art, such as Picasso and Matisse, emerged from the war with their reputations strengthened. Since the Nazis had persecuted modern art, the makers of modern art were now accepted as apostles of freedom. But, in pursuing their own development, men such as these tended more and more to lose touch with what younger painters were thinking and feeling.

In 1945, it seemed that a variety of options were open to European artists with careers and reputations still to make. One of these was a return to realism. This was the solution which many literary intellectuals tried to impose on the visual arts. Painters and sculptors were urged to 'face up to their responsibilities'. The notion of social responsibility played a large part, for instance, in the rise to prominence in England of the so-called 'Kitchen Sink painters', among whom were John Bratby and Jack Smith (both b. 1928). Their most vociferous supporter was the Marxist art critic John Berger. In Italy, too, there was a similar impulse, represented by the work of Renato Guttuso (b. 1912).

In France, however, the impulse towards realism was modified by the impact, not only of Marxism, but of existentialist philosophy. The Swiss sculptor, Alberto Giacometti (1901–66), who had at one time been a prominent member of the Surrealist movement, was later drawn into the orbit of Jean-Paul Sartre and Simone de Beauvoir, and there seems to be little doubt that their thinking had an influence on his work. What began to fascinate him, from about 1940 onwards, was not so much reality itself as the provisional nature of reality. In order to express this feeling of evanescence, he evolved the attenuated, stick-like figures which now seem the most characteristic part of his production. In a cruder sense, the thinness of these figures also seemed to be an expression of existentialist *misérabilisme*, which was also more crudely and superficially articulated in the work of painters such as Bernard Buffet (b. 1928).

But existentialist ideas, though influential, weighed less heavily upon French artists than the accumulated tradition of the École de Paris. The problem was to find a means of developing this great and somewhat oppressive heritage of modernism. If the world looked towards Paris for a new lead in the visual arts, it was unthinkable that Paris should fail to provide it. Of the various solutions proposed, some were more convincing than others.

One was that associated with a group of French painters who were then just entering their forties, among them Maurice Estève, Jean Bazaine (both b. 1904), and Edouard Pignon (b. 1905). None was without talent, but their gifts were unequal to the fierce strain imposed upon them by pressure of public expectation, and most of what they produced was a mere *réchauffage* of pre-war ideas.

Another solution was that proposed by the work of a painter of White Russian origin, Nicolas de Staël (1914–55). De Staël established his reputation in the mid-forties as a gifted abstract painter, using a highly textured, painterly manner which showed the influence of Braque, among artists of the older generation. Abstraction began to dissatisfy him, and gradually he moved closer and closer to figuration. In a series of paintings devoted to the theme of *Football Players*, the claims of abstraction and those of figuration are kept in delicate equilibrium. In the landscapes and still lifes which belong to his final period, the figurative element dominates. These late pictures are triumphs of tact and taste, rather than the expression of an original vision of the world—in this, one can compare them to Whistler's *Nocturnes*.

A contribution of greater originality was made by artists such as Jean Fautrier (b. 1898), Georges Mathieu (b. 1921), Pierre Soulages (b. 1919), and the two German expatriates Wols (Wolfgang Schulze, 1913–51) and Hans Hartung (b. 1904). Fautrier was perhaps the first French painter to commit himself wholly to the seduction of tactility. The series of *Hostages*, with which he established his postwar reputation, has for its starting point a sufficiently tragic theme—the execution of prisoners by the Germans during the war. But what Fautrier really concentrates upon is the quality of the surface which he is able to create. The artist's materials, and his pleasure in handling them, begin to dominate his conception of form; and we see in Fautrier's work the beginnings of what critics were later to dub *art informel*, or 'art without form'.

Hartung and Wols, and in another sense Mathieu, take a slightly different line from Fautrier because their work is more specifically calligraphic, and in this sense provides a parallel for contemporary developments in the United States, though at first without knowledge of what was going on there. Wols, who had studied at the Bauhaus under Moholy-Nagy, had a graphic sensibility which was close to that of Klee. He began as a draughtsman, and only at the very end of his short life transformed himself into a painter. The sensibility already evident in the drawings was carried over into the paintings, but there is about these larger works a sense of desperation which is even more marked, and an indifference to established ways of handling the medium. Wols's work, like Pollock's, is an outpouring of the inner self.

Hartung does not convey the same feeling of desperation, and works to a more limited formula. The bundled sheaves of lines which are characteristic of his work do, however, have a clear resemblance to the technical procedures of many of the American Abstract Expressionists. The resemblance is even more marked in the painting of Mathieu. Mathieu arrived at a technique which resembled Pollock's, in particular, by a process of independent development. Similarly Soulages, also working independently, arrived at a position which was equivalent to that of Franz Kline. Yet none of the three artists I have just named have anything like the impact of their American contemporaries. When we look at a Mathieu, for example, and compare it in our mind's eye to a Pollock of equivalent scale, we are conscious that the Frenchman is a far more superficial artist, whose superficiality is reflected by the curious lack of real suggestiveness in his painting.

Though an artist of the second rank, Mathieu is of greater importance from the historical point of view, as it was chiefly thanks to him that the new American painting made its mark in Europe. For example, it was on his initiative that an exhibition was arranged in 1948 to show the new European and American artists side by side.

The influence of *art informel* was not confined to Paris alone. Painters such as Antonio Tapiés (b. 1928) in Spain and Alberto Burri (b. 1915) in Italy are recognizably part of the same general tendency. Both are artists who lay great emphasis on textures, substances, and surfaces. In the work of Tapiés, we seem to detect a characteristically Spanish preoccupation with commingled luxury and austerity, while Burri's use of sacking and pieces of cloth to form part of the substance of the picture apparently derives from the blood-soaked bandages which he handled as a doctor during the war. But these apparently different starting points produce very much the same kind of art. For a while, informal abstraction became a universal idiom.

There were, however, artists who chose to take a slightly different course. A significant contribution was made by the artists of the Cobra Group, which took its name from the cities which the various participants came from: Copenhagen, Brussels, and Amsterdam. Among the members of the Group were the Dane Asger Jorn (b. 1919), the Dutchman Karel Appel (b. 1921), and the Belgian Alechinsky (b. 1924). The unifying thread in the work produced by the Cobra Group painters was Expressionism. Their work revives and continues the tradition of the German Expressionists of the pre-First World War period, but with greater freedom of expression for unconscious fantasy.

One must also name the totally unclubbable French artist, Jean Dubuffet (b. 1901). In one sense, Dubuffet is a descendant of the Dada movement. Like the original Dadaists, he is fascinated by the notion of the inappropriate and the awkward. This preoccupation also links him to certain important postwar authors, most especially to the playwrights of the Theatre of the Absurd. Much of Dubuffet's work seems to be informed by a despairing, ironic sense of humour. But there is more to it than this—beneath the surface humour lies a covert but extremely persistent attack on the notion of 'good taste'.

Compared to his great predecessors in the École de Paris, Dubuffet is a less powerful artist, marked by an almost crippling self-consciousness. But in range and creative ingenuity he rivals the painters and sculptors of the revolutionary period of Modernism. It is also interesting to compare Dubuffet's work with that of a contemporary, such as de Kooning. In some respects, de Kooning's *Women*, and the paintings of Dubuffet's *Corps de Dames* (Women's Bodies) series are strikingly similar. In each case the painter grotesquely exaggerates the sexual characteristics—these women are earth-mothers, direct descendants of the female images made by palaeolithic man. But where the atmosphere differs is in the emotional tone given to these representations by the two artists. With de Kooning's *Women*, we are always conscious of primitive force, sometimes menacing and sometimes in a strange way coquettish. Dubuffet, on the other hand, produces figures which are slyly funny, and often at the same time grotesque and alien.

Abstract Expressionism, despite its enormous success, was soon to be challenged by stylistic rivals. The first sign of restlessness, in America at least, came with an increasing fascination with the possibilities of collage. If the artist could use paint as freely as he liked, why should he not allow himself the same freedom with objects? It was a freedom which Dubuffet had already seized for himself in Europe, creating sculptures out of lumps of coal and paintings from moth-wings. In 1961, the Museum of Modern Art in New York staged an exhibition under the title 'The Art of Assemblage' which served to canonize the new tendency. Although it included numerous European artists, its consequences were to be felt most especially in the United States.

The reason was that the interest in assemblage was, as far as Americans were concerned, linked to another new current—a revival of interest in Dada, and particularly in Marcel Duchamp's concept of the 'ready-made'—the object which the artist *chose* as a work of art, rather than created *ab initio*. In America, the leading exponents of neo-Dada were Jasper Johns (b. 1930) and Robert Rauschenberg (b. 1925). Both began to establish themselves on the New York scene in the mid-fifties. Rauschenberg, in particular, was influenced in his experimentations by the composer John Cage (b. 1912), whom he met in North Carolina, at the experimental Black Mountain College (Albers also taught there for a while, and it nurtured the poets of the so-called Black Mountain School, such as Charles Olson and Robert Creeley). It was Cage who introduced Rauschenberg to a fusion of Dada and Zen ideas: the point of connection being the acceptance of reality, without the determination to reshape it or to impose oneself upon it. These attitudes led Rauschenberg to the creation of combine-paintings—one contained a working wireless set—and combine-objects which were attempts at a truly flexible response to the contemporary environment.

Johns differed from Rauschenberg in his deliberate exploitation of banality. Instead of inventing a pattern for an abstract painting, Johns would take over a pre-existing design, such as a target, or a set of numerals, or the American flag. His contention was that such patterns were neutral, more neutral in fact than anything personally invented by the artist. True, there was an element of irony to be detected in this, especially when we remember the special loyalty which patriotic Americans feel towards the Stars and Stripes as a national symbol. Nevertheless, by working in this way Johns was able to pose a number of questions—the most important of these being that of the difference between a painting regarded as an object, and the same painting regarded as a representation.

Matters of this kind—ideas connected with what we may label the grammar of representation—were to have an important bearing on the development of Pop Art, the style which was to dominate the art of the 1960s. Though Pop Art became a universal phenomenon, and now has its devotees in France, in Italy, and even in Japan, it was at its beginnings an Anglo-American art movement. The reasons are simple. It was the United States and England which contained the kind of highly industrialized, commercial, and technological environment which provided Pop artists with their most characteristic images. At the same time, a distinction must be made between the forms which Pop Art took in London and in New York.

The first example of Pop is now generally conceded to have been a small collage made by the English painter Richard Hamilton (b. 1922) in 1956. This, entitled *Just What is it that Makes Today's Homes so Different, so Appealing?*, was designed as an entrance display for an environmental exhibition called 'This Is Tomorrow', staged at the Whitechapel Art Gallery. Responsible for the exhibition were a small group of artists, architects, and critics who had already been holding meetings for some time at the premises of the Institute of Contemporary Arts in London. One thing which particularly fascinated the members of the Independent Group (as they labelled themselves) was American popular culture. During the war years, the United States had taken on a fabulous quality for many young Englishmen—it was a land of plenty, a land of dreams. Hamilton formulated English attitudes with great precision when he said, in 1957, that the qualities he now looked for in art were popularity, transience, expendability, wit, sexiness, gimmickry, and glamour. From the intensive study of advertisements (especially those to be found in American magazines such as *Life*), comic-strips, girlie magazines, and technical catalogues, British Pop Art evolved.

In addition to the glamorization of America, there was another powerful impulse behind British Pop. This was nostalgia for the immediate past. In the work of Peter Blake (b. 1932), for instance, we find a preoccupation with the popular culture of the thirties and forties—in fact, with the period of the artist's own childhood and adolescence. Blake finds value in just those artifacts which are in the process of being discarded as ugly and out of date.

British Pop Art, when it burst into full flower at the beginning of the sixties, had a youthful energy and exuberance which were very engaging. The *enfant terrible* of the movement was the young David Hockney (b. 1937), with his owlish glasses, gold lamé jackets, and dyed blonde hair. But the startling façade hid much that was traditional. Hockney's prints in particular—such as the suite of etchings entitled *A Rake's Progress*—reveal his links with the British art of the past, with its penchant for satire and social comment.

In the United States, matters developed rather differently. The American attitude towards modern urban civilization was less romantic, and American commitment to the notion of the *avant-garde* was more dedicated. The chief American Pop artists—Jim Dine (b. 1935), James Rosenquist (b. 1933), Roy Lichtenstein (b. 1923), and Andy Warhol (b. 1930)—differ fairly widely from one another, but none could ever be mistaken for an Englishman. American Pop is more aggressive, more extreme, and more deeply concerned with modernist ideas.

Of the five artists I have just named, Dine is probably the one who can be most directly compared with Rauschenberg and Johns. He, too, makes free use of assemblage, and the concept of the 'ready-made' plays an important part in his work. Typical are the paintings in which some object—a coat, some tools, even a porcelain wash basin—is fastened to a canvas, which is then treated with freely brushed paint.

Oldenburg experiments in a more radical way, both with the notion of the 'ready-made' and with effects of displacement. One of his sources of inspiration are the giant advertising signs which litter America—enormous representations of everyday objects, such as Coca-Cola bottles, slices of cake, and hamburgers. Oldenburg, too, makes everyday objects, which are transformed by a change of scale, or sometimes, too, by a change of material—he will present us with a limp automobile engine made of vinyl sheeting cut and sewn to shape and stuffed with kapok. Rosenquist is also inspired by the more public manifestations of the commercial spirit—but in his case it is hoardings and billboards which fascinate him. He dismembers the images he finds on these and reassembles them, painted on the same scale and according to the same conventions, but deliberately shuffled to make abstract or near abstract compositions.

Lichtenstein is celebrated for basing his paintings on the conventions of the cheaply-printed comic strip, with its hard black outlines, flat colours, and regular screen of dots. These mannerisms have tended to conceal the intellectual quality of his work. Far more than the other artists associated with him, Lichtenstein is a classicist and an ironist. His classicism emerges if we compare his comic-strip compositions with the originals upon which they are based—we can then see that a series of fine adjustments has been made, all of them in the interests of rigour, balance, and harmony. The ironic aspect emerges most positively in paintings which are not directly based upon pop material, but which are commentaries on the artist's contemporaries. The best-known are a series of paintings devoted to the theme of the brush stroke, which take the typical Abstract Expressionist 'mark upon canvas' and translate it into terms of Lichtenstein's own chosen set of conventions.

The most potent figure on the American Pop scene was, however, Andy Warhol. Warhol's characteristic technique is the use of photographic enlargements silk-screened directly on to canvas. These are then given an overlay of crudely applied colour. The method itself is so simple that almost anyone could use it—and it is known that many of Warhol's paintings are the work of assistants. The imagery, too, is simple—there is an intensification of Jasper Johns's concern with the notion of banality, as in the endlessly repeated images of Campbell's soup cans. But other interests are reflected as well—a fascination with the notion of the star, and of star-quality in people, as for example in the images of Marilyn Monroe and Jackie Kennedy; and an equal or greater fascination with death and violence, as in the mug-shots of criminals and the images of race-riots and car crashes. But the intention seems to be to drain these violent scenes of all meaning, all power to affect the spectator—Warhol covers them with washes of sickly colour, or repeats the chosen image endlessly until it loses its impact, and eventually even its identity, like the same word repeated again and again.

In America, Pop artists were not to remain content with conventional formats of expression—the Happening, which was a kind of collage involving people as well as objects, occupied a good deal of energy and inventiveness. Happenings were essentially a revival of the cabaret performances put on by the Russian and Italian Futurists before the First World War, and by the Zürich Dadaists during it. The revival was probably pioneered by John Cage, who was responsible for a 'simultaneous presentation of unrelated events' at Black Mountain College as early as 1952. Among those who took part in it were the choreographer Merce Cunningham and the poet Charles Olson. Jim Dine and Claes Oldenburg were to be especially active as composers and organizers of Happenings in New York, and their work, in turn, had an influence not only upon the legitimate theatre (which began to borrow ideas from the art milieu) but on the development of the visual arts in general—the concept of the Happening and that of so-called Environmental Art were closely related to one another.

Warhol, meanwhile, had become interested in films—in fact, his fascination with film was to lead to his abandonment of painting altogether as a means of creative expression. His early films were an extension of the ideas which he also tried to put into his painting—ideas about inexpressiveness, about boredom, about the banal. Thus, for example, he made a film about a man sleeping, with the camera in a fixed position, which lasted for a merciless six hours. Later, Warhol's preoccupation with the notion of star-quality was to lead him towards a very different kind of film, which depicted a camp, cliquish dream world based on the characters and lives of the people who surrounded him at his New York headquarters, the Factory. Yet even here there is a link to the paintings, since such films are essentially a 'put on'. Warhol's essential question is always: 'How much will you take?'

Pop art did not triumph unopposed in New York. Many of the leading critics—among them the two most influential, Clement Greenberg and Harold Rosenberg—regarded it as a frivolous betrayal of all the gains which American art had made in the years following the war. For them, abstract art was still valid, and indeed they saw it developing more interestingly than ever through the work of certain artists who, though related to Abstract Expressionism, had moved on a stage further. The man who formed a link between Abstract Expressionism and what came to be called 'post-painterly abstraction' was Morris Louis (1912–62). Louis lived in Washington, and was therefore somewhat isolated from the New York scene. However, in 1953, when he was paying a visit to New York, Clement Greenberg introduced him to the work of Helen Frankenthaler (b. 1928), a painter who, while closely related to orthodox Abstract Expressionism, was beginning to work in much thinner washes of paint than were then customary. Louis was impressed by what she had achieved, and by 1954 had arrived at a method of using thinned paint on unprimed cotton duck which enabled him to give the effect of floating veils of colour.

With Louis, and with the artists associated with him, the idea of colour came to dominate the Abstract Impressionist notion of calligraphy. Another artist—and a close friend of Louis's—who adopted the new method of staining rather than painting the canvas was Kenneth Noland (b. 1924). But Noland was not content to let the hues drift freely across the surface; he wanted to subject them to stricter forms of organization. The first motif he hit upon was a target shape of concentric rings, very close in some respects to the targets painted by Johns, but adopted with a very different end in view. Noland wanted to concentrate the effect of the colours he was using, without 'composing' them in the old sense. Later, he was to use other formats—lozenge-shaped canvases with chevrons of colour, an immense horizontal rectangle with lateral stripes. These latter reduce the hues to their simplest relationship, but even so they are deliberately kept separate from one another by the use of narrow bands of unpainted canvas between each colour.

Another painter who was fascinated by stripes was Frank Stella (b. 1936). But Stella is less concerned with colour and colour relationships than he is with the object-quality of the painting itself. Stella's early paintings are monochromes where the field is divided by narrow lines of unpainted canvas into stripes which are the same width as the battens which make up the stretcher that supports the painting. Later, Stella began to employ elaborately shaped stretchers. The work thus becomes more emphatically an object, which interrupts with its shape and colour the smooth regularity of the wall against which it is hung. An almost similar idea can be found at work in recent paintings by the British artist Richard Smith (b. 1931). Smith has pursued a strange but logical course, via Pop Art and a fascination with packaging, to delicately-coloured shaped canvases on three-dimensional stretchers, which often project a good distance from the wall.

Despite the opposition of leading American critics, Pop Art became violently fashionable. The public responded to the familiar images which the artists employed, though usually the irony intended was conveniently ignored. Pop having followed hot on the heels of Abstract Expressionism, people began to think in terms of a dynamic of styles, with each style reacting against and eventually devouring its predecessor. The fashionability of Pop therefore, by a kind of paradox, led to a search for the style which, in turn, was destined to overthrow what was now in favour. The choice fell upon what was promptly labelled Op Art.

The promotion of Op Art in this way was ironic, because research into optical effects was deeply rooted in the modernist tradition—serious interest in the subject can be traced back to experiments made at the Bauhaus in the twenties. In Europe, Victor Vasarely (b. 1908) had long been pursuing his researches into the subject. Vasarely was also the heir to a number of other ideas which originated either with the Bauhaus or with the Russian Constructivists. One of these was the conviction that art must be regarded on the same footing as 'work'—that is, as a practical, totally non-transcendental activity. Another was that the plastic arts formed a unity, and that no distinction could be made between the various categories, such as painting, sculpture, and architecture. Yet a third was the conviction that true art in a technological society should be an art without originals, available to everyone. In a sense, his experimentation with optical patterns was part of an effort to put these broader convictions into effect.

An artist of a very different background, and belonging to a much younger generation, treated optical pattern in a much less impersonal way. This was Bridget Riley (b. 1931), who arrived at her use of these effects through an initial study of Seurat and the pointillists. For Riley, pattern does have an emotional significance, and her assaults on the eye are not made for their own sake, but as a means of conveying feeling. Essentially, however, Riley is an isolated figure on the contemporary scene. Because of the personal, non-technical, lyrical quality of her work (increasingly emphasized as she moved from compositions restricted to black and white to the employment of brilliant colour), it is difficult to find a satisfactory place for her in the development of kinetic art—Op Art being only a small part of this much larger and more complex realm of exploration.

Movement can be present in three ways in a work of art. In the first place, there are objects, either in two or in three dimensions which, though static, seem to move or change—Vasarely's paintings being examples of this. Secondly there are those in which there is random movement—the best-known being the mobiles of Alexander Calder (b. 1898). Thirdly, there are mechanically powered works. After the initial enthusiasm for Op painting, it was works in the third category which began to attract more and more attention, chiefly because they seemed to be representative of a highly technological civilization. Yet it must be said that even the most inventive of these creations, such as those by Takis (Takis Vassilakis, b. 1925) which make fascinating use of electromagnetism to keep apparently weighty objects suspended in mid-air, are not very complex technically—they cling to the coattails of modern science, and pick up crumbs dropped from the researcher's table. Few kinetic artists have been able to express a really personal and positive attitude towards technology, the exception perhaps being Jean Tinguely (b. 1925), whose clumsily-built, juddering, malfunctioning machines are a subtle parody of the whole technological ideal. And when they are regarded simply as sculptors, the kineticists often emerge as men with a much weaker sense of form than those artists who are content to produce static pieces in three dimensions.

I have not discussed sculpture in any detail up to this point because, for quite a long time after the war, the initiative seemed to rest with the painters. Established sculptors, such as Henry Moore (b. 1898), continued to develop their individual styles. In England and in Italy there was a revival of figurative or semi-figurative work, typified by the sculpture of Reg Butler (b. 1913), the British winner of an international competition for a memorial to the Unknown Political Prisoner; and by that of the Italian Marino Marini (b. 1901). In America, sculptors such as Reuben Nakian (b. 1897) seemed to show some influence from Abstract Expressionism in the freely billowing forms which they adopted.

The revolution in sculpture came with the new interest in assemblage. For example, the American sculptor Louise Nevelson (b. 1900) began experimenting with ready-made wooden shapes—fragments of demolished houses, such as banisters and strips of moulding, which she put together within compartments, in a small-scale revival of the techniques Schwitters had used in creating his *Merzbaus*. Other Americans made 'junk sculpture' in metal—among them were men such as John Chamberlain (b. 1927), who used bits and pieces of wrecked automobiles.

The man who gave these impulses a new direction was, however, David Smith (1906–65). In a way, Smith's work was a much subtler reflection of modern technological civilization, and of modern attitudes towards technology, than that of the kinetic artists. Smith began his career as a painter, in the milieu which also produced Arshile Gorky and Willem de Kooning. He turned sculptor in the thirties, already making use of 'found' steel parts. His work, immediately postwar, then went through a linear phase—a kind of drawing with filaments of metal not unrelated to the work of the Spaniard Julio Gonzalez. In the mid- and late fifties, he made a breakthrough to something more personal. He started to make monumental sculptures out of ready-made steel parts—beams, tubes, and girders. The point about these pieces was not their sculptural density, but a grammar of relationships—the way in which each part could be made to rhyme with the others. The items he used were put together as freely and instinctively as the Abstract Expressionists used paint.

Smith's example had an immense impact on the British sculptor Anthony Caro (b. 1924). Caro had begun as figurative artist, whose work had a strongly Expressionist flavour. After a visit to America, during which he saw Smith's work, he too began to use sheet-steel, I-beams, and pieces of metal mesh. He develops Smith's conceptions chiefly by going much further towards abolishing any sense of the monumental. He also has a keener feeling for space, for the way in which a sprawling sculpture, assembled from tubes and girders, extends to embrace the surrounding area; and the way, too, that space flows into the available crevices.

Caro, in turn, exercised a very important influence over the younger British sculptors who began to emerge in the mid-sixties. Most of them were his pupils at the St. Martin's School of Art in London. Among the most interesting of the group were Philip King (b. 1934) and William Tucker (b. 1935). They moved away from metal, though without abandoning it entirely, and began to experiment with other materials, chiefly fibreglass. Colour, which was already an element in Caro's work, started to play a more and more important role in that of his juniors. Sculpture became essentially an indoor thing, meant to be looked at in a neutral but enclosed environment, and at the same time it spread out into the room available until it often seemed to surround and enclose the spectator, offering him chiefly a new kind of space-experience.

Meanwhile, sculpture elsewhere pursued a less easily definable and certainly a less direct course of development. At intervals, throughout the postwar period, artists had arisen who asked the spectator to put the emphasis upon the concept behind the work of art, rather than what was actually there to be seen. The most interesting of these was probably the Frenchman Yves Klein (1928–62), who was associated with the 'New Realism' proclaimed by the critic Pierre Restany. New Realism was in fact a variation upon neo-Dada. Klein, in addition, was both a Rosicrucian and a judo expert. The latter skill gave him some contact with Zen ideas. Perhaps it was this combination of intellectual influences which led him to set a particular value upon the symbolic nature of his actions, rather than upon any kind of end product. One of his exhibitions consisted of a completely empty gallery. Today, he is perhaps best remembered for pictures painted in a completely uniform colour—it was an idea which had also occurred to Rauschenberg during his period at Black Mountain College.

The point about these monochrome canvases, in Klein's case as in Rauschenberg's, was the desire to explore the idea of the minimum—how much could one subtract from the work of art, without destroying its essential character as art? The idea of the minimum was to exert a strong fascination for North American sculptors of the generation that followed David Smith. An important part in this development was played by another artist with the same surname—the ex-architect Tony Smith (b. 1912). Tony Smith abandoned architecture for sculpture because it seemed to him that the architect had no final control over what happened to his work. He did not exhibit his first piece of sculpture until 1963, and his first one-man exhibition was held in 1965. The outstanding characteristic of his work is the employment of unitary forms, but he himself claims that in many cases these forms must be regarded as being 'part of a continuous space grid . . . In this light they may be seen as interruptions in an otherwise unbroken flow of space.' The notion of the work of art as an excerpt taken from an infinitely extensible series was to attract many of the other artists who came to be classified as Minimalists, among them Donald Judd (b. 1928), Carl André (b. 1935), and Sol LeWitt (b. 1923). But they were not to remain content, in some instances, even with the neutrality of the regular geometrical forms employed by Tony Smith. Robert Morris (b. 1931), for instance, moved from hard-edge sculpture to randomly piled pieces of felt (thus approaching the immediately postwar notion of *art informel* from a new and unexpected direction).

From the researches of the Minimalists, there began to develop a broader structure of artistic ideas, which has now come to be labelled Conceptual Art. A number of artists who began in the Minimalist camp, such as Morris, have progressed to the point where the concept behind the work—the structure of thought which informs it—is held to outweigh any visual impact which it may have on the spectator. This has led, on the one hand, to the production of immensely ambitious projects in inaccessible spots—for instance, the *Circular Jetty* built by Robert Smithson (b. 1938) on the shores of the Great Salt Lake in Utah—which are available to most art-lovers only through photographs or films; or, on the other hand, to projects where it is the artist himself and his physical actions or reactions which constitute the work of art. A pioneer in this new cycle of performance pieces (most of them a great deal more esoteric than the Happenings they have replaced) is the Düsseldorf-based German artist, Joseph Beuys (b. 1925).

These very recent manifestations have led many people to question whether or not our society still has a place for the visual arts at all. Certainly the whole system whereby art is purveyed to the public—through dealers, and through exhibitions in galleries, has been called into question.

## II

One cannot, however, make the same judgement about postwar architecture, since architecture has retained, by its very nature, the social connectiveness which painting and sculpture seem to be in the process of losing.

Naturally, the situation in 1945 was very different in the United States to what it was in Europe. In America, the best traditions of the twenties and thirties had continued to develop, very often in the hands of the leading European architects of the pre-war years, most of whom had found their way to the United States—the only country in which they could now hope to practise their profession. There was no break with what had already been achieved. Richard Neutra (b. 1892), Walter Gropius (1883–1969), and Marcel Breuer (b. 1902) created notable buildings on American soil while the conflict was still in progress. Mies van der Rohe had already developed the site plan for one of his most important projects, the Illinois Institute of Technology, in 1939–40, and some of the buildings were erected as early as 1946. This ambitious institutional programme was not, however, altogether typical of America at the beginning of the peace. More in tune with the times was the luxurious Kaufman house built by Neutra at Palm Springs—a symbol, even if it was not designed as such, of American wealth and security. Such a building was something unimaginable in the war-battered Europe of the period, and this is far more important than the fact that the design of this house is not really much in advance of Le Corbusier's Villa Savoye, built some fifteen years earlier.

The one shackle imposed upon architects working in America, both thanks to the resources available to them, and the calm continuity of the architectural tradition which they had inherited, was a certain rigidity of architectural planning. If we compare American architecture, postwar, with what was to happen in Europe, we discover a far greater emphasis on the single, monumental building, rather than upon structures which play their part in a planned environment. The example which most readily comes to mind is Mies van der Rohe's famous Seagram Building in New York (1958). In one sense, the Seagram Building is the masterpiece and culmination of International Modern in architecture. But there are certain disturbing things about it, if one measures it against the buildings put up by the Bauhaus architects in their earlier European phase. One is conscious, for instance, of a degree of hyper-refinement which is not to be found in these predecessors. The detail of the building is so fine as almost to deny the nature of the materials from which it is made. The brute structural qualities are kept well out of sight, not by concealing things in the literal sense, but by polishing every detail until it blinds us with its glitter. We are left in no doubt that such effects are very expensive to achieve. Like an ultra-slim platinum watch, the Seagram Building is one of the more paradoxical examples of conspicuous consumption. Built with an eye on 'prestige', it rather ostentatiously rejects its surroundings. For example, its major gesture towards urban amenity—the broad plaza with its fountains behind which the building stands—is not so much a concession to the psychological needs of enclosed and claustrophobic New Yorkers as a firm statement about the power and wealth of the people who gave the commission.

The severity and refinement—not to speak of the expense—of International Modern in its late phase tended to make its re-adaptation to European conditions difficult. Europe could produce the technical inventiveness required for a new and exciting architecture, as for example in the great span of the exhibition hall in Pier Luigi Nervi's (b. 1891) Palazzo delle Esposizioni in Turin (1948–9). This is the product of an older, and rather different, set of commercial ideals from those which inspired the Seagram Building. The nineteenth century invented great international exhibitions, of the kind which Nervi's building is designed to house. And the Palazzo delle Esposizioni follows Joseph Paxton's example at the Crystal Palace by providing new and daring solutions to the architectural problem they present. But it was not necessarily inventiveness which marked the Europeans off from the Americans: neither side had a monopoly of that. We can guess at the real difference if we look at one of the most original buildings put up in England since the war—the school at Hunstanton in Norfolk by Peter and Alison Smithson (b. 1923 and 1928, respectively). This was designed in 1949 and completed in 1954.

Like airport architecture, school buildings have been peculiarly characteristic of postwar construction. If Eero Saarinen's (1910–61) TWA Terminal at Kennedy Airport in New York is a somewhat fanciful expression of the new mobility, built as it is to look like a bird in flight, Hunstanton makes an equally significant statement about the new and democratic concern for education. It thus takes its place with a great many other excellent school buildings in various European countries. For instance, Arne Jacobsen's (1902–70) Munksgård School in Copenhagen (1952–6) is an equivalent expression of postwar democratic idealism about education. Merely to look at Jacobsen's building tells us much about the kind of society which the Scandinavian countries intended to create, and about the values which their citizens were asked to respect. But the school at Hunstanton goes further than this, in that it deliberately abandons any pretence at architectural refinement. Simultaneously with its design and construction a new label came into use; people began to talk of the New Brutalism. This was the first sign that something different was stirring in European architecture.

One way of looking at the New Brutalism is to regard it as the equivalent, in terms of architecture, of neo-realism in films or in the novel. The Smithsons believed that buildings should be made of what they actually seemed to be made of; and that every function of the building should be clearly visible, and not tucked away out of sight. A grasping for the physical, even at the price of awkwardness, is the thing which makes Hunstanton different from the American architecture which undoubtedly influenced it, such as Mies's work at the Illinois Institute of Technology. But the break with finesse was not only a matter of theory; economic necessity also played its part. The Smithsons simply could not afford, in terms either of time or of money, Mies's meticulous standard of craftsmanship, and postwar building conditions would not, in any case, have allowed them to attain it.

Precisely the same problem faced Le Corbusier, when he built the Unité d'Habitation at Marseilles (1947–52). As an imaginative attempt to solve the acute postwar housing problem, this building exercised an enormous influence on other architects not only through its conception, but through its details. It is built of concrete—a cheap material, as opposed to expensive steel and glass—and the patterns left by the rough shuttering on the concrete are exposed. This was something forced upon Le Corbusier by his inability to obtain really skilled labour. Unable, therefore, to obtain the smooth finish of the Villa Savoye, Le Corbusier turned necessity into a virtue. Roughness became a personal trademark, just as it had with the Smithsons.

Of course, the personal touch is an increasingly slippery criterion by which to judge any building, as the constructions put up since 1945 have tended to prove. As architecture becomes more and more closely knit into a highly organized and bureaucratized social system, 'personal' buildings, in this sense, require a great deal of good luck if they are to be erected at all. When built, they are not by any means always successful in fulfilling their designated functions. Not only have Hunstanton and the Unité been severely criticized from the functional point of view, but a building such as Frank Lloyd Wright's Guggenheim Museum in New York (designed 1943–6, built 1956–9) offers an even clearer example of the way in which expression of personality can triumph over utility. The Museum is the final embodiment of an idea which had fascinated the architect for many years. A truncated cone, narrower at the bottom than at the top, it has a ramp which coils upward within it, expanding as it goes. The whole thing shows a brilliant manipulation of architectural volumes, and gives one the same heightened consciousness of space, and of the energy of space, as can be got from Borromini's churches. But it does not, it seems to me, serve its intended purpose well. It is not a good place in which to show pictures, and it has none of the flexibility which has come to be required of museum buildings by the developments in the visual arts which I have already outlined.

Indeed, any examination of the development of postwar architecture tends to suggest that the dominance of the personal, and certainly of the monumental, building is rapidly coming to an end, and that we shall henceforth have to consider architecture in a new way. In effect, the greatest advances postwar have not been made in 'architecture'—choosing to treat that word in its traditional sense—but in things such as flexible town-planning (the result of a more sophisticated sociology), and in the progress which has been made in the design of temporary or demountable structures, and in techniques of pre-fabrication. According to this line of thought, Buckminster Fuller's (b. 1895) geodesic domes probably have more significance for the future than the Seagram Building. My own belief is that the current decline of interest in the monumental is more than a temporary shift of fashion. If buildings increasingly come to be thought of as flexible, transportable, and temporary—as I am convinced they will be—then architecture, too, like the other visual arts, will have to rethink its order of priorities.

## III

Similarly, postwar music has been in a state of flux, and solid well-established landmarks have become increasingly rare during the last quarter of a century. If we try to find a workable structure for the musical history of the postwar years, then it seems easiest to consider it in terms of two overlapping sections. First, there is the music which bases itself on the discoveries made during the early twentieth century; and secondly there is the search for a completely new means of expression, which in turn has led to some of the most radical gestures and pronouncements to be made by practitioners in any of the arts.

So far as the first category is concerned, the history of postwar music is necessarily dominated by the eternally youthful figure of Igor Stravinsky (1882–1971). Stravinsky's musical activity during the period under review provides us with a sort of guideline to the development of music as a whole. The first works to follow the war show him in fairly familiar neo-classical guise. They include the Symphony in Three Movements (1945), the ballet *Orpheus* (1947), the Mass in G (1948), and the opera *The Rake's Progress* (1950), written on a libretto by W. H. Auden and Chester Kallmann. *Orpheus* does not differ very radically in style from the *Apollo Musagetes* of 1928. It is, however, *The Rake's Progress* which illustrates most clearly the dilemma in which Stravinsky found himself. Stravinsky handles the opera conventions of the eighteenth century very charmingly in it, and the score has enough melody to please the conventional opera-goer, spiced with enough dissonance and rhythmic ingenuity to keep the more sophisticated listener attentive almost in spite of himself. But it is a curiously distant, receding, elusive work—we are always conscious that we are hearing a *tour de force.*

Once he had reached this position, one might have expected Stravinsky to remain there, growing steadily more barren. Instead, his musical development took an unexpected turn. Around 1948, Stravinsky's young assistant Robert Craft had aroused his interest in the music of Anton von Webern, who had died three years previously. The ballet *Agon*—the earliest parts of which date from the end of 1953—shows Stravinsky gradually taking possession of the dodecaphonic style, and making it, in the process, entirely his own. *Agon* looks both forward and back—back even as far as *Le Sacre du printemps* and *L'Histoire du soldat*. There was, however, one characteristic of Stravinsky's new manner which seemed definitely to stem from Webern: the tendency to become very brief. It might be said that Stravinsky started to produce his own version of Minimal Art.

In any case, having achieved this astonishing self-transformation, he went on to produce works quite as fine, given the smallness of scale, as any which he had created during his previous career. Notable among these late works is the wonderful *Threni* (1958), which is the first piece which Stravinsky conceived entirely in twelve-tone technique. Severe, technically very complex, *Threni* is one of the monuments of postwar music. But, by its very austerity, it does something to explain why the music written since the war has had difficulty in establishing itself with a broad public.

Any contemporary music which has succeeded in making a popular impact has usually been the product of special circumstances. Russian music, for example, as much as the other Russian arts, was subject to the discipline of Socialist Realism, and in 1948 a document was issued accusing leading Soviet composers of 'formalistic distortions and anti-democratic tendencies'. A reorganization of the Composers' Union followed. Yet despite their difficulties, Soviet composers continued to produce good work. Besides continuing to work on his opera *War and Peace* (1941–52), and composing ballet scores—*Cinderella* (1945) and *The Stone Flower* (1950, but not performed until 1954)—Serge Prokofiev (1891–1953) wrote his Sixth and Seventh Symphonies (1947 and 1952). Dimitri Shostakovitch's (b. 1906) Ninth Symphony was first performed in 1945, and his Tenth in 1953. These were followed by two more symphonies on revolutionary themes, and then by the Thirteenth Symphony, a symphonic cantata based on poems by Yevtushenko. This received its first performance in December 1962, and was promptly withdrawn for revisions to text and music. Both Prokofiev and Shostakovitch also wrote impressive concertos. Shostakovitch's Violin Concerto (1948, but not heard until 1955) and his Cello Concerto (1959) are especially interesting.

Despite all this activity, Russian music has remained very isolated. The preoccupations of Soviet composers are obviously very different from those of musicians in the west. Robert Craft once remarked that Soviet 'musical logic' is 'at least a light-year away'. Yet, paradoxically enough, the nineteenth-century character of Soviet compositions has made them extremely acceptable to the musical public outside Russia.

British music also tended to be cautious about committing itself to the more extreme developments. Partly, one must attribute this to the genius of Benjamin Britten (b. 1913). Britten has had the musical resources to develop old forms, and make them live anew. He has been particularly successful with opera, by its very nature one of the most conservative species of musical creation. *Peter Grimes* was first heard in 1945. It was followed by *Billy Budd* (1951), *Gloriana* (1953), and *A Midsummer Night's Dream* (1960); and by the 'chamber operas' *The Rape of Lucretia* (1946), *Albert Herring* (1947), and *The Turn of the Screw* (1954). Britten's handling of operatic form has become increasingly unconventional over the years—one can see this not only in the children's operas *Let's Make an Opera* (1949) and *Noye's Fludde* (1958), but in the recent *Curlew River* and *The Burning Fiery Furnace*, both of which were written for church performance. There has also been *Owen Wingrave*, an opera especially composed for television. Meanwhile, Britten's status as a 'national' composer, somewhat in the Russian manner, has been confirmed by the huge success of his *War Requiem* (1962), the words of which were taken from the Latin of the Requiem Mass, and from the poems of Wilfred Owen. This work pleased the public, but made a minority uncomfortable because of its rhetoric. Its reception summed up the difference between those who go to a concert in the hopes of enjoying some perhaps unspecific emotional experience, and those who listen to music searching for intellectual pleasure.

The conflict between the rhetorical and the intellectual has been especially acute among those musicians who still cling to the established traditions of Western music. It can be seen quite clearly, for example, in most of the operas which have been written since the war. The American composer Gian-Carlo Menotti (b. 1911) has offered an extreme version of one particular solution, in works such as *The Medium* (1946) and *The Consul* (1950), where he has sought for a kind of naturalism apparently at odds with the medium. Another very successful composer of operas, Hans Werner Henze (b. 1926), has been less doctrinaire. In a succession of operas—among them *Boulevard Solitude* (1952), *König Hirsch* (1956), *Die Prinz von Homburg* (1960), and *The Bassarids* (1966)—Henze has proved himself to be one of the most flexible and versatile of modern composers, taking what he needs from whatever source seems convenient. *The Bassarids,* to take one instance, is interrupted by an extraordinary intermezzo in eighteenth-century style, in which the classical characters appear in Marie Antoinette costume. Henze's solution, basically that of using whatever means will serve, however apparently incongruous, has been adopted by a number of opera composers in England, such as Richard Rodney Bennett and Malcolm Williamson. Other means have been tried as well. Alexander

Goehr, one of the most interesting of the younger generation of English composers, returned in his first opera, *Arden Must Die* (1967), to the manner of Kurt Weill and Hans Eisler.

The crucial nature of the choices to be made in this medium—perhaps the most difficult that any composer can tackle—can be seen most distinctly of all in Arnold Schoenberg's (1874–1951) unfinished *Moses und Aaron*, which was first performed in 1957, though the composer had actually abandoned work on it in 1932. Here the central character, Moses, does not sing but speaks. It is the untrustworthy Aaron who is allowed the gift of music. Indeed, if one had to pick on a single characteristic of postwar music, one would claim that it was primarily *against eloquence*, and this despite such works as Britten's *War Requiem*, and Schoenberg's own cantata, *A Survivor from Warsaw* (1948). The most influential composers of the postwar years have been interested in the constructive rather than the expressive side of music—in making something, rather than expressing external ideas.

An exception might perhaps be made in the case of Olivier Messaien (b. 1908), certainly one of the most influential musicians where other composers are concerned. Messaien offers something which is in one sense an alternative to the dodecaphonic tradition of Schoenberg, but which at the same time runs parallel to it. Messaien is in many ways a contradiction in terms—a 'figurative' composer in an age which is violently opposed to programme music. He has become more and more obsessed with the world of natural sound, and especially with bird-song. The obsession appears in full force in his recent works, such as *Le Reveil des oiseaux*, *Oiseaux exotiques*, and *Catalogue des oiseaux*. But these three works, strange as they seem at first, are nevertheless the direct descendants of the Impressionism of Debussy. The significant characteristics of Messaien's music can be extended further than this. There is, for instance, a persistent orientalism, derived in particular from Hindu music. This influence, since Messaien first felt it, has come to permeate a great deal of contemporary music—the more advanced and complex type of pop music also shows it. There is, too, something even more personal—the extraordinarily static character of Messaien's musical thought, the way in which his compositions accumulate rather than progress.

Messaien's best-known pupil is undoubtedly Pierre Boulez (b. 1925). Because Boulez made his reputation as a composer (which has now been succeeded by an even more considerable reputation as a conductor), thanks to performances at the modern music festivals at

Darmstadt and Donauschauingen, and—more important still—because he is a serialist, there has been a tendency to think of him as a man who is importing foreign techniques into French music. In fact, his position is more complex than this. On the one hand, he is an explorer—the early First Sonata for Piano (1946) already exhibits deviations from classical serial technique, while *Le Marteau sans maître* (1954) revealed a composer with a fully-established personal vocabulary. But at the same time Boulez is a sharp critic of fellow-innovators and conservatives alike. He once called the Britten *War Requiem* 'vulgar in its realization'—yet he has also had this to say about more self-consciously modern music: 'Webern only organized intervallic relationships; now rhythm, tone colour, and dynamics are all organized, and all serves as fodder for the monstrous poly-organization, from which one must break free if one is not to condemn oneself to deafness.'

Some notion of what Boulez believes to be the task of the modern musician of the second generation, such as himself, can be gathered from what he has had to say about the pioneers:

> These people were in a very difficult position—they had to destroy a certain order completely. But after the destruction they *had* to reconstruct, they *had* to produce something more positive. And the need to be constructive curtailed the scope of their imagination. I myself know only two artists who remain interesting throughout their lives—Webern and Klee. These two attain the kind of freedom which accompanies a search for strictness.

It is this attitude which lies at the root of Boulez's interest in 'aleatory music' (music into which there enters the element of choice or chance):

> One creates one's own labyrinth—one constructs it in exactly the same way as the underground animal that Kafka describes so well constructs his burrow: one is always arranging one's resources in the interests of secrecy, in order to withhold one's knowledge. At the same time, the work must be open to a certain number of possible paths, and in this chance plays the role of a railway point which clicks at the last moment. This idea is not a product of pure chance, but of non-determined choice.

There is one other musician who looms as large as Boulez in the European experimental music of the postwar period—Karl-Heinz Stockhausen (b. 1928). Stockhausen's name has been particularly associated with the development of electronic music which has taken place since 1950. He, like Boulez, is one of Messaien's pupils—he also studied with Darius Milhaud and (in Cologne) with Frank

Martin. Besides his interest in electronics, Stockhausen has concerned himself with several other topics—the chance element, for example, as in the well-known *Piano Piece XI* (1956) which consists of nineteen fragments which the interpreter may play in whatever order his eye falls upon them, using any of a choice of six different tempi, dynamics, and kinds of touch. The single positive instruction is that 'when [the player] has played one fragment three times, the piece must end'.

Another preoccupation of Stockhausen's has been the spatial dimension in music. His *Gruppen* for three orchestras (1955–7) are designed so that the audience is surrounded by three different orchestras, each under its own conductor. Stockhausen describes the music thus:

> [The orchestras] play . . . partially independently in different tempi; from time to time they meet in common rhythm; they call to each other and answer each other; one echoes the other; for a whole period of time one hears only music from the left, from in front, or from the right, the sound wanders from one orchestra to the other. . . . The spatial aspects of the music are functional. One finds oneself listening in the midst of several different temporal-spatial manifestations which together create a new musical *time-space*.

To choose Boulez and Stockhausen as the most interesting representatives of the postwar musical *avant-garde* in Europe may seem to to a grave injustice to a throng of other talents—to Michael Tippett (b. 1905) in England, to Dallapiccola (b. 1904), Malipiero (b. 1882), and Nono (b. 1924) in Italy, and to the composer-architect Iannis Xenakis, who has written music for an IBM computer. My excuse must be that one of the most interesting things about postwar music, in so far as its relationship to the other arts is concerned, is the fact that musicians were the pioneers of certain attitudes towards the creative process, almost indeed of a new approach to the idea of 'art'. Boulez and Stockhausen are very particularly the representatives of this in Europe.

In the United States, the honour belongs—and to an even greater degree—to John Cage. Cage was one of Schoenberg's earliest pupils in America, yet he is more completely and distinctively American than any other living musician. Changing ceaselessly throughout his career, he has never ceased to be radical. From the fifties onwards, he has had an importance which is much more than merely musical. As we have seen, his influence has extended to the other arts, and especially to painting, thanks to his friendship with Robert Rauschenberg and Jasper Johns.

A number of ingredients go to give Cage's music, and his writings, their distinctive character. He is the heir of Dada in an especially American way, in that Dada irrationality is mingled with oriental philosophy. Cage, even more than Stockhausen or Boulez, has been an advocate of aleatory techniques. One can get the best insight into his musical attitudes by going to his own writings. For example, there is his description of experimental music. 'In this new music', he says, 'nothing takes place but sounds; those that are notated and those that are not. Those that are not notated appear in the written music as silences, opening the doors of music to the sounds that happen to be in the environment.' Or again: 'New music: new listening. Not an attempt to understand something that is being said, for, if something were being said, the sounds would be given the shapes of words. Just an attention to the activity of sounds.'

Connected with Cage's interest in silence is his interest in the idea of 'nothing'. He remarks, for instance, in a piece on Erik Satie, that the twelve-tone system has no zero in it, and comments that thus 'there is not enough of nothing in it'. His 'Lecture on Nothing' (1959), perhaps the best-known text he has produced (it is at one and the same time a lecture and a carefully notated score for solo speaker), contains the famous phrase which might be taken as the motto of the new American music: 'I have nothing to say and I am saying it.' Cage and his associates—Morton Feldman, Earle Browne, and Christian Wolfe—form an important, if also a particularly difficult, chapter in the history of the arts since the war, which is why I single them out in preference to Bernstein, Barber, Elliott Carter, Roger Sessions, and other contemporary American composers, whose work can be comprehended in terms which were already established before 1945.

Finally, there is one other aspect of the contemporary music scene which needs to be mentioned—the development of pop. I think it is safe to say that, before the 1960s, pop had no pretensions to be an art form with its own validity, though from time to time the pop world did throw up a composer such as George Gershwin, whose merits were everywhere acknowledged. With the advent of the Beatles, pop began to develop its own aesthetic—often closely linked to the ideas of the international *avant-garde*. In addition, it began to become compartmentalized in the way that 'serious' music already was: some works had universal appeal, others were for *aficionados*. The standard of musical inventiveness rose enormously, and so did the claims made for what was being produced. The most imaginative pop music plundered all the sources open to those who created it—including the ideas of men such as Messaien, Stockhausen, and Cage. The result was to thrust 'serious' music, especially if it was also *avant-garde* music, into a kind of ghetto. It became one of the most specialized and rarefied of art forms.

## IV

By contrast, the least specialized art-form was probably the film, though even here there were signs of the development of a cult mentality—not perhaps surprising in view of the fact that in most countries films were steadily losing their place as the major entertainment medium to television.

One of the other striking characteristics of the postwar film industry was a growing degree of internationalization. An early example of this was the world-wide success enjoyed by Akiro Kurosawa's *Rashomon* (1950). Indian as well as Japanese directors also made their mark—another triumph was scored by Satyajit Ray's *Pather Panchali* (1956). Perhaps the most important international reputation to be built up by a film director from a small country was that of the Swede Ingmar Bergman, with a whole series of films, the best-known of which was *The Seventh Seal* (1956). But the fact remains that one cannot construct a convincing history of the postwar cinema by looking chiefly at the activities of Japanese, Swedish, and Indian film directors. To do this, it is necessary to look first at film-making in France and in Italy. It was here that new attitudes towards the cinema began to develop.

Initially, it was Italy that took the lead, with the neo-realist cinema of Roberto Rossellini, as represented by films such as *Roma, Città Aperta* (*Open City*) (1945). The manner in which this film was created, which was in part forced upon the director by sheer necessity, was to have a good deal of significance for the future. It is in *Roma, Città Aperta* that we meet the use of non-professional actors, of 'real' settings (as opposed to sets built into the studio), which were to be typical of much of the most interesting postwar film-making. The film owes much of its special quality to improvisation. All the materials, in fact, of a truly personal and subjective cinema were already present in Rossellini's work.

The degree to which the cinema was to become personal, subjective—something which put forward a way of looking at reality, rather than what purported to be reality itself—was at first veiled. The kind of subjects which the new generation of Italian directors chose to depict suggested that theirs was a cinema of social concern.

De Sica's *Sciuscia* (*Shoeshine*) (1945), *Bicycle Thieves* (1948), and *Umberto D* (1952), Visconti's *La Terra Trema* (1948), Fellini's *I Vitelloni* (1953): all of these did what Italian painters of the time would also have liked to do. They were films which valued humanity even at its most worthless.

But it is Fellini's career which offers us a slightly different view of things. The Fellini of *I Vitelloni* is not divorced from the Fellini of *Otto e Mezzo* (*8½*) (1962). The ten years which separate these two films simply allowed Fellini to see more clearly what kind of director he was. *I Vitelloni* is set in Rimini, where Fellini was born and brought up, and it seems quite incontestably to contain an autobiographical element. More than this, while there is in Fellini something irrepressibly self-dramatizing, the dramatization is always what we may call conditional—'as if' and 'perhaps' are the things which govern its development. The sprawling *Otto e Mezzo* is the classic example of this. This is a film about a film director who does not know what film he wishes to make. Part dream, part reality; partly a speech shouted from a platform, partly a quietly introverted reverie, *Otto e Mezzo* uses the expensive, elaborate medium of the cinema for insolently private ends. Just as Bergman seems to owe much to his fellow-countryman August Strindberg, so Fellini seems to owe a good deal to Pirandello. Yet the attitudes which he embodies in his recent work are essentially contemporary.

At first sight Fellini's opposite, but in many respects closely related to him in attitude, is Michelangelo Antonioni. The novelist Alberto Moravia gave a sympathetic description of Antonioni's aims and his methods of achieving them in 1961, just after the first showing of *La Notte*. 'The feeling for reality expressed in Antonioni's works', he wrote, 'does indeed constitute something new in Italian cinema. . . . Antonioni's reality is static, inert, visual—circumstantial, one might say. Anguish is the only feeling it inspires, and it is the feeling in which that reality is reflected, as in a mirror. Why this anguish? Because for Antonioni reality seems absurd—that is, composed of objects bound together by no rationally perceptible links. Like a dream, or a totally foreign world.'

At the end of the war, the French cinema did not break as radically with the past as the Italian cinema. Indeed, it seemed to pick up the threads with surprising smoothness. René Clair returned to France and started to make films again; Jean Renoir, too, continued his career. Marcel Carné, whose reputation perhaps stood highest of all, after the success of *Les Visiteurs du soir* and *Les Enfants du Paradis*, had the opportunity to make numerous new creations. Directors such as René Clément and Henri-Georges Clouzot made names for themselves.

Looking back, it seems as if the French cinema of the immediately postwar years was essentially a craftsman's cinema. The things one recalls with most pleasure are films impeccably prepared and shot, but without a trace of the spontaneity which was to come later. Many were films with elaborate period costumes and settings—Clair's elegant *Les Grands Manœuvres* (1955), Renoir's dashing *French Cancan* (1954). Good 'non-period' films mostly fell into well-defined categories: Clouzot's thriller *Le Salaire de la peur* (1953), Jacques Becker's light comedy *Edouard et Caroline*. Exceptions to this rule were, on the one hand, the classically austere films of Robert Bresson, which often seem like Racine translated into the terms of the cinema; and on the other the totally individual work of the veteran surrealist, Luis Bunuel.

Inevitably, there was a revolt against the formality and lack of spontaneity of the immediately postwar years. One of the foyers of the revolution—soon to be dubbed the '*nouvelle vague*', was the magazine *Cahiers du Cinéma*, and the first breakthrough was made by Claude Chabrol, with his film *Le Beau Serge* (1958). But despite his priority in point of time, Chabrol has not proved to be the most interesting director of the group. This honour must be shared equally by François Truffaut and Jean-Luc Godard. It is not too much to say that the dancing, dragon-fly quality of Truffaut's *Jules et Jim* (1961) not only typified one aspect of the new movement, but was actually the signal for a new fashion in behaviour by young people all over the world.

Despite this, Truffaut is arguably a less important figure than Godard, who had his first impact with *À Bout de Souffle* (1959), and has been staggeringly prolific thereafter. Godard's films are a perpetual self-interview, conducted in public. For example, to compare Godard's 'war' films, *Le Petit Soldat* (1960–3) and *Les Carabiniers* (1963), with a film such as Clément's *La Bataille du rail* (1946), is to recognize the extent to which Godard is prepared to disregard the spectator's expectations. He has a special importance as the first major director who deliberately chose to make films for an informed audience. He could afford to do this because almost all his films were low budget. He was also the first film-maker since Bunuel and Dali in the thirties (with the possible and partial exception of Jean Cocteau) to place himself consciously and deliberately within the modernist tradition. Philip French remarks, in an essay on *Une Femme mariée*, that Godard 'is only seeking in the nature of his art what a tradition of artists from Joyce and Picasso to Nabokov and Johns have sought in theirs'. But Godard brings something special and disturbing to the search—the most disturbing thing about him is perhaps the combination of radicalism and self-confessed impotence.

Another group of *nouvelle vague* directors centred round the publishing house Les Editions du Seuil. They included Alain Resnais, Agnes Varda and her husband Jacques Demy, and Chris Marker. Resnais is perhaps the best known thanks to *Hiroshima, Mon Amour* (1959) and *L'Année dernière à Marienbad* (1961). Speaking of *Marienbad*, Resnais said, 'It is possible to imagine a world where everything happens at one and the same time, a way of thinking like that of the bees, where every brain is in perpetual communication with all the rest. In order to try and seize this multiplicity of the universe, one must try and make films which are a synthesis of all the means of artistic expression.'

In English-speaking countries, the experiments made in the cinema have been neither so ambitious nor so rigorous. The one exception has been the so-called 'underground cinema' in America, now very much an overground operation thanks to the popular success enjoyed by the later films of Andy Warhol. After his first period of film-making, in which the films were statements intended to be taken in conjunction with the pictures he was then painting, he became increasingly interested in character and plot—the characters being based on his own entourage of 'super-stars', the plots being perhaps suggested by their real-life actions, or imagined actions. Films such as the recent *Flesh* (1969) and *Trash* (1970) combine a number of apparently disparate elements—an affectionate parody of Hollywood conventions of the thirties, a determination to outrage the susceptibilities of the mass public (which refuses to be outraged), and a running fire of private jokes and allusions. The spectator feels like the outsider who has been allowed to watch—perhaps by mistake—a game of charades being played by a snobbish little group of friends. The film technique remains deliberately rough, as if to snub the world of the commercial cinema—yet many other elements in Warhol's work in this medium pay homage to that very world.

At the same time, the American commercial film has not entirely lost its influence. Hitchcock, in particular, has been the object of much discussion and analysis in intellectual film circles in France and in England. His admirers have discovered subtleties in his work which Hitchcock says are not relevant to his purpose, which is simply to entertain.

Until recently, British films have tended to follow the prevalent fashions in other countries, and have often been based upon successful novels and plays. In the early sixties, some of the best were based on novels which dealt with working-class life. Particularly notable were Karel Reisz's *Saturday Night and Sunday Morning* (1960), based upon Alan Sillitoe's book of the same name, and Lindsay Anderson's *This Sporting Life* (1963), adapted from the book by David Storey. Films by the *nouvelle vague* French directors have, of course, influenced British films. Tony Richardson's *Tom Jones* (1963) was a commercially successful example. The mild extravagances of *Tom Jones* seem, in turn, to have prepared the way for the more lurid ones perpetrated by Ken Russell, in films such as *The Devils* (1971).

Perhaps the two most individual directors working in England have been Joseph Losey, especially in *The Servant* (1963), *Accident* (1967), and *The Go-Between* (1971); and Dick Lester, the director of the two films made by the Beatles, *A Hard Day's Night* (1963) and *Help!* (1966). These two films of Lester's were influenced by the new pop style, of which the Beatles themselves were pioneers. They were also influenced by the developing visual conventions of television. *Help!*, in particular, is like an immensely extended, but still very brilliant, TV commercial.

In any case it is clear that the intellectual, director's cinema, first invented in France and Italy, will soon be as firmly rooted in England and America as it is upon the Continent. At the same time, film will finally surrender its claim to be one of the destined media of mass entertainment, and television will reign unchallenged.

## FOR FURTHER READING

Obviously there is a vast bibliography dealing with the topics covered in this essay. The following books, mostly handbooks of various kinds, seem to me especially useful.

On the visual arts, I recommend Udo Kultermann, *The New Painting* (1969), Jack Burnham, *Beyond Modern Sculpture* (1968), *Figurative Art Since 1945*, a symposium (1971), *Abstract Art Since 1945*, a symposium (1971), and Edward Lucie-Smith, *Movements in Art Since 1945* (1969). All these are heavily illustrated.

Useful background to developments in architecture are to be found in the *Encyclopaedia of Modern Architecture*, ed. Wolfgang Pehnt (1963). This is extremely comprehensive. G. E. Kidder-Smith, *The New Architecture of Europe* (1961) is an outstandingly sensible book, with a refreshingly personal style.

General surveys of music are *Contemporary Music in Europe*, ed. Paul Henry Lang and Nathan Broder (New York, 1965), *European Music in the Twentieth Century*, ed. Howard Hartog (1961), *Twentieth-Century Music*, ed. Rollo Myers (1960), and Joseph Machlis, *Introduction to Contemporary Music* (New York, 1961). None of these is ideal, as most are more or less out of date. Machlis is a mine of information, but his critical comments should be taken with a pinch of salt. John Cage, *Silence* (Middletown, Conn., 1961) is an essential theoretical text for understanding the postwar visual arts, as well as music.

On the cinema, see Roger Manvell, *New Cinema in Europe* (1966) and *New Cinema in Britain* (1969), Roy Armes, *French Cinema since 1946*, 2 vols. (1966), *The New American Cinema*, ed. Gregory Battcock (New York, 1967), and Sheldon Renan, *An Introduction to the American Underground Film* (New York, 1967).

# Index